THE EAST EUROPEAN OPPORTUNITY

The Complete Business Guide and Sourcebook

Marvin Zonis
Dwight Semler

John Wiley & Sons, Inc.

New York • Chichester • Brisbane • Toronto • Singapore

Library of Congress Cataloging-in-Publication Data
Zonis, Marvin, 1936–
    The East European opportunity : the complete business guide and
sourcebook / by Marvin Zonis, Dwight Semler.
      p.   cm.
    Includes index.
    ISBN 0-471-54734-4 (Cloth)
    1. Europe, Eastern—Economic conditions—1989– 2. Europe,
Eastern—Politics and government—1989- I. Semler, Dwight.
II. Title.
HC244.Z593   1992
330.947-dc20   92-992
Printed in the United States of America

10 9 8 7 6 5 4 3 2 1

Preface

The most dramatic year since the close of World War II was 1989. That year must be counted with 1688, 1776, and 1789 as a time of irrevocable transformation. This book recounts the dramatic events of that year in Bulgaria, Czechoslovakia, Hungary, Poland, Romania, and Yugoslavia; each of them, having emerged from Soviet control, now wishes to be part of Central Europe. It also recounts the histories of those countries and how they came to be communist regimes, satellites of the Soviet Union; how they overthrew Soviet control; and how they have gone about recovering their national traditions while creating new democracies and market economies.

Remarkably, the liberators from communism in Eastern Europe did not mimic their masters. Havel and his compatriots huddled in the basement of the Magic Lantern Theater in Prague and discussed what it meant to be democratic. They believed it to be of the utmost importance that they show respect for what they were about to inherit—political power. In nearly every one of the countries, the new revolutionary leadership accepted what they were able to win at the various Round Table talks between themselves and the old communist bosses, who negotiated for the first time without the support of Moscow and demonstrated their utter bankruptcy. Except for Romania, there was no great bloodletting or settling of scores—testimony to the political maturity of the democrats.

Gorbachev never intended that *perestroika* and *glasnost*, his means to reinvigorate communism, would lead to its collapse. Reform was meant to produce not the end of communist authority, but its revitalization through creating new and more savvy and tolerant leadership to replace the corrupt Brezhnevites who clung to their positions of authority and privilege. But the Communist Party of the Soviet Union proved incapable of reform, and the new leaders who acceded to power were not those Gorbachev had in mind.

Even before the collapse of communist authority in the USSR, however, revolution spread throughout Eastern Europe, consuming the opponents of change. Seizing the moment produced by the confusion in the Soviet Union and Gorbachev's obvious preoccupation with his internal challenges, anticommunist forces throughout the six countries went on the offensive. Suddenly, the communist stalwarts in those six countries found themselves on their own—for the first time without the ardent backing of the mother party in the USSR.

The destruction of the Berlin Wall has come to be powerfully symbolic of the outcome of the struggle in Eastern Europe. Within the Soviet Union, the end of the line for the communist system came only with the failure of the August 1991 coup.

But no sooner had the dissidents in Eastern Europe come to power than the gravity of the moment became clear. The "revolutions" turned out to be only the first step. The more profound revolutions still lay ahead—the excruciatingly painful processes of political, economic, and social reform.

Despite different precommunist histories, the peoples of Eastern Europe had shared many common experiences. Prior to World War I they were all, in some way, the subjects of empires. The Ottomans, the Hapsburgs, and the Russians all dominated parts of the area and stunted the rise of indigenous governments and economies. Following the Great War, the similarities continued. Except for Czechoslovakia, none of the newly independent states successfully established a democratic government. None was able to establish effective economic growth. All struggled with the explosive challenge of conflicting nationalisms.

Following the Second World War, a more rigid similarity was imposed by Stalin. During the Cold War the region was nearly a single communist monolith, with only Yugoslavia enjoying relative independence from Moscow. The other satellites were members of the communist military alliance, the Warsaw Pact, and the communist economic bloc, CMEA (the Council for Mutual Economic Assistance). They were all tightly bound to the Soviet Union.

In the postcommunist era, the countries again confront similar challenges. Every state must create a completely new order, from the adoption of a constitution to the fashioning of a tax code to the creation of a civil society. In every country, public property must be sold by the state and made productive in order to compete with world standards. A new legal system that ensures the security of the people and their property must be written. Although the specifics of the challenges differ, Bulgaria, Czechoslovakia, Hungary, Poland, Romania, and Yugoslavia face a future of similar challenges.

Yet the nature of the reforms demonstrates the uniqueness of each of the states of Eastern Europe. More experienced with markets than the others, Hungary was initially the reform leader. But once Hungary instituted a democratic regime, that process bogged down in parliamentary debate. The Poles then took the lead, rallying around the charismatic figure of Lech Walesa. The zloty was dramatically devalued, both eliminating and legalizing the black market. Czechoslovakia's Velvet Revolution seemed dormant for a full year before an avalanche of reforms began in early 1991. Under the ruin of Ceausescu, the pervasive atomization of Romanian society hampered any quick political or economic reform. Bulgaria proceeded quietly, nearly unnoticed—just as under communist rule—and was the first to ratify a postcommunist constitution. Yugoslavia destroyed itself, squandering what was its leading position in terms of experience with a market economy and trade and political relations with the West.

This book is meant to describe and analyze these challenges and reforms, especially for outsiders—those who have not been a part of the historic transformations. It has been written with two kinds of readers especially in mind—businesspersons and travelers. With the initiation of market economies, new opportunities for businesses have been created. Dramatic new possibilities for trade and investment now exist in each of these six countries. In addition, new opportunities have been created for travel to these countries that have been centrally connected to the history of the West.

This book is meant to help the businessperson and the traveler better grasp the significance of these opportunities. The book recounts the precommunist political and economic histories of the countries. It assesses the nature of communist rule, the emergence of the six countries from the control of the Soviets and their indigenous allies, and the efforts of these countries to create new states, economies, and societies while struggling to resume their place in Europe.

The challenges for the peoples of Bulgaria, Czechoslovakia, Hungary, Poland, Romania, and Yugoslavia are formidable. In the process, so are the opportunities.

Acknowledgments

No book is written by its authors alone. This was especially true for this book, given the extraordinary pace of change in the six countries of Central or Eastern Europe. In particular, a cadre of country experts made it possible for us to follow the intricacies of the emergence of these countries from communist control.

We are indebted to Luan Troxel of the University of Michigan for her assistance on politics of Bulgaria. Carl Horne of Indiana University introduced us to the politics of Czechoslovakia. Andrew Hruska of Yale Law School added to our understanding of Hungarian politics, while Thomas P. M. Barnett of Harvard University assisted with the politics of Romania. Mary Jane Osa of The University of Chicago lent her expertise to our grasp of Poland, and Hal Kosiba of Indiana University kept us apprised of the deteriorating situation in Yugoslavia. Scott Lyden of the Department of Economics at The University of Chicago provided expertise on the economies of Czechoslovakia and Hungary.

The staff at Marvin Zonis & Associates was also critical to the successful completion of this project. For the onerous burden of gathering the statistical data, which seemed to change as rapidly as the politics, we owe special thanks to Susan Brady, who oversaw the project, and also to Ronald Wagner. Romeo Qureishi cheerfully bore responsibility for the layout of the data tables and for frequently revising them under unreasonable deadlines. For their editorial expertise, we are indebted to Stephen Gessner and David Murrell. Both made the chapters more concise and infinitely more readable. Christian Stracke, Laurie McDonald, Elise Loukas, Scott Powell, and Maureen Loughnane were all champions at finding facts and statistics that we had concluded were unattainable. Sydney Westerhoff served as controller and confidant, maintaining morale and stimulating quality.

John B. Mahaney, our editor at John Wiley and Sons, was crucial to the completion of this project. For his early recognition of the usefulness of this project and his constant support, we are most grateful.

Finally, Lucy Salenger, the wife of the first of the authors, was the most significant source of support and guidance throughout the most difficult periods in the completion of this work. To her our special gratitude.

But to all our colleagues in this collective venture we are most grateful.

Marvin Zonis
Graduate School of Business, The University of Chicago

Dwight Semler
The Department of Political Science and
Center for the Study of Constitutionalism in Eastern Europe
The Law School, The University of Chicago

Contents

CHAPTER ONE

POLAND

POPULATION:	37,776,725
SQUARE MILES:	120,727
RELIGION:	Roman Catholic, 95.0%
CURRENCY:	zloty
EXCHANGE RATES:	Zl 9,500 : $1
DEBT:	$43 billion

I POLAND

POLITICS, HISTORY, AND ECONOMICS

POLITICS

The rebellions that initiated the political collapse of the communist regimes in Eastern Europe and dramatically shattered the world order began in Poland. The Hungarian uprising of 1956 and the Prague Spring of 1968 were important precursors of those rebellions, but it was the 1980 rise of Solidarity (*Solidarnosc*), Poland's independent trade union, that marked the beginning of the end of communism.

In 1981, Solidarity was crushed by the imposition of martial law by General Wojciech Jaruzelski, and the independent trade union then seemed a historical aberration, destined to take its place alongside other failed uprisings against communism. But senior officials in Moscow, including then KGB chief Yuri Andropov, took Solidarity more seriously. It now appears they understood that economic reform was essential if communist governments were to preserve their rule. Early in the 1980s, years before Mikhail Gorbachev would take center stage, the Kremlin discussed the need for decisive economic innovation. But that innovation was not forthcoming—there was only more repression. Solidarity went underground, only to reappear in 1989 with greatly reduced support but more political experience. By the end of that year, communist rule had effectively collapsed in Poland, leading to the fall of almost every East bloc state.

By 1988, Poland's economy had reached an impasse, and Prime Minister Mieczyslaw Rakowski's government could no longer function. The state budget was bankrupt, the country's hard-currency debt was unserviceable, and labor unrest was threatening a complete industrial standstill. Surprisingly, it was the Minister of Internal Affairs, General Czeslaw Kiszczak, KGB director Andropov's Polish counterpart, who first proposed in 1988 that the government sit down with Lech Walesa, the leader of the still outlawed Solidarity movement. It was crucial for the military government to come to terms with mounting labor unrest. Younger labor leaders had emerged and organized strikes without support from Solidarity. By agreeing to talk with Solidarity, Jaruzelski had elected to negotiate with the lesser of the evils while at the same time undermining the emerging radicals. Once the talks with Solidarity were made public, prospects for the radicals instantly faded. Nonetheless, the government and Solidarity had ample grounds for mutual hatred.

On February 6, 1989, they began official negotiations, termed the Round Table talks. Nine weeks later, on April 9, they concluded an accord, which both sides pledged to maintain until 1995. Interestingly, Walesa was rarely present at the talks except during formal events, choosing instead to let the intellectual leaders of Solidarity work out the agreement. The accord legalized Solidarity, granted minority representation for noncommunists in the government, and set a framework for gradual economic reform.

The Round Table talks also produced a formula for conducting partially free elections in June, 1989. The communist party, formally known as the Polish United Workers' Party (PUWP), was allocated 37.5 percent of the seats in the *Sejm*, the lower but more powerful house of the legislature, with 16.5 percent allotted to the United Peasant Party and 6 percent for the Democratic Party, both long-time "fronts" for the communists. Solidarity

2

was allocated 35 percent of the seats, with the remainder distributed among small Christian parties. Multiple candidates were to be allowed to run for each seat. In addition, an upper house, the Senate, was created but granted few legislative powers. As a result, the communists agreed to allow all seats to be freely contested.

The agreement was a dramatic development. A communist party had granted legal status to an independent party. But it did not appear that the party was doomed. The communists still controlled the instruments of repression. Moreover, the short electoral campaign, from April to June, favored the ruling party, since it commanded the state's organizational apparatus as well as its financial resources. Yet Solidarity moved swiftly. It fielded a national list of candidates. "Citizens' Committees" (*Komitety Obywatelskie, KO*) emerged, without formal structure, to mobilize supporters for the elections and serve as the political arm of the union.

Early on, there was a struggle to determine whether Solidarity candidates would be selected locally through democratic procedures or nominated by a national committee. Lech Walesa favored the latter procedure, arguing that there was insufficient time to organize primaries to choose candidates. Walesa carried the day but in the process generated enemies, who defected and founded the Christian Democratic and other parties. Nevertheless, candidates sponsored by Lech Walesa's Citizens' Committees won the June elections handily, assuming all 35 percent of the seats allotted to them in the Sejm and 99 of 100 seats in the Senate.

But not a single communist candidate was elected. The party had committed a major political blunder. Knowing that the elections were stacked in their favor, PUWP candidates did no significant campaigning until two weeks before the vote. In the process, they appeared arrogant and helped Solidarity to overcome its laggard and disorganized position. The election results were shattering. The voters rejected every PUWP candidate, and the party was forced to field an entirely new list for a runoff election so it could lay claim to its guaranteed 37 percent of the Sejm seats.

No sooner was the second-round election completed and the parliament convened than the communists again showed their political ineptitude. Solidarity formed its deputies into the Citizens' Parliamentary Club (OKP), while the PUWP did nothing. The OKP then immediately engaged in an intense lobbying campaign to win the support of the minority parties as well as the two former "puppet parties," the United Peasant Party and the Democratic Party. That effectively eliminated the guaranteed majority of the communists and forced them to seek Solidarity's approval for the formation of the new government. Following the seating of the parliament, the PUWP managed to accomplish only one of its goals: the election of Jaruzelski as President.

By the end of the summer of 1989, with a communist president and a noncommunist majority in the legislature, the political process was at a deadlock. Lech Walesa brilliantly lobbied the smaller parties, promising them cabinet-level posts in exchange for their support for a Solidarity candidate as Prime Minister. His candidate was a longtime Catholic activist and close friend, Tadeusz Mazowiecki, then editor of the Solidarity Union weekly newspaper, *Tygodnik Solidarnosc*. Allegedly with Gorbachev's assent, Jaruzelski accepted Walesa's demands but preserved some communist representation in the government. The communists were allowed to keep four ministries: the portfolios of Defense, Internal Affairs (police), Transportation, and Foreign Economic Cooperation. Solidarity took all six ministries involving the domestic economy. Of the remaining positions, four were awarded to the Peasant Party, three to the Democratic Party, and the final five ministries were without portfolio.

Walesa and Mazowiecki also pledged that there would be no "witch hunt" of communist party members and promised the communist bureaucrats that their positions were assured if they followed the will of the parliament. Jaruzelski proposed the new government to the Sejm, which accepted it on September 12, 1989. In 1981, when General Jaruzelski imposed martial law, he had personally overseen the imprisonment of Mazowiecki. Eight years later, he appointed Mazowiecki as his prime minister and watched while his own nomination as president was confirmed by only one vote—a carefully arranged insult to the communists. The Round Table compact, which had assured the communists of five additional years of party dominance, had been used to subvert communist rule only five months after its adoption.

The Mazowiecki government lost no time in setting an ambitious political and economic agenda. Mazowiecki was determined to maintain political unity and stability. Yet his zealous pursuit of his economic objectives was certain to threaten the very order he hoped to preserve. The more his program cut into the communist economic system, the more national unity waned.

After three and a half months in power, on January 1, 1990, the new government unleashed an unprecedented program of economic renewal, named after Finance Minister Leszek Balcerowicz. With the help of the IMF, World Bank officials, and Harvard economists Jeffrey Sachs and David Lipton, the five-point program instituted fiscal austerity and private economic development. State expenditures were slashed and easy-credit policies were halted to kill inflation and eradicate shortages. Prices were decontrolled and state subsidies drastically cut to usher in a system of supply and demand. The currency was made domestically convertible through a major devaluation in order to stimulate foreign trade and establish a realistic price structure in congruence with world market prices. Many restrictions on the private sector were abolished, and specific sectors were targeted for rapid demonopolization. Finally, a plan was developed for the rapid privatization of the state's nearly 8,000 industrial enterprises.

In less than six months, the program was a marked economic success. The budget deficit had been eliminated and a surplus produced. The Polish National Bank successfully conducted a tight-money policy. The hard-currency international trade account was more than $1 billion in the black. More than 70,000 private firms had been established. The Polish currency, the zloty, was stabilized and inflation had declined from 2,000 percent to 5 percent on an annual basis. Approximately 90 percent of all prices were freed from state manipulation. Food lines were eliminated, and scarce goods found their way from the black market onto the open market.

The costs, however, had been tremendous. Industrial output fell by more than 30 percent, and unemployment rose above a half million. The state's seven million elderly were forced to find ways to subsidize their meager state pensions. Real income declined by more than 40 percent, leaving six of ten Poles living below their national poverty level.

Yet there had been no protests in response to the hardships. With broad national support, the Mazowiecki government had accomplished what it had promised—the dismembering of the old system. But it had scarcely begun the process of building a new noncommunist economic system. Then, in May, a week-long railroad strike showed that the unity was unraveling in the face of the economic hardships. Walesa intervened and settled the strike, but mass political turmoil appeared ever more likely. Despite these signs of discontent, Mazowiecki thought his government secure. He had been bolstered in May by the first totally free elections for 2,383 town council governments, or communes. Solidarity citizens' committees took 41 percent of the vote, with independents taking 50.5 percent, while the communist party managed to win only 1 percent. No sooner had the prime minister's mandate been endorsed in the elections than Solidarity began to splinter.

The most vocal opposition came from peasant representatives, particularly hard hit by the austerity program. Polish farms are the smallest in Europe, averaging 15 acres per farm and numbering one farm for every seven citizens. Private farms command three-fourths of total farm land and account for more than 80 percent of all agricultural output. Despite their independence, the private farmers had grown accustomed to large state subsidies and guaranteed purchases. Under the original Balcerowicz Plan, no distinction was made between industrial and agricultural policies, so that the burden of conversion to the free market would be shared by all. But Balcerowicz's conception of equality proved unacceptably austere to the peasants.

The end of price supports left the farmers with insufficient funds for equipment, fertilizers, machinery, and energy. Moreover, the dramatic decline in national incomes meant that the average Pole was unable to buy all the newly available produce. The farmers claimed, with considerable justification, that there were no food lines because few could afford the higher food prices. The farmers demonstrated their outrage by disrupting highway traffic in June and July of 1990, while their representatives petitioned for the removal of the agricultural minister. The government avoided a crisis by accepting the minister's resignation while it promised easier farm credits. But the farmers broke from the original anticommunist coalition in the Sejm. The extent of Mazowiecki's loss became clear when the Sejm refused his choice for the new agricultural minister.

Another major factor in the collapse of the government was the man who had bro-kered its very existence—Lech Walesa. After the success of the Round Table talks, it was assumed that Walesa would choose political office. But he remained instead as leader of Solidarity, addressing specific labor concerns while continuing to boost broad support for the new government. By mid-1990, however, Walesa found himself on the periphery of the government's policy-making process. He had been marginalized by Solidarity politi-cal leaders, almost exclusively intellectuals. Equally as troubling, Walesa could no longer expand the membership of Solidarity, only half the size of the former communist trade union. Nor had the economy rebounded after the adoption of the Balcerowicz reforms.

Walesa boldly sought to restore his lagging influence and the status of Solidarity. As the workers became more critical of the government's economic program, he voiced their demands for more effective reforms and for the removal of communists in the government and bureaucracy. Mazowiecki appeared to have been stunned. The reforms were moving as rapidly as any of the Polish or foreign experts deemed possible, and the communists in the government had long since accepted the control of the noncommunists. In July, Mazowiecki accepted the resignations of the communist Ministers of Defense, Interior, and Transportation. Yet the Sejm refused his noncommunist candidates. Solidarity had splintered into factions.

Walesa pressed his attack. He insisted that President Jaruzelski be replaced. As a symbol of the old regime, the general had become a lightning rod for discontent and was a useful scapegoat for disaffection with the hardships caused by the government's austerity. Jaruzelski was forced to resign, and new elections were scheduled for the fall. Walesa was promoted as president by the new editors of the Solidarity weekly and by the Center Accord (*Porozumienie Centrum*), led by Senator Jaroslaw Kaczynski, which was a loose group of parliamentarians who broke from the Solidarity Citizens' Parliamentary Club to promote Lech Walesa's candidacy for president and push a "political acceleration." The Center Accord and Walesa argued that change had to come faster and with less hardship, but they offered few substantive revisions of the Balcerowicz Plan.

The major organization that supported the Mazowiecki government and eventu-ally Mazowiecki himself for president was the Citizens' Movement for Democratic Action (*Ruch Obywatelski–Akcja Demokracja*, ROAD). Its leaders included the long-time worker-activists of the Solidarity trade union, Zbigniew Bujak and Wladyslaw Frasyniuk; the well-known activists Adam Michnik and Henryk Wujec; and the Catholic intellectuals, Jerzy Turowicz and Andrzej Wielowiejski. Democratic Action called for a stable parliamentary democracy that guaranteed civil liberties and equal rights for citizens with only a minimal role for the state. At its founding congress in July, it agreed on the banner "Freedom Without Chaos." ROAD did not call itself a political party, choosing instead to describe itself as "a group that supports the Mazowiecki government—in other words, the rule of law—and the speaking of the truth." The group's platform was only a thinly disguised attack on Walesa and his motives. The presidential campaign turned out to be exciting despite the absence of policy differences between Walesa and Mazowiecki. Mazowiecki defended his government and the pace of reform, insisting that only half of the country's enterprises could be converted to private hands in the next three years. Walesa took the role of populist radical. Mazowiecki, he declared, was too soft on the communists and too slow in pushing reform. In addition, he claimed that the government's tight-money policy stifled potential economic growth. At times, his messages were entirely contradictory, claiming that unemployment would be unacceptable to his government while admitting that unemployment was a necessary evil. More Western investment would be sought, he assured the voters, but Poles would not become cheap labor slaves to the West. Walesa's appeal was, nonetheless, considerable. He carried an immense aura as the founder of Solidarity and the winner of the Nobel Prize. He promised more for less while also promising, finally, to settle the score once and for all with the communists.

But the excitement of the campaign was supplied by Stanislaw Tyminski. Born in Poland, he had left the country as a youth and settled in Canada, where he claimed to have made a fortune in business. For reasons still obscure, he then settled in Peru, where he initiated other business ventures, dabbled in indigenous Peruvian religious rituals, and married a Peruvian woman. Tyminski declared himself a candidate for president. The press focused more on revelations of his private life than on his proposals for the future of the country. His wife spoke not a word of Polish, and it was learned that he entered Poland on seven different occasions in the 1980s with visas obtained in Libya. He funded his entire presidential campaign with his own money and, when asked how much he was spending, replied that his wife was saving all of his expense receipts in a shoe box for a later tally. His staff included former communist security agents and during the campaign he frequently praised Jaruzelski for his contributions to the nation, including the imposition of martial law. His economic recommendations suggested that Poland's future lay in agriculture, that Western investment threatened the sovereignty of Poland, and that the management of enterprises first had to improve before any privatization could take place.

When the election returns were tallied on November 25, 1990, Tyminski won more votes than Mazowiecki, placing second behind Walesa. Mazowiecki took 18 percent of the vote and Tyminski managed 23 percent, while Walesa collected 40 percent. The other three candidates each earned only single-digit percentages. In the runoff election between Walesa and Tyminski on December 9, Walesa won handily with 74 percent of the vote and was sworn in as President of the Republic of Poland at the end of the month.

The conclusion of the election came as a great relief. Mazowiecki's placing third had humiliated him and many Poles as well. Tyminski's candidacy in Poland's first major democratic test had been an embarrassment for many Poles. That he had outpolled the prime minister left many feeling humiliated. Tyminski, many believed, had made Poland the laughingstock of Europe. The Prosecutor-General charged him with slandering the prime minister during the election. Tyminski was required to post a $100,000 bond before leaving the country. He left but vowed his return to vindicate his "good name." Some Mazowiecki supporters blamed Walesa for the farcical election, since he had forced its early date. More important, the presidential election revealed the end of a unified Solidarity. The secular, intellectual dissidents and the more religious, nationalist working-class leadership could no longer work within the same political grouping.

Poland's political situation in 1991 remained bizarre. Its president and its local government officials had been freely elected, but the Sejm had been elected under the fixed quotas of the 1989 Round Table talks. Appreciating that it lacked the legitimacy that a completely democratic election would have produced, the parliament avoided any significant legislation until after new parliamentary elections.

When those elections occured, they were contested by the groups that backed Walesa (Center Accord) and Mazowiecki (ROAD), along with a number of other parties, political clubs, and movements.

Solidarity initially reelected Lech Walesa as its chairman. But after Walesa was elected president, Solidarity chose Marian Krzaklewski, a relatively obscure activist, to head the union. It also agreed to maintain Solidarity as a union, not a political party, and to concentrate on union work and increase membership. Solidarity membership has plummeted from its glory days of 1981, and it still has fewer members than the "official," formerly communist-sponsored, trade union, the National Trade Union Accord (OPZZ).

Solidarity has been hurt by a number of factors. Its successes led to the establishment of alternative organizations for citizen activism. OPZZ is an apt example. Once shunned as the tool of the communists, it has now become a meaningful trade union. Many intellectuals left Solidarity to work in the political Citizens' Committees. Solidarity, moreover, was for a time in the ironic position of discouraging workers from making demands, to facilitate Walesa's transforming the economy. In addition, farmers and peasants established Rural Solidarity to represent their interests, which they believed had been ignored by urban workers in the original union.

Solidarity's political arm, consisting of the Citizens' Committees, was founded to organize and field candidates for the June 4, 1989 elections. The factions of Solidarity have struggled for control of the Committees. Their future is uncertain, but they will no doubt be part of an alliance in the new Sejm.

Among the groups not Solidarity-affiliated, OPZZ is a collection of "official" trade unions established by the communist authorities during the martial law of 1981–82 to replace Solidarity and other outlawed unions. OPZZ Chairman Alfred Miodowicz, a longtime communist, was a member of the last communist Politburo. The OPZZ organization is far from cohesive. Factory activists and rank-and-file members frequently act independently of the national leadership. Membership, however, did not decline after the legalization of Solidarity in 1989. OPZZ still has more members than Solidarity and displayed great hostility towards the Mazowiecki government. Its political position and support from its members could continue to strengthen during the present period of difficult economic conditions.

The Social Democrats of the Republic of Poland (SD-RP) is the new name for the former communist party, the PUWP. Much like the other communist parties in Eastern Europe, the Polish United Workers Party dissolved one day and recreated itself on the next day as a social democratic party. The status of PUWP property remains the center of political dispute. The SD-RP party gave up the Central Committee building, but it claims it should own other PUWP property. The SD-RP won a surprisingly impressive 9 percent of the vote in the presidential election for their candidate Wlodzimierz Cimoszewicz, and they still retain noteworthy influence with many political and economic elites. Walesa's promise to remove all communists from public office suggests a certain political struggle.

The Social Democratic Union, also called the Fiszbach Union, is organized and led by Tadeusz Fiszbach, the former communist party secretary in Gdansk who originally signed the agreement that first created Solidarity. Fiszbach broke off from the SD-RP in February, 1990 to form a progressive left party that repudiated the communists while still espousing social democratic goals. Thus far, his group has commanded minuscule electoral support.

The Labor Party (*Stronnictwo Pracy*, SP) is a reactivated prewar Christian Democratic party, now controlled by former Solidarity members whose candidacies were rejected by the Citizens' Committees. It threw its support behind the Center Accord and Lech Walesa during the presidential campaign. As a small, populist party it has the potential for growth, especially if it allies with Solidarity or the various peasant groups.

The Polish Peasant Party (*Polskie Stronnictwo Ludowe*—PSL) represents the reactivation of the most powerful rural prewar party. All other peasant groups, except Rural Solidarity, gathered under the PSL banner after a "Unification Congress" in May 1990.

The "Wilanow" faction of the Peasant Party joined with Rebirth (*Odrodzenie*), the successor to the United Peasants' Party, which controlled 76 seats in the Sejm during the Mazowiecki government. The unified PSL chairman is Roman Baroszcze, a well-known former Rural Solidarity activist. Baroszcze has urged Rural Solidarity to merge into PSL. Rural Solidarity did split into two factions, one of which merged into the unified PSL. Baroszcze ran under the PSL banner but managed to win only 7 percent of the vote. PSL power, however, has actually grown since the elections. The peasant movement has become increasingly unified and is attracting support from various Christian democratic parties. PSL demands that agricultural development be made the state's chief priority. But Poland will be hard pressed to find markets for its food exports, given EC barriers to food imports. Irrespective of the outcome of the Sejm elections, Lech Walesa can be expected to consolidate his immense political power, based on agreements reached in the Round Table talks in order to accommodate the demands of General Jaruzelski. The first order of business for the next Sejm will be the drafting of a new constitution. Unless the new document curbs the vastly expanded powers of the presidency, Walesa will remain the major figure. While he cannot issue decrees that have the force of law, he does have the power to issue regulations and ordinances. He has not hesitated to exercise the prerogatives of his office. He has done everything possible to make his office the center of decision making at the expense of the government and the Sejm. His staff has grown dramatically, ensuring Walesa's involvement in any matter of political importance. Despite his immense power, Walesa has still not accelerated the pace of economic reform, and for the first time, his popularity has fallen below 50 percent.

In many respects, Poland is better placed for transformation than other reforming states. Its president still retains great charisma, based on his leadership of Solidarity against the communists, and has the authority to impose punishing reforms on his already weary people. In addition, Poland is homogeneous, both culturally and ethnically, and has no ethnic conflicts endemic to the rest of Eastern Europe. Depoliticization of the military and police has gone more smoothly than elsewhere. The approximately 12 million Poles living in the United States are a source of political support and economic investment. The disputed border with the now united Germany has been resolved, and relations with the former Soviet Union improved with Moscow's acceptance of the responsibility for the Katyn massacre.

Yet problems with the former Soviet Union remain. Some 50,000 Soviet troops and their 40,000 dependents are still stationed in Poland. Although a timetable for their exit has been resolved, no payment for their military installations has been finalized. Soviet troops will remain in Poland until 1994–95 to help maintain transit rights across Poland for Soviet troops still in Germany. But the Soviet presence has created serious environmental problems, which Moscow has refused to acknowledge. And given the collapse of the Soviet Union, no single republic can be expected to accept responsibility. Meanwhile, Poland remains dependent on Russia for its oil supplies—some 20% of its total energy needs—and sees the former republics as a market for its argicultural surpluses. The country is in no position to attempt any vigorous settling of scores with any of its neighbors in the former Soviet Union.

Walesa has retained members of Mazowiecki's government, most notably Deputy Prime Minister Leszek Balcerowicz and Foreign Minister Krzysztof Skubiszewski. But his closest advisors are more conservative, staunchly Catholic, and nationalist. They are not the intellectual dissidents with whom Solidarity was forged, and the brief secular drift is over. The Catholic Church, to which 94 percent of the population belongs, with its Polish Pope, has not hesitated to reassert itself in politics. Religious instruction has returned to public schools, and abortions have been banned. The Church continues to warn of the spiritual dangers that accompany the consumerism of market economies. The vision of the Church contradicts that of the devoutly Catholic Walesa, but both sides have chosen to ignore their differences, at least for the time being.

If Walesa attempts to realize his economic manifesto, privatization will be speeded, the banking system will be decentralized, the tax system will be simplified, foreign investment regulations will be further liberalized, and the sale of land will be unrestricted. He can already claim the reduction of Poland's debt. After intense negotiations, the Paris Club agreed, in early 1991, to forgive half the Polish debt. But the country still faces formidable challenges. Its economy may have turned from decline to the beginnings of growth, but hardships remain intense. Walesa no longer enjoys his earlier support and has been challenged in his efforts to provide the leadership crucial for the country's transformation.

HISTORY

Origins to 1900

The earliest origins of the Slavic tribes known as Poles, "field dwellers," are not known. Legend has it that the founding of the state took place in 966 A.D., when King Mieszko I married a Catholic princess of Bohemia and forced his subjects to convert to Catholicism. The forced conversions were probably less a reflection of the faith of the ruler than a political maneuver to stem the advance of crusading and marauding Germans under the sway of the Holy Roman Emperor.

During the next three centuries, sections of the Polish kingdom were seized by the Danes, by the Hungarians, and by the Russians. In 1079, Boleslaw II, known as The Brave, murdered the Bishop of Cracow (St. Stanislaus), and Poland was placed under papal interdict. Later, the Poles defeated various pagan tribes and invaders and gradually expanded the Polish dominions. The kingdom was consolidated during the rule of Wladyslaw I Likietek (1260–1333) of the Piast dynasty. During the second dynasty, Jagiello, the Grand Duke of Lithuania, married Jadwiga, Queen of Poland, and introduced Christianity into Lithuania. The territories of Poland and Lithuania were merged, creating a great Commonwealth in the 15th and 16th centuries, which marked the peak of Poland's power in Europe. The Commonwealth controlled vast territories in Central Europe and the Baltic regions, defeated the Teutonic Knights in 1410, monopolized the Baltic grain trade, and became the breadbasket of Europe.

Then, in the 17th and 18th centuries, Poland went into a long decline just as other European states embarked on an era of expansion. Poland disappeared from the map of Europe in 1795. It was partitioned by three imperial powers—Prussia, Russia, and Austria— and its peoples and territories were incorporated into their empires—unprecedented occurrences in modern European history. Partition was accomplished in three periods: in 1773, in 1793, and completely by 1795.

The Polish-Lithuanian Union suffered from a multitude of internal weaknesses that contributed to its downfall. Conflicts within the Commonwealth between the Duchy of Lithuania and the Kingdom of Poland inhibited attempts at reform. The Commonwealth was a "democracy of nobles," which elected its King. He was, as a result, a weak monarch, subject to outside manipulation as neighboring emperors bought votes for their handpicked candidates. The nobles were also able to exercise what was known as a *liberum veto*. Under that system, a single noble casting a negative vote was sufficient to nullify any measure deemed significant, and taxation, for example, was a particularly important issue. While the democratic ideals of the Polish-Lithuanian Commonwealth were admirable, in practice they produced paralyzing and corrupt weaknesses.

As a result, the state found it impossible to withstand the pressures of its more powerful neighbors. Russian annexations incorporated 63 percent of Poland's territory. Prussia took another 19 percent, and Austria, 18 percent. While Russia absorbed the largest territory, Prussia acquired the majority of the population.

The Poles attempted three uprisings to regain their independence. The first took place in 1794 and aimed to expel the occupying powers and restore the Polish state. Tadeusz Kosciuszko, a Polish hero of the American Revolution, commanded makeshift forces, many of whom were peasants armed with scythes. They fought, and lost to, the imperial armies of Austria and Russia. Their defeat led to the third, and final, partition of 1795. A second revolt occurred in 1830–31. Begun as a plot by Polish cadets in the czarist army, the rebels managed to force the Russian imperial authorities from Warsaw and withstand the attacks of czarist armies for several months. The revolt was eventually crushed and a campaign to "Russify" Polish society was launched. Russification included the mandatory teaching of Russian in the schools and the suppression of local democratic institutions. Finally, the "December Rising" of 1863 was instigated by Polish emigres abroad and fought, again, in the Russian partition. A major repression by czarist authorities followed the revolt, and the Russification of society was accelerated. Rebels were thrown in jail, restrictions were placed on the activities of the Roman Catholic Church, and the Polish language was eliminated from public life.

For over a century, then, economic and cultural development in the partitioned Polish lands owed more to the Central European empires than to Polish nationalist proclivities. Culturally, politically, and economically, eastern Poland was transformed into a Russian province. Considerable economic benefit followed. The Polish regions were more economically advanced than other Russian provinces, and the products of Polish industry became competitive in the vast Russian market.

In the areas of the Prussian partition, urbanization and industrialization Germanized the Poles with minimal social conflict and produced cultural development and prosperity. Yet Bismarck's *Kulturkampf* from 1872 and his German colonization program from 1886 were much resented by the Poles. His tactics provoked bitter nationalist conflict, culminating in the 1901–07 school strikes led by Polish Catholic clergy.

In the Austrian partition of southern and eastern Poland, known as Galicia, conditions for Polish subjects were the most favorable. The Hapsburgs left local institutions and elites intact, demanding only loyalty and taxes. But while Polish literature and art flourished with the support of Polish aristocrats, Galicia itself was economically the most backward of the partitioned territories. Since the region had little industry and was dominated by large landed estates, the majority of Poles were poor peasants who lived in abject poverty.

1900 to 1945

World War I upset the European balance of power and led to the dissolution of its empires. The collapse of the old imperial order and the Russian Revolution created the possibility for a new Poland to emerge after more than a century of nonexistence. Several factors favored the reemergence of a Polish state. Because of the defeat of Prussia and Austria, Russia's withdrawal from the war, and subsequent revolutionary upheavals, the partitioning states were not able to dictate the terms of peace and decide Poland's future. In addition, the military mobilization of Poles during the War by Russia, Prussia, and Austria meant that hundreds of thousands of potential Polish patriots were given arms and training. In the final days of the War, under the leadership of Josef Pilsudski, these men formed military units to fight for Polish independence.

The Second Republic dates from November 11, 1918, the day on which the Regency Council and the Lublin Provisional Government turned over power to Pilsudski, chief military commander of the Polish Legions and head of the Polish Military Organization (POW). The POW was Pilsudski's elite corps, a secret and conspiratorial body designed for diversionary and intelligence operations. Under Pilsudski's direction, the Polish armed forces increased in manpower from a level of 110,000 at the end of the war to 170,000 in 1919 and to one million by early 1920.

The early years of the Republic were ones of military and political struggle as the nation's leaders struggled to carve out the geographical limits of the country. Military conflicts over territory ranged from limited border skirmishes to full-scale war. The Poles fought the Russians, Ukrainians, Lithuanians, Czechs, and Germans. The results of these struggles determined the territorial boundaries of the new Polish state. In addition, social uprisings in Posnania and Silesia resulted in these areas uniting with Poland. From these armed struggles, Poland took shape as one of the larger European states, with an overwhelmingly agrarian economy, many ethnic minorities within its boundaries, and a legacy of hostile neighbors. In short, despite its large army, the conditions of Poland's "rebirth" and its historical legacy left it dependent on its western allies, internally weak, and fragmented.

Poland's population in 1931 was counted at 31.9 million, of whom Poles were 66 percent; Ukrainians, 16.2 percent; Jews, 8.7 percent; Byelorussians, 5.6 percent; Germans, 2.6 percent; Russians, 0.4 percent; Lithuanians, 0.2 percent; Gypsies and others, 0.2 percent; and Czechs, 0.1 percent. But despite constituting two-thirds of the total population, Poles were often the minority in specific regions. Poles were also in the minority in certain professions. But because of the Nazi extermination program and the mass migrations and redrawing of its borders following WW II, Poland emerged from the war as a nation of Poles.

The most numerous ethnic minority had been the Ukrainians, concentrated in southeast Poland and predominantly Catholics of the Greek rite. Some 80 percent of them were peasants who worked small and medium-sized farms. Ukrainian agricultural cooperatives were well developed and expanded significantly during the interwar years. Byelorussian peasants, mainly of the Orthodox faith, lived in northeast and eastern Poland where they made up some 40 percent of the population. They were often landless and worked on estates owned by the Polish nobility. The Jews were a socially distinct group and spread throughout Poland, with more than three-quarters of the Jewish population in towns and cities. Jews were concentrated occupationally, specializing in trade and the free professions. Germans, although the smallest group numerically, had great political and economic influence. They lived mostly in the three western voivodships of Posnania, Pomerania, and Silesia.

The social and occupational structure of the national minorities residing in Poland's Second Republic hampered the economic, social, and political integration of the Polish state. But at root, the "nationalities problem" was not an issue of incompatible cultures. It was connected with the desire of the Poles to translate their numerical majority and political dominance into economic and social power. As a result, economically based social tensions were expressed as national antagonisms. In Silesia, for example, capital was in the hands of Germans and Jews, while the majority of the Poles were laborers. In Pomerania and Wielkopolska, the large agricultural enterprises and cooperatives were run by Germans. In eastern Galicia, there was intense competition for producing and marketing agricultural products between Poles and Ukrainians. And in Middle Lithuania and Byelorussia, Polish landed gentry maintained traditional agrarian relations with Byelorussian peasants. The resulting social disorganization and ethnic antagonisms created many difficulties for the numerous interwar Polish governments.

Constitutional democracy in the Second Republic lasted only from 1921 until 1926. With its social, ethnic, and class divisions, it is not surprising that the twenty years of Polish independence were marked by a competition for power by dozens of political parties, numerous coalition governments, and 31 changes of government. The parties covered the political spectrum. On the left, there were socialists, social democrats, and communists, until they were outlawed in 1926. On the right were nationalists, cryptofascists, and conservative landowners, while various Christian democratic parties occupied the center. For added complication, the agrarian movement and national minorities were represented by parties, factions, and splinter groups. No group or party had a majority. Unstable coalitions and brief tenures compounded the difficulties of government ministers. Weak and short-lived governments were no match for the formidable problems of Poland.

Yet some achievements were won. Many national institutions were created, including an army, a legal system, a civil service, and an education system as well as some state industries. Currency reform was accomplished, and a fledgling private commercial economy was established. The government lacked the authority to institute agrarian reform and could not control the institutions it had created. The civil service was riddled with corruption, and the military became ever more contemptuous of the civilian authorities and democratic procedures.

On May 12, 1926, Marshal Pilsudski staged a military coup and overthrew Poland's legal government. Pilsudski was infuriated by the corruption and incompetence of political leaders and feared that the 1925 Treaty of Locarno failed to guarantee the borders of Poland. He established the *"Sanacja"* regime, named after the slogan of his group calling for a return of Poland's political health. The Parliament continued to function, but the Marshal directed the state through political manipulation, electoral fraud, and repression. The Polish army moved into the provinces to put down or harass separatist Ukrainians, rebellious peasants, and other critics. The nationalist party was suspended in 1933, and military men usurped key government positions. Increasingly, social and political problems were suppressed, rather than solved, in the interest of maintaining order. Meanwhile, Pilsudski and his army took note of Germany's military buildup in the west and the expansion of the Red Army in the east. The Marshal raised with Britain and France the possibility of a preventative war against Hitler, but received no response. Renouncing the possibility of an alliance with either Germany or Russia, Pilsudski instead pressed for a nonaggression pact with both enemies. Poland signed treaties with the Soviet Union in 1932 and with Germany in 1934. In 1935, the country adopted a new, authoritarian constitution.

Pilsudski died in the same year, and the country appeared to confront disaster. The lingering effects of the Great Depression and the Marshal's death exacerbated internal political problems. Military preparations and belligerent rhetoric from Poland's west and east threatened its survival. The Polish economy could not provide the resources necessary for military expansion and modernization. The heightening of international tensions fed domestic tensions and, in turn, enhanced the appeal of various nationalist groups. The German minority turned increasingly to Nazism, while the Jews were increasingly harassed and fearful. The Ukrainians seethed with discontent, and the Poles became both defensive and aggressive.

Events moved rapidly to seal Poland's fate. Hitler annexed the Rhineland in 1936, Austria in 1937, and the Sudetenland of Czechoslovakia in 1938. When Hitler and Stalin signed their nonaggression pact in 1939, the end of Poland's Second Republic was assured. Poland was invaded by the Germans and the Soviets in 1939 and divided into three zones—the new Reich territories, which were incorporated into Germany, including Upper Silesia, East Prussia, and Pomerania; the eastern territories annexed by the Soviet Union, including parts of Galicia, the Ukraine, and Lithuania; and the remainder, labelled *General Gouvernement* (GG), including South and Central Poland.

Conditions were harshest in the territories incorporated into the Reich. They were designated as *Arbeitsbereiche* (work areas) and placed under martial law. Jews were stripped of all rights and forced into ghettos. Non-Germans were subject to deportation, and Polish property was turned over to new German settlers. Food was severely rationed. Polish men born between 1910 and 1924 were forcibly drafted into the German army. All schools except primary schools and some vocational trade schools were closed; the Polish language was forbidden outside of homes; and religious worship was restricted to a minimum, with only one church allowed per county. All associations and organizations were forbidden. No travel was allowed. Bicycles were confiscated, train travel was forbidden, and individuals were assigned specific routes to go to work. Spies and the Gestapo were everywhere. The Nazis liquidated the intelligentsia and the local elites.

Conditions in the territories occupied by the Soviets were little better. Stalin staged elections to demonstrate popular support and the Soviet "commitment to the democratic process." Properties were confiscated, the zloty was taken out of circulation, and savings and bank accounts were blocked. Peasants were ordered to provision the army. Schools were Sovietized, and children were segregated by nationality—Ukrainian, Byelorussian, Polish, Jewish. The NKVD (the forerunner to the KGB) conducted a campaign of terror rivaling the Gestapo's. Mass deportations were the norm. By 1941, one and one-half million people had been sent to work camps in Siberia. Unknown numbers perished in the process.

When the Germans invaded the Soviet Union in June, 1941, Poland was subject to even greater hardships. Hitler ordered Poles moved into the territories of the *General Gouvernement* as a reservoir of labor that would ultimately be murdered following the liquidation of the Jews. Ethnic Germans were moved out into the incorporated territories.

The Nazis conducted a reign of terror. They liquidated the intelligentsia, arrested thousands, expropriated property, and began the extermination of the Jews. Yet survival in the *General Gouvernement* was actually more feasible than elsewhere. Its population was not subject to resettlement. Its families remained intact, and the Polish language was retained. Local government institutions, fiscal machinery, city police, and the Red Cross continued to function. The Bank of Poland operated, although under a different name, as did the Polish Savings Bank and National Economic Bank.

Resistance to Hitler was centered in Warsaw, where thousands of volunteers were involved in conspiracies and sabotage against Nazi operations. The Polish Home Army rose in rebellion to drive the Germans out of Warsaw in August, 1944, as Soviet forces approached the city from the east. But rather than cross the Vistula River to join the Polish forces and defeat the retreating Nazis, the Red Army camped on the river's east bank. They waited for some sixty-three days while the fighting raged. The Nazis killed a quarter of a million people. When the Poles were finally defeated, Hitler ordered his troops to retreat but only after razing Warsaw to the ground. The destruction was systematic, street by street, until the city was left in rubble. When the Germans had finished their work, they retreated to the west. Then the Soviets crossed the river and "liberated" the city.

1945 to 1990

Hounded by the advancing Red army, the Germans retreated across Poland from July, 1944 until May, 1945, leaving the country devastated. The number of Polish casualties was staggering, nearly every Polish city was in ruins, and transport and power systems were destroyed. Most important to Poland's political future, a new Russian occupation of Poland had begun.

As a result of the Potsdam talks between the Great Powers, new Polish borders were drawn. Poland's eastern territories, Western Lithuania (Vilnius) and Western Ukraine (East Galicia), were ceded to the Soviet Union. Poland was granted German territory as compensation—Gdansk (Danzig), East Prussia, Pomerania, and Silesia. An exchange of populations was also agreed upon. Germans were expelled from the Polish side of the Oder–Neisse boundary and Poles were moved from territories east of the Curzon line to the "Recovered Territories." To placate the Polish government-in-exile in London, the Allies called for free elections. However, only Stanislaw Mikolajczyk, former head of the Polish Peasant Party, returned to his homeland to participate in the elections. The communists, using strong-arm tactics to control the opposition, conducted a campaign of deception, intimidation, and fraud. Mikolajczyk was accused of spying for foreign governments, for example, and fled for his life.

The communists appeared to demonstrate flexibility when they agreed to a coalition government in 1946, but their flexibility soon disappeared. As the Marshall Plan was implemented in Western Europe and the Yugoslavs under Marshal Tito broke with Stalin, the Soviet leader tightened his hold on the Eastern bloc. Propelled by his paranoia and fear of aggression, Stalin forced the merger of the "national communists" of the Polish Socialist Party into the Moscow-controlled Polish Workers' Party. Renamed the Polish United Workers' Party (PUWP), the new party would hold power from 1948 until September, 1989.

The onset of Stalinization in 1948 was an effort to recreate in Poland, as well as in Czechoslovakia, Hungary, and the GDR, the main institutions of Stalinist control that had been conceived and implemented in the USSR before the War. The components of Stalinism included Marxism-Leninism as the sole ideology; the establishment of a large conscript army; a command economy based on central planning; an economic structure favoring heavy industry and autarky; strict censorship of the press; and most importantly, the monopoly of power by the communist party.

Boleslaw Bierut presided over the Stalinist period in Poland. He created a cult of personality while he instituted a wave of terror and conducted widespread purges. Konstantin Rokossovsky, a Russian marshal of Polish descent, served as Poland's deputy premier, a member of the Politburo, and the supervisor of the armed forces. All effective power was in the hands of the Politburo and the first secretary who instituted Stalinism in Poland.

An attempt was made to collectivize agriculture. Peasants were moved onto state farms and forced to produce fixed quotas for food delivery to urban areas. New towns and industries were built with peasant labor. The "working masses" were glorified in communist propaganda at the same time the authorities were creating burdensome conditions for worker survival. Coercion, xenophobia, and conformity permeated the society.

By 1949, the Soviet Union moved to institute an international system of the socialist states. A trading bloc, the Council for Mutual Economic Assistance (CMEA) or Comecon, was established. To satisfy Stalin's obsessive concern that the United States was about to attack, an intensive military buildup was initiated throughout the bloc. In 1951, the Warsaw Pact was created, with Poland a founding member.

Despite these developments, Stalinism was not as pronounced in Poland as it was in other communist states. The control of society by the secret police was not as extreme as in Hungary, the GDR, Czechoslovakia, or Romania. The collectivization of agriculture was not as successful as in Hungary and East Germany, and state farms started to break up in Poland as early as 1953. The Catholic Church was repressed, but not forced underground as in Czechoslovakia. "National communists" were put on trial, but not executed. Thus, when the "thaw" started following Stalin's death, and particularly after the revelations of his crimes by Khrushchev at the 20th Party Congress, "national communists" were able to argue for a Polish road to socialism.

Under pressure of bread riots in Poznan in June 1956, the PUWP changed its leadership. Wladyslaw Gomulka, who had been imprisoned by Bierut, became party First Secretary. Soviet "advisors" were invited to leave, and Russian approval for high-level personnel changes was no longer automatically sought. Gomulka and the "national communists" abandoned collectivization and allowed private agriculture to develop. Concessions to the Church were granted, censorship was eased, and intellectuals were allowed some leeway.

After a dangerous confrontation with Nikita Khrushchev, Gomulka convinced the Soviets to allow a "Polish Road to Socialism." Gomulka's actions were interpreted in Poland as defiance of the Soviet Union, earning him wide backing for his reforms. He had actually traded continuing subordination to Moscow—at least in foreign policy—for limited internal autonomy to develop a national brand of communism.

Gomulka remained in power until 1970, a period in which Poland experienced only fitful and limited economic growth, most impressively in agriculture. But the command economy was already breaking down. All the typical defects associated with a state socialist economy became manifest: chronic shortages, shoddy consumer goods, poor worker morale and discipline, arbitrary and capricious management by the "nomenklatura," unpredictable supplies of production inputs, and false reporting to fulfill quotas and "the Plan." In addition, as the terror of the Stalinist period receded, opportunities for free expression and association steadily increased.

In 1968, a mix of faltering economic output and increasing tolerance for expression produced the first significant social unrest since the 1956 Poznan riots that had brought Gomulka to power. Demonstrations by university students and intellectuals were put down by the government's paramilitary forces. Then an anti-Semitic campaign was instigated by a hard-line faction of the party in an attempt to mobilize sentiment for the regime as well as to settle old political scores. Many in the small Polish Jewish community finally fled the country, while the PUWP ordered that many prominent academics and intellectuals be dismissed from their positions. The Church protested. But other social groups and, strikingly, peasants and workers, looked on in silence. Gomulka managed to weather the crisis and hold on to power for two more years.

Shortly before Christmas in 1970, in an effort to recover some of the costs of its subsidies, the government announced food price increases. Riots erupted in several cities, particularly on the Baltic coast. In Gdansk, a march by shipyard workers to PUWP headquarters ended in a bloody confrontation between police and demonstrators. It was widely believed that Gomulka had personally approved the orders to fire. A deep sense of disillusionment and anger spread among workers who believed themselves to have been betrayed by Gomulka, the man who had initially granted some freedoms. With the possibility of unrest spreading, the Politburo took action. The price rises were rescinded, and Gomulka was dropped as first secretary in favor of Edward Gierek.

Gierek began his career as a populist party leader from the Silesia. His strategy was to stimulate the economy, not through structural reforms but through foreign credits and trade. Beginning in 1972, the government borrowed huge sums from foreign banks to buy expensive Western technology, making the country dependent on foreign inputs for production. Substandard manufactured products, however, could not be sold in world markets. Exports never generated hard-currency earnings sufficient to service the debt. At the same time, the government diverted a good portion of its foreign credits to import Western consumer goods to secure social quiescence. Foreign borrowing camouflaged the dimensions of the growing economic crisis.

By the mid-1970s it was clear that the state could not continue to provide the extraordinary subsidies to Polish consumers. The government, mindful of the disturbances that had driven Gomulka from power, nonetheless announced steep price hikes in June, 1976. One day later, work stoppages swept the country. Rail travel was disrupted and railroad tracks were ripped up. Riots spread, and the militia in the city of Radom intervened, leaving casualties. The economic minister hastily appeared on television to announce the withdrawal of price increases "for further consideration." But simultaneously, the government conducted extensive political reprisals against workers.

Gierek weathered the crisis of 1976, but the events of that year spawned the emergence of unofficial opposition groups and *samizdat* (underground publications). The most important of these groups was KOR, the Committee for the Defense of Workers' Rights. A second important opposition group arose as well, the Movement for the Defense of Civil Law and Citizens' Rights (*Ruch Obrony Praw Ciwilnych i Obywatelskich*).

The events of 1976 also revealed the economic difficulties of the country. The foreign debt had risen to $18 billion and loans had begun to come due. Despite efforts to reinvigorate agriculture, grain had to be imported following poor weather in 1975–1976. The country was perilously short of funds.

In 1978, a remarkable event occurred. The Archbishop of Cracow, Karol Wojtyla, was elected Pope of the Roman Catholic Church. As Pope John Paul II, he announced a papal pilgrimage to his homeland and arrived in Poland in June of 1979. The communists remained aloof as they struggled to find a "correct line" to take vis-à-vis this cleric, who had been a thorn in their side for many years. But for the people, Wojtyla's election was a great source of national pride. The stimulus that the Polish Pope was able to provide the Polish people, aided by the faltering economy, contributed to the rise of Solidarity and the transformation of the nation's politics.

The Solidarity period falls into three phases: its formation and growth as a social movement from August 31, 1980, to 1982; martial law and underground Solidarity, 1982 to 1988; and the campaign for the legalization of Solidarity that led to the Round Table talks, 1988–89.

The creation of Solidarity owed much to the gradual development of an organized opposition during the 1970s. The disaffected spanned all social groups—leftist as well as Catholic intellectuals, politicized workers, and patriots resentful of Poland's dependency on the USSR. KOR and other organizations were able to build bridges between intellectuals and workers, and the movement for a civil society was profoundly stimulated when the Church was able to mobilize millions in the welcome and celebration of the Pope's return to his native land. The party and military were at a complete loss in their attempts to control the erosion of their political power.

Another round of price hikes on foodstuffs in 1980 led to strikes. The authorities responded with promises and pay hikes, but the workers escalated their demands to include political issues. The Lenin Shipyard in Gdansk rejected a favorable settlement offer, deciding to remain in *solidarity* with other striking workers. Under duress, government negotiators signed an agreement in Gdansk on August 31, creating the first independent trade union in a communist country. A 37-year-old unemployed electrician who had jumped the Lenin Shipyard fence to lead the strike—Lech Walesa—was elected chairman.

The fifteen months of Solidarity's legal existence resulted in an explosion of social and political activism. Thousands of people joined Solidarity each week, creating union chapters throughout the society. Farmers formed a Rural Solidarity. By the fall of 1981, Solidarity counted ten million members and had transformed itself into a democratic social movement. The union used its right to strike to force concessions from the government. Many PUWP members joined Solidarity. The early euphoria, however, changed to frustration. Solidarity failed to obtain sustainable commitments from the government, which, while on the defensive, was still capable of using force.

Solidarity, finally, concluded that the system was unreformable. At a meeting of its national executive committee in December, 1982, Solidarity leaders asserted the need for free elections and a referendum on Poland's alliance with the Soviet Union. Ten days later martial law was declared. The Polish army moved swiftly to imprison Solidarity leaders and crush the resistance.

Hopes for change were dashed. Workers loyal to Solidarity resisted the army fiercely, especially in the mining regions, where many were killed. Walesa was imprisoned along with thousands of other activists and Solidarity supporters. A curfew was imposed, and gatherings of more than three people were banned. Nevertheless, some key leaders, such as Zbigniew Bujak and Wladyslaw Frasyniuk, managed to elude the police and establish an underground Solidarity structure. Secret presses and radio transmitters disseminated uncensored information about the union and society. Pope John Paul II condemned the crackdown, and Catholic charities organized relief aid for the families of the prisoners. Yet as the repression increased, public protests declined.

Once again there was a turnover at the top of the PUWP. General Jaruzelski became first secretary, replacing Stanislaw Kania, who had in turn briefly replaced Gierek. The regime tried without success to generate some legitimacy for its policies. But the worsening economy and the government's total lack of credibility led instead to work slowdowns and the rationing of food, liquor, tobacco, and gasoline.

When Mikhail Gorbachev was chosen first secretary of the Soviet Communist Party, political conditions in Poland began to change. *Perestroika* (restructuring) and *glasnost* (openness) were eagerly embraced by the Poles, communists and noncommunists alike. Optimism swept the country as Poles came to believe that fundamental changes were possible. With glasnost in place, the extent of the Polish economic and financial crises became known. Poland's foreign debt had grown to staggering totals. Its industries had become hopelessly noncompetitive. Its infrastructure was archaic and crumbling. The entire region had suffered severe ecological damage. Worst of all, the Party appeared to have no idea of how to deal with the multiple crises simultaneously besetting the country.

Solidarity used the new openness to push for radical reforms and stressed the need for political freedom to solve Poland's ills. Slowly, elites on both sides cautiously edged their way toward the Round Table talks to establish a framework for reforms. To the amazement of virtually all Poles, those talks were finally held. Their outcome was to transform the entire Eastern European scene.

DIAGRAM OF GOVERNMENTAL STRUCTURE

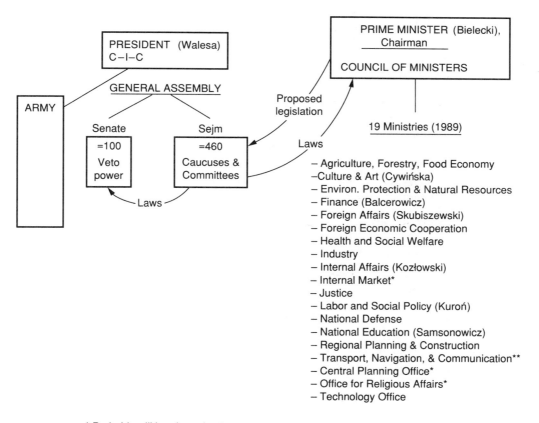

* Probably will be phased out.

** In spring, 1990, split into two ministries: Transport and Telecommunications.

ECONOMICS

Introduction

In December, 1989, Poland adopted the "shock treatment" plan of Finance Minister Balcerowicz to propel it into a market system in one dramatic move. Many economic analysts from Europe and the United States argued that the ambitious program was essential for economic reform but warned that it could plunge Poland into unprecedented economic and political turmoil.

Under the "shock treatment," prices were freed from the control of the state and its central planners. Generous subsidies on food, consumer goods, raw materials, and energy were ended. Restrictions on private economic activity were lifted and the zloty, the Polish currency, was devalued to its international value.

There was little doubt that some significant changes were essential. Inflation had risen to nearly 900 percent in 1989, while real wages and economic output had declined by more than 40 percent. Living standards had fallen below those of a decade earlier. Faced with the magnitude of the crisis and the harshness of the cure, observers expected social turmoil, at best. Yet only six months after the adoption of the Balcerowicz Plan, Poland had turned the corner towards economic recovery. By the summer of 1990, the economy had bottomed out and was showing signs of a modest recovery.

The reform process is still far from complete, but the conditions for sustained economic growth appear to have been created. Fears that reform would hurl Poland into chaos have disappeared. The value of the zloty has been stabilized, and the renowned black market, especially in currency speculation, has been eliminated. Public trust has been restored and appears sufficiently sturdy to support the next major reform steps— the privatization of approximately 8,000 state enterprises and the implementation of new banking, tax, and commercial codes. Even with much yet to be accomplished, the Polish reform program is the most comprehensive example of the transition from a command to a market economy, surpassing the steps taken by Hungary. Because of the speed and depth of its reforms and the size of its domestic markets, Poland has become the model for other, more reluctant, reforming states.

Despite its early accomplishments, Poland is steeped in problems common to the East bloc. The communications infrastructure is as primitive as in Prague or Budapest. Problems of securing raw materials and distributing finished products are endemic. Bureaucratic obstruction and even worker resistance can still be found. The government wrestles with the practical issues of the transition and with the burden of the foreign debt, approximately $22 billion after the near-50 percent write-off by the Paris Club.

Poland is distinguished from other former communist satellites, not only by the abruptness of its transition but also by its possibilities for future economic development. The country boasts a large, skilled labor force with average wages between $80 and $120 per month and a sizable domestic market for goods and services. Over 1000 joint ventures were registered by the newly established Foreign Investment Agency in 1990. While the ventures are small in dollar terms, they indicate the growing interest of foreign investors.

Current Economic Reforms

In September 1989, the immediate and critical problem facing Solidarity Prime Minister Tadeusz Mazowiecki, chosen by Lech Walesa to lead the new Solidarity government, was the problem of macroeconomic stabilization. Hyperinflation threatened the economy, and the foundations of a market economy had to be established. On January 1, 1990, Mazowiecki instituted a program of drastic economic reform and austerity, based on proposals by IMF and World Bank officials and his foreign economic advisers.

Finance Minister Balcerowicz developed the five-point initiative for the transition. First, the government would eliminate the budget deficit and end easy-credit policies in order to eradicate shortages and eliminate inflation. Second, prices would be decontrolled and subsidies diminished, instituting the principle of supply and demand in prices and market allocation. Third, the zloty would be made convertible to encourage foreign trade, thus "importing" a realistic price structure. Fourth, restrictions on the private sector would be immediately abolished and specific sectors targeted for rapid demonopolization. Finally, a plan to encourage the rapid privatization of most of the state's 8,000 industrial enterprises would be initiated.

From the outset, the reformers were determined to eliminate any inhibitions to Western trade and internal investment so as to establish a realistic price structure and create a competitive domestic market. The forthright nature of the resulting legislation has proven exceptionally attractive to Western investors and has also attracted a number of Western financial support programs, which have provided just under $10 billion in assistance. Since early 1989, the new government has instituted legal changes covering international trade agreements, foreign investment, joint ventures, duty-free zones, currency convertibility, and the partial and eventual full repatriation of profits.

The new foreign exchange laws set a realistic valuation for the zloty and allowed for the full internal convertibility of the zloty for Poles as well as foreigners. The rate of exchange was established at Zl 9,500 to $1, representing a full 50 percent devaluation. That exchange rate effectively eliminated hyperinflation and remained effective throughout 1990. The new exchange provisions have been supported by a $1 billion stabilization fund granted to Poland by Western governments. Existing hard-currency bank accounts are being phased out, and all foreign exchange transactions must be conducted at banks whose hard-currency reserves are buttressed by the National Bank. Hard-currency retail stores, set up for communist party members, were phased out by the end of 1990, and the zloty was made the universal commercial currency. As a result of all these measures, the zloty acquired both economic and symbolic value.

Poland first legalized joint ventures in 1976, but not a single foreign investor was attracted by the legislation. A new joint venture law was adopted in 1986, yet it was considered excessively restrictive and far less attractive than comparable laws in China and Hungary. The current law, the Polish Foreign Investment Law, was originally drafted in December, 1988, further amended in December, 1989, and came into force in January, 1990. Appropriate to Poland's strategy of attracting foreign investment, the new code has generous terms and promises a speedy resolution of all applications. Through the Foreign Investment Agency, the Polish Chamber of Foreign Commerce, the Warsaw branch office of the United Nations Industrial Development Organization, and the Overseas Private Investment Corporation (OPIC), interested investors may obtain lists of Polish enterprises seeking Western joint venture partners.

The law allows foreign companies, foundations, banks, and individuals to operate businesses in the form of joint stock companies or limited-liability firms. Wholly foreign-owned subsidiaries may also be established in Poland and will be treated as Polish firms under the Commercial Code of 1934, presently under considerable revision. Joint stock and limited-liability firms may be owned by foreigners alone or with Polish partners. A sole foreign investor or group of investors can also establish a limited-liability company in which foreign capital amounts to 100 percent of the new company's shares, or they may, with permission from the Foreign Investment Agency, raise equity by public subscription of shares. Stock may be purchased by foreigners in already existing joint stock or limited-liability firms. The law does require that the foreign investment in a joint stock firm account for at least 20 percent of the total equity or at least Zl 25 million. Besides convertible currency, equipment and technology may also satisfy the 20-percent-of-total-invested-capital requirement.

Income from a joint venture is taxed at the rate of 40 percent, and standard deductions, including depreciation, are allowed. All joint ventures are entitled to a three-year tax holiday, which may be extended for another three years if the investment is a "priority" venture. Construction, agriculture and food processing, pharmaceutical production, telecommunications, electronics and electronic products, printing machines and office equipment, metallurgical products, transport, tourism, and environmental protection are all considered priority sectors by the government. For firms with sizable exports, additional tax breaks are available.

All joint ventures are subject to an annual audit by the Ministry of Finance and must make yearly contributions of 8 percent of after-tax profits to the obligatory Reserve Fund, an account used to cover wages and financial obligations to other Polish firms in case of bankruptcy. The payments must continue until the Fund equals at least 4 percent of the joint venture's annual operating expenses. Firms must now convert 100 percent of export proceeds, but the joint venture can buy back its convertible currency. Joint ventures and foreign businesses also have the right to repatriate 100 percent of their after-tax hard-currency profits, but only 15 percent of their zloty profits. The U.S.–Polish business treaty of March, 1990, stipulates that the ceiling for repatriation will rise to 20 percent at the end of 1992, continuing to 100 percent repatriation by 1996. Walesa is likely to speed full repatriation to attract more foreign investors.

Joint ventures seeking to hire non-Polish workers require special authorization. A 30 percent withholding tax is levied on the salaries of foreign employees, though the U.S.–Polish Economic Treaty provides certain exemptions. Joint ventures must pay all social service taxes—pension funds and other benefits—for both Polish and foreign workers. Personnel already employed by foreign companies outside of Poland need no permission to work in the country. They require only residency papers for housing purposes. The foreign labor that is hired must be paid in zlotys but may convert their earnings when leaving the country. Polish labor law applies to Polish workers, who are paid according to contracts established with the joint ventures. The commercial code requires that firms have an Assembly of shareholders, with representation proportional to capital investment. The Assembly's chairman may be foreign. Unanimity among shareholders is required for resolving "fundamental questions," the nature of which must be defined in the founding charter of the joint venture.

Joint ventures must be certified by the Foreign Investment Agency. Applicants must submit a detailed draft of the founding document of the joint venture; evidence of its financial condition, legal status, and backgrounds of the founding members; and a feasibility study of the proposed project. For its part, the Investment Agency must decide on the application in no more than two months. If permission is granted, the venture must then register with the courts, after which time it may begin to hire workers, rent office space, and begin normal operations. If changes in the founding charter are desired or its shares are sold or transferred, then a report must be sent to the Investment Agency. If a joint venture is liquidated, the Polish partners retain the first opportunity to purchase the assets of the venture. Joint venture partners may specify the laws of a third country in cases when arbitration is necessary.

The foreign investment law is less attractive to foreign firms than the codes of Hungary, although new legislation is expected to improve the climate. The Investment Agency has full power to refuse a venture's application, and it can revoke permission for an operating joint venture if it finds questionable practices. In addition, foreign partners cannot appeal the findings of the Agency, whose assessment of the value of the Polish contribution to the venture is essential to the venture's application. Also, permits are required to change the charter of a joint venture or transfer equity interests among joint venture partners or to third parties. Legal problems also stem from the continued use of the 1934 Commercial

Code. But recent amendments to contract law have followed continental practice largely as a result of the dominance of German joint ventures.

Banking has also been opened to foreigners. Foreign banks may open branches or representative offices overseen by the Finance Ministry, and joint stock banks may be created with National Bank approval. General banking activity has been opened to public and private banks. A joint stock bank must have $6 million in initial capital, but investments in Polish banks do not require the 20 percent minimum investment called for in other foreign ventures. Tax holidays for banks are not covered in the new law and must be individually negotiated. Several Western banks have begun talks with Polish authorities, but none of these ventures have yet to become operational.

Besides joint ventures and banks, foreign investors also have the option of operating in numerous duty-free zones, initiated in 1988. Such zones now exist in border cities and ports as well as in cities in the interior of the country. The zones are treated as foreign territory for purposes of trade turnover, and exports and imports to and from the zones destined for ultimate export are exempt from export/import licenses, from customs duties, and from all taxes. The zones are managed by both civil law and the 1934 Commercial Code, and the initiators of a zone have the legal right to manage the duty-free area as they please. There are few restrictions on the kinds of economic activity allowed in a zone, other than activity of a "military nature." Financial transactions between the zones and Polish firms must be conducted in convertible currency. The zones have all been established as separate Polish stock companies and may be contracted with directly, bypassing government authorities. The law also provides for the establishment of additional duty-free zones, which, as in the joint venture law, require feasibility studies, specifications of management, and a minimum of $50,000 or its equivalent as the initial investment.

The foreign investment laws and the terms of the duty-free zones were strengthened in March, 1990, when the U.S.–Polish Business and Economic Treaty was signed. Poland had already signed similar bilateral agreements to protect and enhance foreign investments with West Germany, Italy, Austria, Belgium, the United Kingdom, and China. But the agreement was the first for the United States with any former socialist state. The treaty puts American investors on equal footing with all domestic and foreign investors in Poland and provides for internationally recognized protections. Specifically, the treaty guarantees that American firms will have the right to market goods and services at the wholesale and retail level; have access to public utilities and financial institutions; obtain commercial space and materials on a nondiscriminatory basis; obtain necessary permits and licenses expeditiously; and conduct market studies and distribute commercial information of any kind without discrimination. Nondiscrimination is also guaranteed in matters of investment procedure. Poland's application of investment laws guarantees U.S. investors automatic entry into the market within sixty days unless the investor is given reasons for the denial in writing. Environmental standards for U.S. investments will be identical to standards applied to domestic firms. U.S. investors will not be restricted because of Polish economic interests, except in specified and rare situations, which do not include limitations on competition. A number of formal entry permits required of foreign investors will be reviewed for elimination. The treaty also provides for Poland's adherence to internationally recognized standards regarding intellectual property, as outlined by the Paris Act of the Berne Convention. Computer software, integrated circuit layout designs, proprietary information, and the production and processing of pharmaceuticals and chemicals are now all protected. In dispute resolutions, U.S. firms may go to international arbitration after six months, and in cases of expropriation, prompt payment at a fair market value is promised. The U.S.–Polish agreement reaffirms that the repatriation level of zloty profits will be raised to 100 percent by 1996.

Smaller foreign investors have been quick to respond to the new opportunities. Poland has close to 3,000 registered joint ventures led by firms from Germany, Sweden,

Austria, the United States, the UK, and France. But few of the investments exceed $1 million, averaging only slightly more than $150,000. Only slightly more than $100 million has been invested by foreign firms and investors, compared to $800 million in Hungary. Many larger foreign investors have been fearful that Poland's revolution was made by workers and would retain its "socialist" leanings to protect its power base from the hardships of the transition to capitalism. But the government, under the former electrician Lech Walesa, has continuously demonstrated its commitment to a speedy transition. As the legal system has been revised to match that commitment, a burst of new foreign investment is expected.

The foundation of the second stage of Poland's economic reform began with a series of new privatization laws and the creation of a Ministry of Ownership Transformation (MOT) in September, 1990. State firms are to be converted into joint stock or limited-liability firms with 100 percent of their equity held by the State Treasury. Equities are then sold at open auction or by other "competitive" and "public" means within two years of the Treasury's acquisition of the firm. In order to satisfy the demands of workers for a management role, employees have the exclusive right to purchase up to 20 percent of their firm's equity shares at a 50 percent discount. Workers also have the right to appoint one-third of the members of the firm's board of directors until all shares are sold, at which point the shareholders acquire the privilege. In order to satisfy farming interests, farmers too will have the right to discounted share purchases in firms with which they have "long-standing" associations. Foreign purchases of any one firm's equities cannot exceed 10 percent, although the Foreign Investment Agency can allow specific exceptions. (In Hungary, 100 percent foreign ownership is allowed of any firm.)

Shares not bought by workers or foreigners are to be sold to the general public or other Polish firms with MOT permission. Yet other than the former communist elites, few Poles have the funds to buy common stocks. To broaden the base of share ownership, the legislature has proposed discounts for equity purchases and the distribution of vouchers, which can be redeemed for shares to all citizens resident in the country. French financial experts have been retained to create a stock market at which the newly distributed shares can be traded.

The first state enterprises to be sold are the most profitable ones, usually engaged in export for hard currency, and the smallest ones, such as restaurants and shops, which are being sold to their managers. The most unprofitable firms will be dissolved and their plant and equipment sold. Privatization has moved slowly. Only six firms were sold by mid-1991, and the voucher system to provide citizens the opportunity to buy shares has yet to be inaugurated. The government has promised to speed privatization, but without quick returns the government will find itself under continued pressure.

Before his electoral defeat, Mazowiecki's economic successes had been impressive. Inflation had dropped to 5 percent. The zloty had been stabilized at a rate of 9,500 to $1 and had become domestically convertible to hard currencies. Food processing and retailing had been demonopolized. The state budget registered a surplus. The cost of the shock approach, however, especially tight credit, was more severe than anticipated. The economy remains in a deep recession. Living standards have fallen dramatically, and for the first time in postwar history, Poland is experiencing unemployment, already above 1.2 million persons at the close of 1990.

Balcerowicz and his Western advisers disputed the severity of the recession. They argued that there had been price rises, but that at the controlled prices of the communists, no goods had been available. They also argued that economic statistics do not include the private sector or the gray markets, whose output grew by 50 percent in 1990 and accounted for 18 percent of national income, up from slightly more than 10 percent in 1989.

By the inauguration of the presidency of Lech Walesa, the Polish economy was poised for the resumption of rapid economic growth. Credit was loosened, money from the national budget was freed for infrastructure and housing investment, strict wage controls were eased, and the 5,000-item tariff list was cut in half. The results have been positive.

Contrary to earlier predictions, President Walesa has not veered appreciably from Mazowiecki's economic program. He had promised to quicken the pace of change but discovered that even more rapid change would prove unbearable. But he has not sought to reverse Mazowiecki's bold course. Since Walesa's inauguration, unemployment has grown to 8 percent, headed to over 11 percent. Inflation reemerged and, coupled with a drop in hard-currency exports to the West, prompted another zloty devaluation, to Zl 11,000 to $1. Because of the strong dollar, the zloty exchange rate is being maintained against a basket of Western currencies. In the face of these economic pressures, Solidarity's unity has collapsed and Walesa's popularity has plummeted. Walesa's greatest challenge is to maintain his political support until economic reform and privatization yield more widespread material benefits. He has proved to be an exceptionally skilled politician, and he has strong international support. Foreign aid, totaling some $8–$10 billion, will facilitate Poland's transition.

But the processes of transformation and growth will take time, and it is not clear how much time Walesa has. Farmers have demonstrated for subsidies, and workers have protested the coming inevitable bankruptcies. The government has responded by refusing to declare any actual insolvency. Poland is also threatened by the demand of the Soviets for hard currency for their oil. Poland could respond by burning more coal, which already accounts for 79 percent of total domestic energy use. The alternatives—ballooning foreign exchange deficits versus increased environmental damage—are both unpalatable. Despite Walesa's desire for a Polish solution to his nation's problems, he will need a greater Western presence in his economy if he is to maintain the course towards a market economy with economic growth.

Current State of the Economy

Both Poland and Romania incurred massive foreign debts in the 1970s in order to purchase machinery and technologies, which, it was hoped, would boost exports while fostering domestic productivity. The strategy failed in both countries, but each chose a different course for dealing with its debt problems. Ceausescu chose to pay Romania's debts. He deprived the Romanian people of foodstuffs and other goods to increase exports while cutting imports dramatically and forcing the industrial sector into the Stone Age. At great cost to the country, and ultimately to himself, he succeeded in eliminating the country's foreign debts.

Poland's Prime Minister Gierek responded less vigorously. He reduced the import of intermediate and capital goods and made half-hearted efforts to increase exports. But despite a trade surplus with the West after 1981, Poland's foreign debt continued to spiral upward. From 1983 to 1986, the country produced a trade surplus of over $1 billion per year, increasing to over $1.5 billion in 1987 and 1988. But interest arrears from 1981 to 1987 had mounted to over $10 billion. Some $3 billion was needed in each of 1987 and 1988 for debt servicing. Expressed differently, Poland's total exports could grow 4 percent annually. But that was less than half the growth necessary to reach balance of payments equilibrium.

No other factor so thoroughly dominated and dictated the urgency of Poland's reform as did its more than $43 billion hard-currency debt. In the final decade of Polish communism, General Jaruzelski sought to make state enterprises self-dependent, self-financed, and self-managed, all within the structure of a regulated market—an impossible set of goals. The economic managers used their new power to raise prices. In order to appease their workers, they used the new revenues to raise wages. Investment was virtually eliminated—totally in agriculture. Inflation soared and productivity plummeted.

When it became clear that Poland could not repay its debt, international creditors withdrew from Poland. Jaruzelski's legitimacy and authority eroded. In 1988, the General adopted a new course. Driven by massive state printing of zlotys, the government increased investment in industry. Industrial production responded and grew by 5.4 percent. Electronics and electrical engineering showed the strongest growth. But even steel and coal managed 1 percent growth. Goods for export grew by 8 percent. That part of the economy most important to the average consumer—housing and agriculture—did poorly. A general shortage of building supplies, coupled with delivery bottlenecks, reduced housing completions to a record low. Agricultural output declined by 2.3 percent in 1987. In 1988, potato output declined by over 4 percent while grain output declined by 6 percent, the result of sparse spring rains. Sugar beets managed an increase of less than 1 percent, and livestock production grew by slightly more than 1 percent in response to higher state purchase prices.

But accompanying the higher production of goods was rampant inflation. Consumer prices grew by 26 percent in 1987 and jumped over 60 percent in 1988. In the face of a 153 percent increase in government food subsidies in 1988, food prices for the consumer were raised 50 percent while non-food prices were increased by 65 percent. The growth of money produced widespread shortages. In 1988 for example, for every 1,000 zlotys of income, the market delivered goods worth 830 zlotys, down from 880 zlotys in 1987. More telling was the black market exchange rate of zlotys for dollars. In 1987 the average monthly worker's salary in zlotys could purchase only $40 of goods.

In comparison to the early 1980s, 1987 and 1988 were years of modest economic growth. Yet in comparison to the economic needs for debt servicing, the demands of the people for greater economic well-being, and the economy's performance of the 1970s, the end of the 1980s appeared an economic disaster. In 1987, for example, national income was only slightly more than 90 percent of the 1978 total, while national income per capita was less than 90 percent of the 1978 level. The foreign borrowing of the 1970s appeared to have done nothing to improve output in the 1980s. In the final year of communism, Rakowski's year of "freedom, equality, and competitiveness," the economy faltered. Production declined by 3.5 percent. Every branch of industry declined from 2 percent to 8.5 percent, except for light industry, which managed a 0.5 percent increase. The extractive industries dropped over 4 percent, and metal production fell more than 5 percent, with steel output falling over 10 percent. State construction fell 8 percent, while total construction fell only 2 percent because of an 8 percent gain by newly emerging private construction firms. Agricultural output jumped 10 percent, but none of the increased production was sold to the state. It went instead to the gray markets. Foreign trade faltered as well, 1989 being the first year since 1983 without a trade surplus. Accelerating hard-currency imports and interest payments thoroughly eroded the hard-currency account.

By the end of 1989, the regime had lost any semblance of financial control. In the midst of its final political crisis the government lost control of its budget. In 1988, the deficit had reached 66 billion zlotys. By mid-1989, it stood at over 3.5 trillion zlotys, rising to more than 5 trillion by the end of the year. With no other device for satisfying public demands, the government printed money, generating an inflation rate for the year between 850 percent and 1,000 percent. Nominal wages actually grew faster than inflation. But putting new bills into circulation did nothing to produce additional foodstuffs, consumer goods, or services. Instead, living standards plummeted below the level of a decade earlier.

The troubled finances of the state were not the result of its commitment to raising workers' wages. Rather, they were the result of the drain of money and resources demanded, as always, by heavy industry. In its final year under communism, heavy industry absorbed a state subsidy in excess of $8 billion, producing goods for export but consuming three times more energy per unit of output than its Western counterparts. The per capita productivity of the Polish industrial worker was only one-sixth that of the average

Swedish worker, and, according to official Polish government sources, over 60 percent of the workforce lived below the poverty line. More than 40 years of communist economics had exacted a heavy price.

As a result of the strict stabilization program instituted by Prime Minister Mazowiecki, the economy declined dramatically in 1990, with only agriculture managing to produce some growth. The shrinking economy was a mark of the swiftness and seriousness of the reform process. But by the final quarter of 1990, economic gains were recorded relative to the first three quarters. The economy appears to have stabilized and inflation ended through government austerity, the two devaluations of the zloty, the decontrol of prices, the elimination of government subsidies, and the capping of wages. But robust economic growth is still in the future.

The very success of the program has had a devastating effect on both industry and agriculture. The interactive effects of the end of industrial subsidies and the fall in consumer spending as a result of the wage cap and the increasingly erratic energy supplies from the Soviet Union proved especially devastating for many firms. Total economic output declined by 15 to 20 percent. Light industry and food processing registered declines of more than 40 percent. Metallurgy and engineering fell by more than 20 percent, chemicals were off 25 percent, and construction supplies and wood output both registered 27 percent declines. Some of the larger state firms were not as badly hit by the reforms, because they were able to offset decreased subsidies with higher prices through their monopolist positions. While a new antitrust law will allow the government to break the monopolies in the future, they were unchecked in 1990.

But state output figures do not include the production of the emerging private sector, which grew by at least 20 percent—according to some economists, by more than 50 percent—in 1990. The wide variations in the data makes a precise assessment of the impact of the private sector impossible. Yet there has been sensational growth. Best estimates are that the private sector provided jobs for more than 2 million people and expanded from 10 percent to nearly 18 percent of national income by the close of 1990.

While per capita national income remains very low, the purchasing power of the average Polish citizen has improved. By the end of 1990, the average monthly worker's salary expressed in dollars could buy three times what it bought in 1987. Yet the most surprising results of the reform program were evident in the government budget and foreign trade. The state cut its subsidies by more than half, while taxes on profits were larger than expected, leaving the state with a Zl 9 billion surplus used for loans in construction and the food industry. Trade turnover had a staggering turnaround and produced a $3.5 to $4 billion hard-currency surplus.

For the first time in its postwar history, Poland's trade with the West was greater than with the East. Imports were cut more drastically from Poland's former CMEA partners (down some 40 percent) than from the West (down some 20 percent). Exports to the West increased by more than 20 percent, while they fell 10 percent to the East. Some of the $4 billion trade surplus was necessary to pay for the country's oil imports. But the rest was used to service the debt—thus attracting more foreign investment—and for capital goods investment. Consistent with Poland's commitment to establish a productive and modern economy, imports of capital from the West increased by some 20 percent. Other imports fell. Intermediate goods imports fell 20 percent, while imports of consumer goods fell by 30 percent.

Budgetary discipline did more than sober the economy. It also attracted significant Western aid and debt renegotiation as well as grants and trade concessions. Debt relief has come from the World Bank, the IMF, the European Community, the Paris Club, and the United States, but not from the commercial banks. The Paris Club, holding just under 70 percent of the total hard-currency debt, met in early 1990 and rescheduled all past-due principal and interest payments over 14 years, including 8 years of grace on the principal. Interest for the period March 1990 to March 1991 was deferred until 1991 and will likely be deferred again. In 1991, the Paris Club agreed to write off half the Polish debt it holds. New funding from the World Bank includes loans in excess of $2.5 billion, with the IMF adding another $725 million from the Standby Program. The International Finance Corporation, a World Bank subsidiary for private enterprises, has already invested in several Polish firms and has extended credit to the Export Development Bank for funding small-scale enterprises. The International Bank for Reconstruction and Development (IBRD) has granted two loans worth $360 million in the form of an Industrial Export Loan and an Agricultural Industries Export Development Loan, with another $340 million planned for projects in environment, energy, and transport. To aid the currency stabilization program, the United States and West European nations have provided $1 billion in funds, while the European Community has added another $1.3 billion in loans and grants, having already forgiven $3 billion in debt.

Poland has not been successful in its debt renegotiations with commercial banks. In 1989, it paid only 15 percent of the interest due on its commercial debt and made no interest payments in 1990. Discussions have been held with the London Club, the consortium of Western bank lenders, on the $8.8 billion outstanding commercial debt. The banks have indicated a willingness to reschedule the debt, but they refuse to forgive for fear of the precedent.

The United States has added several independent initiatives to the collective aid effort. One program, SEED I, is worth over $850 million and includes $245 million for the enterprise investment fund, $200 million for the Trade Credit Insurance Program, a special export loan fund, and $200 million for the stabilization fund. SEED II took effect in 1991 and added additional funds to SEED I, as well as allowing funds to be targeted for specific national needs and adding another $250 million to the Eastern Europe Development Bank. The U.S. Export-Import Bank provides short-term credit insurance for U.S. exports to Poland, while the Overseas Private Investment Corporation (OPIC) provides insurance and finance. The U.S. Trade and Development Program provides feasibility studies of industrial projects for U.S. exporters and investors. Trade possibilities may also be explored through the ongoing trade missions sponsored by the Department of Commerce. Missions have already included the electric power, food processing, telecommunications, and coal sectors, and there are plans for missions covering energy conservation, technologies, tourism, pollution control, and aerospace. To further encourage U.S. exports, The Coordinating Committee on Export Controls (COCOM) announced in 1990 that it will relax its licensing curbs on the export of telecommunications equipment, computers, and machine tools and will shorten the license review period from 12 to 8 weeks. Taken as a whole, the new U.S. programs are certain to maintain Poland's position as the largest Eastern European importer of U.S. goods.

Polish economic growth should also be stimulated by a new network of offices to assist small private businesses. In 1989, Solidarity established the Economic Foundation to "facilitate the implementation of the radical, free market–oriented economic reform." While this new branch of Solidarity exists on meager funds, its network is extensive. The organization is establishing its own bank, Bank Solidarnosc, S.A., with an American partner, to make loans for small businesses and do personal banking. With the assistance of Western businessmen, the Foundation provides free consulting services and low-cost loans to Polish workers committed to start new businesses. Business management courses are offered in conjunction with local universities. There are plans for business schools in Gdansk and Wroclaw as well as for centers to train workers in the skills of modern industries. The Foundation has also collected data on all state firms committed to establishing joint ventures with Western investors. No other Eastern European state, except Hungary, has produced such information. While still crude by Western business standards, the data reflect the intense efforts of Solidarity to move Poland towards a market economy based on a bedrock of small private firms.

Economy from Origins to 1945

The industrialization of the Polish economy occurred in the 18th century while it was partitioned by Russia, Prussia, and Austria. Prior to the partition, the economy had been dominated by agriculture and mining. After World War I, the economy of independent Poland was stunted by backwardness relative to its neighbors and by the world depression. Of the northern Soviet satellites—Poland, Czechoslovakia, and East Germany—only Poland was truly transformed by Stalin. It emerged from Soviet control as an industrialized state, while its economic development resembled that of its former communist compatriots in the Balkans.

Because of its long relationship with more developed states and its political tradition of partial civil liberties, Poland's agriculture had been prosperous for centuries. As early as the mid-15th century, grain from the Vistula river basin was shipped from the port of Danzig, now Gdansk. The trade encouraged the development of commerce and banking. It also strengthened the hold of the large landowners on the land, while stimulating a host of small manufacturing concerns for processing, transporting, and trading grain. The first surpluses of corn and rye coincided with the formation of political unity and encouraged an influx of foreign, mostly Dutch, merchants. The internal market grew rapidly as did foreign trading relationships. European ships brought manufactured goods, fuels, tools, alcohol, fish, and salt. Overland, the Germans traded metals and tools from Silesia, and the Russians traded cattle hides and fur pelts, all in exchange for Polish corn, rye, wool, timber, metals, and flax.

By the mid-17th century, after two hundred prosperous years, foreign demand for Polish grain diminished as European states developed their own agricultural production. Diminishing returns on serf-operated manors and an upsurge of wars contributed to the century-long decline.

In the 1750s, despite the absence of fundamental economic change, landlords and feudal barons began a process of improving their estates by raising the technological level of cottage industries. The partitioning powers, however, developed both the agricultural and the industrial sectors, leaving Poland an industrialized country following World War I.

When independence came, Poland could not take full advantage of its prewar prosperity, because it had accumulated the legacies of three distinct imperial systems. In every sector of the economy, three different ways of doing business prevailed. The effort to centralize the state was frustrated because the partitioners conducted tariff wars among themselves, leaving Poland almost always the loser in their struggles.

A classic example of the legacy of partition can be seen in the extensive railroad system inherited by Poland. At the outbreak of the First World War, Poland could boast trains with three different braking systems and two different track gauges. Forty of the fifty lines of track that ran from Prussia and Austria into Poland did not continue into Russia. The fragmented transportation system was illustrative of the economy as a whole. Yet Poland might still have succeeded in strengthening its fledgling industrial base if its territory had not been the primary killing grounds of two world wars.

Silesia, now in northern Poland, was ruled by Prussia and was the mining and manufacturing center of the partitioned territories. Because the territory was rich in salt, coal, lead, zinc, and silver, it became of great importance to the Germans, second only to the Ruhr, and was developed solely as an adjunct of the German economy. The benefits to Poland were limited to jobs for Polish workers. In the Prussian territory, referred to as Greater Poland and Pomerania, agriculture was as prosperous as industry. It, too, enriched only the Germans.

Serfdom was abolished in 1850, and property rights were granted to Polish peasants, but, protected by high tariffs and finding a ready market for their foodstuffs in the German industrial centers, the peasants lacked incentives to become efficient producers. At the same time, in hopes of maintaining large German-dominated estates, Prussia provided

German landowners with easy credit. Over time, the farming regions came to resemble a German colony. Poles provided the labor while Germans were the owners and managers, creating a system that came to dominate not only the Prussian-held territories but the other two partition territories as well.

In contrast to the robust economic health of Silesia, the poorest of the partition regions was Galicia, held by Austria. Although serfdom had been abolished there in 1848, the small peasant landholdings, coupled with the low return on agricultural products, kept life at subsistence levels. The region never became self-sufficient in food, and industry was barely present. Salt and coal were mined but little else developed, as a result of a limited home market, a shortage of capital, and the stunting effect of more powerful industries in the Czech and Austrian territories. Until the discovery of oil and gas in the 1850s, the entire region was more of a liability to Austria than an asset. But with English and Canadian drilling, the region was producing more than 2,000 tons oil by the 1880s, rising to over 2 million tons in the first decade of the 20th century. For Europe the reserves were significant, less important only than the fields of Russia and Romania. As so often in Polish history, war brought tragic destruction. As it retreated in 1915, the Russian army destroyed the wells. Postwar oil production did not approach preindependence levels until the 1960s.

The third section of Poland, known as the Kingdom of Poland or as the Congress Kingdom (since partition was conducted by the Congress of Vienna), was under the tutelage of the Russian empire. In economic terms, its development fell somewhere between the wealthier, industrialized Silesia and the impoverished, agricultural Galicia. But unlike the Prussian or the Austrian partitions, in the Congress Kingdom Polish entrepreneurs played a significantly larger role.

In the first half of the 19th century, lacking capital and an industrial base, the Polish Kingdom had only modest success in its efforts to promote industrial development on the back of its semi-feudal society. During the second half of the century, however, aristocratic landowners took the initiative. Largely because of its location, Poland began to be drawn into the wider European market as the link between the advanced German market and the backward domains of Russia. European capital, machinery, trade, and skilled labor flowed freely through the territory after the 1860s, combining with the earlier private Polish initiatives and stimulating a flurry of activity in textiles, mining, and metallurgical industries.

Textiles developed in the area of Lodz and Bialystok. Mining and heavy industry developed in the Dabrowskie region, and food processing, engineering, and textiles grew in the greater Warsaw area. Textile manufacturing grew the most rapidly to supply the Russian market. Poland exported other manufactured goods as well in exchange for Russia's raw materials. By the end of the 19th century, more than 70 percent of Poland's trade was with Russia. Generous protective tariffs, when they were granted, safeguarded the Russian market for Polish industries against German and Austrian competition. Not that the Russians were beyond removing the safeguards. In the 1830s, the tariffs were removed, and Polish industry stagnated until the tariffs were restored in 1850. After the 1850s, Polish textiles outstripped the German and Austrian competition. As growth became more constant, small Polish firms evolved into larger and larger joint stock firms, driven by foreign management and foreign capital. In the process, they established Polish textiles as a major European producer.

Yet the Kingdom of Poland was not yet an industrialized state. Even at the height of its industrialization, its agriculture was dominant and the vast majority of Poles continued to cultivate the land. But they could never grow enough food to feed their population. The inputs for a more sophisticated agriculture were present. Cheap labor was plentiful, machinery and fertilizers were also available, but low prices for food lowered agricultural profits, discouraging investment and preserving the antiquated agricultural system. Food imports from Russia became the norm.

Although the agricultural system did not drive the national economy, it nonetheless was responsible for the emergence of thousands of small and medium-sized firms, whose sustenance was related to the agricultural sector and which were built with limited home capital. Mining and manufacturing enterprises were major contributors to economic well-being, but the most important share came from small, local enterprises—sawmills, tanneries, breweries, paperwork, and most importantly, food processors. Throughout the 19th century, from the beginning of industrialization until the last decade before World War I, these were the major sources of employment for Polish workers, and they produced the only true Polish entrepreneurial class.

Yet being capital-poor, these small firms never produced an industrial base sufficient to employ the expanding population. As a consequence, waves of migration sent Poles streaming westward from all the partitioned territories. Over a million Poles left their homelands between 1870 and 1910, while another 500,000 left in 1912 and 1913. Most left for the United States and Canada, but many chose work in Germany.

The disruptions of those migrations did not compare to the mass destruction and carnage of World War I. During the war, both the Russians and the Germans looted the cities and the countryside. Besides the destruction from battle, the retreating Russian army removed whole industrial plants and instituted a scorched-earth policy over what was left. For the Germans, the policy of taking war booty was slightly different. They continued to operate some factories, pushing all mining and raw material production to breakneck capacity to supply German factories. Metal ores, coal, copper, cotton, wool, wood, and machines were all plundered for German industrial consumption. The cost of the war to the Polish economy was estimated in excess of 70,000 million French francs. So thorough was the damage that as late as 1920, only the oil and coal industries were operating at more than 50 percent of prewar levels. Employment in 1918 was not more than 15 percent of what it had been in 1914.

In the aftermath of the War, Poland did gain its political unity and its independence. But the challenges of the postwar era consumed the strength of the new government. It had to deal with the ruin of war and forge one nation and one infrastructure from territories that had been distributed among three empires for more than a century.

Ironically, the war with the newly declared Soviet Union, fought in late 1919 and 1920, was the most important stimulus to postwar economic recovery. The war was short and not destructive. The industries that were geared up for military production were speedily converted consumer goods. More importantly, however, the extraordinary demand for production led to the creation of many new firms, breaking the power of the cartels. The nature of industrial production changed as well, as factories produced for the domestic markets rather than those of the former empires. Both the mining and textile industries declined while the mineral and chemical, food-processing, and, especially, building and construction–related industries were developed. The economic changes reflected a system undergoing the painful process of rationalization to fulfill the needs of the newly unified state.

Before 1920, the Polish mark traded for the dollar at the ratio of 9 to 1. In the early 1920s, it took 15,000,000 marks to buy $1, a rate that makes the Polish inflation of 1989 and 1990 seem trivial. Remarkably, in the 1920s the Polish government stabilized its currency and even attracted Western loans as investments in industry and public works. No sooner did recovery seem assured than the world depression devastated the weaker world economies. On the eve of the Nazi occupation of 1939, neither gross industrial production nor steel, coal, and oil output had yet reached their 1913 levels. The percentage of the workforce employed in industry was actually lower than at the turn of the century. Two decades of independence had proved insufficient to make good on the prior century of division, destruction, and exploitation.

Economy from 1945 to 1990

The communist control of Poland was similar, at least in one crucial respect, to the earlier period of partition. Communist rule was more brutal and its economic system was different. But in both periods, the economy of Poland was made to serve the needs of the dominant state. The economic policies proved destructive for Poland itself.

Converting the entire economy to state ownership and management was, of course, economically absurd for all the satellites. What made it particularly alien in Poland was the industrial sector, which had been established during the period of Polish independence. A small but growing entrepreneurial class had used the mineral and energy wealth of the country to build small and medium-sized firms to satisfy the demands of a domestic market.

But the industrialization forced on Poland by Stalin flew in the face of the history of Polish economic development. Add to that the inefficiencies and irrationalities inherent in Stalinist economic policies, as well as the long history of pervasive mutual hatred between Poles and Russians, and the result was the overall failure of Bolshevik industrial policies in Poland.

The Nazi occupation had actually facilitated the communists' task of converting Poland to a planned economy because of the vast destruction caused by the German and Soviet occupations. Moreover, the German military government had nationalized and consolidated Polish industry into conglomerates. The foundation for a planned economy had been prepared before the communists arrived on the scene.

In the initial stages of the German occupation in 1939, Polish industry, predominantly in Warsaw, was only marginally damaged. The Nazis chose to continue to operate the factories using Polish labor. The most technically efficient plants and machinery, usually brought on-line in the late 1930s, were dismantled and shipped to the German heartland. But the rest of Polish industry remained and was restructured to fulfill the needs of the German army. A division of labor was imposed by the Germans, requiring small and medium-sized firms to consolidate, destroying nearly all the artisan and trade shops, which were the life blood of the young economy. Consolidation meant the collapse of over 65 percent of the firms in Warsaw, with consumer industries being hardest hit.

For the Germans, the new system worked well. In the firms operated for the German army, especially those in mining, oil, and raw materials, output was significantly raised. For the Poles it meant the complete exhaustion of their industrial facilities, as the Nazis worked the industrial plant around the clock with little maintenance and no replacement of equipment.

As a result, by 1943 economic decline had begun. Soon after, the retreating Reich, following the old Russian tactic, destroyed everything it could not relocate to Germany. Other than the Soviet Union, no other country experienced such tremendous human and economic losses as did Poland. More than 40 percent of its population was either killed in concentration camps, resettled as forced labor, or displaced because of the fighting. In economic terms, the propertied members of the population were liquidated, including the entire Jewish community, and the better part of those who were the entrepreneurs. It is estimated that World War I had destroyed approximately 10 percent of Poland's property. World War II destroyed nearly 40 percent of the nation's wealth.

The 1945 Yalta settlement partially compensated Poland, in which it acquired industrialized areas of Germany. However, these industries were in dilapidated condition and linked totally to the German and not the Polish economy. Furthermore, for those Polish firms left standing, the entrepreneurial relationships forged among firms during the Polish independence had been destroyed, replaced with an alien Nazi form.

The Soviets participated more directly in the reconstruction and development of the economy of Poland than in that of any other state. Poland had no other sources of capital investment or trade, and the result was total Soviet economic dominance. Having no transportation connections with any other country, for example, Poland imported exclusively from the Soviets.

The first order of communist business was to nationalize the vast majority of firms, specifically those owned by Germans, controlled by Germans in joint stock arrangements, run by anyone who had fled to the side of the enemy, or staffed by at least 50 employees. Employment in state-operated firms exceeded 85 percent of the labor force by 1947, increasing to 90 percent in 1949. Priority industries were mining, heavy industry (with an emphasis on processing mined goods such as chemicals, coal, and oil) and most importantly, mechanical engineering.

From the very beginning it was apparent that Moscow intended the Polish economy to focus on producer goods. More than 75 percent of all investment capital was allocated to the producer goods industry. Agriculture was ignored.

But Polish heavy industries were grossly inefficient in terms of energy and raw materials consumption. Czechoslovakia and East Germany were already producing the goods that Polish factories were instructed to make, and Poland found itself competing with its two strongest CMEA partners from an inferior position. Still, the commitment to heavy industry never changed. In the late 1950s, machinery accounted for 20 percent of exports, growing to slightly less than 40 percent in 1970, and totaling more than 50 percent of all exports to other socialist countries. The production of engines, machinery, and processed goods grew two to three times faster than the production of the primary goods that supplied these industries. Poland's raw material supplies were soon exhausted.

During the first decade under communism, Soviet engineers and specialists oversaw the construction of almost all of Poland's industrial complexes, merging them into the Soviet military-industrial complex. The industries built in the first decade remained dominant throughout the communist era. In the 1980s they still accounted for one-third of Poland's industrial production, including close to 60 percent of the steel production and almost all of the oil and iron production. The focused effort naturally yielded tremendous growth, spawning a host of industries related to the processing and machinery industries. Automobile, shipbuilding, and aircraft industries were developed. Yet growth was produced overwhelmingly by increasing the factors of production through greater investment and higher levels of employment. The increases were not generated by enhancing the technological sophistication of the production processes. By the 1970s, Poland was the first East bloc state to be in an obvious economic crisis.

Polish agriculture had its own crisis. It had developed in an entirely different way from other East bloc states. Agriculture recovered very quickly following the war, and as a result, planners assumed that targets for the sector could be set unreasonably high without appreciable new investment. Along with setting higher output targets, planners forced collectivization to "rationalize" the farm and free up surplus labor for industrial projects. Collectivization called for destroying the farm buildings that dominated the countryside and ending the "horse and plow" system of farming.

The communist system totally disrupted traditional agriculture. Food shortages quickly developed. The state demanded that peasants increase their grain deliveries. Instead, farmers withdrew their grain, destroyed it in protest, or simply stopped working. Peasant resistance only quickened the resolve of communist planners. In 1950 there were 2,200 cooperative farms. By 1956, there were over 10,500. Those few cooperatives that managed to secure reasonable machinery produced relatively high yields of grain. Individual farms, still a majority of the land in 1956, proved superior at producing potatoes and sugar beets and at conducting husbandry. In 1956, in the face of continued food shortages, the planners retreated and authorized the dissolution of the nonproductive cooperative farms.

The results were dramatic. In less than one year the number of cooperatives dropped from 10,500 to less than 1,700. The majority of the cooperative land was returned to individual farmers. In addition, there was a concerted effort to increase investments in industries producing farm machinery and fertilizers. But the revision of the cooperative system proved a failure as well. Private agriculture was restored, but the state continued to impose strict limits on individual farmers. They were required to fill quotas of various foodstuffs, but they were not free to hire additional labor or use fertilizers or other inputs except as specified by the state.

Private farming in Poland became an extension of the planned economy. By splitting the difference between cooperative farming and private farming, the state guaranteed the worst of both worlds.

Faced with these crises, the government chose to embark on a Western-financed modernization program. The scheme seemed ideal—to finance modernization with Western funds, which would be paid back with the revenues from exports generated by the new technologies. Bankers were willing to lend on the assumption that Poland, and all the satellites, were implicitly being underwritten by the Soviets. The credits financed a flow of imports, which became an addiction. Licenses for technology were bought from Germany, France, and the United States. Huge quantities of machinery were imported to raise the capacity of Poland's traditional heavy industries. The amount of capital formation as a portion of national income was higher than at any other period in Poland's communist history.

New investment projects, however, threw good money after bad and bore no relationship to the needs or the capacities of the domestic economy. In the early 1970s optimism had abounded. Living standards were rising and consumer goods were readily available. But from the start of the Western borrowing, there was no economic reform. Western capital was allocated not on the grounds of economic efficiency but on the basis of power within the planning bureaucracy. The investment in the largest conglomerates strained Poland's capacity to supply raw materials and energy resources, creating shortages that were felt throughout the economy. Thus, by the end of the 1970s, the "modernization" had left Poland more dependent on imports of raw materials and semi-finished goods. Energy demand grew more than sevenfold during the decade, and the economy became more centralized. At the time of the imposition of martial law, a mere 10 percent of Poland's enterprises were providing over 60 percent of total industrial production. Yet none were generating the levels of production necessary to pay back the borrowed funds.

By the middle of the 1970s, debt servicing was absorbing over a third of export income. By the early 1980s, debt service exceeded foreign earnings by more than 150 percent. Poland was effectively bankrupt, but the planners were not deterred. Long after the rise of Solidarity, communist planners were implementing over 1,600 investment projects. For the rest of the decade, living standards fell as quickly as Poland's credit rating. The communist system was about to collapse.

FURTHER READING

Ascherson, Neal. *The Polish August*. New York: The Viking Press, 1982.

Ash, Timothy Garton. "Eastern Europe: Après le Deluge, Nous." *The New York Review of Books* 37, no. 13 (August 16, 1990): 51–7.

Davies, Norman. *Heart of Europe*. Oxford: Oxford University Press, 1986.

———. *God's Playground: A History of Poland*. 2 vol. New York: Columbia University Press, 1982.

Sachs, Jeffrey, and David Lipton. "Poland's Economic Reform." *Foreign Affairs* 69, 3 (Summer 1990): 47–69.

DATA AND VITAL STATISTICS

5. Principal trading partners
4. Index of import and export prices, and terms of trade
5. Major imports and exports
6. Trade with western countries
7. Trade with the USSR, by commodity
8. Trade with the United States, by commodity

Note: Where possible and relevant, Poland is compared to Spain, because they are of comparable population. Also, data for the United States, France, USSR, and other East European countries is provided for comparison where relevant.

I. AGRICULTURE

TABLE 1.I.1 Land use, 1990

		(Percent)			
Arable Land	Permanent Crops	Forest and Woodland	Meadows and Pastures	Other	Irrigated Land
46	1	28	13	12	Negligible

Source: U.S. Central Intelligence Agency, *The World Factbook,* 1991.

TABLE 1.I.2 Agriculture production index (Poland and selected countries)

	(1980 = 100)				
Country	1965	1970	1980	1986	1990
Poland	81	100	100	130	125
USSR	83	99	100	120	118
United States	79	81	100	107	112
France	77	81	100	105	105[a]

[a] 1989 data.

Source: U. S. Central Intelligence Agency, *Handbook of Economic Statistics,* 1991.

TABLE 1.I.3 Selected indicators of agricultural development, 1970–1985

	1971–1975	1976–1980	1981–1985
Agricultural land use[a]			
Arable	14,586	14,440	14,394
Natural grassland	4,196	4,077	4,069
Other agricultural land	552	534	417
Crop structure[b]			
Grain	57	56	58
Maize	N/A	N/A	N/A
Oilseeds	2	2	2
Fodder roots, silage maize	4	6	5
Cultivated grassland	11	12	13
Beet	3	4	3
Potatoes, vegetables	20	18	17
Other	3	2	2

[a] In thousands of hectares; 1 hectare = 2.471 acres.

[b] Percent of sown area.

(continued)

TABLE 1.I.3 *(continued)*

	1971–1975	1976–1980	1981–1985
Total outputs[c] 1982 prices			
Gross[d]	3.2	.6	−0.5
Net[d]	.1	−2.9	−0.5
Arable output[c]			
Total (gross) 1982 prices	2.4	−0.3	1.2
Grain	4.1	−1.5	2.7
Oilseeds	1.0	2.7	1.6
Coarse fodder	6.7	4.4	−2.3
Livestock output[c]			
Total (gross) 1982 prices	4.1	1.7	−2.0
Meat	4.7	2.5	−3.3
Milk	1.8	.9	−1.0
Eggs	3.1	2.4	−.8

[c] Annualized percentage changes between five-year periods.
[d] Gross output is total yield before harvest. Net output reflects losses following processing.
Source: UN, *Economic Survey of Europe in 1987–1988.*

TABLE 1.I.4 Total grain production[a] (Poland and selected countries)

	(Million Metric Tons)				
	1960	1970	1980	1985	1990
Poland	14.30	16.26	18.34	23.74	28.02
USSR[b]	125.49	186.80	189.09	191.67	238.00
United States	181.26	186.72	269.68	347.01	312.14
France	23.02	31.29	47.36	55.07	55.38

[a] Data are for the following products where they are produced: barley, corn, oats, rice, rye, sorghum, and wheat.
[b] Includes miscellaneous grains and legumes. For comparative purposes, an average discount of 11% should be applied because USSR totals include excess moisture, unripe and damaged kernels, weed seeds, and other trash.
Source: U. S. Central Intelligence Agency, *Handbook of Economic Statistics,* 1989, 1990, 1991.

TABLE 1.I.5 Principal crops

	(Thousand Metric Tons)		
	1985	1987	1989
Potatoes	36,546	36,252	34,390
Sugar Beets	14,644	13.989	14,374
Wheat	4,461	7,942	8,462
Rye	7,600	6,816	6,216
Barley	4,086	4,335	3,909
Mixed Grain	2,751	3,314	3,466
Oats	2,682	2,428	2,185
Cabbages	1,570	1,793	1,617
Rapeseed	1,073	1,186	1,586
Carrots	682	771	756

Source: The Europa World Year Book, 1989, 1990, 1991.

TABLE 1.I.6 Yields for selected crops (Poland and selected countries)

| | | (ql/ha)^a | | |
		1985	1987	1989
Wheat	Poland	34.3	37.2	38.5
	Bulgaria	28.7	38.2	47.7
	Czechoslovakia	49.3	50.8	51.2
	Hungary	48.3	43.7	52.4
	Romania	23.4	28.0	35.8^b
	Yugoslavia	36.0	36.0	42.0^b
	Soviet Union	15.5	17.8	19.4
Barley	Poland	32.9	33.7	33.3
	Bulgaria	30.7	37.0	43.6
	Czechoslovakia	44.3	42.3	47.2
	Hungary	37.3	38.2	46.8
	Romania	25.9	36.0	44.8
	Yugoslavia	27.0	24.0	28.0^b
	Soviet Union	16.0	19.1	17.5
Maize	Poland	43.0	46.0	47.8
	Bulgaria	30.7	37.2	40.0
	Czechoslovakia	54.4	56.4	52.7
	Hungary	62.9	61.3	62.2
	Romania	38.5	27.0	24.7
	Yugoslavia	41.0	40.0	34.0^b
	Soviet Union	32.1	32.4	37.1
Rye	Poland	24.7	25.8	27.3
	Bulgaria	14.9	16.6	20.4
	Czechoslovakia	34.0	34.9	40.5
	Hungary	19.3	19.5	27.3^b
	Romania	15.0	14.9	16.2
	Yugoslavia	17.0	17.0	19.0^b
	Soviet Union	16.5	18.6	18.6
Oats	Poland	27.0	28.4	27.2
	Bulgaria	13.9	14.8	27.0
	Czechoslovakia	37.4	37.3	32.3
	Hungary	29.6	23.9	32.5
	Romania	12.8	15.7	15.9
	Soviet Union	16.3	15.7	15.7
Potatoes	Poland	174	187	185
	Bulgaria	109	86	137
	Czechoslovakia	184	171	186
	Hungary	196	160	186
	Romania	204	129	124
	Yugoslavia	88	81	70^b
	Soviet Union	113	121	120
Sugar beets	Poland	336	332	340
	Bulgaria	168	188	246
	Czechoslovakia	377	355	352
	Hungary	379	363	440
	Romania	223	201	265
	Yugoslavia	418	380	349^b
	Soviet Union	241	266	291

^{a}ql: quintal = 100 kg (220.46 lbs); ha: hectare = 10,000 m^2 (2.471 acres).
^{b}1988 data.

Source: EUROSTAT, *Central and Eastern Europe 1991,* 1991; *Comecon Data 1989,* 1990.

TABLE 1.I.7 Livestock (Poland and selected countries)

		(Thousand Head)		
		1980	**1985**	**1989**
Horses	Poland	1,780	1,324	992[a]
	Bulgaria	120	120	119
	Czechoslovakia	45	46	42
	Hungary	120	98	76[a]
	Romania	555	672	663
	Yugoslavia	N/A	N/A	N/A
	Soviet Union	5,563	5,782	5,920
Cattle	Poland	11,337	11,774	10,277
	Bulgaria	1,843	1,735	1,600
	Czechoslovakia	5,002	5,066	5,129
	Hungary	1,918	1,766	1,698
	Romania	6,485	6,692	6,291
	Yugoslavia	5,474	5,034	4,759[a]
	Soviet Union	115,057	120,888	118,429
Dairy cows	Poland	5,666	5,331	4,964
	Bulgaria	723	682	633
	Czechoslovakia	1,902	1,860	1,795
	Hungary	765	688	646
	Romania	2,670	2,901	2,468
	Yugoslavia	3,086	2,915	2,858[a]
	Soviet Union	43,389	42,863	41,716
Pigs	Poland	18,734	19,170	18,686
	Bulgaria	3,808	3,912	4,353
	Czechoslovakia	7,894	6,651	7,498
	Hungary	8,330	8,280	7,661
	Romania	11,542	13,631	11,671
	Yugoslavia	7,867	7,821	7,396[a]
	Soviet Union	73,382	77,772	79,033
Sheep	Poland	3,490	4,720	4,196
	Bulgaria	10,433	9,724	7,973
	Czechoslovakia	910	1,087	1,051
	Hungary	3,090	2,465	2,068
	Romania	15,865	17,342	15,435
	Yugoslavia	7,384	7,693	7,564[a]
	Soviet Union	141,573	14,850	138,443
Goats	Poland	10	10	10
	Bulgaria	467	460	433
	Czechoslovakia	57	53	50[a]
	Hungary	15	16	16
	Romania	347	828	1,070[a]
	Yugoslavia	N/A	N/A	N/A
	Soviet Union	5,925	6,480	6,974
Hens	Poland	76.1	66.2	55.6
	Bulgaria	39.9	37.9	37.3
	Czechoslovakia	45.3	45.4	46.6
	Hungary	61.0	56.7	52.8
	Romania	97.8	120.1	114.0
	Yugoslavia	N/A	N/A	N/A
	Soviet Union	967.3	1,109.9	1,151.0

[a] 1988 data.
[b] In millions.

Source: EUROSTAT, *Central and Eastern Europe 1991,* 1991; *Comecon Data 1989,* 1990.

TABLE 1.I.8 Slaughterings and production of selected animal products (Poland and selected countries)

		Production of Selected Animal Products (Thousand Tons)				Slaughterings (Thousands)		
		1980	1985	1989		1985	1987	1989
Beef	Poland	866	900	789	Cattle	4,290	4,049	3,425
	Bulgaria	167	163	159	and	704	651	601
	Czechoslovakia	468	467	460	calves	1,804	1,710	1,733
	Hungary	215	180	170		525	471	435
	Romania	285	240	230[a]		1,772	1,570	1,510
	Yugoslavia	344	352	301[a]		N/A	N/A	N/A
	Soviet Union	7,367	8,278	8,780		36,659	41,800	43,300
Pork	Poland	1,526	1,773	1,880	Pigs	16,169	19,082	19,210
	Bulgaria	390	434	482		4,582	5,086	5,364
	Czechoslovakia	853	891	971		8,180	8,495	9,124
	Hungary	1,100	1,113	1,112		11,301	11,589	11,830
	Romania	975	900	840		12,500	11,539	11,218
	Yugoslavia	461	526	546[a]		N/A	N/A	N/A
	Soviet Union	5,835	6,299	6,737		72,248	77,000	78,000
Mutton	Poland	39	47	43	Sheep	1,347	1,654	1,580[a]
and	Bulgaria	126	116	112	and	5,705	5,907	5,481[a]
goat	Czechoslovakia	12	13	12	lambs	1,380	1,457	1,500[a]
meat	Hungary	23	18	21		429	261	285
	Romania	81	70	67[a]		4,412	3,880	4,700[b]
	Yugoslavia	59	63	70[a]		N/A	N/A	N/A
	Soviet Union	827	905	993		52,646	56,579	57,600[b]
Poultry	Poland	290	345	381	Goats	23	15	15
	Bulgaria	158	169	188		385	413	404[a]
	Czechoslovakia	172	194	233		1,700	1,875	1,562[a]
	Hungary	405	469	445		50	54	53[a]
	Romania	475	425	390		468	508	547
	Yugoslavia	277	299	329[a]		N/A	N/A	N/A
	Soviet Union	2,811	3,116	3,357		N/A	N/A	N/A
Milk	Poland	16,446	15,543	16,429				
	Bulgaria	2,357	2,590	2,512				
	Czechoslovakia	6,942	6,982	7,150				
	Hungary	2,729	2,833	2,942				
	Romania	5,411	5,165	4,667				
	Yugoslavia	4,352	4,682	4,638[a]				
	Soviet Union	98,608	103,743	108,529				

[a] 1988 data.
[b] Inlcuding goats.

Source: EUROSTAT, *Central and Eastern Europe 1991,* 1991; *Comecon Data 1989,* 1990.

TABLE 1.I.9 Agricultural labor force and tractors, 1988 (Poland and selected countries)

	Percent of Labor Force in Agriculture	Population per km^2 of Arable Land	Output per Worker in $	Tractors per 10 km^2
Poland	22.2	261	1,957	33.4
USSR	14.2	125	3,830	45.3
United States	2.5	131	33,519	10.8
OECD average	8.1	809	23,334	18.2

Source: The Economist, *Book of Vital World Statistics,* 1990.

TABLE 1.I.10 Agricultural output, 1988 (Poland and selected countries)

	(Thousand Tons)			
	Cereals	**Meat**	**Vegetables**	**Fruit**
Poland	24,504	2,894	5,505	2,173
OECD average[a]	12,362	1,830	3,685	3,272
East bloc average[b]	19,125	2,024	3,523	2,582

[a]Excluding the United States.

[b]Excluding Albania.

Source: The Economist, *Book of Vital World Statistics*, 1990.

TABLE 1.I.11 Growth per capita in agriculture and food, 1977–1988 (Poland and selected countries)

	Agriculture	**Food**
Poland	.1	.1
USSR	.4	.5
United States	1.4	1.4
France	1.3	1.3

Source: The Economist, *Book of Vital World Statistics*, 1990.

II. COMMUNICATIONS AND TRANSPORT

TABLE 1.II.1 General facts, 1990

1. Communications

Telecommunications
  Stations   30 AM, 28 FM, 41 TV
  Televisions (1987)   9,868,000 (1 per 3.8 persons)
  Radio receivers (1987)   10,845,000 (1 per 3.5 persons)
  Telephones (1987)   4,618,000 (1 per 8.2 persons)

2. Transport

Railroads
    27,041 km total (1989)
    24,287 km 1.435-meter standard gauge
    11,016 km electrified, government-owned
     8,987 km double track
     2,357 km narrow gauge
       397 km 1.524-meter broad gauge

Highways
   299,887 km total, of which
   130,000 km improved hard surface (1985)

Inland
  Waterways
     3,997 km navigable rivers and canals (1989)

Pipelines
     1,986 km crude oil
       360 km refined products
     4,500 km natural gas (1987)

Airports
       160   total, including
        85   with permanent-surface runways

Source: U.S. Central Intelligence Agency, *The World Factbook*, 1991; *The Europa World Yearbook*, 1990.

TABLE 1.II.2 Radio and television receivers (Poland and selected countries)

| | (per Thousand Inhabitants) | | | |
	1970	1975	1980	1986–88
Poland				
Radios	174	239	244	294
TVs	130	190	224	263
USSR				
Radios	390	481	490	686
TVs	143	217	305	314
United States				
Radios	1,415	1,857	1,989	2,120
TVs	413	560	684	811
France				
Radios	315	326	743	995
TVs	216	269	354	333[a]

[a]1987 data.

Source: UN, *Statistical Yearbook,* 1988; UN, *Human Development Report 1991,* 1991.

TABLE 1.II.3 Percentage of households owning various consumer durables, 1986–1988[a] (Poland and selected countries)

| | (Percent) | | | |
	Televisions	Radios	Refrigerators	Vacuum Cleaners
Poland	70	79	91	15
USSR	45	96	N/A	N/A
United States	98	99	100	N/A
France	98	98	97	88

[a]Means data for each country may refer to 1986, 1987, or 1988.

Source: The Economist, *Book of Vital World Statistics,* 1990.

TABLE 1.II.4 Daily newspapers (Poland and selected countries)

Country	1970	1975	1979	1986–88
Poland	43	44	44	45
USSR[a]	639	691	N/A	723[b]
United States	1,763	1,775	1,787	1,657
France[c]	106	92	90	92

[a]Data include nondaily newspapers.

[b]1984 data.

[c]Data shown for 1975 and 1979 refer to 1976 and 1978 respectively.

Source: UNESCO, *Statistical Yearbook,* 1989.

TABLE 1.II.5   Transport traffic

	1980	1987	1989
Road traffic			
Passengers (millions)			
(excl. municipal buses)	2,379	2,487	2,564
Freight (million metric tons)	237	105	95
Passenger-km (billions)	49.2	54.0	58.1
Ton-km (millions)	11,106	9,712	9,476
Railway traffic			
Passengers (millions)	1,215	1,102	1,047
Freight (million metric tons)	482	429	389
Passenger-km (billions)	51.3	53.9	60.9
Ton-km (billions)	134.7	121.4	111.1
Inland waterway traffic[a]			
Passengers (millions)	9.4	6.6	5.8
Freight (million metric tons)	22.2	14.8	14.0
Passenger-km (millions)	126.6	80.1	67.7
Ton-km (millions)	2,325	1,519	1,193
Sea traffic			
Passengers (millions)	.3	.4	.7
Freight (million metric tons)	39.6	30.2	28.3
Passenger-km (millions)	272	234	251
Ton-km (billions)	257	197	212
Air traffic			
Passengers (thousands)	1,828	1,858	2,305
Freight (thousand metric tons)	17.2	9.2	12.1
Passenger-km (millions)	2,714	3,340	4,887
Ton-km (millions)	30.1	19.5	39.8

[a]On domestically registered ships.

Source: EUROSTAT, *Central and Eastern Europe 1991,* 1991.

TABLE 1.II.6   Railroad freight, (Poland and selected countries)

Country	1960	1970	1985	1989
Poland				
Billion metric ton-km	66.5	99.3	120.6	110.2
Million metric tons carried	286.9	382.3	419.4	428.0
Poland as a percent of				
Eastern Europe[a]				
Billion metric ton-km	35.6%	35.0%	32.8%[b]	N/A
Million metric tons carried	30.8%	30.9%	27.2%[b]	N/A
USSR				
Billion metric ton-km	1,504.3	2,494.7	3,718.4	3,924.8[c]
Million metric tons carried	1,884.9	2,896.0	3,951.0	4,000.0
United States				
Billion metric ton-km	868.5	1,141.0	1,288.3	1,473.9
Million metric tons carried	1,180.5	1,426.3	1,567.0	1,792.0
France				
Billion metric ton-km	56.9	70.4	58.5	52.7
Million metric tons carried	227.0	260.0	193.0	174.0

[a]Eastern Europe includes: Bulgaria, Czechoslovakia, East Germany, Hungary, Poland, and Romania.

[b]Latest available data.

[c]1988 data.

Source: U.S. Central Intelligence Agency, *Handbook of Economic Statistics,* 1989, 1990.

TABLE 1.II.7 Air cargo, 1986–1988[a] (Poland and selected countries)

Country	Freight (in km-tons[b])
Poland	14
Spain	598
USSR	2,721
United States	13,829
OECD average	1,622

[a] Means data for each country may refer to 1986, 1987, or 1988.
[b] Of national origin.

Source: The Economist, *Book of Vital World Statistics,* 1990.

TABLE 1.II.8 Road traffic

| | (Thousand Vehicles) | | |
	1986	1987	1989
Passenger cars	3,962	4,232	4,846
Trucks[a]	827	866	977
Buses	86	87	91
Motorcycles and scooters	1,515	1,470	1,411

[a] Including nonagricultural tractors.

Source: The Europa World Yearbook, 1989, 1990, 1991

TABLE 1.II.9 Ownership of vehicles and automobiles, 1985–1988[a] (Poland and selected countries)

| | (Thousands) | |
Country	Vehicles[b]	Automobiles
Poland	5,528.0	4,519.0
Spain	12,475.0	10,500.0
United States	183,468.0	140,655.0
USSR	21,500.0	12,500.0

[a] Means data for each country may refer to 1985, 1986, 1987, or 1988.
[b] Vehicles include: Passenger cars, goods vehicles, and buses and coaches.

Source: The Economist, *Book of Vital World Statistics,* 1990.

TABLE 1.II.10 Number of persons per automobile, 1986–1988[a] (Poland and selected countries)

Country	
Poland	9.0
Spain	3.8
OECD	2.6
USSR	22.8
United States	1.8

[a] Means data for each country may refer to 1986, 1987, or 1988.

Source: The Economist, *Book of Vital World Statistics,* 1990.

TABLE 1.II.11 Post, telephones, and telex lines, 1986–1988[a]

Country	Post Offices	Letters per Person	Persons per Telephone Line	Persons per Telex Line
Poland	8,405	37.36	8.5	1,219
Spain	12,985	100.22	4.1	740
USSR	98,445	217.81	10.3	162,875
Unites States	40,117	645.48	1.3	N/A

[a] Means data for each country may refer to 1986, 1987, or 1988.

Source: The Economist, *Book of Vital World Statistics,* 1990.

III. ECONOMY

TABLE 1.III.1 Economic profile, 1990 (Poland and selected countries)

	Poland	USSR	United States	France
Gross national product				
Billion 1990 U.S. $[a]	167.1	2,660.0	5,456.2[b]	873.6[b]
Percent real growth	−8.9	−2.4 to −5.0	1.0	2.8
Per Capita (1990 U.S. $)	4,400	9,140	21,830	15,490
Industrial production[c]	−23.0	−2.8	1.0	1.1
Trade (billion U.S. $)				
Exports, f.o.b.	28.5[d]	109.3[d]	393.9	216.6
Imports, c.i.f.	24.4[d]	114.7[d]	516.2	234.4
Trade balance	4.1[d]	−5.4[d]	−122.3	−17.8
Living standard indicators				
Automobile registrations (per thousand persons)	106[e]	46[e]	571[f]	395[e]
Energy consumption[g]	23[d]	35[d]	57[d]	29[d]

[a] At U.S. purchasing power equivalents.
[b] Gross domestic product
[c] Percent growth.
[d] 1989 data.
[e] 1987 data.
[f] 1988 data.
[g] Barrels oil equivalent per capita.

Source: U.S. Central Intelligence Agency, *Handbook of Economic Statistics,* 1991.

TABLE 1.III.2 Estimated real gross national product (Poland and selected countries)

	(Billion 1990 U.S. $)				
Country	1970	1980	1985	1989	1990
Poland	117.0	165.9	171.1	172.4	149.4
USSR	1,726.9	2,257.0	2,440.9	2,663.7[a]	1,465.9[a]
United States	2,985.8	3,916.0	4,513.0	5,198.4	5,465.6
France	491.7	680.6	733.9	818.5	819.6

[a] The 1989 GNP figure for the USSR is based on CIA statistics, while the 1990 GNP figure is based on PlanEcon statistics. The great disparity between the Soviet GNP in 1990 and 1988 is due to extremely high estimates by the CIA during the 1980s.

Source: U.S. Central Intelligence Agency, *Handbook of Economic Statistics,* 1989, 1990; "PlanEcon Report," vol. 6, no. 52, December 28, 1990.

TABLE 1.III.3 Real gross national product growth (Poland and selected countries)

Country	Percent Average Annual Rate of Growth		Percent	
	1971–1980	1981–1985	1989	1990
GNP growth				
Poland	3.6	1.8	−2.0	−8.9
USSR[a]	2.4	1.8	1.5	−2.4 to −5.0
United States[b]	2.8	3.0	2.5	1.0
France[b]	3.6	1.5	3.6	2.8
GNP per capita growth				
Poland	3.0	1.0	−2.0	−8.9
USSR	1.5	.8	.7	−2.9 to −5.5
United States[b]	1.7	1.8	1.5	.3
France[b]	3.0	1.0	3.1	2.4

[a] At factor cost.
[b] GDP growth.
Source: U.S. Central Intelligence Agency, *Handbook of Economic Statistics,* 1990, 1991.

TABLE 1.III.4 GNP per capita in dollars[a] 1990 (Poland and selected countries)

Country	(U.S. $)		
	Commercial	Purchasing Parity	Free Market
Poland	2,340	3,910	2,350
USSR	2,560	5,060	1,299
United States	21,732	21,732	21,732
West Germany	24,210	16,310	24,210

[a] Based on exchange rate, purchasing power parity, and free market rate.
Source: "PlanEcon Report," vol. 6, no. 52, December 28, 1990.

TABLE 1.III.5 GDP per capita as a percentage of OECD average, 1988 (Poland and selected countries)

Country	(Percent of OECD)
Poland	10.1
Spain	50.9
USSR	12.1
United States	116.3

Source: The Economist, *Book of Vital World Statistics,* 1990.

TABLE 1.III.6 Exchange rate

	1987	1988	1989	Jan 1990	Feb 1991
	(Zloty per $; Period Averages)				
Commercial	265	431	1,439	9,500	9,688[a]

[a] The devaluation was the result of continued inflationary pressure.
Source: U.S. Central Intelligence Agency, *The World Factbook,* 1990; EIU, "Poland, Country Report," No. 1, 1991.

TABLE 1.III.7 Savings

(Million Zl)				
1984	1986	1987	1988	1989
1,237,263	2,091,111	2,482,301	3,695,381	7,971,323

Source: Comecon Data 1990, 1991.

TABLE 1.III.8 Money in circulation

(Million Zl)			
1980	1985	1988	1989
296,684	1,030,676	2,728,146	12,778,400

Source: Comecon Data 1990, 1991.

TABLE 1.III.9 Growth of GNP by producing and consuming sectors

	(Percent Average Annual Rate of Growth)		
	1985	1987	1989
GNP	1.0	−2.0	−1.6
Producing sector			
Industry	1.6	−1.0	−3.5
of which Machinery	4.3	−11.3[a]	N/A
Agriculture and forestry	0.3	−7.3	0.2
Construction	−2.4	1.2	−2.0
Transportation and communications	−0.2	1.1	−2.5
Trade	2.9	0.3	−6.7
Services	−2.3	6.5	5.8
Other	2.6	1.0	0.3
Consuming sector			
Personal consumption	0.5	3.0	−4.3[b]
Government	2.1	2.3	0.9[b]
Gross investment	−7.2	−3.8	7.7[b]
Residual	−8.2	−7.4	0.3[b]

[a] 1986 data.
[b] 1988 data.

Source: U.S. Central Intelligence Agency, "Eastern Europe: Long Road Ahead to Economic Well-Being," May, 1990.

TABLE 1.III.10 Growth of GNP inputs and productivity

	(Percent Average Annual Rate of Growth)			
	1980	1985	1987	1989
GNP	−2.4	1.0	−2.0	−1.6
Combined inputs	2.0	1.3	1.1	1.8
Capital stock	5.4	2.9	3.3	5.0
Labor	0.8	0.7	0.3	0.6
Combined productivity	−4.4	−0.2	−3.1	−3.2
Capital productivity	−7.4	−1.8	−5.2	−6.2
Labor productivity	−3.2	0.4	−2.3	−2.1

Source: U.S. Central Intelligence Agency, "Eastern Europe: Long Road Ahead to Economic Well-Being," May, 1990.

TABLE 1.III.11 Consumer spending on various items as a percentage of personal income, 1989 (Poland and selected countries)

	Total per Head $	Percent Food/ Drink	Percent Clothing	Percent Energy	Percent Household Goods	Percent Health	Percent Transport
Poland	931	53.4	9.0	4.9	7.0	9.0	7.7
USSR	2,820	43.2	19.0	7.0	8.0	2.7	2.9
United States	12,233	13.3	6.5	19.5	5.7	14.7	14.8
France	9,635	20.0	7.0	18.8	8.3	8.8	16.7

Source: The Economist, *Book of Vital World Statistics,* 1990.

TABLE 1.III.12 Cost-of-living price index[a]

Index Group	(1985 = 100)		
	1984	1987	1989
Total	87	147	812
Food and consumer goods	88	146	831
Food	87	139	860
Alcoholic beverages	96	150	888
Other consumer goods	86	151	785
Services	82	156	686

[a] Annual average.

Source: EUROSTAT, *Central and Eastern Europe 1991,* 1991.

IV. EDUCATION

TABLE 1.IV.1 Schools, students, and teachers

	1980–1981	1987–1988	1989–1990
Schools			
General schools[a]	14,259	18,747	18,954
Vocational schools[b]	3,274	3,167	3,129
Technical colleges[c]	7,146	5,743	5,719
Universities	91	92	98
Students (thousands)			
General-school pupils[d]	4,602	5,479	5,623
Vocational-school pupils	749	781	823
Technical-college students[e]	1,044	818	862
Day pupils	689	609	669
Pupils per 10,000 population	292	217	227
Technical-college graduates	277.2	158.8	189.2

[a] Includes general lower secondary schools and combined lower/upper secondary schools. General schools include the compulsory primary/lower secondary school (7–10 years' schooling) and an upper secondary stage of 2–4 years.

[b] Pupils here receive a job-oriented education.

[c] Includes distance-learning institutions for teaching certificates; technical colleges to train technicians, technical colleges to improve the qualifications of workers' and similar for craftsmen.

[d] Includes both day and evening school pupils and also those on correspondence courses.

[e] Includes pupils involved in distance learning to gain teaching certificates, at technical colleges for technicians, at technical colleges to improve the qualifications of workers and craftsmen.

(continued)

TABLE 1.IV.1   (*continued*)

	1980–1981	1987–1988	1989–1990
University undergraduates	454	343	361
Day students	299	265	275
Pupils per 10,000 population	127	91	95
University graduates	84.0	55.3	48.0
Teachers (thousands)			
General-school teachers[f]	238	353	358[h]
Technical-college lecturers[g]	66.2	71.2[i]	N/A
University academic staff	54.7	58.4	61.1

[f] Includes general schools and combined lower/upper secondary schools; teaching staff includes those members of staff with secondary or higher education who work as teachers, instructors, and technical instructors in the school workshops.

[g] 1989–1990 data.

[h] The academic staff includes those members of staff with secondary or higher education, as well as staff seconded from industry (such as engineers, technicians, or craftsmen).

[i] For the years 1985–1986.

Source: EUROSTAT, *Central and Eastern Europe 1991,* 1991.

TABLE 1.IV.2   Public expenditures on education

Year	Zloty	As a Percent of GNP	Percent of Total Government Expenditures
1985	497,497,000	4.9	12.2
1986	603,548,000	4.8	12.2
1987	744,955,000	4.6	12.5
1988	1,010,655,000	3.6	10.1

Source: UNESCO, *Statistical Yearbook,* 1989.

TABLE 1.IV.3   Expenditures and pupils per teacher, 1989 (Poland and selected countries)

Country	Percent of GNP	Pupils per Teacher Primary/Secondary
Poland	4.4	16/11
USSR	7.3	17/N/A
United States	6.7	21/13
France	5.7	19/17

Source: The Economist, *Book of Vital World Statistics,* 1990.

TABLE 1.IV.4   Distribution of teachers and pupils by educational level, 1987

Educational Level	Teachers	Percent Female	Pupils	Percent Female
Preschool	82,531	99	1,409,012	N/A
First level	321,615	83	5,036,114	49
Second level	160,076	55	1,688,997	50
General	31,250	70	372,604	72
Teacher training	N/A	N/A	26,352	91
Vocational	N/A	N/A	1,290,041	43
Third level[a]	N/A	N/A	458,585	56
Total	N/A		10,281,705	

[a] Includes evening and correspondence courses.

Source: UNESCO, *Statistical Yearbook,* 1989.

TABLE 1.IV.5 Mean years of schooling[a], 1980
(Poland and selected countries)

Country	Total
Poland	7.3
USSR	7.6
United States	12.2
France	9.4

[a]For adults over 25 years old.

Source: UN, *Human Development Report 1991,* 1991.

TABLE 1.IV.6 School enrollment ratios[a]

Year	Primary (Ages 7–14)	Secondary (Ages 15–18)	Third Level (Ages 20–24)
1975	100	72	16.8
1980	100	77	17.6
1987[b]	101[c]	80	17.8

[a]Percent total enrollment of all ages divided by the population of the specific age groups that correspond to the age groups of primary and secondary schooling.

[b]1987 data represent new age ranges in the following categories: First Level (Ages 6–13) and Second Level (Ages 14–17).

[c]Ratios exceeding 100 reflect instances in which the students at a given level are not necessarily in the age group delineated for that level.

Source: UNESCO, *Statistical Yearbook,* 1989.

TABLE 1.IV.7 School enrollment, 1989 (Poland and selected countries)

	(Percent)					
	Primary			Secondary		
	Total	Male	Female	Total	Male	Female
Poland	101	101	101	80	78	82
USSR	106	N/A	N/A	98	N/A	N/A
United States	100	101	100	98	99	99
France	113	114	113	92	89	96

Source: The Economist, *Book of Vital World Statistics,* 1990.

TABLE 1.IV.8 Books, newspapers, and library book loans, 1989 (Poland and selected countries)

	(Thousands)			
	Books Published per Year	Newspaper Circulation	Library Books Loans per Year	Volumes Stock
Poland	10,416	7,480	158,645.0	129,710
Spain	38,302	2,910	N/A	14,040
USSR	83,011	12,982	2,634.3[a]	1,523,071
United States	48,793	62,502	197,328.1	523,493

[a]Soviet library regulations rarely allow the loaning of books, thus the low figure.

Source: The Economist, *Book of Vital World Statistics,* 1990.

V. ENERGY AND RESOURCES

TABLE 1.V.1 History of primary energy production (Poland and selected countries)

Energy Type	Country	(Thousand Barrels per Day of Oil Equivalent) 1970	1980
Coal	Poland	1,788	2,318
	USSR	6,080	6,370
	United States	7,359	9,785
	France	523	284
Crude oil	Poland	8	7
	USSR	7,060	12,030
	United States	11,380	10,170
	France	68	51
Natural gas	Poland	88	104
	USSR	3,270	7,170
	United States	10,686	9,838
	France	118	129
Hydro/nuclear	Poland[a]	11	17
	USSR	660	1,170
	United States	1,394	2,774
	France	317	665

[a] Poland has no nuclear power facilities. The only nuclear construction site was halted in September 1990 by a vote of the legislature.

Source: U.S. Central Intelligence Agency, *Handbook of Economic Statistics*, 1990.

TABLE 1.V.2 Complete energy use (production, consumption, export/import, Soviet portion of import)

	Year	(Thousand Metric Tons) Production	Consumption[a]	Export	Import	Soviet Portion of Imports (%)[b,c]
Crude oil[e]	1985	196	13,908	0	13,712	12,960 (95)
	1988	163	15,129	0	14,966	13,540 (90)
	1990	150	13,158	0	13,008	10,837 (83)
Refined oil products	1985	14,067	17,082	461	3,476	2,250 (65)
	1988	15,008	17,497	793	3,282	2,218 (68)
	1990	12,860	13,511	1,641	2,300	1,607 (70)
Motor and aviation gas	1985	2,311	2,867	0	556	N/A
	1988	2,824	3,643	49	868	N/A
	1990	2,191	2,946	10	765	N/A
Diesel oil	1985	4,842	5,761	300	1,219	N/A
	1988	5,174	6,394	106	1,326	N/A
	1990	3,880	4,879	112	1,156	N/A
Fuel oil	1985	2,399	3,513	32	1,146	N/A
	1988	2,512	3,354	213	1,055	N/A
	1990	3,092	2,294	975	177	N/A
Other refined products	1985	4,515	4,941	129	555	N/A
	1988	4,498	4,106	425	33	N/A
	1990	3,747	3,397	552	202	N/A

[a] Poland is the 11th largest energy consumer in the world.

[b] Soviet portion of imports as a percent.

[c] To the nearest 1%.

[e] Poland is ranked fourth in the world among nations whose energy is generated from solid fuels. It is the fifth-largest producer, the sixth-largest exporter, and the fifth-largest consumer of coal in the world; and the eleventh-largest producer in terms of total energy produced in the world.

(*continued*)

TABLE 1.V.2 *(continued)*

	Year	Production	Consumption[a]	Export	Import	Soviet Portion of Imports (%)[b,c]
		(Thousand Metric Tons)				
Other refined	1985	4,515	4,941	129	555	N/A
products	1988	4,498	4,106	425	33	N/A
	1990	3,747	3,397	552	202	N/A
Natural gas	1985	6,390	12,288	0	5,988	5,979 (100)
(million cm³)	1988	5,713	13,199	1	7,487	7,483 (100)
	1990	3,866	12,276	0	8,410	8,410 (100)
Hard coal[d]	1985	191,642	156,547	36,155	1,060	1,077 (100)
(including	1988	193,015	161,967	32,177	1,129	1,129 (100)
anthracite)	1990	147,600	120,256	27,904	506	639 (N/A)
Brown coal[d]	1985	57,746	57,545	201	0	0
(including	1988	73,489	73,489	0	0	0
lignite)	1990	67,600	67,600	0	0	0
Coke[d]	1985	15,996	14,357	1,639	0	0
	1988	17,071	14,227	2,844	0	0
	1990	13,730	10,388	3,332	0	0
Electricity	1985	137,717	135,605	7,568	5,456	800 (15)
(million kWh)	1988	144,344	148,820	7,980	12,456	6,382 (51)
	1990	136,250	135,550	10,500	9,800	1,579 (16)

[a] Poland is the 11th largest energy consumer in the world.

[b] Soviet portion of imports as a percent.

[c] To the nearest 1%.

[d] 1 metric ton = 8.03 barrels of oil.

Source: "PlanEcon Report," vol. 7, March 6, 1991.

TABLE 1.V.3 Electricity production[a] (Poland and selected countries)

Country	1970	1980	1985	1989
	(Billion Kilowatt-Hours)			
Poland	64.52	121.87	137.72	146.96
USSR	740.93	1,293.88	1,544.20	1,722.00
United States[b]	1,742.73	2,437.82	2,634.65	2,970.21
France	146.97	243.29	325.73	378.00

[a] Data are for total (gross) production at generating centers and therefore include transmission losses and station use.

[b] Beginning in 1980, data are for public utilities only.

Source: U.S. Central Intelligence Agency, *Handbook of Economic Statistics*, 1990.

TABLE 1.V.4 Installed electricity-generating capacity[a] (Poland and selected countries)

Country	1970	1980	1985	1986[b]
	(Million Kilowatts)			
Poland	13.89	24.77	29.10	29.80
USSR	166.15	266.71	315.00	322.00
United States	360.33	630.94	656.12[c]	674.14[c]
France	36.22	63.66	85.56	92.48

[a] All plants for both public and industrial use.

[b] Latest available data for Poland.

[c] Data are for public utilities only.

Source: U.S. Central Intelligence Agency, *Handbook of Economic Statistics,* 1990.

TABLE 1.V.5 Commercial energy use by sector[a], 1985 (Poland and selected countries)

		(Percentage of Commercial Energy Used)			
	Industry	Transport	Agriculture	Commercial and Residential	Other[b]
Poland	47	8	0	45	0
USSR	60	13	0	27	0
United States	31	35	1	30	4
France	33	26	2	35	3

[a] Includes all solid, liquid, and gaseous fuels, as well as primary and secondary electricity.
[b] "Other" includes nonenergy uses, military uses, and nonspecified uses.

Source: From *World Resources, 1988–89.* Copyright © 1988 by the World Resources Institute and the International Institute for Environment and Development in collaboration with the United Nations Environment Programme. Reprinted by permission of Basic Books, a division of Harper Collins Publishers Inc.

TABLE 1.V.6 Proved reserves of crude oil, natural gas, and coal, 1989 (Poland and selected countries)

Country	Crude Oil (Billion Barrels)	Natural Gas (Trillion Cubic Feet)	Coal (Million Metric Tons)
Poland	Negligible	5	30,000
USSR	50–80	1,450	182,000
United States	26	165	205,000
UK	4	21	4,200
France	0.03	0.18	1,070

Source: U.S. Central Intelligence Agency, *Handbook of Economic Statistics,* 1990; U.S. Department of Energy, Energy Information Administration, *International Energy Annual,* 1988; UN, *Energy Statistics Yearbook,* 1986.

TABLE 1.V.7 Mineral production

	(Tons)		
Mineral	1985	1987	1989
Aluminum, primary	47,000	47,000	47,800
Barytes	91,215	59,300	N/A
Bentonite	85,200	88,600	93,098
Cadmium	610	620	485
Coal, bituminous	191,642,000	193,012,000	178,000,000
Coal, brown	57,746,000	73,194,000	71,800,000
Copper			
Mine production of	432,000	438,000	401,000
Smelter production of	380,000	367,300	460,519
Production of refined	387,000	390,200	390,268
Feldspar	60,100	57,600	N/A
Ferro alloys, blast furnace			
Spiegeleisen	1,900	2,500	906
Ferro-manganese	99,400	95,300	90,267
Ferro-alloys, electric furnace			
Ferro-chrome	49,000[e]	35,900	28,222
Ferro-manganese	4,000[e]	4,800[e]	1,427
Ferro-silicon	52,000[e]	77,100	83,210
Other ferro alloys	60,000[e]	60,000[e]	60,718
Silicon metal	10,500[e]	10,000[e]	10,000[e]
Gypsum	235,900	260,900	N/A
Iron ore	11,300	6,300	7,200

[e] Estimated.

(*continued*)

TABLE 1.V.7 (*continued*)

Mineral	(Tons) 1985	1987	1989
Iron, pig	9,707,000	10,476,000	9,488,000
Kaolin	55,200	60,300	61,604
Lead, mine production of	51,300	48,800	66,000
Lead, production of refined	87,300	89,800	78,200
Magnesite	19,200	22,300	24,133
Natural gas[a]	6,390	5,781	5,377
Petroleum, crude	194,000	149,000	159,000
Salt, rock	1,198,000	1,231,000	994,000
Salt, other	3,667,000	4,944,000	3,700,000[e]
Silver[b]	831,000	831,000	1,003,000
Steel ingots and castings	16,126,000	17,145,000	15,094,000
Sulphur and pyrites			
Frasch	4,876,000	4,966,000	4,864,000
Recovered	170,000[e]	170,000[e]	150,000[e]
Anhydrite	20,000[e]	20,000[e]	20,000[e]
Zinc	190,900	185,800	204,000
Zinc, slab	180,000	176,500	163,727

[a] Million m^3.
[b] Kilograms.
[e] Estimated.

Source: British Geological Survey, *World Mineral Statistics,* 1984–88; *World Mineral Production, 1985–89.*

VI. GOVERNMENT AND DEFENSE FORCES

TABLE 1.VI.1 State budget

	(Million Zloty) 1985	1987	1988	1989
Revenue				
Total				
of which	4,043,453	5,850,497	10,088,700	30,108,500
Central government	2,809,709	3,928,672	6,702,200	19,394,000
Local authorities	1,233,744	1,921,825	3,386,500	10,759,500
Expenditure				
National economy	1,600,200	2,527,200	4,196,800	11,941,400
Science	31,300	10,300	68,600	109,100
Education	405,597	607,255	1,010,655	4,342,528
Culture	59,580	89,393	164,191	638,779
Public health	358,449	647,651[a]	1,093,259	4,015,807
Social welfare	44,429	N/A	N/A	N/A
Physical culture and				
tourism	17,716	24,871	51,735	199,492
Social insurance	350,300	436,386	432,700	2,344,400
National defense	315,200	467,600	742,200	2,118,000
Public administration and				
jurisdiction	218,800	330,300	541,000	1,997,900
Current expenditure				
(incl. others)	3,487,600	5,030,600	8,430,600	29,617,500
Investment expenditure	591,000	942,600	1,579,600	4,069,600
Total				
of which	4,078,600	5,973,200	10,010,200	33,687,100
Central government	2,732,700	3,824,600	6,315,300	20,933,500
Local authorities	1,345,900	2,148,600	3,694,900	12,753,600

[a] Public health and social welfare were combined for 1987–1989.
Source: The Europa World Year Book, 1989, 1990, 1991.

TABLE 1.VI.2 Hard-currency debt

	(Billion U.S. $)			
	1980	1985	1988	1989
Gross debt				
of which	25.0	29.3	38.5	39.8
Government	10.1	18.7	26.6	26.3
Commercial	14.9	10.6	11.9	13.4
Other	N/A	N/A	N/A	N/A
Reserves	N/A	0.9	2.1	2.3
Net debt	N/A	28.4	36.4	37.5
Debt service ratio[a]	N/A	65%	70%	74%

[a]Debt service ratio is calculated as the share of principal and interest payments to total hard currency earnings.

Source: U.S. Central Intelligence Agency, "Eastern Europe: Long Road Ahead To Economic Well-Being," May 1990.

TABLE 1.VI.3 Armed forces totals, 1991

Total armed forces	305,000 (191,000 conscripts)[a]
Branches	
Army	199,500 (127,500 conscripts)
Navy	19,500 (11,600 conscripts)
Air Force	86,000 (52,000 conscripts)
Total reserves	507,000
Army	420,000
Navy	17,000 (to age 50)
Air Force	70,000 (to age 60)
Manpower	292,769 men reach the military age of 19 annually
Budget	23,274.70 billion zlotys ($2.11 billion)[b]

[a]Active duty personnel is estimated to decline to 250,000 in 1992.
[b]Budget based on 9,500 zlotys = $1.

Source: The International Institute for Strategic Studies, *The Military Balance 1991–1992,* 1991. Copyright IISS.

TABLE 1.VI.4 Components of defense force, 1989

Army
  Organization
    3 military districts
    3 armored divisions
    8 mechanized divisions
    1 airborne division
    3 artillery brigades
    3 antitank regiments
    4 surface-to-surface brigades with Scud
    1 air defense brigade
    1 amphibious assault division
  Major equipment (1986)
    3,450 medium tanks
      110 light tanks
    3,300 armored personnel carriers
        130mm multiple rocket launchers
        Frog-7 and Scud surface-to-surface missiles

(continued)

TABLE 1.VI.4 *(continued)*

Navy
    Organization
        Naval bases at Gdynia, Hel, Swinoujscie, Kolobrzeg, and Ustka
    Major equipment
        3 W-class submarines
        1 Kotlin destroyer
        3 Tarantul corvettes
        13 Osa I-class fast attack craft
        18 motor torpedo craft
Air Force
    Organization
        33 interceptor squadrons
        18 fighter/bomber squadrons
        6 reconnaissance squadrons
        2 transport regiments
        3 helicopter regiments
    Major equipment (1986)
        150 MiG-17 fighter/bomber/interceptor aircraft
        400 MiG-21/-23 interceptors
        149 helicopters
        300 trainers

Source: Reprinted with permission from *World Defense Forces,* 2nd edition, published by ABC-CLIO, 1989.

TABLE 1.VI.5 Military expenditures

	1979	1985	1987	1988
Million zlotys	70,780	315,200	424,490	542,000
Constant price figures (million U.S. $)[a]	2,426	2,510	2,294	1,952
Military expenditures as a percent of GDP				
Poland	2.9%	3.0%	2.5%	N/A
USSR	12.9	13.0	12.5	N/A
United States	5.0	6.6	6.4	6.0
France	3.9	4.0	4.0	3.8

[a]1986 exchange rates and prices.

Source: SIPRI Yearbook, 1989: *World Armaments and Disarmamament,* Stockholm International Peace Research Institute, 1989

VII. INDUSTRY

TABLE 1.VII.1 Industrial production index[a] (Poland and selected countries)

Country	1960	1970	(1980 = 100) 1980	1986	1987	1989	1990[b]
Poland	34	67	100	96	94	91	73
USSR[c]	38	68	100	113	116	118	115
United States	45	73	100	113	119	129	130
France	47	75	100	100	102	110	111

[a]Indexes for the noncommunist countries are value-added weighted indexes of industrial intermediate and final products. Industry includes manufacturing, mining, and, in most countries, public utilities. The indexes for the communist countries are estimates constructed by the U.S. Central Intelligence Agency, as nearly as possible on the same basis as the indexes for Western countries, and include manufacturing, mining, and public utilities.
[b]Preliminary
[c]Index of gross values of output for individual commodities and branches are aggregated by 1982 value-added weights. This index is as comparable with the index of U.S. industrial production of the U.S. Federal Reserve Board as data will permit.
Source: U.S. Central Intelligence Agency, *Handbook of Economic Statistics,* 1991.

TABLE 1.VII.2 Industrial production index (official and adjusted)

	1960	1970	1980	1986	1987	1989[a]
			(1980 = 100)			
Official	22	48	100	99	102	104
Adjusted	34	68	100	95	95	92

[a] Preliminary.

Source: U.S. Central Intelligence Agency, *Handbook of Economic Statistics,* 1990.

TABLE 1.VII.3 Production of selected industrial items

	(Metric Tons Unless Noted)	
	1985	1987
Agricultural and forestry products		
Sausages and smoked meat	692,000	777,000
Refined sugar[a]	1,708	1,671
Margarine	173,000	204,000
Wine and mead[b]	2,675	2,600
Beer[b]	11,708	11,900
Cigarettes[c]	90,021	98,700
Cotton yarn	183,900	198,000
Flax and hemp yarn	30,100	28,600
Wool yarn	84,200	79,900
Mechanical wood pulp	118,000	116,000
Newsprint	82,000	69,100
Other paper	989,000	1,089,000
Paperboard	221,000	221,000
Fuels, minerals, metals, and chemicals		
Synthetic rubber	126,100	117,000
Ethyl alcohol[b]	2,680	2,730
Sulfuric acid, 100%[a]	2,863	3,149
Nitric acid, 100%[a]	1,883	2,136
Caustic soda, 96%	431,000	440,000
Soda ash, 98%	939,000	930,000
Nitrogenous fertilizers[a]	1,253.7	1,543
Phosphate fertilizers[a]	888.8	942
Plastics and synthetic resins	603,000	641,000
Gasoline[a]	3,771	4,039
Distillate fuel oils[a]	4,883	4,981
Residual fuel oils[a]	2,434	2,321
Petroleum bitumen-Asphalt[a]	1,129	N/A
Hard coal briquettes[a]	858	N/A
Coke-oven coke[a]	15,585	17,100
Gas coke[a]	411.2	N/A
Cement[a]	14,990	16,100
Pig-iron[a]	9,807	10,476
Rolled steel products[a]	11,845	12,410
Aluminum, unwrought	47,000	47,500
Refined copper, unwrought	387,000	390,000
Refined lead, unwrought	87,300	89,800
Zinc, unwrought	180,100	177,000

[a] Thousand metric tons.
[b] Thousand hectoliters.
[c] Million units.

(continued)

TABLE 1.VII.3 (*continued*)

	(Metric Tons Unless Noted)	
	1985	1987
Machinery and equipment		
Merchant ships launched[d]	307,800	N/A
Trucks[e]	49,114	45,600
Motorcycles[e]	35,500	N/A
Manufactured consumer goods		
Woven cotton fabrics[f]	831,000	749,000
Linen and hemp fabrics[f]	82,000	83,800
Woven woollen fabrics[f]	105,000	99,500
Woven fabrics of cellulosic fibers[f]	59,768	N/A
Leather footwear[g]	70,300	65,600
Passenger motor cars[e]	283,000	233,000
Domestic washing machines[e]	739,000	779,000
Domestic refrigerators[e]	578,000	506,000

[d] Gross registered tons.
[e] Units.
[f] Thousand meters.
[g] Pairs.
Source: The Europa World Year Book, 1989.

TABLE 1.VII.4 Production change by industry branch[a]

	(Percent Change on Year Earlier Period)
Fuel and energy	−11.5
Metallurgy	−20.9
Electrical and mechanical engineering	−23.9
Chemicals	−25.9
Construction materials	−27.1
Wood and paper	−27.0
Light industry	−38.7
Food industry	−30.9
Others	−37.6
State industry total	−27.1

[a] State sectors only.
Source: EIU, "Poland, Country Report," No. 4, 1990.

TABLE 1.VII.5 Rank of industry, manufacturing, and service share of GDP[a], 1990 (Poland and selected countries)

	Rank
Poland	6
Brunei	1
Angola	20
USSR	9

[a] All former East bloc countries rank in the top 10 except Hungary. No OECD country is in the top 20. Additionally, no East bloc state, nor the Soviet Union are among the top 20 countries in terms of manufacturing share of GDP or services share of GDP. This chart indicates the significant role of extractive industries in Eastern Europe and the USSR.
Source: The Economist, *Book of Vital World Statistics,* 1990.

TABLE 1.VII.6 Industrial waste generation (Poland and selected countries)

Country	Year of Estimate	Total (Thousand Metric Tons per Year)	Per National Land Area (Metric Tons per km² per Year)
Poland	1985	274,885	901.3
USSR	1985	306,258	13.8
United States	1985	613,000	66.9
France	1980	32,200	59.0

Source: From *World Resources 1988–1989.* Copyright © 1988 by the World Resources Institute and the International Institute for Environment and Development in collaboration with the United Nations Environment Programme. Reprinted by permission of Basic Books, a division of Harper Collins Publishers Inc.

TABLE 1.VII.7 Emissions of air pollutants, 1988 (Poland and selected countries)[a]

	Nitrogen Oxides		Sulfur Dioxide		
	Emissions (Thousand Tons)	Emissions per Unit GNP (Grams)	Emissions (Thousand Tons)	Emissions per Unit GNP (Grams)[c]	Greenhouse Index[b]
Poland[d]	1,550	7	4,180	20	2.9
USSR[e]	4,510	2	18,584	10	3.4
United States[f]	19,800	4	20,700	4	5.3
France	1,615	2	1,226	1	2.4

[a] Preliminary data.

[b] Carbon heating equivalents, metric tons per capita. 1988–89 data.

[c] East European countries have a significantly higher emissions per unit GNP because of inefficient production. For example, on average, these countries use 50–100 percent more energy than the United States to produce a dollar of GDP, and 100–300 percent more than Japan.

[d] The very high pollution rates in Poland have had deleterious consequences for the population. Studies have shown that illnesses such as tuberculosis, pneumonia, bronchitis, and leukemia are more common in heavily polluted areas. In addition, the Institute for Environmental Engineering and the Environment Center in Berlin have found that there is 155 percent more circulatory illness, 30 percent more cancer, and 47 percent more respiratory illness in the heavily polluted Upper Silesia region than the national average. Lastly, the effect of such pollution has explained to researchers why life expectancy for Polish men between ages 40 and 60 has fallen back to 1952 levels.

[e] Stationary sources only. 1987 data.

[f] Sulfur data are for sulfur oxides.

Source: State of the World 1991, A Worldwatch Institute Report on Progress Toward a Sustainable Society, 1991; UN, *Human Development Report 1991,* 1991.

TABLE 1.VII.8 Environmental summary, 1991

	Poland	Spain	USSR	United States	France
Energy					
Energy production					
Solids[a]	4,500	452	14,299	20,736	365
Liquids[a]	8	41	24,139	17,297	145
Gas[a]	136	58	25,541	16,280	115
Biomass[a]	29	20	742	1,150	97
Nuclear[b]	0	56,124	213,001	529,352	303,928
Hydroelectric[b]	3,761	19,530	222,803	272,023	51,158

[a] Trillion BTUs.

[b] Gigawatt-hours.

(*continued*)

TABLE 1.VII.8 (continued)

Energy consumption					
Total[a]	4,795	2,696	52,027	69,469	6,119
Per capita[c]	128	83	193	307	149
Per capita (global rank)	27	38	12	7	22
Energy intensity					
BTUs/$1987 GNP	76,374	10,173	N/A	15,787	8,784
Global rank	7	117	N/A	99	120
Waste					
Access to sanitation services					
Urban population	100%	100%	100%	N/A	100%
Rural population	100%	100%	100%	N/A	100%
1988 greenhouse emissions					
Carbon dioxide[d]	140,000	57,000	1,200,000	1,400,000	96,000
Methane[d]	2,700	1,700	35,000	40,000	2,800
CFCs[d]	7	35	110	190	50
Share of world emissions	1.4%	1.1%	13.6%	17.3%	1.7%
Global rank[e]	34	46	14	7	41

[c] Million BTUs.
[d] Thousand tons.
[e] Per capita.

Source: From *The 1992 Information Please Environmental Almanac*. Reprinted by permission of the Houghton Mifflin Company.

VIII. LABOR FORCE

TABLE 1.VIII.1 Workforce by selected areas of the economy

	(Percent)		
	1980	1986	1989
Total (thousand)	17,874.5	17,789.6	17,705.1
Material production	83.6	81.1	79.1
of which			
Manufacturing industry	38.9	37.1	37.2
Agriculture and forestry	29.7	28.5	26.4
Transport and communications	6.6	6.2	5.8
Distributive trades and restaurants,			
wholesale purchasing	7.7	8.9	8.9
Nonmaterial production	16.4	18.9	20.9

Source: EUROSTAT, *Central and Eastern Europe 1991,* 1991.

TABLE 1.VIII.2 Average monthly earnings by economic sector[a,b]

	(Zloty)			
	1980	1985	1989	1990[c]
Total of which	6,040	20,005	206,758	816,519
Agriculture	6,052	20,104	206,896	762,444
Manufacturing sector	6,536	22,566	235,352	913,164
Construction	6,784	22,205	201,577	793,337
Transports	6,591	19,428	192,173	793,552

[a] State and cooperative sector; the average monthly wages and salaries of manual and nonmanual workers are calculated by taking 1/12 of total annual wages and salaries and dividing it by the average number of registered manual and nonmanual workers.
[b] Net earnings, including bonuses. From 1985 onwards, includes compensatory payments paid in conjunction with rises in prices.
[c] Average of first six months of the year.

Source: EUROSTAT, *Central and Eastern Europe 1991,* 1991.

TABLE 1.VIII.3 Economically active population by sex and industry (1988 census)

	Males	Females	Total
Total	10,070,005	8,382,225	18,452,230
Agriculture and forestry[a]	54.0%	46.0%	5,133,826
Mining, manufacturing, utilities[b]	64.6	35.4	5,652,938
Construction	84.4	15.6	1,456,071
Trade and Restaurants	27.7	72.3	1,493,045
Transport, storage, and communications	71.0	29.0	1,042,838
Other services[c]	34.2	65.8	3,664,512

[a] Including fishing from inland waters.
[b] Including sea fishing.
[c] Remaining branches of activity, including hotels.

Source: The Europa World Year Book, 1991.

IX. POPULATION AND HEALTH

TABLE 1.IX.1 Geography and demographic profile, 1990

Population
  Population in 1990   37,776,725
  Population by 2000   39,900,000 est.
  Population by 2020   42,400,000 est.
  Current annual percent increase   0.5%
  Population density per sq km   121.1
  Net migration rate   −5 migrants/1,000
  Urban/Rural   62%/38%
Ethnic division
  Poles   97.6%
  Germans   1.3%
  Other   1.1%
Religion
  Roman Catholic   95% (75% est. practicing)
  Russian Orthodox   5%
Geography
  Total area   312,680 sq km (120,726 sq mi)
  Land area   304,510 sq km (117,571 sq mi)
  Coast line   491 km (305 mi)
  Land borders with
    Czechoslovakia   1,309 km (813 mi)
    Germany   456 km (283 mi)
    USSR   1,215 km (755 mi)
  Disputes
    Border question with Germany resolved

Source: The Economist, Book of Vital World Statistics, 1990; U.S. CIA, Atlas of Eastern Europe, August 1990; Population Reference Bureau, 1989 World Population Data Sheet (Washington, D.C.: Population Reference Bureau, Inc., 1989); U.S. CIA, The World Factbook, 1990.

TABLE 1.IX.2 Population (Poland and selected countries)

	(Million People at Midyear)				
	1960	1970	1980	1985	1990
Poland	29.6	32.5	35.6	37.2	37.8
Spain	30.6	33.9	37.5	38.5	39.3
USSR	214.3	242.8	266.4	278.9	290.9
United States	180.7	205.1	227.8	239.3	250.4
France	45.7	50.8	53.9	55.2	56.4

Source: U.S. Central Intelligence Agency, Handbook of Economic Statistics, 1990, 1991.

TABLE 1.IX.3 Population by age (Poland and selected countries)

Age	Poland (1987) Total	Percent	Spain (1987) Total	Percent	United States (1987) Total	Percent	USSR (1987) Total	Percent
<19	12,237,495	32.5	11,854,078	30.5	70,857,000	29.1	92,267,217	32.8
20–44	14,089,306	37.4	13,718,564	35.3	97,413,000	40.0	99,559,765	35.4
45–64	7,753,021	20.6	8,447,716	21.8	45,293,000	18.6	64,009,456	22.8
65+	3,583,934	9.5	4,811,904	12.4	29,836,000	12.3	25,501,353	9.0
Total	37,663,756	100.0	38,832,262	100.0	243,400,000	100.0	281,337,791	100.0

Source: UNESCO, *Statistical Yearbook,* 1989.

TABLE 1.IX.4 Population of major cities, 1989

Warsaw	1,655,100
Lodz	851,700
Cracow	748,400
Wroclaw	642,300
Poznan	588,700
Gdansk	464,600
Szczecin	412,100
Bydgoszcz	380,400
Katowice	367,000
Lublin	349,600

Source: The Europa World Year Book, 1991.

TABLE 1.IX.5 Health indicators, 1990 (Poland and selected countries)

Birth rate	15.0/1,000
United States	15.0/1,000
USSR	18.0/1,000
Death rate	10.0/1,000
United States	9.0/1,000
USSR	10.0/1,000
Infant mortality rate	17.5/1,000
OECD and United States	9–10/1.000
USSR	25.0/1,000
Maternal mortality rate[a]	11/100,000
OECD and United States	10/100,000
USSR	48/100,000
Life expectancy	68 male/76 female
OECD	72 male/78 female
Fertility rate	2.1 children/woman
United States	1.9 children/woman
USSR	2.4 children/woman
Suicides[b]	13.5/100,000
OECD and United States	14.6/100,000
USSR	19.8/100,000

[a]Figures refer to live births.   1980–87 figures.
[b]1987–88 figures.

Source: Population Reference Bureau, *1989 World Population Data Sheet* (Washington, D.C.: Population Reference Bureau, Inc. 1989); The Economist, *Book of Vital World Statistics,* 1990; UN, *Human Development Report 1991,* 1991.

TABLE 1.IX.6 Registered illnesses and fatalities by selected causes of death

Illness	1984	1986	1988
Influenza	2,452,000	1,579,000	629,000
Mumps	214,516	156,683	67,427
Bacterial food poisoning	16,791	29,459	40,979
Streptococcal angina and scarlet fever	14,613	15,223	34,994
Diarrhea[a]	28,292	28,768	26,859
Salmonella infection	18,442	25,282	26,254
Viral hepatitis	52,287	28,880	21,827
Pulmonary tuberculosis	21,233	19,447	17,492
Bacillary dysentery	8,243	5,480	11,321

Cause of Death	1984	1986	1988
Circulatory illnesses	181,964	193,052	193,333
of which			
Arteriosclerosis	72,702	77,052	80,295
Ischemic heart diseases	32,984	35,781	37,273
Acute myocardial infarction	24,688	28,064	28,632
Illnesses of the cerebrovascular system	22,912	24,892	24,816
Hypertonia and hypertensive heart diseases	8,352	8,068	7,464
Malignant neoplasms	66,067	68,082	71,025
of which			
Windpipe, bronchi, and lungs	14,391	15,242	16,330
Stomach	8,550	8,026	7,777
Mammary gland	3,792	3,844	4,045
Liver	3,318	3,191	3,168
Colon	2,206	2,411	2,611
Leukemia	1,959	2.037	1,962
Bronchitis, emphysema, and asthma	11,239	11,166	9,057
Diabetes mellitus	5,617	5,840	5,918
Pneumonia	6,659	7,349	5,908

[a]In children under two years.

Source: EUROSTAT, *Central and Eastern Europe 1991,* 1991.

TABLE 1.IX.7 Life expectancy by sex, 1990
(Poland and selected countries)

Poland	
Male	69
Female	77
USSR	
Male	65
Female	74
United States	
Male	72
Female	79
France	
Male	74
Female	82

Source: U.S. Central Intelligence Agency, *The World Fact-book,* 1991.

TABLE 1.IX.8 Medical Care, 1983–1988 (Poland and selected countries)

	Doctors	Dentists	Pharmacists	Beds (Thousands)	Total Health Expenditure[a]
			(Number per Million)		
Poland[b]	1,933.0	461.0	424.0	6.9	4.0
Spain	3,547.0	187.0	827.0	5.2	6.0
USSR[b]	4,124.0	N/A	321.0	12.8	3.2
United States	2,035.0	560.0	641.0	5.9	11.2
OECD	2,199.5	453.8	559.2	8.0	8.3

[a] As a percent of GDP. 1987 figures.

[b] Figures for the former communist countries are clearly misleading. According to the Soviet Ministry of Health, 1.2 million beds are in facilities with no hot water, 1/6 of the beds are in hospitals with no water, and 30 percent of the hospitals have no indoor toilets. Source: *Literaturnaya Gazeta,* February 3, 1988; and see also *World Affairs,* vol. 152, no. 1, Summer 1989.

Source: Population Reference Bureau, *1989 World Population Data Sheet* (Washington D.C.: Population Reference Bureau, Inc. 1989); The Economist, *Book of Vital World Statistics,* 1990; UN, *Human Development Report 1991,* 1991.

TABLE 1.IX.9 Abortion rates (Poland and selected countries)

Country	Number of Abortions per Year	Rate per Thousand Women Age 15–44	Ratio per 100 Known Pregnancies	Total Rate[a]
Poland (1987)	122,600	14.9	16.8	N/A
Spain (1987)	63,900	8.0	N/A	N/A
USSR (1987)	6,818,000	111.9	54.9	N/A
United States (1985)	1,588,600	28.0	29.7	797

[a] The number of abortions that would be experienced by 1,000 women during their reproductive lifetimes, given present age-specific abortion rates.

[b] In contrast to women from Western European and English-speaking countries, who are young, unmarried women seeking to delay a first birth, women from Eastern Europe are married with two or more children using abortion for spacing and ending childbirth. In addition, high rates in Eastern Europe, except Romania, may be attributed in part to the very liberal abortion laws, where abortion has been used as a form of birth control since the 1950s.

Source: Adapted with the permission of The Alan Guttmacher Institute from Stanley K. Henshaw and Evelyn Morrow, *Induced Abortion: A World Review 1990 Supplement,* 1990.

X. TRADE

TABLE 1.X.1 Exports and imports, by commodity group

Commodity Group	1970	1980	1986	1988
		(Million U.S. $)		
Exports				
Machinery and equipment	1,366	7,807	12,475	19,372
Fuels, minerals and metals	848	4,473	4,696	4,305
Agricultural and				
forestry products	600	1,754	2,219	1,537
Manufactured consumer goods	571	2,684	2,990	4,280
Other	163	825	982	1,246
Total	3,548	17,543	23,362	30,750
Imports				
Machinery and equipment	1,306	6,443	7,809	9,580
Fuels, minerals and metals	960	6,127	8,188	9,314
Agricultural and				
forestry products	772	4,118	2,610	3,193
Manufactured consumer goods	231	1,261	2,097	2,396
Other	339	1,753	1,607	2,129
Total	3,608	19,702	22,311	26,612

Source: U.S. Central Intelligence Agency, *Handbook of Economic Statistics,* 1990.

TABLE 1.X.2 Main destinations of exports and origins of imports, 1990.

Country	(Percent of Total)
Destinations of exports:	
Germany	25.3
USSR	15.3
UK	7.0
Switzerland	4.6
Czechoslovokia	4.0
Austria	3.9
Origins of imports:	
Germany	22.0
USSR	18.7
Italy	7.2
Switzerland	5.9
Austria	5.7
U.K.	5.5

Source: EIU, "Poland, Country Report," No. 4, 1991.

TABLE 1.X.3 Principal trading partners

	(Percent)			
	Imports from		Exports to	
	1985	1987	1985	1987
United States	1.3	1.3	2.1	2.8
USSR	34.4	27.5	28.4	24.8
Western Europe				
Austria	3.2	3.9	2.3	3.1
Belgium	1.3	1.3	1.0	1.1
Denmark	0.4	0.6	1.2	1.3
Finland	0.4	0.8	1.7	1.4
France	1.8	2.5	2.4	2.4
Italy	2.1	2.9	2.3	2.9
Netherlands	1.8	2.0	1.8	1.9
Norway	0.2	0.4	N/A	N/A
West Germany	9.0	11.5	8.7	10.8
Spain	N/A	N/A	0.7	0.6
Sweden	1.3	1.4	1.9	2.5
Switzerland	3.4	3.9	1.1	2.2
UK	3.5	3.7	4.3	4.4
Eastern Europe				
Bulgaria	2.0	2.0	2.7	2.2
Czechoslovakia	6.0	6.2	6.2	6.0
East Germany	6.1	5.4	4.9	4.2
Hungary	3.0	2.5	3.2	2.4
Romania	2.6	1.9	2.6	1.5
Yugoslavia	3.9	3.8	3.4	2.9

(*continued*)

TABLE 1.X.3 (*continued*)

	(Percent) Imports from		Exports to	
	1985	1987	1985	1987
Other				
Argentina	0.8	0.2	N/A	N/A
Australia	0.8	1.2	N/A	N/A
Brazil	1.3	2.1	1.4	1.1
Canada	0.2	0.1	N/A	N/A
China	1.8	3.2	2.3	3.4
India	0.6	1.4	0.5	0.6
Iran	0.5	0.2	N/A	N/A
Iraq	N/A	N/A	1.4	0.6
Japan	0.7	1.2	N/A	N/A
Libya	N/A	N/A	1.5	1.2
Turkey	N/A	N/A	1.2	0.8
Total incl. others	100.0	100.0	100.0	100.0
Total (million zlotys)	1,594,889	2,875,586	1,690,994	3,236,528

Source: The Europa World Year Book, 1989.

TABLE I.X.4 Index of import and export prices and terms of trade (Poland and selected countries)

	(1980 = 100)			
	1984	1986	1987	1989
Poland				
Import prices	139	198	279	1,281
Export prices	127	189	275	1,516
Terms of trade	91	95	99	118
Bulgaria				
Import prices	128	125	124	112
Export prices	111	110	112	110
Terms of trade	86	88	90	98
Czechoslovakia				
Import prices	134	146	142	137
Export prices	112	119	119	129
Terms of trade	84	81	83	93
Hungary				
Import prices	125	136	139	163
Export prices	116	120	124	153
Terms of trade	93	88	89	94
Romania				
Import prices	135	130	127	N/A
Export prices	124	114	114	N/A
Terms of trade	92	88	90	N/A
Yugoslavia				
Import prices	116	108	109	124
Export prices	108	107	108	123
Terms of trade	93	99	100	99
USSR				
Import prices	115	112	110	113[a]
Export prices	130	114	110	103[a]
Terms of trade	113	102	100	100[a]

[a]1988.

Source: Comecon Data 1989, 1990, 1991.

TABLE 1.X.5 Major imports and exports[a]

Import Goods/Categories	(Thousand U.S. $)		
	1987	1988	1989
Live animals other than fish	20,490	26,032	34,365
Meat and meat preparations	99,881	45,059	44,813
Fish, etc. and preparations thereof	36,686	45,059	44,813
Vegetables and fruit	95,280	119,764	135,147
Oil seeds and oleaginous fruits	17,810	14,725	49,426
Cork and wood	30,726	35,451	37,836
Crude animal and vegetable materials[c]	23,854	24,999	29,668
Coal, coke, and briquettes	118,690	92,546	96,513
Petroleum, petroleum products, and related materials	37,145	31,977	65,263
Cork and wood manufactures (excl. furniture)	13,696	15,239	24,178
Nonmetallic mineral manufactures[c]	25,107	35,146	34,151
Iron and steel	54,130	80,283	136,144
Nonferrous metals	198,696	279,905	284,621
Manufactures of metals[c]	43,875	61,306	68,443
Power-generating machinery and equipment	7,139	11,486	21,589
Electrical machinery, apparatus, and appliances[c]	11,768	30,338	38,181
Furniture and parts therof; bedding, etc.	55,645	78,061	86,846
Articles of apparel and clothing accesories	205,811	235,176	247,400
Footwear	23,425	24,957	24,675

Export Goods/Categories	1987	1988	1989
Meat and meat preparations	2,010	23,549	103,296
Cereals and cereal preparations	47,516	35,054	210,656
Feeding stuff for animals (not incl. unmilled cereals)	19,876	32,248	32,779
Beverages	2,544	4,259	33,340
Organic chemicals	77,020	91,047	74,233
Dyeing, tanning, and coloring materials	28,401	33,329	31,627
Medical and pharmaceutical products	52,555	60,898	56,110
Plastics in primary forms[b]	N/A	56,916	58,612
Chemical materials and products[c]	N/A	99,596	12,834
Textile yarn, fabrics, made-up articles, and related products[c]	131,647	160,865	198,530
Iron and steel	50,241	87,087	112,840
Manufactures of metals[c]	29,675	33,675	52,467
Machinery specialized for particular industries	47,142	154,018	221,053
Metalwork machinery	56,427	70,019	87,128
General industrial machinery and equipment[c]	119,966	161,901	193,827
Office machines and automatic data-processing machines	17,354	14,351	29,500
Telecommunications and sound-recording and -reproducing apparatus and equipment	6,995	10,116	33,724
Electrical machinery, apparatus, and appliances[c]	63,146	62,219	77,577
Road vehicles (incl. air-cushion vehicles)	45,904	78,222	173,824
Professional instruments and apparatus[c]	42,225	52,972	56,412

[a] According to SITC headings.

[b] Classification changed in 1988, figures for previous years not applicable.

[c] Not elsewhere specified.

Source: EUROSTAT, *Central and Eastern Europe 1991*, 1991.

TABLE 1.X.6 Trade with Western countries[a] (monthly averages)

| | (Million U.S. $) | | | | | |
| | Importing Countries | | | Exporting Countries | | |
	1985	1988	1989	1985	1988	1989
Austria	19.4	28.6	27.4	17.4	25.1	33.0
Belgium/Luxembourg	10.1	13.8	10.9[c]	8.7	11.4	15.4[c]
Denmark	14.4	19.9	18.4	7.2	9.0	13.6
Finland	16.3	17.7	20.7	4.5	6.8	6.0
France	24.6	31.1	33.4	16.8	26.7	31.7
West Germany	88.3	138.0	159.2	81.0	136.8	198.4
Italy	25.4	36.9	44.3	20.5	31.3	39.5
Netherlands	17.4	24.6	31.1	14.4	22.6	26.9
Norway	4.1	4.9	6.5	2.6	6.7	5.9
Spain	8.4	6.5	8.2	3.0	4.4	4.4
Sweden	18.6	26.3	25.3	12.4	18.0	20.7
Switzerland	4.6	5.9	6.0	10.2	16.6	17.0
Turkey	4.1	6.6	8.4[c]	2.9	6.5	5.3[c]
UK	34.6	48.6	45.0	19.9	26.0	26.8
United States	18.3[b]	31.5[b]	32.3[b]	26.5	25.3	34.5
Yugoslavia	23.3	36.2	44.0	25.3	41.0	35.6

[a] Figures from Western countries' trade accounts.

[b] Imports, f.o.b.

[c] January–October

Source: EIU "Poland, Country Report," No. 4, 1990.

TABLE 1.X.7 Trade with the USSR, by commodity

| | (Million Rubles) | |
Imports from the USSR	1987	1988
Machinery and transport equipment	885.1	913.3
Metal cutting machine tools	64.7	68.9
Mining, hoisting, excavating machinery	108.6	112.3
Tractors	97.9	96.5
Motor vehicles and garage equipment	168.9	172.3
Coal and coke	58.7	62.2
Petroleum products	2,464.0	2,098.8
Metal ores and concentrates	249.9	228.5
Pig iron	108.4	105.8
Rolled ferrous products and pipes	102.4	99.4
Chemicals	187.5	177.1
Wood, paper and manufactures	113.8	106.4
Textile fibers and yarn	136.2	141.1
Raw cotton and waste	133.9	138.5
Television sets	54.6	70.4
Domestic appliances, clocks, and cameras	149.1	146.7
Total, including other items		
Million rubles	6,542.2	6,298.0
Million U.S. $	10,867.4	10,290.8

(*continued*)

TABLE 1.X.7 (*continued*)

Exports to the USSR	(Million Rubles)	
	1987	1988
Metal-cutting machine tools and presses	130.5	126.4
Power-generating equipment	75.7	90.2
Electrical equipment	324.8	369.0
Equipment for mining	173.8	206.3
Hoisting and conveying equipment	134.9	166.3
Excavators	95.9	91.1
Pipelines	41.0	82.9
Instruments and laboratory equipment	226.9	134.3
Computer equipment	125.0	162.0
Agricultural machinery	88.1	96.9
Railway rolling stock	194.5	195.8
Motor vehicles and garage equipment	175.9	176.5
Ships and boats	301.4	275.5
Other machinery and transport equipment	885.3	1,184.9
Coal and coke	533.7	663.1
Rolled ferrous products	198.4	195.4
Textiles, clothing, and footwear	431.4	432.1
Total, including all other items		
Million rubles	6,329.3	7,109.3
Million U.S. $	10,513.8	11,616.5

Source: EIU, "Poland, Country Report," No.4, 1990.

TABLE 1.X.8 Trade with the United States, by commodity

Imports from the United States	(Thousand U.S. $)	
	1987	1988
Foodstuffs	82,245	114,818
Cereals and products	78,296	111,837
Tobacco and manufactures	6,919	7,181
Hides and skins, undressed	2,555	3,484
Textile fibers and waste	14,940	23,280
Animal and vegetable oils and fats	701	N/A
Chemicals	29,179	32,378
Machinery, including electric	32,159	36,139
Transport equipment	3,328	6,135
Scientific instruments, etc.	3,794	6,436
Total, including other items	237,399	300,785

Exports to the United States	1987	1988
Foodstuffs	157,793	137,194
Meat and products	121,129	112,030
Chemicals	11,062	29,029
Textile yarn, cloth, and manufactures	10,928	21,419
Nonmetallic mineral manufactures	10,167	10,949
Iron and steel	20,086	24,878
Nonferrous metals	3,821	21,276
Metal manufactures	13,714	13,856
Machinery, including electric	17,090	35,470
Transport equipment	4,754	9,188
Furniture	5,247	9,198
Clothing and footwear	28,073	46,226
Scientific instruments, etc.	1,410	1,796
Total, including all other items	296,156	377,576

Source: EIU, "Poland, Country Report," No.4, 1990.

CHAPTER TWO

CZECHOSLOVAKIA

POPULATION: 15,683,234
SQUARE MILES: 48,440 mi^2, 125,460 km^2
RELIGION: Roman Catholic, 50%; Protestant, 20%; other, 30%
CURRENCY: koruna (Kcs)
EXCHANGE RATES: Kcs 17.95 : $1
DEBT: $7.9 billion

I CZECHOSLOVAKIA

POLITICS, HISTORY, AND ECONOMICS

INTRODUCTION

The events in late 1989 that brought an end to the rule of the Communist Party in Czechoslovakia have come to be known, appropriately, as the Velvet Revolution. Czechoslovakia had fallen to the communists in 1948 in much the same way, in an abduction of power that has been termed the Elegant Takeover. Prague seemingly fell into and out of communism abruptly and with hardly a shot being fired. Moreover, while other East bloc communist parties rallied their troops for a last ditch effort at retaining power, the communists in Prague quickly abandoned their control. Of course, there had been Round Table negotiations between the opposition and the Party with fierce bargaining, as in other bloc states. But the talks had lasted only a matter of days before the Party utterly surrendered.

Seen in the context of its precommunist history, the dramatic political turnabout was not surprising. Czechoslovakia was the only central European state with a solid democratic tradition, one that drew its strength from a prominent middle class, in contrast to the more aristocratic political systems of Poland and Hungary. At its independence in 1918, Czechoslovakia inherited the best of the crumbling Austro-Hungarian empire and used those resources to develop a strong and dynamic economy. At the time of its occupation by Hitler in 1939, its national wealth and annual productivity ranked sixth in the world. At the end of World War II, it was the only state to be incorporated into the East bloc with an economy superior to that of the Soviet Union. Czechoslovakia's peaceful transition to democracy is also rooted in the history of its efforts at reform. It was the first bloc state to attempt to reform its Communist Party. *Perestroika*, or *Prestavba* as it is known in Czech, did not originate in Moscow in 1985 with the ascension of its new, reforming party chief. Genuine reform of communism had begun in Prague in 1968 and lasted through August of that year. The "Prague Spring," as Gorbachev acknowledged, had been a key antecedent of his own reforms.

The Czechoslovak Communist Party was then under the direction of Alexander Dubeček, who believed it possible for a communist government to operate with democratic principles. Brezhnev understood the alternatives differently and replaced Dubeček with Gustáv Husák, a hard-liner. During Husák's tenure, the slightest criticism of Party rule was answered with criminal prosecution, propelling Czechoslovakia into a twenty-year-long decline of political and economic stagnation. But the period of stagnation did not eliminate the reformers who had gathered around Dubeček. Many of the most capable party leaders became dissidents and went underground, turning against both Husák and communism. When Husák needed political support, he could find it neither in Prague nor in Moscow.

The leadership that came to power in December 1989 stands in stunning contrast to the previous rulers. None of Husák's senior colleagues survived. Prague, instead, is guided by a band of former dissidents and political outcasts, led by the playwright Václav Havel, himself no stranger to prison. His team is a collection of competent experts and advisors, nearly all of whom were associated with the Charter 77 Movement, the leading dissident movement in the East bloc during the 1980s. Most were grouped under the umbrella organizations Civic Forum, in the Czech Republic, and Public Against Violence, its sister organization in the Slovak Republic.

These organizations have fragmented since the first free elections, in June 1990, but their successors have maintained absolute agreement on the need to eliminate the Party from state functions and to restore the government to its precommunist democratic traditions. Less agreement exists on the pace of economic reform, though the leading economists would follow the Polish model. The postcommunist era has been marked by increased ethnic tension between the Czechs and Slovaks. The two-thirds of the total population who are Czechs spent the better part of 1990 trying to preserve the fragile democratic state, while the Slovak minority, the other one-third, tried to win significant autonomy. The issue remains so salient that major economic legislation has been stymied as the nationality question has raged. The greatest challenge for the new democratic leadership is to devise political and economic arrangements under which both Czechs and Slovaks can flourish.

POLITICS

For years, a legend has circulated in Bohemia, the westernmost region of Czechoslovakia, that upon the canonization of Agnes of Bohemia, who lived in the thirteenth century, great and miraculous things would happen. Agnes, daughter of Ottokar I, King of Bohemia, and of Queen Constance of Hungary, declined offers of marriage from both Holy Roman Emperor Frederick II and England's Henry III. She chose instead to preserve her purity and joined the Poor Clare order. During her life she built a hospital for the poor, a Franciscan friary, and the Poor Clare abbey, all in Prague. After she was beatified in 1874 by Pius IX, Bohemia awaited her canonization. The Vatican chose to canonize Agnes on November 12, 1989. Five days later, Prague was engulfed in political unrest. Less than six weeks later, Václav Havel had become the president of a democratic Czechoslovakia.

When the Berlin Wall fell on November 9, 1989, the Prague communists remained remarkably firm, resolved to stand against the general wave of reform in Eastern Europe. The collapse of communism in East Germany must, however, have produced alarm. East Germany, especially with Honecker at the helm, had been its major ally preserving traditional communist rule. But even after the dramatic days in Berlin, the party in Prague continued to appeal to the communist faithful to broaden their "socialist activities" while initiating trials for antistate behavior.

Only a few days later, the momentous events of November 17 would sweep Czechoslovakia and mark the demise of the entire system. Since 1945, the 17th of November has been a day of commemoration for Czechoslovak students. On that day in 1939, Hitler's Gestapo attacked Czech students and murdered at least one of them, Jan Opletal. The 1989 commemoration was to be especially significant, as it marked the fiftieth anniversary of that attack. Students actually managed to obtain permission from the communists to gather at Opletal's grave. The hard-line communists were worried over the possibility of political protests but were outvoted by those who argued that the consequences of canceling the ceremonies outweighed their threat. The ceremonies went on.

Following the graveside service, close to 30,000 students, either by design or spontaneously, marched to Wenceslas Square, where they were joined by another 20,000 protestors. A bitterly antigovernment rally was then held, demanding freedom, elections, and the overthrow of the government. Their challenge was answered by heavily armed riot police and the Red Berets, the security police, who charged the protestors, reportedly killing at least one and arresting many.

Rather than intimidating the populace, the physical violence backfired. More massive demonstrations hastily convened to protest the brutality of the security forces and demand the resignation of the government. News of the events spread rapidly throughout Prague and the country, and the rally was immediately referred to as a "massacre," while the day itself was labeled "Bloody Friday."

The very next day, at the Realistic Theatre, students met with elements of the radical theater community to plan a general strike and draft a list of demands against the Party. The following day, at the Magic Lantern Theatre, Václav Havel and a collection of dissidents known as Charter 77 convened and decided to form the Civic Forum to speak on behalf of the disenfranchised Czechoslovak public. Charter 77 was a longstanding outlawed group of intellectual, literary, and artistic dissenters who had been meeting since 1977, when it had issued its "Charter" of demands—thus its name. The day following, a similar organization formed in Bratislava, Public Against Violence (PAV), the Slovak version of the Civic Forum. The Velvet Revolution had begun without its leaders being aware of what they had inaugurated. They could not have imagined that within a few weeks Civic Forum and PAV would comprise the majority voice in the new government.

This account of the fall of communism is now the received wisdom of the transition to democracy in Czechoslovakia. Yet recent disclosures suggest that the fall of the Party depended on more than a peaceful protest turned ugly. Since 1987, the Party had been under considerable pressure, both overt and covert, from Moscow. As early as January, 1987, Gorbachev had called for reform in Czechoslovakia at a Moscow communist party speech, and in April, 1987, he visited the country and again called for reform. That visit deeply unsettled the Czechoslovak communists. Gorbachev's spokesman, Gennadi Gerasimov, held a press conference at Hradcany Castle, Party headquarters. He was asked by reporters to explain the difference between Czechoslovakia's great attempt at reform—the 1968 Prague Spring—and the one that was taking place in the Soviet Union under Gorbachev's *perestroika* and *glasnost*. Gerasimov responded, "Nineteen years." With those two words he both championed Alexander Dubeček's 1968 reform agenda and, more importantly, questioned Husák's entire tenure in office as the quintessential antireform communist.

Gerasimov made it clear that Mikhail Gorbachev was not yet prepared to denounce the 1968 Red Army invasion and that he preferred a reformed Communist Party in Prague rather than political instability. But Husák concluded that while he was out of favor in Moscow, he could still outmaneuver Moscow's allies in Prague. In December, 1987, he resigned as communist party chief and arranged its transfer to the woefully inept Milos Jakes. Gorbachev had preferred the prime minister and Politburo member Lubomir Strougal, known for favoring gradual and controlled reform. To enhance his chances, Strougal had been called to Moscow shortly before Husák's resignation. But he and his allies were outmaneuvered.

The Soviet Union found the new leadership totally unacceptable. Husák's despised clique had been moved aside, but the reactionary stance of the government was as strong as ever. Husák himself remained at the political center, becoming Czechoslovak president. Many of Jakes' lieutenants were free of the taint of crushing the 1968 uprising, yet they were the products of Husák's repressive rule. The same was not true of Jakes. He had been the head of the Control Commission, which undertook the massive purge and general political crackdown following the Prague Spring.

Throughout 1988 and 1989, Jakes refused reform, turning instead to traditional methods of preserving communist rule. Moscow issued consistent challenges to Jakes, frequently in the form of statements favoring liberalization that made their way into the Czechoslovak press. The statements emboldened ever larger numbers of Czechoslovaks to make increasingly strident demands of the Party. The new challenges became even more daring than the earlier ones of Charter 77. New groups sprang up, some legal but mostly not. On occasion they won permission to hold public demonstrations, where they invariably issued demands far beyond what they had pledged to the authorities. Typically, the leaders quashed the larger and more embarrassing protests but chose to ignore the rest.

In 1988, the Party issued public warnings against the growing strength of the anti-socialist forces, which they identified. Charter 77 headed the list, along with the Catholic Church, which in 1987 had begun a campaign for religious freedom, as well as an ecology group, the Jazz Section, and a civil rights group, the Committee for the Unjustly Persecuted. However, the Party never mentioned a host of new groups. Friends of Soviet Perestroika, Readers Club of the Soviet Press, Peace Club of John Lennon, Club for Socialist Renewal, Democratic Initiative, Czechoslovak–Helsinki Committee, and Movement for Civil Freedom had all been established in 1988 and gained support as they gained attention.

The most impressive opposition moves came in August and October of 1988, months of remarkable tension for the communist authorities. Protests against the 1968 Soviet invasion had conventionally been held in August, while celebrations recognizing the 1918 founding of the Czechoslovak republic had been regularly held in October. What distinguished the celebrations of 1988 were the massive crowds. More than 10,000 marched in the August protest—an unheard-of number in Prague—and at least 5,000 marched in October. The authorities responded to both demonstrations with brutal police force.

More demonstrations were nonetheless held in January 1989 to commemorate the death of Jan Palach, the protestor who 20 years previously had committed public self-immolation to denounce the 1968 Soviet occupation. The police arrested the protest leaders. Václav Havel was seized and put on trial for antistate activities. He was convicted and imprisoned, though released a few months later when the resolve of the Party began to weaken.

Thus Jakes and the Communist Party, still refusing the slightest liberalization, entered 1989 on the defensive. Throughout the year, the voice of public protest grew louder, while the Party found itself increasingly surrounded by reformist movements in neighboring communist states, including the Soviet Union. Havel's conviction had generated public outrage and international scorn. A new group issued a petition, known as "Just a Few Sentences," which called for democratic reforms. It was released with 1,800 signatures, but within a month more than 10,000 Czechoslovaks had put their names to the appeal—a bold gesture of defiance, since the signatories knew full well they were inviting arrest. The authorities obliged with mass arrests but could not stem the tide of public defiance.

Once again in August and October of 1989, as in 1988, commemorations of the Prague Spring and the founding of democratic Czechoslovakia brought thousands into the streets. Again they were met by police violence. The government was embarrassed by the international coverage of the demonstrations by the Western press. The regime was further embarrassed when it became public that the police had beaten and arrested several Hungarians, creating a minor international incident between the still "fraternal allies."

Ultimately, pressures from neighboring countries proved to be a crucial ingredient in the fall of the Party. Hungary, whose democratic reform movement was more developed, had challenged Jakes throughout the year. In April of 1989, Hungarian television, widely watched in Czechoslovakia, ran an extensive interview with Dubeček. Despite repeated protests from Prague, he was allowed freely to criticize both the current Czech regime and the Soviet one, which had placed it in power. In September, the Hungarians aired an interview with former Soviet Politburo member, Kiril Mazurov, which shocked the Czechoslovaks. Mazurov condemned the 1968 invasion as a disastrous error and urged the current rulers to step down. By this time, condemnation of the 1968 invasion was hardly startling news, even from the Soviets. But Mazurov revealed that it was he who had actually led the 1968 invasion, under the name of General Trofymov. Poland also created difficulties for Prague. In July 1989, an unofficial Solidarity delegation met with Dubeček, Havel, and other notable dissidents. Their joint public statements incensed Czechoslovak communists by calling for all Warsaw Pact nations to condemn the 1968 invasion as a means to prod the country to reform. In October, the legislatures in both Hungary and Poland did just that–condemned their nations' participation in quelling the Prague Spring. Moscow seconded the condemnation in late December, but only after it was clear that the ruling Czechoslovak Communist Party had fallen.

In the summer of 1989, *Pravda* and *Izvestia* repeatedly published articles critical of the Czechoslovak regime as well as giving coverage to Dubeček and other supporters of the Prague Spring. In September, a Soviet television crew showed up in Bratislava, in southern Czechoslovakia, to interview the "nonperson" Dubeček. The discussion was never broadcast in Czechoslovakia, but the public knew of it and understood the significance of Moscow's recognition of a man who was not recognized in his own country.

Two years of political unrest, then, had preceded the events of November 17, 1989. By then, the Party was intellectually and morally spent. It had no idea of how to maintain its power and seemed unsure of whether it was entitled to do so. The demonstrations, and the brutality of the security forces, appeared no different that day than during countless earlier protests. But these protests became larger and more menacing, drawing more people to the streets than ever before.

The Czechoslovak regime, moreover, could no longer look to its traditional support-ers, its former "fraternal allies" in Eastern Europe and the Soviet Union. Another powerful contributor to the paralysis of the Jakes government was the attitude of Mikhail Gorbachev. By November 17, only two weeks remained before Gorbachev's summit meeting with Pres-ident George Bush at Malta. Gorbachev desperately wanted a favorable climate for what he intended to be the first post–Cold War summit and feared the consequences of discord and repression in the satellites.

Months after the Communist Party had fallen and Civic Forum had investigated the events of November 17th, it was found that Gorbachev had taken direct action to unseat Jakes. Throughout the bloc, Gorbachev had apparently played a role in moving the reform process. But in Prague, his role was remarkably direct. The day before the November 17th protest, Jan Fojtik, a ranking Czechoslovak Party member, was summoned to Moscow and informed that the protest was not to be thwarted by Jakes. Accepting the warning, Ladislav Adamec, then the prime minister, took rather suddenly to his bed, claiming illness. Jakes left town, retiring to his residence on Lake Orlik. Command of the riot police was turned over to General Tislenko, who was neither Czech nor Slovak but Soviet. Once the protestors moved from the cemetery to Wenceslas Square, Czech and Soviet agents posing as students are reported to have stirred the crowd to move directly into the police, thus provoking violence. Furthermore, the "student" allegedly killed by the police turned out to be neither a student nor a victim. He was a police agent who was seen in Prague days later, perfectly well. But he had played an important role. The uprising, though spontaneous in origin, was encouraged by a plan.

What followed, however, appears to have taken on a life of its own, beyond the reach of Moscow and the Party in Prague. Havel and the Charter 77 members who formed the Civic Forum gathered in the Magic Lantern Theatre and decided on four simple demands of the government. None of the demands was especially bold, considering political developments elsewhere in the bloc. Civic Forum never even demanded a role in the government. Rather, they called for the resignation of all of those responsible for destroying the Prague Spring of 1968 and the 20 years of "devastation" that followed, which naturally included President Husák and Party head Jakes. They also called for the resignation of Frantisek Kincl, Interior Minister, and Miroslav Stepan, head of the Party in Prague, both of whom were considered directly responsible for the police action on November 17th. Finally, they sought a special and independent investigation of the circumstances of the 17th of November and for the immediate release of all political prisoners.

The specific demands drafted by the Forum were presented to Prime Minister Adamec on November 23rd, in the first talks between the opposition and the ruling order.

The Party had entered the talks when it realized it was losing all control over Prague. This was occurring largely because after the 17th, the Forum managed to secure the balcony of the Socialist Party publishing house in the middle of Wenceslas Square to use as a speech platform. Each day, more than 100,000 people gathered to hear speakers criticize the government. In addition to the daily demonstrations, the Forum pursued other tactics to force the hand of the regime. It announced its refusal to negotiate with representatives of the Party but only of the government, thereby diminishing the legitimacy of the Party. The tactic had the additional effect of dividing the upper echelons of the Party. Several Party members had cast their lot with the reformers at the political expense of the governing Party members. Civic Forum also formed an alliance with Public Against Violence, its Slovakian counterpart. This solidarity with the Slovak minority preempted the Party's stratagem of alternatively favoring the Czechs or the Slovaks at the expense of the other.

Another crucial factor was the success of labor leader Petr Miller in persuading the workers to join the Forum protests. Without labor, none of the Forum's protests would ever have brought the nation to a complete standstill. With labor, the Forum managed to bring under its wings every major social force except the Party. With Miller's help, demonstrations went from hundreds of thousands to millions throughout the country's industrial centers.

On November 24, as the demonstrations grew out of control, Jakes and the rest of the Party leadership resigned, with Karel Urbanek becoming the new head of the Party. Only a few days later, the party experienced its first mass defections. More than 50,000 resigned to establish the Forum of Democratic Communists and declare their support for Civic Forum. Having seized the political initiative, the Forum now demanded an end to the "leading role of the Party," the legalization of other parties, a timetable for free elections, the drafting of a new constitution, the establishment of an independent judiciary, and the freeing of the economy. The Forum backed up its demands with a successful nationwide general strike on November 27th, affecting every urban center in the country.

The following day, Havel and Adamec met again, with Adamec promising to name a new government, "a broad representative coalition," to remove the "leading role of the Party," and to lift a ban on previously censored books. The hated Interior Minister, Miroslav Stepan, resigned. The National Assembly met, officially renounced the leading role of the Party, and ended the teaching of Marxism-Leninism in schools. East Germany added to the momentum by announcing an apology for its participation in the 1968 invasion, which was followed by the issuance of a similar apology from the Czechoslovak Communist Party.

As he had promised, Adamec announced his new "broad coalition" government on December 3. The new cabinet was neither broad nor a coalition. Of its 21 members, 16 were communists, with the rest unknown independents. The Forum was outraged at their betrayal. On the following day the largest crowds ever to have gathered in the country heard Forum demand the formation of a new government in one week.

Adamec and Urbanek were called to Moscow to meet Gorbachev, just returned from the Malta summit. Again, the Czech communists were caught in the larger issues of East–West relations. The leaders of the Warsaw Pact were also called to Moscow, where they renounced the Pact's invasion of August 1968. Adamec and Urbanek returned to Prague and resigned on December 7th.

Round Table talks were immediately convened between the party, Civic Forum, and Public Against Violence. In less than 48 hours, they had reached an agreement on a new government, tilted in favor of the Forum. The prime minister was to be the communist Marian Calfa, who immediately resigned from the Party, while there were to be eight communist ministers and 12 Forum members. On December 10, President Husák swore the new Forum-dominated government into office and then resigned.

The new regime was named the Government of National Understanding and was to stand until free elections could take place in June, 1990. The new government read like a

Who's Who of Czechoslovak political dissent. Jan Čarnogurský, a Slovak lawyer nationally famous for defending human rights cases, was released from prison just two weeks before becoming the first deputy premier and assigned responsibility for overseeing the security apparatus. Under him, Czechoslovakia became the first state in Eastern Europe to remove control of the security services from the Party. Jiri Dienstbier, a major actor in Charter 77 and no stranger to prison, went from coal shoveler to foreign minister. The four major thinkers of the Institute for Economic Forecasting of the Academy of Sciences took the leading economic posts. Valtr Komarek, Institute director, was made deputy prime minister. His assistant, Vladimir Dlouhy, was appointed chief of state planning. Václav Klaus, widely known as the Czechoslovak Milton Friedman, headed the Ministry of Finance. Tomás Jezek, a free-market theorist, became a senior economic advisor. In little more than a week, the economists had already laid out a plan for market conversion and economic renewal. Blacksmith and labor leader Petr Miller was made labor and social affairs minister. Miroslav Kusy, a dissident philosopher and Charter 77 member, was charged with overseeing the press and information ministry. Besides the premiership, the communists were left with two deputy premierships and the ministries of defense, foreign trade, energy, transportation, and metallurgy.

For the new government, however, one matter still remained unresolved: the presidency vacated by Husák. In a mini–Round Table, Civic Forum convened the Communist Party, the former rump parties, and Public Against Violence, and won the presidency for Havel, whom Adamec just weeks before had called "a nobody—an absolute zero." On November 28, Dubeček was elected Chairman of the National Assembly, a position of marginal political power but immense symbolism, and by the end of January, the communist majority had resigned from the Assembly. At the outset of the new year, Civic Forum had won control of the government and the National Assembly. In less than six weeks, it had secured more than had been so arduously won in Hungary and Poland.

Civic Forum appreciated the irony of its position—a democratic government never democratically elected—and proceeded to govern cautiously with broad public debate, being especially careful not to exacerbate Czech–Slovak tensions. Nonetheless, before the June elections, it passed over 60 reform laws, ranging from human rights and election procedures to legalizing private businesses and reducing compulsory military service.

In order to gain a listing on the national ballot for the June elections, a party had to demonstrate that it had at least 10,000 members. For local elections, however, parties needed only 1,000 members. More than 100 parties had managed to meet the requirements for local listing, and 20 met the requirements for national listing by the time of the June elections. To counter the charges that it stood only for vague generalities—pluralist democracy and returning Czechoslovakia to Europe—Civic Forum published an election program that presented an austere scenario for the country's economic future. "We should avoid the temptation of increasing our consumption," the program declared, calling instead for higher investment and debt repayment. Clearly a product of Václav Klaus, the program advocated the speedy introduction of a market economy.

The elections were to decide the composition of both the national and regional legislatures. The federalist system recognizes the two major ethnic groups, the Czechs and the Slovaks, and establishes a centralized government tolerable to both. The National Assembly is bicameral. Representation in the Assembly of the People reflects population, but in the Assembly of the Nations, the approximately five million Slovaks have representation equal to that of the approximately ten million Czechs. The National Council is a regional legislature for each of the Czech and Slovak constituent republics. The Slovaks and the Czechs each have separate ministries, while the Ministries of Foreign Affairs and Defense, for example, are joint federal ministries. The statewide ministries report to the National Assembly, while the regional ministries are responsible to the National Councils.

The big electoral winners among the Czechs was the Civic Forum and for the Slovaks, the Public Against Violence. They were widely popular as heirs of the Velvet Revolution. As umbrella organizations rather than true political parties, they contained the largest collection of political groups under their informal structure. The Forum and PAV won a majority of 170 out of the 300 seats in the National Assembly. The Liberal Democratic Party, a founding member of Forum, pulled out following the election, taking its two seats with it and leaving the Forum–PAV majority at 168. The Communist Party won slightly more than 13 percent of the popular vote and took 47 seats. A coalition Christian Democratic Party, made up of the People's Party, the Christian Democratic Party, and the Slovak Christian Democratic Movement, gained 40 seats. The Slovak National Party won 15 seats, and the Association for Moravia and Silesia took 16 seats. The Hungarian Christian Democratic Movement won 12 seats.

The results of the regional National Council elections were slightly different. The Civic Forum won a majority in the Czech National Council, followed by the Communist Party, which managed to gain a 13 percent share. In the Slovak National Council, the Public Against Violence fell short of a majority. It managed only 30 percent of the vote, followed by the Christian Democrats with 19 percent, and the Slovak Nationalist Party and the Communist Party each winning 13 percent of the vote. The poorer showing of the PAV was a clear indication of Slovak discontent with the federal structure and a fear that reforms emanating from Prague would fall more severely on Slovakia.

The combined representation of the Forum and the PAV provided substantial majorities in both chambers of the Federal Assembly. But President Havel, appreciating the two-thirds majority necessary to change the constitution, sought to base the new government on a broad coalition. The Civic Forum ruled out only the Communists and the Slovak National Party as coalition partners. No sooner were the elections completed when the Forum–PAV umbrella structure began to dissolve. At the federal level, the Forum–PAV dissolved into a right and center, and in Slovakia the PAV factionalized, losing support to nationalist parties.

But having emerged victorious in the country's first postwar democratic elections, the Havel government had to deal with three challenges whose resolution will define Czechoslovakia's future—Slovak nationalism, the economic transformation of the country, and the political future of the Civic Forum.

Czech–Slovak Relations

The election results at the federal and national levels indicated that the Slovaks were to some extent rejecting the Forum's agenda. Two new parties with regional, ethnic appeals have appeared in Slovakia. The Slovak National Party is decidedly militant, while the Christian Democratic Movement, like the Christian Democrats in Germany, represents conservative and Catholic views. Its leader is Jan Čarnogurský, the First Deputy Prime Minister at the federal level and, as of April, 1991, the Slovak Prime Minister. He is respected in Prague as a reasonable voice for Slovak aspirations, but he is increasingly viewed in Slovakia as too moderate to realize those aspirations. Frustrated by the nationalists' impeding the government reform agenda, Čarnogurský threatened to resign in April 1991.

Slovak nationalist sentiment has been a central issue in all political debate. Slovaks have attempted to assert the supremacy of Slovak laws over those of the federation, and economic reform has been sidetracked. The government has sought to appease the separatists by decentralizing power and encouraging national autonomy. Several ministries have been abolished and their powers transferred to the republics. In November, 1990, after heated negotiations, it was agreed that the nation would remain a federal state, but with the republics gaining control over taxation, budgets, and property ownership. Yet with each concession, some Slovak group wanted more.

Most threatening, demands for an independent Slovakia have not abated. Havel, the consummate democrat, has made it clear that if the Slovaks wish to leave the union, he will not stand in their way. But every poll through the summer of 1991 indicates that a strong majority of Slovaks favor remaining in a union that allows them significant autonomy. The government is left facing a major constitutional predicament. When the first round of talks for drafting new federal and republican constitutions was called for in February, 1991, the Slovaks demanded a state treaty between the republics before the writing of a constitution. The Slovaks sought to codify their rights before yielding any powers to the federal government. But the leadership in Prague has feared that more concessions to the Slovaks would push the federal system into irrelevance.

Czech–Slovak tensions were aggravated in April, 1991, by the collapse of the Slovak government. Vladimir Meciar, the populist prime minister, grew increasingly hostile to the federal economic program as disproportionately harsh on Slovakia. He broke from the PAV and formed the PAV–For a Democratic Slovakia. The PAV retaliated by opening an investigation into his use of police files against political opponents and eventually replaced him with Čarnogurský. Unless the economy improves dramatically before the June, 1992, election, Meciar and his new party can be counted on to be a disruptive, nationalist political force.

Another major challenge stems from the nearly 600,000 ethnic Hungarians in the southern fringe of Slovakia along the border with Hungary. The federal government has sought to accord them full civil rights within the state. But the Slovak National Council actually restricted some of their rights. As a result, the Hungarians living in Slovakia have serious problems, and relations between Prague and Budapest are strained.

Economic Problems

There are positive indications for the Czechoslovak economy. Basic consumer goods are relatively abundant, and the state foreign debt is not unbearably large, though it is nearing $10 billion. International sympathy for the Civic Forum in Europe and the United States has led to the widespread availability of credits.

But economic reform has moved with glacial slowness, reflecting deep divisions within the government. Since the political transformation had been painless, many believed that economic transformation could be achieved with as little cost. But the initial economic legislation failed to improve the economy, while the unraveling of the communist bureaucracies added to its decline. The Slovak political challenge has diverted attention from economic reform. As the economy declined, even Forum supporters retreated from their commitment to rapid economic reform.

Václav Klaus, the charismatic Minister of Finance, refocused public debate on rapid change at the end of 1990, but only at the expense of the unity of Civic Forum. Since the Forum's accession to power, the political stature of the Finance Minister had skyrocketed. In the 1990 election, he won more votes than any other candidate, and in the early fall he managed to win the chairmanship of the Forum, declaring that he would make it a right-of-center political party. As his power increased, he became ever less popular with left-leaning Forum members, who resented his devout commitment to a free market. In early 1991 the Forum split over the issue of "'Klauskrieg' economics," raising the possibility of a Klaus premiership after the 1992 elections.

Klaus has been determined to force a program of substantial privatization to attract more foreign and domestic investment. The Czech koruna was made internally convertible, and foreign investors offered more substantial protection. A sweeping privatization program for the approximately 3,000 largest firms in the country was ratified, and the controversial property restitution bill was completed. As if to seal Czechoslovakia's new economic direction, Klaus secured the largest privatization deal to date in Eastern Europe. Skoda, the Czech automobile manufacturer, sold a 70 percent stake to Volkswagen for DM 1.4 billion. While his popularity has become second only to President Havel, Finance Minister Klaus must demonstrate continuous economic victories to retain that support.

The Survival of the Civic Forum

The third major challenge is to maintain the Forum as the country's dominant democratic political force. Like Solidarity in Poland, Civic Forum and Public Against Violence are heterogeneous political groupings, gathered around the banner of opposition to the old order. While the overthrow of the old order was an achievement of magnificent proportions, it was in many ways simple in comparison with the complexities faced by the new regime. To paraphrase the motto of the 1968 Prague Spring reform movement, Czechoslovakia must now create "capitalism with a human face," but the country is riven with disputes as to the humanity of the market.

Civic Forum/Public Against Violence has changed radically since the 1990 elections. Václav Klaus formed a conservative party, the Civic Democratic Party, while the more liberal members formed the Civic Movement, still claiming to be an umbrella organization rather than a party. The most left-leaning Forum members have gone over to the already existing leftist faction—the Social Democrats, joined by the Agrarians and Greens. The liberals of the Civic Movement have slowed Klaus's ability to realize his agenda and argue that welfare and jobless benefits must be maintained. But all the Forum's factions generally agree that overall unity is crucial in order to adopt a new constitution while holding off the threat of Slovak separatism. The adoption of a constitution is likely to result in the breakdown of the Forum's unity and the establishment of new political groupings to compete in the 1992 elections.

Clearly, the Forum is unlikely to repeat its 1990 electoral triumph in 1992. Recent polls indicate promising prospects for the Klaus group, for the Green Party, and, in Slovak politics, for the Christian Democrats, who have overtaken Public Against Violence and the PAV–For a Democratic Slovakia. A Socialist Party, competing with the Communist Party, and a Farmers' Party are likely to be more formidable political competitors.

Other government challenges appear less threatening. The collapse of the USSR in August 1991 appears to pose no immediate threat. All Soviet troops withdrew from Czechoslovakia by June, 1991, and bilateral relations have been amicable. Havel and the Forum, unlike the Hungarians, have not aggressively claimed compensation from the former Soviet Union for military housing and cleanup expenses. They even maintained their reserve when it was revealed, in the spring of 1991, that Moscow maintained at least three secret nuclear weapons depots in the country at Prague's expense. The people and the government are aware of their continued need for oil, raw materials, as well as markets from the former Soviet republics. Only Bulgaria had more trade with the USSR during the communist period, and Prague will do nothing to jeopardize its relations, at least until it has been able to reorient its trade.

The future role of the Communist Party is another concern. The 1990 elections made it clear that the Party will continue to play a political role. They received 13 percent of the votes, second only to the Civic Forum. But it is possible that the disintegration of the Forum will leave the communists with the largest single party. Membership has declined dramatically, but many Party leaders are still popular at the local level. If the economy deteriorates sharply, the communists could regain a larger following.

But perhaps the most formidable challenge is a moral one. More than the other revolutions in Eastern Europe, the Velvet Revolution was a moral phenomenon, driven by the words and ideas repressed by the communists for more than two decades. The intellectuals, poets, and artists of Charter 77 had been reduced to sweeping shop floors and shoveling coal. Their victory was a triumph for the moral imperatives to which they were committed. Yet the future of the country seems likely to be driven more by political than moral concerns. The ability of the leaders of Czechoslovakia to make the transition to the politics of compromise will determine their future and that of the party they ousted.

Czechoslovakia's foreign trade is a case in point. For the past 15 years the country collected nearly 50 percent of its foreign earnings through the sale of arms. Upon coming to power, the Forum declared its intention to cease trading in weapons. But desperately short of foreign exchange, the government now trades arms for oil in the Middle East. Klaus has vigorously defended the trade, stating that market economies do the same. Little wonder that Havel has expressed the desire not to make politics a career.

Nearly all of the major political actors agree that civil order is the desired end, even if that requires forming a very loose federation between the republics to accommodate the ethnic and nationalist demands of the Slovaks. But many, especially former Charter 77 leaders, fear the costs of establishing a demand-driven, market-oriented economy. Yet others forcefully press for a full and rapid conversion, arguing their case on the grounds of ultimate economic prosperity. The tension between moral and political imperatives will continue to dominate much of Czechoslovak political life.

HISTORY

Origins to 1900

The first Slavic tribes began to move into the area that is now Czechoslovakia in the sixth century A.D., gradually displacing Celtic and Germanic tribes. As they settled, the Slavs developed two distinct regional identities, with the peoples of what is now Bohemia and Moravia in the western part of the territory becoming known as Czechs and the people in the eastern part known as Slovaks. The two groups have never differentiated decisively and to this day retain strong cultural and linguistic ties. In the ninth century, Moravia was the area's center of power. At that time, Prince Mojmir and his successor Rotislav consolidated Moravia, Slovakia, and much of Bohemia into the first Slavic union. Rotislav's successor Svatopluk continued the expansion of greater Moravia into Magyar territories. The Magyars resisted, however, and conquered Slovakia but not Bohemia. Slovakia remained under Hungarian control until the dissolution of the Austro-Hungarian Empire after World War I. With the demise of the Moravian kingdom, power in the area shifted to Bohemia around the castle of Prague, the residence of the Premysl dynasty. The most renowned ruler of this period was the Christian martyr King Wenceslas, of Christmas carol fame. His brother, Boleslav the Cruel, murdered him more for power than religious conviction, yet a cult developed around St. Wenceslas. He is Bohemia's national saint, whose Czech name, Václav, is given frequently to firstborn males (including President Havel and Finance Minister Klaus) and for whom the Prague square, the site of the crucial November 1989 demonstrations, is named.

In 962, the Pope restored the Holy Roman Empire by crowning the German Otto as Emperor. Bohemia was then incorporated into the loosely organized empire and prospered as a result of the immigrants who had left the more heavily populated regions of Germany. The German immigrants turned empty Bohemian lands into productive farms, founded thriving merchant businesses in the towns, and brought mining skills to the region's substantial gold and silver deposits. Becoming a powerful force in Bohemia, the Germans developed a wealthy burgher class in the towns and, except for the Czech nobility, remained more prosperous than the Czechs. (It was the descendants of these Germans that Hitler incorporated into the Third Reich when he annexed the Sudetenland.)

In the early fifteenth century, a hundred years before Martin Luther's Protestant Reformation, a number of Czechs embraced Jan Hus's liberal teachings of church reform and a return to more genuine Christian life. But their religious practices, which threatened the established Catholic powers, was violently disrupted when Ferdinand I, a Catholic and Austrian Hapsburg, was crowned King of Bohemia in 1527. He set out to drive the Hussites, as Hus's followers were known, from Bohemia and restore the power of the monarchy by weakening the nobles and merchants. Under his sway, many Hussites converted to Catholicism. He also successfully crushed the power of the lords and burghers who opposed him. With the nobility greatly weakened, the townships lost nearly all the political privileges they had previously won. In 1558, Ferdinand I was elected Holy Roman Emperor, making Prague again the center of the Empire.

But religious tensions persisted, as many of the former Hussites had since adopted the teachings of Luther. Following a Protestant rebellion in Bohemia, the new Emperor, Ferdinand II, defeated the Protestants once and for all in 1620 and forced their renewed conversion to Catholicism. These forcible conversions left the Czechs less fervently Catholic than the Slovaks, one of the critical differences that has continued to this day.

Over the following two hundred years, Bohemia and Moravia lost much of their independence as they were incorporated into the Hapsburg Empire. The emperors allotted land, wealth, and political power to the Germans in Bohemia, while the majority of the Czechs became serfs working for the German or the Czech nobility. German became the popular language among bureaucrats, merchants, and universities. Austrian influences penetrated and spread throughout Czech culture.

By the beginning of the nineteenth century, the Hapsburg Empire—the Austro-Hungarian Monarchy, as it had come to be called—included territories now a part of eight European countries, from Poland in the north to Italy and Yugoslavia in the south, and from Austria in the west to the Soviet Union in the east. The core of the Monarchy, however, centered on the lands that make up present-day Austria, Czechoslovakia, and Hungary. The Czechs and their language continued to be subordinate to the Germans, with the majority living as serfs, the subjects of feudal lords. Others were small freeholders or petty tradespeople in towns and cities. Among the urban population of Bohemia and Moravia, Germans remained the majority of the landholding aristocracy. As a Czech nationalist movement formed, its leaders were drawn from predominantly modest origins. To enhance their status, the Czechs sought the assistance and protection of their Slav brother to the East, Russia. Russophile sentiments would also prove to play a similar role in the later development of Slovak nationalism.

In the spring of 1848, revolutions shook the capitals of Europe. The Austro-Hungarian Monarchy was no exception, but by 1850 the only apparent change was the abolition of serfdom. In 1867, the Hungarians managed to forge a compromise with the Hapsburgs, receiving broad autonomy in deciding the affairs of the eastern half of the Empire. The elevation of Hungarian status, however, created a critical demarcation between the Czech and Slovak regions. This new constitutional order confirmed German predominance in the western half of the Empire, the Czech region, while the Slovak region was subordinated to the Hungarians.

In the latter nineteenth century, industrialization made rapid progress in Bohemia and Moravia, which were particularly rich in natural resources. For example, a machine shop established in 1859 grew into the giant Skoda industries, producing large machinery, locomotives, and, beginning in 1886, armaments, for which the firm became notorious. In the twentieth century, the firm began producing tanks and the Skoda automobile, now commonplace throughout Eastern Europe.

With industrialization, urbanization naturally followed. The cities and towns gained a larger and larger portion of Czech inhabitants as numerous Czech laborers and shopkeepers moved to the developing urban areas, taking up residence alongside the German populace. Paralleling the development of a modern society in Bohemia and Moravia, modern political parties grew to articulate economic interests and ideological viewpoints—the Social Democrats represented the industrial workers; Agrarians, the farmers and peasants; and the People's Party, the Catholics.

1900 to 1945

Over the decades, the various Czech parties were able to extract significant concessions, such as the right to use the Czech language in public life, from successive governments in the imperial capital of Vienna. By 1914, as a result of their growing national movement rooted in industrialization and urbanization, the Czechs had made major strides toward economic, social, and even political equity with the ethnic Germans (later termed Sudeten Germans). Though spread throughout Bohemia and Moravia, the majority of the Germans were concentrated in the mountainous border districts, where they constituted a majority of the population.

In contrast to the dynamic growth and development occurring in the Czech lands, the industrialization of Slovakia began to occur much later, at the turn of the century. Slovak society remained predominantly rural, with Slovaks living as peasants and the Hungarians as the nobility. Slovak nationalists enjoyed sympathetic support but remained a small group, with only limited political success. At the turn of the century, new voices emerged advocating greater cooperation between Czechs and Slovaks, but such ideas had little impact on either people. By the beginning of World War I, the Slovaks had only begun the process of establishing differentiated political parties. While the Catholic Father Anrej Hlinka was recognized as the leader of the Slovak nationalist movement, independence was far from the mainstream of political thought at the outbreak of World War I. The redrawing of the map of Europe following that war, however, was to transform the region.

Like the Russian empire of the Romanov dynasty and the German empire of the Hohenzollerns, the Hapsburg empire was unable to withstand the strains of the First World War. Tensions among the nationalities were exacerbated by economic deprivation and a war of great savagery and duration. During the war, each of the Czech parties came to favor autonomy or an independent state including the Slovaks. Soon after the outbreak of fighting, Tomás G. Masaryk and Edvard Benes laid the groundwork among the Entente Powers—Britain, France, Italy, Russia, and later the United States—for recognizing a revolutionary Czechoslovak government-in-exile. By late October 1918, the Austro-Hungarian Empire was near collapse, and a Czech uprising seized power in Prague, the capital of Bohemia. The new government hastily mobilized regiments to put down an attempt by the Sudeten Germans to create their own state. Establishing the power of the new government in Slovakia proved a slower process. The Paris Peace Conference of 1919–1920 drew a new map for Eastern Europe, joining the Czechs and Slovaks together to form almost two-thirds of the total population of Czechoslovakia and including three-quarters of a million Hungarians and the Sudeten Germans, all compounding the ethnic problems facing the new state.

The constitution of the Czechoslovak Republic drew primarily on European and American models. The National Assembly was to be elected by universal suffrage, and since it was empowered to appoint the president, it became the central institution of the new state. To guarantee representation of smaller parties and the national minorities, seats in the National Assembly were allotted by proportional representation. National minorities were guaranteed extensive cultural and local autonomy, more than was enjoyed in other Central and East European countries, and their rights were largely respected. But the new state structure was highly centralized rather than a federal state, strengthening the Czech parties, the prime architects of the constitution, and undermining Slovak interests.

Postwar independence exacerbated wartime scarcities and produced greater economic dislocation. The Bolshevik seizure of power in Russia radicalized the Czechoslovak Social Democratic Party, whose left wing formed the Communist Party in 1920. The Czechoslovak communists operated legally throughout the interwar period, setting them apart from their sister communist parties, banned and forced underground in the other countries of Eastern Europe.

While never a member of the government, the Czechoslovak Communist Party had substantial membership, though only in the cities. As a result of land reform, the communists could not successfully recruit in the countryside. The land reform also crippled the aristocracy by transferring most of its holdings to peasants and smallholders. Because they administered the land reform program, the Agrarian Party had rich opportunities for patronage that produced substantial political power.

The 1920s were Czechoslovakia's "golden days." Bolstered by international stability, the country's economy boomed. Of the three main successor states to the Hapsburg Monarchy—Czechoslovakia, Hungary and Austria—Czechoslovakia was the most industrialized and the most stable.

Yet the Slovaks became increasingly alienated. Companies established in Slovakia were forced to compete with well-established competitors in Bohemia and Moravia, though they had lost their prewar markets in Hungary. Because laissez-faire capitalist thinking dominated the state, no particular measures were taken to ameliorate the economic dislocations that followed. The nationalist and separatist Slovak People's Party steadily gained adherents. The Catholic Slovaks were also offended by the relatively clear separation of church and state favored by President Masaryk and the majority of Czechs. The Slovak People's Party, led by Father Hlinka, capitalized on the offended religious sensibilities of the Slovaks and demanded greater Slovak autonomy.

The other main political force in Slovakia was the Slovak wing of the Agrarian Party, which, together with the four Czech parties which supported the constitution of 1920, made up the Pětka, or "Fivesome." The Pětka constituted the club of political insiders. Its members were invariably part of one or another of the coalition governments of the interwar period. Its leaders consulted each other informally on political issues. While individual governments fell and were reformed, the Pětka contributed greatly to stability. But the stability produced by Pětka insiders was achieved by ignoring significant problems— the discontent of the Slovaks, the Sudeten Germans, and treatment of the Hungarian minority in southern Slovakia.

Until 1926, the Czechoslovak Social Democrats were the Agrarian Party's major partners in the center-left coalition governments. In that year the Agrarians formed a new, center-right governing coalition with both the Czech and Slovak People's Parties. The coalition also included the Sudeten German Clerical and Agrarian parties and for the first time, Slovak and German parties entered the government. Negotiations followed for constitutional reform that would decentralize power to the benefit of the Slovaks. But the reform failed, a failure which was to return to haunt the country in later decades.

While the 1920s were a decade of stable politics and expanding prosperity, the 1930s were a disaster. The worldwide depression devastated the economic and social fabric of Czechoslovakia. The ascendancy of fascist and authoritarian regimes across Europe gave impetus to the rise of antidemocratic elements within the Slovak People's Party. The same processes occurred among the Germans of Bohemia and Moravia with the rise of Konrad Henlein's Sudeten German Party, which supported the Third Reich.

When Masaryk retired from the presidency in 1935, Edvard Benes, who had been foreign minister through the ebb and flow of the coalitions, was elected president. Despite the disturbing trends of the early 1930s, Czechoslovakia did not seem endangered. Its political life was relatively stable, civil, democratic, and free of corruption. Anti-Semitism played no major role in public life—in contrast to neighboring countries—and national minorities were not persecuted. The Communist Party was not outlawed. The Czechoslovak army was large, disciplined, and well-equipped, and the country had a system of defensive treaties with France.

But at the Munich conference in September, 1938, Britain and France abandoned their Czechoslovak ally to Hitler, spelling the end of the interwar Republic. Slovakia became a nominally independent German client state under the Slovak People's Party.

But by March 1939, the Czech lands were incorporated into the Third Reich. Some acts of protest occurred in Bohemia and Moravia, and in the fall of 1939 university students seemed on the verge of launching massive protests. To prevent them, large numbers of German Gestapo and SS members rampaged through the Prague student hostels on November 17th, 1939. Many of the Czech students who were not killed were sent to concentration camps, and all Czech universities were closed. During the war, communists in Slovakia formed an underground Party organization that helped organize the most notable instance of anti-Nazi resistance anywhere in Czechoslovakia, the Slovak National Uprising in the fall of 1944.

1945 to 1990

When Czechoslovakia emerged from the Second World War, Edward Benes once again became president, but the rest of the nation's circumstances and its political complexion had been irretrievably altered. Before returning to Prague from his exile in London, Benes went to Moscow to sign a friendship treaty with Stalin. Benes saw Czechoslovakia as a strong state in Central Europe, neither East nor West. He was certainly no communist, but neither did he see his country as a member of the emerging Western camp that had betrayed Czechoslovakia at Munich.

But there was to be no Central Europe following World War II, and the friendship treaty gave the Czechoslovak communists an immense advantage, strengthened by the massive population resettlements begun near the end of the war. The three million Sudeten Germans who had lived in western Czechoslovakia before the war migrated west or were expelled to Germany. Benes requested permission from the Allied Powers to expel the Hungarian minority but this was denied. Nevertheless, the expulsion of the Germans, more than a fifth of the total population, proved a major stimulus to the rise of the communists. Communist Party members were well placed in the bureaucracy and were able to control the distribution of the property of the departing Germans, making them widely popular.

As in World War I, wartime deprivation, limited as it was relative to the other states of Eastern Europe, served to radicalize sentiment on the left. On the center and right many were dispirited. They understood the failure at Munich as somehow discrediting the entire political system of the interwar Republic. Some of the conservative parties, most notably the strong prewar Agrarian Party, were banned outright. The fact that President Roosevelt had honored his agreement with Stalin to allow Soviet troops to "liberate" Czechoslovakia in 1945 gave the Czechoslovak left additional prestige by its association with Moscow. The communists especially resurrected and played on Russophile traditions and themes, as well as exploiting the fact that the West had sold out Czechoslovakia at Munich while the Soviets had saved the country from the Fascists.

Elections in 1946 gave the communists a strong position in the National Front, the coalition government of four parties from the Czech territory and two from Slovakia. The communists held the Ministry of the Interior, in charge of the police, and the Ministries of Agriculture, Social Welfare, Information, and Education. Moreover, Prime Minister Zdenek Fierlinger, a Social Democrat, was sympathetic to the communists and took the head of the Communist Party, Klement Gottwald, as one of his four major deputies.

The likelihood of a weaker showing in the forthcoming elections, however, led the communists to stage a "coup from within" in February 1948. Prior to the election, it had become clear to the communist leadership that their popularity was fading. The realities of reconstruction had overtaken the postwar sentiment that had made the Party a popular force. Commissioning a survey of Czechoslovak public opinion, the Party found that their supporters numbered just slightly more than a quarter of the voters. The communists decided on a speedy takeover. Minister of the Interior Václav Nosek fired his noncommunist police commissioners and refused a cabinet demand that the officers be reinstated. The entire cabinet resigned in protest, expecting to engineer the fall of the government and early elections, which they knew the communists would lose.

But the elections never took place. With overt support from Moscow, the Communist Party bullied Benes into suspending the elections and appointing their members to fill the government vacancies. The democratic leadership either fled the country, was forced into internal exile, or was quietly eliminated. President Benes died in September, 1948, allowing Klement Gottwald to assume the presidency. The takeover had taken less than seven months. Like Czechoslovakia's political crisis of 1968, the changing of the guard was startlingly rapid.

After seizing power, the Communist Party adhered rigidly to the Soviet model. Centralized planning and huge heavy industries dominated the economy. Large-scale industrialization was brought to Slovakia, significantly less developed than Bohemia and Moravia. The pattern of intensive development continued into the early 1960s, when its failures became overwhelmingly clear.

In 1962, reform economists tried to decentralize economic decision making, but, fearing that dispersing economic control would lead inevitably to the erosion of communist power, Antonin Novotny, who had become party secretary following Gottwald's death in 1953, resisted.

Challenges to Novotny's rigid Stalinism came from all sides as economic stagnation became impossible to ignore. After 20 years of unfulfilled promises, the Slovak Communist Party began to express previously repressed Slovak nationalist sentiments, demanding a genuine federation. The intellectual and cultural elites outside the party demanded the restoration of civil liberties.

Open attacks on the hard-line leadership burst onto the scene at the Congress of Czech Writers in June 1967. Authors and poets took the podium to condemn the Novotny government. They accused it of betraying true socialist principles and maintaining oppressive censorship. Novotny responded with an immediate crackdown. But many within the party had grown weary of the general secretary's heavy hand and sympathized with the writers. The desire for liberalization was strengthened because Khrushchev had undertaken his de-Stalinization campaign years before in 1956. But no relaxation of the Czechoslovak political climate had yet appeared in Prague.

In November 1967, a group of students and intellectuals organized demonstrations against poor housing conditions, which soon grew into general political protest. With support from Moscow, the Central Committee replaced the Stalinist first secretary in early 1968. Brezhnev's choice to replace Novotny was Alexander Dubeček, the first secretary of the Slovak Communist Party. How disastrously Brezhnev had miscalculated Dubeček's intentions for Czechoslovakia became stunningly clear after only a few months.

Dubeček's legendary but brief term in office is now referred to as the Prague Spring. In April, Dubeček announced an Action Program, which called for the restoration of civil liberties in a democratic socialism. The Action Program pledged to initiate significant economic reform and amend the constitution to provide autonomy for Slovakia. A rehabilitation law was passed calling for the retrial of anyone convicted of political crimes.

Czechoslovakia's 1968 reforms differed from those in the rest of Eastern European efforts because the principal impetus for change came from within the Communist Party. The changes in Hungary in 1956 were in opposition to the Party. In still earlier and lesser known uprisings in East Germany and Poland, the challenges came from within and without the party. The Prague Spring was even more unnerving for the Kremlin because it came as Leonid Brezhnev was tightening his grip on power to erase the last vestiges of Nikita Khrushchev's reforms.

Dubeček and his fellow reform leaders were nonetheless traditional communists in their rejection of any role for other political parties. The Communist Party was to become democratic, allowing open discussion and enduring factional divisions. Fuller participation from below would enable the Party to synthesize a wide range of political viewpoints. A noncensored press would criticize the Party but not threaten it, because the Party would function democratically. The Party would then lead through its responsiveness to its members and society rather than by dictating from above. The Action Program was widely popular, and many Czechs and Slovaks believed they were on the road to creating "socialism with a human face."

Ultimately, the Kremlin could not accept the Action Program because of its reformulation of the role of the Party. When Dubeček allowed political "clubs" to form outside the Communist Party, Brezhnev reached the limits of his tolerance. The Prague leaders reassured Moscow that Czechoslovakia would remain a loyal member of the Warsaw Pact. Many of the reformers around Dubeček believed their reforms would strengthen communism and the international socialist system. They had no desire to break from the East bloc. But for Moscow, the threat from Prague, unlike the earlier threat from Budapest, was not the dissolution of the Warsaw Pact. The threat came from Dubeček's redefinition of the leading role of the Party. The ultimate result, so it seemed to Brezhnev, was to threaten the very rule of the Communist Party.

When the Czechoslovak Communist Party called a Congress formally to approve the Action Program and to purge the remaining advocates of traditional communist rule, the USSR decided to use force. The Soviet Army, with token units from its "fraternal socialist" allies Poland, East Germany, Hungary, and Bulgaria, (but not Romania) invaded Czechoslovakia on the night of August 20, 1968, seizing the reform leaders. The Czechoslovak army was ordered not to resist. But the Czechoslovak people resisted courageously and nonviolently, succeeding in slowing but not preventing the reimposition of political orthodoxy.

Dubeček was replaced by another Slovak, Gustáv Husák, who proceeded to liquidate the Prague Spring. The only reform to survive was federalization—the granting of considerable autonomy to Slovakia—a move that now haunts the postcommunist government. The positive regard that the Soviets had enjoyed from their liberation of Czechoslovakia from Nazi Germany was replaced by the hostility common throughout the East bloc.

From the crushing of the Prague Spring to the fall of communist rule in 1989, Czechoslovakia was governed by the vigorous reassertion of Stalinist rule, completely different from Hungary after its 1956 uprising. Hungary had been subjected to brief repression to remove the ranking reformers, and Janos Kadar then instituted a program of controlled liberalization. But in Czechoslovakia Husák restored Stalinist controls, obliterating any hint of a civil order while sapping the economy of any remaining vigor. He increased his political strength with the help of hard-liners such as Vasil Bilák and Alois Indra and then, in 1970, conducted an unprecedented party purge. The purge was deep and changed both the nature of the party and the relationship between the Czech and Slovak republics. He ousted some 500,000 party members, nearly all Czechs, a full third of the total membership. By differentially punishing the Czechs, the Slovak Husák greatly damaged the already strained relations between the two peoples. In the 20 years following the purge, the relationship never improved, as Husák continued to favor Slovaks over Czechs. Disproportionately higher investments were directed to Slovakia, and larger numbers of Slovaks were promoted to national office, traditionally filled by the more numerous Czechs.

Though Husák's purges did not lead to executions, they were otherwise classically Stalinist. Stalin had directed his first purge at the "Old Bolsheviks," the founders whose loyalties were more to the Party than to Stalin. Husák's purge was similar. His mission was not simply to favor Slovaks over Czechs, but to decimate the party, as Stalin had done, and then reconstitute it with cadres loyal to him personally. Managers and factory directors, senior research scientists and engineers, competent bureaucrats, and labor leaders were all purged. They and their families, as well as their close associates, were given menial jobs as janitors, miners, construction workers, or common shop laborers.

The purge had devastating effects on the party and the state. Those promoted to replace the purged officials were largely incompetent. The effectiveness of the political and economic bureaucracies plummeted. The entire social fabric of the society was demoralized following the defeat of the Prague Spring. During Husák's tenure, the Soviets, as they had done in Hungary, tried to buy "Normalization" by offering credits and consumer goods. In this sense, "Normalization" was successful. Even during the Velvet Revolution, consumer goods and basic foodstuffs were more available in Czechoslovakia than anywhere in the bloc save Hungary. But the availability of consumer goods did not produce the tolerance found elsewhere. Rather, the vast majority of the Czechs and the Slovaks appeared to shun the party whenever possible, showing that respect minimally necessary while withdrawing into the few pockets of private life still allowed.

The most important event during Husák's 20-year regime, however, was not a function of his party or the Soviet Union or even, for that matter, the declining economy. It was the emergence of the powerful, though extremely small, voice of dissent known as Charter 77. After the signing of the Helsinki Accords in 1975, a group of isolated intellectuals and former cultural leaders began to meet. In January 1977 (hence the name Charter 77), with no more than 240 supporters, the group released its first Charter, a public challenge to the government. The statement, carefully framed within Czechoslovak communist orthodoxy, called for the government to abide by its own laws and international agreements, particularly the human rights provisions of the Helsinki Accords. The protest was particularly unsettling to the government, since it demanded only the fulfillment of pledges that the government had publicly made.

Charter 77 was immediately denounced in a major propaganda campaign, typical of Husák, and many of its members were arrested and prosecuted or put under the surveillance of the police. But Charter 77 continued to exist throughout Husák's entire tenure, periodically issuing protest statements. The group's activities were given wide international coverage by other European Helsinki watch groups and human rights organizations, making it virtually impossible for Husák to do more than harass Charter 77 members while rotating them in and out of prison. The group steadfastly maintained that its activities were legal, that it did not seek the overthrow of the government, that it would never use violence as a means of protest, and that its members would maintain high ethical and principled standards. At no time did it directly threaten Husák's regime, although it was a constant annoyance. Although the group remained small, with at most two thousand members, it became the hero of Czechoslovak political dissent. It stimulated other groups into action and maintained public awareness of issues of human rights and democracy. Charter 77 served as the leading moral force for change in all of Eastern Europe.

In the only significant shift of power prior to its fall, the party replaced Husák as first secretary with Milos Jakes in December 1987. The move was not meant to appease the small but simmering dissident movement but to placate Gorbachev's grumbling over the slow pace of change in Prague. Husák was given the presidency, a figurehead position, and Jakes sent a number of Husák's cronies into retirement. But Jakes appointed no reformers and introduced no reforms because of profound disagreements within the Party on how to maintain its dominance. While communist parties were falling in neighboring states, Jakes and his colleagues could agree only on an all-or-nothing stand. With no capacity for internal reform, the impetus for major change in late 1989 came from outside the Party. Charter 77, the voice of dissent for over 10 years, was to fill the ranks of the newly formed democratic government.

DIAGRAM OF GOVERNMENTAL STRUCTURE

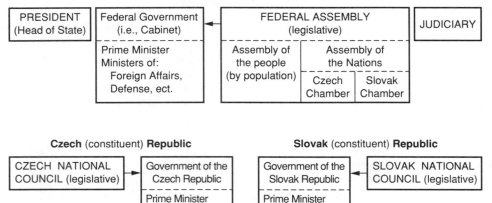

Czechoslovak Republic (federal)

| PRESIDENT (Head of State) | Federal Government (i.e., Cabinet) | FEDERAL ASSEMBLY (legislative) | JUDICIARY |

Prime Minister Ministers of: Foreign Affairs, Defense, ect.

Assembly of the people (by population)

Assembly of the Nations — Czech Chamber | Slovak Chamber

Czech (constituent) **Republic**

CZECH NATIONAL COUNCIL (legislative) ► Government of the Czech Republic

Prime Minister Ministers of: Education, Culture, etc.

Slovak (constituent) **Republic**

Government of the Slovak Republic ◄ SLOVAK NATIONAL COUNCIL (legislative)

Prime Minister Ministers of: Education, Culture, etc.

ECONOMICS

Throughout its history, Czechoslovakia has been characterized as a nation "at the cross-roads." Geographically, culturally, politically, and economically it has continually been at the center of a contest of larger forces. As time-worn as that characterization is, it has never been more apt. Tied economically to the USSR but committed to the West, Czechoslovakia has been distressingly slow to institute a new economic system. Moreover, Czechoslovakia faces a more formidable challenge in restoring the economy to private ownership than the other East European countries. With the exception of Albania, the communists nationalized the Czechoslovak economy more thoroughly than any other bloc country.

It is now apparent that to meet that challenge, Václav Klaus, Minister of Finance, and Vladimir Dlouhy, Minister of the Economy, and their supporters had early on formulated an economic agenda, in hopes that it could be introduced systematically with the settling of the country's political disputes. The earliest reform legislation, not unlike that of Poland and Hungary, sought only to break the state's monopoly on economic activity. Since that goal was accomplished before the June, 1990, elections, other more significant changes were held in check. The most important new laws legalized private entrepreneurial activity. But even during the conflict between the republics, general agreement on national economic policy was reached. Rather than attempting a complete and sweeping privatization, Czechoslovakia produced a plan for the privatization of small firms along with a limited rehabilitation of confiscated property. In the summer of 1991, a scheme for larger-scale privatizations was introduced, and the highly controversial rehabilitation of agricultural property began. By mid-1991 Hungary, which had initiated such legislation considerably earlier, had made no greater progress because of disputes over the restoration and compensation of properties seized by the communists. Unable to determine the conditions for returning church property, the entire program was held up. Czechoslovakia also stumbled over similar issues, but it determined to postpone the church issue and proceed with the rehabilitation of property on which agreement had been reached. Czechoslovakia is seriously behind Hungary and Poland in the area of foreign investment. Of the 1,500 industries overseen by the Czech Ministry of Industry, only 35 had attracted foreign capital by mid-1991. Finding no reform legislation in the country in 1990, foreign investment went to Warsaw and Budapest. At this critical stage of its new economic order, Czechoslovakia is now disinclined to quibble over the demands of foreign investors.

Current Economic Reforms

After the Prague Spring, the government of Czechoslovakia pursued traditional communist economic policies. The fall of the Party did not, however, produce immediate economic reform. The challenge of Czech–Slovak relations became paramount. As a result, the country fell considerably behind Poland and Hungary, at least temporarily. For example, the "Law Concerning Entrepreneurship of Individuals," which secures the right of Czechoslovaks to enter free enterprise, was not adopted until May 1, 1990. Privatization, the cornerstone of the transformation to a market economy, did not begin until 1991. Even then, while Poland rushed forward in its commitment to rapid conversion, major segments of the Czechoslovak economy remained in limbo, with some key industries subject to government fiat and others allowed an ill-defined autonomy.

By the summer of 1991, some of the necessary legislation finally had been codified and made operational, and there were clear signs of a newly emerging market order. Yet the details of the transition have remained highly controversial. The Slovaks have demanded revisions of the national program at every legislative juncture, delaying its adoption. But Václav Klaus, pressing for a complete transition, has made few concessions. A program has been adopted, but there is little sense of assurance that the Slovaks will actually carry it out, while Prague has only limited means to enforce it. The full conversion of Czechoslovakia to a market economy demands resolute leadership. By the summer of 1991, having been challenged in the Civic Forum and provoked by Slovak demands, President Havel finally lent his prestige to the reform agenda.

The first concrete step toward reform had been the adoption of the Law Concerning Entrepreneurship of Individuals. Immediately after, the provisions for joint stock firms were legalized under the Joint Stock Companies Law. In the first nine months after the law took effect, more than 500,000 businesses were registered and operating. All citizens 18 years of age, without a criminal record relevant to their proposed business, were free to engage in private business in manufacturing, trade, and services. There is no limit on the number of employees hired, the amount of property acquired, or the number of businesses a person establishes. Tax requirements are also standard—income and pension taxes, social security, and insurance. Though the act refers to "citizens," it does not prohibit foreign sole proprietorships, and foreigners may acquire property for business use, although still not for personal use.

The law does not cover businesses requiring professional licenses, such as medicine or law, nor farming. Those activities are still directed by government certification agencies. New firms formed for exporting must be on record with the Trade Registry. If a private business has more than 25 employees and the owner's annual gross income exceeds $0.5 million, then registration in the corporate registry is required. The law does specify that foreigners register their operations in the city where their enterprise is to be located and in the republic where operations are contemplated. Registration in both republics is required for firms operating on a national scale.

The joint stock law provides for all business firms to convert to share companies and to "go public" if their management wishes. A stock market should be operational before the end of 1992.

The most significant legislation following the June elections concerned the partial rehabilitation of property confiscated by the communists. Ratified in October, 1990, and subsequently expanded and amended, the rehabilitation law was the first effort by any former communist state to return illegally seized property. At first the government sought to restore to their former owners some 70,000 small properties seized between 1955 and 1961. The amended legislation, the Law on Extrajudicial Rehabilitation, provided for the rehabilitation of larger properties, both as a means to strengthen the privatization process and to provide greater equity to all former property holders. Neither act includes agricultural land, but the two together cover more than 10 percent of the property owned by the state.

In order to acquire nationalized property, the owners or their heirs generally must hold Czechoslovak citizenship. Those seeking to reclaim property must also prove their status as former owners by title and other supporting documents. The government has maintained extensive records useful for title documentation, but the potential for litigation remains tremendous. The state may refuse to return the property of successful claimants. In cases where the property has been extensively altered or developed, or if a joint venture operates on the property, the former owners may be compensated in either stock or money. It is anticipated that most claims will be paid in vouchers, which can be traded for shares in newly privatized firms. Former owners who insist on reclaiming their property may have to pay, rather than be paid, for the property if it is deemed to have been substantially improved after its seizure. To allow the expeditious settlement of ownership disputes, all claims were to have been filed by November, 1991. Claims are unlikely to be settled before the end of 1992.

When the process began, Václav Klaus announced that returning property could cost in the range of $10 to $11 billion, a sum equivalent to 20 percent of the GNP, an unprecedented transfer of wealth. But he insisted that the rehabilitation be done, for both economic and moral reasons.

Small-scale privatization of some 100,000 small and medium-sized firms was begun in 1991 to establish a mid-level business cadre. Czechoslovak communist law had forbidden the private possession of even small businesses, while such shops were commonplace in Hungary and Poland. With the privatization, a large number of private owners and operators were created. Small firms set for rehabilitation to former owners were excluded from the privatizations. In order to foster the republics' autonomy, their governments were empowered to implement the privatizations and split the profits from the sales, with 70 percent to the republics and 30 percent to local authorities. Only Czechoslovak citizens can participate in the first round of an auction, and prospective buyers must be present at the actual auction. Those who work for or manage businesses to be auctioned are not given special auction rights, but all bidders are treated equally.

Foreigners may participate in the privatization as an investor with Czechoslovak citizens but are prohibited for two years from buying newly privatized firms. Firms not sold at first auction may be bought by foreigners at a second-round auction now set for early 1992. At the second round, Czechoslovak citizens can buy at rates discounted by as much as 80 percent of assessed value. Full payment for auctioned property is required in 30 days. Privatization sales have ranged from as low as $200 to as high as $1 million.

The first privatization auctions occurred in January, 1991. As their opponents had predicted, prices for even small establishments were quickly bidded up beyond the means of ordinary citizens. However, the government has steadfastly refused to reconsider its strategy.

Legislation providing for the privatization of more than 3,000 large-scale firms took effect in April, 1991. Unlike the Poles, the Czechoslovaks have subordinated the pace of privatization to economic efficiency and have set a 10-year framework for the process. Most large firms will be restructured, divided, and converted to joint stock firms before being sold. This will slow the process, but as a result, the profitable portions of large firms will operate more efficiently once privatized.

Vouchers costing 2,000 korunas ($70) will be offered to all adult Czechoslovaks, who can then exchange the vouchers for corporate shares. The vouchers will have an arbitrary value of 1,000 "points." The shares offered by firms will also have a "point" value, allowing the buyer to assess the value of any firm's offering. Additional vouchers representing "points" may be purchased, but at substantially higher prices. Much like the rehabilitation act, this aspect of the privatization act is novel. Of all the Eastern European privatization programs, none has attempted to guarantee the widespread distribution of state property.

Substantial Western advice is being sought for the privatization of the large firms and, in general, Western investment is being broadly encouraged. No restrictions have been put on foreign share purchasing, but the state retains ultimate discretion over the percentage of its shares a firm will trade for vouchers and sell to foreign investors. Some one-fifth of the 3,000 large-scale firms slated for privatization will be offered for complete foreign acquisition. State authorities have promised that state firms already involved in joint ventures will not be affected by the privatization. Newly privatized firms are free to seek joint venture partners.

The politically difficult challenge to the state is the need to balance the interests of its citizens with the desires of prospective Western purchasers. Foreign investors seek to acquire control of the most profitable Czechoslovak firms. But the government cannot leave the least desirable firms to its own citizens.

Privatization legislation in May, 1991, sought to address the highly controversial issue of agricultural land. Breaking up the 1,660 huge cooperatives and the 245 state farms, however, proved too great a challenge. Instead, the legislation aimed at rehabilitating a portion of previously seized land. As many as 3.5 million people could make claims for land. A maximum of 150 hectares (370 acres) of agricultural land or 250 hectares (620 acres) of general-purpose land will be given to successful claimants. The state may substitute land for the original property, where rehabilitation would seriously disrupt cooperative farming or in highly developed areas. Also, according to government sources, documenting land ownership will prove difficult because land records have been poorly maintained. They estimate that only about one-third of the land covered by the legislation will actually be returned to its claimants. Nor does the law cover all the disputed land. It has denied demands for restitution by Sudeten Germans, Hungarians, and Americans.

Additional legislation will be required for those claiming lands greater than the 150-hectare limit, for the restoration of Church property, and for the dissolution of state farms and cooperatives. Given the strength of the communists and socialists in rural areas, drafting an acceptable law for either state farms or cooperatives will be extremely difficult. State farms, which control approximately 30 percent of all farm land, will likely be the first agricultural lands to be privatized. They are owned by the state rather than by the cultivators, and the state should be able to privatize those relatively small properties. Large cooperative farms, controlling more than 60 percent of the acreage under cultivation, are a more formidable political challenge. Those farms, at least theoretically, are owned by their members, and their huge size makes the resolution of land claims formidable. In the short term, the government is hoping that competitive pressures will spur the cooperatives into increasing their economic efficiency. One course may be to reformulate the cooperatives as voluntary units. Moreover, there appears to be only limited interest in small farming, which is generally considered uneconomic. Any new legislation is likely to favor agricultural concentration.

Restrictive joint venture laws dating back to the Husák regime have been broadly relaxed. The "Law Concerning Enterprises with Foreign Capital Participation" allows for complete foreign ownership of firms as well as the participation of individual Czechoslovaks in the operation of such firms. Establishing a venture now requires only three steps—an investment of at least 100,000 korunas (approximately $3,500), a company charter, and registration with the federal Ministry of Finance. The law permits various structures, including corporations and partnerships. Joint stock companies may issue debt and common and preferred stock, and firms may create employee stock ownership plans. Joint ventures are specifically exempted from the dictates of the central planners.

Despite this liberalization, it is clear that Czechoslovakia still lags behind the other reforming states in attracting joint ventures. As of mid-1991 there were approximately 1,200 in operation. Several represent investments in excess of $1 million. But the majority of ventures are very small and employ few, with investment of no more than $20,000 to $30,000. More than three-quarters of the joint ventures and the investment capital are located in the Czech republic.

The law sets the tax rate lower on joint venture corporate profits than on indigenous companies. Joint ventures with one-third foreign capitalization are taxed at 20 percent on the first Kcs 200,000 of profit and 40 percent thereafter. Income from copyrights, rents, interest, and dividends is taxed at 25 percent. Firms may apply for tax abatements and tax holidays for the first two years of their operation. Tax relief appears to be granted on the grounds of Czechoslovak national priorities. Firms doing environmental cleanup, for example, are being enticed with offers of tax holidays extending beyond two years. Taxes on wages are still unclear. As the law now stands, there is a 50 percent tax on wages paid, though here, as with the tax on profits, variations and exemptions are specified. New laws on taxation are expected in the future.

All firms are required to maintain a so-called "reserve fund" to cover losses. A minimum of 5 percent of after-tax profit or 10 percent of capitalization, whichever is larger, must be paid annually into this fund. Any firm intending to lay off employees for whatever reason must give them three months' notice, as well as provide an explanation for the layoffs to the relevant unions. A firm may be allowed to transfer currency abroad as well as purchase hard currency, but joint venture laws still limit the complete repatriation of profits and the disposition of foreign currencies. At least for the foreseeable future, the state bank has few funds to allow transfers, and hard-currency shortages can delay large import purchases for as much as three months. Permission of the Czechoslovak State Bank is not required for foreign-denominated accounts or foreign currency borrowings, and foreign employees' wages may be repatriated without restriction. Enterprises are also required to offer 30 percent of their foreign currency earnings for sale at official exchange rates. Convertibility restrictions will be lifted when the koruna is made fully convertible, promised for late 1992. But Czechoslovakia will likely remain behind Poland and Hungary in its ability to earn a hard-currency trade surplus. It was hard hit by the loss of its markets in East Germany, and it imports substantially more Soviet oil, for which it now pays hard currency and world prices. In preparation for partial convertibility of the Czechoslovak koruna, subsidies on many food items have been reduced. The average monthly grocery bill has risen by 25 percent, and some basic items rose in excess of 100 percent. With 85 percent of all prices already freed and remaining controls scheduled for elimination, the cost of living will rise dramatically. To ease the burden on consumers, the government has instituted temporary lump-sum compensation packages. But the true test of freeing prices is whether the higher prices result in more goods finding their way to market, as happened in Poland.

The American government, intent on fostering the transition to a market economy, has signed a U.S.–Czechoslovak trade agreement. The agreement extends Most-Favored-Nation status to Czechoslovakia, facilitates repatriation of profits, allows American firms in Czechoslovakia the same access to banking services and other goods and services as Czechoslovak nationals, and secures protection for intellectual property rights. The Board of Directors of the Export-Import Bank of the United States has approved extension of all its lending and insurance activities to support trade with Czechoslovakia.

Czechoslovakia has been the first Eastern European country to receive substantial backing from the International Monetary Fund. The IMF offered a credit line of almost $2 billion in January, 1991—a resounding endorsement of Czechoslovakia's fiscal health and of its strict monetary and fiscal policies. IMF action is expected to attract additional international financing.

Current State of the Economy

For 1990, Czechoslovak GNP fell by 4 percent, and as the reforms strike deep into the state sector in 1991, GNP is expected to fall by more than 10 percent. Even in the face of this, Czechoslovaks continue to enjoy a fairly high standard of living by East bloc standards and promise to make a vigorous transition to a flourishing market economy.

Though all bloc states maintained centralized economies, Prague's was among the most heavily concentrated. The degree of concentration, as in the USSR, was especially great in heavy industry, such as chemicals and weapons. As a result, it was most intense in the Slovak republic, where postwar industrialization had been based entirely on Soviet-style mammoth installations. Slovakia must now bear more of the brunt of the transition to new forms of economic organization than the Czech lands. But throughout the country private ownership of even the smallest businesses had been prohibited, in contrast to Hungary, and in the countryside private cultivation was forbidden, in contrast to Poland. Thus, Czechoslovakia's conversion to a market economy started with virtually no elements of a market in place. The country began its structural transformation minus the service sector of Hungary, the farming sector of Poland, or their experience with Western trade. Under those conditions, the economy faced a steep decline. By the middle of 1991, more than half of the country's firms were de facto insolvent.

Despite the failure of the leadership to drive the pace of the transition, the private sector began to flourish in the second half of 1990, replacing some of the economic performance lost by the declining state sector. The economy remains in a state of limbo, having neither a plan nor a market. Yet, by and large, the economy has held up. Food and other day-to-day consumption items are still plentiful compared to other Eastern European economies. Inflation, at 6 to 10 percent, also remained under control. In comparison, Hungary had an inflation rate estimated at almost 30 percent and Poland more than 500 percent.

Moreover, there are favorable indications for the maintenance of the comparative well-being of the Czechoslovaks. The hyperinflation that ravaged Poland and Yugoslavia is unlikely to occur. The past abundance of consumer goods and tightly controlled wages meant little "forced savings"—money accumulated for lack of anything to spend it on. When prices are fully freed from state control, there will be no massive "koruna overhang," as there is a massive "ruble overhang" in the USSR. As a result, prices are unlikely to be driven up by consumers seeking to exchange bank notes for goods, as has been the case elsewhere in the East bloc. To maintain low inflation, the government, and particularly Finance Minister Klaus, have declared its intention of maintaining a policy of tight money.

The long-standing policy of the government to disproportionally favor the industrialization of Slovakia narrowed the income differential between the republics dramatically. But Slovakia's relative prosperity was accomplished by building heavy industry and trading with the socialist bloc. Slovakia now possesses an energy- and raw material–intensive industrial base, as well as major military industries. Its industrial base was founded on the presumption of cheap oil and raw material imports from the Soviet Union. As a result, the transition has had a greater impact on the Slovaks than on the Czechs. The USSR no longer sends abundant and inexpensive raw materials or petroleum. The collapse of CMEA trade has deprived Slovak industry of its markets. The international decrease in weapons sales has also hurt. Unemployment in Slovakia is twice the rate in the Czech lands. In the spring of 1991, there were more than 44,000 job vacancies in the entire country, but only slightly more than 7,000 of them were in Slovakia. Prices were 10 percent higher and industrial production 10 percent lower in Slovakia than the national average. It is not surprising that public opinion polls show that 50 percent of the Czechs favor speeding economic reform while 65 percent of Slovaks favor slowing the process. At this critical stage, the transition could be thwarted by the resistance of the Slovaks.

Another impediment to reform that is solely a phase in the transition to a market is a shortage of skilled labor. Like all other shortages in a socialist economy, the labor shortage is a function of the system. Because the Communist Party was committed to full employment, most industries were forced to hire more laborers than warranted by efficiency criteria. Now that the insistence on "full employment," better understood as institutionalized underemployment, has been eliminated, the apparent labor shortage will disappear. Large numbers of unemployed are being produced, estimated now to be in excess of 220,000 and likely to double by early 1992, representing an 8 percent unemployment rate. The government is totally unprepared to deal with substantial unemployment, with only a limited system of unemployment compensation and no labor retraining programs. But the labor force necessary for the market economy will be available.

Another apparent characteristic of the labor force in Eastern Europe is its high education level. The educational level of Eastern European workers is, indeed, high relative to the per capita incomes of their countries. But their educational attainments are not nearly as high as those of the labor force of Western Europe. For example, 61 percent of the labor force in OECD countries have a secondary school or higher education. Less than 30 percent of the Czechoslovak workforce have comparable educations. The competitiveness of the former satellites is correspondingly less.

Yet another factor diminishing the competitive position of all the former communist states of Eastern European is the deplorable state of their economic infrastructure. While Czechoslovakia possesses the strongest transportation and communications capabilities in the East bloc, it is quite limited in comparison to Western Europe. For example, Czechoslovakia has 33 percent more kilometers of roads per capita than Hungary, but 83 percent less than Austria. With about 246 telephones per thousand inhabitants, Czechoslovakia is tied for first place with Hungary in the CMEA. (OECD countries average more than twice this number of telephones.) The government has already taken action to improve telecommunications, awarding substantial contracts to American firms for state-of-the-art equipment and service.

The country also confronts a materials challenge. Czechoslovakia had imported nearly all its petroleum, all of its natural gas, and close to 70 percent of its coal from the Soviets. The failure of the country to adapt to the post-1973 energy reality is revealed by the sale of gasoline in Prague through 1990 for 50 cents per gallon. The need to make hard-currency payments for oil has proved as painful for Czechoslovakia as for all the former satellites, which on average consume fully twice as much energy per dollar of GNP as the developed economies of Western Europe.

Like Hungary, the country's economic future has been slightly brightened by the speed with which its trade has been reoriented away from the USSR and other CMEA countries and towards the West. In 1988, only 20 percent of the country's trade was with Western countries. In 1989, the proportion nearly doubled, and West Germany surpassed East Germany as a trading partner. The state had provided incentives for hard-currency trade to Czechoslovak exporters. The koruna had been substantially devalued against major hard currencies, and new laws allowed Czechoslovak firms to retain a portion of their hard-currency earnings. Meanwhile, trade with the former CMEA countries has plummeted in excess of 25 percent in 1991, while trade with the Soviet Union is likely to fall by as much as 70 percent.

Czechoslovakia has never been a major trading partner of the United States. In 1988, it was the world's 113th largest importer of U.S. products and the world's 88th largest exporter to the United States. (U.S. exports to Czechoslovakia are understated to the extent that sales occurred through European intermediaries.) The increasing influence of Germany has made Czechoslovakia especially receptive to non-German investments. Americans are the partners of choice, as Czechoslovakia seeks to escape what it has come to believe is the possibility of renewed German domination.

One of Czechoslovakia's greatest advantages in its transition to a market economy is its relatively low hard-currency debt. At the end of communism, its debt to the West stood at $7.8 billion, as compared to $10 billion for Bulgaria, $16.2 billion for Yugoslavia, $20.7 billion for Hungary, $21.2 billion for East Germany, and $39.8 billion for Poland. Only Romania, after years of Ceausescu's oppression to suppress living standards and generate a surplus to pay off its foreign obligations, had a smaller debt, of $400 million. Borrowing by the Havel government burgeoned in late 1990 and 1991, resulting in a debt topping $11 billion. Even with the increased borrowing, Czechoslovakia has retained its relative creditworthiness and secured a 1991 IMF loan for nearly $2 billion. Finally, and perhaps more important than many specific economic details, Czechoslovakia has a certain tradition that sets it apart form the rest of the former East bloc. Before the communist takeover, it had both a liberal democratic order and a robust economy. Democracy is not alien to the Czechoslovak people, and their new democracy will likely continue to function smoothly. Relative to many of its neighbors, Czechoslovakia's nationalities have relatively harmonious relations. The Slovaks and even the Moravians continue to espouse separatist sentiments, but acrimony comparable to the hatred of the Serbs and the Croats or the Romanians and the Hungarians is absent. In fact, ethnic friction between Czechs and Slovaks is less now than in 1938, when many Slovaks, alienated by the economic domination of the Czechs, supported the Nazi invasion. Certainly Slovak sentiments will not easily be appeased, and it can be anticipated that modifications of the national economic program will be made for their special circumstances. But in the immediate future, the challenge of reviving the country's economy is likely to take precedence.

Economy from Origins to 1945

At the end of World War I, Czechs and Slovaks led by Tomás Masaryk seized the opportunity presented by the defeat of the Austro-Hungarian Empire to declare themselves a nation. However much these two peoples shared culturally, they differed considerably in their economic endowments. The Czech lands in the west, consisting of Bohemia, Moravia and part of Silesia, were a major industrial center. They contained almost all of the sugar-refining and glass- and porcelain-producing capacity of the Empire as well as considerable capacity in the textile, mining, metal, and machinery industries. In the east, Slovakia and Ruthenia were still emerging from 1,000 years of Hungarian domination. They had primitive agrarian economies, with little industry and a per capita income approximately two-thirds that of their Czech countrymen. In addition to agricultural goods, Slovakia produced forest products and textiles, while near the Slovak capital of Bratislava, chemical and machinery industries existed on a modest scale. Ruthenia, the most backward region of the new Czechoslovakia, was absorbed into the Ukraine by the Soviets at the end of the Second World War.

Czechoslovakia had been spared great destruction during the First World War, and the new nation proceeded immediately to build on its already substantial economic base. The country inherited a highly developed communications infrastructure. Indeed, on a track-mile per capita basis, Czechoslovakia and Hungary were in approximate parity with Western Europe. The rest of Eastern Europe lagged far behind.

The Hapsburgs had financed the late phases of World War I at the printing press. Consequently, the nations of the former Austro-Hungarian Empire suffered severe inflation after the war. The Czechoslovak finance ministry established an independent currency, the koruna, and instituted a severely progressive tax on wealth, amounting to expropriation, in order to reduce the money supply in circulation. In addition to these initial efforts to control the price level, the monetary authorities also intervened in foreign exchange markets to stabilize the value of the koruna. Czechoslovakia's monetary policy was heavy-handed, but at least it was more effective in controlling inflation than those of much of the rest of postwar Europe.

Early in the Republic's history, the parliament turned from its conservative beginnings. A new liberal majority adopted an eight-hour workday, unemployment and sickness benefits, and land reforms. At the start of the Republic, 35 percent of Czech and Slovak lands were held by 0.1 percent of the population. The land reform of April 16, 1919 forced the sale of land in estates larger than 150 hectares (371 acres). By 1928, 1.2 million hectares (2,965,200 acres) had been transferred to the cultivators.

Public education, particularly significant in relatively poorly educated Slovakia, was given high priority. Under the Austro-Hungarian Empire, Slovaks could obtain elementary instruction in their own language only from a few private, denominational schools. In 1918, there were 276 such schools, with a total of only 390 teachers. By 1926, the number of Slovak language primary schools and teachers had increased by a factor of 10. Significant progress was made in all levels of education. Slovakia's first university was founded in 1919. A second university was opened in the Czech lands to complement Prague's Charles University, established in 1348.

In 1930, 95.9 percent of the total Czechoslovak population were literate, an unparalleled rate in Eastern Europe. Slovakia's illiteracy rate was 8 percent of its population over age ten. While this was high by Western European standards, it was as low or lower than any East European nation. Only Hungary had a literacy rate comparable to Slovakia, while only Poland could boast sections of its country that matched the 95.9 percent literacy rate of the Czech lands.

Cooperatives were an important form of economic activity during the Republic. They were particularly prevalent in agriculture, where financial institutions, warehouses, and processing plants were organized on cooperative principles. During the Depression, the national administrative apparatus of the cooperatives was transformed into a virtual monopoly clearinghouse for agricultural products. This was accomplished with the encouragement of the government, which also tolerated industrial cartels. By the end of the interwar period, many industries were dominated by government-recognized cartel agreements. The Skoda Works, the precommunist progenitor of the enterprise that has become the centerpiece of modern Czechoslovak industry, was the preeminent engineering and armaments concern in Eastern Europe. When it concluded an agreement with its principal domestic competitor in 1935, Skoda effectively secured complete cartel control of one of Czechoslovakia's leading industries. The situation was similar in steel, another mainstay of the nation's industry. Virtually all of the steel produced in the interwar period was marketed through a central joint-marketing clearinghouse.

In this favorable climate, Czechoslovakia's national economy grew impressively in the 1920s. Czechoslovakia consolidated its status as the only truly industrial economy in the region. In 1921, Czechoslovakia had 33.7 percent of its working population engaged in agriculture and 37.7 percent in industry. By 1930, the economy had shifted further to industry. Only 28.3 percent of the labor force was still employed in agriculture, while industry employed 40.4 percent of the labor force. By contrast, in the 1920s roughly 75 percent of Polish workers and 80 percent of Bulgarian and Yugoslav workers were employed in agriculture. Only Hungary, where 58.2 percent of the labor force worked in agriculture in 1920, came even remotely near to rivaling Czechoslovakia.

The Republic's economic progress was not without its setbacks. The tremors of the worldwide recession of 1920–1921 had reached Czechoslovakia and were exacerbated by the deflationary monetary policies of the finance ministry. Later, in the middle of the decade, tariff wars with neighboring countries led to disruption of one of the nation's most lucrative export businesses, sugar beet farming and sugar refining. Consequently, sugar, which in the mid-1920s had constituted upwards of 14 percent of exports, fell to about 5 percent in 1929 and by 1937 had declined to 2 percent. In part, however, sugar's declining share of trade was the result of steady growth in industrial exports. Metal and metal products increased their share from 6.5 percent in 1921 to almost 20 percent in 1937. Export growth in machinery and leather goods such as shoes was also dramatic. Overall growth in industrial output was impressive. Over the period 1925 to 1929, generation of electricity increased from about 2 to 3 million kilowatt-hours, steel output increased 50 percent, and the annual production of motor vehicles tripled from 5,000 to 15,000. Modern principles of factory organization were embraced by technologically sophisticated captains of industry, such as the renowned Batá family. In the mid-1920s, they applied conveyor belt–driven assembly line techniques to transform the manufacture of shoes. In 1927, shoe output was increased 75 percent, while the labor force increased by only 35 percent.

The rural economy also prospered. Prior to World War I, wheat yields were already above the European average. The war caused little disruption of Czechoslovak agriculture and insignificant losses of farm implements and herds. After the war, all of Eastern Europe undertook radical land reform, but the reforms in Czechoslovakia were more orderly and less destructive of agricultural output. Agricultural output was also enhanced by soil improvements and the introduction of greater mechanization. The nation maintained the highest agricultural yields in Eastern Europe for all major crops. Like other measures of well-being, agricultural output was not evenly distributed across the Republic. Farming in the Czech lands was far more capital-intensive than in the eastern provinces. As late as 1930, Slovakia still had a higher fraction of its population engaged in agriculture than before the war.

The overall Czechoslovak economy grew rapidly in the 1920s, partly through a major expansion in exports. By 1928, nearly one-third of the country's GNP was derived from exports. There was never a more dangerous time to be so exposed to the fortunes of the world economy. The Great Depression brought a collapse in Czechoslovakia's exports, which in turn brought on a general economic collapse.

The government attempted to counter the effects of the depression through the widespread distribution of unemployment benefits and the maintenance of agricultural price supports. But recovery was agonizingly slow, as it was throughout Eastern Europe. Industry fell into an apparently endless and severe contraction. Industrial production decreased 50 percent over the period 1929 to 1933. Meanwhile, output of many farm crops increased during the depression due to import restrictions and price supports, somewhat mitigating the industrial collapse.

When Hitler annexed the heavily industrialized Sudeten territory of Czechoslovakia following the Munich crisis in 1938, the economy had not yet reached predepression levels. With the seizure of the Republic's industrial heartland and the subsequent occupation of the remainder of the country, the Germans forcibly converted Czechoslovakia into a captive industrial vassal. To supply the wartime needs of the Nazis, the heavy industry of the Czech lands and the agriculture and forests of Slovakia were exploited to their limits.

Economy from 1945 to 1990

When civil authority was reasserted after the German expulsion, the communists had the upper hand. They were popular because of their prominent role in the resistance and their association with the Soviet liberators. Their platform called for the expulsion of almost three million citizens of German origin suspected of collaborating with the Nazis, the nationalization of their property and of major industries, and the banning of all political parties that had collaborated with the enemy.

Limited central planning was instituted for 1947 and 1948. With a large fraction of the owners of capital and land already dispossessed and the memory of the depression still a fresh reminder of the turbulence of unfettered capitalism, a political consensus appeared to favor such a policy. The plan relied on market prices for guidance in resource allocation and succeeded in restoring the economy to its prewar level by 1948. The principal instruments of the central planners were the allocation of investment resources and advisory output quotas.

The government chose an investment strategy that favored heavy industry. By 1948, manufacturing had more than exceeded its 1937 level, with a marked shift towards heavy industry, while the value of mining output was 13 percent greater than in 1937. The output of metal and metal products was 18 percent greater than its prewar value. Textiles and processed agricultural goods, reflecting their disfavor in the eyes of the central planners, were nearly one-quarter below their 1937 values.

Among Eastern European countries in 1948, only Poland could claim more troubled agriculture than Czechoslovakia. Yet Czechoslovakia had suffered far less war damage. The failure of agriculture to rebound to prewar levels reflected a decades-long pattern of investment neglect and organizational failure. In February 1948, the communists exploited a parliamentary crisis and seized control of the government in a bloodless coup. By the time of the coup, Czechoslovakia, alone in Eastern Europe, had a thriving industrial base and a solid economic infrastructure. Its rail network was more extensive than that of Western Europe, while its network of roads, some 90 percent of the Western European level, was the only one in the region to approach international standards.

The country's economic success had been achieved in the face of severe macroeconomic shocks. Two world wars and the Great Depression, as well as tensions resulting from regional disparities of wealth, all had been significant threats to Czechoslovakia's prosperity. But its greatest challenges, which, like its Eastern European neighbors, it never managed to overcome, were to be faced in the decades of communist rule.

In contrast to the two-year plan adopted by the democratically elected government, the first communist five-year plan of 1949 to 1953 did away entirely with market forces. Economic goals, which had been determined by political consensus in the Central Planning Commission, were now set by decree of the State Planning Office. By eliminating the role of freely determined prices, the planners hopelessly complicated their task. The Depression, the recovery, the World War, and the postwar recovery had all been phases of economic activity for the two decades preceding the communist takeover. As a result, there had been no "normal" period of economic activity for 20 years, and the planners had no conventional level of economic activity to use in guiding their decisions.

By February 1948, the state had nationalized virtually all large industrial enterprises. By 1950, the smaller pockets of private enterprise that remained had been forced into cooperatives. The state had been able to determine their fate by withholding resources, including labor, from smaller enterprises and by restricting their access to markets, which had by that time come under government control.

The first five-year plan called on Czechoslovakia, as the industrial powerhouse of the region, to supply massive amounts of capital goods for the industrialization of other East bloc countries. In effect, the war economy of 1939–1945 continued after the communist seizure of the economic system. Not only was the production of Czechoslovakia's economy largely dictated by another country, but its output remained remarkably similar to that demanded by the Germans. Once again, the output of Czechoslovak industry served to bolster the industrial systems of other states and was pressed to produce armaments. Periodically, the industrial targets set by the original plan were revised upwards for no reason other than the economic demands of the Soviets. Time and again the planners issued quotas utterly heedless of economic possibilities, producing major economic distortions as enterprises hoarded vast quantities of productive resources in anticipation of new production quotas.

The first five-year plan set the tone for the economic future of Czechoslovakia under central planning. By concentrating on heavy industry and neglecting other parts of the economy, such as the consumer goods and agricultural sectors, Czechoslovakia set out on a path of unbalanced growth. Ultimately, the Czechoslovak economy collapsed under the weight of its heavy industry. Engineering steadily and more greedily devoured massive investment resources while making no commensurate contribution to raising the standard of living. Beginning in the late 1950s and continuing through the 1960s, Czechoslovakia invested a far higher proportion of its GDP in productive assets than did the countries of Western Europe. Yet Czechoslovak growth levels never exceeded those of the Western countries. Even while industry showed significant growth in the 1950s, living standards changed little. By the late 1980s, the investment gap had narrowed. Czechoslovakia was investing roughly a quarter of its GDP in productive assets, while OECD countries were investing slightly less than 20 percent. But the Czechoslovak economy continued to grow considerably slower than the OECD countries.

The central authorities underestimated the information required to plan an economy. The planners never had a sound basis on which to estimate, for example, the level of output that could be expected from a given plant or the increase in productivity that could be expected from a given investment. Their efforts were complicated by three factors. The planners had to operate without the economic signals of market prices. Neither could they look back to periods of "normal" economic activity to establish comparable base lines. Finally, the entire effort was effectively sabotaged by plant managers, who sought to enhance their performance and rewards by understating the output capacities of their plants while overstating their needs for resources. Their commitment to operating under conditions of abundant resources and constricted outputs would help bring about the downfall of the communist system.

In the 1980s, machinery and equipment made up more than 60 percent of Czechoslovakia's exports to socialist countries. By linking its fate to mechanical engineering, the economy required continual technical advances and a plentiful supply of raw materials. Yet the inability to develop new technologies has been a widespread failing of planned economies, and raw materials, especially iron ore, were in chronic short supply in the resource-poor country. Even before the conclusion of the 1950s, the quality of Czechoslovak machinery began to lag behind the West.

Initially, the Soviets had insisted that Czechoslovakia be largely self-sufficient in raw materials. Massive investments were wasted in an attempt to extract sufficient amounts of iron ore and other materials from the country's stingy mines. The Soviets eventually began to supply raw materials, but shortages continually plagued Czechoslovak industry.

By the end of the first five-year plan in 1953, the distortions of Czechoslovakia's unbalanced development had already begun to trouble planners. Wages had increased faster than the supply of consumer goods. As a result, black market trade was flourishing, and many household goods were being rationed. In two successive one-year plans adopted for the years 1953–1955, planners retreated somewhat from the policy of industrialization for industrialization's sake. Resources were assigned relatively more to consumption and away from investment. The government also took strong measures to reduce consumer demand. In 1953, a currency "reform" expropriated individual savings while raising the prices of consumer goods.

The failure of the one-year plans to increase the supply of consumer goods and renewed pressures from the Soviet Union for higher levels of industrial production led, in the second five-year plan of 1955 to 1960, to the pattern established in the first five-year plan. Breakneck industrialization was once again the order of the day in Czechoslovakia.

Shipments of raw materials from the Soviet Union increased during the second five-year plan. The year 1956, which was to witness searing criticism and repression in both Poland and Hungary, passed quietly in Prague. From 1948 to 1959, the industrial production of producer goods grew at an average annual rate of 10.1 percent, as compared to an average of 6.1 percent for the production of nonagricultural consumer goods.

Czechoslovakia's industry grew at roughly the same rate as that of the Soviet Union, Hungary, and Poland. But output per employee grew at a higher annual average rate in Czechoslovakia, which spurred more intensive industrial development and achieved greater gains in efficiency. In the period 1948–1959, industry in Czechoslovakia and in the EEC grew at approximately equal rates. With the exception of that period, however, Czechoslovak industry never grew faster than the EEC countries, despite its pursuit of industrial development and the relative neglect of other sectors of its economy.

The impressive growth rates of the second plan period appeared to portend the triumph of communism. Similar successes in the USSR had led the Soviet Premier, Nikita Khrushchev, to predict that his country would "bury" the West. In this heady era of communist optimism, Czechoslovakia was "promoted" from a "peoples' democracy" to become the Czechoslovak Socialist Republic.

Yet the optimism of the 1950s quickly gave way to frustration. The third five-year plan period, 1961–1965, brought a deep recession in 1962 and 1963, considered unthinkable in a planned economy. GNP declined a full percentage point in 1963. In response, a movement for a change of economic policy developed within the Party and the plan was abandoned. Economist Ota Sik was appointed to head a commission charged with making recommendations for change. His group was accorded extraordinary freedom of discussion as they considered alternative reform schemes. The recommendations of Sik's panel, called the "New Economic Model," were incorporated into a new five-year plan, the fourth, of 1966–1970.

The "New Economic Model" made some economic changes. But in the Czech tradition, they were largely at the margins of the economy. For example, firms were allowed greater freedom to dispose of after-tax net income, but they were not permitted to pay higher wages. The government feared that wage increases that outpaced the growth in consumer goods would produce hidden inflation and other distortions. They had as of yet no means of increasing the supply of goods to the consumer sector. In addition, Sik's plan specified higher prices for agricultural outputs relative to the prices for inputs. Direct access to foreign markets was extended to other agencies beyond the foreign trade ministry, and a training school was established to teach enterprise management.

Sik and his group understood the central problem of the planned economy—prices that did not reflect demand and supply and thus could not serve as signals for the allocation of resources. They called for a modest and phased decontrol of some prices. The Sik reforms hardly constituted a thoroughgoing restructuring of the economy. Nevertheless, resistance in the state bureaucracies to any reform subverted many of the proposals in the "New Economic Model."

Divisions within the government also arose over other fundamental issues, such as the limits of freedom of expression, and political reform. The reformers prevailed and Alexander Dubeček replaced Antonin Novotny as First Secretary of the Communist Party. To great popular acclaim, Dubeček instituted the reforms of the "Prague Spring." Czechoslovakia enjoyed a brief period of relatively free public expression, comparable to what the Soviets came to call *glasnost*. But in 1968 the Soviets called it counterrevolution, and on August 21, 1968, led an invasion of Warsaw Pact troops. The invasion not only did away with the political reforms; it ended the economic reforms as well.

Central control over all details of production and enterprise management was restored, and the modest freeing of prices and wages was ended. Consumers, the Czech people, were given a simple bargain enforced by Warsaw Pact weapons—an exchange of political docility in return for higher levels of consumption. Heavily subsidized imports of raw materials from the Soviet Union plus borrowing from the West put more goods on the shelves. Trade deficits with both East and West rapidly accumulated.

The post-1968 increase in centralization ensured that Czechoslovakia missed out on the high-tech revolution of the "information age." Planners devoted more investment resources to high-technology industries, especially the manufacture of chemicals and electronics. But there was no change in the mechanisms for setting prices and wages from the center. The system never managed to structure incentives to elicit independent initiative, and the new investments were doomed to failure.

In the 1970s era of detente and petrodollars, the West willingly granted trade credits to East European countries. Many of the satellites, Poland in particular, borrowed extensively to import Western technology. But post-1968 Czechoslovakia was deterred both by its own hardliners and by the political realities of a hostile West from looking to the capitalist world for technology. Given the structural distortions in the economy, however, the technological transplants would have by and large failed to take root just as they had failed to take root in Poland. The result was that Czechoslovakia was spared the accumulation of the vast foreign debt amassed by other East European states.

Czechoslovakia also spurned another favored method of importing Western technology—the joint venture. Many countries had made their first serious efforts to court joint ventures in hopes of importing technology without building additional debt. But Czechoslovakia's renewed central control precluded foreign equity participation and made joint ventures very difficult. No Western firms showed any interest in initiating such ventures.

Czechoslovakia's per capita GNP had respectable growth in the first half of the 1970s, but only Bulgaria and Poland, in severe economic and political difficulties, had slower GNP growth rates in the latter years. The planners had shifted toward production of housing and consumer goods and away from heavy machinery. That policy was aimed at quieting the restive populace and was also a response to the fall in market share of East bloc machinery, even in communist countries, to the higher-quality offerings of the West. Agriculture, especially meat production, contributed to the greater availability of consumer goods. Higher farm prices for outputs relative to inputs were one of the few elements of the reforms of the late 1960s that were allowed to continue. Largely as a result, Czechoslovak farm output grew 17 percent from the late 1960s to the late 1970s. Over the same period, farm output in East Germany had increased by 9 percent; Hungary and Bulgaria, 7 percent; while Poland's production stagnated.

The seventh five-year plan, 1981–1985, ushered in the "Set of Measures for the Improvement of the System of Planned Management of the National Economy after 1980." Far from a break with communist orthodoxy, this timid package of economic adjustments followed the adoption of a very similar program in the Soviet Union. The "Set of Measures" called for greater discretion at the plant level. The central planning authorities would still set binding quotas, but firm management was allowed to determine how the annual quotas would be met. Managers were also given somewhat more discretion in their use of bonus and investment funds. Under the new law, enterprise performance was to be evaluated by a new criterion, the "value added" by any firm. But, of course, with prices set by the central authorities, there was little economic significance to the value added by any given productive activity. Nevertheless, Czech planners adopted the measure, hoping that it would encourage greater attention to the quality of output.

By the early 1980s, Czechoslovakia's trade deficit, although smaller than that of other East bloc countries, had grown menacingly large for the comfort of its leaders. Poland had already experienced embarrassing difficulties with its Western creditors, which served as a warning to Czechoslovak officials of the dangers of massive Western debts.

The seventh five-year plan called for resolving the debt issue while maintaining the standard of living. Trade accounts with the West were quickly restored to the black, largely by reducing imports. With the exception of glassware and wood products, efforts to increase exports to the West were not successful. The actual composition of Czechoslovak exports to the West belies its reputation as a relatively advanced industrial economy. During the 1980s, over 40 percent of its exports to nonsocialist states were fuels and basic raw materials, while machinery and equipment made up only 30 percent of exports.

Trade relations with the Soviets were not as easily repaired as economic relations with the West. Czechoslovakia's dependence on raw material and energy imports had been increasing steadily since the 1950s. The country had been spared the consequences of the OPEC oil embargo of 1973 and the doubling of oil prices following the ouster of the Shah of Iran, through the willingness of the Soviets to maintain generous supplies of heavily subsidized oil. Not that the Soviets were entirely happy with the arrangement. They adjusted the formula used to set the petroleum transfer price to reflect changes in world oil prices. They complained about the low quality of the industrial goods they were receiving in exchange for their oil. They urged their socialist trading partners to seek other supplies and to economize on energy use.

Czechoslovakia, for its part, incorporated measures in its seventh five-year plan to reduce its energy imports through conservation and the greater consumption of coal. It also advanced its already ambitious nuclear energy program. By the mid-1980s, nuclear energy accounted for 30 percent of all electricity generation, and the planners called for massive increases in nuclear energy production. Despite these efforts, Czechoslovakia's trade deficits with the Soviets continued to mount. By the early 1980s, when the effects of the world oil price shocks of the 1970s began to be reflected in the price Czechoslovakia was paying for Soviet oil, fuel, and raw materials constituted roughly 45 percent of its imports from socialist states. Finally in 1988, buoyed by increased prices for its exports, notably construction materials and chemicals, Czechoslovakia's trade account with the socialist states returned to a surplus. The Soviet oil-pricing formula, which smoothed global price fluctuations, began to reflect the lower world price of oil in the mid-1980s. But despite its trade balance with the USSR, Czechoslovakia ended communist rule critically dependent on subsidized raw material imports from the Soviets.

The main source of growth in the Czechoslovak economy under communism had been steady increases in the supply of inputs—both human and material. But because of very low birth rates and the aging of the population, the size of the labor force had stopped increasing. Because of Soviet reductions in energy supplies and the amount by which they subsidized their oil exports, the availability of material inputs declined as well. As a result, Czechoslovak GNP growth stagnated in the 1980s. The regime responded with renewed efforts to conserve energy. But Czechoslovak industry continued to consume energy and raw materials at rates disproportionately huge compared to the most inefficient consumers in the West. Communist officials refused to deal with the heart of the problem—the maintenance of rigid central planning controls.

Trade statistics provide another clue to the sorry state of the Czechoslovak economy at the end of communism. In 1989, only Bulgaria conducted a larger proportion of its foreign trade with the USSR. Czechoslovakia never succeeded in weaning itself from Soviet energy supplies, which could be obtained by barter, and never managed to find export markets besides the USSR for its substandard goods. Its machinery exports outside the Soviet bloc declined 37 percent from 1980 to 1985. The performance of its leading industry is devastating testimony to the state of the Czechoslovak communist economy.

FURTHER READINGS

Ash, Timothy G. *The Magic Lantern*. New York: Random House, 1990.

Johnson, Owen V. *Slovakia 1918–1938: Education and the Making of a Nation*. Boulder, CO: East European Monographs, 1985.

Skilling, H. Gordon. *Czechoslovakia's Interrupted Revolution*. Princeton: Princeton University Press, 1976.

Teichova, Alice. *The Czechoslovak Economy, 1918–1980*. London: Routledge, 1988.

Wallace, William V. *Czechoslovakia*. Boulder, CO: Westview Press, 1976.

II CZECHOSLOVAKIA

DATA AND VITAL STATISTICS

I. Agriculture

1. Land use, 1991
2. Agriculture production index
3. Selected indicators of agricultural development, 1970–1985
4. Total grain production
5. Principal crops
6. Yields for selected crops
7. Livestock
8. Slaughterings and production of selected animal products
9. State farms and collectives 1985
10. Agricultural labor force and tractors, 1988
11. Agricultural output, 1988
12. Growth per capita in agriculture and food, 1977–1988

II. Communications and Transport

1. General facts, 1990
2. Radio and television receivers
3. Percentage of households owning various consumer durables, 1986–1988
4. Daily newspapers
5. Transport traffic
6. Railroad freight
7. Air cargo, 1986–1988
8. Road traffic
9. Ownership of vehicles, 1985–1988
10. Number of persons per automobile, 1985–1988
11. Post, telephones, and telex lines, 1986–1988

III. Economy

1. Economic profile, 1990
2. Estimated real gross national product
3. Real gross national product growth
4. GNP per capita in dollars, 1990
5. GDP per capita as a percentage of OECD average, 1988
6. Exchange rate
7. Savings
8. Money in circulation
9. Growth of GNP by producing and consuming sectors
10. Growth of GNP inputs and productivity
11. Consumer spending on various items as a percentage of personal income, 1989
12. Cost-of-living price index

IV. **Education**
1. Schools, students, and teachers
2. Public expenditures on education
3. Expenditures and pupils per teacher, 1989
4. Distribution of teachers and pupils by educational level, 1987
5. Mean years of schooling, 1980
6. School enrollment ratios
7. School enrollment, 1989
8. Books, newspapers, and library book loans, 1989

V. **Energy and Resources**
1. History of primary energy production
2. Complete energy use
3. Electricity production
4. Installed electricity-generating capacity
5. Commercial energy use by sector, 1985
6. Proven reserves of crude oil, natural gas, and coal, 1989
7. Mineral production

VI. **Government and Defense Forces**
1. State budget
2. Hard-currency debt
3. Armed forces totals, 1991
4. Components of defense force, 1987
5. Military expenditures

VII. **Industry**
1. Industrial production index
2. Industrial production index (official and adjusted)
3. Production of selected industrial items
4. Rank of industry, manufacturing, and service sectors as a percent of GDP, 1990
5. Industrial waste generation
6. Emissions of air pollutants, 1988
7. Environmental summary, 1991

VIII. **Labor Force**
1. Workforce by selected areas of the economy
2. Average monthly earnings by economic sector
3. Economically active population by sex and industry, 1988
4. Structure of employment by republic, 1989

IX. **Population and Health**
1. Geography and demographic profile, 1990
2. Population
3. Population by age
4. Population of major cities, 1989
5. Population by nationality and republic, 1987
6. Health indicators, 1990
7. Registered illnesses and fatalities by selected causes of death
8. Life expectancy by sex, 1991
9. Medical care
10. Abortion rates

X. **Trade**
1. Exports and imports by commodity group
2. Main destinations of exports and origins of imports, 1989

3. Principal trading partners
4. Index of import and export prices, terms of trade
5. Major imports and exports
6. Trade with western countries
7. Trade with the USSR, by commodity
8. Trade with the United States, by commodity

Note: Where possible and relevant, Czechoslovakia is compared to the Netherlands, because they are of comparable population. Also, data for the United States, France, USSR, and other East European countries is provided for comparison where relevant.

I. AGRICULTURE

TABLE 2.I.1 Land use, 1991

		(Percent)			
Arable Land	Permanent Crops	Forest and Woodland	Meadows and Pastures	Other	Irrigated Land
40	1	37	13	9	1

Source: U.S. Central Intelligence Agency, *The World Factbook*, 1991.

TABLE 2.I.2 Agriculture production index (Czechoslovakia and selected countries)

			(1980 = 100)		
Country	1965	1970	1980	1986	1990
Czechoslovakia	66	80	100	111	115
USSR	83	99	100	120	118
United States	79	81	100	107	112
France	77	81	100	105	105[a]

[a] 1989 figure.

Source: U.S. Central Intelligence Agency, *Handbook of Economic Statistics*, 1991.

TABLE 2.I.3 Selected indicators of agricultural development, 1970–1985

	1971–1975	1976–1980	1981–1985
Agricultural land use (thousand ha[a])			
Arable	4,950	4,866	4,791
Natural grassland	1,749	1,709	1,662
Other agricultural land	352	364	374
Crop structure[b]			
Grain	56	57	55
Maize	3	4	4
Oilseeds	1	2	3
Fodder roots, silage maize	9	9	10
Cultivated grassland	21	20	21
Beets	4	4	4
Potatoes, vegetables	7	6	5
Other	2	2	2
Total output[c], 1977 prices			
Gross[d]	3.8	2.7	3.4
Net[d]	1.4	0.1	−0.5

[a] 1 hectare = 2.471 acres.
[b] Percent of sown area.
[c] Annualized percentage changes between five-year periods.
[d] Gross output is total yield before harvest. Net losses reflects output following processing.

(continued)

TABLE 2.1.3 (*continued*)

	1971–1975	1976–1980	1981–1985
Arable output[c]			
Total (gross) 1980 prices	1.1	0.9	2.5
Grain	5.8	1.6	1.7
Oilseeds	9.3	7.6	11.4
Coarse fodder	3.7	2.4	2.8
Livestock output			
Total (gross) 1980 prices	3.7	2.0	1.4
Meat	3.9	2.5	1.1
Milk	2.7	1.0	2.5
Eggs	5.0	1.9	2.3
Consumption per capita (kg)			
Cereals	110	107	109
Meat (including fat)	77	83	84
Milk (excluding butter)	207	223	242
Eggs (number)	292	308	330
Potatoes	105	87	79
Vegetables	74	71	74

[c] Annualized percentage changes between five-year periods.

Source: UN, *Economic Survey of Europe in 1987–1988.*

TABLE 2.1.4 Total grain production[a] (Czechoslovakia and selected countries)

	(Million Metric Tons)				
	1960	1970	1980	1985	1990
Czechoslovakia	4.84	7.20	10.70	11.77	12.42
USSR[b]	125.49	186.80	189.09	191.67	238.00
United States	181.26	186.72	269.68	347.01	312.14
France	23.02	31.29	47.36	55.07	55.38

[a] Data are for the following products, where they are produced: barley, corn, oats, rice, rye, sorghum, and wheat.

[b] Includes miscellaneous grains and legumes. For comparative purposes, an average discount of 11% should be applied, because USSR totals include excess moisture, unripe and damaged kernels, weed seeds, and other trash.

Source: U.S. Central Intelligence Agency, *Handbook of Economic Statistics,* 1990, 1991.

TABLE 2.1.5 Principal crops

	(Thousand Metric Tons)		
	1985	1987	1989
Sugar beet[a]	7,747	6,698	6,390
Wheat and spelt	6,023	6,154	6,356
Barley	3,538	3,551	3,550
Potatoes	3,450	3,072	3,167
Maize	1,114	1,160	1,000
Rye	620	496	708
Apples	379	308	552
Oats[b]	473	406	330
Rapeseed	285	337	387
Cabbages	261	296	306

[a] Including sugar beet seed.
[b] Including mixed crops of oats and barley.

Source: The Europa World Year Book, 1989, 1990, 1991.

TABLE 2.I.6   Yields for selected crops (Czechoslovakia and selected countries)

| | | (ql/ha^a) | | |
		1985	1987	1989
Wheat	Czechoslovakia	49.3	50.8	51.2
	Bulgaria	28.7	38.2	47.7
	Hungary	48.3	43.7	52.4
	Poland	34.3	37.2	38.5
	Romania	23.4	28.0	35.8^b
	Yugoslavia	36.0	36.0	42.0^b
	Soviet Union	15.5	17.8	19.4
Barley	Czechoslovakia	44.3	42.3	47.2
	Bulgaria	30.7	37.0	43.6
	Hungary	37.3	38.2	46.8
	Poland	32.9	33.7	33.3
	Romania	25.9	36.0	44.8
	Yugoslavia	27.0	24.0	28.0^b
	Soviet Union	16.0	19.1	17.5
Maize	Czechoslovakia	54.4	56.4	52.7
	Bulgaria	30.7	37.2	40.0
	Hungary	62.9	61.3	62.2
	Poland	43.0	46.0	47.8
	Romania	38.5	27.0	24.7
	Yugoslavia	41.0	40.0	34.0^b
	Soviet Union	32.1	32.4	37.1
Rye	Czechoslovakia	34.0	34.9	40.5
	Bulgaria	14.9	16.6	20.4
	Hungary	19.3	19.5	27.3
	Poland	24.7	25.8	27.3
	Romania	15.0	14.9	16.2^b
	Yugoslavia	17.0	17.0	19.0^b
	Soviet Union	16.5	18.6	18.6
Oats	Czechoslovakia	37.4	37.3	32.3
	Bulgaria	13.9	14.8	27.0
	Hungary	29.6	23.9	32.5
	Poland	27.0	28.4	27.2
	Romania	12.8	15.7	15.9
	Yugoslavia	N/A	N/A	N/A
	Soviet Union	16.3	15.7	15.7
Potatoes	Czechoslovakia	184	171	186
	Bulgaria	109	86	137
	Hungary	196	160	186
	Poland	174	187	185
	Romania	204	129	124
	Yugoslavia	88	81	70^b
	Soviet Union	113	121	120
Sugar beets	Czechoslovakia	377	355	352
	Bulgaria	168	188	246
	Hungary	379	363	440
	Poland	336	332	340
	Romania	223	201	265
	Yugoslavia	418	380	349^b
	Soviet Union	241	266	291

^{a}ql: quintal $=$ 100 kg (220.46 lbs).
^{b}1988 data.
Source: EUROSTAT, *Central and Eastern Europe 1991*, 1991; *Comecon Data 1989*, 1990.

TABLE 2.I.7   Livestock (Czechoslovakia and selected countries)

| | | Thousand Head | | |
		1980	1985	1989
Horses	Czechoslovakia	45	46	42
	Bulgaria	120	120	119
	Hungary	120	98	76[a]
	Poland	1,780	1,324	992[a]
	Romania	555	672	663
	Yugoslavia	N/A	N/A	N/A
	Soviet Union	5,563	5,782	5,920
Cattle	Czechoslovakia	5,002	5,066	5,129
	Bulgaria	1,843	1,735	1,600
	Hungary	1,918	1,766	1,698
	Poland	11,337	11,774	10,277
	Romania	6,485	6,692	6,291
	Yugoslavia	5,474	5,034	4,759[a]
	Soviet Union	115,057	120,888	118,429
Dairy cows	Czechoslovakia	1,902	1,860	1,795
	Bulgaria	723	682	633
	Hungary	765	688	646
	Poland	5,666	5,331	4,964
	Romania	2,670	2,901	2,468
	Yugoslavia	3,086	2,915	2,858[a]
	Soviet Union	43,389	42,863	41,716
Pigs	Czechoslovakia	7,894	6,651	7,498
	Bulgaria	3,808	3,912	4,353
	Hungary	8,330	8,280	7,661
	Poland	18,734	19,170	18,686
	Romania	11,542	13,631	11,671
	Yugoslavia	7,867	7,821	7,396[a]
	Soviet Union	73,382	77,772	79,033
Sheep	Czechoslovakia	910	1,087	1,051
	Bulgaria	10,433	9,724	7,973
	Hungary	3,090	2,465	2,068
	Poland	3,490	4,720	4,196
	Romania	15,865	17,342	15,435
	Yugoslavia	7,384	7,693	7,564[a]
	Soviet Union	141,573	14,850	138,443
Goats	Czechoslovakia	57	53	50[a]
	Bulgaria	467	460	433
	Hungary	15	16	16
	Poland	10	10	10
	Romania	347	828	1,070[a]
	Yugoslavia	N/A	N/A	N/A
	Soviet Union	5,925	6,480	6,974
Hens (million)	Czechoslovakia	45.3	45.4	46.6
	Bulgaria	39.9	37.9	37.3
	Hungary	61.0	56.7	52.8
	Poland	76.1	66.2	55.6
	Romania	97.8	120.1	114.0
	Yugoslavia	N/A	N/A	N/A
	Soviet Union	967.3	1,109.9	1,151.0

[a] 1988 data.

Source: EUROSTAT, *Central and Eastern Europe 1991,* 1991; *Comecon Data 1989,* 1990.

TABLE 2.I.8 Slaughterings and production of selected animal products (Czechoslovakia and selected countries)

		Production of Selected Animal Products (Thousand Tons)				Slaughterings (Thousand Tons)		
		1980	1985	1989		1985	1987	1989
Beef	Czechoslovakia	468	467	460	Cattle	1,804	1,710	1,733
	Bulgaria	167	163	159	and	704	651	601
	Hungary	215	180	170	calves	525	471	435
	Poland	866	900	789		4,290	4,049	3,425
	Romania	285	240	230[a]		1,772	1,570	1,510
	Yugoslavia	344	352	301[a]		N/A	N/A	N/A
	Soviet Union	7,367	8,278	8,780		36,659	41,800	43,300
Pork	Czechoslovakia	853	891	971	Pigs	8,180	8,495	9,124
	Bulgaria	390	434	482		4,582	5,086	5,364
	Hungary	1,100	1,113	1,112		11,301	11,589	11,830
	Poland	1,526	1,773	1,880		16,169	19,082	19,210
	Romania	975	900	840		12,500	11,539	11,218
	Yugoslavia	461	526	546[a]		N/A	N/A	N/A
	Soviet Union	5,835	6,299	6,737		72,248	77,000	78,000
Mutton and goat-meat	Czechoslovakia	12	13	12	Sheep and lamb	1,380	1,457	1,500[a]
	Bulgaria	126	116	112		5,705	5,907	5,481[a]
	Hungary	23	18	21		429	261	285
	Poland	39	47	43		1,347	1,654	1,580[a]
	Romania	81	70	67[a]		4,412	3,880	4,700[b]
	Yugoslavia	59	63	70[a]		N/A	N/A	N/A
	Soviet Union	827	905	993		52,646	56,579	56,600[b]
Poultry	Czechoslovakia	172	194	233	Goats	1,700	1,875	1,562[a]
	Bulgaria	158	169	188		385	413	404[a]
	Hungary	405	469	445		50	54	53[a]
	Poland	290	345	381		23	15	15
	Romania	475	425	390		468	508	547
	Yugoslavia	277	299	329[a]		N/A	N/A	N/A
	Soviet Union	2,811	3,116	3,357		N/A	N/A	N/A
Milk	Czechoslovakia	6,942	6,982	7,150				
	Bulgaria	2,357	2,590	2,512				
	Hungary	2,729	2,833	2,942				
	Poland	16,446	15,543	16,429				
	Romania	5,411	5,165	4,667				
	Yugoslavia	4,352	4,682	4,638[a]				
	Soviet Union	98,608	103,743	108,529				

[a] 1988 data.
[b] Including goats.

Source: EUROSTAT, *Central and Eastern Europe 1991,* 1991; *Comecon Data 1989,* 1990.

TABLE 2.I.9 State farms and collectives, 1985

	State Farms	Collectives
Gross output per ha, korunas (Kcs)	13,283	16,400
Gross output per worker (Kcs)	111,623	102,209
Profit per ha (Kcs)	1,462	2,359
Grants and subsidies per ha (Kcs)	665	217
Average monthly wage (Kcs)	2,968	2,635
Agricultural land per worker (ha)	8.4	6.2
Hectare yields (tons)		
Wheat	4.51	5.69
Barley	4.15	4.66
Potatoes	18.87	19.54
Sugar beet	34.52	38.25

Note: In 1987 there were 1,664 collectives with a total work force of 698,118. Members of these cooperatives are officially termed "peasants." There were 235 state farms with 167,946 employees (defined officially as "workers").

Source: EIU, *Czechoslovakia, Country Profile,* 1988–1989.

TABLE 2.I.10 Agricultural labor force and tractors, 1988 (Czechoslovakia and selected countries)

	Percent of Labor Force in Agriculture	Population per km² of Arable Land	Output per Worker in $	Tractors per 10 km²
Czechoslovakia	10.0	312	3,532	8.2
USSR	14.2	125	3,830	45.3
United States	2.5	131	33,519	10.8
OECD average	8.1	809	23,334	18.2

Source: The Economist, *Book of Vital World Statistics*, 1990.

TABLE 2.I.11 Agricultural output, 1988 (Czechoslovakia and selected countries)

	(Thousand Tons)			
	Cereals	Meat	Vegetables	Fruit
Czechoslovakia	11,861	1,616	1,129	1,005
OECD average[a]	12,362	1,830	3,685	3,272
East Bloc average[b]	19,125	2,024	3,523	2,582

[a]Excluding the United States.
[b]Exluding Albania.
Source: The Economist, *Book of Vital World Statistics*, 1990.

TABLE 2.I.12 Growth per capita in agriculture and food, 1977–1988 (Czechoslovakia and selected countries)

	Agriculture	Food
Czechoslovakia	0.9	0.9
USSR	0.4	0.5
United States	1.4	1.4
France	1.3	1.3

Source: The Economist, *Book of Vital World Statistics*, 1990.

II. COMMUNICATIONS AND TRANSPORT

TABLE 2.II.1 General facts, 1990

1. Communications
    Telecommunications
        Stations 58 AM, 16 FM, 45 TV
        Radios (1988) 4,257,556 (1 per 3.7 persons)
        Televisions (1988) 4,387,144 (1 per 3.6 persons)
        Telephones (1987) 3,838,000 (1 per 4.1 persons)

2. Transport
    Railroads
        13,103 km total, of which
        12,855 km 1.435-meter standard gauge
            146 km narrow gauge
            102 km broad gauge
         3,798 km electrified, government-owned (1988)
    Highways
        73,540 km total, of which
            517 km is superhighway (1986)

(continued)

TABLE 2.II.1 *(continued)*

Inland Waterways
    475 km (1988)
Pipelines
    1,448 km crude oil
    1,500 km refined products
    8,100 km natural gas
Airports
    158 total, including
        40 with permanent-surface runways
        19 with runways 2,440–3,659 m
        37 with runways 1,220–2,439 m

Source: U.S. Central Intelligence Agency, *The World Factbook,* 1991; *The Europa World Yearbook,* 1990.

TABLE 2.II.2 Radio and television receivers (Czechoslovakia and selected countries)

	(Per Thousand Inhabitants)			
	1970	**1975**	**1980**	**1986–88**
Czechoslovakia				
Radios	269	264	291[a]	577
TVs	216	249	280	281
USSR				
Radios	390	481	490	686
TVs	143	217	303[a]	314
United States				
Radios	1,415	1,857	1,989	2,120
TVs	413	560	684	811
France				
Radios	315	326	743	995
TVs	216	269	354	333[b]

[a] 1979 data.
[b] 1987 data.

Source: UN, *Statistical Yearbook,* 1988; UN, *Human Development Report 1991,* 1991.

TABLE 2.II.3 Percentage of households owning various consumer durables, 1986–1988 [a] (Czechoslovakia and selected countries)

	(Percent)			
	Televisions	**Radios**	**Refrigerators**	**Vacuum Cleaners**
Czechoslovakia	95	75	90	49
USSR	45	96	N/A	N/A
United States	98	99	100	N/A
France	98	98	97	88

[a] Means data for each country may refer to 1986, 1987, or 1988.

Source: The Economist, *Book of Vital Statistics,* 1990.

TABLE 2.II.4 Daily newspapers (Czechoslovakia and selected countries)

Country	1970	1975	1979	1986
Czechoslovakia	28	29	30	30
USSR[a]	639	691	N/A	723[b]
United States	1,763	1,775	1,787	1,657
France[c]	106	92	90	92

[a]Data include nondaily newspapers.
[b]1984 data.
[c]Data shown for 1975 and 1979 refer to 1976 and 1978 respectively.
Source: UNESCO, *Statistical Yearbook,* 1989.

TABLE 2.II.5 Transport traffic

	1980	1987	1989
Road traffic			
Passengers (million)	2,135	2,333	2,320
Freight (million metric tons)	337	338	329
Passenger-km (billion)	33.8	38.7	39.7
Ton-km (million)	10,802	12,533	13,247
Railway traffic			
Passengers (million)	416	416	411
Freight (million metric tons)	286	291	284
Passenger-km (billion)	18.0	20.0	19.7
Ton-km (million)	66.2	68.0	66.3
Inland-waterway traffic[a]			
Passengers (million)	2.1	2.4	2.1
Freight (million metric tons)	10.5	14.3	13.5
Passenger-km (billion)	35.1	47.3	37.3
Ton-km (million)	3,593	5,067	5,099
Sea traffic			
Passengers (million)	N/A	N/A	N/A
Freight (million metric tons)	1.7	1.6	2.0
Passenger-km (million)	N/A	N/A	N/A
Ton-km (billion)	12	9	17
Air traffic			
Passengers (thousand)	1,678	1,368	1,493
Freight (thousand metric tons)	25.2	26.6	29.1
Passenger-km (million)	1,814	2,443	2,627
Ton-km (million)	42.4	63.0	66.1

[a]On domestically registered ships.
Source: EUROSTAT, *Central and Eastern Europe 1991,* 1991.

TABLE 2.II.6 Railroad freight (Czechoslovakia and selected countries)

Country	1960	1970	1985	1989
Czechoslovakia				
Billion metric ton-km	47.4	61.0	73.6	72.0
Million metric tons carried	194.1	236.9	293.2	283.9
Czechoslovakia as a percent of Eastern Europe[a]				
Billion metric ton-km	25.4%	21.5%	20.0%[b]	N/A
Million metric tons carried	20.9%	19.1%	18.9%[b]	N/A

[a]Eastern Europe includes Bulgaria, Czechoslovakia, East Germany, Hungary, Poland, and Romania.
[b]Latest available data.

(continued)

TABLE 2.II.6 (continued)

Country	1960	1970	1985	1989
USSR				
Billion metric ton-km	1,504.3	2,494.7	3,718.4	3,924.8[b]
Million metric tons carried	1,884.9	2,896.0	3,951.0	4,000.0
United States				
Billion metric ton-km	868.5	1,141.0	1,288.3	1,473.9
Million metric tons carried	1,180.5	1,426.3	1,567.0	1,792.0
France				
Billion metric ton-km	56.9	70.4	58.5	52.7
Million metric tons carried	227.0	260.0	193.0	174.0

[b]Latest available data.

Source: U.S. Central Intelligence Agency, *Handbook of Economic Statistics,* 1990.

TABLE 2.II.7 Air cargo, 1986–88[a]
(Czechoslovakia and selected countries)

Country	(Freight in Km Tons[b])
Czechoslovakia	17
Netherlands	1,882
USSR	2,721
United States	13,829
OECD average	1,622

[a]Means data for each country may refer to 1986, 1987, or 1988.
[b]Of national origin.

Source: The Economist, *Book of Vital Statistics,* 1990.

TABLE 2.II.8 Road traffic

	(Number of Vehicles)		
	1986	1987	1989
Passenger cars	2,812,357	2,903,947	3,122,307
Buses	36,786	36,595	39,382
Trucks	400,824	412,969	446,725
Motorcycles and scooters	567,937	555,252	551,497

Source: The Europa World Year Book, 1990, 1991.

TABLE 2.II.9 Ownership of vehicles, 1985–1988[a] (Czechoslovakia and selected countries)

Country	Thousand Vehicles[b]	Thousand Passenger Cars
Czechoslovakia	3,175.0	2,750.0
Netherlands	5,788.8	5,250.6
United States	183,468.0	140,655.0
USSR	21,500.0	12,500.0

[a]Means data for each country may refer to 1985, 1986, 1987, or 1988.
[b]Vehicles include passenger cars, trucks, and buses.

Source: The Economist, *Book of Vital World Statistics,* 1990.

TABLE 2.II.10 Number of persons per automobile, 1985–1988[a] (Czechoslovakia and selected countries)

Country	
Czechoslovakia	5.7
Netherlands	2.9
OECD	2.6
USSR	22.8
U.S.	1.8

[a]Means data for each country may refer to 1985, 1986, 1987, or 1988.

Source: The Economist, *Book of Vital World Statistics,* 1990.

TABLE 2.II.11 Post, telephones, and telex lines, 1986–1988[a] (Czechoslovakia and selected countries)

Country	Post Offices	Letters per Person	Persons per Telephone Line	Persons per Telex Line
Czechoslovakia	5,972	91.55	2.6	1,397
Netherlands	2,291	342.22	1.6	376
USSR	98,445	217.81	10.3	162,875
United States	40,117	645.48	1.3	N/A

[a]Means data for each country may refer to 1986, 1987, or 1988.

Source: The Economist, *Book of Vital World Statistics,* 1990.

III. ECONOMY

TABLE 2.III.1 Economic profile, 1990 (Czechoslovakia and selected countries)

	Czechoslovakia	USSR	United States	France
Gross national product				
Billion 1990 U.S. $[a]	126.8	2,660.0	5,465.2[b]	873.6[b]
Percent real growth	−2.9	−2.4 to −5.0	1.0	2.8
Per capita (1990 U.S. $)	8,100	9,140	21,830	15,490
Industrial production[c]	−3.3	−2.8	1.0	1.1
Trade (billion U.S. $)				
Exports, f.o.b.	13.2[d]	109.3[d]	393.9	216.6
Imports, c.i.f.	13.0[d]	114.7[d]	516.2	234.4
Trade balance	0.2[d]	−5.4[d]	−122.3	−17.8
Living standard indicators				
Automobile registrations (per thousand persons)	175[e]	46[e]	571[f]	395[e]
Energy consumption[g]	37[d]	35[d]	57[d]	29[d]

[a]At U.S. purchasing power equivalents.
[b]Gross domestic product.
[c]Percent growth.
[d]1989 data.
[e]1987 data.
[f]1988 data.
[g]Barrels oil equivalent per capita.

Source: U.S. Central Intelligence Agency, *Handbook of Economic Statistics,* 1991.

TABLE 2.III.2   Estimated real gross national product (Czechoslovakia and selected countries)

Country	(Billion 1990 U.S. $)				
	1970	1980	1985	1989	1990
Czechoslovakia	83.2	109.3	116.1	123.2	124.3
USSR	1,726.9	2,257.0	2,440.9	2,663.7[a]	1,465.9[a]
United States	2,985.8	3,916.0	4,513.3	5,198.4	5,465.6
France	491.7	680.6	733.9	818.5	819.6

[a]The 1989 GNP figure for the USSR is based on CIA statistics, while the 1990 GNP figure is based on PlanEcon statistics. The great disparity between the Soviet GNP in 1990 and 1988 is due to extremely high estimates by the CIA during the 1980s.

Source: U.S. Central Intelligence Agency, *Handbook of Economic Statistics,* 1989, 1990; and "PlanEcon Report," vol. 6, no. 52, December 28, 1990.

TABLE 2.III.3   Real gross national product growth (Czechoslovakia and selected countries)

Country	Percent Average Annual Rate of Growth		Percent		
	1971–1980	1981–1985	1985	1989	1990
GNP growth					
Czechoslovakia	2.8	1.3	0.7	1.1	−2.9
USSR[a]	2.4	1.8	0.9	1.5	−2.4 to −5.0
United States[b]	2.8	3.0	3.8	2.5	1.0
France[b]	3.6	1.5	1.9	3.6	2.8
GNP per capita growth					
Czechoslovakia	2.3	1.0	0.4	0.9	−3.2
USSR	1.5	0.8	0.1	0.7	−2.9 to −5.5
United States[b]	1.7	1.8	2.8	1.5	0.3
France[b]	3.0	1.0	1.5	3.1	2.4

[a] At factor cost.
[b] GDP growth.
Source: U.S. Central Intelligence Agency, *Handbook of Economic Statistics,* 1990, 1991.

TABLE 2.III.4   GNP per capital in dollars[a], 1990 (Czechoslovakia and selected countries)

Country	(U.S. $)		
	Commercial	Purchasing Parity	Free Market
Czechoslovakia	2,684	7,940	1,701
USSR	2,560	5,060	1,299
United States	21,732	21,732	21,732
West Germany	24,210	16,310	24,210

[a]Based on exchange rate, purchasing power parity, and free market rate.
Source: "PlanEcon Report," vol. 6, no. 52, December 28, 1990.

TABLE 2.III.5   GDP per capita as a percentage of OECD average, 1988 (Czechoslovakia and selected countries)

Country	(Percent of OECD)
Czechoslovakia	16.1
Netherlands	90.5
USSR	12.1
United States	116.3

Source: The Economist, *Book of Vital World Statistics,* 1990.

TABLE 2.III.6   Exchange rate (Czechoslovakia)

	1987	1988	1989	1990	Jan. 1991
	(Korunas per $; Periods Averages)				
Commercial	13.69	14.36	15.05	17.95	27.65

Source: U.S. Central Intelligence Agency, *The World Factbook*, 1991.

TABLE 2.III.7   Savings

1984	1987	1988	1989
(Million Kcs)			
203,717	249,752	263,429	274,694

Source: Comecon Data 1990, 1991.

TABLE 2.III.8   Money in circulation

1980	1985	1988	1989
(Million Kcs)			
41,578	53,967	58,648	68,059

Source: Comecon Data 1990, 1991.

TABLE 2.III.9   Growth of GNP by producing and consuming sectors

	1985	1987	1989
	(Percent Average Annual Rate of Growth)		
GNP	0.7	1.1	1.0
Producing sector			
Industry	1.9	1.5	0.7
of which			
Machinery	5.2	3.8[a]	3.8[a]
Agriculture and forestry	−0.4	1.5	1.4
Construction	−3.8	−0.7	2.1
Transportation and communications	2.2	0.9	−0.3
Trade	1.7	1.6	1.7
Services	1.4	3.1	3.3
Other	1.4	0.9	1.0
Consuming sector			
Personal consumption	1.9	2.6	1.9[b]
Government	1.6	1.1	1.1[b]
Gross investment	−3.1	4.1	0.8[b]

[a] 1986 data.
[b] 1988 data.

Source: U.S. Central Intelligence Agency, "Eastern Europe: Long Road Ahead to Economic Well-Being," May, 1990.

TABLE 2.III.10 Growth of GNP by inputs and productivity

	(Percent Average Annual Rate of Growth)			
	1980	1985	1987	1989
GNP	2.4	0.7	1.1	1.0
Combined inputs	2.1	1.8	1.8	2.0
Capital stock	5.4	4.7	4.5	5.2
Labor	0.7	0.6	0.7	0.7
Combined productivity	0.3	−1.1	−0.7	−0.9
Capital productivity	−2.8	−3.9	−3.3	−3.9
Labor productivity	1.7	0.1	0.3	0.3

Source: U.S. Central Intelligence Agency, "Eastern Europe: Long Road Ahead to Economic Well-Being," May, 1990.

TABLE 2.III.11 Consumer spending on various items as a percentage of personal income, 1989 (Czechoslovakia and selected countries)

	Total per Head $	Percent Food/ Drink	Percent Clothing	Percent Energy	Percent Household Goods	Percent Health	Percent Transport
Czechoslovakia	5,088	38.0	6.8	4.1	13.0	5.5	6.0
USSR	2,820	43.2	19.0	7.0	8.0	2.7	2.9
United States	12,233	13.3	6.5	19.5	5.7	14.7	14.8
France	9,635	20.0	7.0	18.8	8.3	8.8	16.7

Source: The Economist, *Book of Vital World Statistics,* 1990.

TABLE 2.III.12 Cost-of-living price index[a]

Index Group	(Jan. 1977 = 100)		(Jan. 1984 = 100)	
	1983	1985	1986	1988
Manual workers	118	120	103	103
Foods	115	115	100	100
Beverages	125	149	126	126
Industrial goods[b]	118	120	102	102
Services	120	121	99	101
Cooperative farmers	117	120	103	103
Foods	114	114	100	100
Beverages	125	150	126	126
Industrial goods[b]	119	122	102	102
Services	116	118	99	100
Pensioners	116	102	102	103
Foods	114	114	100	100
Beverages	124	151	126	127
Industrial goods[b]	115	119	102	103
Services	122	123	99	100

[a] Annual average.

[b] Including tobacco and tobacco products.

Source: EUROSTAT, *Central and Eastern Europe 1991,* 1991.

IV. EDUCATION

TABLE 2.IV.1 Schools, students, and teachers

	1980–1981	1987–1988	1989–1990
Schools			
General schools[a]	7,094	6,585	6,557
Vocational schools[b]	2,089	1,090	957
Technical colleges[c]	578	556	563
Universities	36	36	36
Students (thousand)			
General-school pupils[d]	2,087	2,200	2,115
Vocational-school pupils	393	422	513
Technical-college students[e]	331	260	274
Day pupils	243	215	240
Pupils per 10,000 population	216	167	175
Technical-college graduates	77.6	65.1	66.6
University undergraduates	197	170	174
Day students	152	140	138
Pupils per 10,000 population	128	109	111
University graduates	31.0	32.5	29.5
Teachers (thousand)			
General-school teachers[f]	99	108	109
Technical-college lecturers[g]	17.3	17.4	18.6
University academic staff	18.31	20.4	20.3

[a] Includes general lower secondary schools and combined lower/upper secondary schools. General schools include the compulsory primary/lower secondary school (7 to 10 years' schooling) and an upper secondary stage of 2 to 4 years.

[b] Pupils here receive a job-oriented education.

[c] Includes distance-learning institutions for teaching certificates; technical colleges to train technicians, technical colleges to improve the qualifications of workers and similar for craftsmen.

[d] Includes both day and evening school pupils and also those on correspondence courses.

[e] Includes pupils involved in distance learning to gain teaching certificates, at technical colleges for technicians, and at technical colleges to improve the qualifications of workers and craftsmen.

[f] Includes general schools and combined lower/upper secondary schools; teaching staff includes those members of staff with secondary or higher education who work as teachers, instructors, and technical instructors in the school workshops.

[g] The academic staff includes those members of staff with secondary or higher education, as well as staff seconded from industry (engineers, technicians, craftsmen, etc.).

Source: EUROSTAT, *Central and Eastern Europe 1991*, 1991.

TABLE 2.IV.2 Public expenditures on education

Year	Korunas	As Percent of GNP	Percent of Total Government Expenditures
1975	19,104,801,000	4.7	7.0
1980	23,180,783,000	4.8	N/A
1985	28,201,234,000	5.1	7.9
1986	29,466,873,000	5.2	8.1
1987	30,548,501,000	N/A	8.0

Source: UNESCO, *Statistical Yearbook*, 1989.

TABLE 2.IV.3   Expenditures and pupils per teacher, 1989 (Czechoslovakia and selected countries)

Country	Percent of GNP	Pupils per Teacher Primary/Secondary
Bulgaria	5.2	21/10
USSR	7.3	17/N/A
United States	6.7	21/13
France	5.7	19/17

Source: The Economist, *Book of Vital World Statistics,* 1990.

TABLE 2.IV.4   Distribution of teachers and pupils by educational level, 1987

Educational Level	Teachers	Percent Female	Pupils	Percent Female
Preschool	50,385	100	659,592	N/A
First-level	97,733	83	2,062,215	49
Second-level	34,335	52	351,199	63
General	11,634	57	136,243	61
Teacher training	669	68	8,006	98
Vocational	22,032	48	206,950	62
Third-level	26,514	28	170,550	42
Total	208,967		3,243,556	

Source: UNESCO, *Statistical Yearbook,* 1989.

TABLE 2.IV.5   Mean years of schooling[a], 1980 (Czechoslovakia and selected countries)

Country	Total
Czechoslovakia	7.8
USSR	7.6
United States	12.2
France	9.4

[a]For adults over 25 years old.

Source: UN, *Human Development Report 1991,* 1991.

TABLE 2.IV.6   School enrollment ratios[a]

Year	First Level (Ages 6–14)	Second Level (Ages 15–18)	Third Level (Ages 20–24)
1975	96	35	12.1
1980	92	44	17.1
1987[b]	96	38	16.2

[a]Percent total enrollment of all ages divided by the population of the specific age groups which correspond to the age groups of primary and secondary schooling.

[b]1987 data represent new age ranges in the following categories: First Level (ages 6–13) and Second Level (ages 14–17).

Source: UNESCO, *Statistical Yearbook,* 1989.

TABLE 2.IV.7 School enrollment, 1989 (Czechoslovakia and selected countries)

| | (Percent) | | | | | |
| | Primary | | | Secondary | | |
	Total	Male	Female	Total	Male	Female
Czechoslovakia	96	95	96	38	27	49
USSR	106	N/A	N/A	98	N/A	N/A
United States	100	101	100	98	99	99
France	113	114	113	92	89	96

Source: The Economist, *Book of Vital World Statistics*, 1990.

TABLE 2.IV.8 Books, newspapers, and library book loans, 1989 (Czechoslovakia and selected countries)

	Books Published per Year	Newspaper Circulation (Thousand)	Library Book Loans per Year (Thousand)	Volumes Stock (Thousand)
Czechoslovakia	10,565	5,139	100,125.5	56,577
Netherlands	13,329	4,518	168,604.0	39,572
USSR	83,011	12,982	2,634.3[a]	1,523,071
United States	48,793	62,502	197,328.1	523,493

[a]Soviet library regulations rarely allowed the loaning of books—thus the low figure.

Source: The Economist, *Book of Vital World Statistics*, 1990.

V. ENERGY AND RESOURCES

TABLE 2.V.1 History of primary energy production (Czechoslovakia and selected countries)

| Energy Type | Country | (Thousand Barrels per Day of Oil Equivalent) | |
		1970	1980
Coal	Czechoslovakia	861	899
	USSR	6,080	6,370
	United States	7,359	9,785
	France	523	284
Crude oil	Czechoslovakia	4	2
	USSR	7,060	12,030
	United States	11,380	10,170
	France	68	51
Natural gas	Czechoslovakia	18	9
	USSR	3,270	7,170
	United States	10,686	9,838
	France	118	129
Hydro/nuclear	Czechoslovakia	23	53
	USSR	660	1,170
	United States	1,394	2,774
	France	317	665

Source: U.S. Central Intelligence Agency, *Handbook of Economic Statistics*, 1990.

TABLE 2.V.2 Complete energy use

	Year	Production	Consumption[a]	Exports	Imports	Soviet Portion of Imports (%)[b,c]
			(Thousand Metric Tons)			
Crude oil[d]	1985	123	16,761	290	16,928	16,640 (98)
	1988	143	16,657	500	17,014	16,421 (97)
	1990	145	15,095	750	15,700	12,960 (83)
Refined oil products	1985	16,744	16,290	1,234	780	370 (47)
	1988	16,660	15,567	1,866	773	382 (49)
	1990	15,020	14,470	1,500	950	145 (15)
Motor and aviation gas	1985	1,473	1,827	100	454	N/A
	1988	1,743	2,153	100	550	N/A
	1990	1,540	2,170	50	680	N/A
Diesel oil	1985	3,647	3,563	91	7	N/A
	1988	4,469	3,408	1,077	16	N/A
	1990	4,236	3,451	871	85	N/A
Fuel oil	1985	7,362	6,497	970	105	N/A
	1988	6,014	5,441	614	41	N/A
	1990	5,170	4,785	480	95	N/A
Other refined products	1985	4,262	4,403	73	214	N/A
	1988	4,474	4,565	75	166	N/A
	1990	4,074	4,064	100	90	N/A
Natural gas (million cm³)	1985	724	11,117	418	10,811	9,384 (87)
	1988	944	12,357	624	12,037	10,673 (89)
	1990	830	13,510	1,750	14,430	12,662 (88)
Hard coal (including anthracite)	1985	26,223	28,233	2,676	4,686	3,241 (69)
	1988	25,503	28,137	2,147	4,781	3,015 (63)
	1990	22,900	25,540	2,250	4,800	3,299 (69)
Brown coal (including lignite)	1985	100,387	98,291	2,832	736	0
	1988	98,318	97,327	1,968	977	0
	1990	84,180	82,280	2,500	600	0
Coke	1985	10,237	9,080	1,157	0	0
	1988	10,586	9,201	1,385	0	0
	1990	9,743	8,263	1,480	0	0
Electricity (million kWh)	1985	80,629	84,166	2,537	6,076	4,000 (66)
	1988	87,374	90,421	2,950	5,997	4,300 (72)
	1990	86,600	89,700	5,400	8,500	6,773 (80)

[a] Czechoslovakia is the 18th largest energy consumer in the world.
[b] Soviet portion of imports as a percent.
[c] To the nearest 1%.
[d] 1 metric ton = 8.03 barrels of oil.
Source: "PlanEcon Report," vol. 7, March 6, 1991.

TABLE 2.V.3 Electricity production[a] (Czechoslovakia and selected countries)

Country	1970	1980	1985	1989
		(Billion Kilowatt-hours)		
Czechoslovakia	45.16	72.73	80.63	89.64
USSR	740.93	1,293.88	1,544.10	1,722.00
United States[b]	1742.73	2,437.82	2,634.65	2,970.21
France	146.97	243.29	325.73	378.00

[a] Data are for total (gross) production at generating centers and therefore include transmission losses and station use.
[b] Beginning in 1980, data are for public utilities only.
Source: U.S. Central Intelligence Agency, *Handbook of Economic Statistics,* 1990.

TABLE 2.V.4 Installed electricity-generating capacity[a] (Czechoslovakia and selected countries)

Country	(Million Kilowatts)			
	1970	1980	1985	1989
Czechoslovakia	10.81	16.65	20.32	21.70[c]
USSR	166.15	266.71	315.00	346.00
United States	360.33	630.94	698.10[b]	683.99[b]
France	36.22	63.66	86.56	100.62[c]

[a] All plants for both public and industrial use.
[b] Data are for public utilities only.
[c] 1988 data.

Source: U.S. Central Intelligence Agency, *Handbook of Economic Statistics,* 1990.

TABLE 2.V.5 Commercial energy use by sector[a], 1985 (Czechoslovakia and selected countries)

	(Percentage of Commercial Energy Used)				
	Industry	Transport	Agriculture	Commercial and Residential	Other[b]
Czechoslovakia[c]	52[d]	7	41[e]	N/A	N/A
USSR	60	13	0	27	0
United States	31	35	1	30	4
France	33	26	2	35	3

[a] Includes all solid, liquid, and gaseous fuels as well as primary and secondary electricity.
[b] Other includes nonenergy uses, military uses, and nonspecified uses.
[c] 1986 data from *Comecon Data 1989,* 1990.
[d] Industry and construction.
[e] Households, agriculture, trade, and other consumers.

Source: From *World Resources 1988–89.* Copyright © 1988 by the World Resources Institute and the International Institute for Environment and Development in collaboration with the United Nations Environment Programme. Reprinted by permission of Basic Books, a division of Harper Collins Publishers Inc.

TABLE 2.V.6 Proven reserves of crude oil, natural gas, and coal, 1989 (Czechoslovakia and selected countries)

Country	Crude Oil (Billion Barrels)	Natural Gas (Trillion Cubic Feet)	Coal (Million Metric Tons)
Czechoslovakia	0.002	0.035	55,792
USSR	50–80	1,450	182,000
United States	26	165	205,000
UK	4	21	4,200
France	0.03	0.18	1,070

Source: U.S. Central Intelligence Agency, *Handbook of Economic Statistics,* 1990; U.S. Department of Energy, Energy Information Administration, *International Energy Annual,* 1988; UN, *Energy Statistics Yearbook,* 1986.

TABLE 2.V.7 Mineral Production

Mineral	1985	(Tons) 1987	1989
Alumina	138,000	149,917	204,615
Primary aluminum	31,725	32,366	28,500
Antimony	782	931	839
Asbestos	N/A	194	147
Barytes	60,000[e]	60,000[e]	62,438
Burtonite	N/A	152,656	156,719
Coal			
Bituminous	26,223,000	25,736,000	25,071,000
Lignite	3,682,000	3,639,000	N/A
Brown	98,634,000	98,347,000	93,908,000
Cobalt metal[a]	N/A	N/A	N/A
Copper			
Mine production	10,100	9,400	8,000
Smelter production	33,400	34,415	36,832
Production of refined	26,414	27,202	26,920
Ferro alloys, electric furnace			
Ferro-chrome	25,178	29,018	29,844
Ferro-manganese	62,358	59,252	63,518
Ferro-silico-manganese	31,000[e]	33,000[e]	28,000[e]
Other ferro alloys	9,000[e]	9,000[e]	8,000[e]
Silicon metal	4,500[e]	5,000[e]	5,000[e]
Fluorspar	95,000[e]	95,000[e]	95,000[e]
Graphite	15,000[e]	12,763	14,676
Gypsum	771,600	771,998	N/A
Iron ore	1,859,000	1,798,000	1,780,000[e]
Iron, pig	9,562,000	9,788,000	10,000,000[e]
Kaolin	548,000	581,000	N/A
Lead, mine production	2,718	2,849	2,670
Lead, production of refined	21,437	26,008	26,008
Magnesite	654,000	671,000	630,000[e]
Manganese ore, 17%[b]	950[e]	900[e]	900[e]
Mercury[c]	158,000	164,000	131,000
Natural gas[d]	705	785	865
Nickel, smelter/refinery			
production of	4,000[e]	3,700[e]	3,460
Perlite	44,000[e]	42,305	45,396
Petroleum, crude	123,000	147,000	144,000
Salt	349,174	337,985	N/A
Sillimanite minerals	75,000[e]	75,000[e]	75,000[e]
Silver[f]	32,000[e]	34,000[e]	20,000[e]
Steel ingots and castings	15,036,000	15,356,000	15,463,000
Sulfur and pyrites			
Pyrites, 42%	62,000	60,000[e]	N/A
Recovered	41,866	38,023	60,182
Sulfur ore	6,000	6,000e	N/A
Tin, mine production of	250	500	300
Tin, smelter production of	507	545	562
Tungsten, mine production of	50[e]	45[e]	N/A
Zinc, mine production of	7,200	6,900	6,600

[a] Czechoslovakia is thought to recover cobalt from materials imported from Cuba. Exact figures are N/A.

[b] Average estimated content of manganese.

[c] Manganiferous iron ore.

[d] Kilograms.

[e] Estimated.

[f] Millon m^3.

Source: British Geological Survey, *World Mineral Statistics,* 1984–88; *World Mineral Production,* 1985–89.

VI. GOVERNMENT AND DEFENSE FORCES

TABLE 2.VI.1   State Budget

	(Millon Kcs)			
	1985	1987	1988	1989
Revenue				
State budget	233,473	245,191	258,400	259,607
From socialist economy	258,183	276,747	291,387	308,252
Taxes and rates	47,245	35,121	36,423	2,159
Other receipts	2,064	2,762	3,000	4,412
Minus grants and subsidies to local administrative organs	74,019	69,439	72,410	55,216
Budgets of local administrative organs	126,219	138,541	145,645	155,825
Total	359,692	383,732	404,045	415,432
Expenditure				
State budget	233,402	245,191	258,400	263,107
National economy	90,179	94,891	103,638	86,801
Science and technology	9,133	9,731	9,754	9,636
Money-order and technical services	6,432	6,393	6,740	6,715
Culture and social welfare	96,121	101,320	104,447	11,765
Defense	27,393	28,496	29,236	43,784
Administration	4,144	4,360	4,585	4,406
Budgets of local administrative organs	124,626	136,960	142,799	151,839
Total	358,028	382,151	401,199	414,946

Source: The Europa World Year Book, 1990, 1991.

TABLE 2.VI.2   Hard-currency debt

	(Billion U.S. $)			
	1980	1985	1988	1989
Gross debt	5.0	3.8	6.1	7.8
of which				
Government	0.9	1.0	1.3	1.9
Commercial	4.1	2.8	4.8	5.9
Other	N/A	N/A	N/A	N/A
Reserves	N/A	1.0	1.7	1.6
Net debt	N/A	2.8	4.4	6.2
Debt service ratio[a]	N/A	17%	15%	25%

[a]Debt service ratio is calculated as the share of principal and interest payments to total hard-currency earnings.

Source: U.S. Central Intelligence Agency, "Eastern Europe: Long Road Ahead To Economic Well-Being," May, 1990.

TABLE 2.VI.3 Armed forces totals, 1991

Total armed forces	154,000 (87,000 conscripts)[a,b]
Branches	
Army	87,300 (69,000 conscripts)
Navy	None. Landlocked.
Air Force	44,800 (18,000 conscripts)
Total reserves	495,000
Army	450,000
Navy	None. Landlocked.
Air Force	45,000
Manpower	137,733 reach military age annually.
Budget	26.5 billion Kcs ($2.80 billion)[c]

[a]Czechoslovakia reduced its active duty personnel in 1990 and will continue to cut until the mid-1990s. Reductions are moving towards a 33% total cut. Total active duty personnel will be on the order of 35,000. Tank divisions are slated for a 25% reduction.

[b]Includes Internal Defense.

[c]Budget based on 27.88 Kcs = $1.

Source: The International Institute for Strategic Studies, *The Military Balance 1991–1992,* 1991. Copyright IISS.

TABLE 2.VI.4 Components of defense force, 1987

Army
  Organization
        1 Army Headquarters and 2 Military divisions
        5 tank divisions
        5 motorized rifle divisions
        1 airborne regiments
        1 artillery division
        1 airborne regiment
        6 engineer brigades
        5 Civil Defense regiments
  Major equipment (1987)
  3,500 tanks
  4,900 armored fighting vehicles, including
  1,250 OT-65A BRDM reconnaissance vehicles
    900 heavy mortars
    320 multiple rocket launchers
    575 air defense guns
     71 surface-to-surface missiles

Navy
  None

Air Force
  Organization
        2 air armies
        4 air divisions
       14 combat regiments
  Major equipment (1987)
    145 fighter/ground attack aircraft
    including 50 Su-7
              40 MiG-23M
              30 MiG-21
              25 Su-25
    275 interceptor aircraft including MiG-21s and MiG-23s
     45 reconnaissance aircraft
     51 transport aircraft
    250 surface-to-air missiles

Source: Reprinted with permission from *World Defense Forces,* 2nd edition, published by ABC-CLIO, 1989.

TABLE 2.VI.5 Military expenditures

	1979	1980	1985	1987
Million korunas	21,380	22,900	27,393	29,260
Constant price figures (billion U.S. $)[a]	3,019	3,142	3,449	3,479
Military expenditures as a percent of GDP:				
Czechoslovakia[b]	3.3%	3.3%	3.6%	3.7%
USSR	12.9	13.0	12.5	N/A
United States	5.0	5.4	6.6	6.0
France	3.9	4.0	4.0	4.0

[a] 1986 exchange rates and prices.

[b] Percent of gross national product (GNP).

Source: SIPRI Yearbook 1989: World Armaments and Disarmament, Stockholm International Peace Research Institute, 1989; *World Military Expenditures and Arms Transfers*, 1987.

VII. INDUSTRY

TABLE 2.VII.1 Industrial production index[a] (Czechoslovakia and selected countries)

Country	1960	1970	(1980 = 100) 1980	1986	1987	1989	1990[b]
Czechoslovakia	46	72	100	111	112	115	110
USSR[c]	38	68	100	113	116	118	115
United States	45	73	100	113	119	129	130
France	47	75	100	100	102	110	111

[a] Indexes for the noncommunist countries are value-added weighted indexes of industrial intermediate and final products. Industry includes manufacturing, mining, and, in most countries, public utilities. The indexes for the communist countries are estimates constructed by the U.S. Central Intelligence Agency as nearly as possible on the same basis as the indexes for Western countries, and include manufacturing, mining, and public utilities.

[b] Preliminary.

[c] Index of gross values of output for individual commodities and branches are aggregated by 1982 value-added weights. This index is as comparable with the index of U.S. industrial production of the U.S. Federal Reserve Board as data will permit.

Source: U.S. Central Intelligence Agency, *Handbook of Economic Statistics*, 1991.

TABLE 2.VII.2 Industrial production index (official and adjusted)

	1960	1970	(1980 = 100) 1980	1986	1987	1989[a]
Official	32	57	100	112	114	118
Adjusted	46	72	100	111	113	115

[a] Preliminary.

Source: U.S. Central Intelligence Agency, *Handbook of Economic Statistics*, 1990.

TABLE 2.VII.3 Production of selected industrial items

	Thousand Metric Tons (Unless Otherwise Noted)		
	1985	1987	1988
Agricultural and forestry products			
Wheat flour	1,334	1,384	1,427
Refined sugar	969	895	702
Margarine[a]	34,123	37,419	38,937
Wine[b]	1,763	1,403	1,422
Beer[b]	22,354	22,228	22,670
Cigarettes[c]	23,840	25,365	25,502
Cotton yarn, pure and mixed[a]	142,166	145,157	147,220
Wool yarn, pure and mixed[a]	57,711	55,397	55,617
Chemical wood pulp	840.3	850.9	884.9
Newsprint	72.0	64.7	73.9
Other paper	891.5	917.9	900.1
Fuels, minerals, metals, and chemicals			
Chemical fibres	193.2	196.5	204.0
Synthetic rubber	69,600	76,488	77,078
Sulfuric acid	1,298	1,264	1,249
Hydrochloric acid	236.2	246.4	247.4
Caustic soda	331.1	344.1	337.1
Soda ash	112.0	102.7	112.2
Nitrogenous fertilizers	582.1	596.4	596.4
Phosphate fertilizers	353.3	277.0	313.0
Plastics and synthetic resins	1,100	1,150	1,192
Liquefied petroleum gas	138	142	126
Gasoline	1,500	1,664	1,678
Kerosene and jet fuel	426	418	416
Distillate fuel oils	3,648	4,075	4,469
Residual fuel oils	7,363	6,925	6,014
Petroleum bitumen (asphalt)	1,086	1,057	1,146
Coke-oven coke	10,237	10,586	10,586
Cement	10,265	10,369	10,974
Pig iron	9,562	9,788	9,706
Crude steel	15,036	15,416	15,380
Rolled steel products	11,040	11,364	11,420
Aluminum, unwrought[a]	31,725	32,366	31,435
Refined copper, unwrought[a]	26,414	27,202	27,076
Lead, unwrought[a]	21,437	26,008	26,045
Electricity energy[d]	80,627	85,825	87,374
Manufactured gas[e]	7,500	7,270	6,782
Machinery and equipment[f]			
Electric locomotives	126	99	132
Diesel locomotives	530	524	507
Trams	955	950	685
Tractors	5,184	35,274	33,558

[a] Metric tons.
[b] Thousand hectoliters.
[c] Millions.
[d] Million kilowatt-hours.
[e] Million cubic meters.
[f] Number of units.

(continued)

TABLE 2.VII.3 *(continued)*

| | Thousand Metric Tons (Unless Otherwise Noted) | | |
	1985	1987	1988
Manufactured consumer goods			
Woven cotton fabrics[g]	606,355	599,900	591,240
Woven woolen fabrics[g]	60,161	58,178	58,669
Leather footwear[h]	57,887	53,815	55,320
Rubber footwear[h]	6,119	5,163	4,809
Other footwear[h]	67,316	60,449	58,959
Rubber tires[i]	5,015	5,316	5,519
Radio receivers (radiograms excluded)[f]	242,348	199,807	183,570
Television receivers[f]	432,338	506,743	481,897
Passenger cars[f]	183,701	172,355	163,834
Goods vehicles[f]	47,956	51,194	50,498
Motorcycles (100 cm^3 and larger)[f]	157,257	134,573	136,160
New dwellings completed[f]	104,524	N/A	N/A

[g] Thousand meters, after undergoing finishing processes.
[h] Thousand pairs.
[i] Thousands.
Source: The Europa World Year Book, 1989, 1990.

TABLE 2.VII.4 Rank of industry, manufacturing, and service sectors as a percent of GDP[a], 1990 (Czechoslovakia and selected countries)

	Rank
Czechoslovakia	3
Brunei	1
Angola	20
USSR	9

[a] All former East Bloc countries rank in the top 10 except Hungary. No OECD country is in the top 20. Additionally, no East Bloc state nor the Soviet Union is among the top 20 countries in terms of manufacturing share of GDP or services share of GDP. This chart indicates the significant role of extractive industries in Eastern Europe and the USSR.

Source: The Economist, *Book of Vital World Statistics,* 1990.

TABLE 2.VII.5 Industrial waste generation (Czechoslovakia and selected countries)

Country	Year of Estimate	(Thousand Metric Tons per Year) Total	(Metric Tons per km^2 per Year) per National Land Area
Czechoslovakia	1982	80,910	647.3
USSR	1985	306,258	13.8
United States	1985	613,000	66.9
France	1980	32,200	59.0

Source: From *World Resources 1988–89.* Copyright © 1988 by the World Resources Institute and the International Institute for Environment and Development in collaboration with the United Nations Environment Programme. Reprinted by permission of Basic Books, a division of Harper Collins Publishers Inc.

TABLE 2.VII.6 Emissions of air pollutants, 1988[a] (Czechoslovakia and selected countries)

	Nitrogen Oxides		Sulfur Dioxide		
	Emissions (Thousand Tons)	Emissions per Unit GNP (Grams)	Emissions (Thousand Tons)	Emissions per Unit GNP (Grams)[c]	Greenhouse Index[b]
Czechoslovakia[d]	950	8	2,800	24	3.3
USSR[e]	4,510	2	18,584	10	3.4
United States[f]	19,800	4	20,700	4	5.3
France	1,615	2	1,226	1	2.4

[a] Preliminary data.

[b] Carbon heating equivalents, metric tons per capita. 1988–89 data.

[c] East European countries have a significantly higher emissions per unit GNP because of inefficient production. For example, on average, these countries use 50 to 100 percent more energy than the United States to produce a dollar of GDP, and 100 to 300 percent more than Japan.

[d] The very high pollution rates in Czechoslovakia have had deleterious consequences for the population. According to the Institute of Hygiene and Epidemiology, there is a correlation between high air pollution and elevated rates of a number of health problems, including acute respiratory illnesses. Children in these regions exhibit retarded bone development, diminished immunity, and a higher incidence of enlarged lymph nodes and cranial infections.

[e] Stationary sources only. 1987 data.

[f] Sulfur data are for sulfur oxides.

Source: State of the World 1991, A Worldwatch Institute Report on Progress Toward a Sustainable Society, 1991; UN, *Human Development Report 1991,* 1991.

TABLE 2.VII.7 Environmental summary, 1991

	Czechoslovakia	Netherlands	USSR	U.S.	France
Energy					
Energy production					
Solids[a]	1,643	0	14,299	20,736	365
Liquids[a]	6	153	24,139	17,297	145
Gas[a]	26	2,146	25,541	16,280	115
Biomass[a]	14	2	742	1,150	97
Nuclear[b]	24,578	4,022	213,001	529,352	303,928
Hydroelectric[b]	4,274	41	222,803	272,023	51,158
Energy consumption					
Total[a]	2,589	2,738	52,027	69,496	6,119
Per capita[c]	180	189	193	307	149
Per capita (global rank)	16	14	12	7	22
Energy intensity					
BTUs/$1987 GNP	52,278	12,380	N/A	15,787	8,784
Global rank	17	110	N/A	99	120
Waste					
Access to sanitation services					
Urban population	100%	100%	100%	N/A	100%
Rural population	100%	100%	100%	N/A	100%
1988 Greenhouse emissions					
Carbon dioxide[d]	70,000	36,000	1,200,000	1,400,000	96,000
Methane[d]	900	1,300	35,000	40,000	2,800
CFs[d]	2	13	110	190	50
Share of world emissions	0.7%	0.6%	13.6%	17.3%	1.7%
Global rank[e]	21	32	14	7	41

[a] Trillion BTUs.

[b] Gigawatt hours.

[c] Million BTUs.

[d] Thousand tons.

[e] Per capita.

Source: From *The 1992 Information Please Environmental Almanac.* Reprinted by permission of the Houghton Mifflin Company.

VIII. LABOR FORCE

TABLE 2.VIII.1 Workforce by selected areas of the economy

| | (Percent) | | |
	1980	1986	1989
Total (thousand)	7,473	7,806	7,911
Material production	79.9	78.8	77.8
of which			
Manufacturing industry	48.3	48.0	47.9
Agriculture and forestry	13.4	12.3	11.5
Transport and communications	6.6	6.5	6.5
Distributive trades and restaurants,			
wholesale purchasing	10.6	10.8	10.7
Nonmaterial production	20.1	21.2	22.2

Source: EUROSTAT, *Central and Eastern Europe 1991*, 1991.

TABLE 2.VIII.2 Average monthly earnings by economic sector[a]

| | (Korunas) | | | |
	1980	1985	1989	1990[b]
Total	2,637	2,883	3,123	3,144
of which				
Agriculture	2,567	2,936	3,258	3,334
Manufacturing sector	2,723	3,037	3,272	3,276
Construction	2,932	3,236	3,516	3,484
Transports	3,093	3,292	3,543	3,477

[a] State and cooperative sector; the average monthly wages and salaries of manual and nonmanual workers are calculated by taking 1/12 of total annual wages and salaries and dividing it by the average number of registered manual and nonmanual workers.
[b] Average of first six months of the year.

Source: EUROSTAT, *Central and Eastern Europe 1991*, 1991.

TABLE 2.VIII.3 Economically active population by sex and industry, 1988

| | (Percent) | | |
	Males	Females	Total (Thousand)
Agriculture, forestry, fishing and hunting	14.1	9.9	966
Mines, quarries	4.1	0.9	204
Manufacturing	36.3	32.7	2,766
Electricity, gas, and water	2.0	0.8	115
Construction	14.3	2.6	684
Commerce, restaurants, and hotels	5.6	18.3	947
Transportation, storage, and communication	8.3	4.6	519
Finance, insurance, real estate, and business			
services	3.4	3.9	290
Community, social, and personal services	11.8	25.9	1,498
Other activities	0.2	0.3	22
Total	4,086,000	3,925,000	8,011,000

Source: The Europa World Year Book, 1990.

TABLE 2.VIII.4   Structure of employment by republic, 1989

	(Percent)	
	Czech Republic	Slovak Republic
Agriculture, forestry, and water	11.1	14.4
Industry	38.9	33.5
Construction	8.2	10.4
Transport and communications	6.6	6.5
Science, education, culture services, and welfare	18.9	19.8
Others	16.2	15.5

Source: EIU, "Czechoslovakia, Country Profile," 1988–1989.

IX. POPULATION AND HEALTH

TABLE 2.IX.1   Geography and demographic profile, 1990

Population	
Population in 1990	15,683,234
Population by 2000	16,200,000 est.
Population by 2020	17,100,000 est.
Current annual percent increase	0.2%
Population density per sq km	122.3
Net migration rate	Negligible
Urban/Rural (1988)	75.7%/24.3%
Ethnic division	
Czech	62.9%
Slovak	31.8%
Hungarian	3.8%
German	0.3%
Polish	0.5%
Ukrainian	0.3%
Russian	0.1%
Jewish, Gypsy, Other (combined)	0.3%
Religion	
Roman Catholic	50%
Protestant	20%
Orthodox	2%
Other	28%
Geography	
Total area	127,870 sq km (49,371 sq mi)
Land area	125,460 sq mi (48,440 sq km)
Coast line	None
Land borders with	
Austria	548 km (341 mi)
Germany	815 km (506 mi)
Hungary	676 km (420 mi)
Poland	1,309 km (813 mi)
USSR	98 km (61 mi)
Disputes	
Nagymaros Dam project with Hungary	

Source: The Economist, *Book of Vital World Statistics,* 1990; U.S. CIA, *Atlas of Eastern Europe,* August 1990; Population Reference Bureau, *1989 World Population Data Sheet* (Washington, D.C: Population Reference Bureau, Inc., 1989); U.S. CIA, *The World Factbook,* 1990.

TABLE 2.IX.2 Population (Czechoslovakia and selected countries)

| | (Million People at Midyear) | | | | |
	1960	1970	1980	1985	1990
Czechoslovakia	13.7	14.3	15.3	15.5	15.7
Netherlands	11.5	13.0	14.1	14.5	14.9
USSR	214.3	242.8	266.4	278.9	290.9
United States	180.7	205.1	227.8	239.3	250.4
France	45.7	50.8	53.9	55.2	56.4

Source: U.S. Central Intelligence Agency, *Handbook of Economic Statistics,* 1990, 1991.

TABLE 2.IX.3 Population by age (Czechoslovakia and selected countries)

| | Czechoslovakia (1987) | | Netherlands (1987) | | United States (1987) | | USSR (1987) | |
Age	Total	Percent	Total	Percent	Total	Percent	Total	Percent
<19	4,846,331	31.2	3,945,168	26.9	70,857,000	29.1	92,267,217	32.8
20–44	5,689,747	36.6	5,915,928	40.4	97,413,000	40.0	99,559,765	35.4
45–64	3,269,359	21.1	2,981,906	20.3	45,293,000	18.6	64,009,456	22.8
65+	1,728,089	11.1	1,822,038	12.4	29,836,000	12.3	25,501,353	9.0
Total	15,533,526	100.00	14,665,040	100.0	243,400,000	100.0	281,337,791	100.0

Source: UNESCO, *Statistical Yearbook,* 1989.

TABLE 2.IX.4 Population of major cities, 1989

Praha (Prague)	1,214,885
Bratislava	440,629
Brno	390,986
Ostrava	331,219
Kosice	235,729
Plzen (Pilsen)	174,666
Olomouc	106,684
Usti nad Labem	106,463
Liberec	104,142
Hradec Kralove	101,082

Source: The Europa World Year Book, 1991.

TABLE 2.IX.5 Population by nationality and republic, 1987

| | Czech Socialist Republic | | Slovak Socialist Republic | | Total | |
	(Thousands)	(Percent)	(Thousands)	(Percent)	(Thousands)	(Percent)
Czech	9,742	94.1%	62	1.2%	9,804	62.9%
Slovak	412	4.0	4,541	86.7	4,953	31.8
Magyar (Hungarian)	22	0.2	575	11.0	597	3.8
German	51	0.5	3	0.1	54	0.3
Polish	70	0.7	3	0.1	73	0.5
Ukrainian and Russian	15	0.1	40	0.7	55	0.3
Others and unspecified	38	0.4	13	0.2	51	0.3
Total	10,350	100.0	5,237	100.0	15,587	100.0

Source: The Europa World Year Book, 1990.

TABLE 2.IX.6 Health indicators, 1990 (Czechoslovakia and selected countries)

Birth rate	14.5/1,000
of United States	15.0/1,000
of USSR	18.0/1,000
Death rate	11.5/1,000
of United States	9.0/1,000
of USSR	10.0/1,000
Infant mortality rate	13.1/1,000
of OECD and United States	9-10/1,000
of USSR	25.0/1,000
Maternal mortality rate[a]	10/100,000
of OECD and United States	10/100,000
of USSR	48/100,000
Life expectancy	68 male/75 female
of OECD	72 male/78 female
Fertility rate	2.0 children/woman
of United States	1.9 children/woman
of USSR	2.4 children/woman
Suicides[b]	19.4/100,000
of OECD and United States	14.6/100,000
of USSR	19.8/100,000

[a] Figures refer to live births. 1980–87 figures.

[b] 1987–88 figures.

Source: Population Reference Bureau, *World Population Data Sheet* (Washington, D.C: Population Reference Bureau, Inc., 1989); The Economist, *Book of Vital World Statistics,* 1990; UN, *Human Development Report 1991,* 1991.

TABLE 2.IX.7 Registered illnesses and fatalities by selected causes of death

	1984	1986	1988
Illness			
Streptococcal angina and scarlet fever	24,056	20,253	27,151
Salmonella infections	17,389	21,139	16,768
Bacillary dysentery	7,818	26,100	14,040
Viral hepatitis	9,284	6,520	8,513
Gonococcal infections	10,936	9,465	8,409
Pulmonary tuberculosis	5,458	3,935	3,098
Other forms of tuberculosis	730	640	610
Syphilis	474	304	415
Cause of death			
Circulatory illnesses	100,256	101,703	96,659
of which			
Ischaemic heart diseases	44,382	46,411	43,109
Illnesses of the cerebrovascular system	30,595	31,458	29,092
Acute myocardial infarction	21,204	22,290	21,946
Arteriosclerosis	13,632	11,733	12,680
Hypertonia and hypertensive heart diseases	1,317	1,431	1,677
Malignant neoplasms	35,979	37,097	38,156
of which			
Windpipe, bronchi, and lungs	7,716	7,920	7,938
Stomach	3,844	3,428	3,311
Colon	2,417	2,634	2,959
Mammary gland	2,381	2,480	2,469
Leukemia	1,045	1,089	1,142
Pneumonia	6,528	6,448	4,880
Bronchitis, emphysema, and asthma	5,335	4,916	4,119
Diabetes mellitus	2,886	3,046	3,063

Source: EUROSTAT, *Central and Eastern Europe 1991,* 1991.

TABLE 2.IX.8 Life expectancy by sex, 1991 (Czechoslovakia and selected countries)

Czechoslovakia	
Male	69
Female	77
USSR	
Male	65
Female	74
United States	
Male	72
Female	79
France	
Male	74
Female	82

Source: U.S. Central Intelligence Agency, *The World Factbook,* 1991.

TABLE 2.IX.9 Medical care, 1983-1988 (Czechoslovakia and selected countries)

	(Number per million)				
	Doctors	Dentists	Pharmacists	Beds (thousand)	Total Health Expenditure[a]
Czechoslovakia[b]	3,577.0	N/A	465.0	10.1	4.2
Netherlands	2,517.0	514.0	142.0	12.0	7.2
USSR[b]	4,124.0	N/A	321.0	12.8	3.2
United States	2,035.0	560.0	641.0	5.9	11.2
OECD	2,199.5	453.8	559.2	8.0	8.3

[a] As a percent of GNP. 1987 figures.

[b] Figures for the former communist countries are clearly misleading. According to the Soviet Ministry of Health, 1.2 million beds are in facilities with no hot water, 1/6 of the beds are in hospitals with no water, and 30% of the hospitals have no indoor toilets. Source: *Literaturnaya Gazeta,* February 3, 1988; and see also *World Affairs,* vol. 152, no. 1, Summer 1989.

Source: Population Reference Bureau, *1989 World Population Data Sheet* (Washington, D.C.: Population Reference Bureau, Inc., 1989); The Economist, *Book of Vital World Statistics,* 1990; UN, *Human Development Report 1991,* 1991.

TABLE 2.IX.10 Abortion rates (Czechoslovakia and selected countries)

Country	Number of Abortions	Rate per Thousand Women 15–44	Ratio per 100 Known Pregnancies	Total Rate[a]
Czechoslovakia (1987)[b]	156,600	46.7	42.2	1,400
Netherlands (1985)	18,300	5.3	9.0	155
USSR (1987)	6,818,000	111.9	54.9	N/A
United States (1985)	1,588,600	28.0	29.7	797

[a] The number of abortions that would be experienced by 1,000 women during their reproductive lifetimes, given present age-specific abortion rates.

[b] In contrast to women from Western European and English-speaking countries, who are young, unmarried women seeking to delay a first birth, women from Eastern Europe are married with two or more children, using abortion for spacing and ending childbirth. In addition, high rates in Eastern Europe, except Romania, may be attributed in part to the very liberal abortion laws, where abortion has been used as a form of birth control since the 1950s.

Source: Adapted with the permission of The Alan Guttmacher Institute from Stanley K. Henshaw and Evelyn Morrow, *Induced Abortion: A World Review 1990 Supplement,* 1990.

X. TRADE

TABLE 2.X.1 Exports by commodity group

Exports by Commodity Group	(Million U.S. $)			
	1970	1980	1986	1989[a]
Machinery and equipment	1,911	7,673	21,261	6,359
Fuels, minerals, and metals	705	2,624	4,508	2,104
Agricultural and forestry products	277	1,312	2,163	1,288
Manufactured consumer goods	629	2,426	5,792	2,047
Other	270	1,220	2,933	1,383
Total	3,792	15,255	36,657	13,181[b]
Imports by Commodity Group	**1970**	**1980**	**1987[a]**	**1988**
Machinery and equipment	1,234	5,681	13,900	4,962
Fuels, minerals and metals	868	4,921	13,491	1,313
Agricultural and forestry products	890	2,499	3,988	1,988
Manufactured consumer goods	314	916	2,124	1,156
Other	389	1,506	3,761	3,591
Total	3,695	15,523	37,264	13,010[b]

[a] Preliminary.

[b] The sharp decline is mainly attributable to a decline in the koruna exchange rate.

Source: U.S. Central Intelligence Agency, *Handbook of Economic Statistics*, 1990.

TABLE 2.X.2 Main destinations of exports and origins of imports, 1989

Country	(Percent of Total)	(Country)	(Percent of Total)
Destinations of exports:		Origins of imports:	
USSR	30.5	USSR	29.7
Germany	14.9	Germany	17.1
Poland	8.5	Poland	8.6
Austria	4.6	Austria	5.5
EC	18.2	EC	17.8
Socialist states	60.8	Socialist states	62.3
Nonsocialist states	39.2	Nonsocialist states	37.7

Source: EIU, "Czechoslovakia, Country Report," No. 4, 1991.

TABLE 2.X.3 Principal trading partners

	(Percent)			
	Imports from		Exports to	
	1984	1988	1984	1988
USSR	46.8	31.3	43.4	33.6
United States	0.3	N/A	N/A	N/A
Western Europe				
Austria	2.0	5.3	2.6	4.2
Belgium	0.4	0.8	N/A	N/A
France	0.8	1.6	0.8	1.6
Netherlands	0.7	1.2	0.8	1.3
West Germany[a]	4.2	9.3	4.7	7.7
Switzerland	2.1	3.5	0.9	1.5
U.K.	1.2	2.2	1.1	2.1

[a] Excluding imports to and exports from West Berlin.

(continued)

TABLE 2.X.3 *(continued)*

	(Percent) Imports from		(Percent) Exports to	
	1984	1988	1984	1988
Eastern Europe				
Bulgaria	2.8	2.5	2.8	2.8
East Germany	10.4	8.2	8.9	7.0
Hungary	5.6	4.4	5.0	4.2
Poland	7.2	8.2	7.1	8.1
Romania	2.0	1.8	1.7	1.6
Yugoslavia	3.4	3.3	4.1	3.2
Other				
Brazil	0.4	0.5	N/A	N/A
China	0.7	2.6	0.9	2.9
Cuba	0.9	0.7	1.3	0.9
Iran	0.8	0.3	0.3	N/A
Iraq	N/A	N/A	0.8	0.4
Japan	0.4	0.6	N/A	N/A
Libya	N/A	N/A	1.1	0.2
Syria	N/A	N/A	1.6	0.3
Turkey	N/A	N/A	0.6	0.5
Total including others	100.0	100.0	100.0	100.0
Total (million Kcs)	113,737	209,554	114,230	213,887

Source: The Europa World Year Book, 1990.

TABLE 2.X.4 Index of import and export prices, terms of trade (Czechoslovakia and selected countries)

	(1980 = 100)			
	1984	1986	1987	1989
Czechoslovakia				
Import prices	134	146	142	137
Export prices	112	119	119	129
Terms of trade	84	81	83	93
Bulgaria				
Import prices	128	125	124	112
Export prices	111	110	112	110
Terms of trade	86	88	90	98
Hungary				
Import prices	125	136	139	163
Export prices	116	120	124	153
Terms of trade	93	88	89	94
Poland				
Import prices	139	198	279	1,281
Export prices	127	189	275	1,516
Terms of trade	91	95	99	118
Romania				
Import prices	135	130	127	N/A
Export prices	124	114	114	N/A
Terms of trade	92	88	90	N/A
Yugoslavia				
Import prices	116	108	109	124
Export prices	108	107	108	123
Terms of trade	93	99	100	99
Soviet Union				
Import prices	115	112	110	113[a]
Export prices	130	114	110	103[a]
Terms of trade	113	102	100	100[a]

[a] 1988.

Source: Comecon Data 1989, 1990, 1990, 1991.

TABLE 2.X.5 Major imports and exports[a]

Import Goods/Categories	(Thousand U.S. $)		
	1987	1988	1989
Meat and meat preparations	45,903	45,150	56,861
Vegetables and fruit	23,420	33,941	33,835
Cork and wood	56,565	60,996	58,388
Pulp and waste paper	16,785	19,536	21,892
Crude fertilizers and crude minerals	24,950	26,266	29,205
Metalliferous ores and metal scrap	12,208	16,707	18,711
Coal, coke and briquettes	80,884	65,293	68,709
Petroleum, petroleum products and related materials	117,553	98,992	125,434
Organic chemicals	55,834	80,446	58,072
Plastics in primary form[b]	N/A	42,255	46,029
Cork and wood manufactures (excl. furniture)	28,392	28,042	29,247
Paper, paper board, and articles of paper pulp	21,819	20,450	27,237
Textile yarn, fabrics, made-up articles and related products[c]	94,504	89,396	83,059
Nonmetallic mineral manufactures[c]	45,369	54,664	57,891
Iron and steel	115,123	143,712	153,779
Manufactures of metals[c]	13,970	15,948	19,523
General industrial machinery and equipment[c]	15,004	18,887	21,896
Road vehicles (incl. air-cushion vehicles)	14,332	17,300	19,348
Furniture and parts thereof; bedding, etc.	29,600	31,975	35,250
Articles of apparel and clothing accessories	81,509	80,073	78,600

Export Goods/Categories	(Thousand U.S. $)		
	1987	1988	1989
Sugars, sugar preparations and honey	701	741	28,709
Feedingstuff for animals (not incl. unmilled cereals)	19,101	32,784	25,285
Organic chemicals	71,970	77,437	72,208
Inorganic chemicals	20,377	25,625	24,380
Dyeing, tanning and coloring materials	31,385	33,109	34,000
Chemical materials and products[c]	40,008	43,934	46,255
Textile yarn, fabrics, made-up articles, and related products[c]	52,409	52,839	52,195
Iron and steel	47,236	24,465	28,395
Non-ferrous metals	16,463	23,164	26,485
Manufactures of metals[c]	49,394	38,843	34,853
Goods for complete production plants, Div. 84, 85, 87	9,358	5,133	26,774
Power-generating machinery and equipment	15,505	22,285	30,272
Machinery specialized for particular industries	236,476	220,925	225,809
Metalwork machinery	99,697	75,322	90,881
General industrial machinery and equipment[c]	186,931	196,862	183,058
Office machines and automatic data-processing machines	27,353	34,012	48,112
Electrical machinery, apparatus, and appliances[c]	74,491	75,497	76,100
Road vehicles (incl. air-cushion vehicles)[c]	24,109	75,429	73,234
Professional instruments and apparatus[c]	63,509	75,429	73,234

[a] According to SITC headings.

[b] Classification changed in 1988, figures for previous years not applicable.

[c] Not elsewhere specified.

Source: EUROSTAT, Central and Eastern Europe 1991, 1991.

TABLE 2.X.6   Trade with western countries[a]

	Imports		
Countries	1985	1988	1989
Austria	33.76	40.83	40.27
Belg/Lux	4.64	7.70	8.57
Canada	4.80	5.30	5.17
Denmark	5.67	5.65	5.42
Finland	4.96	8.93	9.69
France	13.10	20.80	21.47
West Germany	71.60	104.30	103.10
Italy	18.10	28.10	30.20
Netherlands	9.96	13.30	15.50
Spain	3.11	6.46	6.90
Sweden	6.37	9.33	9.08
Switzerland	6.60	9.46	9.96
Turkey	3.25	2.32	5.81
UK	13.00	22.00	21.12
Yugoslavia	32.87	37.73	49.33
United States	6.35	7.30	6.67
Countries	1985	1988	1989
Austria	15.76	31.65	26.55
Belg/Lux	5.27	7.60	6.90
Canada	1.39	.80	.90
Denmark	2.37	5.10	3.98
Finland	3.71	5.53	6.77
France	10.90	19.20	18.63
West Germany	68.30	115.40	108.17
Italy	14.60	23.50	19.63
Netherlands	8.21	13.00	12.60
Spain	2.53	3.62	4.75
Sweden	6.64	9.89	8.10
Switzerland	10.52	20.23	15.74
Turkey	1.19	2.94	1.93
UK	10.90	19.30	16.80
Yugoslavia	28.52	44.06	39.92
United States	5.22	4.60	4.50

[a] Monthly averages from Western countries' trade accounts, in million U.S. $.
[b] Imports, f.o.b.

Source: EIU, "Czechoslovakia, Country Report," No. 4, 1990.

TABLE 2.X.7   Trade with the USSR, by commodity

Imports from the USSR	(Million Rubles[a]) 1987	1988
Power-generating equipment	178.8	204.7
Mining, hoisting, excavating machinery, etc.	63.9	76.8
Tractors and agricultural machinery	70.6	59.4
Railway rolling stock	33.6	33.8
Motor vehicles and garage equipment	75.6	80.5
Aircraft	33.6	100.5
Other machinery and transport equipment	278.4	288.5
Coal and coke	134.9	124.2
Petroleum and products	2,675.6	2,258.6
Fuel gas and electricity	1,281.4	1,164.4
Metal ores and concentrates	279.1	257.5
Pig iron and ferro alloys	81.4	81.3
Rolled ferrous products and pipes	18.5	19.7
Chemicals	165.9	178.3
Wood, paper, and manufactures	68.5	55.8
Domestic appliances, clocks, and cameras	18.6	25.2
Televisions and radios	45.0	80.7
Total, including other items		
Million rubles	6,776.7	6,384.6
Million U.S. $	11,257.0	10,432.4

Exports to the USSR	1987	1988
Metal-cutting machine tools and presses	219.0	195.9
Power-generating equipment	187.4	167.0
Rolling mill equipment	126.2	107.2
Hoisting and conveying equipment	124.3	133.0
Equipment for food industry	135.5	126.0
Equipment for textile industry	374.2	309.8
Equipment for chemical industry	134.9	139.3
Equipment for road building	45.7	53.5
Instruments and laboratory equipment, including medical	99.3	97.1
Agricultural machinery	209.4	181.5
Railway rolling stock	406.3	394.5
Motor vehicles and garage equipment	670.1	704.7
Ships and Boats	74.5	71.1
Other machinery and transport equipment	1,295.7	1,251.2
Ores, base metals, and manufactures	445.1	431.2
Chemicals	245.9	244.2
Building materials	35.3	35.3
Textiles, clothing, and footwear	779.1	777.4
Furniture	140.7	149.5
Total, including other items		
Million rubles	6,907.4	6,817.3
Million U.S. $	11,474.1	11,139.4

Note: Commodity totals are additions of items in the trade accounts and may be incomplete.

[a]Noncommercial rate: end 1987 0.602 rubles = $1.00, end 1988 0.612 rubles = $1.00.

Source: EIU, "Czechoslovakia, Country Report," No. 2, 1990.

TABLE 2.X.8 Trade with the United States, by commodity

Imports from the United States	(U.S. $ Millions) 1987	1988
Grains	82	143
Tobacco	2,808	2,079
Crude metals	0	0
Hides	14,945	13,942
Pulp	180	466
Crude minerals	1,702	148
Coals	0	0
Petro products	3	0
Chemicals	8,951	3,311
Metal manufactures	234	180
Machinery	12,338	22,442
Road vehicles	27	51
Scientific instruments	2,830	5,954
Total	43,470	48,716

Exports to the United States	1987	1988
Meat and fish	3,263	3,012
Dairy	460	315
Tobacco	0	0
Crude rubber	0	0
Textiles	5,700	6,188
Crude animal and vegetable materials	0	1
Crude petroleum and petro products	0	2
Chemicals	2,621	2,813
Paper	10	83
Semi-finished nonferrous	0	0
Fibres	0	0
Steel	8,440	13,984
Machinery	9,595	12,798
Transport	776	856
Furniture	2,352	2,063
Clothing	6,995	8,156
Footwear	9,426	11,072
Total, including other items	49,637	61,433

Source: U.S. Central Intelligence Agency, "Selected Countries' Trade with the USSR and Eastern Europe," 1990.

CHAPTER THREE

HUNGARY

POPULATION:	10,568,686
SQUARE MILES:	35,653 mi^2, 92,340 km^2
RELIGION:	67.5% Roman Catholic; 25% Protestant
CURRENCY:	forint (HUF)
EXCHANGE RATES:	61,449 HUF: $1
DEBT:	$21 billion

I   HUNGARY

POLITICS, HISTORY, AND ECONOMICS

POLITICS

Introduction

Hungary is a political enigma. It was the first communist country in Eastern Europe that both tolerated some political opposition and began significant economic reforms. By granting notable latitude to the press and freedom of movement to the citizens, the government relaxed its enforcement of two crucial methods of communist control, relative to other Eastern European states. Uniquely, in Hungary the impetus for reform by and large came from within the communist party.

Charter 77 in Czechoslovakia and Solidarity in Poland were opposition groups. In Hungary, the idea-makers and the challengers to one-party rule were mostly younger, but ranking and influential, party members. Dissent existed in Hungary, though never as a unified or widely prevailing force, and much of what would have been considered political dissent in the other communist states was actually entertained in Hungary's communist party. Moreover, the party had a remarkable capacity to overcome any opposition by staying ahead of it. But it did not tolerate all forms of opposition. As late as 1988, public demonstrations were forcefully quelled.

The party's reformist notions had their roots in the economic reforms of 1968. They were primarily economic and institutional and came to be termed "goulash communism." Because the reforms were depoliticized and avoided any hint of being anti-Soviet, the party in Budapest was spared any potential retaliation from Moscow through the application of the Brezhnev Doctrine. In the end, however, the party could not contain its own reformist inclinations. It bargained with the newly emerging opposition but ultimately split into several distinct factions. Some discontented members left the party to join the opposition. Among those who remained, there was little unity and a diminishment of their mutual commitment to preserve the communist party. Even in this they could not reach agreement; the party split again on the question of whether its role should be as the dominant political force or as a party among equals. By the end of 1990 the debate made little difference, since in the wake of the reforms initiated by the party, there were, ironically, few if any communists remaining in power. The party, unable to preempt indefinitely a reform movement, was finally consumed by it.

While the pace of political transformation since 1988 has been rapid, both the communist party and the newly elected democratic government adopted reform legislation at an agonizingly slow pace. Poland, with only a semi-democratically elected legislature, briskly formulated and implemented its impressive reform program. Yet Hungary's legislature, freely elected in 1990, procrastinated, bickering over seating arrangements in the new parliament. It was not, however, simply petulance. Having won the right to govern freely, the leadership was at a loss as to where to begin the reforms. The most crucial reforms have been mired in political jousting while the legislature adopts legislation in relatively peripheral areas.

A new civil order has definitely formed, but it remains to be seen whether the new democracy will spawn durable institutions that speak to the needs of Hungary or whether it will simply be carried by events. The government is still struggling to get its political bearings while the economy, in mid-1991, appears to have bottomed and to be on the rebound with only limited political guidance. The markets may well have turned the corner to self-sustaining growth in the absence of direct government intervention. But even if that is not the case, Hungary can claim, with Poland, to be the leader in economic reform and transformation.

Current Politics

On June 16, 1989, in Budapest's Square of Heroes, Hungarians celebrated the reburial of Imre Nagy from an anonymous plot to a marked grave in the Rakoskeresztur Cemetery. The ceremony accorded full honors to Nagy, the martyr of the failed 1956 Revolution and the symbol of Hungary's thirst for independence, and marked Hungary's dismissal of its communist order. The reburial ceremony also demonstrated the total breakdown of party discipline. Some Politburo members attended the ceremony, but only in their roles as state officials, since the party, along with the Red Army, had been found guilty for the events of 1956. At the time of the ceremony, however, it was not yet clear to party leaders that their willingness to restore Nagy's status had become irrelevant. The party would not long survive his restoration.

The ceremony in the Square of Heroes unleashed Hungary's "Quiet Revolution," a peaceful and spontaneous outpouring of the long-simmering opposition to the 40-year rule of the Hungarian Socialist Workers' Party (HSWP, the communist party). Although party maverick Imre Pozsgay had for years been urging his fellow communists to enact significant reforms, by 1989 the opportunity for communist reform had been lost. Given the rising tide of social disillusionment, the emergence of numerous unofficial associations later to become political parties, and the increasing fragmentation of the party, the transition to a multi-party political system could at most have been postponed, not prevented. Through compromise and negotiation, the HSWP tried to create some form of government that would retain for the party its position of significance, but the manipulations were clumsy and ineffectual, due to an indecisiveness—the result of strategic disagreements over how best to maintain power—which had first fallen upon the party years before Nagy's reburial. The ceremony at Rakoskeresztur was in a sense a dual interment, for the corpse of Nagy and for the communist party.

It is difficult to mark the beginning of the end for the HSWP, since the party was able to maintain the appearance of unity as it was disintegrating. Hungary never witnessed a highly visible grand opposition to the party on the model of Solidarity. Until the mid-1980s, Hungary was prosperous compared with its fellow Soviet satellites. The communist party took the credit based on its modest economic liberalizations of 1968 and 1978. In the middle of the 1980s the economy soured, and every change instituted by communist party head Janos Kadar seemed to cripple the economy. In many respects, Kadar's final reform efforts were similar to those attempted in 1990 by the new democratically elected government. But his reforms introduced only partial market measures. Wholesale and retail prices were raised while price supports for food were reduced. A bankruptcy law was introduced in 1986, foreign trade was somewhat decentralized, and small private businesses were allowed. When the country's hard-currency account grew worse, Kadar retrenched and introduced income and value-added taxes—unheard of revenue-raising devices in communist countries.

In the process he managed to impose considerable austerity, but he did not increase efficiency or convert the state sector, merely tinkering at the edges of the command system. The reforms, along with a tolerated black market and private garden plots, produced consumer goods uncommon in other Bloc states. Still, for the average Hungarian, reform came to mean working harder to stay even, and by the end of the decade, all that work had resulted in negative income growth. The Czechs and East Germans, whose communist regimes had instituted no economic reforms, actually had higher living standards.

The deteriorating economy was a major contributor to ending the rule of the aging Kadar. In a sense, his 32 years as party secretary general seemed a lengthy process of redemption for his collusion with the Soviet invasion of 1956. That redemption, and also his survival, had taken the form of an economic leniency, which continually stimulated and fed the population's rising expectations. After more than three decades in power, though, he had run out of ideas. He and his compatriots failed to recognize the rumblings among their comrades and fell victim to a party purge in the spring of 1988. Inspired by a 1987 confidential party report stressing the party's rapidly deteriorating political position, a group of HSWP reformers assumed power, promoting Kadar to an entirely ceremonial position as party president while dumping more than a third of the more conservative members of the Central Committee and Politburo. Kadar died a year later, but not before suffering the further humiliation of losing even his new powerless post.

Ironically, the reform faction that took power in May, 1988, was led by a man not known for liberal leanings, Karoly Grosz. He was joined by Imre Pozsgay, a leading reformer, and Rezso Nyers, the designer of the first economic reform blueprint of 1968, later demoted in 1972 for going too far with his reform ideas. Although Pozsgay and Nyers remained in the party, both were also involved in the unofficial associations that emerged as rival political parties by the end of 1988. The combination of Grosz's supporters and Pozsgay's reformist faction was sufficiently powerful to oust Kadar. But their deep differences soon shattered their alliance. For six months, their dissension was largely masked by the euphoria of Kadar's ouster; the passage of promising, first-step, economic liberalization reforms; and the international accolades won by Grosz from President Reagan and other heads of state.

Yet all the while, Grosz was being undermined by both party reformers and conservatives. The reformers became increasingly resentful of his reform plans, while conservative and centrist party members abhorred his sudden acceptance of reform. Grosz lost more support when he refused to censure Ceausescu's repression of Romania's Hungarian minority. By the end of 1988, the differences within the party had become public, while various quasi-official democratic groups, no longer fearing reprisals from the party or the government, came out in open opposition. Though officially in power for another six months, the reformers would discover early in 1989 that even they could not control the new forces they had unleashed.

The inability of Grosz and Pozsgay to continue working together came to a head over the party's official position towards the 1956 Revolution. For 32 years the party had officially maintained that the uprising had been a counterrevolution led by Imre Nagy. The Soviet Army was invited by the "true" government of Hungary to put down the "illegal" uprising and restore the people's will—a communist government allied with Moscow. But over the past three decades the truth of 1956 had spread throughout the country, and few, if any, believed the official party version. Party reformers felt the need to rectify the fallacious party version of history even if it meant undermining the party's already emaciated political legitimacy.

Pozsgay proved adept at turning the truth of 1956 to his political advantage. In 1988, the party had already conducted a rather cryptic study of the 1956 Revolution and was planning to release its findings. Before the party publicized its official revisions of the 1956 events, it declared that Nagy and other 1956 leaders were to be exhumed for proper burials. By announcing the exhumations before revealing the contents of its own study, the party managed to announce its intention to alter its position on the Revolution. Yet Pozsgay and others knew that the still unpublished report was far from a full confession of the party's role. Pozsgay announced the substance of the study but went considerably beyond its conclusions by declaring the party's full responsibility for the Soviet invasion and subsequent repression. In a nationwide radio interview, Pozsgay referred to 1956 as a "popular uprising." More importantly, he used the case of 1956 to declare the inevitable failure of one-party political systems and called for the transformation to a multi-party democratic structure. Grosz, already disturbed at how far the reformers had gone in criticizing the party, was enraged.

Since the faction in the party loyal to Grosz outnumbered the partisans of Pozsgay, most party members assumed that Pozsgay would be punished. Yet he emerged from the radio interview stronger than ever. The party endorsed Pozsgay's position by declaring that the new constitution would no longer support a "leading role" for the party and would provide for free and contested elections. His radio broadcast had proved to be a dramatic and decisive event. From that point forward the conservatives could only disrupt events, not control them.

Throughout 1989, Grosz's position declined with every passing day. The man who had the political foresight to seize power when Janos Kadar had been weakened failed to understand and control the opposition to his own rule. His foreboding and animus for having let events control him were never more apparent than in the summer of 1989, when he still refused to accept the factual account of the 1956 Revolution. Even if an opportunist, Grosz remained a party *apparatchik* to the end.

In November 1988, Miklos Nemeth had become prime minister. As a technocrat who lacked the political clout to be an independent leader for reform, his pragmatism lent additional support to the party reform leaders. His government and the legislature did not hesitate to endorse the political changes that enacted free, multi-party elections. The "associations," some of which had emerged as early as 1987, were legalized by the Law of Association of January, 1989, and began to form independent political parties. They were joined by two precommunist parties of 1948, the Smallholders' Party and the National Peasant Party, and by various rump parties that withdrew their loyalty to the HSWP. The number of independent parties and associations grew slowly at first, but after Nagy's reburial in the summer of 1989, they multiplied to more than 100 as more than four decades of official communist political quiescence gave way to exuberant activism. The party remained in disarray, but the Nagy debate clearly defined its real divisions.

Pozsgay, meanwhile, had engineered a partial consolidation of power in February, 1989. The press, old and new, basking in its pristine freedoms, wasted no time. It printed volumes of material on the Revolution of 1956, the economy, the party, and Kadar, who died during the summer. The press also tore down the last wall of self-censorship, criticized the Soviet Union for its long repression of Hungary, and demanded the immediate withdrawal of Soviet armed forces. In effect, the press was publicizing a demand already made by the communist party. The communist legislature also gained a measure of courage and declared its commitment to the reformist wing of the party.

In April 1989, Pozsgay met with a group of liberals, who threatened to bolt the party unless economic reform and democratic transformation were immediately initiated. The following month the liberals formed a "reform circle" and proposed that the HSWP dissolve itself in favor of a democratic socialist party. A majority of the party backed the reform circle's agenda. In June, the Central Committee again met, and in an effort to preserve itself, dissolved the Politburo in favor of a Political Executive Committee composed of reformers. Grosz was stripped of his power as General Secretary and given a powerless position on the new Presidium. Power in the Presidium lay with its new head, Rezso Nyers, and with Imre Pozsgay and Miklos Nemeth. Imre Pozsgay also received the party's nomination as its presidential candidate in the election scheduled for 1990. The early nomination of Pozsgay, who had become the most popular figure in the HSWP and probably in the country, was an attempt by the party to preempt support for candidates to be proposed by the other parties.

Nevertheless, by making the nomination before coming to terms with the emerging opposition, the Party clearly revealed its direction. The reformers had wrested control and intended a democratic conversion of the Hungarian political system. Discussions among the various political forces were essential to defining the process of conversion, yet the appropriation of power by the reformers seemed to make the process a foregone conclusion.

In June, just prior to the HSWP's Central Committee meetings, Round Table talks were convened with the emerging parties in an effort to reach a consensus on a new political structure for the country. The legislature agreed to enact into law whatever the round table produced, as well as promising not to take advantage of the inevitable political vacuum during the period between the talks and their actual implementation. It took months of bargaining before the actual negotiations could be convened. Conservative party members still had the strength to obstruct the talks, while the opposition could not reach agreement, given their diverse agendas. In Hungary, there were no neat lines as there were in Poland, where dialogue occurred between a unified Solidarity and the communist party. Fragmentation occurred in Poland after its Round Table talks, while in Hungary it had been an aspect of political life for at least two years leading up to the talks.

Eventually, the format and agenda were established. The participants grouped into three major camps, none of which were unified. The HSWP, led by Pozsgay, comprised one fairly moderate group. Another camp consisted of representatives of former communist organizations—youth groups, trade unions, and the former rump parties of the HSWP—an exceptionally diverse group of both reformers and conservatives. The third camp brought together nine newly created political parties, the most important of which were the Democratic Forum, the Alliance of Free Democrats, the Independent Smallholders' Party, and the Alliance of Young Democrats.

By and large, the negotiators demonstrated unusual tolerance and civility. Those who sat at the Round Table were not new faces. They were the nonparty elite, with whom the communist party reformers had been in contact for years prior to the talks. The familiarity of the negotiators did not make the debate over practical issues any easier except in one respect. There was quick agreement that no revenge would be extracted from the HSWP and that there would be no communist bloodletting. At least partially because of that agreement, the political transformation of Hungary proceeded more smoothly than in other former satellites. Yet the substantive negotiations were intense and bitter, lasting three months before an accord that actually blurred the political battle lines was finally produced.

With the signing of the accord on September 18th, the monopolistic position of the HSWP was finally ended. A multi-party system was confirmed, with an elaborate electoral scheme that guaranteed no legislative seats for the communist party. Several months after the Round Table, it was reported that some of its most sophisticated participants never fully understood the scheme. The new formula ensured that no one party could dominate the legislature, by guaranteeing representation to parties that won even small percentages of the national vote. While the new formula guaranteed that minorities would be heard, it also made it difficult for a single party to win a majority in the parliament, thus ensuring the need for coalition rule.

For Pozsgay personally, the most important issue at the talks was the call for presidential elections in November, 1989. Several of the parties understood Pozsgay's strategy— early elections would favor his chances. As a result, three of the political parties refused to accept the Round Table accord, and a fourth endorsed only portions of the agreement. But none of the parties exercised their right to veto the accord.

After the Round Table, events continued to unfold at a dizzying pace. With support from a majority of the delegates to the Fourteenth Party Congress, held in October, 1989, Pozsgay and his allies forced a vote to dissolve the communist party. Of the 1,202 delegates,

1,005 immediately elected to reconstitute the HSWP into the Hungarian Socialist Party (HSP). The name change was intended to close the book on the communist past and allow former communists to be reborn as socialists, at least for the upcoming elections. The party assented to giving up nearly all its wealth, returning its assets to the state, and elected a Presidium void of conservatives. The reformers attempted, but failed to win support for their plan to terminate the network of the party, permeating every workplace and every organization.

No sooner had the party congress adjourned when the legislature, still controlled by the HSWP, accepted the Round Table, declared Hungary a democratic republic, and rejected the HSWP's right to maintain its organization of party cells. The cells were ordered to disband within three months. Party conservatives panicked, rejected the formation of the Hungarian Socialist Party, and joined together to maintain the HSWP and carry on a communist Hungary. They did not leave the new socialist party, however, until the reformers in the party had been thoroughly damaged by the conservatives' presence.

Despite the political maneuvering in the party congress, Pozsgay maintained his dominant position in the presidential election, set for November. The newly minted HSP campaigned especially hard for Pozsgay, assuming that an HSP president would do much to transform their tainted reputations and help them win more seats in parliament. But Pozsgay underestimated the growing strength of the independent political groups. The upstart Alliance of Free Democrats knew that Pozsgay, in conjunction with the largest new party, the Democratic Forum, had orchestrated early elections for the presidency to favor an HSP victory. Using the new law on referenda, they gathered over 200,000 signatures to bring the question of the schedule of the presidential election to a popular vote. They proposed that the new president not be popularly elected but chosen by the new parliament, whose election was already set for March, 1990. Additionally, their referendum proposed that the Workers' Militia (the political army of the HSWP) be disbanded rather than turned over to the state; that the HSWP, now HSP, should give an account of its far-flung assets; and that all party cells be removed from the workplace. On November 26, 1989, the electorate, in its first experience with free elections since 1945, approved all of the propositions of the Free Democrats by the slimmest of margins, 50.1 percent to 49.9 percent. Pozsgay had lost his only advantage—a short election campaign.

Pozgay's rebuff provided the new parties more time to organize for the elections. The communist credential, which had been an indispensable ticket to power, became an albatross. In the face of Pozsgay's failure to maintain the election schedule, and torn by internal dissent brought on by Prime Minister Miklos Nemeth's resignation over economic issues, the HSP quickly lost ground to the new independent parties. They, in turn, proved much more adept at running a political campaign than had been imagined just months before.

The first round of parliamentary voting on March 25, 1990, presented the Hungarian electorate with twelve political parties arrayed across the political spectrum from the unrepentant HSWP holdouts to the unabashedly pro-Western Alliance of Free Democrats. The Hungarian Democratic Forum (HDF) emerged from the vote with a 24.7 percent plurality, followed by the Alliance of Free Democrats (AFD) with 21.4 percent; the Independent Smallholders' Party (ISP), 11.8 percent; the Hungarian Socialist Party (HSP), 10.9 percent; the Federation of Young Democrats (FYD), 8.9 percent; the Christian Democratic People's Party (CDPP), 6.5 percent; the Hungarian Socialist Workers' Party (HSWP), 3.7 percent; the Social Democrats (FZDP), 3.5 percent; and other smaller parties.

The election laws stipulated that in order to move into the second round of voting a party must win at least 4 percent of the total vote. Only six parties, in the first round, qualified to compete in the second round of elections on April 8, 1990, leaving the communist HSWP out of the running.

The Democratic Forum garnered a substantial plurality in the second round, with 42.7 percent of the vote and 165 seats in the new parliament. The Forum proved to be the general second choice for those voters who had chosen one of the nearly 50 parties that failed to win 4 percent of the total vote in the first round. Forum leader Jozsef Antall, while not in the least charismatic, proved a capable politician. His statesmanlike foreign travels between the two elections, and the Forum's effective mudslinging against the AFD in a mutually demeaning campaign, proved effective. But the key to the Forum's victory appears to have been its ability to present itself as the party of compromise—a politics without vendettas and economic reforms without shocks. The populist and conservative appeal was clear. The AFD managed to increase its share of the votes in the second round only marginally to 23.8 percent, winning 92 seats. The ISP actually lost ground, winning only 11.1 percent of the votes and 43 seats. The HSP lost more than two percentage points with 8.5 percent and 33 seats. The Young Democrats and Christian Democrats both fared badly, their totals shrinking to 5.4 percent and 21 seats for each. The remaining eleven seats went to independent candidates.

In theory, the victorious Hungarian Democratic Forum draws heavily on the Christian Democrat traditions of western Europe. Its conservative agenda, however, puts it to the right of most European Christian Democratic parties. The Forum was founded as a political discussion group in September, 1987, at a meeting attended by none other than the communist reformer, Imre Pozsgay. Its leaders, Jozsef Antall, Geza Jeszenszky, and Sandor Keresztes, favor a transfer to a free-market economy "in a reasonable and socially controlled process," which is to say, at a pace considerably slower than sought by most other parties. Its platform and policies provide for gradual and strictly monitored privatization, with a significant role for worker-stock ownership. Its position on land reform also followed this incremental pattern. Though officially supporting Hungarian neutrality in foreign policy, the Forum has received funds from European Christian Democratic parties.

At its base, however, the popular appeal of the Forum depends on its nationalist and populist commitments including its concern for the civil rights of the Magyars outside Hungary, especially those in Romania. Antall can perhaps be best described as a Christian Democratic populist, having forced out of the HDF those who had argued for a "Third Way"—moderate socialism between capitalism and communism.

During the elections, Antall was generally effective at channeling populist sentiment onto the issue of Magyar mistreatment abroad. But the Forum used more negative tactics as well. In Budapest, the HDF attempted to discredit the Free Democrats by reminding the voters that AFD leaders were urban intellectuals from Jewish backgrounds. Tapping into the anti-Semitism of the countryside, the Forum framed its rivalry with the Free Democrats as Magyars against Jews, a disturbing manipulation of a not-so-latent Hungarian chauvinism.

Antall vigorously denied that the Forum was anti-Semitic, and after the election he appointed a Jew to the position of Speaker of the Parliament. Yet during the campaign he never distanced himself from the anti-Semitic elements of his party, and he has dealt openly with the anti-Semitic base of the Forum's widespread, grassroots support. As the son of a prominent leader in the postwar Independent Smallholders' Party which had won 57 percent of the vote in the last free election in 1945, Antall claims the mantle of democratic continuity in Hungarian politics. It made him an exceptional candidate in the first postcommunist election, but it remains to be seen whether he will survive what is still a transition process.

The Forum's chief rival, the Alliance of Free Democrats (AFD), sprang out of the dissident movement of the 1970s and 1980s, making contacts with Solidarity in Poland and Charter 77 in Czechoslovakia. It rose to political prominence when its last-minute campaign to force a referendum on the presidential election succeeded in the fall of 1989. The leaders include the philosopher Janos Kis, expelled from the HSWP in 1973 on ideological grounds; the writers Gyorgy Konrad and Miklos Haraszti; the former underground publisher Gabor Demszky; the sociologist Balint Magyar; and the son of a renowned purged communist leader, Laszlo Rajk. The Free Democrats style themselves as Western liberals in the classic sense, supporting freedom of the press, constitutionality, respect for minority rights, and free enterprise. The AFD's social agenda gives them the appearance of a European social democratic party, but they are vociferous believers in the free market. Their economic platform was candid, too bold, as it turned out, for the exhausted electorate. They proposed an immediate cut in subsidies and the national budget and quick-paced privatization, coupled with deep cuts in personal and corporate taxes to encourage economic growth. They acknowledged that these measures would lead to double-digit inflation and unemployment for at least three years. The AFD painted an honest and sobering picture of the austerity necessary to invigorate the economy, but that picture did little to attract working-class voters. Instead, it captured the support of the more educated electorate, who were persuaded that reform measures similar to those applied in Poland were indispensable. The AFD's inability to increase its votes in the second round of elections seems to indicate that no more than a quarter of the voting public is in favor of an abrupt and painful economic transformation. But as support for the dominant Forum waned in 1991, the AFD gained some ground.

The social backgrounds of the AFD won them little popularity. They are primarily educated professionals, most living in Budapest with a smattering from other cities. They were portrayed by the other parties, especially the Forum, as a group of "urbanite," intellectual Jews. This depiction, though accurate, made the AFD seem more European than Hungarian and less concerned with Magyar rights and the lot of the common worker. The Free Democrats did little to help its cause when it counterattacked and charged the Forum with being rural and illiterate. The AFD campaign slogan—"We can, we dare, we do"—came to be widely perceived as arrogant, further alienating the voters.

A reincarnation of the post–World War II majority party, the Independent Smallholders' Party (ISP) concentrated almost exclusively on the issue of returning agricultural land to its precollectivization owners. The ISP draws on many of its prewar constituents in the villages and among the elderly for support. It is correspondingly rural, Christian, and vehemently anticommunist. Reactivating itself in late 1988, it was the only precommunist party that managed a respectable showing in the 1990 election. Many of the same men who led the party in the 1940s head the new version, in particular Tobor Partay, Jozsef Torgyan, Vince Voros, Istvan Prepeliczay, and Pal Dragon. This old guard has purged its ranks of young firebrands, like the independent publisher Ivan Baba, and seems intent on returning Hungary to its precommunist past. Ironically, its highly vocal call for a return to private land ownership is actually based on a communist scheme. Land ownership in 1945 was highly concentrated. Between 1945 and 1947, the communists drastically subdivided the land, giving every peasant a modest plot. The communists rapidly collectivized that same land in 1948 when they were in full control of the government. The ISP insists that the communist seizures be repealed and the land returned to its 1945–1947 owners, but not to the owners of the large estates before that period.

It is highly unlikely that the ISP will ever realize its land ownership goals. Much agricultural land has been converted to industrial development, and many urban voters find the issue irrelevant. Moreover, in 1991 the Constitutional Court repeatedly found the legislature's laws on land return unconstitutional, because the laws did not return all property and thus were deemed discriminatory. Nonetheless, the ISP is evolving into the major party concerned with agricultural and rural issues.

The Hungarian Socialist Party (HSP), led by Imre Pozsgay and Rezso Nyers, the author of the 1968 New Economic Mechanism, is the reformed successor to the HSWP. While membership is down sharply from the days of communist rule, the HSP is still somewhat popular among officials and industrial workers. It appears to be consigned to an opposition role, advocating social democratic policies and pushing for a mixed economy. It did, however, vote with the Forum for the gradual introduction of economic reforms.

Like many of the other parties, its economic platform is contradictory, inasmuch as it advocates a conversion to the market economy but warns against selling Hungary to the foreigners.

During the dismemberment of the HSWP, opinion polls showed Pozsgay to be the most popular figure in Hungary. But when he ran for the legislative election as an HSP candidate, he was whipped by a political unknown. In the second round of voting he managed to secure a parliamentary seat on the HSP county list. Primarily on account of his declining influence in the new HSP and his failed presidential attempt, Pozsgay resigned his HSP seat after only five months and declared he would remain in the parliament as an independent. In the end, like so many he had forced from office, Pozsgay was a transitional figure, as is the HSP, the party he left behind. It will have limited influence, either as an opposition force or as a supporter of the Forum on an array of economic issues.

The Federation of Young Democrats (Fidesz), led by Viktor Orban, Tamas Dutsch, and Gabor Fodor, began as an independent alternative to the state communist youth organization. In 1989 it grew into a full-fledged political party, with membership restricted to young people. No one over 35 may join. The ideology of Fidesz is nearly identical with that of the Free Democrats, except for a greater emphasis on youth issues and Hungary's growing environmental problems. Because of the unique way Fidesz came into being as a youth group and not as a political organization, many Young Democrats also belong to the AFD, with whom they compete for the votes of the young intelligentsia. During the election campaign, Fidesz went to great lengths to distance itself from the AFD. But their economic platforms are virtually identical. Like the AFD, Fidesz favored a rapid privatization process with full disclosure to the electorate of the severe social costs of economic conversion.

Fidesz had very limited resources to field candidates, but ran a very sophisticated campaign. Nonetheless, they managed to win only 21 seats in the legislature. As a party, Fidesz is a youthful version of the AFD, with a high concentration of professional elites. Its members appear to comprise the future leadership of Hungary, both in government and business.

The Hungarian Socialist Workers' Party (HSWP), led by Karoly Grosz and Gyula Thurmer, is the conservative rump of the old HSWP after the majority of the party followed the reformers into the HSP in October 1989. The HSWP advocates a return to socialism with state control of the economy and warns of the dangers of inviting capitalism into Hungary. The new HSWP has virtually no supporters outside hard-line proponents of the old regime.

A number of other small parties won seats in the legislature but are likely to disappear by merging into the more successful parties. Among those parties are: the Christian Democratic People's Party, the smallest of the reborn precommunist parties; the Social Democratic Party of Hungary, a resurrected pre-war party along with the ISP, forced to merge with the Communists in 1948; the Hungarian People's Party, a populist centrist party that considers itself the successor to the pre-1948 National Peasant Party (NPP); the Entrepreneurs' Party, supporting the economic rights of a small but growing class of entrepreneurs; the Patriotic Election Coalition, the remains of the Patriotic People's Front, a powerless quasi-representative body that existed under the communists and was headed for many years by Imre Pozsgay; and the Agrarian Federation, a leftist coalition of cooperative farm leaders, which opposes the ISP's demand to return the land to the pre-1947 owners. All of these parties won at least a seat in the second round of voting.

The surprisingly solid electoral showing by the Democratic Forum gave it a strong hand in forming a coalition while avoiding the necessity of reaching an alliance with their main rival, the Free Democrats, who are now combined with the Young Democrats, in the major opposition block. The Forum chose its partners from the Smallholders and Christian Democrats, creating a 72-seat majority in the legislature. It also took under its wing the People's Party, which failed to win any seats. The dilemma of the Forum was that its 58 percent majority precluded its enacting a program, since the rules of the non-communist legislature required a two-thirds majority. In an auspicious act of compromise, the Forum and the Free Democrats agreed to amend the two thirds rule, replacing it with a simple majority rule except in major constitutional and security matters. In return, Antall agreed to give the presidency, a position of modest political power, to Arpad Goncz, a leading AFD figure.

Initially, the Forum seemed assured of adopting its reform legislation. All three parties in its coalition were conservative, had a rural national base, and had agreed on a gradual transition to the market. But the Forum's plurality within its coalition proved flawed from the start. In order to bring in the Smallholders' Party, the Forum gave it the ministries of Agriculture and Labor, which the ISP used single-mindedly to attempt the restoration of the land to its 1945–1947 owners. Refusing to compromise, the ISP paralyzed the government until it finally produced a draft law for returning a portion of the land and a scheme to compensate former owners whose property was now too developed to return. But when the Constitutional Court declared the law unconstitutional, the government was essentially returned to paralysis.

By the end of 1990, Antall had replaced the Agriculture minister, and the ISP finally acquiesced to a limited compensation plan and the gradual splitting up of state and collective farms. In 1991, however, new rural legislation was also overturned by the Court, seriously straining the coalition's relationship. The issue of land ownership is far from resolved, and the ISP is committed to pursue the issue as long as it remains in the coalition.

Political wrangling was equally apparent on nonagricultural issues. Typical of Antall's style of attempting to govern without creating controversy or enemies was his appointment of independents rather than Forum members to the key economic ministries. The result was that economic reform legislation was hopelessly delayed and economic decline accelerated as Hungary's economy remained poised between its old command form and a new market form. No legislative initiatives were made despite the fact that all the major parties had agreed to give the Forum-led government a 100-day "grace period" to develop and establish its own national economic program.

By mid-1990, the state budget for the entire year had already been expended. By the fall, a mounting deficit led the IMF to suspend support until more fiscal restraint was applied. Privatization had begun, but only at a snail's pace, and nothing had been done to alleviate the hard-currency debt, which at more than $2,000 per capita is twice that of Poland. Moreover the government's penchant for raising prices rather than cutting subsidies nearly brought about its collapse at the end of the year, as it raised fuel prices by more than 60 percent to prepare for paying hard currency to the Soviet Union for its energy supplies. But Hungary's taxi and truck drivers demonstrated in the streets and were joined by the general public in what became a near-national strike, halting all transportation for several days. The government rescinded the price increases. The strike was more than a protest over prices. It was an indication of the public's displeasure with the Forum-led government.

Through it all, Antall continued to claim that Hungary would not go through "shock therapy" as did Poland. Even this decision did not, however, come easily. After no more than a few months in power, Antall's chief economic advisor, Gyorgy Matolcsy, concluded that more rapid reform was essential, putting him in open conflict with the independent Finance Minister, Ferenc Rabar, who saw no reason for drastic measures. By the end of 1990, both men had resigned, and more government reshuffling was necessary. One Hungarian economist observed that the government was paralyzed in its attempts to create anything new, while the old system had atrophied. As a result, all that the Hungarians were getting from their new democracy was shock and no therapy.

At the outset of 1991, most Hungarians survived the transition from communism despite their new, democratically elected government. Basic necessities are still provided by the declining old state sector and by the more than 500,000 workers who pioneered private businesses under communism in the 1980s. Many of the best public officials left political activity altogether, choosing instead to join the numerous joint ventures or the better state firms, which are first in line for privatization. In the long run, their presence in the private sector will undoubtedly hasten prosperity. But in the short run, the Forum party is noticeably short of skilled professionals who can manage essential structural changes.

Despite these problems, and despite Hungary's having more experience with a market-like economy than all the other former communist states combined, Antall and his HDF are generally reluctant to speed the transition to a market economy.

One explanation for the HDF's immobility can be found in its understanding of the nation's exhausted social condition. Hungarians work the longest hours in Europe, and it became commonplace in the late communist period for workers to take on a third job rather than just a second. The cost of such ambition has been tremendous. Hungary has the highest death rate among working-age men and the highest suicide rate in Europe—both are twice the European average—and life expectancy has dropped dramatically in the last decade. Few of the newly elected political figures have been willing to state that Hungary must endure further economic decline before it can experience economic recovery, especially in the midst of the highly fragmented democratic political structure. Antall especially fears the social dislocation of deep and abrupt reform.

Almost begrudgingly, the Forum has found just enough resolve to implement some austerity. Strong fiscal and monetary policies, which impressed both the IMF and OECD, were instituted in 1991. The Program for National Renewal, the Forum's official agenda for the next three years, calls for gradual privatization with no dramatic changes. The new Finance Minister, Mihaly Kupa, has promised a mixed economy for Hungary for at least a decade before developing the Austrian economic model.

Perhaps because of its relative paralysis, the Forum began to lose support after only six months in power. But it managed to keep its hold on power and initiated a minimal reform program. Yet the Forum was decisively defeated in local elections in the fall of 1990. The city of Budapest is now controlled by the opposition Free Democrats, and a majority of small townships reelected their former communist officials as independent candidates. Where the communists did not win, the Young Democrats did, effectively blocking any extension of Forum support beyond the national legislature.

What the government has failed to do at home, it has more than accomplished on the international scene. Hungary remains the darling of the West, demonstrated by the fact that more than half of the total private investment in the East bloc and Soviet Union since the beginning of 1990 has been directed to Hungary. There are many reasons for Hungary's unusually warm reputation in the West. The country has long invited Western businesses to participate in the Hungarian economy.

The country also adopted daring political positions long before the dissolution of the other communist regimes. Hungary openly challenged Romania over the treatment of its large Hungarian minority. The feud highlighted the collapse of the unity of the socialist states. In addition, Hungary tore down its border fences with Austria, allowing thousands of East Germans to travel through Hungary, supposedly on vacation, and then to enter Austria to escape into West Germany. It also canceled a major dam project with Czechoslovakia out of environmental concerns, an explanation otherwise unheard-of among socialist states. And just before the fall of the Czech communist government, Hungarian state radio broadcast interviews and materials from the 1968 uprising in Prague.

Hungary has also been willing to challenge the Soviet Union, first challenging the Soviet view of the 1956 uprising, but more recently publicly insisting that Soviet troops withdraw from its territory. To most Hungarians, who rival only Poland in their anti-Soviet attitudes, the most repellent aspect of communism was not poverty but Russian domination. Hungary was the first of the Warsaw Pact states to insist on withdrawing from the military alliance, and then it managed to force a Soviet agreement for the departure of its troops in March 1990. By early June 1991, more than two weeks ahead of schedule, Hungary was free of Soviet forces for the first time since 1944.

While its relations with the Czechs and the former East Germans have improved since the collapse of the East bloc, problems persist with Romania. Though Magyar treatment is better than what was seen under Ceausescu, the 1.8 million Hungarians living in Romania are still treated as second-class citizens, and the Forum government will undoubtedly keep the pressure on Bucharest, straining their relations. There is also potential for trouble in Yugoslavia, where another 400,000 Magyars live in the Autonomous Province of Vojvodina. The dissolution of Yugoslavia as a nation-state could exacerbate the nationalist tensions of its neighbors and engross Hungary.

Hungary's willingness to challenge other satellites, but especially the Soviet Union, has been noted and appreciated in the West. As a result, despite Antall's incoherent policy making, Hungary is likely to continue to enjoy the fervid and patient support of the West. Given the challenges of its transformation to a market economy, that support is likely to prove crucial.

HISTORY

Origins to 1900

The Magyar-speaking people arrived in the upper Danube basin, the territory which would become modern Hungary, in the late ninth century A.D. as part of the great migration of peoples from the steppes of eastern Russia. A tribe of nomadic horsemen, the Magyars terrorized their neighbors and launched pillaging expeditions through most of Western Europe before being contained by a group of German princes, at which time they finally settled into an agricultural way of life. In 1222, rebellious nobles forced the Magyar ruler to adopt limits on his rule, the Golden Bull, which mandated election of kings by the nobles and permitted minimal resistance to royal orders.

A Mongol invasion in 1241 laid the country waste, fostering an early fear of marauders from the East. These fears were well founded as, throughout the fifteenth century, Hungary suffered attacks from the expanding Ottoman Empire. In 1526 at the Battle of Mohacs, the Turks annihilated the paltry army of the Hungarian King Louis II, and captured the bulk of Hungarian possessions east of the Danube. The remainder of the kingdom fell to the Austrian Hapsburgs, who revoked the Golden Bull.

The rigid Hapsburg rule sparked several rebellions. In Transylvania, a region regained from the Turks in 1691, Ferenc II (1703–11) seized power, and the Hungarian Diet, a body of nobles, declared Hungary independent of the Hapsburgs in 1707. In return for granting broad rights to the Hungarian nobility, the Hapsburgs consolidated their rule in 1711 with the Treaty of Szatmar, and in 1723 with the Pragmatic Sanction, Hungary was established as an integral and indivisible part of the empire.

Speaking a language markedly different from those of their Central European neighbors, the Slavs and the Germans, the Magyars, as the Hungarians continue to call themselves, maintained a distinct ethnic identity despite these periodic conquests and devastations. Within Magyar culture, three distinct classes emerged—a small Upper Nobility, controlling 2,000 large estates that comprised 25 percent of Hungary, a larger Lower Nobility, composed of 1,000 families holding smaller estates, and the vast bulk of peasants. Those Hungarians who did not fit into this three-tiered social scheme were mostly foreigners, mainly Germans and Jews who controlled the country's finance and modern technology. The class structure reflected and reinforced a markedly rural country with little industry. Social tensions eventually arose because of the perpetuation of peasant poverty, the presence of large numbers of non-Magyars, and the marginality of the Lower Nobility.

Despite attempts to reform Hapsburg rule and to rationalize the Hungarian bureaucracy in the early nineteenth century, the Magyar nobility, led by Lajos Kossuth, revolted against Austrian rule in 1848, joining the wave of revolutionary unrest sweeping Europe. During their brief hold on power, the revolutionaries promulgated a democratic political program, radical for its time, and emancipated the peasants. These reformers, however, while demanding Magyar independence, notably failed to mention the nationalist aspirations of the kingdom's substantial non-Magyar regions. With the help of some 200,000 Russian troops, the Austrian Emperor Franz Joseph eventually suppressed the rebellion, driving Kossuth and his men into exile.

Stricter Austrian rule followed the failed uprising. Yet the nationalistic political climate developing in Europe limited the absolute authority of the Hapsburgs. Franz Joseph came to accept the Compromise of 1867, which established a dual Austro-Hungarian monarchy, with Hungarian autonomy in all matters except finance and foreign affairs.

Despite increasing political reform, a mere 27 percent of adults gained the franchise before World War I, and the Upper Nobility continued to hold sway, checking the influence of both the King and the restive non-Magyar nationalities. As Hungary slowly industrialized, a new political force emerged from the small urban proletariat: the General Workers Association, which represented about 15 percent of the population. Founded in 1868, it was the forerunner of the Hungarian Social Democratic Party.

History from 1900 to 1945

Unlike the other states of East Central Europe, Hungary began the new century not only as a sovereign power, but as an imperial domain holding sway over a vast territory. Despite its apparent power, Hungary was in fact dependent on a series of foreign mentors—Austria, France, Germany, and the Soviet Union, each of which in turn beguiled, manipulated, and betrayed Hungary.

Intent on filling the power vacuum in Southeastern Europe left by the retreat of the Ottoman Empire, Hungary entered WW I as the ally of its Austrian imperial partner. But Hungary emerged from the war as the greater loser. Not only did the Magyars sustain 2.1 million killed and wounded among its 3.6 million troops, but the humiliating Trianon Treaty, which the victorious Allies forced on them, left Hungary with little of its former greatness. It lost two-thirds of its prewar territory, three-fifths of its total population, and one-third of its Magyar population, leaving millions of Magyars now subject to the vengeful successor states of Czechoslovakia, Yugoslavia, and the victorious Romania.

If the political losses were punishing, the economic losses were disastrous. With the lost land went 58 percent of the railroads, 60 percent of the roads, 84 percent of the timber, 43 percent of the arable land, and 83 percent of the iron ore. An overly centralized prewar economy caused Hungary to retain much of its limited heavy industrial capacity but lost the raw materials to feed it as well as the guaranteed markets, which the empire had ensured.

Yet before the end of the war, Hungary had abandoned both its Austrian partner and its German ally. The Western sympathizer, Count Mihaly Karolyi, seized power in a bloodless revolution on October 31, 1918, and pulled Hungary out of the war twelve days before Germany agreed to an armistice. Karolyi hoped that by abandoning the alliance with Germany he could gain an understanding with France, which would allow Hungary to retain its empire. Furthermore, by offering Hungarians universal suffrage, Karolyi hoped to enhance the image of Hungary as a democratic nation.

But Karolyi's five-party coalition could deliver neither the French support nor the domestic political strength to maintain power. Each of the parties had its own weaknesses. Karolyi's own Party of Independence had no organizational base. The Democrats enjoyed no following outside Budapest and were mostly Jewish, alienating the strongly anti-Semitic populace. The Smallholder Party, while voicing no clear program, was opposed to land reform that would hurt their constituents, small landowners. The Radical Party eventually recognized the connection between Magyar land reform and non-Magyar aspirations for autonomy. But their recognition came too late to bring new supporters to the Party or the coalition.

Only the Social Democrats (SDs), who drew on the membership of the 700,000-strong trade unions for support, commanded political respect. But the Social Democrats also failed. The Party rejected the demand of the peasants for land, limiting their appeal in a country more than 55 percent rural.

But the SDs could not maintain their principal base, the trade unions, which had been infiltrated by communists. Many had spent the war as Hungarian POWs in Russian camps where they were recruited by the Soviets. Bela Kun was one such former prisoner who led some 10,000 communists in Budapest and 20,000 in smaller towns. The Soviets funded the revolutionaries, who were armed with an incendiary newspaper, Voros Ujsag, and 35,000 rifles. Power was to fall into Kun's lap. While SD leaders were organizing to crush the communists, Kun's dual appeal to patriotism and revolution seduced away many SD supporters.

On March 20, 1919, French Lt. Colonel Vyx delivered a note to the Karolyi government demanding still more territory from defeated Hungary. This was to be the last straw. Karolyi's liberals fell and Kun's communists, who had just succeeded in co-opting the SD leadership, stepped into the void. Betrayed by France, Hungary, at Kun's urging, threw in its lot with the Soviet Union. In the spring of 1919, the USSR seemed the spearhead of an inevitable world communist revolution.

Kun quickly struck against those who had benefited from Hungary's defeat. Hungarian armies flooded into Slovakia on May 20, 1919, and stopped only at France's threat of direct military intervention. Next, Kun turned west in an abortive attempt to foment revolution in Austria. Finally, in a move that would prove his undoing, Kun attacked Romania on July 19, 1919, to regain Transylvania. More than any other lost region, Transylvania has fired Magyar politics and imagination as an integral part of the Hungarian state. Despite initial success, the attack failed because of both treason by officers unreconciled to communist rule and demoralization in the ranks.

Communist policies had run into trouble at home as well. Instead of gaining support for the regime by parceling out large estates to land-hungry peasants, Kun had expropriated the estates and placed them under state ownership. Then Kun threw the economy into crisis by outlawing private commerce—an order he later rescinded—and then issuing an unbacked "white" currency, which Hungarians refused to recognize.

On August 2, 1919, Kun's government succumbed to overwhelming pressures and was replaced by a socialist government, which lasted only four days before falling to invading Romanian forces, which looted and burned the capital. During this period of leftist ascendancy, the right had been busy. Count Gyula Karolyi, cousin of Mihaly, and Admiral Miklos Horthy had assembled counterrevolutionary troops in the southern border town of Szeged. They swept into Hungary on the heels of the victorious Romanians. Both the vengeful Romanians and the anticommunist Hungarians set out to liquidate all vestiges of Kun's regime with a "white terror" which surpassed the brutality of Kun's red terror.

Horthy supported the strongly anti-Bolshevik government of Istvan Friedrich, which had benefited from the Romanian occupation. At Allied insistence, on November 25, 1919, Friedrich gave way to the more moderate administration of Karoly Huszar, which accepted the ignominious Trianon terms and called for general elections to be held January 25, 1920.

The elections, carried out in the midst of continuing white terror, returned a conservative parliament, many of whose members favored restoring the dynasty. As a compromise between the old political elite, which wanted a Hapsburg restoration, and the Allies, who wanted a representative, non-Hapsburg government, Horthy himself took control as "regent," with kinglike powers, on March 1, 1920. Horthy remained the titular head of state almost until the end of the Second World War.

But Horthy did not govern alone. He used the parliamentary parties in various coalitions to support his choice for premier, the active leader of the country. After the 1920 election, itself marred by political violence, the Government Party used open balloting in the countryside and other pressures in the cities to return strong majorities through the interwar years. The Government Party emerged as a marriage of convenience between the Smallholder Party, the largest in parliament, and the deeply conservative Christian National Union, arranged by Count Istvan Bethlen, who would govern Hungary with Horthy's assent for the next decade.

Bethlen's political program deliberately avoided divisive issues, essentially trying to return the country to its prewar status. In foreign policy, Bethlen's government schemed to regain the lost Trianon territories. At home, he attempted to revive the previous social system. A sham land reform law of December 7, 1920 redistributed so little land that the recipients collected less than an acre apiece.

The Social Democrats reluctantly consented to Bethlen's program as the price of survival. In return for a pledge not to hold strikes or to recruit peasants, the SDs received full legal status and the right to organize trade unions.

Bethlen's economic program initially fitted comfortably with his political objectives. First, he solicited international financial investment. Hungary's admission to the League of Nations in September 1922 paved the way for $50 million in reconstruction loans in July 1924. Loans continued to be granted in the 1920s until by 1930 Hungary claimed the highest foreign debt per capita in Europe. Bethlen tried, with little success, to use these funds to encourage industrial development and to secure materials for Hungary's industry, cut off from supplies in the Trianon lands. Bethlen also stimulated inflation through 1923, in an effort to shift the financial burden of reconstruction off the gentry, and then stabilized the economy in 1924, establishing a National Bank.

The global depression of the 1930s dealt a severe blow to the Hungarian economy. Hungary had remained an agricultural nation, with over half its population still engaged in farming in 1930. Plummeting food prices, combined with the evaporation of foreign credits, plunged Hungary into a spiral of unemployment and financial chaos. Industrial unemployment rose from 5 percent in 1928 to more than 35 percent in 1933. Credit contracted, making it impossible to fund new enterprises.

As in Germany, this economic turmoil fueled the growth of the radical right. In October 1930, a group of radical right deputies defected from Bethlen's governing coalition to form a new party. Although Bethlen won the July 1931 elections, he resigned the next month, sensing that the tide of public opinion was turning against him. Count Gyula Karolyi's conservative government maintained its hold for a year before Gyula Gombos took power promising to "break up finance capitalism."

Gombos had led the "white" troops under Horthy until Allied objections to Gombos's pronounced pro-German views forced his dismissal. As Hitler rose to eminence in Germany, Gombos's dedication to militarism and fanatical anti-Semitism increased. He used the Spring 1935 elections to purge the Government Party of members of the old elite and install deputies loyal to himself. Mass resignations in the Army over a League of Nations investigation gave Gombos a convenient pretext to position his men in the military as well. For a time Gombos struck a deal with Jewish financiers to fund his party anonymously in exchange for muffling his anti-Semitism. In October 1936, just as he was about to implement some of his most dangerous programs, he suddenly died.

Following Gombos, Horthy appointed a series of premiers whose will to resist encroaching German domination gradually diminished, descending into full-scale Hungarian participation in the Nazi war effort. Kalman Daranyi, premier from October 1936 through May 1938, tried to drive the hardest bargain with Germany, trading Hungarian cooperation for return of the lost Trianon lands and German revitalization of Hungarian industry. He eventually fell out of favor with Berlin and was succeeded by other premiers, progressively more subservient to Germany until Hungary became a political and economic vassal of Germany. Hungary declared war on the United States and sent 200,000 combat troops to serve on the Eastern Front.

Domestically, the war years saw the enactment of several anti-Semitic laws, which, though less extreme than the Final Solution, abused and bankrupted the sizable Jewish minority. The war also witnessed the rise of a small-scale antigovernment communist insurgency, which included, among others, Laszlo Rajk and Janos Kadar. These events, along with the almost complete annihilation of Hungarian forces in the aftermath of Stalingrad, swung popular and government opinion against the war in which Hungary now found itself a captive.

When Hitler discovered that Horthy's premier, Miklos Kallay, had established contacts with the Allies to discuss Hungarian withdrawal from the war, the Germans invaded Hungary in March, 1944. Soon afterward, in October, 1944, finding Horthy's regime unreliable in continuing to supply men and matériel for the war, Hitler supported Ferenc Szalasi's Arrow Cross Party in a coup. Szalasi, even more rabidly pro-Nazi than Gombos, aided Hitler in exterminating Hungary's remaining Jews and ensured Hungary's dedication to the losing cause until the bitter end.

Red Army troops entered Hungary in December 1944 and proclaimed a National Independent Front government, including the Hungarian Communist Party (HCP), the Hungarian Social Democratic Party (HSDP), the Independent Smallholder Party (ISP), several smaller parties, and the free trade unions. Though granted only 30 percent of the representatives in this ad hoc body, the HCP benefited greatly from the support of the invading Red Army. After house-to-house fighting for Budapest in December 1945, the Nazis were finally forced out of Hungary in April and the Arrow Cross deposed.

History from 1945 to 1990

In 1945, the Soviets occupied most of the country, and Hungary once again came under the sway of a victorious great power, as it had many times since the Turkish conquest of the sixteenth century. The Soviets had agreed at Yalta to share control equally with the Western Allies, and Stalin allowed Hungary to hold elections on November 4, 1945. The Independent Smallholder Party won a majority with 57 percent of the vote and gained some 245 of 409 legislative seats. A distant second, the HSWP garnered 17.4 percent; the HCP a mere 17 percent; the National Peasant Party (NPP) 6.9 percent; and the urban, Western-leaning Citizen Democrats 1.6 percent. Despite winning an absolute majority, the ISP stood by a preelection pledge to preserve the coalition regardless of the election results. Nevertheless, the outcome marked a clear failure for the communists, despite their Soviet sponsorship and an ambitious land reform program announced in January 1945 by Agriculture Minister Imre Nagy. While some 150,000 peasants had joined the HCP, most had flocked to the leftist-radical NPP and the centrist ISP.

Unwilling to serve merely as the loyal opposition, the HCP leader Matyas Rakosi, with Stalin's connivance, began to whittle down the noncommunist authorities. Rakosi formed tactical alliances with the left wings of the ISP and the HSWP, dividing his opposition and lessening their ability to resist Communist encroachments. He used Soviet influence to guarantee the HCP vital government posts, most prominently the Interior portfolio, through which Rakosi himself effectively ruled the country. Finally, using the Interior Ministry's secret police, the AVO, which later became the AVH, Rakosi arranged the ouster of noncommunist politicians and bureaucrats on pretexts of both political conspiracy and economic redundancy.

In this climate, on September 5, 1947, new elections, marked by coercion and fraud, gave the HCP 22.3 percent of the vote, trailed by the ISP (15.4 percent), the HSWP (14.9 percent), and the National Peasant Party (8.3 percent). The ISP's image had suffered from two years of fruitless coalition management and its impotence in the face of Soviet demands. Bolstered by an HCP plurality, Soviet support, and the formation of communist regimes across Eastern Europe, Rakosi schemed to eliminate all opposition to his rule.

His power play climaxed on June 12, 1948, with the shotgun marriage of the HCP to the HSWP after the Socialists had purged their more right-wing members. The hybrid entity became the Hungarian Workers' Party (HWP) in name, but in fact remained the Communist Party under General Secretary Rakosi, who gradually eradicated the former HSWP leadership from its ranks. A communist-inspired constitution followed in August 1949, proclaiming Hungary a "People's Democracy" and guaranteeing the HWP the "leading role" in Hungarian society—code words for the establishment of a one-party state.

Rakosi also controlled the influence of the Catholic Church and its combative Cardinal Mindszenty. Two-thirds of the population practiced Roman Catholicism and one-quarter Calvinism, most of them sending their children to parochial schools. Mindszenty had fought communism at each step, condemning land reform, which cost the church dearly in support from the peasants, and secular intrusion upon religious education. In June 1948, the HWP nationalized all religious schools. That virtually the entire HWP Central Committee was Jewish helped fuel traditional Hungarian anti-Semitism. Cardinal Mindszenty retaliated by denouncing communism and the HWP and its leadership and by excommunicating Catholic officials who supported the law.

Having become too great a thorn in Rakosi's side, Mindszenty was arrested by the AVH on Christmas Day 1948 and condemned to life imprisonment after a 1949 show trial accusing him of espionage and currency speculation. The Calvinist ministry, though more receptive to communist orders, was similarly purged in 1952. (Mindszenty was briefly liberated during the 1956 uprising only to seek cover from the communists again in the U.S. embassy, where he lived until 1971. Then he was allowed to depart for the Vatican, where he died in 1975. Expressing a desire to be buried in his native land only after "the red star of faithless Moscow falls," his remains were moved to Budapest in early May, 1991, just five weeks before all Soviet troops left Hungary.)

With power now firmly in the hands of the HWP, Rakosi used the conflict between Stalin and Tito to stamp out all opposition within the party. Laszlo Rajk, a wartime underground leader and deputy secretary-general of the HWP, had lobbied for faster "communization" of Hungary than Stalin deemed appropriate. Rajk's independence and popularity threatened the ruling clique of Rakosi, Erno Gero, Mihaly Farkas, and Jozsef Revai, all wartime exiles in Moscow. At these men's bidding, the AVH arrested Rajk in June 1949. At his show trial in September he admitted to spying for the implausible "fascist-imperialist" partnership of Horthy, Heinrich Himmler, Allen Dulles, and Tito. Following Rajk's hanging in October, the AVH executed 2,000 HWP members and imprisoned 150,000 more, while 350,000 were expelled from the party. Through this bloody purge, Rakosi won totalitarian control of the country and the absolute hatred of ordinary Hungarians.

Rakosi now had a free hand to turn Hungary, for centuries an agrarian nation and food exporter, into a "country of iron and steel." Following Stalin's lead, Rakosi embarked on the nationalization of industry and the collectivization of agriculture. Coal mines had been nationalized as early as December, 1945. On March 25, 1948, the government expropriated all factories with more than 100 employees. In January 1950, the HWP introduced the nation's first five-year plan, which allocated 48 percent of total investment to industry, almost all of it heavy, particularly iron, steel, and coal. Though industrial productivity increased, the farms languished, receiving a mere 13 percent of total investment. Compulsory collectivization, though strongly resisted, further damaged agricultural productivity, and with it the standard of living.

In the elections of May 7, 1953, the HWP claimed to have won 98.2 percent of the vote. Whatever the actual total, the country was clearly gripped by growing discontent.

Rakosi's Stalinist economic goals had squeezed the country, and his political agenda had fallen out of step with the post-Stalin Soviet leadership. Under pressure from Moscow, on June 28, 1953, the HWP Central Committee criticized Rakosi for his excesses and "personality cult." Though Rakosi remained General Secretary, the reformer, Imre Nagy, became Premier and began to usher in his "new course." The June Resolutions shifted the economic emphasis away from heavy industry. Consumer industries were developed, and peasants were allowed to leave the collectives. Within months, 130,000 peasants out of a total 380,000 (by official figures) had fled.

Nagy set about liberalizing every aspect of economic and political life, and his reforms between 1953 and 1956 are heralded as a model for post-Communist reorganization. Economically, Nagy concentrated on consumer industries and decollectivizing agriculture. Politically, he encouraged open debate, religious toleration, and popular participation. The new course won popular support but enraged the party traditionalists. In February 1955, Khrushchev ousted his rival Giorgiy Malenkov, Nagy's political mentor and Soviet protector. In April, the HWP Central Committee, at Rakosi's behest, followed suit by expelling Nagy. Nagy then joined the informal, but tolerated, opposition group of intellectuals, the Petofi Circle, named for the 1848 revolutionary.

Hungary's anti-Stalinist movement was encouraged by the uprisings in neighboring Poland and Austria's escape from Soviet occupation. In July 1956, Khrushchev discovered that Rakosi planned to crush the anti-Stalinists. He immediately deposed Rakosi, installing Erno Gero, Rakosi's deputy, as secretary general. The Petofi Circle and other opposition groups then organized resistance to Gero, joining dissident intellectuals with rebellious workers. On October 22, 1956, students in Budapest adopted a sixteen-point resolution calling for, among other things, withdrawal of Soviet troops, free general elections, and full civil liberties.

On the very next day, events mushroomed out of control. Hundreds of thousands of Hungarians took to the streets to demand Gero's ouster and Nagy's return. AVH men protecting the state radio station opened fire on the crowd, but army units called in to reinforce the AVH joined the demonstrators. The HWP Central Committee, fearing revolution, urged the Kremlin to send Soviet troops to restore order. Soviet forces stationed in Hungary suppressed the lightly-armed students, but halted their intervention when they found the workers in sympathy with Nagy.

On October 24, 1956, Nagy returned as Premier with near-universal popular support. On the next day, Janos Kadar replaced Gero as General Secretary of the HWP. Kadar had been an underground leader during the war and a jailed "Titoist" under Rakosi. On October 27, Nagy proclaimed his desire for the withdrawal of Soviet troops and the reinstatement of a multi-party system. He formed a "People's Patriotic Government," which included two former Smallholder leaders, and began dismantling the Stalinist system, seemingly with Soviet acquiescence.

While Khrushchev may have been ready to countenance Hungary's domestic political pluralism, he drew the line at the abrogation of Warsaw Pact commitments. When on November 1, 1956, Nagy issued a statement withdrawing Hungary from the Warsaw Treaty Organization and requesting United Nations protection, the Soviets responded with massive force. On the morning of November 4, Soviet tanks attacked Budapest while thousands of Soviet troops streamed across the Russian border to crush the revolution, just as Tsarist troops had done in 1848. Nagy fled to the Yugoslav Embassy, from which he was eventually kidnapped, despite a promise of safe passage, and later executed. The architect of the Soviet invasion was the HWP General Secretary, Kadar, who had split with Nagy and his "People's Patriotic Government" and formed a "Revolutionary Worker-Peasant Government" in Uzhgorod, a town on the Soviet border.

Kadar returned to Budapest on November 7, 1956, determined to remove supporters of both Nagy and Rakosi and to reestablish communist authority through the rechristened

Hungarian Socialist Workers' Party (HSWP). The thwarted revolution had cost 25,000 lives and sent 200,000 into exile. Exhausted by fighting, Kadar judged the Hungarian people ready to strike a deal. His "alliance policy" amounted to a compromise among the Hungarians, the Kremlin, and his own government. Kadar reformed both political and economic policy in exchange for popular obedience, while the Soviets allowed domestic reform in Hungary in return for faithful adherence to its international policies.

Initially, the alliance policy produced promising results. Rather than being coerced, the peasants were offered financial incentives to join collectives. As a result, collective membership rose from 6.1 percent of the agricultural population in 1957 to 75 percent in 1962. Kadar permitted a wide range of artistic expression, even some critical of economic conditions, though he drew the line at outright political opposition. Amnesty was granted to the "counterrevolutionaries" of 1956, at least to those not killed by the Soviets.

But economic growth was soon stymied by socialist, bureaucratic inefficiency. To combat the disappointing statistics, the HSWP authorized Finance Minister Rezso Nyers to outline a program of further economic liberalization. Approved in 1967, this "New Economic Mechanism" (NEM) went into effect on January 1, 1968, allowing individual enterprises greater responsibility in setting wages and prices and in determining capital investment.

The NEM was soon attacked by orthodox communists, the "workers' opposition," who resented the growing social inequalities and were threatened by the new small enterprises. In November, 1972 under trade union pressure, the Central Committee approved a wage hike for 1.3 million workers, taking the steam out of the NEM. For the remainder of the 1970s, Hungary's economy wallowed in inefficiency and heavy dependence on Soviet raw materials. This combination forced Kadar to borrow money in the West to make up the trade imbalance and to curtail both domestic reform and international contacts to please the increasingly conservative Brezhnev. Political retrenchment became obvious in 1973, when many intellectuals, including Janos Kis, were expelled from the party for "antisocialist tendencies." Economic dependence on the Soviets also was costly. A tax increase was decreed in 1977 as the hard-currency debt mounted to $7 billion.

Nevertheless, Western bankers and governments saw in Hungary a liberal opening of the Soviet bloc. Admission to the IMF and World Bank in 1982 cleared the way for more loans, ostensibly for economic restructuring. Actually the thriving "black" and "gray" markets and Western credits did more than the NEM to shore up the Hungarian economy.

But creeping steps toward political pluralism in the 1980s secured greater Western support. In 1985, the People's Patriotic Front, a communist-dominated political "umbrella" organization headed by communist reformer Imre Pozsgay, held parliamentary elections with no fewer than two candidates for each seat, though all candidates had to pledge to support HSWP policies. The loans kept coming, and the hard-currency debt grew to $13 billion.

In a seeming repeat of 1956, economic stagnation at home and political reform in the Soviet Union combined to force political change. The aging Kadar was ousted as General Secretary and elevated to the ceremonial chairmanship of the HSWP in June 1987. His successor, Karoly Grosz, a longtime party stalwart, mouthed the language of reform but quickly clashed with the more liberal Imre Pozsgay. In May 1988, Pozsgay and his allies, Miklos Nemeth and Reszo Nyers, forced the HSWP Central Committee to expel Kadar from the party, thus striking a blow against Grosz.

In contrast to the violence of 1956, the Revolution of 1989 came quietly. The HSWP voted to dissolve itself in October 1989. In order to "disassociate itself from the sins and the mistaken methods of the HSWP," it immediately reconstituted itself as the Hungarian Socialist Party.

DIAGRAM OF GOVERNMENTAL STRUCTURE

President
Arpad Goncz
(AFD)

(Ceremonial)

Prime Minister
Jozsef Antall
(Democratic Forum)

The Parliament:

Governing Coalition	
Democratic Forum	165 seats
Independent Smallholders	45
Christian Democrats	21

Opposition Parties	
Alliance of Free Democrats	92 seats
Socialist Party	33
Young Democrats	21
Independents	11

Local Councils in each of 176 Constituencies

ECONOMICS

Hungary is as much an economic enigma as a political enigma. No East bloc state was more determined to be free of the Soviets and yet has been so slow to deepen economic reform following their ouster. Hungary will have full currency convertibility no sooner than 1993, has moved very slowly in privatizing its state enterprises, and has the highest per capita hard-currency debt among former bloc states. As late as the summer of 1991, the legislature had yet to act on a host of bills essential to establishing a legal basis for a market economy. Yet these facts can be deceiving. The economic transformation of the country began before the revolutionary uprisings that swept the region in 1989. Because Hungary began an economic reform program first, even as it maintains a gradualist policy, it still finds itself a leader in economic performance.

Serious economic change began in 1968, when central planning, the major device for controlling the economy, was freed from total control. There was a partial recentralization in the early 1970s, but by and large the process of liberalization was never fully reversed, resulting in major changes in the 1980s. Early in the decade, private business in services, construction, and light industry were legalized, along with several realignments of consumer prices. Soon after, other market institutions were introduced, while the central plan became increasingly general and less intrusive. Many state firms came to develop quasi-independent status, entering into international contracts and retaining control of their hard-currency earnings. A small bond market was established in 1983, some independent banks with limited capital began operation, a bankruptcy law came in 1986, and stock sales at banks were introduced in 1988, the same year the foreign investment law was significantly liberalized. All the while, in a generally more liberal environment that included Western contact, a thriving black market developed.

These changes did not establish a market economy, but they introduced elements of a market. As a result, Hungarians are more comfortable with market ideas, especially the notion of a private sector, than their counterparts in other Eastern European states. Western investors have been comfortable as well. Since Hungary under communism already had a Western presence, the fall of the HSWP led to more foreign capital. The number of joint ventures tripled in 1990, bringing roughly 11 percent of all Hungarian firms into business relationships with Western firms. More than half of all hard-currency investments in all former communist states and the Soviet Union as of 1991 were in Hungary, for a total in excess of $1.5 billion.

Thus, while the coalition government of Jozsef Antall has been slow to adopt a faster reform pace, many elements of a market economy have taken root. The opposition Free Democrats argue that Hungary will lose its leading position if deeper legal reforms are not forthcoming, and they are by and large correct. The coming year, 1992, will determine whether Hungary is able to sustain its transformation.

Current Economic Reforms

Overarching all of Hungary's economic reforms is one auspicious proviso. Article 9 of the constitution states that Hungary has a market economy. No other former communist state has made so bold a claim, and Hungary is having a difficult time living up to it. The government has achieved only mixed results in fulfilling its pledge to reform. The transfer of Hungary's public assets to private control is the most obvious example. A wave of "spontaneous" privatizations had occurred in the waning days of the communist government. Act XIII of 1989, the Transformation of Economic Organizations and Economic Associations Act (hereafter referred to as the Privatization Act), was passed in July to govern those spontaneous privatizations. The law has legally been supplanted by Act VII of 1990, which grants direct regulatory control and intervention to the State Property Agency (SPA). But the original law nevertheless continues to serve as the SPA's point of departure and so, in the absence of alternative directives, Article XIII of 1989 continues to function as the overall guideline for privatization in Hungary.

The attempted impromptu privatization of the Hungar Hotel chain is a classic example of the problems with this first Privatization Act. The Swedish-based Quintus hotel chain attempted to buy controlling interest in Hungar for U.S. $100 million. The bid was widely believed to be grievously inadequate and was met with considerable public outrage. Hungary's Constitutional Court heard the case and ruled invalid the conversion of Hungar Hotels into a stock corporation. The company was, in effect, renationalized.

Act VII granted broad control over privatization transactions to the State Property Agency. The Agency was removed from the direct control of the parliament and empowered to prevent assets from being sold at below-market prices by officials who stood to gain by offering such discounts. The tide of privatizations has slowed to a trickle in the absence of legislation clarifying the process for the SPA and the 2,200 firms it oversees. In the absence of legislation, there is increased scope for destructive arbitrariness. An even greater threat to privatizations has been the SPA revelation that after selling property for more than 100 billion forints, it had only 5 billion forints of net profit.

The government announced its three-year economic program in a "white book," issued in September 1990. The "Program for National Renewal" set as its main goal the privatization of Hungary's productive resources and the auctioning of between 20 and 25 state enterprises every three or four months. In a three-year period, the share of state ownership was scheduled to fall to under 50 percent, an extraordinarily modest goal in view of the rapid growth of production outside the state sphere and the inevitable contraction of state production as resource-wasting state plants are closed. According to PlanEcon estimates, private sector output increased 25 to 30 percent in the first half of

1990, continuing to grow at nearly the same pace in 1991, while overall industrial and agricultural output declined 7 percent over the year.

Shortly after adopting the new economic program, a law was passed directing the SPA to auction approximately ten thousand small shops and restaurants. Auctions have since been held for many of these properties, which generated higher than expected sale prices and the formation of a large number of individual entrepreneurs at one stroke. Foreigners were forbidden from bidding directly on these small businesses. The auction results were complicated by the need to seek the approval of local councils before the consummation of each sale.

The government is preparing to auction 20 of the most successful Hungarian enterprises, only 3 of which were designated open to 100 percent foreign ownership. (Hungar Hotels is slated to be auctioned off in this first round.) Later legislation broadened foreign participation, but the present status of 100 percent foreign ownership on the privatized properties is still murky. In the summer of 1991 the Finance Minister attempted to dispel fears of foreigners acquiring Hungarian assets at fire sale prices. He noted that foreign investment amounted to no more than 3 to 4 percent of total investment in the nation's firms.

Hungary passed new tax legislation. For the calendar year 1990, profits in excess of HUF 3,000,000 (HUF, the international designation of the Hungarian forint) were taxed at a 40 percent rate. Profits of 3 million forints (about U.S. $46,000 at 1990 exchange rates) or less were taxed at 35 percent. These rates are lower than their 1989 levels of 50 and 40 percent, respectively. (Firms with a foreign stake greater than 20 percent of assets, or HUF 5,000,000, pay a maximum rate of 32 percent.) Manufacturing and hotel joint ventures with total assets of at least HUF 25,000,000 and foreign ownership of at least 30 percent may be granted a top rate of 16 percent for the first five years of operation and a top rate of 24 percent thereafter.

The Act on Foreign Investment enumerates certain priority industries, which may be granted a full tax holiday for the firm's first five years, followed by a maximum marginal rate of 16 percent thereafter. Broadly speaking, these preferred areas include electronics, automation equipment, vehicle and machine tool engineering, packaging technology, food processing, forestry, pharmaceuticals, energy conservation technology and equipment, animal husbandry equipment, and essentially any line of business that is likely to increase Hungary's export earnings. For tax purposes, losses can be carried forward for two years. By mid-1991 more than 5,000 joint ventures had been established, representing more than $1.3 billion in investments.

In addition to the profit tax, a value-added tax of 25 percent is carried by most products, while some "non-basic" services are taxed at 15 percent of value added. The "basic" services, certain other products chosen for subsidization by the government, and exports are all exempt from the value-added tax.

Personal income taxes have also been instituted. For foreign employees and investors, Hungary has reciprocal taxation treaties with all the major industrialized countries. Domestic residents with incomes between 55,000 and 90,000 forints in 1990 paid a straight 15 percent tax. Taxes rise progressively with higher incomes, with maximum rates for incomes above HUF 500,000. Employers must contribute a sum equal to 43 percent of wages and salaries of employees to the social insurance fund, and employers must withhold 10 percent of wages and salaries as a contribution to the national pension system.

The Law on Economic Associations, better known as the Companies Act (Act VI of 1988), is the core of the Hungarian business code. The law limits companies to six basic legal forms and regulates general business practices. The Hungarians have, in some respects, modeled their business code after those of their former partner in empire, the Austrians. The limited liability company (LLC) is thus somewhat similar to the Austrian and German GmbH or an incorporated partnership, while the company limited by shares (CLS) is something like the Austrian and German AG form. There were approximately 4,500 LLCs in

1989, increasing to more than 18,000 in 1990. The total number of private firms operating in 1991 exceeded 30,000, and more than a quarter of these enjoyed foreign investment.

Profits may be repatriated at the prevailing official exchange rate. However, if inflation continues at its approximately 30 percent annual rate, the market value of the currency will diverge significantly from the official exchange rate unless the government either continues to devalue or allows the market to set the exchange value of the forint. In the face of rising inflation in the summer of 1991, the government refused to allow another devaluation.

Minority foreign interest in a firm requires only regular business registration. Majority foreign ownership requires an application being filed with the Ministry of Finance. Grounds for acceptance or rejection of such an application have not been announced, but a response is guaranteed within 90 days of filing. If no response is received in that time, the silence of the regulators may be taken as approval.

The statute sets the minimum operating capitalization for LLCs at one million forints, which at the 1990 exchange rate would be a little more than U.S. $15,000. The CLS form requires a larger minimum capitalization of ten million forints, or more than U.S. $150,000. Preferred shares or convertible bonds can comprise up to half of the firm's capital. As is common in European securities law, firms are significantly restricted in their ability to buy back stock. No more than one-third of outstanding securities can be repurchased, and they must be sold by the company within three years of the repurchase.

The Company Act sets out some of the minimal functions of the boards of directors and stockholders meetings for LLCs and CLSs. In the case of the CLS, the law requires that one-third of the board of directors must be elected by the workforce in firms with more than 200 employees.

The Company Act applies to foreigners and citizens alike, whereas the Act on Foreign Investments in Hungary (Act XXIV of 1988) relates only to the investments of foreigners. One of the main purposes of the law was to assure foreign investors that any actions such as nationalization or expropriation by the government will be fully compensated "at real value and without delay" in the currency in which the initial investment was made. For those requiring more assurance than this, OPIC, the U.S. Overseas Private Investment Corporation, offers insurance against political risks to American investors.

Foreign partners in joint ventures must pay the cash component of their investment in hard currency. The balance can take the form of intangible assets, such as licenses and marketing expertise, as well as equipment and materials. One of the major incentives to foreign ownership is that the law permits duty-free importation of capital equipment and materials equal to the value of the amount of the hard-currency contribution of the foreign partner.

All of the legal forms of business may be operated from duty-free areas, which the Hungarians call "customs-free zones." Foreigners may establish or participate in these ventures on an equal footing with citizens. While these firms enjoy duty-free status with respect to customs and foreign exchange, they are still subject to the full corporate taxation.

Hungary has also codified stock trading. With extensive foreign assistance, a stock market was opened in June 1990 and was subject to tighter trading rules in January 1991. Daily turnover is small, ranging from $100,000 to $1 million, and on any given day only about 12 to 15 issues are traded. The vast majority of share companies have gone private, and more Hungarian shares are traded in Vienna than Budapest. But over its first year of operation, trading has increased sixfold. As is the case in other economic matters, Hungary is ahead of its Eastern European counterparts, at least in terms of experience.

Hungary's foreign debt casts a pall over economic reform. The government has vowed not to reschedule its $20 billion debt, but it has not spelled out how it intends to remain current on its international financial obligations. It has offered only vague and not entirely convincing pledges of fiscal austerity. The "Program for National Renewal" released in September 1990 is equally vague on various matters of social policy, including the health care system, housing, unemployment insurance, and personal taxes. Of these, it is essential to begin some sort of restrictions on unemployment insurance and social security, which are major drains on the state's resources. The government realizes the expense but fears the public outcry if it restricts the benefits.

The ambiguity of Prime Minister Antall's economic reform program reflects the deep divisions over economic policy within his government. The divisions surfaced only a few months after the unveiling of the "Program for National Renewal" when Ferenc Rabar, the Minister of Finance, and Gyorgy Matolcsy, Prime Minister Antall's chief economic advisor, took radically different public positions regarding the pace with which Hungary should pursue reform. Matolcsy had been one of the prime movers in urging legislation authorizing the privatization of small businesses. His views were broadly consistent with the "Program for National Renewal," but he set a much more abrupt timetable for its implementation. He also called for the rapid elimination of subsidies and the creation of a social welfare program to support and retrain unemployed workers. To promote job creation and growth, Matolcsy advocated generous tax incentives for investment.

The Finance Minister and other key economic officials rejected Matolcsy's program as too radical. In the acerbic debates that followed, Matolcsy was accused of improperly enriching himself in a privatization transaction, and both Matolcsy and Rabar ended up resigning their posts. The Antall government is no closer to a consistent economic program than it was before the debate, but the transition continues despite the lack of a coherent agenda.

Antall confronts a menacing choice. A rapidly disintegrating economy demands rapid change, but popular pressures are on the side of stability and caution. His government was challenged by nationwide strikes following his attempts to increase energy prices, and his party lost the recent local elections to his principal rivals. The government's paralysis worsens as the need for resolute action grows ever more pressing. In his public speeches, Antall has come down firmly on the side of muddling through. He has enjoyed some success in using fiscal austerity to combat inflation, which has run at an annual rate of 30 to 40 percent in 1991, and, as a result, he has advanced the date for full convertibility to 1993. But it remains unclear whether the pressure of a rapidly deteriorating economy will cause Antall to step up the pace of reform.

Current State of the Economy

Hungary's vaunted reform of 1968 was a major disappointment in terms of GNP growth. According to the Research Project on National Income in East Central Europe, Hungary had the lowest growth rate of GNP of all the East European economies in the 1965–1978 period. For the 1980s, growth was never more than 2 percent, and since 1988 it has been negative. Gross investment was negative for seven of the 10 years. The current account in hard currency was negative seven of the last 10 years and only positive in nonhard-currency accounts since 1985. Despite positive nominal earnings, real earnings were also negative for seven of 10 years.

Not surprisingly, the economy fell into its deepest decline following the 1989 revolution. In 1990, GDP fell by 5 percent and will have fallen further in 1991 by roughly 8 percent. Industrial output also fell 5 percent and will have more than doubled its decline in 1991. Agriculture was also hard hit, mostly because of drought. It declined nearly 9 percent. Crop losses were estimated by Hungarian sources to be in the range of $500 million. Gross investment fell more than 12 percent and even private investment, as best it can be counted, fell by more than 4 percent.

Unemployment remains around 3 percent, representing about 150,000 workers. But the government is bracing for at least 6 percent unemployment by the end of 1991. Labor Minister Gyula Kis has estimated that some half million laborers are employed by firms exporting to the former socialist countries. Many are likely to be bankrupt by the end of 1991. In the first half of 1991, Soviet imports had been cut by 40 percent over the comparable period of 1990. There is no indication that the decline will soon be reversed.

Yet the Hungarian picture is more complex than these numbers would indicate. There is general agreement that the quality and variety of goods produced in Hungary have improved immensely relative to its neighbors. One indicator of that improvement is that Hungary's share of hard-currency trade with OECD has declined the least of all the East European nations over the 1978–1989 period. Recently, the decline has been reversed. Hungary and Czechoslovakia have slightly increased their share of trade with OECD countries between 1986 and 1989. Additionally, the output of the burgeoning black market has been undercounted in the national figures. As a result, the performance of the Hungarian economy post-1968 has not been as bleak as GNP figures alone would suggest.

Furthermore, Hungary is the traditional consumption capital of Eastern Europe. The widespread availability of consumer goods can be partially attributed to Hungary's hard-currency borrowings. Yet Hungarian production of consumer goods has been increased by allowing the profit motive a limited role in determining production. There is a good bit of truth to the old joke that East Europeans all shop in Hungary, while Hungarians shop in Austria. Hungary's current economic structure more closely resembles an optimal free-market structure than other Eastern European countries.

Hungary's high consumption of consumer goods is especially impressive, because in 1989 Hungary's GNP per capita ranked third among eastern European countries. East Germany led the bloc with a per capita income of $9,670. Czechoslovakia followed with $7,900 and Hungary with $6,090. (The per capita GNP of France was $14,590, and for South Korea it was $4,920, roughly the same as the figure for Poland.)

Hungary suffered relatively mild inflation in 1990—27.5 percent as compared to 40 percent for Bulgaria, 5.8 percent in Czechoslovakia (which had yet to institute reforms), 535 percent in Poland, and almost 1,000 percent in Yugoslavia. Hungarian inflation in 1991 is unlikely to be higher than 40 percent.

If Hungarians differ from their East European neighbors as consumers, they are even more distinctive as producers. They are far more likely to work in the private sector than are the workers of any other East European country. Only Poland, with its large number of private small farmers, comes close to Hungary. Virtually every working Hungarian participates at least to some extent in the nonsocialized economy, and a good many pensioners and underaged children assist family businesses as well. In 1986, an astounding 44 percent of the total hours worked in Hungary were dedicated to the private sector, legal and illegal, full and part-time.

The private sector has expanded and contracted with the changes in the political climate, but it has always contributed a significant portion of national production, particularly in agriculture and in the relatively highly developed service sector. Consequently, there are a number of people in Hungary with many years of entrepreneurial and private business experience. A major reason for the great declines in the national economy in 1991 are a direct result of more workers fully abandoning their state jobs in favor of full-time private sector work.

Without question, this is Hungary's greatest advantage in the transition to capitalism. The work ethic, at least in respect to the private sector, remains powerful. The East bloc adage, "They pretend to pay us, and we pretend to work," is scarcely applicable to the private sector in Hungary. Hungarians also boast considerable managerial experience, which will prove significant to operating businesses in the coming free-market economy. Managers of small business cooperatives and professional partnerships, called business work partnerships, have taken great risks in leaving the security of the state sector in pursuit of profits. Having improvised means of financing and supplying their operations, often under highly adverse circumstances, they have survived through will and ingenuity. Western businesses have flocked to Hungary because of these qualities.

Additionally it should be noted that this pool of talent comes, not primarily from the ranks of the communist party, but from the ranks of those who spurned it before 1989. In Poland and Czechoslovakia, in contrast, much social tension has been engendered because communist bureaucrats appear the best able to prosper from the advent of markets. This has both dampened enthusiasm for reform and led to calls for government intervention to prevent enrichment of the "wrong" people. Hungary should be spared such anguish.

Eastern bloc countries have virtually eliminated illiteracy. But this does not mean that their workers are well educated. Educational attainment in the former communist states is not nearly as high as it is in Western Europe. The fraction of the Hungarian workforce with a secondary or higher education is 34 percent, slightly more than half the average for the OECD countries.

While the skills and industry of its people are its greatest advantage in the transition to the market, Hungary's greatest disadvantage is its hard-currency debt, which has more than doubled since 1985. In 1990, gross hard-currency indebtedness stood at approximately $20 billion and was closer to $21 billion in 1991, roughly the same level as the hard-currency debt of the former German Democratic Republic. The difference, of course, was that East Germany was a more prosperous country. The GDR's debt constituted 13 percent of its GNP, compared to approximately 30 percent for Hungary. Indeed, Hungary's hard-currency debt is the largest relative to GNP of all the former satellites. (Poland ranks second, with debt equivalent to 25 percent of annual GNP, while Bulgaria ranks third with debt of approximately 20 percent of GNP.)

Hungarian debt is trading at substantial discounts on secondary markets in the West, suggesting that the financial community does not believe Hungary can maintain debt payments averaging $2.4 billion per year over the period 1991 to 1994. There are two major reasons for the belief. Prime Minister Antall has been slow in producing fiscal arrangements to satisfy international lenders. Hungary, a member of the IMF and World Bank since 1982, managed only to elicit a $228 million line of credit in March of 1990. Only in February 1991 did it manage to win a three-year, $1.6 billion loan. Poland, by contrast, received $780 million in credits, with more aid promised for 1991, while Czechoslovakia parlayed its relatively solid debt position into a $1.8 billion loan in January 1991.

A second reason for the discounts is the widespread belief that the 1990 improvement in Hungary's current account will be difficult to repeat. The first three quarters of 1990 produced a $300 million surplus, compared to a 1989 deficit of $1.3 billion. But in 1991 Hungary has had difficulties paying the USSR hard currency for its energy imports. For all of 1991 the current account will show an estimated $800 million deficit. The IMF granted additional aid of $500 million to defray energy expenses, nearly the same amount Hungary lost because of the rising price of oil during the Gulf crisis.

All Eastern European economies have been hard hit. Yet Hungary's energy and debt-servicing payments drain more than 90 percent of its foreign earnings, making its exchange position especially difficult. The country has little alternative but to hasten its industrial restructuring.

Although rescheduling of debt payments appears inevitable, the situation is not desperate. Hungary's goods have been relatively competitive in world markets. But the difficult debt situation will result in the postponement of much-needed infrastructure investments. Roads, bridges, airports, water mains, sewers, telecommunications systems, and electrical grids and production plants are pitifully inadequate throughout the former bloc. Hungary is no exception. Most OECD countries have at least 3.5 times as many telephones per capita as are in use in Hungary. The CIA, moreover, estimates that 20 percent of all telephone calls result in wrong connections.

There are two positive aspects to Hungary's foreign currency crisis. The country was directing over 40 percent of its exports to the demanding markets of the developed Western economies in 1989–1990, giving it valuable foreign trade experience and market share. Hungary has a head start in developing products for the world market and adjusting to the wrenching shift in the flow of trade from the socialist bloc to hard-currency trade. Total socialist trade declined by more than 24 percent in 1989, and in 1990 no more than 19 percent of Hungary's trade was with the Soviet Union. Conversely, in 1987 about 29 percent of purchased machinery was from the West, while in 1990 this portion grew to nearly 45 percent.

Hungary's relationship with Western economies should aid the transition. The country managed to strike an agreement for association with the EC in May 1991, the first for any East European country. The OECD has signed a cooperation memorandum that prepares the country for full membership. The European Trade Association has agreed to lower quotas and duties beginning in 1992.

Second, under intense fiscal pressures, the government has made the difficult decision to liquidate resource-inefficient industrial operations. Domestic banks, still entirely owned by the state, have been asked to initiate bankruptcy proceedings against some inefficient state-owned firms while government subsidies are being slashed.

Economy from Origins to 1945

As early as the 13th century, the Kingdom of Hungary was an economically vibrant and prosperous state. As a center of trade along the Asiatic land routes, Hungary was an important commercial center and a meeting place for Italian, German, Walloon, Jewish, Muslim, and Russian traders. In exchange for finished goods such as textiles, weapons, and tiles, the Hungarians offered furs, leather, and, most importantly, copper and silver from the mines in northern Hungary. During this period of prosperity Hungary went through an important process of urbanization in the royal towns, the commercial centers of the kingdom. Hungary had all the signs of becoming a major economic and political European power, much like the prosperous states of Bohemia or even France.

That prosperity and importance, however, was lost in just two years because of the Mongol invasion. In 1241 Genghis Khan's armies swept through Eastern Europe and into the poorly defended kingdom of Hungary. The invaders swept to the Adriatic sea, looting and pillaging as they passed. In the ensuing reorganization of the country, the king and the merchants in the towns lost significant power to the clergy and nobility, who formed large estates. These estates were the main centers of economic activity. Seeking work, peasants moved to the estates as serfs, establishing feudalism throughout the kingdom and an almost exclusively agricultural economy in the wake of the Mongol invasion.

During the 14th century the monarchy and some nobility experienced something of a renaissance. Gold, extremely scarce in Europe, was discovered in the north and provided considerable wealth for the king and the nobility who owned the mines. But the new wealth was not invested to provide the base of a productive economy. Rather, the proceeds from the sale of gold were spent on foreign luxury items. The wealth stayed within the courts, while the country remained little changed.

A vigorous but largely unsuccessful attempt to return to commercial activity was seen in the 15th century. Gold output declined just when there was a need for substantial revenues to finance war with the Ottoman Empire and later with Bohemia. Hungary's King Sigismund encouraged the establishment of trading cities. Offering tax privileges and freedom from feudal obligations, Sigismund tried to attract serfs and foreigners into the towns. But Hungary had long since become geographically unimportant. The trade routes to the east had shifted to the Mediterranean and to the sea route around Africa. The country also had little to trade. Sigismund and his successors were able to attract only few foreign merchants.

Over the next two hundred years, Hungary's economy suffered during the period of Ottoman occupation. By the first half of the 16th century, the Ottomans had conquered all of southern and central Hungary, including Buda, the capital. In the north a portion of the kingdom remained under the control of the king, but it was constantly threatened by Ottoman invasion. Under Ottoman rule, most of Hungary's feudal estates were dismantled, while the cities became backwaters. Feudal lords and the urban bourgeoisie fled the Ottoman invasion for royal Hungary, destroying the traditional economic structure.

In royal Hungary, conditions were better. The wars had cost many lives and the ensuing scarcity of labor led the nobility to forgive the obligations of the serfs in return for their labor. In the cities the merchants prospered to an extent because of the trade with Ottoman Hungary.

Later in the Ottoman occupation, Hungary was decimated by wars and the bubonic plague. Transylvania, for example, is estimated to have lost 50 percent of its population. To compound Hungary's difficulties, Europe suffered a long economic depression in the first half of the 17th century.

Royal Hungary was revived during the second half of the 17th century as Europe began to recover. The nobles reestablished the agricultural estates, reinstated feudal obligations, and repopulated the countryside. The progress made by the serfs over the previous century, the trend towards commercialization, and the establishment of manufacturing were reversed.

The Ottomans were finally driven from the country, and by 1711 Hungary was incorporated into the Hapsburg empire of Austria and Bohemia. This period was one of great economic progress in the rest of Europe, and the demand for traditional Hungarian goods like cattle, grains, copper, and wool had never been greater. However, Hapsburg policy required that Hungarian products first be offered for sale inside the empire, creating a virtual embargo on trade. Only with the revolution of 1848 did the modern economic history of Hungary begin.

In March of that year, Hungary joined the other territories of the Hapsburg Empire in revolt. Under the leadership of the radical Lajos Kossuth, the Hungarians, although badly divided along class and ethnic lines, succeeded in holding the Hapsburg army at bay until the Russian Tsar entered the conflict on the side of the Hapsburgs. The revolt ended when the Hungarian army suffered defeat at Vilagos in August 1849.

The Hapsburg Emperor responded by brutally asserting his absolute rule over the prodigal territory. But the reimposition of Hapsburg rule eventually brought the benefits of legal reform, the imposition of Austrian commercial, tax, and criminal laws, the abolition of serfdom, and the elimination of tariff barriers between the Austrian and Hungarian territories. Hungary's long delayed transition from feudalism to capitalism was forced from outside, avoiding a longer and more turbulent internal struggle. In terms of the rapidity of its transition, Hungary enjoyed a profound advantage compared to Rumania, Yugoslavia, and parts of Poland.

Reliable economic data for mid-19th century Hungary are hard to come by, but the broad outline of the country's economic condition is fairly clear. The economy was almost entirely agricultural and in a very primitive state. Manufacturing accounted for only 8 percent of national income. Farm land was largely concentrated in the hands of the great estates. After the reforms, approximately half the farm land passed to the peasants.

In 1870 the illiteracy rate was still around 70 percent. Ethnic Magyars comprised only 40 percent of the total population of about 14 million. Romanians were the largest minority at about 17 percent, while Slovaks, Germans, Croats, and Serbs also constituted large fractions of the population.

Amidst all the backwardness, the first hopeful signs of economic development began to appear. By 1848, 200 kilometers of railroad track had been laid. This was the beginning of a rail system which, before the end of the century, connected all the major agricultural, mining, and industrial centers to the major urban markets of the Austro-Hungarian Empire. As early as 1851 Budapest and Vienna were connected by rail, but Hungary still lagged well behind Western Europe in the construction of railroads. In 1850, Hungary had 2 km of track for every 100,000 people, 25 percent of the level of Austria and about 5 percent of the level of England. But over the period 1851–1870, 3,255 km of track were added. (The Austrian Rothschilds owned, or had an interest in, 97 percent of all the track laid in Hungary before 1873.) Hungary's metals industry grew with this surge in rail construction, increasing over the period 1847–1867 at an annual average rate of 8.6 percent. Exports of grain and flour grew at an annual average rate of 6.6 percent over the same period.

The Hungarians remained restive after their abortive revolution in 1849. In 1866, with the Habspurgs weakened by military defeat at the hands of the Prussians, the Hungarians exploited the opportunity to press demands for greater independence from Vienna. The result was the "Compromise of 1867," under which the Hapsburg Empire was transformed into the dual Austro-Hungarian Empire, with largely autonomous seats of government in Vienna and Budapest.

Except for a brief interruption during the worldwide recession of 1873 and a longer slowdown at the end of the century, the Compromise of 1867 ushered in a period of dramatic industrialization. Manufacturing output increased on average by almost 4 percent annually from 1874 to 1913.

In the year following the Compromise, public education was made mandatory for school-aged children. By World War I the literacy rate had more than doubled to close to 70 percent. This growth in human capital was matched by large inputs of foreign, and especially Austrian, financial capital. The Rothschilds founded their Credit Bank in 1867 and were followed in rapid succession by other foreign investors, creating four additional major banks. In all, the assets of banks increased more than threefold between the Compromise of 1867 and the banking panic of 1873. After the recession, the influx of foreign capital continued unabated. From 1873 to 1913 both the number of credit institutions and their capitalization increased approximately tenfold. Foreigners consistently held the majority of the securities issued by the Hungarian government between the early 1870s and 1913. Foreign ownership was particularly remarkable since, following the crash of 1873, the Hungarian government took ownership of the railroads from their foreign owners.

Hungary's greatest era of railroad construction began in the early 1880s. From then until the outbreak of the First World War, kilometers of track increased more than threefold. By 1913 Hungary's railway network had achieved a level of density comparable to that of Austria. Formerly isolated territories were opened to trade and development.

Naturally, agriculture was the first economic sector to benefit from the new-found accessibility of the Austrian markets. Hungary's agricultural exports grew rapidly. By 1913 it was annually exporting over 1.5 million tons of grain, compared to total agricultural exports of 0.5 to 0.75 tons per year before the era of railroad building. The mechanization of agriculture kept pace. By 1913, the number of steam threshers was 30,000, some twelve times the 1871 level. Yet Hungary's agricultural yields were still poor. Compared with Western European countries, Hungary ranked ninth in wheat yields per hectare between 1909 and 1912. Its production was only slightly more than one-third of Denmark's, which ranked first.

The construction of the railroads not only opened new markets, it also created them. Heavy industry first appeared in Hungary to supply the needs of the railroad builders. The development of the iron industry is the foremost example. From 1830 to 1913 the ferrous metal industry grew at an average annual rate of over 5 percent. The iron and steel industries grew not only in the volume of their output but also in the sophistication of their product, expanding from simple objects like rails to more complex products such as railroad cars and locomotives. Hungary embraced electrical technology quickly, even by Western standards, and made important technological advances. While Edison stubbornly insisted on using primitive direct-current technology, engineers at the Ganz works in Budapest invented the alternating-current transformer, which made long distance transmission of alternating current practical.

For much of the late 19th century, milling, especially of flour, was Hungary's major industry. Flour milling was for Hungary what machine building was for the Czech lands. From 1850 to 1875, total exports of flour increased twentyfold. In the next twenty-five years, they multiplied by an additional five times. In 1898, flour comprised fully a quarter of all industrial production. By 1913 food processing still made up roughly 40 percent of manufactured output, with refined sugar taking up some of the slack of declining rates of flour production.

Prewar Hungary offers an example of successful economic development primarily brought about by foreign capital. Investors contemplating a similar role in the modern Hungarian economy can take encouragement from a study of this period. However, it is important to remember that after WW I, Hungary repudiated its debt to Austria, equal to 20 percent of Hungary's prewar annual GNP.

The dawn of the period between the two world wars was something of a golden age for much of Eastern Europe. Nations that had long been dominated by imperial powers, including Hungary, reveled in their independence as the global economic boom of the 1920s fostered their development. Hungary had an altogether different experience. Vanquished in World War I, Hungary was forced by the Trianon Treaty to cede two-thirds of its territory to the "Successor States." The demoralization and destruction wrought by that humiliating defeat sent the country reeling into economic and political turmoil.

The nation's industrial structure was ill suited to postWar Hungary. Before the War, Hungarian manufacturers had enjoyed duty-free access to the tariff-protected markets of both the Austrian and the Hungarian territories of the former empire. After the War, Hungary was left with only one-third of its former territory. Isolated from national sources of raw materials and markets, Hungary became more dependent on foreign trade. Yet three of the four neighbors were openly hostile. Romania, Yugoslavia, and Czechoslovakia, distrustful of the territorial ambitions of the Magyars, formed the "Little Entente," an alliance largely aimed at checking Hungarian influence. Only Austria could be counted as a friendly neighbor. Austria, however, was saddled with heavy war reparations and was preoccupied with the reconstruction of its ravaged economy. To make matters worse, Hungary's increased dependence on trade came at a time when all the countries of Europe were taking refuge from foreign competition behind rising tariff barriers. Consequently, Hungarian trade languished after the war. Agricultural exports were about 20 percent of prewar levels in 1920 and had increased to only 40 percent in 1921. Industrial exports were slightly more robust, at roughly 40 percent of prewar levels in 1920 and 60 percent in 1921.

At the outset of the 1920s, Hungary was still a predominantly agricultural nation. Some 58 percent of the labor force was engaged in farming, compared with 76 percent in Poland, 34 percent in Czechoslovakia, and 32 percent in Austria. With the loss of its territory, the share of Hungary's workforce in agriculture would drop ten percentage points. Yet the country still contained much prime agricultural land, and the mechanization of agriculture proceeded rapidly. Tractors were first introduced to Hungarian farming in the 1920s. By 1925, 1,189 were in use. By the time the Depression hit, the number had increased almost sixfold. The Depression, however, virtually arrested the further introduction of capital equipment.

Hungary's wheat yields during the 1920s and 1930s were second only to Czechoslovakia in Eastern Europe. However, all Eastern European yields were significantly lower than Western European and stagnant across time. Husbandry, which accounted for approximately 40 percent of rural incomes between the wars, showed no growth. Herd populations never regained their prewar levels. In Austria and Czechoslovakia there were about twice as many head of cattle per farm area, while in Poland there were four times as many.

The Austro-Hungarian central bank had financed the late stages of the war at the printing press, and Hungary began the 1920s suffering from hyperinflation. The price level increased about 42 times between July 1914 and July 1921. By July 1924 the price level had shot up to 2,295 times the prewar level. Yet as a loser in the war, Hungary's financial crisis evoked little sympathy from the Allies, and international assistance was slow in coming. In 1924, the League of Nations floated the government a loan while insisting on strict fiscal controls, including a rapidly balanced budget and creation of an independent central bank. These were quickly implemented under the scrutiny of the League. The hyperinflation came to a dramatic halt in July 1924.

After the stabilization, deposits at commercial banks flooded back. In 1925 alone the value of deposits at commercial banks more than doubled. From 1925 until the onset of the Great Depression deposits further increased almost fourfold. Capital from abroad also came streaming in as foreign investors gained confidence in the country's future.

The Depression hit Hungary's rebounding economy particularly hard. Prices for agricultural output fell precipitously. In Hungary the price of a 60-pound bushel of wheat fell from U.S. $1.58 to 60 cents from January 1929 to January 1932. For a great many, conditions on the farms were desperate, especially on the numerous small parcels of land, where even in the best of times conditions were harsh.

During the twenty-five year period preceding World War II, light industry, principally textiles, gained in importance, while the food industry declined. Heavy industry maintained a fairly constant share of industrial output, which showed only sluggish growth. Hungary's industry was relatively resilient during the Depression, with industrial production increasing 30 percent from 1929 to 1937. In Poland the figure was 11 percent, and in Czechoslovakia, where the Depression devastated industry, output declined by 4 percent. The relative buoyancy of its industry during the Depression was just about Hungary's only stroke of economic good fortune during the interwar years.

Economy from 1945 to 1990

Hungary was devastated by the war. In 1944-1945 fierce fighting moved to Hungary as the Germans attempted to repel the advancing Red Army. The nation's transportation infrastructure was particularly hard hit. Over three-fourths of the railroad rolling stock was destroyed, damaged, or removed from the country, compounding the problems wrought by massive damage to roads, rails, bridges, and waterways.

By 1947 agricultural production was still almost 40 percent below its already low prewar levels. Livestock herds, decimated in the war, recovered very slowly. The pig and sheep populations stood at 64 percent and 32 percent, respectively, of their 1939 levels. Production of ferrous metals, which would be vital for reconstruction, was only at its 1936 level and still below pre-depression standards. Adding to the burden, the Soviet Union exacted staggering war reparations from its former enemy, making Hungary contribute to the Soviets' own recovery efforts. The Soviets even drafted an army of Hungarian peasants to serve as forced labor brigades to do some of the most back-breaking work of Soviet reconstruction. Moreover, they claimed as war booty all German factories on Hungarian territory. Entire plants were dismantled and shipped to the USSR.

By 1946, inflation had assumed astronomical dimensions, and the old currency, the pengo, collapsed. Food and other commodities served as the means of exchange. In an attempt to stabilize the currency, a new unit of money was introduced, the forint.

Hungary had introduced many elements of central planning in order to direct war production. Price controls, rationing, and a system of state requisitions had already been established. Nationalization of major enterprises was, therefore, not such a large step to take. Mining, tightly controlled during the war, was nationalized first. Absorption of large-scale heavy industry followed quickly. In November 1947, the major banks, together with the firms under their control, were forced into the state's portfolio. By December 1949, all enterprises with more than 10 employees were taken over. With the exception of small retailers, nationalization was effectively completed by the end of 1949.

The first three-year plan was introduced on August 1, 1947, with the nationalization of industry still incomplete. That plan did not set mandatory production quotas but channeled resources to postwar reconstruction. The results were impressive. By the end of 1948, mining output had reached a level 50 percent higher than that attained in 1938. Likewise, rail freight was up 50 percent and trucking freight was up 30 percent.

A sweeping land reform was carried out in 1945. Giant estates were nationalized, while smaller parcels were doled out to the peasants or incorporated into state farms. In all, 35 percent of the postwar territory was distributed. In response, agricultural production quickly revived. From 1947 to 1948, agricultural production increased by 50 percent. Only Poland instituted a more far-reaching land redistribution program, but its agricultural output was static. Hungary's increase was the largest of all of the East bloc states, returning the production almost to prewar levels.

The successes of the first three-year plan, together with what was thought to be the necessity of preparing for war with the West, led planners to set very ambitious goals in the first five-year plan, covering 1950 to 1954. A drastic revision of the plan in 1951 doubled the originally targeted 13 percent annual growth for industrial production. To achieve their objectives, the plans called for a massive diversion of resources to investment in heavy industry and away from consumption. Industrial capital grew at an annual rate of 9 percent, compared to 4 percent in farming. Consumption suffered even more. Because of the investments in heavy industry, per capita personal consumption did not surpass 1938 levels until 1959.

Under the plan, virtually every detail of the economy was dictated by the central economic authorities in quarterly plan directives to managers. Problems developed immediately as the quality and assortment of products produced never matched demand. The central authorities could not adequately anticipate demand nor control production. Managers had quickly realized that their bonuses depended only on the fulfillment of a few simple quantitative quotas. The planners responded with a proliferation of regulations that attempted to specify quotas for quality and assortment. Regulations relating bonuses to performance in these areas multiplied. The size and intrusiveness of the economic bureaucracy grew by leaps and bounds.

Officials had been careful not to push collectivization too hard in the late 1940s as the peasantry was a very strong factor in Hungarian politics. However, General Secretary Rakosi, his grip on power apparently secure, chose to force collectivization during the first five-year plan. The effort was a disaster. Most peasants, having so long hungered for their own plot of land, were not about to give up what they had won in 1945. Others abandoned their farms and joined the ranks of the relatively better-off industrial labor force rather than give in to the bullying of the communist authorities. Few joined the cooperative farms.

The situation in the countryside grew steadily worse until, following the death of Stalin, Imre Nagy, a former agricultural official who had displaced Rakosi, retreated from the hard-line position. He allowed peasants to leave the cooperative farms and channeled more resources into consumption. This respite from breakneck industrialization and collectivization did not last long, however. Rakosi returned as head of the government in February 1955. He and his successor Erno Gero resumed the pace of collectivization and industrialization called for by the first five-year plan. The alienation and frustration of both the peasantry and the urban population were to serve as the basis for the uprising of October, 1956.

Following the consolidation of communist control, Kadar instituted some economic changes. In industry, some prices were realigned, and minor experiments in industrial management were tried. In agriculture, there was more of a pretense of reform. The Kadar government eliminated many compulsory supply quotas, raised some agricultural prices, and, to a very limited extent, allowed prices to adjust to reflect scarcity. However, conditions in the rural economy continued to decline relative to the industrial sector. When the collectivization campaign was resumed in the late 1950s and early 1960s, a more sophisticated incentive system was employed. The inducements to join included compensation for land contributed to the collective; promises of greater investment by the state in farming equipment, housing, and amenities; private plots for families to farm independently; retention by the peasants of their livestock; and a say in the management of the collective. By these means, collectivization was effectively completed.

From 1949 to 1967, Hungary's GNP grew at an average rate of 4.5 percent. Industry grew at 6.8 percent, agriculture at 2.1 percent, and housing at only 1.3 percent. Overall, there was a significant downturn in economic activity leading up to the reform year of 1968.

The mid-1960s were a period of economic soul searching in eastern Europe generally. A decade earlier, economists such as Janos Kornai had brought to light many of the inadequacies of the Stalinist model of central planning. Kornai did a case study of the effects of central planning on light industry, a task requiring great personal courage. He confronted Hungarian economic officialdom, which was accustomed to dealing in the comfortable abstractions of Marxist-Leninist theory, with cold, hard data.

He showed that every time the center tried to spell out quotas for industry, managers devised ingenious ways to meet them, compromising the social value of the product in the process. If the output quota for cloth was stated in terms of area of woven fabric, for example, managers would respond by weaving very thin cloth. If the quota were stated in kilograms, producers would use the heaviest materials available. In general, stating quotas in terms of gross output led producers to massive inefficiencies through the use of too many expensive resources. When planners responded with rules designed to conserve resources, producers would respond by skimping so much on materials that their output was worthless to anybody.

By a series of such examples, Kornai portrayed a bleak pattern of stimulus and response that suggested that the only way to elicit rational, value-maximizing responses from producers was for the central planners to allow for the operation of market forces. Kornai's litany of examples showed that economic salvation was not to be sought in the direction of greater centralization. More directives and more inspections by central authorities, aimed at closing all the loopholes, would themselves create further distortions. Nor was economic salvation to be had simply by granting firms greater autonomy in the context of the existing planning system. That would only leave the loopholes that planners had attempted to close in the first place. Something had to be substituted for the central directives, and that something was the market.

In 1956, Kornai served as head of a group of economists at the Institute of Economics of the Hungarian Academy of Sciences, which drafted a proposal for reform of the economy based on these ideas. Their proposal and others like it were shelved once Kadar consolidated his power. But in the mid-1960s, the topic of economic reform once again rose to the fore.

Economic officials in Yugoslavia, Czechoslovakia, Poland, and even the Soviet Union were propounding ideas very much like those raised a decade earlier in Poland and Hungary. Indeed, the degree to which the proposals of Ota Sik and his group in Czechoslovakia resembled those adopted in Hungary is striking. Clearly, the reformers in each country were watching each other closely.

But the Soviets had already condemned Yugoslavia's moves toward worker self-management as heretical. Any imitation of the Yugoslav example was out of the question.

In any case, the economic reformers of Hungary and Czechoslovakia reached different conclusions—that year-to-year plan output quotas must be eliminated; prices should be determined by the market to the extent possible; and firms should be given greater control over the disposition of retained earnings so that they could select the most effective investment projects and use the remaining funds to motivate employees.

The reforms began in agriculture as early as 1965, when limits were placed on planners' setting agricultural output quotas. Farm prices were raised to stimulate supply. Cooperative farms and individuals farming private plots were given greater independence in comparison to state collective farms, ensuring that the bulk of farm production would be in the hands of people who had an interest in the efficiency and profitability of their farms. Private plot farming received a special boost from the reforms, in part to check pilfering of supplies from the collectives, but also to promote a form of agriculture that produced far higher yields than that in the state sector. The reformers made farm supplies more accessible to private cultivators and even made small amounts of capital available for investment in private plots.

With the advent of prices that bore some relation to scarcity, and with production, procurement, marketing, and investment decisions left to the farmers, Hungarian agriculture faced a reasonable approximation of a market.

Encouraged by the results achieved in agriculture, officials extended the limited application of market forces with the unveiling of the "New Economic Mechanism" (NEM) in January, 1968. Prices of goods were given more latitude to fluctuate, while prices of certain key industrial materials and agricultural goods were still centrally set. Once it was determined that price decontrol worked, the list of products outside the price-setting mechanisms increased markedly until 1972, when communist ideologues and disgruntled planners rallied their forces and rolled back some of the reforms.

As prices were freed from central control by NEM, so were firms freed from the dictates of the annual plans. Managers, still appointed by the central planners, were instructed to choose their production plans to maximize net revenues. Managers were given greater discretion over the uses of retained earnings, deciding between investment projects and bonuses for workers.

The reforms of the late 1960s led to a slowing in the rate of production growth in the 1970s, notable since Hungary was insulated from the oil shocks and subsequent world recessions of the decade. The Soviets heavily subsidized Hungarian imports of electricity and oil, but from 1965 to 1978, Hungary's GNP growth was the slowest of the other eastern European countries. Hungary's GNP grew by 47 percent, while Bulgaria's GNP grew 76 percent, Czechoslovakia's and the GDR's grew about 52 percent, and Poland's grew 83 percent. Czechoslovakia, which had introduced reforms very similar to those of Hungary only to have the reforms reversed at gunpoint, grew faster.

When the economy faltered after the introduction of the NEM, Hungarian economic officials attempted to maintain consumption and investment through imports financed by borrowing. Net indebtedness in hard currency rose steadily until it reached the $6 to 7 billion range in 1982, where it remained until the mid-1980s, when it began to soar again. Hungary's trade position was exacerbated by several factors. Hard-currency imports were subsidized by the state. The quality of Hungarian goods deteriorated in comparison to Western goods. Also, the global economic slowdown of the 1970s dampened demand for Hungarian exports. It became difficult for the Hungarians to raise hard currency.

The 1980s was a decade of continual flux, as the rules of the economic game, tax rates, investment restrictions, export subsidies, and most other economic parameters were changed constantly by officials in their frantic attempts to find solutions to Hungary's mounting economic problems.

The government instituted a major realignment of consumer prices in July 1979, followed by a similar adjustment of producer prices in January 1980. There was an attempt to link producer prices to those prevailing in market economies, eliminating some of the distortions that had accumulated following the recentralization of 1972.

More far-reaching reforms were implemented in 1981 and 1982 when new forms of private enterprise were legalized. Nonfarm cooperatives with memberships of 100 or fewer were legalized and granted limited liability. The cooperatives formed in light industry and construction have had a major effect on stimulating economic growth out of all proportion to their small total numbers. Small business work partnerships up to 30 members and professional partnerships were also legalized and became common in service industries. Their activities range from software design to matchmaking services. Business work partnerships had 70,000 members in December 1986.

A further form of private enterprise organization was created, in part, to allow state enterprises to compete with the growing private sector. Enterprise business work partnerships allow state enterprises to subcontract state industrial work out to groups of employees, who freely negotiate their compensation. Participation in this necessarily part-time form of private enterprise was significant, reaching nearly 300,000 workers by the end of 1987.

More economic difficulties and the mounting foreign debt led to another round of reform legislation. In 1983, efforts were made to create a capital market as state and cooperative enterprises were allowed to issue bonds. Competition in the banking industry was initiated by the establishment of a handful of tiny rivals to the behemoths, the Hungarian National Bank and the National Savings Bank. These banks acted as venture capitalists to small private sector enterprises, but were so small as not to have a major effect. Later, in a further effort to introduce competition to the capital market, the Hungarian National Bank was divested of its commercial banking functions, those functions being taken up by smaller banks.

Reformers also attempted to address some of the fundamental problems at the enterprise level. In 1985, an attempt was made to limit the power of the central planners by forming company councils composed of representatives elected by management and labor. Hiring, firing, and compensation of officers now fell under the jurisdiction of company councils. In practice, this produced chaos and the scope of the councils' actions were curtailed.

In 1986, a bankruptcy act was passed in an attempt to improve the performance of marginal firms and to close down enterprises that were a drain on the state treasury. Again, practice fell short of principle, as few resource-squandering enterprises were actually subjected to enforcement of this law. Further changes in the areas of commercial banking and taxes followed in 1987 and 1988, but it was all too little, too late. At a communist party conference in May, 1988, reformist forces, emboldened by Moscow, staged the dramatic ouster of Janos Kadar and many of his closest comrades. Karoly Grosz replaced Kadar as General Secretary, and reformers occupied the majority of the seats in the newly reconstituted Politburo. The political and economic transformation of Hungary had begun.

FURTHER READINGS

Heinrich, Hans-Georg. *Hungary: Politics, Economics, and Society.* Boulder: L. Reinner, 1986.

Hoensch, Jorg K. *A History of Modern Hungary 1867–1986.* (trans. Kim Traynor) New York: Longman, 1988.

Rothschild, Joseph. *East Central Europe between the Two World Wars.* Seattle: University of Washington Press, 1974.

_____, *Return to Diversity: a Political History of East Central Europe since World War II.* Oxford: Oxford University Press, 1989.

Rupnik, Jacques. *The Other Europe.* New York: Pantheon,1989.

Sugar, Peter F. ed. *A History of Hungary.* Bloomington: Indiana University Press, 1990.

I HUNGARY

DATA AND VITAL STATISTICS

IV. **Education**
  1. Schools, students, and teachers
  2. Public expenditures on education
  3. Expenditures and pupils per teacher, 1989
  4. Distribution of teachers and pupils by educational level, 1987
  5. Mean years of schooling, 1980
  6. School enrollment ratios
  7. School enrollment, 1989
  8. Books, newspapers, and library book loans, 1989

V. **Energy and Resources**
  1. History of primary energy production
  2. Complete energy use
  3. Electricity production
  4. Installed electricity-generating capacity
  5. Commercial energy use by sector, 1985
  6. Proven reserves of crude oil, natural gas, and coal, 1989
  7. Mineral production

VI. **Government and Defense Forces**
  1. State budget
  2. Hard-currency debt
  3. Armed forces totals, 1991
  4. Components of defense force, 1987
  5. Military expenditures

VII. **Industry**
  1. Industrial production index
  2. Industrial production index (official and adjusted)
  3. Production of selected industrial items
  4. Industrial waste generation
  5. Basic structure of industry
  6. Rank of industry, manufacturing, and service share of GDP, 1990
  7. Emissions of air pollutants, 1988
  8. Environmental summary, 1991

VIII. **Labor Force**
  1. Workforce by selected areas of the economy
  2. Average monthly earnings by economic sector
  3. Economically active population by sex and industry, 1988

IX. **Population and Health**
  1. Geography and demographic profile, 1990
  2. Population
  3. Population by age
  4. Population of top ten cities, 1990
  5. Health indicators, 1990
  6. Registered illnesses and fatalities by selected causes of death
  7. Life expectancy by sex, 1990
  8. Medical care, 1983–1988
  9. Abortion rates

X. **Trade**
  1. Exports and imports, by commodity group
  2. Main destinations of exports and main origins of imports, 1990

3. Principal trading partners
4. Index of import and export prices, terms of trade
5. Major imports
6. Major exports
7. Trade with western countries
8. Trade with the USSR, by commodity
9. Trade with the United States, by commodity

Note: Where possible and relevant, Hungary is compared to Belgium, because they are of comparable population. Also, data for the United States, France, USSR, and other East European countries is provided for comparison where relevant.

I. AGRICULTURE

TABLE 3.I.1 Land use, 1991

Arable Land	Permanent Crops	Forest and Woodland	Meadows and Pastures	Other	Irrigated Land
			(Percent)		
54	3	18	14	11	2

Source: U.S. Central Intelligence Agency, *The World Factbook*, 1991.

TABLE 3.I.2 Agriculture production index (Hungary and selected countries)

Country	1965	1970	1980	1986	1990
			(1980 = 100)		
Hungary	63	76	100	106	105
USSR	83	99	100	120	118
United States	79	81	100	107	112
France	77	81	100	105	105[a]

[a] 1989 figure.

Source: U.S. Central Intelligence Agency, *Handbook of Economic Statistics*, 1991.

TABLE 3.I.3 Selected indicators of agricultural development, 1970–1985

	1971–1975	1976–1980	1981–1985
Agricultural land use (thousand ha[a])			
Arable	5,157	5,055	5,025
Natural grassland	1,279	1,299	1,272
Other agricultural land	383	338	273
Crop structure[b]			
Grain	66	63	62
Maize	29	27	24
Oilseeds	4	6	9
Fodder roots, silage maize	6	7	7
Cultivated grassland	14	14	12
Beet	2	2	2
Potatoes, vegetables	6	6	5
Other	2	2	3

[a] ha: hectare = 10,000 m^2 (2.471 acres).
[b] Percent of sown area.

(continued)

TABLE 3.1.3 *(continued)*

	1971–1975	1976–1980	1981–1985
Total output[c] 1981 prices			
Gross[d]	3.1	2.9	2.1
Net[d]	−0.4	0.3	2.0
Arable output[c]			
Total (gross) 1981 prices	2.6	2.1	1.8
Grain	6.5	2.1	2.7
Oilseeds	10.9	14.1	11.9
Coarse fodder	−1.1	3.0	0.9
Livestock output[c]			
Total (gross) 1981 prices	3.9	3.9	2.4
Meat	5.6	2.6	3.3
Milk	0.3	5.3	3.8
Eggs	4.9	4.9	−0.6
Consumption per capita (kg)			
Cereals	121	118	112
Meat (including fat)	64	70	75
Milk (excluding butter)	117	149	179
Eggs (number)	264	316	318
Potatoes	68	62	58
Vegetables	85	84	77

[c]Annualized percentage changes between five-year periods.
[d]Gross output is total yield before harvest. Net output reflects losses following processing.
Source: UN, *Economic Survey of Europe in 1987–1988.*

TABLE 3.1.4 Total grain production[a] (Hungary and selected countries)

	(Million Metric Tons)				
	1960	1970	1980	1985	1990
Hungary	6.90	7.62	14.01	14.54	12.48
USSR[b]	125.49	186.80	189.09	191.67	238.00
United States	181.26	186.72	269.68	347.01	312.14
France	23.02	31.29	47.36	55.07	55.38

[a]Data are for the following products, where they are produced: barley, corn, oats, rice, rye, sorghum, and wheat.
[b]Includes miscellaneous grains and legumes. For comparative purposes, an average discount of 11 percent should be applied, because USSR totals include excess moisture, unripe and damaged kernels, weed seeds, and other trash.
Source: U.S. Central Intelligence Agency, *Handbook of Economic Statistics,* 1990, 1991.

TABLE 3.1.5 Principal crops

	(Thousand Metric Tons)		
	1985	1986	1989
Maize	6,818	7,261	6,996
Wheat	6,578	5,793	6,540
Sugar beet	4,073	3,760	5,301
Potatoes	1,378	1,264	1,332
Apples	954	1,253	959
Sunflower seed	676	862	699
Barley	1,046	857	1,340
Grapes	466	691	580
Legumes	216	241	433
Rye	166	172	267

Source: The Europa World Year Book, 1989, 1990, 1991.

TABLE 3.I.6   Yields for selected crops (Hungary and selected countries)

| | | (ql/ha^a) | | |
		1985	1987	1989
Wheat	Hungary	48.3	43.7	52.4
	Bulgaria	28.7	38.2	47.7
	Czechoslovakia	49.3	50.8	51.2
	Poland	34.3	37.2	38.5
	Romania	23.4	28.0	35.8^b
	Yugoslavia	36.0	36.0	42.0^b
	Soviet Union	15.5	17.8	19.4
Barley	Hungary	37.3	38.2	46.8
	Bulgaria	30.7	37.0	43.6
	Czechoslovakia	44.3	42.3	47.2
	Poland	32.9	33.7	33.3
	Romania	25.9	36.0	44.8
	Yugoslavia	27.0	24.0	28.0^b
	Soviet Union	16.0	19.1	17.5
Maize	Hungary	62.9	61.3	62.2
	Bulgaria	30.7	37.2	40.0
	Czechoslovakia	54.4	56.4	52.7
	Poland	43.0	46.0	47.8
	Romania	38.5	27.0	24.7
	Yugoslavia	41.0	40.0	34.0^b
	Soviet Union	32.1	32.4	37.1
Rye	Hungary	19.3	19.5	27.3
	Bulgaria	14.9	16.6	20.4
	Czechoslovakia	34.0	34.9	40.5
	Poland	24.7	25.8	27.3
	Romania	15.0	14.9	16.2^b
	Yugoslavia	17.0	17.0	19.0^b
	Soviet Union	16.5	18.6	18.6
Oats	Hungary	29.6	23.9	32.5
	Bulgaria	13.9	14.8	27.0
	Czechoslovakia	37.4	37.3	32.3
	Poland	27.0	28.4	27.2
	Romania	12.8	15.7	15.9
	Yugoslavia	N/A	N/A	N/A
	Soviet Union	16.3	15.7	15.7
Potatoes	Hungary	196	160	186
	Bulgaria	109	86	137
	Czechoslovakia	184	171	186
	Poland	174	187	185
	Romania	204	129	124
	Yugoslavia	88	81	70^b
	Soviet Union	113	121	120
Sugar beets	Hungary	379	363	440
	Bulgaria	168	188	246
	Czechoslovakia	377	355	352
	Poland	336	332	340
	Romania	223	201	265
	Yugoslavia	418	380	349^b
	Soviet Union	241	266	291

^{a}ql: quintal = 100 kg (220.46 lbs)
^{b}1988 data.

Source: EUROSTAT, *Central and Eastern Europe 1991,* 1991; *Comecon Data 1989,* 1990.

TABLE 3.1.7 Livestock (Hungary and selected countries)

		(Thousand)		
		1980	1985	1989
Horses	Hungary	120	98	76[a]
	Bulgaria	120	120	119
	Czechoslovakia	45	46	42
	Poland	1,780	1,324	992[a]
	Romania	555	672	663
	Yugoslavia	N/A	N/A	N/A
	Soviet Union	5,563	5,782	5,920
Cattle	Hungary	1,918	1,766	1,698
	Bulgaria	1,843	1,735	1,600
	Czechoslovakia	5,002	5,066	5,129
	Poland	11,337	11,774	10,277
	Romania	6,485	6,692	6,291
	Yugoslavia	5,474	5,034	4,759[a]
	Soviet Union	115,057	120,888	118,429
Dairy cows	Hungary	765	688	646
	Bulgaria	723	682	633
	Czechoslovakia	1,902	1,860	1,795
	Poland	5,666	5,331	4,964
	Romania	2,670	2,901	2,468
	Yugoslavia	3,086	2,915	2,858[a]
	Soviet Union	43,389	42,863	41,716
Pigs	Hungary	8,330	8,280	7,661
	Bulgaria	3,808	3,912	4,353
	Czechoslovakia	7,894	6,651	7,498
	Poland	18,734	19,170	18,686
	Romania	11,542	13,631	11,671
	Yugoslavia	7,867	7,821	7,396[a]
	Soviet Union	73,382	77,772	79,033
Sheep	Hungary	3,090	2,465	2,068
	Bulgaria	10,433	9,724	7,973
	Czechoslovakia	910	1,087	1,051
	Poland	3,490	4,720	4,196
	Romania	15,865	17,342	15,435
	Yugoslavia	7,384	7,693	7,564[a]
	Soviet Union	141,573	14,850	138,443
Goats	Hungary	15	16	18
	Bulgaria	467	460	433
	Czechoslovakia	57	53	50[a]
	Poland	10	10	10
	Romania	347	828	1,070[a]
	Yugoslavia	N/A	N/A	N/A
	Soviet Union	5,925	6,480	6,974
Hens (million)	Hungary	61.0	56.7	52.8
	Bulgaria	39.9	37.9	37.3
	Czechoslovakia	45.3	45.4	46.6
	Poland	76.1	66.2	55.6
	Romania	97.8	120.1	114.0
	Yugoslavia	N/A	N/A	N/A
	Soviet Union	967.3	1,109.9	1,151.0

[a] 1988 data.

Source: EUROSTAT, *Central and Eastern Europe 1991,* 1991; *Comecon Data 1989,* 1990.

TABLE 3.I.8 Slaughterings and production of selected animal products (Hungary and selected countries)

		Production of Selected Animal Products (Thousand Tons)				Slaughterings (Thousands)		
		1980	1985	1989		1985	1987	1989
Beef	Hungary	215	180	170	Cattle	525	471	435
	Bulgaria	167	163	159	and	704	651	601
	Czechoslovakia	468	467	460	calves	1,804	1,710	1,733
	Poland	866	900	789		4,290	4,049	3,425
	Romania	285	240	230[a]		1,772	1,570	1,510
	Yugoslavia	344	352	301[a]		N/A	N/A	N/A
	Soviet Union	7,367	8,278	8,780		36,659	41,800	43,300
Pork	Hungary	1,100	1,113	1,112	Pigs	11,301	11,589	11,830
	Bulgaria	390	434	482		4,582	5,086	5,364
	Czechoslovakia	853	891	971		8,180	8,495	9,124
	Poland	1,526	1,773	1,880		16,169	19,082	19,210
	Romania	975	900	840		12,500	11,539	11,218
	Yugoslavia	461	526	546[a]		N/A	N/A	N/A
	Soviet Union	5,835	6,299	6,737		72,248	77,000	78,000
Mutton	Hungary	23	18	21	Sheep	429	261	285
and	Bulgaria	126	116	112	and	5,705	5,907	5,481a
goatmeat	Czechoslovakia	12	13	12	lamb	1,380	1,457	1,500[a]
	Poland	39	47	43		1,347	1,654	1,580[a]
	Romania	81	70	67[a]		4,412	3,880	4,700[b]
	Yugoslavia	59	63	70[a]		N/A	N/A	N/A
	Soviet Union	827	905	993		52,646	56,579	57,600[b]
Poultry	Hungary	405	469	445	Goats	50	54	53[a]
	Bulgaria	158	169	188		385	413	404[a]
	Czechoslovakia	172	194	233		1,700	1,875	1,562[a]
	Poland	290	345	381		23	15	15
	Romania	475	425	390		468	508	547
	Yugoslavia	277	299	329[a]	N/A	N/A	N/A	N/A
	Soviet Union	2,811	3,116	3,357		N/A	N/A	N/A
Milk	Hungary	2,729	2,833	2,942				
	Bulgaria	2,357	2,590	2,512				
	Czechoslovakia	6,942	6,982	7,150				
	Poland	16,446	15,543	16,429				
	Romania	5,411	5,165	4,667				
	Yugoslavia	4,352	4,682	4,638[a]				
	Soviet Union	98,608	103,743	108,529				

[a] 1988 data.
[b] Including goats.

Source: EUROSTAT, *Central and Eastern Europe 1991*, 1991; *Comecon Data 1989*, 1990.

TABLE 3.I.9 Agricultural labor force and tractors, 1988 (Hungary and selected countries)

	Percent of Labor Force in Agriculture	Population per km^2 of Arable Land	Output per Worker in $	Tractors per 10 km^2
Hungary	12.7	210	6,768[a]	8.2
USSR	14.2	125	3,830	45.3
United States	2.5	131	33,519	10.8
OECD average	8.1	809	23,334	18.2

[a] Reflects Hungary's private plot agriculture. They were the largest such plots in the former East Bloc.

Source: The Economist, *Book of Vital World Statistics*, 1990.

TABLE 3.I.10 Agricultural output, 1988
(Hungary and selected countries)

| | (Thousand Tons) | | | |
	Cereals	Meat	Vegetables	Fruit
Hungary	14,635	1,607	2,041	1,859
OECD average[a]	12,362	1,830	3,685	3,272
East Bloc average[b]	19,125	2,024	3,523	2,582

[a] Excluding the United States.
[b] Excluding Albania.
Source: The Economist, *Book of Vital World Statistics,* 1990.

TABLE 3.I.11 Growth per capita in agriculture and food, 1977–1988 (Hungary and selected countries)

| | (Percent Growth) | |
	Agriculture	Food
Hungary	0.9	0.9
USSR	0.4	0.5
United States	1.4	1.4
France	1.3	1.3

Source: The Economist, *Book of Vital World Statistics,* 1990.

II. COMMUNICATIONS AND TRANSPORT

TABLE 3.II.1 General Facts, 1990

1. Communications
  Telecommunications
    Stations — 13 AM, 11 FM, 21 TV
    Radios (1988) — 5,500,000 (1 per 3.7 persons)
    Televisions (1988) — 3,500,000 (1 per 3.6 persons)
    Telephones (1988) — 1,609,465 (1 per 6.6 persons)

2. Transport
  Railroads
    7,765 km total, of which
    7,508 km 1.435-meter standard gauge
    222 km narrow gauge
    35 km broad gauge
    1,147 km double track
    2,161 km electrified, government-owned (1988)

  Highways
    130,014 km total, of which
    29,715 km national highway system (1988)

  Inland Waterways
    1,622 km (1988)

  Pipelines
    1,204 km crude oil
    630 km refined products
    3,895 km natural gas (1986)

  Airports
    90 total, including
    20 with permanent-surface runways
    2 with runways over 3,659 m
    10 with runways 2,440–3,659 m
    15 with runways 1,220–2,439 m

Source: U.S. Central Intelligence Agency, *The World Factbook,* 1991; *The Europa World Yearbook,* 1990.

TABLE 3.II.2 Radio and television receivers (Hungary and selected countries)

| | (per Thousand Inhabitants) | | | | |
	1970	1975	1980	1983	1986–88
Hungary					
Radios	N/A	N/A	499	540	590
TVs	N/A	N/A	N/A	371	402
USSR					
Radios	390	481	490	514	686
TVs	143	217	305	308	314
United States					
Radios	1,415	1,857	1,989	2,043	2,120
TVs	413	560	684	790	811
France					
Radios	315	376	743	860	995
TVs	216	269	354	375	333[a]

[a] 1987 data.

Source: UN, *Statistical Yearbook,* 1988; UN, *Human Development Report 1991,* 1991.

TABLE 3.II.3 Percentage of householders owning various consumer durables, 1986–1988[a] (Hungary and selected countries)

| | (Percent) | | | |
	Televisions	Radios	Refrigerators	Vacuum Cleaners
Hungary	21	40	90	85
USSR	45	96	N/A	N/A
United States	98	99	100	N/A
France	98	98	97	88

[a] Means data for each country may refer to 1986, 1987, or 1988.

Source: The Economist, *Book of Vital World Statistics,* 1990

TABLE 3.II.4 Daily newspapers (Hungary and selected countries)

Country	1970	1975	1979	1986
Hungary	27	27	27	29
USSR[a]	639	691	N/A	723[b]
United States	1,763	1,775	1,787	1,657
France[c]	106	92	90	92

[a] Data include nondaily newspapers.
[b] 1984 data.
[c] Data shown for 1975 and 1979 refer to 1976 and 1978 respectively.

Source: UNESCO, *Statistical Yearbook,* 1989.

TABLE 3.II.5 Transport traffic

	1980	1987	1989
Road traffic			
Passengers (million)	2,413	2,974	2,828
Freight (million metric tons)	232	223	203
Passenger-km	21.9	23.3	22.0
Ton-km (million)	6,012	6,892	7,623
Railway traffic			
Passengers (million)	389	333	323
Freight (million metric tons)	130	115	105
Passenger-km (billion)	14.7	12.3	12.7
Ton-km (million)	24.4	21.3	19.8
Inland-waterway traffic[a]			
Passengers (million)	4.0	4.3	3.6
Freight (million metric tons)	3.5	3.8	3.7
Passenger-km (million)	76.3	78.5	67.2
Ton-km (million)	1,875	2,046	2,139
Sea traffic			
Passengers (million)	N/A	N/A	N/A
Freight (million metric tons)	0.8	1.0	1.6
Passenger-km (million)	N/A	N/A	N/A
Ton-km (million)	6	8	13
Air traffic			
Passengers (thousand)	922	1,320	1,472
Freight (thousand metric tons)	14.4	12.0	8.3
Passenger-km (million)	1,076	1,286	1,577
Ton-km (million)	28.3	15.9	12.2

[a]On domsetically registered ships.

Source: EUROSTAT, *Central and Eastern Europe 1991,* 1991.

TABLE 3.II.6 Railroad freight (Hungary and selected countries)

Country	1960	1970	1985	1989
Hungary				
Billion metric ton-km	13.3	19.8	22.3	19.8
Million metric tons carried	96.0	117.4	117.4	104.5
Hungary as a percent of Eastern Europe[a]				
Metric ton-km	7.1%	6.9%	6.0%[b]	N/A
Metric tons carried	10.3%	9.5%	7.6%[b]	N/A
USSR				
Billion metric ton-km	1,504.3	2,494.7	3,718.4	3,924.8[c]
Million metric ton carried	1,884.9	2,896.0	3,951.0	4,000.0
United States				
Billion metric carried	868.5	1,141.0	1,288.3	1,473.9
Million metric ton carried	1,180.5	1,426.3	1,567.0	1,792.0
France				
Billion metric ton-km	56.9	70.4	58.5	52.7
Million metric ton carried	227.0	260.0	193.0	174.0

[a]Eastern Europe includes Bulgaria, Czechoslovakia, East Germany, Hungary, Poland, and Romania.

[b]Latest available data.

[c]1988 data.

Source: U.S. Central Intelligence Agency, *Handbook of Economic Statistics,* 1989, 1990.

TABLE 3.II.7 Air cargo, 1986–88[a] (Hungary and selected countries)

Country	(Freight in km Tons[b])
Hungary	6
Belgium	651
USSR	2,721
United States	13,829
OECD average	1,622

[a] Means data for each country may refer to 1986, 1987, or 1988.
[b] Of national origin.

Source: The Economist, *Book of Vital World Statistics,* 1990.

TABLE 3.II.8 Road traffic

| | (Number of Vehicles) | | |
	1985	1986	1989
Passenger cars	1,435,937	1,538,877	1,732,385
Buses and coaches	24,854	25,920	23,793
Goods vehicles	167,136	179,272	208,306
Motorcycles and scooters	395,622	399,447	412,390[a]

[a] 1988

Source: The Europa World Yearbook, 1990, 1991.

TABLE 3.II.9 Ownership of vehicles and automobiles, 1985–1988[a] (Hungary and selected countries)

Country	Thousand Vehicles[b]	Thousand Automobiles
Hungary	1,968.8	1,789.6
Belgium	3,936.6	3,573.3
United States	183,468.0	140,655.0
USSR	21,500.0	12,500.0

[a] Means data for each country may refer to 1985, 1986, 1987, or 1988.
[b] Vehicles include passenger cars, trucks, and buses.

Source: The Economist, *Book of Vital World Statistics,* 1990.

TABLE 3.II.10 Number of persons per automobile 1985–1988[a] (Hungary and selected countries)

Country	
Hungary	6.4
Belgium	2.8
OECD	2.6
USSR	22.8
United States	1.8

[a] Means data for each country may refer to 1985, 1986, 1987, or 1988.

Source: The Economist, *Book of Vital World Statistics,* 1990.

TABLE 3.II.11 Post, telephones, and telex lines 1986–1988[a] (Hungary and selected countries)

Country	Post Offices	Letters per Person	Persons per Telephone Line	Persons per Telex Line
Hungary	3,222	149.02	16.2	887
Belgium	1,838	262.73	2.2	359
USSR	98,445	217.81	10.3	162,875
United States	40,117	645.48	1.3	N/A

[a] Means data for each country may refer to 1986, 1987, or 1988.

Source: The Economist, *Book of Vital World Statistics,* 1990.

III. ECONOMY

TABLE 3.III.1 Economic profile, 1990 (Hungary and selected countries)

	Hungary	USSR	United States	France
Gross national product				
Billion 1990 U.S. $[a]	64.2	2,660.0	5,465.2[b]	873.6[b]
Percent real growth	−5.7	−2.4 to −5.0	1.0	2.8
Per capita (1990 U.S. $)	6,100	9,140	21,830	15,490
Industrial production[c]	−7.9	−2.8	1.0	1.1
Trade (billion U.S. $)				
Exports, f.o.b.	20.2[d]	109.3[d]	393.9	216.6
Imports, c.i.f.	18.6[d]	114.7[d]	516.2	234.4
Trade balance	1.6[d]	−5.4[d]	−122.3	−17.8
Living standard indicators				
Automobile registrations (per thousand persons)	157[e]	46[e]	571[f]	395[e]
Energy consumption[d,e]	22[d]	35[d]	57[d]	27[d]

[a] At U.S. purchasing power equivalents.
[b] Gross domestic product.
[c] Percent growth.
[d] 1989 data.
[e] 1987 data.
[f] 1988 data.
[e] Barrels oil equivalent per capita.

Source: U.S. Central Intelligence Agency, *Handbook of Economic Statistics,* 1991.

TABLE 3.III.2 Estimated real gross national product (Hungary and selected countries)

	(Billion 1990 U.S. $)				
Country	1970	1980	1985	1988	1990
Hungary	46.4	60.3	62.3	64.6	62.6
USSR	1,726.9	2,257.0	2,440.9	2,663.7[a]	1,465.9[a]
United States	2,985.8	3,916.0	4,513.3	5,198.4	5,465.6
France	491.7	680.6	733.9	818.5	819.6

[a] The 1989 GNP figure for the USSR is based on CIA statistics, while the 1990 GNP figure is based on PlanEcon statistics. The great disparity between the Soviet GNP in 1990 and 1988 is due to extremely high estimates by the CIA during the 1980s.

Source: U.S. Central Intelligence Agency, *Handbook of Economic Statistics,* 1989, 1990; and "PlanEcon Report," vol. 6, no. 52, December 28, 1990.

TABLE 3.III.3 Real Gross National Product growth (Hungary and selected countries)

Country	Percent Average Annual Rate of Growth		Percent		
	1971–1980	1981–1985	1985	1989	1990
GNP growth					
Hungary	2.6	0.5	−2.5	−2.2	−5.7
USSR[a]	2.4	1.8	0.9	1.5	−2.4 to −5.0
United States[b]	2.8	3.0	3.8	2.5	1.0
France[b]	3.6	1.5	1.9	3.6	2.8
GNP per capita growth					
Hungary	2.5	0.6	−2.3	−2.3	−5.6
USSR	1.5	0.8	−0.1	0.7	−2.9 to −5.5
United States	1.7	1.8	2.8	1.5	0.3
France[b]	3.0	1.0	1.5	3.1	2.4

[a] At factor cost.
[b] GDP growth.
Source: U.S. Central Intelligence Agency, *Handbook of Economic Statistics,* 1990, 1991.

TABLE 3.III.4 GNP per capita in dollars[a], 1990 (Hungary and selected countries)

Country	Commerical	(U.S. $) Purchasing Parity	Free Market
Hungary	2,943	5,320	2,661
USSR	2,560	5,060	1,299
United States	21,732	21,732	21,732
West Germany	24,210	16,310	24,210

[a] Based on exchange rate, purchasing power parity, and free market rate.
Source: "PlanEcon Report," vol. 6, no. 52, December 28, 1990.

TABLE 3.III.5 GDP per capita as a percentage of OECD average, 1988 (Hungary and selected countries)

Country	(Percent of OECD)
Hungary	15.4
Belgium	90.4
USSR	12.1
United States	116.3

Source: The Economist, *Book of Vital Statistics,* 1990.

TABLE 3.III.6 Exchange rate

	1987	1988	(Forints per $; Period Averages) 1989	1990	Dec. 1990
Commercial	46.97	50.41	59.07	63.21	60.95

Source: U.S. Central Intelligence Agency, *The World Factbook, 1991.*

TABLE 3.III.7 Savings

(Million FHO)			
1984	1986	1988	1989
219,401	274,900	311,100	333,000

Source: Comecon Data 1990, 1991.

TABLE 3.III.8   Money in circulation

(Million FHO)			
1980	**1985**	**1988**	**1989**
79,800	116,700	153,700	164,400

Source: Comecon Data 1990, 1991.

TABLE 3.III.9   Growth of GNP by producing and consuming sectors

	(Percent Average Annual Rate of Growth)		
	1984	**1987**	**1989**
GNP	2.6	0.7	−1.3
Producing sector			
Industry	2.8	3.2	−3.4
Agriculture and forestry	6.3	−6.0	−2.0
Construction	−3.4	3.9	3.1
Transportation and communications	0.9	2.4	−1.4
Trade	−0.1	5.7	−1.3
Services	1.4	3.3	9.4
Other	1.5	1.5	1.2
Consuming sector			
Personal consumption	0.3	3.0	−4.3[a]
Government	1.7	2.3	0.9[a]
Gross investment	−2.9	−3.8	7.7[a]
Residual	0.9	−7.4	0.3[a]

[a] 1988 data.

Source: U.S. Central Intelligence Agency, "Eastern Europe: Long Road Ahead to Economic Well-Being," May, 1990.

TABLE 3.III.10   Growth of GNP inputs and productivity

	(Percent Average Annual Rate of Growth)			
	1980	**1985**	**1987**	**1989**
GNP	1.0	−2.5	0.8	−1.3
Combined inputs	1.5	0.9	1.2	1.8
Capital stock	5.8	3.6	3.8	5.6
Labor	−0.6	−0.5	−0.1	−0.1
Combined productivity	−0.5	−3.3	−0.4	−2.7
Capital productivity	−4.5	−5.9	−2.9	−6.2
Labor productivity	1.7	−2.0	0.9	−0.9

Source: U.S. Central Intelligence, "Eastern Europe: Long Road Ahead to Economic Well-Being," May, 1990.

TABLE 3.III.11   Consumer spending on various items as a percentage of personal income, 1989 (Hungary and selected countries)

	Total per Head $	Percent Food/ Drink	Percent Clothing	Percent Energy	Percent Household Goods	Percent Health	Percent Transport
Hungary	1,616	40.5	8.0	6.3	7.0	6.0	9.0
USSR	2,820	43.2	19.0	7.0	8.0	2.7	2.9
United States	12,233	13.3	6.5	19.5	5.7	14.7	14.8
France	9,635	20.0	7.0	18.8	8.3	8.8	16.7

Source: The Economist, *Book of Vital World Statistics,* 1990.

TABLE 3.III.12 Cost-of-living price index[a]

Index Group	(1980 = 100)		
	1985	1987	1989
Total	139	159	215
Foods	136	151	206
Beverages and tobacco	132	158	201
Clothing	146	176	249
Heating, domestic energy	146	161	202
Consumer durables	124	134	171
Other industrial goods	144	161	229
Services	148	176	241

[a] Annual average.

Source: EUROSTAT, *Central and Eastern Europe 1991*, 1991.

IV. EDUCATION

TABLE 3.IV.1 Schools, students, and teachers

	1980–1981	1987–1988	1989–1990
Schools			
General schools[a]	3,893	3,815	3,820
Vocational schools[b]	268	284	299
Technical colleges[c]	271	333	382
Universities	57	54	57
Students (thousand)			
General-school pupils[d]	1,287	1,403	1,319
Vocational-school pupils	154	177	202
Technical-college students[e]	209	196	213
Day pupils	114	134	157
Pupils per 10,000 population	195	185	202
Technical-college graduates	43.1	41.1	41.0
University undergraduates	101	99	101
Day students	64	67	72
Pupils per 10,000 population	95	93	95
University graduates	26.9	24.1	24.8
Teachers (thousand)			
General-school teachers[f]	82	100	100
Technical-college lecturers[g]	8.8	10.5	11.8
University academic staff	13.9	15.3	16.3

[a] Includes general lower secondary schools and combined lower/upper secondary schools. General schools include the compulsory primary/lower secondary school (7–10 years' schooling) and an upper secondary stage of 2–4 years.

[b] Pupils here receive a job-oriented education.

[c] Includes distance-learning institutions for teaching certificates; technical colleges to train technicians, technical colleges to improve the qualifications of workers, and similar for craftsmen.

[d] Includes both day and evening school pupils and also those on correspondence courses.

[e] Includes pupils involved in distance learning to gain teaching certificates, at technical colleges for technicians, and at technical colleges to improve the qualifications of workers and craftsmen.

[f] Includes general schools and combined lower/upper secondary schools; teaching staff includes those members of staff with secondary or higher education who work as teachers, instructors, and technical instructors in the school workshops.

[g] The academic staff includes those members of staff with secondary or higher education, as well as staff seconded from industry (engineers, technicians, craftsmen, etc.).

Source: EUROSTAT, *Central and Eastern Europe 1991*, 1991.

TABLE 3.IV.2 Public expenditures on education

Year	Forints	As Percent of GNP	Percent of Total Government Expenditures
1975	19,325,492,000	4.1	4.2
1980	33,099,379,000	4.7	5.2
1985	54,061,000,000	5.4	6.4
1986	59,469,000,000	5.7	6.4
1988	73,035,000,000	5.4	6.4

Source: UNESCO, *Statistical Yearbook,* 1989.

TABLE 3.IV.3 Expenditures and pupils per teacher, 1989 (Hungary and selected countries)

Country	Percent of GNP	Pupils per Teacher Primary/Secondary
Hungary	5.6	14/16
USSR	7.3	17/N/A
United States	6.7	21/13
France	5.7	19/17

Source: The Economist, *Book of Vital World Statistics,* 1990.

TABLE 3.IV.4 Distribution of teachers and pupils by educational level, 1987

Educational Level	Teachers	Percent Female	Pupils	Percent Female
Preschool	33,896	100	398,325	48
First level	90,925	83	1,277,257	49
Second level	N/A	N/A	426,932	49
General	8,646	65	105,976	66
Teacher training	N/A	N/A	5,045	100
Vocational[a]	N/A	N/A	315,911	43
Third level[b]	15,302	31	99,025	53
Total	N/A		2,201,539	

[a] Data include full-time apprenticeship training.
[b] Includes evening and correspondence courses.

Source: UNESCO, *Statistical Yearbook,* 1989.

TABLE 3.IV.5 Mean years of schooling[a], 1980 (Hungary and selected countries)

Country	Total
Hungary	8.6
USSR	7.6
United States	12.2
France	9.4

[a] For adults over 25 years old.

Source: UN, *Human Development Report 1991,* 1991.

TABLE 3.IV.6 School enrollment ratios[a]

Year	First Level (Ages 6–13)	Second Level (Ages 14–17)	Third Level (Ages 20–24)
1975	99	63	11.7
1980	96	69	12.9
1987	97	70	15.2

[a]Percent total enrollment of all ages divided by the population of the specific age groups which correspond to the age groups of primary and secondary schooling.

Source: UNESCO, *Statistical Yearbook,* 1989.

TABLE 3.IV.7 School enrollment, 1989
(Hungary and selected countries)

	(Percent)					
	Primary			Secondary		
	Total	Male	Female	Total	Male	Female
Hungary	97	97	97	70	69	70
USSR	106	N/A	N/A	98	N/A	N/A
United States	100	101	100	98	99	99
France	113	114	113	92	89	96

Source: The Economist, *Book of Vital World Statistics,* 1990.

TABLE 3.IV.8 Books, newspapers, and library book loans, 1989 (Hungary and selected countries)

	Books Published per Year	Newspaper Circulation (Thousand)	Library Books Loans per Year (Thousand)	Volumes Stock (Thousand)
Hungary	9,111	2,778	48,766.0	49,704
Belgium	8,327	2,186	N/A	24,100
USSR	83,011	12,982	2,634.3[a]	1,523,071
United States	48,793	62,502	197,328.1	523,493

[a]Soviet Library regulations rarely allow the loaning of books, thus the low figure.

Source: The Economist, *Book of Vital World Statistics,* 1990.

V. ENERGY AND RESOURCES

TABLE 3.V.1 History of primary energy production (Hungary and selected countries)

Energy Type	Country	(Thousand Barrels per Day of Oil Equivalent)	
		1970	1980
Coal	Hungary	182	138
	USSR	6,080	6,370
	United States	7,359	9,785
	France	523	284
Crude oil	Hungary	39	41
	USSR	7,060	12,030
	United States	11,380	10,170
	France	68	51

(continued)

TABLE 3.V.1 *(continued)*

Energy Type	Country	(Thousand Barrels per Day of Oil Equivalent) 1970	1980
Natural gas	Hungary	56	99
	USSR	3,270	7,170
	United States	10,686	9,838
	France	118	129
Hydro/nuclear	Hungary	1	1
	USSR	660	1,170
	United States	1,394	2,774
	France	317	665

Source: U.S. Central Intelligence Agency, *Handbook of Economic Statistics,* 1989, 1990.

TABLE 3.V.2 Complete energy use

	Year	(Thousand Metric Tons) Production	Consumption[a]	Exports	Imports	Soviet Portion of Imports (%)[b,c]
Crude oil[d]	1985	2,012	8,708	557	7,253	6,910 (95)
	1988	1,947	8,917	0	6,970	6,920 (90)
	1990	1,978	7,948	0	5,970	4,819 (81)
Refined oil	1985	9,348	9,718	1,524	1,894	1,460 (77)
products	1988	9,029	9,074	1,486	1,531	1,434 (94)
	1990	8,156	8,564	1,190	1,598	1,531 (96)
Motor and	1985	1,162	1,303	210	351	N/A
aviation	1988	1,345	1,365	323	343	N/A
gas	1990	1,274	1,616	145	487	N/A
Diesel oil	1985	3,512	3,616	660	764	N/A
	1988	3,537	3,451	845	759	N/A
	1990	2,793	2,859	710	776	N/A
Fuel oil	1985	2,339	2,891	0	552	N/A
	1988	1,693	1,914	0	221	N/A
	1990	1,856	1,946	0	90	N/A
Other refined	1985	2,335	1,908	654	227	N/A
products	1988	2,454	2,344	381	208	N/A
	1990	2,233	2,143	355	245	N/A
Natural gas	1985	7,456	11,444	21	4,009	4,008 (100)
(million cm^3)	1988	6,272	11,620	23	5,371	5,308 (99)
	1990	4,885	11,209	23	6,347	6,316 (100)
Hard coal	1985	2,639	4,920	483	2,764	692 (25)
(including	1988	2,355	4,436	181	2,362	1,234 (52)
anthracite)	1990	1,734	3,126	150	1,542	1,403 (91)
Brown coal	1985	21,403	21,785	294	676	0
(including	1988	18,620	19,523	15	918	0
lignite)	1990	16,000	16,712	15	727	0
Coke	1985	607	1,793	0	1,186	480 (40)
	1988	996	1,765	0	769	477 (62)
	1990	1,027	1,565	0	538	333 (62)
Electricity	1985	26,725	37,533	1,924	12,732	10,500 (82)
(million kWh)	1988	29,183	40,475	2,322	13,614	11,050 (81)
	1990	28,220	39,880	2,000	13,660	11,598 (85)

[a] Hungary is the 33rd largest energy consumer in the world.
[b] Soviet portion of imports as a percent.
[c] To the nearest 1%.
[d] 1 metric ton = 8.03 barrels of oil.

Source: "PlanEcon Report," vol. 7, March 6, 1991.

TABLE 3.V.3 Electricity production[a] (Hungary and selected countries)

Country	(Billion Kilowatt-hours)			
	1970	1980	1985	1989
Hungary	14.54	23.87	26.73	29.90
USSR	740.93	1,293.88	1,544.10	1,722.00
United States[b]	1,742.73	2,437.82	2,634.65	2,970.21
France	146.97	243.29	325.73	378.00

[a]Data are for total (gross) production at generating centers and therefore include transmission losses and station use.
[b]Beginning in 1980, data are for public utilities only.
Source: U.S. Central Intelligence Agency, *Handbook of Economic Statistics,* 1989, 1990.

TABLE 3.V.4 Installed electricity-generating capacity[a] (Hungary and selected countries)

Country	(Million Kilowatts)			
	1970	1980	1985	1989
Hungary	2.61	5.25	6.35	7.09[c]
USSR	166.15	266.71	315.00	346.00
United States	360.33	630.94	656.12[b]	683.99
France	36.22	63.66	86.56	100.62[c]

[a]All plants for both public and industrial use.
[b]Data are for public utilities only.
[c]1988 data.
Source: U.S. Central Intelligence Agency, *Handbook of Economic Statistics,* 1989, 1990.

TABLE 3.V.5 Commercial energy use by sector [a], 1985 (Hungary and selected countries)

	(Percentage of Commercial Energy Used)				
	Industry	Transport	Agriculture	Commercial and Residential	Other[b]
Hungary	31	12	6	30	21
USSR	60	13	0	27	0
United States	31	35	1	30	4
France	33	26	2	35	3

[a]Includes all solid, liquid, and gaseous fuels, as well as primary and secondary electricity.
[b]Other includes nonenergy uses, military uses, and nonspecified uses.
Source: From *World Resources 1988–1989.* Copyright © 1988 by the World Resources Institute and the International Institute for Environment and Development in collaboration with the United Nations Environment Programme. Reprinted by permission of Basic Books, a division of Harper-Collins Publishers Inc.

TABLE 3.V.6 Proven reserves of crude oil, natural gas, and coal, 1989 (Hungary and selected countries)

Country	Crude Oil (Billion Barrels)	Natural Gas (Trillion Cubic Feet)	Coal (Million Metric Tons)
Hungary	0.018	0.47	44,633
USSR	50–80	1,450	182,000
United States	26	165	205,000
UK	4	21	4,200
France	0.03	0.18	1,070

Source: U.S. Central Intelligence Agency, *Handbook of Economic Statistics,* 1990; U.S. Department of Energy, Energy Information Administration, *International Energy Annual,* 1988; UN, *Energy Statistics Yearbook,* 1986.

TABLE 3.V.7 Mineral production

Mineral	1985	(Tons) 1987	1989
Alumina	798,000	857,000	881,505
Aluminum, primary	73,859	73,500	75,200
Bauxite (and aluminum)	2,814,791	3,101,000	2,644,000
Bentonite	59,853	102,000	105,432
Coal			
Bituminous	2,639,103	2,360,056	2,127,359
Lignite	7,387,123	7,223,032	5,882,957
Brown	14,016,288	13,261,262	12,019,527
Copper, smelter production of	33,400	34,415	36,832
Copper, production of refined	23,018	23,251	13,137
Ferro-alloys, electric furnace			
Ferro-silicon	10,578	9,342	10,224
Other ferro-alloys	2,000[d]	2,000[d]	1,000[d]
Silicon metal	2,000[d]	2,000[d]	2,000[d]
Gold, mine production of[a]	600[d]	600[d]	500[d]
Gypsum	20,000[d]	84,438	N/A
Iron ore	311,000	N/A	N/A
Iron, pig	2,095,152	2,107,000	1,954,000
Kaolin	35,523	38,468	28,612
Lead, mine production of	575	N/A	N/A
Manganese ore	62,294	69,964	84,247
Natural gas[b]	7,456	7,126	6,175
Perlite	94,460	112,410	108,678
Petroleum, crude	2,012,000	1,914,000	1,966,000
Silver[c]	500	N/A	N/A
Steel ingots and casting	3,646,000	3,621,000	3,317,000
Sulfur and pyrites			
Pyrites	2,000	1,000	N/A
Recovered	9,000	10,000	N/A
Talc	1,756	1,685	1,041
Zinc, mine production of	1,606	N/A	N/A

[a] Kilograms.
[b] Million m^3.
[c] Estimated average content.
[d] Estimated.

Source: British Geological Survey, *World Mineral Statistics,* 1984–1988; *World Mineral Production,* 1985–1989.

VI. GOVERNMENT AND DEFENSE FORCES

TABLE 3.VI.1 State budget

	1985	(Billion Forints) 1987	1988	1989
Revenue				
Payments made by enterprises (cooperatives) and agricultural cooperatives	407.5	469.5	423.6	443.2
Consumers' turnover tax	92.2	122.3	210.5	230.7
Payments made by the population	61.5	79.3	154.7	209.4
Payments made by organizations financed by state budget	51.0	63.7	80.9	138.8
Other receipts	20.6	25.9	28.5	41.6
Total revenue	632.8	760.6	898.2	1,063.7

(continued)

TABLE 3.VI.1 *(continued)*

	(Billion Forints)			
	1985	1987	1988	1989
Expenditure				
Investment	82.4	99.9	108.8	115.5
Industrial enterprises (cooperatives)				
and agricultural cooperatives	119.1	150.7	143.8	115.7
Supplement to consumers' prices	50.2	66.7	44.5	44.1
Budgetary institutions	204.9	242.7	304.4	386.5
Health and social welfare	35.0	42.2	55.1	74.7
Culture	62.9	73.5	93.0	127.6
Defense	37.6	45.4	59.0	62.0
Legal and security order	2.6	3.2	4.6	6.3
Administration	8.7	10.5	15.9	23.0
Economic tasks	48.9	54.5	64.3	71.2
Others	9.2	13.4	12.5	21.7
Social security	131.5	154.7	216.6	269.5
Others	58.5	80.3	91.1	181.1
Total expenditure	646.6	795.0	908.4	1,112.4

Source: The Europa World Year Book, 1989, 1990, 1991.

TABLE 3.VI.2 Hard-currency debt

	(Billion in U.S. $)			
	1980	1985	1988	1989
Gross debt, of which	9.1	11.8	18.0	20.7
Government	0.3	0.8	1.0	3.2
Commercial	8.8	9.8	15.6	15.7
Other	0.0	1.2	1.4	1.8
Reserves	N/A	3.1	1.4	1.0
Net debt	N/A	8.7	16.6	19.7
Debt service ratio[a]	N/A	58%	43%	34%

[a]Debt service ratio is calculated as the share of principal and interest payments to total hard currency earnings.

Source: U.S. Central Intelligence Agency, "Eastern Europe: Long Road To Economic Well-Being," May, 1990.

TABLE 3.VI.3 Armed Forces totals, 1991

Total armed forces	84,500	(45,900 conscripts)[a,b]
Branches		
Army	66,400	(36,000 conscripts)
Navy	None[c]	
Air Force	20,100	(9,500 conscripts)
Total reserves	210,000	
Army	192,000	
Navy	None	
Air Force	18,000	(to age 55)
Manpower	86,481	men reach the military age of 18 annually.
Expenditures	54.4	billion forints ($1.23 billion)[d]

[a]Hungary is reducing its active duty personnel by 30 percent. Active duty personnel will fall to approximately 70,000. Its tank divisions will be demobilized by 1992.

[b]Excludes interior forces. Border Guards 18,000 (13,000 conscripts).

[c]Small flotilla included in army totals.

[d]Budget based on 72.50 forints = $1.

Source: The International Institute for Strategic Studies, *The Military Balance 1991–1992,* 1991. Copyright IISS.

TABLE 3.VI.4 Components of defense force, 1987

Army
  Organization
        1 tank division
        5 motorized rifle divisions
        1 airborne battalion
        1 artillery brigade
        4 surface-to-air missile regiments
        1 surface-to-surface missile brigade
  Major equipment (1987)
    1,300 tanks
      100 light tanks
      750 reconnaissance armored fighting vehicles
    1,000 armored personnel carriers
      485 guns/howitzers
       50 multiple rocket launchers
       33 surface-to-surface missiles

Navy
  None

Air Force
  Organization
        3 fighter regiments
        1 transport regiment
        1 reconnaissance squadron
        1 helicopter regiment
  Major equipment (1985)
      130 fighter aircraft, including
          120 MiG-21
           10 MiG-23M
       15 Su-25 fighter/ground attack aircraft
       15 Su-22 reconnaissance aircraft
       26 transport aircraft
       95 helicopters
      120 surface-to-air missiles

Source: Reprinted with permission from *World Defense Forces,* 2nd Edition, published by ABC-CLIO, 1989.

TABLE 3.VI.5 Military expenditures

	1979	1980	1985	1987
Million forints	16,200	17,700	37,700	53,340
Constant price figures (million U.S. $)[a]	499	500	767	947
Military expenditures as a percent of GDP				
Hungary	2.4%	2.5%	3.6%	4.3%
USSR	12.9	13.0	12.5	N/A
United States	5.0	5.4	6.6	6.4
France	3.9	4.0	4.0	4.0

[a] 1986 exchange rates and prices.

Source: SIPRI Yearbook 1989: World Armaments and Disarmament, Stockholm International Peace Research Institute, 1989.

VII. INDUSTRY

TABLE 3.VII.1 Industrial production index[a] (Hungary and selected countries)

Country	1960	1970	1980	1986	1987	1989	1990[b]
				(1980 = 100)			
Hungary	44	79	100	109	110	106	97
USSR	38	68	100	113	116	118	115
United States	45	73	100	113	119	129	130
France	47	75	100	100	102	110	111

[a] Indexes for the noncommunist countries are value-added weighted indexes of industrial intermediate and final products. Industry includes manufacturing, mining, and, in most countries, public utilities. The indexes for the communist countries are estimates constructed by the U.S. Central Intelligence Agency, as nearly as possible on the same basis as the indexes for Western countries, and include manufacturing, mining, and public utilities.

[b] Preliminary.

[c] Index of gross values of output for individual commodities and branches are aggregated by 1982 value-added weights. This index is as comparable with the index of U.S. industrial production of the U.S. Federal Reserve Board as data will permit.

Source: U.S. Central Intelligence Agency, *Handbook of Economic Statistics,* 1991.

TABLE 3.VII.2 Industrial production index (official and adjusted)

	1960	1970	1980	1987	1988	1989[a]
			(1980 = 100)			
Official	32	62	100	116	114	110
Adjusted	44	79	100	111	110	106

[a] Preliminary.

Source: U.S. Central Intelligence Agency, *Handbook of Economic Statistics,* 1989, 1990.

TABLE 3.VII.3 Production of selected industrial items

	(Thousand Metric Tons)	
	1985	1988
Agricultural and forestry products		
Canned fruit	288	302[a]
Canned vegetables	370	386[a]
Margarine	29	29[a]
Refined sugar	483	421
Fuels, minerals, metals, and chemicals		
Pig iron	2,095	2,093
Crude steel	3,646	3,583
Rolled steel	2,863	2,793
Aluminum	74	74
Cement	3,678	3,873
Nitrogenous fertilizers	684	574
Phosphatic fertilizers	252	238
Electric power (million kWh)	26,735	29,183

[a] 1987 data.

(continued)

TABLE 3.VII.3 *(continued)*

	(Thousand Metric Tons)	
	1985	**1988**
Machinery and equipment		
Buses and trucks (number)	13,982	13,740[a]
Semiconductors (million units)	119	199[a]
Computers (small units)	2,735	12,592[a]
Manufactured consumer goods		
Cotton fabrics (thousand sq meters)	309,715	311,602
Leather footwear (thousand pairs)	45,169	35,683
Woolen cloth (thousand sq meters)	36,100	29,649
Television receivers (thousands)	407	433
Washing machines (thousand units)	263	239[a]

[a] 1987 data.

Source: Hungarian Statistical Yearbook, 1986; *The Europa World Year Book,* 1989, 1990; EIU, *Hungary, Country Profile,* 1988–89.

TABLE 3.VII.4   Industrial Waste Generation

Country	Year of Estimate	Total[a]	Per National Land area[b]
Industrial waste			
Hungary	1985	21,146	229.8
USSR	1985	306,258	13,8
United States	1985	613,000	66.9
France	1980	32,300	59.0
Hazardous and special waste			
Hungary	1985	7,081	77.0
USSR	1985	N/A	N/A
United States	1985	250,000	27.3
France	1980	2,000	3.7

[a] Thousand metric tons per year.
[b] Metric tons per km^2 per year.

Source: From *World Resources 1988–1989.* Copyright © 1988 by the World Resources Institute and the International Institute for Environment and Development in collaboration with the United Nations Environment Programme. Reprinted by permission of Basic Books, a division of Harper-Collins Publishers Inc.

TABLE 3.VII.5   Basic structure of industry

	(Percent Share)								
	Output			Employment			Fixed Assets		
	1975	**1980**	**1987**	**1975**	**1980**	**1987**	**1975**	**1980**	**1987**
Total heavy industry	67.8	68.6	69.6	58.6	59.1	60.6	75.4	74.1	77.2
Mining	9.2	8.1	6.9	7.2	7.1	7.7	9.0	8.1	10.8
Electric energy	5.1	5.7	6.0	2.2	2.2	2.9	15.2	14.7	19.9
Metallurgy	10.0	9.1	8.0	6.0	6.0	5.7	10.8	9.6	9.0
Engineering	24.0	23.6	25.9	31.6	32.0	32.3	17.6	18.5	17.0
Machinery	6.1	5.5	5.8	8.7	7.9	8.5	4.0	4.3	3.8
Vehicles	6.9	6.8	7.1	6.2	6.4	6.4	5.6	5.6	5.0
Electrical engineering	3.1	3.2	3.3	3.4	3.9	3.8	2.1	2.2	2.0
Telecommunications	2.7	3.3	4.7	5.6	6.2	6.5	2.6	2.9	3.0
Precision engineering	1.7	2.0	2.5	3.3	3.6	3.6	1.3	1.5	1.5
Metal products	3.4	2.7	2.4	4.4	3.7	3.5	2.0	1.7	1.6
Building materials	3.2	3.5	3.3	4.8	4.9	4.5	6.9	6.9	5.3
Chemicals	16.3	18.6	19.5	6.8	6.9	7.5	15.9	16.3	15.2
Light industry	14.4	13.7	12.9	26.4	25.3	22.7	12.2	12.0	9.9
Miscellaneous	1.0	1.0	.9	3.6	3.4	2.5	1.1	1.1	.6
Food	16.8	16.7	16.6	11.4	12.2	14.2	11.3	12.8	12.3

Source: Hungarian Statistical Yearbook; U.S. Department of State, "Hungarian Economic Reform: Status and Prospects," Sept. 1989.

TABLE 3.VII.6 Rank of industry, manufacturing, and service sector share, GDP,[a] 1990 (Hungary and selected countries)

	Rank
Hungary	(not in top 20)
Brunei	1
Angola	20
USSR	9

[a] All former East Bloc countries rank in the top 10 except Hungary. No OECD country is in the top 20. Additionally, no East Bloc state, nor the Soviet Union, is among the top 20 countries in terms of manufacturing share of GDP or services share of GDP. This chart indicates the significant role of extractive industries in Eastern Europe and the USSR.

Source: The Economist, *Book of Vital World Statistics,* 1990.

TABLE 3.VII.7 Emissions of air pollutants, 1988[a] (Hungary and selected countries)

	Nitrogen Oxides		Sulfur Dioxide		
	Emissions (Thousand Tons)	Emissions per Unit GNP (Grass)	Emissions (Thousand Tons)	Emissions per Unit GNP[c] (Grams)	Greenhouse Index[b]
Hungary[d]	259	4	1,218	17	1.8
USSR[e]	4,510	1	18,584	10	3.4
United States[f]	19,800	4	20,700	4	5.3
France	1,615	2	1,226	1	2.4

[a] Preliminary data.

[b] Carbon heating equivalents, metric tons per capita. 1988–1989 data.

[c] East European countries have a significantly higher emissions per unit GNP because of inefficient production. For example, on average, these countries use 50–100 percent more energy than the United States to produce a dollar of GDP, and 100–300 percent more than Japan.

[d] The very high pollution rates in Hungary have had deleterious consequences for the population. Health problems include a higher incidence of heart disease, cancer rates, congenital birth defects, and asthma, rising mortality rates, and shorter life spans. In addition, children living in highly polluted areas develop twice as many diseases in the upper respiratory system than do those living in areas with clean air. Finally, the National Institute of Public Health has discovered that 1 out of every 24 disablements and 1 out of every 17 deaths in Hungary is caused by air pollution.

[e] Stationary sources only. 1987 data.

[f] Sulfur data are for sulfur oxides.

Source: State of the World 1991, A Worldwatch Institute Report on Progress Toward a Sustainable Society, 1991; UN, *Human Development Report 1991,* 1991.

TABLE 3.VII.8 Environmental summary, 1991

	Hungary	Belgium	USSR	United States	France
Energy					
Energy production	1,111,111	1,111,111	1,111,111	1,111,111	1,111,111
Solids[a]	211	92	14,299	20,736	365
Liquids[a]	98	0	24,139	17,297	145
Gas[a]	220	0	25,541	16,280	115
Biomass[a]	26	6	742	1,150	97
Nuclear[b]	13,889	41,218	213,001	529,352	303,928
Hydroelectric[b]	155	366	222,803	272,023	51,158
Energy consumption					
Total[a]	1,076	1,588	52,027	69,496	6,119
Per capita[c]	120	187	193	307	149
Per capita (global rank)	29	15	12	7	22
Energy intensity					
BTUs/$1987 GNP	51,394	12,097	N/A	15,787	8,784
Global rank	18	111	N/A	99	120
Waste					
Access to sanitation services					
Urban population	100%	100%	100%	N/A	100%
Rural population	100%	100%	100%	N/A	100%
1988 Greenhouse emissions					
Carbon dioxide[d]	24,000	28,000	1,200,000	1,400,000	96,000
Methane[d]	440	490	35,000	40,000	2,800
CFSs[d]	1	9	110	190	50
Share of world emissions	0.2%	0.4%	13.6%	17.3%	1.7%
Global rank[e]	54	26	14	7	41

[a] Trillion BTUs.
[b] Gigawatt hours.
[c] Million BTUs.
[d] Thousand tons.
[e] Per capita.

Source: From *The 1992 Information Please Environmental Almanac*. Reprinted by permission of the Houghton Mifflin Company.

VIII. LABOR FORCE

TABLE 3.VIII.1 Workforce by selected areas of the economy

	(Percent)		
	1980	1986	1989
Total (thousand)	5,073.6	4,892.5	4,813.6
Material production	81.0	79.9	77.4
of which			
Manufacturing industry	41.4	38.5	37.4
Agriculture and forestry	22.0	21.8	20.0
Transport and communications	8.0	8.2	8.3
Distributive trades and restaurants,			
wholesale purchasing	9.6	10.4	10.8
Nonmaterial production	19.0	20.1	22.6

Source: EUROSTAT, *Central and Eastern Europe 1991*, 1991.

TABLE 3.VIII.2 Average monthly earnings by economic sector[a]

	(Forints)			
	1980	**1985**	**1989**	**1990**
Total	3,987	5,887	10,180	10,985
of which				
Agriculture	3,822	5,617	10,156	10,064
Manufacturing sector	3,883	5,836	10,709	11,165
Construction	3,883	5,836	10.709	11,165
Transport and communications	4,163	5,921	9,989	10,899

[a] State and cooperative sector; the average monthly wages and salaries of manual and nonmanual workers are calculated by taking 1/12 of total annual wages and salaries and dividing it by the average number of registered manual and nonmanual workers.

Source: EUROSTAT, *Central and Eastern Europe 1991*, 1991.

TABLE 3.VIII.3 Economically active population by sex and industry, 1988

	(Percent)		
	Males	**Females**	**Total (Thousand)**
Agriculture, hunting, forestry, and fishing	61.2	38.8	978.6
Mining, quarrying, manufacturing, electricity, gas, and water	57.1	42.9	1,481.4
Construction	80.7	19.3	342.4
Trade, restaurants, and hotels	34.6	65.4	519.7
Transport, communication, and storage	71.4	28.6	400.2
Financing, insurance, real estate; business, community, social, and personal services	37.2	59.2	1,153.0
Activities not adequately defined[a]	0.5	96.6	243.0
Total	2,616.8	2,452.9	5,069.7

[a] Including persons in receipt of child care allowance.

Source: ILO Yearbook of Labour Statistics, 1989, 1990.

IX. POPULATION AND HEALTH

TABLE 3.IX.1 Geography and demographic profile, 1990

Population	
Population in 1990	10,568,686
Population by 2000	10,500,000 est.
Population by 2020	10,300,000 est.
Current annual percent increase	−0.2%
Population density per sq km	113.9
Net migration rate	0/1,000
Urban/Rural (1988)	75.7%/24.3%
Ethnic division	
Hungarian	96.6%
German	1.6%
Slovak	1.1%
South Slav, Romanian, Gypsy, Other (combined)	0.7%
Religion	
Roman Catholic	67.5%
Calvinist	20.0%
Lutheran	5.0%
Atheist, Other (combined)	7.5%

(continued)

TABLE 3.IX.1   *(continued)*

Geography
  Total area   93,030 sq km (35,919 sq mi)
  Land area   92,340 sq km (35,653 sq mi)
  Coast line   None
  Land borders with
    Austria   366 km (227 mi)
    Czechoslovakia   676 km (420 mi)
    Romania   443 km (275 mi)
    USSR   135 km (84 mi)
    Yugoslavia   631 km (329 mi)
  Disputes with
    Transylvania question with Romania
    Nagymaros Dam project with Czechoslovakia

Source: The Economist, *Book of Vital World Statistics,* 1990; U.S. CIA, *Atlas of Eastern Europe,* August 1990; Population Reference Bureau, *1989 World Population Data Sheet* (Washington, D.C.: Population Reference Bureau, Inc., 1989); U.S. CIA, *The World Factbook,* 1990.

TABLE 3.IX.2   Population (Hungary and selected countries)

| | (Million People at Midyear) | | | | |
	1960	**1970**	**1980**	**1985**	**1990**
Hungary	10.0	10.3	10.7	10.6	10.6
Belgium	9.1	9.6	9.8	9.9	9.9
USSR	214.3	242.8	266.4	278.9	290.9
United States	180.7	205.1	227.8	239.3	250.4
France	45.7	50.8	53.9	55.2	56.4

Source: U.S. Central Intelligence Agency, *Handbook of Economic Statistics,* 1989, 1990, 1991.

TABLE 3.IX.3   Population by age (Hungary and selected countries)

| Age | **Hungary (1987)** | | **Belgium (1984)** | | **United States (1987)** | | **USSR (1987)** | |
	Total	Percent	Total	Percent	Total	Percent	Total	Percent
<19	2,979,623	28.1	2,627,171	26.6	70,857,000	29.1	92,267,217	32.8
20–44	3,763,611	35.5	3,526,973	35.8	97,413,000	40.0	99,559,765	35.4
45–64	2,512,257	23.7	2,354,231	23.9	45,293,000	18.6	64,009,456	22.8
65+	1,357,250	12.7	1,346,997	13.7	29,836,000	12.3	25,501,353	9.0
Total	8,957,638	100.0	9,855,372	100.0	243,400,000	100.0	281,337,791	100.0

Source: UNESCO, *Statistical Yearbook,* 1989.

TABLE 3.IX.4   Population of top ten cities, 1990

Budapest	2,016,132
Debrecen	212,247
Miskolc	196,449
Szegeda	175,338
Pecs	170,119
Gyor	129,356
Nyiregyhaza	114,166
Szekesfehervar	108,990
Kecskemet	102,528
Szombathely	85,451

Source: The Europa World Year Book, 1991.

TABLE 3.IX.5 Health indicators, 1990 (Hungary and selected countries)

Birth rate	11.6/1,000
of United States	15.0/1,000
of USSR	18.0/1,000
Death rate	13.4/1,000
of United States	9.0/1,000
of USSR	10.0/1,000
Infant mortality rate	17.3/1,000
of OECD and United States	9-10/1,000
of USSR	25.0/1,000
Maternal mortality rate[a]	26/100,000
of OECD and United States	10/100,000
of USSR	48/100,000
Life expectancy	67 male/74 female
of OECD	72 male/78 female
Fertility rate	1.8 children/woman
of United States	1.9 children/woman
of USSR	2.4 children/woman
Suicides[b]	45.8/100,000
of OECD and United States	14.6/100,000
of USSR	19.8/100,000

[a] Figures refer to live births. 1980–87 figures.

[b] 1987–88 figures.

Source: Population Reference Bureau, *1989 World Population Data Sheet,* (Washington, D.C.: Population Reference Bureau, Inc., 1989); The Economist, *Book of Vital World Statistics,* 1990; UN, *Human Development Report 1991,* 1991.

TABLE 3.IX.6 Registered illnesses and fatalities by selected causes of death

Illness	1985	1987	1989
Mumps	24,493	43,881	22,458
German measles	25,545	20,667	20,043
Measles	20	23	17,555
Salmonella enteritis	9,192	15,073	13,791
Streptococcal angina and scarlet fever	6,023	8,698	8,599
Viral hepatitis	3,183	2,238	3,359
Bacillary dysentery	2,854	4,488	2,804
Bacterial meningitis	321	192	245[a]

Cause of Death	1984	1986	1988
Circulatory illnesses of which			
Ischaemic heart diseases	27,374	28,158	28,006
Diseases of the cerebrovascular system	23,427	22,462	21,047
Acute myocardial infarction	14,648	14,508	14,251
Arteriosclerosis	11,912	12,627	10,597
Hypertonia and hypertensive heart diseases	5,112	5,570	5,298
Malignant neoplasms of which	28,523	29,454	29,859
Windpipe, bronchi, and lungs	5,864	6,300	6,397
Stomach	3,327	3,079	2,976
Mammary gland	1,839	2,015	2,021
Prostate	1,219	1,324	1,218
Leukemia	877	1,154	882
Chronic liver disease and cirrhosis	4,599	4,559	4,651
Suicide	4,900	4,817	4,377

[a] 1988 data.

Source: EUROSTAT, *Central and Eastern Europe 1991,* 1991.

TABLE 3.IX.7   Life expectancy by sex, 1990
(Hungary and selected countries)

Hungary	
Male	68
Female	76
USSR	
Male	65
Female	74
United States	
Male	72
Female	79
France	
Male	74
Female	82

Source: U.S. Central Intelligence Agency, *The World Factbook,* 1991.

TABLE 3.IX.8   Medical care, 1983–1988 (Hungary and selected countries)

	Doctors	Dentists	Pharmacists	Beds (Thousands)	Total Health Expenditure[a]
	(Number per Million)				
Hungary[b]	3,279.0	N/A	429.0	9.1	3.2
Belgium	3,119.0	629.0	1,112.0	8.9	7.2
USSR[b]	4,124.0	N/A	321.0	12.8	3.2
United States	2,035.0	560.0	641.0	5.9	11.2
OECD	2,199.5	453.8	559.2	8.0	8.3

[a] As a percent of GDP. 1987 figures.

[b] Figures for communist countries are clearly misleading. According to the Soviet Ministry of Health, 1.2 million beds are in facilities with no hot water, 1/6 of the beds are in hospitals with no water, and 30 percent of the hospitals have no indoor toilets. Source: *Literaturnaya Gazeta,* February 3, 1988; and see also *World Affairs,* vol. 152, no. 1, Summer 1989.

Source: Population Reference Bureau, *1989 World Population Data Sheet,* (Washington, D.C.: Population Reference Bureau, Inc., 1989); The Economist, *Book of Vital World Statistics,* 1990; UN, *Human Development Report 1991,* 1991.

TABLE 3.IX.9   Abortion rates (Hungary and selected countries)

Country	Number of Abortions	Rate per Thousand Women Aged 15–44	Ratio per 100 Known Pregnancies	Total Rate[a]
Hungary (1987)[b]	84,500	38.2	40.2	1,137
Belgium (1985)	15,900	7.5	12.2	N/A
USSR (1987)	6,818,000	111.9	54.9	N/A
United States (1985)	1,588,600	28.0	29.7	797

[a] The number of abortions that would be experienced by 1,000 women during their reproductive lifetimes, given present age-specific abortion rates.

[b] In contrast to women from Western European and English-speaking countries, who are young, unmarried women seeking to delay a first birth, women from Eastern Europe are married with two or more children, using abortion for spacing and ending childbirth. In addition, high rates in Eastern Europe, except Romania, may be attributed in part to the very liberal abortion laws, where abortion has been used as a form of birth control since the 1950s.

Source: Adapted with the permission of The Alan Guttmacher Institute from Stanley K. Henshaw and Evelyn Morrow, *Induced Abortion: A World Review 1990 Supplement,* 1990.

X. TRADE

TABLE 3.X.1   Exports and imports, by commodity group

Commodity Group	(Million U.S. $)			
	1970	1980	1986	1989[a]
Exports:				
Machinery and equipment	755	4,495	5,905	6,623
Fuels, minerals and metls	334	1,490	1,780	310
Agricultural and forestry products	619	3,190	3,867	5,014
Manufactured consumer goods	494	2,073	2,864	3,264
Other	115	1,396	1,763	5,001
Total	2,317	11,644	16,179	20,212
Imports:				
Machinery and equipment	774	3,872	4,843	3,463
Fuels, minerals and metls	591	3,406	4,629	3,267
Agricultural and forestry products	611	2,346	2,553	985
Manufactured consumer goods	193	971	1,763	1,082
Other	336	2,018	2,684	9,113
Total	2,505	12,613	16,472	18,630

[a] Preliminary.

Source: U.S. Central Intelligence Agency, *Handbook of Economic Statistics*, 1990.

TABLE 3.X.2   Main destinations of exports and main origins of imports, 1990

Country	(Percent of Total)
Destinations of exports:	
USSR	20.0
Germany	19.9
Austria	7.8
EC	33.0
CMEA	30.0
Efta	11.9
Origins of imports:	
Germany	23.3
USSR	19.1
Austria	9.9
CMEA	33.0
EC	31.0
Efta	15.2

Source: EIU, "Hungary, Country Report," No. 1, 1992.

TABLE 3.X.3 Principal trading partners

	(Percent)			
	Imports from		Exports to	
	1985	1988	1985	1988
United States	3.0	2.2	2.3	3.0
USSR	30.0	25.0	33.6	27.6
Western Europe				
Austria	6.4	7.2	5.4	5.7
Belgium and Luxembourg	1.1	1.5	0.4	0.8
Finland	0.6	0.8	0.5	0.9
France	1.8	1.9	1.3	2.0
Greece	N/A	N/A	0.5	0.6
Italy	2.8	3.1	2.9	4.2
Netherlands	1.3	1.8	0.9	1.2
West Germany	11.4	13.9	7.8	10.9
Spain	0.5	0.4	N/A	N/A
Sweden	1.1	1.5	0.7	1.2
Switzerland and Liechtenstein	2.0	2.6	2.0	2.0
UK	1.9	1.8	1.5	1.9
Easter Europe				
Bulgaria	1.5	1.4	1.4	1.3
Czechoslovakia	5.0	5.1	5.7	5.4
East Germany	6.5	6.4	6.1	5.3
Poland	4.7	4.1	3.8	3.3
Romania	1.8	1.8	1.7	1.7
Yugoslavia	3.5	2.9	3.6	2.8
Other				
Algeria	N/A	N/A	1.3	0.6
Brazil	1.7	1.7	N/A	N/A
China	0.9	1.7	1.3	1.9
Cuba	N/A	N/A	0.9	0.5
Egypt	N/A	N/A	0.9	0.6
Indonesia	0.2	0.4	N/A	N/A
Iran	0.7	0.4	1.3	0.1
Iraq	N/A	N/A	1.2	0.2
Japan	1.7	1.5	0.3	1.0
Libya	0.6	0.0	1.1	0.3
Nigeria	N/A	N/A	0.8	0.4
Turkey	N/A	N/A	0.6	1.0
Total including others	100.0	100.0	100.0	100.0
Total (million forints)	410,128	472,485	424,601	504,069.5

Source: The Europa World Year Book, 1989, 1990.

TABLE 3.X.4 Index of import and export prices, terms of trade (Hungary and selected countries)

	(1980 = 100)			
	1984	1986	1987	1989
Hungary				
Import prices	125	136	139	163
Export prices	116	120	124	153
Terms of trade	93	88	89	94
Bulgaria				
Import prices	128	125	124	112
Export prices	111	110	112	110
Terms of trade	86	88	90	98
Czechoslovakia				
Import prices	134	138	134	137
Export prices	112	115	115	129
Terms of trade	84	84	86	93

(continued)

TABLE 3.X.4 *(continued)*

	1984	1986	1987	1989
		(1980 = 100)		
Poland				
Import prices	139	198	279	1,281
Export prices	127	189	275	1,516
Terms of trade	91	95	99	118
Romania				
Import prices	135	130	127	N/A
Export prices	124	114	114	N/A
Terms of trade	92	88	90	N/A
Yugoslavia				
Import prices	116	108	109	124
Export prices	108	107	108	123
Terms of trade	93	99	100	99
Soviet Union				
Import prices	115	112	110	113[a]
Export prices	130	114	110	103[a]
Terms of trade	113	102	100	100[a]

[a] 1988.

Source: Comecon Data 1990, 1991.

TABLE 3.X.5 Major imports[a]

Import Goods/Categories	1987	1988	1989
	(Thousand U.S. $)		
Meat and meat categories	80,761	90.597	119,472
Vegetables and fruit	77,185	78,068	89,761
Metalliferous ores and metal scrap	16,593	23,946	25,308
Crude animal and vegetable materials[c]	51,559	50,116	44,631
Petroleum, petroleum products, and related materials	67,537	53,564	62,504
Organic chemicals	31,237	26,625	24,741
Plastics in primary form[b]	N/A	22,886	23,050
Cork and wood manufactures (excl. furniture)	17,003	18,973	18,946
Textile yarn, fabrics, made-up articles, and related products [c]	31,055	32,762	34,154
Nonmetallic mineral manufactures[c]	19,581	23,820	26,604
Iron and steel	54,662	63,524	71,327
Nonferrous metals	30,874	40,066	45,908
Manufactures of metal[c]	42,960	41,417	41,888
Power-generating machinery and equipment	14,430	20,280	24,738
Machinery specialized for particular industries	36,763	42,557	51,964
General industrial machinery and equipment[c]	30,979	35,890	47,861
Telecommunications and sound-recording and -reproducing apparatus and equipment	8,764	18,034	20,600
Electrical machinery, apparatus, and appliances[c]	38,121	41,033	52,234
Furniture and parts thereof; bedding, etc.	33,578	39,716	40,106
Articles of apparel and clothing accessories	192,345	204,132	212,879
Footwear	37,927	56,514	69,379

[a] According to SITC headings.

[b] Classification changed in 1988, figures for previous years not applicable.

[c] Not elsewhere specified.

Source: EUROSTAT, *Central and Eastern Europe 1991,* 1991.

TABLE 3.X.6 Major exports[a]

Export Goods/Categories	(Thousand U.S. $) 1987	1988	1989
Feeding stuff for animals (not incl. unmilled cereals)	18,891	29,059	31,214
Organic chemicals	81,737	86,664	83,783
Inorganic chemicals	27,119	30,669	29,414
Dyeing, tanning, and coloring materials	34,600	39,100	35,836
Medical and pharmaceutical products	16,500	17,585	25,828
Essential oils, etc.; cleaning preparations, etc.	17,289	20,052	20,366
Plastics in primary forms[c]	N/A	54,974	51,137
Chemical materials and products[c]	48,027	41,991	39,959
Leather, leather manufactures, and dressed fur skins[c]	35,615	32,675	43,730
Paper, paperboard, and articles of paper pulp	35,086	39,623	47,684
Textile yarn, fabrics, made-up articles, and related products[c]	162,111	158,422	163,957
Machinery specialized for particular industries	171,335	139,708	183,189
Metalwork machinery	39,303	30,390	35,712
General industrial machinery and equipment[c]	155,128	155,001	175,872
Office machines and automatic data-processing machines	27,906	34,181	37,038
Electrical machinery, apparatus, and appliances[c]	103,801	123,305	143,335
Road vehicles (incl. air-cushion vehicles)	64,524	60,877	234,788
Professional instruments and apparatus[c]	41,820	45,412	58,354
Nonmetallic mineral manufactures	24,787	26,789	28,890
Iron and steel	49,838	54,687	60,240
Nonferrous metals	30,652	21,958	23,445
Other metals	42,102	42,406	48,167
Power-generating machinery and equipment	20,786	21,986	23,946
Telecommunications and sound-recording and -reproducing apparatus and equipment	30,795	29,818	41,783
Articles of apparel and clothing accessories	39,123	39,601	45,938

[a] According to SITC headings.
[b] Classification changed in 1988, figures for previous years not applicable.
[c] Not elsewhere specified.

Source: EUROSTAT, *Central and Eastern Europe 1991*, 1991.

TABLE 3.X.7 Trade with Western countries[a]

	Importing Countries (US $ Million) 1985	1986	1987	1988	1989
Austria	34.46	36.29	40.72	42.98	49.21
Belg/Lux	2.74	4.69	6.70	6.70	8.00[c]
Canada	2.07[b]	2.52[b]	3.00[b]	3.50[b]	3.15[bd]
Denmark	3.30	3.77	3.83	3.76	3.13
Finland	3.81	4.43	6.22	7.73	8.22
France	12.90	17.40	21.80	24.40	28.50
West Germany	64.30	80.30	100.30	107.20	118.90
Italy	25.50	27.00	33.70	40.30	42.26[d]
Netherlands	6.73	8.47	9.50	9.90	11.02[d]
Spain	1.92	2.31	3.30	3.94	5.39
Sweden	5.91	6.91	8.72	10.45	10.54[e]
Switzerland	11.91	12.56	13.29	13.34	12.66
Turkey	4.47	3.22	5.83	7.74	6.26[e]
UK	9.10	9.44	11.30	14.60	14.30
Yugoslavia	16.33	21.88	20.67	24.62	49.05[d]
United States	18.20[b]	18.81[b]	23.20[b]	24.50[b]	20.08[be]

[a] Monthly averages from Western countries' trade accounts, in million $ U.S..
[b] Imports, fas.
[c] January–September.
[d] January–November.
[e] January–October.

(continued)

TABLE 3.X.7 *(continued)*

	Exporting Countries (US $ Million)				
	1985	1986	1987	1988	1989
Austria	37.14	42.60	43.66	46.06	52.49
Belg/Lux	6.80	9.44	10.80	10.70	15.20[c]
Canada	.98	.64	1.00	.40	.48[d]
Denmark	2.84	3.40	4.14	4.50	5.20
Finland	3.92	4.17	5.04	5.70	6.10
France	14.00	16.70	18.30	18.60	21.60
West Germany	87.70	115.30	134.70	131.00	162.00
Italy	19.60	22.40	25.40	26.60	30.23[d]
Netherlands	9.81	14.00	14.90	15.60	16.73[d]
Spain	3.31	3.94	2.87	2.47	2.66
Sweden	6.70	8.71	10.10	12.20	10.57[e]
Switzerland	11.37	14.90	17.79	18.52	19.63
Turkey	.31	1.04	1.55	2.07	1.87[e]
UK	11.60	12.42	13.84	19.50	16.10
Yugoslavia	16.25	22.11	19.77	21.29	21.79
United States	7.90	8.20	7.90	6.50	9.69[e]

[a] Monthly averages from Western countries' trade accounts, in million $ U.S..
[b] Imports, fas.
[c] January–September.
[d] January–November.
[e] January–October.
Source: EIU, "Hungary, Country Report," No. 4, 1990.

TABLE 3.X.8 Trade with the USSR, by commodity

Imports from the USSR	(Million Rubles[a])	
	1987	1988
Power-generating equipment	106.7	121.1
Mining, hoisting, excavating machinery	37.8	41.2
Tractors and agricultural machinery	84.2	73.7
Motor vehicles and garage equipment	263.1	244.0
Aircraft	24.0	31.0
Other machinery and transport equipment	128.6	146.9
Coal and coke	87.0	108.1
Petroleum and products	1,333.7	1,113.9
Fuel gas and electricity	846.5	871.6
Metal ores and concentrates	51.3	38.4
Pig iron and ferro alloys	39.6	43.9
Rolled ferrous products and pipes	177.7	167.3
Chemicals	259.2	251.4
Wood, paper, and manufactures	242.3	246.9
Textile fibres and yarn	62.1	81.8
Raw cotton waste	50.3	70.8
Domestic appliances, clocks, and cameras	37.3	46.7
Total, including other items		
Million rubles	4,600.0	4,484.3
Million U.S. $	7,641.2	7,327.3

[a] Noncommercial rate: end 1987 0.602 rubles = $1.00, end 1988 0.612 rubles = $1.00

(continued)

TABLE 3.X.8 *(continued)*

Exports to the USSR	(Million Rubles)[a]	
	1987	**1988**
Metal-cutting machine tools & presses	42.6	33.5
Power-generating equipment	54.9	47.8
Rolling mill equipment	19.1	16.4
Hoisting and conveying equipment	106.0	65.8
Equipment for food industry	86.9	93.7
Equipment for textile and clothing industry	36.7	39.4
Equipment for chemical industry	28.2	20.5
Instruments and laboratory equipment, including medical	170.8	191.5
Agricultural machinery	95.4	116.0
Railway rolling stock	34.5	31.8
Motor vehicles and garage equipment	977.7	947.2
Ships and boats	33.9	30.1
Other machinery and transport equipment	915.4	852.9
Ferrous metal manufactures	54.5	39.3
Chemicals	401.5	398.7
Fruit, vegetables, and products	237.2	233.4
Beverages	110.3	72.5
Clothing and footwear	396.3	325.9
Cereals	85.9	107.8
Meat	270.4	253.3
Total, including other items		
Million rubles	5,080.3	4,943.2
Million U.S. $	8,439.0	8,077.1

Note: Commodity totals are additions of items in the trade accounts and may be incomplete.

[a]Noncommercial rate: end 1987 0.602 rubles = $1.00, end 1988 0.612 rubles = $1.00

Source: EIU, "Hungary, Country Report," No. 4, 1990.

TABLE 3.X.9 Trade with the United States, by commodity

Imports from the United States	(Thousand U.S. $) 1987	1988
Foodstuffs (including tobacco)	19,950	4,366
Tobacco	3,753	1,740
Animal and vegetable oils	0	0
Hides	1,374	916
Pulp	0	38
Farm chemicals	9,356	2,770
Coal	0	0
Petroleum products	5	6
Chemicals (inc. farm chemical)	19,070	18,465
Semi-finished, nonferrous metals	106	188
Steel	498	6
Metal manufactures	707	373
Road vehicles	12,675	10,242
Farm machines	2,154	2,463
Engines	68	166
Trains	8	0
Aircraft and parts	242	462
Ships	1,786	1,734
Scientific instruments	3,975	6,124
Machinery-general (incl. above categories)	22,494	24,560
Total	95,291	77,521

Exports to the United States	1987	1988
Meat and fish	49,923	38,682
Dairy	1,730	3,501
Grains	640	1,928
Crude materials (incl. hides, rubber, etc.)	2,271	1,260
Petro products	698	823
Chemicals	27,640	22,525
Medicines	21,546	12,841
Steel	7,573	10,616
Textiles	18,263	23,522
Clothing	46,454	48,001
Footwear	14,116	17,895
Furniture	5,563	7,474
Transport	35,165	35,899
Machinery (general, incl. other categories)	36,266	35,969
Semi-finished, nonferrous metals	12,476	16,975
Total	280,504	277,911

Source: U.S. Central Intelligence Agency, "Selected Countries' Trade with the USSR and Eastern Europe," 1990.

CHAPTER FOUR

ROMANIA

POPULATION:	23,273,285
SQUARE MILES:	88,934 (237,500 sq km)
RELIGION:	Romanian Orthodox 70%, Roman Catholic 6%, Greek Catholic (Uniate) 3%, Protestant 6%, unaffiliated 15%
CURRENCY:	Leu
EXCHANGE RATES:	Lei 60 : U.S. $1
DEBT:	U.S. $400,000,000

I ROMANIA

POLITICS, HISTORY, AND ECONOMICS

POLITICS

In contrast to Bulgaria, which had been the most loyal Soviet ally, Romania became the most unreliable member of the East bloc. Nicolae Ceausescu eagerly abandoned communist solidarity for the sake of his and the nation's power. Had it not been for the fact that Romania was surrounded by communist states and was of limited strategic value, its irritation of Moscow may have been met by a response similar to the fate of Hungary in 1956 or Czechoslovakia in 1968. The role of the USSR in Ceausescu's overthrow remains unclear. But Romania's fate has always been a function of internal design more than foreign intervention.

Romania arrived at the fall of communism in Eastern Europe behind the other satellites and remains there to this day. While the other states tore down the communist order, Romania fell short of a complete revolution. Its long-standing assertion of at least partial independence from Moscow had not been accompanied by a loosening of its internal totalitarian order. From the early 1970s forward, in fact, state control deepened until the 1980s, when a Maoist-like system was imposed. So cruel was Ceausescu's tenure that it is little wonder that the revolt of December 1989 exploded so quickly and took such a bloody form. It is also no wonder that the brief revolt failed to remove all vestiges of the totalitarian system, for Romania had been de-Sovietized by Ceausescu but, in the process, re-Stalinized. Such a system would not quickly crumble even with its leader dead. Thus, the new rulers of Romania are drawn from the communist party with a different name: the National Salvation Front.

The NSF has partially restrained the state's security forces, the *Securitate,* who have been less conspicuous than under the ousted dictator. Still, at times it has shown little resolve in restraining the mobs of "miners" and "laborers" who in 1990 ravaged the streets of Bucharest and Timisoara, practicing their own style of violent, vigilante justice. There has also been nationalist violence directed against the Hungarian minority (some 8.5 percent of the total population, but largely concentrated in Transylvania), as well as against the smaller minorities—Serbs, Turks, Bulgarians, Ukrainians, Jews, and Gypsies.

Romania's dismal internal situation has dampened European sympathy for the country's plight. As a result of these suspicions—over the nature of Ceausescu's overthrow, over the commitment of the NSF to democratic and market reforms, over the use of mobs to impose NSF rule, and over the eruption of Romanian nationalism against its own minorities—Romania has received only limited Western benefits. In comparison to Poland, Hungary, and Czechoslovakia, the country has received relatively little aid for investment, foreign investment insurance, or improved tariff treatment. Unless the present government initiates a meaningful transformation of Romania's internal order, the country is likely to receive little attention from the West and sink into even greater poverty and isolation.

Current Politics

Within hours of General Secretary Nicolae Ceausescu's hasty departure from Bucharest on December 22, 1989, a new political group calling itself the National Salvation Front (NSF) claimed provisional power as the leading force of the spontaneous uprising begun several days before. But the events surrounding Ceausescu's overthrow and subsequent execution did not lend much credence to the official NSF accounts. It now appears that the initial uprising was entirely spontaneous, while the seizure of power by the NSF was decidedly planned. The initial events, however, which provided the NSF with its opportunity were not of its own making.

The uprising began in Timisoara, distant from the control of the capital of Bucharest and, ironically, through the deeds of a Hungarian, Laszlo Tokes. As a Reformed Calvinist minister, Tokes had a history of challenging the Ceausescu regime for both its human rights violations and its harassment of Christians. On December 15, the government attempted to evict him from his parish. But the community of Timisoara, Romanians as well as Hungarians, in a rare moment of civil disobedience, surrounded the parish and held the Securitate at bay. A near citywide rebellion followed for two days. On December 17, under Ceausescu's direct order, security forces crushed the mini-revolt, with considerable bloodshed.

Assuming the event was an isolated occurrence and that he was still in complete control, Ceausescu departed for a scheduled visit to Iran. In his absence, word of the Timisoara uprising and its brutal end spread throughout the country and beyond. Ceausescu returned abruptly to Bucharest and, on December 21, staged a rally to demonstrate the public's broad support for his rule. What followed was one of the most staggering turns in a year of staggering developments. Rather than showing support, the thousands who had been assembled in the Palace Square turned on Ceausescu, booing and hissing him until he fled inside the palace. The entire spectacle was broadcast live on national television, stimulating other protests, mostly by students. Devastating street fighting followed as the security forces attempted to quell the disorder. But by nightfall many of the government forces had joined the opposition.

It is now clear that at this stage NSF conspirators were heavily involved. On the following day, December 22, the streets of Bucharest and other urban centers were flooded by protesters. Ceausescu fled the Party's Central Committee headquarters in fear for his life. He was quickly apprehended and held by military troops outside the capital, while pockets of street fighting continued. On Christmas Day, the nightmare, at least in part, came to an abrupt end. Ceausescu and his wife Elena were secretly "tried" and summarily executed, with the news quickly announced to the nation. Street fighting continued into January, until the NSF managed to restore order.

From the start, the NSF's leadership consisted largely of former senior communist party officials who had fallen from Ceausescu's favor. Despite their earlier distance from the hated dictator, the Romanian people were uncertain whether the NSF had truly brought changes to their country. The NSF has been reluctant to remove ranking Ceausescu cronies, other than a few of his most senior officials, and they have refused to disband the Securitate.

Initially, there were many puzzling questions. Who gave the order to execute the Ceausescus? How had they been misled into fleeing Bucharest when the street fighting did not appear to threaten their security? Was the NSF's rise to power the result of a popular revolution against communism? If it were, how could the NSF have organized so quickly? Or was the overthrow merely a coup d'état against Ceausescu for the sake of preserving the bulk of the communist party elite with a new name? It now appears that the NSF staged a coup to preserve the essentials of communist rule. If that interpretation is correct, then the answers to the other questions appear certain. The events that came after the demonstration in the Palace Square were the work of the NSF.

Western observers have long been pessimistic about the possibility of establishing a genuine civil society out of what remained of the society so brutalized by Ceausescu. After the violent uprising and coup, the NSF had the unenviable task of reestablishing social order among a population finally able to release their pent-up anger after years of Ceausescu's repression. The NSF did not shun heavy-handed methods to restore political order. In the process, it fostered new resentments among the people. As Romania enters the 1990s with the Front in the leading political position, the survival of Romania's fledgling democracy will depend on how effectively the NSF allows the various opposition groups legitimate means to offer rival agendas. The opposition was promised a voice in the government. But as of the cabinet shuffle of May 1991, no opposition members had been allowed to participate in the government.

The leadership of the Front adopted the fallen dictator's political infrastructure. Its control of the vast resources of the state, especially mass communications, proved an immense advantage for the NSF in the May 1990 national election. Hamstrung by the short interval between the execution of Ceausescu and the election, the smaller parties scrambled for facilities and equipment, while the NSF campaigned effectively. Two of the three leading presidential candidates had been living in exile for years. They had fled to escape Ceausescu's relentless persecution of any independent thought, but they were branded outsiders and never became popular. There were simply too few democratic leaders who had survived the rule of Ceausescu. This too was an advantage for the Front, which managed to recruit the anti-Ceausescu forces during the revolution, greatly reducing the chances that an effective opposition could emerge.

The NSF triumphed handily in the elections, winning some 70 percent of the seats in the new parliament, while its presidential candidate, Ion Iliescu, won 85 percent of the vote. The defeated parties complained of ballot stuffing and intimidation, yet Western observers declared the elections to be generally fair, leaving the weak and disorganized opposition parties with no alternative but to accept their stunning defeat.

The NSF had won the broad support of workers and peasants, who credited it with ending Ceausescu's repression. It was the known entity and had promised a deliberate restructuring of Romania's devastated economy that would not threaten living standards. In contrast, most voters were unfamiliar with the other parties, the Liberals and the Peasants' Party, both of which advocated a rapid move toward a market economy. Clearly, the majority of Romanians had chosen the more predictable future. The Front's popularity has clearly declined since the election, yet any credible alternative is still to emerge.

The post-Ceausescu political system is based on the French model. There are two distinct centers of power. The president is elected directly by the people. Through his advisers, called the Presidential Council, the president develops national policies for the government and acts as the focus of national unity. The president, however, does not have direct control over government ministries. He is the head of state and the commander-in-chief, but the foreign and defense ministers report to parliament. The president is not responsible to the legislature, yet if his party holds a majority, the president can wield tremendous power over that body from his "bully pulpit." So long as the NSF controls parliament, the current president, Ion Iliescu, has the potential to be a powerful executive and influence the economic reform process and the drafting of a new constitution.

The prime minister, as the head of the government, occupies the other center of power and oversees the cabinet of ministers. The prime minister, presently Petru Roman of the NSF, is responsible to the bicameral parliament, which consists of a 395-seat National Assembly and a 119-seat Senate. Each chamber is elected directly from the country's 40 counties and Bucharest. The parliament's first major challenge is to forge a new constitution, scheduled for the end of 1991 but not likely to appear before the end of 1992, followed by new presidential and parliamentary elections tentatively set for the same year.

The greatest shortcoming of the present system appears to be the potential for conflict between the president and prime minister. In May and June of 1990, for example, student demonstrators protested President Iliescu's past ties to the Ceausescu regime. Without direct control over the police or military, Iliescu was unable to disperse the embarrassing protesters. For his part, Prime Minister Roman was either unwilling or unable to end Iliescu's dilemma, forcing the president to look outside the government for support. A rampaging mob of miners, brought into the capital by NSF officials, violently attacked the demonstrators. The use of the miners to protect the president, and their use of violence against the people, remain the principal blight on the National Salvation Front government.

Another example of the possibilities of structural conflict in the political system was demonstrated in the fall of 1990. Roman had decided to escalate the pace of economic reform. President Iliescu and his Council, however, remained committed to a slower timetable. The new constitution may alter the structure of the government, but for the time being there is great danger of a breakdown.

As stated earlier, the National Salvation Front has a near-monopoly over politics in postcommunist Romania. With the majority of the nation's elite as members, the NSF appears, by default, to be the only political group now capable of national leadership. Its plans are likely to be government policy for the indefinite future. Originally, the NSF suggested a 6- to 8-year transition to a market economy. But by October 1990, Prime Minister Roman, following a tactic used by Gorbachev, requested emergency powers from the legislature to "accelerate" the process of reform.

His change of mind had both a domestic and an international component. Nine months after Ceausescu's demise, Roman understood that neither private nor public Western investment would be forthcoming if his government remained too far behind the other reforming East European states. It was likewise clear that the economy was in such poor condition that a drawn-out transition would only accelerate its deterioration.

Yet under the control of the NSF, there are reasons to doubt the nature of the transition to a market. The Front has committed the government to a safety net to protect the most vulnerable. This commitment is likely to preclude the adoption of the "shock therapy" approach of Poland. Equally as important, there is the concern that the Front's dominance will cripple the country's transformation to a multi-party democracy. Throughout 1990 and 1991, NSF leaders have used state resources to consolidate their control. If this continues, Romania may once again become a one-party state, lessening the chances for Western support.

The second largest party to emerge from the 1990 elections was the Hungarian Democratic Union (HDU). The party's surprisingly strong showing indicates the cohesiveness of the Hungarian minority and their restlessness under the NSF. Ceausescu restricted the cultural and educational rights of the Hungarian minority, which is centered in Transylvania and comprises 10 percent of the total population. The HDU is pressing hard for the restoration of those rights, especially the right to use the Hungarian language. In order to highlight their demands, the HDU refused to join the NSF's ruling coalition after the elections. Now that Eastern Europe's borders are open, citizens from neighboring Hungary will provide important support to the HDU, making it a still more formidable force in Romanian politics and ensuring that relations between Hungary and Romania remain strained in the foreseeable future.

The National Liberal Party is the descendant of one of Romania's precommunist parties. Although the Liberals placed a close third behind the HDU in the 1990 elections, it was an unexpectedly poor showing for this traditional party of the urban middle class. The Liberals are led by bankers and businessmen. Their leading figure is Radu Campeanu, 66, who returned to Romania to contest the elections after a 17-year exile in Paris. In 1990 and 1991 he sought, without success, to bring Liberal Party members into the government.

Of the major political parties, the Liberals are the most supportive of a rapid transition to a market economy and a Western-style political system. They favor foreign investment and closer ties to the West. They are the party of choice for intellectuals critical of the NSF, and their internationalism moderates the nation's historical tendency toward xenophobia.

Given Ceausescu's total disregard for the environment, it is not surprising that the Ecological Movement achieved a promising, if modest, showing in the 1990 elections. While winning only 12 seats in the National Assembly, the Romanian "Greens" are likely to become more powerful. Because Ceausescu's industrialization drive emphasized quantity over quality, the technological level of Romanian industry remains 15 to 20 years behind the West, and pollution controls are nonexistent, rendering many industrial areas uninhabitable by Western standards. Romanian laborers endured horrible working conditions under Ceausescu and will no longer remain silent on such issues in the postcommunist era.

The National Peasant Party is another prewar party that resurfaced for the 1990 elections. Its presidential candidate was Ion Ratiu, 72, a shipping magnate who spent the entire communist reign exiled in England. The party's official leader is Corneliu Coposu, a longtime political dissident. Like the Liberals, the Peasants' Party advocates a rapid move toward market economics while calling for the complete privatization of Romania's collective farms. While one-third of the arable land has already been turned over to citizens, ownership remains unclear. The Front has promised a comprehensive solution to the issue in the near future, but peasants are unlikely to be satisfied with anything short of full privatization. Romanian agriculture has been a major source of export earnings in the past, and the NSF understands that it would be unwise to alienate the peasantry.

More than 100 other parties and political groups also compete for the attention of the public. Most are led by young political activists and suffer from a lack of financial resources, access to the mass media, and political experience. Collectively, these smaller parties won 50 Assembly seats and 4 Senate seats in the 1990 elections. Their legislative influence will remain minimal so long as the NSF keeps its strong majority.

Immediately following Ceausescu's death, the communist party's labor organization, the General Union of Romania's Trade Unions (GURTU) disbanded and reformed the same day as the National Confederation of Romania's Free Trade Unions (NCRFTU). The new union, with nearly all the former officers from the old organization, occupied the old union's offices, continued to operate its press under a new name (Romania Muncitoare) and, most importantly, gained access to the former union's financing—all with the support of the NSF. The membership in the NCRFTU, however, dropped by two-thirds, leaving an estimated 2.5 million members.

The other 5 million former members have formed into new unions and more than 2,000 other independent groups. The groups offer an alternative to the NSF. The most prominent new labor groups include The Brotherhood of Workers and Peasants (Fratia), Banateana, The 15 November Movement (a name derived from a 1987 protest against Ceausescu), the Intertrade Union Alliance, and Alfa (or The Cartel), which is an umbrella organization for several unions in the dominant industries.

All of the new unions shun political demands, preferring instead to press their professional demands. But there is an inevitable political component to their agenda. They insist on dismantling the communist bureaucracy, especially the internal security forces, and they protest the favorable treatment of the quasi-official NCRFTU by the NSF. The new unions, like the political parties, lack access to facilities and financing and hold conflicting notions of how best to transform the economy.

Directly following the 1990 elections, several splinter groups broke from both the Liberal Party and Peasant Party. The leadership of the two parties then acknowledged that a coordinated effort was the only means of challenging the NSF. They created two umbrella opposition groups—the Democratic Anti-Totalitarian Forum (DAF) and the Civic Alliance, a "noninstitutional" organization formed from several student and pro-democracy groups.

The two groups differ on reform but agree on the need for a genuine pluralist democracy, an end to the former communist security organs, and a link with Europe. Although the groups are dominated by intellectuals, students, and dissidents, they have already begun to attract workers and have won support from the independent trade unions, Alfa and Fratia. The umbrella organizations still lack the resources to challenge the NSF. But new elections are scheduled for 1993, and the groups may then be a major political force.

Since the NSF holds a commanding position, the most influential political figure in Romania today is clearly the 60-year-old president, Ion Iliescu. As a young man he studied at Moscow State University, where he was supposedly acquainted with a fellow student, Mikhail Gorbachev. Iliescu has denied they are friends, and little is known about their relationship. But Ceausescu banished Iliescu from Bucharest during the 1987 visit of the Soviet leader. Iliescu spent his entire career climbing the communist party hierarchy, eventually becoming Ceausescu's heir apparent. Iliescu voiced his criticism of the leader's policies, fearing the establishment of a Ceausescu cult. For the next two decades, Ceausescu consigned Iliescu to a series of meaningless posts. His overwhelming electoral victory appears to demonstrate that the vast majority of citizens do not consider his association with Ceausescu and his allegiance to the communist party to be a significant handicap.

The second most influential figure in the new regime is the activist prime minister, Petru Roman. Roman, 44 years old, studied engineering in France. At the time of the December Revolution, as it has come to be called, Roman was a professor of engineering at Bucharest's prestigious Polytechnical University. In recent years he became involved with a group of party technocrats, who met twice a month to discuss science and technology. Ion Iliescu was a regular visitor to those meetings, and, like the new president, Roman is basically a pragmatic intellectual. He is fluent in Spanish and French, projects an aristocratic air, and appears comfortable with West European political figures. Following the 1990 elections, the prime minister named a new slate of ministers, many of whom are young technocrats from his university.

During the early months of the provisional regime, Silviu Brucan asserted himself as the NSF's ideologue and was described as the "brains" of the NSF or the "power behind the throne." A former ambassador to Washington, the elderly Brucan was the driving force in the NSF's formation. Although he is now distancing himself from Iliescu's government, Brucan remains a potent intellectual force within the Front. Formerly a committed Stalinist and now a convinced socialist, he has warned against slavishly copying the West's economic and political models, and he wants to synthesize a new model that contains the "best of both worlds." He has declared that given Romania's unique revolutionary experience, the country must move "beyond" the multi-party democracies of the West. Political debate, he has argued, must be unrestricted but should occur under the umbrella of the Front. The Front's rule, which serves for "all the people's interests," should not be questioned, because of its leading role in the December uprising. Likewise, Brucan sees Romania's economic future along capitalist lines, but divided into state and private sectors. Given the NSF's dominant position and cautious approach to marketization, Brucan should be able to exert considerable influence on the political scene.

Three other political figures deserve mention in any discussion of Romania's political future. The first is Bishop Laszlo Tokes of the Reformed Church of Romania, the Hungarian cleric whose resistance to Ceausescu's repression ignited the December Revolution. His recent elevation to bishop makes him the spiritual leader of the country's Hungarian minority.

The second figure is Marian Munteanu, leader of Bucharest's boisterous student population. The students have proven to be harsh and constant critics of the NSF government, demonstrating on a regular basis in the streets of the capital and showing themselves to be capable of organization. Given their ability to disrupt Bucharest's political scene, Iliescu's government will be forced to deal with student demands.

Another key figure may yet be Romania's exiled King Michael. Since the 1989 Revolution he has tried without success to secure a visa so that he could reenter the country he fled over forty years ago. Refused permission by the NSF government, he chose to enter the country without a visa in 1990. Making his way through Bucharest customs, he was intercepted by the security forces on the way to the ruling family's cemetery and expelled from the country. While a return to a constitutional monarchy still seems farfetched, Michael commands respect from a significant portion of the population. This was especially true in late 1990 and 1991, as his popularity grew in proportion to the decline of the NSF. Even if he fails to regain his throne, the crown has become a symbol of opposition to the NSF. As a result, Michael may succeed in playing a significant political role.

Three institutions also stand out for their potential future influence. The first is Romania's military, whose defection from Ceausescu's regime was the crucial turning point in the December Revolution. Prior to World War II, General Antonescu formed a military dictatorship, offering a historical precedent to the senior officers. More likely is the military's playing a key role in any future political crisis.

Another key institution is the newspaper *Romania Libera,* the national showcase for critics of the NSF government, which regularly publishes the programs of the opposition parties. In a country where journalists were, until recently, nothing more than cogs in the state propaganda machine, this is a startling development. With a skyrocketing circulation, *Romania Libera* has done much to expand the political debate in Romania.

Finally, the Bucharest human rights organization known by its acronym, LADO, will play a key role in monitoring the government's treatment of its political opponents. It insists that it is nonpolitical, but civil liberties are central to the contemporary political debate in Romania. Given that the organization has been expanding its network throughout the country, it is likely to become a more significant force.

Iliescu's government faces numerous challenges. The overarching challenge is to draft a new constitution. But the most explosive are the relations between the Romanians and the minorities. Anti-Semitism has long been a staple of Romanian society. So few Jews remain that recent anti-Semitic outbursts have been described as "anti-Semitism without Jews." The Hungarian minority is most likely to be the victim of a pogrom. In March of 1990, armed clashes occurred between ethnic Romanians and Hungarians in Transylvania. In the worst incident, 2,000 Romanians attacked a demonstration of 5,000 Hungarians and hundreds were injured in pitched battles, with both sides using firearms. Even more disturbing, a neofascist group, Vatra Romaneasca, has sprung up among ethnic Romanians in Transylvania. Not surprisingly, relations between Bucharest and Budapest are strained as a result of the heightened tension.

Social unrest is equally possible if the Iliescu government fails to maintain an ample food supply. While this seems axiomatic for all of Eastern Europe, the danger point for Romanians is probably much lower than for their counterparts elsewhere. Ceausescu cruelly deprived the population of basic amenities during his eight-year drive to eliminate the country's foreign debt. Consequently, much of the popular anger expressed during the December Revolution stemmed from the dictator's austerity program. Thus far, the Iliescu government has been most sensitive to the food issue, rapidly importing U.S. $1 billion of food. Ironically, Romania's lack of a foreign debt will facilitate the country's ability to finance future food and consumer goods imports to ensure its domestic stability.

One of Ceausescu's most bitter legacies was his devastation of the health system. The dictator's nightmarish campaign to increase the population has saddled the new regime with somewhere between 15,000 and 30,000 abandoned children. As a result of the old Romanian practice of giving each newborn a blood transfusion, a shockingly large number — estimated between 1,000 to 2,000–of these orphans suffer from AIDS. But the country's health system is in a state of complete disrepair. While humanitarian assistance from abroad has met a portion of Romania's immediate needs, the situation remains acute.

Hunting down members of the old order will remain a political mania for the near future. Ceausescu had constructed a pervasive police and spy system, penetrating every social institution and destroying any vestige of civil society. Numerous members of the dreaded Securitate remain at large. Many of these officials of the old regime are likely to be tried as war criminals or collaborators. The Iliescu government must walk a fine line, neither appearing too easy on former officials nor allowing the present regime to become too tainted by association with them.

Another crucial challenge concerns the newly independent Moldova, formerly the Republic of Moldavia. The majority of Romanians believe that the former republic, which contains the traditional territory of Bessarabia and Northern Bukovina, is rightly part of Romania. As they see it, the Soviet Union was not only guilty of unlawfully seizing the area in 1940 and artificially dividing the nation at the River Prut, but equally as guilty of vigorously Russifying it over the past fifty years. The Moldavian language, for all practical purposes, was nothing more than Romanian and Ukranian with Cyrillic characters. Because ethnic Romanians remain the majority in Moldova—Moldavians 63 percent, Ukranians 14.2 percent, and Russians 12.8 percent—many nationalists in the mother country under the Moldavian Popular Front (now Moldova Popular Front) banner demand at least the establishment of cultural ties and, in the long run, reunification. The NSF remains noticeably restrained on the subject for fear of legitimizing Hungary's continuing interest in Transylvania and in hopes of maintaining good relations with Moscow. Iliescu has publicly acknowledged that the loss of Romanian territory was "a historical injustice," but that redrawing the borders would not be in Romania's present interest. The issue is further complicated by Ukrainian independence; thus Romania must now concern itself with relations between Russia and Ukraine. Popular pressures for closer ties and even reunification are bound to grow as free travel between Romania and Moldova becomes more common.

Relations between Romania, Ukraine, and Russia have been complicated by Serpents' Island, the only island in the Black Sea. It was formerly of strategic value; now it is important because of offshore oil drilling rights. Formerly, the Soviet Union controlled the island, having seized it during World War II. Yet the Romanians assert that Moscow has no legitimate basis to retain it. All three nations will continue to press their claims because of the oil deposits in the region.

Of all the East European states, the direction of change is still the least clear in Romania, and the political situation is still highly unstable. For the time being, the NSF dominates the political landscape, allowing it to shape not only the economic future of Romania but also its constitutional future. It controls the largest portion of the press and communications and, equally as important, the largest trade union. The NSF has not shown itself comfortable with pluralism, and its failure to improve the economy has cost support. The small, but increasingly organized and bold, opposition continues to challenge the legitimacy of the NSF. Yet the opposition has yet to gather sufficient strength to challenge the ruling party. Opinion polls in 1991 indicated public support only for the army and the church and very little for any political party. It will be necessary to reverse these public commitments in order to create a civil order.

HISTORY

From Origins to 1900

Romanians have historically viewed their nation as a "Latin island surrounded by a sea of Slavs and Magyars (Hungarians)." As the name "Romania" suggests, the country traces its lineage to the Roman Empire. Ethnic Romanians stress this Latin connection as the starting point of their unique cultural development, while the Roman legacy is the cornerstone of Romanian territorial claims to the regions of Walachia, Moldavia, and Transylvania.

Transylvania is widely considered by Romanians as the cradle of the nation. The region was settled by Thracian tribes from Greece well before the birth of Christ. The resulting kingdom of Dacia grew steadily until it was absorbed by the expanding Roman Empire late in the first century A.D. Dacia remained a prosperous Roman province for two centuries, and the Roman period, although historically brief, left a significant cultural imprint on the region. Romanization of the native population included the Latin basis of the language, exposure to Christianity, and a legacy of cultural identity called "Daco-Roman."

Starting in the third century, Eastern barbarians periodically ravaged the region in a series of brutal invasions, culminating with the Mongols in the 13th century. Historians believe that in this dark period, the Daco-Romans fled the vulnerable plains of Walachia and Moldavia for the protection of Transylvania's mountains and the Danube river basin. Almost nothing is known about the Daco-Romans during these centuries, but most scholars believe that the Vlachs, Latin speakers who eventually resettled the plains in the 11th century (hence the name Walachia), were descendants of the Daco-Romans.

It was at this time that the historical path of Transylvania began to differ from those of Walachia and Moldavia. While Transylvania was firmly under Hungarian control by the 11th century, Walachia and Moldavia developed into semi-independent principalities by the 14th century. The situation, however, did not last for long, as the continued expansion of the Ottoman Empire led to Turkish dominance over all three regions by the 16th century. Yet an important difference separated Transylvania from the other principalities. Each region was forced to submit to Turkish authority and pay tribute to the Ottoman throne. Transylvania, though, was ruled by Hungarian princes, while native Romanians reigned in Walachia and Moldavia. Over time Hungary's grip on Transylvania was strengthened by the infusion of Hungarian settlers in the region.

Two of Romania's most important historical figures emerged during the Turkish period. Both were Walachian princes who successfully defied the advancing Turks for brief periods. Prince Vlad IV (1456–1462), known as "Vlad the Impaler," became infamous for his torture of Turkish prisoners. His reputation for cruelty became the inspiration for Bram Stoker's *Dracula* legend. Romania's leading national hero is Prince Michael the Brave (1593–1601), who briefly united the three principalities in a single kingdom for the first time since the Dacian era.

As the power of the Ottoman Empire declined, Russian influence grew. In a series of wars during the 18th and early 19th centuries, St. Petersburg forced the Turks to grant increasing amounts of independence to Walachia and Moldavia. While Transylvania eventually fell into the orbit of the Austro-Hungarian empire, Walachia and Moldavia developed the political foundations of the modern Romanian state. The Russian Tsars, who schemed to separate the principalities from the Ottoman Empire, encouraged the creation of modern state administration. In 1848, a peasant revolt in Transylvania set off intense nationalist movements in Walachia and Moldavia. Although the Russians and Turks joined forces to quell the unrest, the growing Romanian national consciousness did not subside.

At the end of the Crimean War in 1856, Europe's Great Powers established a collective protectorate over Walachia and Moldavia. In 1859 the two principalities, while still acknowledging Ottoman authority, were allowed to form a permanent union under the name of Romania. Romania's full independence came in 1881, when it was recognized as a sovereign kingdom and a German prince was crowned as King Carol I. By the end of the 19th century, Romania had a formal constitution, an elected parliament, and political parties. However, much political power remained in the hands of the landed gentry. A major peasant revolt in 1907 revealed the fragility of the young state. Romania entered the 20th century much as it now enters the dawn of the 21st: independent, but with an underdeveloped economy and a brittle political system.

History from 1900 to 1945

Romania's geographic location at the crossroads of empires has always had a decisive effect on its domestic politics. In the early 1900s, political groups were defined by their choice of foreign allies and, as appears true now, political parties used other nations as models for Romania's political development. The Liberals, who favored the formation of a strong middle class, promoted an alliance with republican France. Conservative landowners, seeking to maintain their dominant political position, preferred close ties with autocratic Russia. King Carol and some conservatives, however, pushed for closer relations with the Central Powers. Primarily driven by a fear of Russian expansion, Carol attempted to promote industrial development through the infusion of German capital.

Territorial questions were at the heart of Romania's foreign concerns. The oppressed Romanian minority in Transylvania produced strained ties between Romania and the Austro-Hungarian Empire, despite Carol's efforts at friendship with Germany's ally. Similar tensions developed with Greece and Bulgaria. Ties with St. Petersburg also soured as a result of Russia's absorption of Bessarabia, once part of Romania, after Russia's last war with the Ottomans in 1878. The two Balkan Wars of 1912 and 1913 provided opportunities for Romanian expansion, but King Carol pursued a cautious strategy. Feeling increasingly threatened by Russian ambitions, Carol renewed his secret 1883 treaty with the Central Powers on the eve of World War I, reflecting his wish to recover lost Romanian lands. To him, Russia's control over Bessarabia was worse than Austria's control over Transylvania.

Many Romanians disagreed with Carol's priorities since Transylvania was considered the cradle of Romanian culture and had a more developed economy than Bessarabia. These differences divided political leaders at the outset of WW I, leading to Carol's decision to declare the country's armed neutrality. Carol, distressed over his inability to honor his treaty commitments, died in late 1914, but both the Central and Allied Powers tempted his son, Ferdinand, with promises of territory if Bucharest joined the war. A crucial factor in the new king's decision was the influence of his wife, who was granddaughter to England's Queen Victoria and cousin to Russia's Tsar Nicholas II. In August 1916, Romania declared war on the Central Powers.

Romania suffered heavy losses from the start, and Bucharest was occupied by the Central Powers in December of that year. When the Bolshevik Revolution of 1917 led to the collapse of the Russian war effort, Ferdinand had no choice but to sign an armistice, and the Central Powers imposed extremely harsh terms, designed to turn Romania into a virtual economic fiefdom. By late 1918, Ferdinand was confronted with economic collapse and revolution. Aware that the Central Powers would soon be defeated, Romania reentered the war on Nov. 10, 1918, and quickly conquered most of Bessarabia and Transylvania. At war's end, these two provinces, as well as Bukovina, voted to join the Romanian kingdom. By virtue of the collapse of the Austrian and Russian Empires, the dream of a united Romania had finally been realized.

The addition of the new territories presented the regime with formidable administrative and economic challenges. The country more than doubled in size and population, with national minorities approaching 30 percent of the total population. During the 1920s, the Hungarians, Germans, and Jews were systematically excluded from the political system by the ruling Liberals, who fashioned a strongly centralized constitutional monarchy. The Liberals, like most of the Romanian elite, believed that economic development was the key to continued independence, and they pursued that goal through strict protectionism. They succeeded in reducing foreign influence over the economy, but at the cost of economic growth. When the National Peasant Party won control of the government in 1928, it quickly removed restrictions on foreign investment. But the Great Depression coincided with the new strategy, and Romania's economic situation deteriorated over the course of the 1930s. Communist leaders, particularly Ceausescu, reinforced by their wish to avoid repeating the hardships of the 1930s, would later repeat the Liberals' policy of economic nationalism by reducing dependency on the Soviet bloc.

Romania's economic woes exacerbated the regime's political fragility. King Ferdinand had died in 1927, but his son Carol II was unable to succeed him, having disavowed his claim on the throne two years earlier. The prince had kept a Jewish mistress, Magda Lupescu, in a country where anti-Semitism was widespread. Forced to choose between love and the crown, Carol accepted exile. A regency was formed for Carol's young son, Prince Michael, but after the Great Depression disabled the economy, Carol II was invited back in 1930. Originally, Carol had agreed to forsake his mistress as part of his political bargain with Premier Iuliu Maniu, though no sooner was the promise made than Carol recanted. To protest the mistress, Maniu resigned and the government collapsed. Carol emerged from these events determined to break the power of the major political parties.

The king's plans for disrupting the political system were facilitated by the world-wide economic crisis. The rise of fascism encouraged similar developments in Romania. In Moldavia, the fascist group known as the Iron Guard called for the renewal of the nation through racial purity. Following a policy of terror, the Iron Guard succeeded in assassinating the Liberal premier in 1933. Carol made little effort to suppress the fascist group, which was outlawed by the new premier. The fascists simply regrouped under a new name and continued their activity, with financial support from Hitler's Nazi party. In effect, Carol schemed to have the fascists fulfill his plan to destroy the democratic parties. By the end of the decade, his scheme backfired.

Romania's relations with its neighbors were tense throughout the interwar period. The USSR had overtly threatened war over Bessarabia in the mid-1920s. Relations were strained between Hungary and Bulgaria, who also resented having lost territories to Romania. Despite this dangerous environment, the interwar period is still considered by many Romanians as the country's "golden age." Much of this impression stems from Bucharest's active involvement in the League of Nations. Nicolae Titulescu, foreign minister from 1927 to 1936, is considered a national hero for his valiant diplomatic work in defense of Romania's independence. His promotion of Europe's "collective security" was later echoed by Ceausescu in the East-West security conferences of the 1970s.

Under Titulescu's guidance, Romania entered into a web of interlocking alliances designed to guarantee its security from those states eager to dismember it. But by 1938, King Carol found himself in the same predicament that had confronted Carol I. Following in the footsteps of his grandfather, Carol II sought closer ties to Germany to counterbalance Russian and Hungarian threats. Rapprochement with Hitler also gave Carol a freer hand in dealing with Romanian fascists, whose political power began to rival his own. After Carol put the nation's large oil reserves at the disposal of Hitler's war machine, the Nazis looked the other way as he cracked down mercilessly on the Iron Guard. When the King established a single-party state based on his personal dictatorship, his victory over his domestic enemies seemed complete.

Carol's political triumph, however, marked the beginning of the end for Greater Romania. After the 1938 Munich Conference allowed Hitler to dismember Czechoslovakia, Romania lost an important ally against Hungarian challenges. In desperation, Carol obtained a joint French-British guarantee of Romania's territorial integrity, while at the same time Romanian diplomats pushed for a similar agreement among the two European powers and the USSR concerning Poland. Instead, Stalin chose to sign the Nazi-Soviet nonaggression pact in August, 1939. In it, Hitler promised Bessarabia and northern Bukovina to the Soviets, who waited until June, 1940, to seize the provinces. Soon after, Hitler forced Carol to give Transylvania to Hungary, plus a further section to Bulgaria. In a dramatic reversal of fortune, Romania had lost 40 percent of its territory and 50 percent of its population. The era of Greater Romania, if not the dream, had ended.

The resurgent Iron Guard focused the nation's anger on the king, forcing his abdication in September, 1940. Carol's 19-year-old son assumed the throne as Michael I, but the true leader behind the throne was General Ion Antonescu, whom Carol designated as de facto ruler before he left. Under intense pressure from Hitler, Antonescu was forced to accept Iron Guard leaders into his cabinet. Within weeks, Romania was declared a "national legionary state" of the Nazi empire, and a German military mission arrived to direct the war effort. When the Iron Guard attempted a complete seizure of the government in early 1941, Antonescu dissolved the group. With Berlin's blessing, the Romanian general formed a military dictatorship. Antonescu adopted the historical Romanian title of *Conducatorul,* or "the leader." This rank, equivalent to Hitler's *"Der Führer,"* was not to be used again until Ceausescu revived it in the 1970s.

Romania participated in the Nazi invasion of Russia in June, 1941, with Antonescu commanding the national forces. Romanian troops fought alongside the German army over the next three years, even taking part in the battle of Stalingrad. After that turning point in the war, the Soviet Army launched a counteroffensive, which moved it deep within Romanian territory by the summer of 1944. King Michael had deferred to Antonescu and Berlin throughout the war, a fact that taints his reputation to this day. But in August, 1944, he finally took command of the situation by overthrowing the dictator's regime. With the support of the nation's political and military leaders, Michael formed a coalition government and quickly concluded an armistice with the Soviets. Under the communist regime, August 23 became the national holiday. Romania's liberation from Antonescu's fascism signaled the beginning of Soviet dominance. Over the next years, Romania would pay dearly for its status as a former "enemy state."

Under the conditions of the armistice, Romania was forced to pay substantial reparations to Moscow as well as accept occupation by the Red Army until the final peace settlement. The new regime was also compelled to reenter the war on the Soviet side. There was little doubt that Stalin intended to rule over the Balkan countries. However, in the case of Romania, the Soviets were hindered by the lack of a strong socialist movement. The Romanian communist party had not achieved any stature in the prewar period nor organized any substantial resistance movement during the war. Consequently, the Soviets had to start from scratch in creating a satellite regime.

Because Romanian communist leaders lacked popular standing, few made it into the first postfascist coalition governments. Until the Soviets interfered openly in the political process, the cabinets were dominated by the traditional Liberal and Peasants' Parties. In the last months of the war, Romanian communists set about establishing power bases in the trade unions and political fronts. In the fall of 1944, the communists united several smaller leftist parties to form the National Democratic Front. On a trip to Moscow in January, 1945, two communist leaders, Gheorghe Gheorghiu-Dej, who spent the war in jail, and Ana Pauker, who had spent many years in Moscow, were ordered to force a decisive confrontation with King Michael's regime. Regardless of their lack of power, the communists held the ultimate political trump card—Soviet troops.

Within a month of their return from Moscow, the communist leaders provoked a clash with government forces, and several protesters were killed. Moscow used the violence as an excuse to intervene on the communists' behalf. Soviet Deputy Foreign Minister Andrei Vyshinsky was sent to Bucharest to force King Michael to form a new government led by the National Democratic Front. A Soviet sympathizer named Petru Groza was installed as prime minister, while communists dominated the cabinet. Having effectively captured the government by peaceful means, the ruling communists spent the next three years jailing and killing their political opponents. The traditional parties were banned, while leftist groups were absorbed into the newly formed Romanian Workers' Party. The final step in the communist takeover occurred in late 1947, when King Michael was forced to abdicate and leave the country.

Romania's territories were reconfigured by the war. Bucharest regained control over Transylvania, where the substantial Hungarian minority did not welcome the renewal of Romanian rule. Over the subsequent decades, Hungary often criticized its socialist ally over its treatment of its fellow nationals. The Soviets retained the Moldavian provinces of Bessarabia and Bukovina. Stalin grouped the two provinces together to form the Soviet Republic of Moldavia, still largely populated by ethnic Romanians. In the process, Stalin fostered crosscutting territorial claims on the part of Romania, Hungary, and the USSR, restricting any revisionist ambitions held by Bucharest.

History from 1945 to 1990

Under Stalin's direction, the new Romanian regime was transformed into a copy of the Soviet Union. Red Army troops remained in Romania after the peace settlement to supply local communists with the power needed to impose a Soviet-style transformation. These measures included a socialist constitution, collectivization of agriculture, nationalization of industry, a repressive police system, and centralized economic planning. In 1948, the communist-led Democratic Front fielded the sole slate of candidates in national elections and won overwhelming control of the government. During the same year, a "Treaty of Friendship and Cooperation" with Moscow cemented Romania's status as a satellite.

As in the days of Ottoman domination, a foreign power determined which "princes" ruled Romania. Beginning in 1951, the country was convulsed by a series of political show trials, in which noncommunist politicians were systematically eliminated. During the Stalinist terror, the so-called "Moscow communists," led by Ana Pauker and Vasile Luca, held sway over those who had spent the war in Romania, led by Gheorghiu-Dej. While Pauker controlled the top government posts, Gheorghiu-Dej established his power throughout the Romanian Workers' Party. Following Stalin's own career path, Gheorghiu-Dej became general secretary in 1945. He then spent the following years installing his followers throughout the party's nationwide apparatus. This strategy paid off in 1952, when Gheorghiu-Dej toppled Pauker's faction from power. Romania was once again ruled by nationalists committed to increasing the country's autonomy.

Stalin's death in 1953 enhanced the confidence of Gheorghiu-Dej in his belief that he alone could determine Romania's path. Before he could assert the individuality of Romanian socialism, however, Gheorghiu-Dej needed to reduce Moscow's influence over the political system. By carefully eliminating all alternatives to his rule, Gheorghiu-Dej was able to withstand the region's wave of political instability in the mid-1950s. While avoiding open hostility to Khrushchev's policy of de-Stalinization, the Romanian leader placated Moscow by making his Stalinist regime a model of stability. This achievement, buttressed by Bucharest's support of Moscow's Hungarian invasion, was rewarded when Khrushchev removed Soviet troops from Romania in 1958. The withdrawal of Moscow's military presence served as the cornerstone of Romania's campaign for autonomy.

Like Stalin before him, Gheorghiu-Dej firmly believed that his regime's socialist future depended on the forced growth of heavy industry. However, Khrushchev's plans for the Soviet bloc's economic community, the Comecon, foresaw a division of labor among the East Europeans. According to Khrushchev's vision, Romania, whose economy was based on agriculture and oil, would become the bloc's "breadbasket and gas station." But Gheorghiu-Dej would brook no resistance to his development strategy and opposed Khrushchev's efforts to impose Comecon planning. When, in the early sixties, Moscow stepped up its pressures on Bucharest, Gheorghiu-Dej unveiled the policies that would define Romania's independent path over the next three decades.

In the domestic realm, Gheorghiu-Dej instituted a series of political campaigns that erased much of Moscow's imprint on the socialist regime. For example, the compulsory study of the Russian language was ended. The Romanian language was subtly altered to emphasize its Latin roots, while streets and public places that had been renamed for Soviet heroes were given back their original designations. Romanian history and culture were increasingly glorified at Russia's expense. The country remained neutral during Khrushchev's dispute with Mao and openly courted good relations with Beijing. At the same time Bucharest became more open to the West. If the Kremlin would not sanction Romania's development strategy, then Gheorghiu-Dej was determined to pursue it through increased trade with capitalist nations.

A milestone in Romania's growing assertiveness came in April, 1964. The Romanian leader understood that he could withstand Soviet pressure only if the party remained united behind him. To foster such unity, he cast himself as the protector of Romanian independence. At a communist party meeting, the leadership issued a strongly worded statement concerning relations between socialist states. This statement, which came to be known as Romania's "Declaration of Independence," rejected Moscow's direction of socialist development in other states. By denying Moscow's authority, Gheorghiu-Dej increased his regime's autonomy by linking anti-Sovietism with Romanian nationalism. His example served as an essential lesson for the succeeding party head: Nicolae Ceausescu. Following Gheorghiu-Dej's death in early 1965, Ceausescu took care to preserve Romania's autonomous stance.

It took Ceausescu approximately four years to consolidate his personal control over the renamed Romanian Communist Party. During these early years, Ceausescu was something of an enigma. While he mirrored his predecessor's commitment to industrialization and an independent foreign policy, the new leader likewise displayed populist tendencies unusual for a communist ruler. In the late sixties, Ceausescu's image was that of a pragmatic progressive, not unlike Mikhail Gorbachev in the mid-eighties. Like Gorbachev, Ceausescu was relatively young when he assumed power, being only 47 years old in 1965. Ceausescu also opened up political debate and participation for the masses, much in the manner of Soviet *glasnost*. The new Romanian ruler travelled widely around the country and "pressed the flesh" with ordinary citizens. The early years of Ceausescu's rule raised the hopes of many Romanians that a new, more relaxed, political era had dawned.

Ceausescu proved as daring in foreign policy as his predecessor Gheorghiu-Dej. When Soviet tanks rolled into Czechoslovakia in 1968, Ceausescu's vehement denunciation of the invasion shocked the world. Romania refused to participate in the invasion, and Ceausescu called upon the Romanian people to be ready to resist Soviet aggression. Bucharest had quarreled with Moscow for years over trade issues, but never had it openly challenged the Kremlin's military domination of Eastern Europe. Romania's relations with the USSR underwent a deep chill, and it reduced its contacts with the Warsaw Pact, even to the point of withdrawing from joint military exercises. Ceausescu also remodeled Romanian military strategy in order to complicate any Soviet invasion plans. The Romanian leader took his cue from Marshal Tito of Yugoslavia, leading many in the West to wonder if Romania would follow its neighbor's breakaway path.

Like many pragmatic rulers before him, Ceausescu realized that Romania's geographic position made complete independence from foreign domination impossible. As in the long era of Turkish rule, Bucharest was willing to pay the foreign power the tribute needed to maintain its semi-autonomous standing. However, it vehemently refused to let that foreign power decide how the country should conduct its affairs. When the Ottomans brought Greek merchants to rule the provinces, Romanians rallied around the princes who fought back. When Stalin imposed his "Moscow communists" on Bucharest, Romanian communists rallied around the leader who fought back. Then, when the Brezhnev

Doctrine proclaimed Moscow's right to replace a neighbor's political leadership, Romanians once again rallied around the leader who fought back. Ceausescu's popularity soared as he stood up to the Russians, and his resistance became the centerpiece of his burgeoning cult of personality.

Many Romanians look back upon the late 1960s as one of the nation's proudest moments. Beyond his progressive policies and daring anti-Sovietism, Ceausescu was determined to thrust Romania onto the world's diplomatic stage. Projecting Romania as the bloc's maverick, Ceausescu opened trade ties with major capitalist countries. It was the first bloc member, after the Soviet Union, to establish formal state relations with West Germany in 1967, and it contravened bloc policy by maintaining diplomatic ties with Israel after the 1967 war. In effect, Ceausescu sought to raise Romania's section of the Iron Curtain with the West. By forging new diplomatic and economic bonds, he hoped to reduce Moscow's ability to intervene in his increasingly dictatorial regime. Remembering Gheorghiu-Dej's lesson, Ceausescu promoted the idea that Romanian autonomy depended on his continued rule.

While Ceausescu was the leading political figure in the country, his power lay mostly within the party apparatus. The situation would change dramatically in the early 1970s, however, following a visit to China and a strengthening of ties with Beijing. It is likely that Ceausescu was inspired by the cult of Mao and took it upon himself to attempt the same in Romania. Whatever the inspiration, by the Tenth Party Congress in 1974, Ceausescu had pushed aside top government leaders and created for himself the special post of President of the Republic. His cult of personality reached unprecedented dimensions, surpassing even that of Stalin. The Romanian leader was portrayed everywhere as omnipotent, infallible, and all-knowing, refered to as "the Danube of thought" and "the genius of the Carpathians." His wife Elena became the regime's second-leading figure, also achieving cult status as Romania's "greatest scientific genius." Over time, Ceausescu's numerous relatives were given powerful posts throughout the regime, effectively making them Romania's royal family. Not surprisingly, they began to act as if they owned the country. The quasi-break from Moscow, coupled with the perverse development of the Ceausescu cult, largely explain how Romania was both independent and yet completely removed from any general political liberalization.

In 1973, Ceausescu launched the economic campaign that was to define the rest of his reign. During a party meeting, he officially redefined Romania as a "developing socialist country." This new conception gave Ceausescu the authority to launch an ambitious industrialization campaign. Like any Stalinist dictator, Ceausescu sought to maintain the society in a constant state of flux. So long as the people were preoccupied with slavish obedience to orders from the state, there would be little capacity for political dissent. By linking rapid industrialization to the goal of protecting Romania's autonomy, Ceausescu appealed to deep feelings of nationalism and anti-Sovietism. According to official propaganda, anyone who opposed "Ceausescuism" also opposed Romania's development, independence, and autonomy from Moscow.

There were other reasons why the "developing" claim was useful to Ceausescu's grand scheme of a "Multilaterally Developed Socialist Society." By portraying Romania as a needy developing country, Ceausescu obtained concessional trade provisions from many Western nations. Ceausescu's status as a maverick was an essential component of this strategy, as he cleverly crafted his image for sympathetic Western leaders. In effect, he asked to be rewarded for his resistance to Moscow's influence like any other Third World leader. The "developing" status likewise permitted Ceausescu to present Romania as a natural ally of Third World countries. This factor was crucial in expanding Romania's ties with the Middle East and the import of raw materials from the Third World. Bucharest also extended large amounts of aid to Third World countries and became deeply involved in issues of global development.

Over the course of the decade of the 1970s, Ceausescu's strategy paid important dividends. Romania's economy grew vigorously, and Ceausescu was feted the world over as a courageous statesman. By the end of the 1970s, however, the dictator's plans had gone awry. Bucharest had imported large amounts of industrial goods on credit from the West. Foreign exchange was desperately necessary to pay his foreign bills. Yet Ceausescu had limited his options by massively expanding the country's petrochemical industries. With Romania's once-large oil supplies dwindling, the economy became precariously dependent on foreign oil. Unless Bucharest could import Middle Eastern oil at favorable prices, its petrochemical exports would shrink and the country's financial burden would become insupportable. It was precisely this dire condition that occurred. The combination of OPEC price shocks, the Iranian Revolution, and the Iran–Iraq war proved devastating for the country. Romania's industrial productivity plummeted, and its foreign debt ballooned to $16 billion.

In 1977, a large miners' strike in the Jiu Valley signaled labor's growing unrest. Romania's economic crisis contributed to Ceausescu's declining legitimacy. Much of the dictator's popular standing had been dependent on his image as mastermind of Romania's economic growth. As his grand scheme faltered, Ceausescu increased political repression to sustain his political power. When Poland was rocked by the rise of the independent trade union Solidarity, the Romanian strongman feared that his country would be next. He believed that Poland's huge foreign debt had played a significant role in its economic collapse, which in turn had forced a change in the country's leadership. Ceausescu, fearing for his own power, became convinced that Romania's foreign debt had to be erased quickly, whatever the cost. To some appreciable degree, the debt had accumulated because of economic mismanagement. The self-described "Genius of the Carpathians" became obsessed with destroying the evidence.

In 1982, Ceausescu declared that Romania's foreign debt would be eliminated by the end of the decade. However, the dictator also demanded that the pace of economic growth be maintained. Both goals could be accomplished only if the population's standard of living was severely depressed. Ceausescu wrapped his policies, like his anti-Sovietism of the late 1960s, in the mantle of defending Romania's sovereignty. But the harsh and inequitable nature of his austerity program meant that ordinary Romanians were paying with their lives for what increasingly seemed their leader's paranoia. Ceausescu succeeded in rapidly reducing the foreign debt, but the rationing of food, basic amenities, and energy produced virtual wartime conditions. Exiled dissidents estimated that at least 15,000 Romanians died annually from malnutrition, cold, and lack of medical care. Meanwhile, Ceausescu's ruling clan continued to live like Roman emperors, awash in luxury and decadence.

By 1989, the year of revolution, Ceausescu was hated by his people, ostracized by his fellow socialist leaders, and vilified in the West. Intense international criticism greeted his plan of "systemization," whereby thousands of rural villages were to be razed and replaced with huge, prisonlike apartment complexes. Still, Ceausescu's grip on power remained tight to the very end. So certain was he of his power, it should be recalled, that in the middle of the Timisoara uprising he left for Iran on a diplomatic mission. While the masses went without food and heat, the autocrat built his mammoth presidential palace and kept his dreaded security police well-fed so that they would crush dissent wherever it arose. But in the end, the Romanian people, facing another winter of deprivation and emboldened by events elsewhere, finally rose up to exact fatal revenge on the dictator.

DIAGRAM OF GOVERNMENTAL STRUCTURE

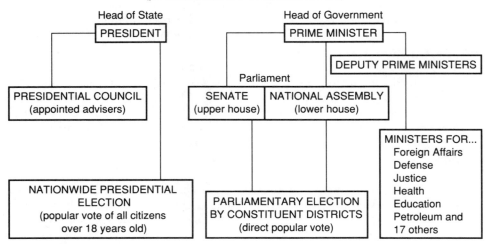

ROMANIA'S POLITICAL SYSTEM
(provisional until new constitution of 1991)

ECONOMICS

Of the Eastern European states, only the utterly backward Albania was less developed than Romania as it began its transformation from communism. In the other communist states of Eastern Europe, the groundwork for economic reform was initiated by leaders seeking to bring their countries into conformity with Mikhail Gorbachev's *perestroika* (restructuring) and *glasnost* (openness). Those leaders also, of course, sought to preserve their power by positioning themselves at the head of reform processes. But Ceausescu resisted to the bitter end any retreat from his Stalinist economic model. Even in 1991, Romania remained the most centralized command economy in Eastern Europe, with an industrial infrastructure in complete decay. Per capita gross domestic product is now only half that of 1989 East Germany, and consumer goods are generally nonexistent.

Ironically because of Ceausescu's socialist independence in the late 1960s, Romania had been the country least integrated in the Council of Mutual Economic Assistance. The country also had the largest trading relationship with the West of any of the East bloc states, yet it managed to remain the most oblivious to market phenomena.

The new government of the National Salvation Front (NSF) has expressed its intention of joining other former satellites in a reorientation to a market economy. But regardless of its intentions, there is a widespread consensus that Romania, more than its neighbors, faces the greatest difficulties in the transition. Because of Ceausescu's human rights violations and suspicions that his overthrow was less the product of a popular uprising than a long-planned coup with at least initial backing from the KGB, the government is largely isolated, both from the newly reforming East and the West. Only by mid-1991 did that isolation begin to break as the IMF entertained the possibility of a $1 billion loan.

Even without all the advantages enjoyed by the other states, Romania still has an economic edge: Romania began the reform process with a clean debt slate. It is also true that many manufacturing plants will be relatively easy to close, or at least to convert. In the process of clearing Romania's debt, Ceausescu banned imports and, in the process, froze the technological level of his factories, leaving them hopelessly outdated, so there is little left to salvage. Furthermore, Romania possesses abundant natural resources: over 80 percent of Eastern Europe's oil and a considerable base of coal, nonferrous ores, minerals, gas, salt, and timber. (Russia invaded the Romanian principalities over fourteen times in their history, usually to gain access to those minerals.) For the Western investor, however, superseding all of these concerns is Romania's markedly lower standard of living. When and if the economy stabilizes and reform takes root, the opportunity for selling energy-efficient capital goods and consumer goods of any kind will be tremendous.

Current Economic Reforms

There were no tentative steps towards economic reform under Ceausescu. In the late 1980s other Eastern European states were in the process of decentralizing their economies, especially in agriculture, while Ceausescu was in the process of recentralizing the farming sector into huge industrial-like agrarian complexes. As a result, the new government has no foundation of reform on which to build. The reform process is utterly new, and the National Salvation Front is split over how quickly Romania can or should change. Iliescu favors the creation of a highly circumscribed market. If he prevails, Romania will remain unattractive for Western investors. Petru Roman and his advisors have demonstrated a commitment to a more rapid transition to a freer market, but the more ardent reformers appear outnumbered.

The most important and easiest decisions taken by the interim government ended Ceausescu's grandiose construction projects, the further centralization of agriculture, and the destruction of villages. On these matters there was no disagreement. The dictator's "prestige projects" were consuming vast quantities of raw materials and engineering resources without hope of economic returns. The export of foodstuffs and petrochemical products to earn foreign exchange was dramatically slowed to make some food, medicines, plastics, and detergents available for the domestic market. In addition to these goods, the Front announced an expansion of hard- and soft-currency imports of meats, fruits, and baby food to satisfy immediate short-term needs. Overarching these changes was the promise that centralized management of the economy would likewise end. The early focus of legislation has not been on dismantling the planning bureaucracy, but on allowing limited private property in the form of joint stock companies, cooperatives, and smaller businesses as well as private farming on a portion of the formerly collectivized land. In many respects, such reform had been instituted years before in Hungary.

The NSF understood that Romania could not hope to be economically self-sufficient as Ceausescu had desired and that his policy of "many-sided industrialization" required conversion to a program of highly selective investment. Total reliance on heavy industry was no way to prosperity, and encouraging light industry as well as small shops was essential. The NSF fell into bitter debate about the implementation of these issues.

A decree in February 1990 allowed for limited free enterprises in hopes of raising the production of desperately needed consumer goods. Though still heavily controlled by the state, the enterprises may employ up to twenty workers, including already employed, moonlighting state employees and pensioners. Private firms may charge prices only 10 percent above state-controlled prices. Export of output still requires the assistance of foreign trade organizations, but 50 percent of hard-currency profits may be kept in interest-bearing hard currency, with the remaining receipts held in lei (plural of leu, the Romanian unit of currency) at the official exchange rate. State factories are no longer required to operate through the foreign trade offices and are free to conduct direct purchases and sales on foreign markets.

By 1991, as many as 40,000 private firms had become operational, the vast majority were in food- and service-related activities, 7,500 were in small industrial ventures, and another 2,500 were in construction. The greatest constraints on the new enterprises appear to be in finding work space and reliable suppliers, all of whom are still state-operated and reluctant to sell to private firms.

A very cautious set of reform proposals was adopted for agriculture in late January, 1990. Private plots were expanded. Farmers cultivating hilly terrain were allotted plots of any size as long as the family can cultivate the land without hiring outside labor. In the plains, farmers were allowed 0.5 hectares for their personal use. Anyone entering farming was promised the same sized plot. The decree further stipulated that urban dwellers could own private plots so long as they were cultivated. The area of the private plot, including the house, front yard, and garden, can now be bought and sold or passed on as an inheritance. Produce from the private plot may be sold at any price on the open market. It is also now legal to purchase agricultural machinery and tractors. The state has promised to open agencies to offer credits to private agriculture. The current laws also elevated the social standing of farmers. They no longer are liable for forced transfer to other farms or to factories or construction sites.

For the most part the agricultural reforms have been very limited. The Christian Democratic Party and the National Peasant Party protested, insisting that a complete privatization of agriculture was essential. But it is highly unlikely that the present government will break up the larger, cereal-producing state farms. They fear that the result of small farms will be sharply diminished agricultural output. The state farms, however, have been ordered to reduce their costs through agricultural sales or risk closure.

Peasants and farmers have been opposed to complete privatization as well. Many cultivators have claimed land significantly larger than allowed by law. The government has been stymied by the rural resistance and reluctant to reclaim the larger plots for the state.

Other legislation has diminished the overvalued exchange of the leu. The old commercial rate of 14.2 lei to $1 was raised to 21 lei to $1 and later raised again to 35 lei to $1. Still throughout 1990, the black market ranged between from 85 and 150 lei to $1. In hopes of attracting IMF funds, another devaluation took place in April 1991, lowering the leu to 60 to $1. By this point the black market rate had rocketed to 200 lei to $1. Like its other decrees, the government's attempt to establish an exchange rate reveals its reluctance to conform to market realities. For the moment, that ensures that black market activity will continue to thrive, whereas in Poland it has all but disappeared.

Legislation for joint ventures was vastly improved in 1990 by Decree 96, "Concerning Some Measures for the Attraction of Foreign Capital Investments into Romania." It is an ambitious first attempt to attract foreign investment and will undoubtedly continue to be amended. The few Western investors who participated in joint ventures under the previous 1972 legislation were forced to rely on barter and other counter-trade arrangements, still common in the USSR. In his final year, Ceausescu is reported to have said that Western joint ventures had no place in Romania's future, insisting instead on plans for Third World investment. It was never clear whether he thought the Third World was intending to invest in Romania or vice versa.

While the new legislation makes foreign investment more attractive, there are other major obstacles. The overall condition of the economy will continue to inhibit foreign participation. So will the Romanians' utter lack of experience in dealing with Western firms, a legacy of their past isolation. In addition, the new legislation is brief, containing only 18 articles, and leaves the rights of foreign investors essentially undefined. Nonetheless, several potential investors who have negotiated with the government point out that since many issues are not covered by the law, they have had broad latitude to negotiate exceptional terms for themselves. Others have revealed that the government's desire to attract Western investment has resulted in more favorable terms than allowed by law.

Decree 96 allows fully-owned foreign subsidiaries to be approved by the Office of the Prime Minister. For joint ventures not wholly foreign-owned as well as other companies, property and land may be rented, with the approval of the relevant economic ministry. A foreign venture must have approval from the ministry most relevant to the proposed economic activity, and the relevant ministry must seek advice from the Ministry of Finance and Foreign Trade. Proposals involving industrial activity must further gain the approval of the Ministry of National Economy. Obviously, the process is time-consuming even if all the relevant ministries are favorably inclined.

Contributions and receipts of the venture must be specified separately, according to the foreign currency, with all foreign capital contributions exempt from custom duties. Joint ventures still have to negotiate all purchases, both in Romania and abroad, by contract, not by the market. The contracts do, however, allow the joint venture's management to negotiate the prices for all of its input supplies and labor, including wages, taxes, and social security contributions. Sales prices, both foreign and domestic, must be set by contract. The law provides for unlimited repatriation of foreign-currency profits. If the foreign partner's profit share is not met through hard-currency sales, the foreign partner may convert into hard currency up to 8 percent of the financial share of his or her capital through the Romanian Bank of Foreign Trade for transfer abroad. Clearly, the limited repatriation of leu profits into hard currency and the artificial exchange rate have both damped the interest of those firms intending to market their products in Romania.

All ventures are free of taxes for two years, and a three-year 50 percent reduction in profit taxes may be negotiated with the Ministry of Finance. Profits reinvested in the venture, or in any other firm in Romania, will be taxed at a 50 percent reduced rate for up to five years. Foreign investment is forbidden in the defense, munitions, and drug industries. Foreign land ownership is also restricted. The government has expressed the desire to attract foreign investment in almost every industry, but particularly in chemicals, petrochemicals, energy, steel, engineering, communications, food, textiles, paper, ceramics, wood, glass, and transportation, as well as in insurance, banking, and foreign trade. In addition, the government is in the process of creating an insurance system for investors. There has been foreign interest. French and German firms have signed agreements for steel and industrial packaging concerns. Canadian, British, U.S., Swedish, Swiss, Korean, Spanish, and Japanese firms are all engaged in the joint venture process, raising the number of ventures to nearly 150 by the end of 1990. More than likely, the current legislation will be amended once the government appreciates its lack of competitiveness with other Eastern European states.

Yet the intentions of the NSF remain obscure. The Front won the election on a platform that assured workers that job security and a minimum salary would be guaranteed. Iliescu clearly has no intention of undertaking the kind of radical reform seen in Poland. In his inauguration speech, he announced that while market reforms would go forward, the process would require at least a decade. He has repeatedly stressed the need for a market economy of which the state would be a major part alongside the private sector. Large state firms will become joint stock enterprises, yet the state's role will remain substantial. Petru Roman, in contrast, has expressed his intention to introduce legislation within two years to break the power of the planning bureaucracy and establish an environment conducive to entrepreneurship. Gathered around him is a group of young technocrats who are in agreement on a hastened reform pace, most notably Adrian Severin, a senior assistant, and Eugen Dijmarescu, the economic minister. Despite being a minority within the NSF, the reformers have managed to drive through legislation that does speed the transformation. But, given the fear of rapid change on the part of most Romanians, it is unlikely that the NSF will tolerate any widespread increase in the pace of reform.

The NSF implemented a staged price liberalization aimed at freeing all prices in 1992. Energy for home use, basic foods, and rents remained fixed through 1991. Prices on goods and services originating from more than three firms were freed and, at least in theory, are open to market determination, while all other prices were raised by over 100 percent and were fully freed in October 1991. As prices were increased, the government announced a wage freeze to damp inflation. The new policies provoked immediate rioting and were met by a partial government backdown on prices. Roman and the reformers have proposed a host of additional reforms, but they have been checked by the reluctance of the NSF to risk its popularity.

Instead, the government has proceeded with piecemeal steps. The leu has been devalued again. The National Bank, still highly centralized and centrally controlled, is in the process of conversion to a central bank and has planned leu auctions and a weekly revision of the leu against hard currencies. To reduce the excess of paper money, the old leu is to be replaced by a new currency—possibly still termed a leu—at a rate of 10 old lei to one new unit. However, full convertibility is still years away. A stock market is in development, and a program for floating state bonds may appear in 1992.

Under the direction of Petru Terzi, the National Agency for Privatization has compiled a list of state holdings and drafted legislation for the conversion of state firms into joint stock companies. The state intends to maintain possession of natural resources, power facilities, forests, transportation, and military industries for the foreseeable future. But Roman declared his desire to privatize half of the capital stock in the rest of industry and agriculture by the end of 1991, with smaller firms, service industries, and agriculture going promptly into private hands. That timetable has proved wildly optimistic, but the legislature has approved a system whereby workers will be given vouchers, to be redeemed for shares at no cost, and also may buy shares in their own enterprises or in other firms. The law forbids the sale of shares for the first year. But privatization has been delayed by a basic issue—determining the share price. The bulk of Romanian industry is limited in competitiveness and capital stock.

President Iliescu still seems to think he can have it both ways. In order to stave off unrest, he has expressed a desire for more foreign investment, but at the same time, he has insisted on "protecting the national market" and the state system. A minimum income has been assured and consumer and producer subsidies have been increased. To meet its obligations, the government appears to be printing lei, further heightening inflationary pressures. The president appears to have strong support in the largest labor union, among the miners and enterprise managers, and among the people outside the major cities. It is apparent that the popular mood will not tolerate a Polish-style reform. Roman and his advisors have adopted much of what the opposition proposed during the election, but this has not translated into support. The government opposition still resents the communist backgrounds of all the members of the NSF. But even with reform, the appalling legacy of Ceausescu will not be quickly overcome, leaving Romania indefinitely as one of the poorest nations in Europe.

Current State of the Economy

Romania ranks below its former socialist allies in every economic sector, revealing the wholly inefficient and obsolete nature of its economy, which in the last communist decade came to reflect the growing madness and near-total isolation of its leader. In late 1988 Ceausescu announced plans for a 1991–1995 five-year plan that were disastrous. Gross output was to grow at 40 to 50 percent over the five years, while only alternative energy sources such as wind and solar were to drive the growth. As previously, one third of national income was to be directed toward investment, primarily for the production of export goods. Foreign trade was to grow at 40 percent for 1991–1995 and by 80 percent for 1996–2000. Agriculture would increase by expanding irrigation to another 7 million hectares. Considering the near paralysis of the economy, the plan was utter folly.

Ceausescu's isolation from reality was reflected in his personal setting of production targets. One of his favorite factories produced locomotive engines. He set its output target at 12,000 engines, despite the fact that all other European countries combined produced less than 10,000 engines. Actual output was 1,200 engines. Several hundred of them were never sold for lack of buyers.

Besides the isolation of the ruler, these accounts demonstrate the problematic quality of Romanian economic statistics. Even those closest to Ceausescu were incapable of knowing the extent of Romania's problems. To the end, Ceausescu devoted vast quantities of resources to useless construction projects while the industrial sector continued to operate with decades-old machinery, leaving the entire country without heating oil, lighting, and basic drugs.

The forced industrialization of the country and the high levels of industrial investment produced economic growth. Romanian GNP had increased by 5 percent annually for three decades while industrial output had increased at an annual rate of 10 percent. The sustained increase in GNP was accompanied by a precipitous decline in the living standards of the people and by the failure of the system to produce more skilled managers and workers. As a result, economic growth required ever-increasing inputs of raw materials per unit of output, making Romania similar to other communist states. Nonetheless, the economy remained vigorous until the major earthquake of March 1977, from which the economy never recovered. The entire decade that followed was a total economic loss.

The most telling illustration of Romania's economic condition was revealed when the National Salvation Front came to power. Staggering shortages of energy supplies and food were immediately apparent. The NSF lessened strict central control of energy resulting in a 50 percent jump in household consumption in one year, achieved through a drastic cut in industrial consumption and by increasing imports of oil and gas from the Soviet Union and West Germany. Data from 1985 indicate that household consumption of energy was then only one-fifth of the household consumption registered in 1979, confirming the magnitude of the hardships imposed by Ceausescu.

Decades ago Romania was self-sufficient in energy, but it is now highly vulnerable due to the fall in local oil production and the development of energy-inefficient industries in steel, chemicals, and oil refining. All the socialist states are characterized by industrial structures of extraordinary energy inefficiency. Yet, as is true of every other economic indicator, the problem is most severe in Romania. In Ceausescu's last year, imports of raw materials and energy represented slightly less than 50 percent of all soft-currency imports and nearly 80 percent of all hard-currency imports. The oil shock of 1973 put Romania on notice that its industrial base was inappropriate. Nevertheless, energy-hungry industries were actually expanded after the first oil price shock and became the foremost source of Romania's accumulation of foreign debt.

The vulnerability of the entire industrial sector became patently clear in 1990. Industrial production in that year fell by more than 26 percent and declined by more than 30 percent in 1991. Shorter working hours for labor, strikes, and energy diversion to households are partial explanations. But a fall in production of energy has been a major problem. Crude oil production fell by 11 percent in 1989 and by another 10 percent in 1990. Natural gas fell 20 percent, while coal declined more than 40 percent and electrical generation was off by 12 percent in 1990. The effects of these declines became dramatically apparent in the energy-intensive industrial sector. For 1990, the chemical industries reported a decline in output of 37 percent, steel fell by 27 percent, lead fell by 48 percent, copper was off by 26 percent, aluminum reported a drop of 35 percent, synthetic rubber production fell 31 percent, nonferrous metals declined nearly 50 percent, and rolled ferrous metals were off by 16 percent. To make up the energy shortfall the Soviets agreed to deliver 5 million tons of oil on top of increased deliveries of natural gas, electricity, and coal. This was a significant gesture considering that the Soviets did not guarantee deliveries to other East bloc states. In 1990, the country imported 30 percent of its gas, 20 percent of its oil, and 10 percent of its electricity from the Soviet Union. But as of 1991, Soviet generosity carried a heavy price in hard-currency payments—more than U.S. $2 billion. Romania originally counted on Iraq solving its energy problem. Iraq is Romania's largest foreign debtor and was scheduled to repay its obligations through oil supplies, a prospect ended by the imposition of international sanctions against Iraq. If there is anything positive to Romania's energy problem, it is that the shortage has reinforced the view in official circles that reform will require closing of the most energy-inefficient enterprises, development of energy-efficient manufacturing, and massive increases in energy exploration.

Since January 1990 three new gas fields have been discovered, and the government is contemplating opening the country to Western energy firms. The government is also seeking to convince Canada to resume the construction of five Canadian Candu nuclear reactors at Cernavoda. Their construction was halted in November, 1989, when inspectors from Atomic Energy Canada, Ltd. discovered the serious falsification of construction records. Begun in 1979 at a cost of $700 million, the project was to have been completed in 1984, providing an estimated 30 percent of the country's electrical needs. In a best-case scenario, revisions to those estimates predict the completion of only one of the five reactors by 1995, with the other four becoming operational between 1996 and 2002. When and if the entire project is complete, it will provide no more than 14 percent of Romania's electrical needs, at a construction cost of an additional $500 million, which Romania hopes to borrow from Canada. In return for Canadian assistance, the government has offered to turn the management of the reactors over to Canada as well as to conduct construction properly.

Compared to industry, the situation in agriculture is not as serious. Ceausescu reported the 1989 grain harvest as 60,000,000 tons. The NSF government announced the actual total as slightly less than 17,000,000 tons. Total agricultural output declined by more than 4 percent in 1989 and by 8 percent in 1990. Although the export of food was halted and domestic supplies instantly rose by 20 percent, the new government was forced to reinstate rationing. Food aid was sent by UN relief organizations and the EEC, and the government has imported foodstuffs. Still, the agricultural sector has the potential to make the country self-sufficient. In fact, actual yields may now have reached that level, but upwards of 20 percent of total output is lost in transport and storage. In addition, current statistics are misleading. Agriculture, like the rest of the economy, is in the course of transformation. Corn, sugar beet, and soybean production are in decline, while labor-intensive vegetable crops and animal products are showing reverse trends—an early indication that private farming is taking hold. At the close of the year there were unconfirmed reports that food output was actually increasing. Over 63 percent of the land is used in some agricultural capacity, and 41 percent of the land is arable.

The troubles in farming are the direct result of Ceausescu's complete disregard for agriculture and its supporting infrastructure. This has been true since his consolidation of power, save a brief period in the early 1980s, when investment in agriculture increased for the sake of exports. The more immediate reason for shortages is a function of the farming policies of 1988–1990, when Ceausescu undertook a systematic destruction of village communities—primarily Hungarian villages—for the purpose of gathering small farmers into huge agro-cities. That destruction has been ended, but violence between Hungarians and Romanians, provoked by the agro-city policy, has persisted. The settling of scores, exacerbated by the ethnic rivalries, has yet to run its course, and the NSF has shown little resolve in stopping the fighting. But with the end of Ceausescu's programs and the restoration of private plots, increased agricultural production awaits adequate supplies of fertilizers and farming equipment.

Revelations on the state of the environment have been startling. In Copsa Mica in southern Transylvania, a layer of black residue of carbon-black production covers an area with a 30-kilometer radius. Chemical factories still expel arsenic, lead, and copper at levels 70 to 90 times greater than the already generous Romanian legal limit. These poisons are widely present in workers, in populations near the factories, and in farm animals and produce. Except for Albania, Romania has the lowest life expectancy rate and the highest infant mortality rate in Europe. Ecologists have reported that of the country's 40 counties, not one is without a concentration of polluting industries, and there are over 625 centers of serious pollution. Ill-conceived expansion of farms and irrigation projects have destroyed over 20 percent of the Danube delta, as has the dumping of industrial pollution from Western Europe, which Ceausescu accepted in return for lucrative hard-currency contracts. In the absence of the capacity to store or dispose of these wastes properly, most were indiscriminately dumped into the ground, the Danube, and the Black Sea. It is impossible to assess the severity of the damage, and the government, fearing any further erosion of public confidence, hesitates to make additional comments while remaining committed to eradicating the problem. While environmental damage is endemic throughout Eastern Europe, Romania, as is the case with so many other indices, again has the dubious distinction of leading the other states.

The most positive aspect of the economy is the absence of foreign debt. At the end of 1989, according to the Bank for International Settlements, Romania was a net creditor, holding $1.7 billion and had a total hard-currency surplus of $2.6 billion. It was also a creditor in terms of its CMEA partners, and less-developed country (LDC) debt to Romania was claimed to be in the range of $3 billion. Under Ceausescu, LDCs were required to make payments on debt in hard currency. The new government, in need of raw materials and finished goods, has agreed to allow future debt repayment in products. Libya is making payments with oil; Guinea with mineral ores, fruit, and coffee; and Egypt with food, textiles, and detergents. However, these repayments in kind are insufficient to meet the country's needs. As a result of imports of energy and foodstuffs, Romania's hard-currency surplus had evaporated by the middle of 1990. Hard-currency imports had increased in 1990 by more than 65 percent over the comparable period in 1989. Exports dropped nearly 50 percent in 1990, producing a $2 billion trade deficit. It improved marginally to $1.3 billion in 1991. Romania cannot long sustain borrowing for consumer and industrial needs without a deepening of its reform process to produce goods for export.

As the poorest nation in the bloc, the government faces formidable challenges. Society is atomized, and the ethnic tension exploited by Ceausescu has yet to be resolved. The regime is reliant on coal from miners, whose penchant for violence and strikes has been obvious, and on trade unions, whose members are restless. As a whole, the people are reluctant to endure additional hardships for some promised future prosperity. In an effort to appease the people, the wage cap was removed and wages were increased by more than 16 percent in 1990. The government printed bank notes to meet the new wage demand; this spurred new inflationary pressures, to which the government responded by reimposing the wage freeze. Unemployment is at least 700,000, and another million are classified as only partially employed. With industrial capacity showing serious decline and little prospect of increased production on the horizon, unemployment is certain to increase substantially.

It would be premature, however, to write off Romania. Even under poor leadership, the nation has shown an impressive capacity for survival. Although Romania withdrew from U.S. Most Favored Nation trade status in 1988 and the United States had not restored it as of 1992, new markets with Italy, West Germany, and France have replaced the lost trade. Relations with Hungary and Yugoslavia are at an all-time low over the treatment of their nationals and pollution issues, but in less than six months under the new government, agreements for extensive trade with the Soviet Union have materialized at a time when the Soviets are not making similar promises to the other East European states. With proper financing, Romania may prove an excellent market, inasmuch as it is in need of every kind of consumer goods and a complete remaking of its industries.

For example, telecommunications have been practically absent from Romania since early 1970 because Ceausescu was so determined to restrict contact, internally and externally. The study of communications engineering was forbidden, and the country has only

111 telephones per 1,000 inhabitants, while Bulgaria has 248 per 1,000 and Hungary has 152 per 1,000. This is an extreme example, but representative, of the opportunities for knowledge-based industries should the government enhance its commitment to reform. While the population as a whole is averse to a rapid change, a large segment of the population has entered entrepreneurial activities for profit. For its part, the government must realize its promises for reforms in banking, prices, and privatization if the country is to have a chance of breaking the cycle of declining output coupled with rising hard-currency debt.

Economy from Origins to 1945

The political and economic history of Romania has been a mix of conflicting impulses, true even today. Of all the Balkan states, none was more blessed with an abundance of natural resources, a large territory, and a sizable population. At independence, Romania was poised to be the dominant Balkan state and, as such, a consequential European state. But never was the potential of a nation more unequivocally squandered by shortsighted policies and a desire to realize its national identity as Greater Romania. Paradoxically, this characterization appears valid both for precommunist as well as communist Romania. For centuries the idea of a "Romanian Land," imbued with Byzantine traditions, has seduced Romania's leadership. Initially, Romania led all the Balkan states—Bulgaria, Greece, and Serbia (Yugoslavia)—in industrial production. But even though domestic economic development was a much-touted political theme, that vision was lost in favor of an unattainable goal of national greatness. When communism took hold seventy years later, the remnants of this national dream were resurrected.

Although Romania's economy was predominately agricultural at independence in 1877, it possessed the requisites of industrial development. The agricultural sector was prosperous, and the natural resource base was extensive. Romania had a host of minerals, huge forests, salt, gas, ferrous and nonferrous ores, and coal, and most importantly, an abundance of oil. More importantly, at independence Romania already had a government administration in place, integrated into the European system. The two principalities constituting Romania (Moldavia and Walachia) had functioning governments before their 1859 unification.

The new Romania inherited from the two principalities not only an established administration but also policies facilitating industrial development. Decades before the other Balkan states had even been established, let alone thought to encourage economic development, the principalities of Romania were granting privileges to domestic industries. As early as the 1830s, consumer goods industries were receiving government assistance and tax exemptions, and as larger factories formed, monopoly status was granted. The discovery of oil and the use of steam power twenty years later further stimulated growth. In 1850, over 5,000 industries were registered, growing to 13,000 by 1863. Of course, the vast majority of these industries were primitive and scattered throughout the hill country, but the industrial diversity and self-sufficiency of the region were impressive. Peasant industries undertook metal working, tanning, brewing, food processing, flour milling, saw milling, and all sorts of crafts.

Economic development was additionally served by the principalities' foresight in infrastructure construction. Moldavia had concentrated its efforts on road construction and canalization. By the 1860s both principalities were directing their efforts to building railroads, which were connected to the Hapsburg empire, facilitating commercial relations with the capitals of Europe. In 1880, Romania had 921 kilometers of track, compared with Bulgaria with 224 kilometers and Greece with a mere 12 kilometers. Built with German money and English engineering, the railroads had the added effect of attracting skilled foreigners into Romania as well as linking the country to European trade.

Romania had a comparable advantage in terms of land. The land reform of 1864 preserved the dominant position of the landlord boyars at the expense of the peasants, but it allowed for agricultural concentration. Similar to the Russian reform of 1861, the Romanian peasant was given a portion of the former huge landholdings. Nevertheless the majority of the land, particularly the most productive land as well as the pasture and grazing lands, remained in the hands of the barons and were not broken into small, unproductive plots. Part of the conditions of the peasants' obtaining land was that they remain on the estates, working the large fields as a form of redemption. Preserving the feudal system was unjust for the peasants but had the effect of increasing cereal production, Romania's chief export.

Preserving the old land system had the additional effect of stimulating peasant industries. With an abundance of raw materials and a shortage of land, the peasants tended to organize small rural factories. As commercial ties with Europe increased and domestic capital grew scarce, these firms collapsed, but they were critical to Romania's initial development.

At independence, Romania was quick to unify the resources, communications, and bureaucracies of the former principalities. In the initial years of independence, agricultural exports, particularly cereals, were the major exports. Landlords seized the opportunity, abandoning their traditional pursuits of horse breeding and cattle raising, to grow land-intensive crops. Within little more than a decade of independence, Romania had the highest proportion of cereal area to cultivated area (81 percent) in all of Europe. The figure grew to 86 percent by 1910. Wheat and corn accounted for 80 percent of the grain totals, with half of the wheat going for export while the other half was consumed by Romania's rapidly growing population. For at least three decades, cereal growth was phenomenal. Romania was surpassed only by Argentina, Canada, and the United States.

The factors that most contributed to the rapid growth were at the root of later problems, most notably peasant discontent, ending in revolt. The quick return on cereal production encouraged the landlord boyars and the peasants to grow only grains at the expense of other crops and even the preservation of the land. Pasture lands used for raising horses and cattle were converted to grain cultivation, and the soils became exhausted. So focused was the countryside on grain production that the once famous export of Romanian horses was ended and the country found itself importing horses for plow teams.

The high returns on cereals had the added effect of strengthening the landlords vis-à-vis the peasants. As the peasant population grew, some formed small shops and industries, yet the vast majority continued to desire land. The landlords offered more land through sharecropping and were able to extract high prices for it as peasants tended to bid for the dwindling space. In 1905, over 51 percent of peasant farmers held no land or plots of less than five acres, while over half of the total land was held by the landlords whose holding, on average, exceeded 100 acres. The peasants revolted in 1907. The government sent the military, which inflicted 10,000 peasant deaths. By 1913, the percentage of peasants without land had grown to 60 percent.

Despite its reliance on agricultural exports, the government did little to support the agricultural sector, never spending more than 5 percent of its budget on the rural areas. Vulnerable to the more developed agricultural sectors of Germany, Poland, and Russia, Romania had little success protecting its exports once world grain prices fell. Instead it chose to develop its industries. The country had always strived to create a positive environment for industries. Initial legislation was well conceived, and it promoted industries where Romania had a strong resource base, creating a climate of confidence for Romanian and foreign investors. The 1840 commercial code of the former principalities was revised at independence and offered firms tax reductions, duty exemptions, free land, reduced railroad rates, free water power, and tariff protection as well as tariff reductions for the import of manufacturing machinery. Tariff protection in the 1880s was quite high, but four-fifths of Romania's imports were still finished goods, providing the necessary technologies to process Romania's raw materials. Even before this legislation, paper- and lumber-milling firms were being given free lumber, and sugar producers were receiving a direct 15 percent subsidy on their production. Expansion of the state's railroads stimulated related industries, such as metallurgy and iron works.

One of the more intriguing aspects of Romania's economic growth was the special place played by its capital, Bucharest, and to a lesser degree its other urban centers. The other Balkan states lacked skilled labor and concentrated urban centers; their domestic demand was always insignificant. Romania, in contrast, had both. Bucharest was a "boom town," attracting foreign wealth and skilled laborers from central Europe and Romanian boyar landlords, who increasingly left the management of their estates to trusted overseers. Four times larger than Belgrade or Sofia for all of the nineteenth century, Bucharest had a population in excess of 350,000 inhabitants by 1914. The influx of wealth and talent had a tremendous effect on Romania's development. The boyar families who moved to the capital brought huge financial resources and set out about constructing palatial homes. The lumber, glass, and cement industries boomed, trying to satisfy the desires of the elite as well as fulfilling lucrative state contracts for constructing regal government buildings in the capital. Ceausescu was not the first to determine that Bucharest was to be a showplace.

The concentration of wealth and talent had the added effect of attracting large-scale industries. Romania was the only Balkan state where firms grew large enough to enjoy economies of scale and profitable enough to attract capital away from banks. Well over half of all industries within Romania situated themselves within the city limits of Bucharest.

The capital was equally attractive as a banking center. The Romanian National Bank was the only Balkan bank to successfully set and maintain the European gold standard, albeit not without lapses. Romania had joined the standard in 1890 in hopes of attracting foreign investment, but having little gold, the bank spent the majority of its time protecting its reserves. Since there was no intention of allowing gold to leave the country, the need to support the leu with a trade surplus of cereals was an ongoing concern. Serving more as a symbol of political independence than a source of economic development, the bank failed as a source of international borrowing. But foreign investment did occur. Per capita foreign ownership was many times greater in Romania than elsewhere in the Balkans, primarily due to the attractiveness of Bucharest for foreign banks. Operating with no restrictions, foreign banks were a significant source of support for industries and manufacturing. They underwrote stock issues for enterprises and were actively involved in turning manufacturing and mining firms into joint stock firms. With direct bank participation, by 1913 one-third of Romania's industries were joint stock firms, representing over 60 percent of total industrial production. Only Romania among the Balkan states opened itself to foreign business to the extent that it learned more productive forms of finance and management.

Foreign investment played the largest role in the oil industry. Until the turn of the century, over 80 percent of the wells were hand-dug. But in 1895, new American technology for mechanized drilling became available, and the government passed a generous mining law to encourage foreign investment. The results were immediate. Standard Oil and Royal Dutch Shell wasted no time in establishing a network of drilling and refining facilities. No sooner were they operating, however, than German banks, having the financial resources to drive out the Americans and the English, moved in and bought up a majority of the oil operations. To the Germans, Romanian oil was exceptionally attractive, since it was the closest source of supply. The German banks went directly into the oil business, buying and managing firms, while Romania enjoyed immense new revenues, financed by foreign capital.

By and large, independent Romania enjoyed significant economic development. Due to its abundant raw materials, a large domestic market, access to European markets, and sufficient government commitment, economic development proceeded rapidly. Before the outbreak of WWI, it had higher per capita output and income than either Bulgaria or Serbia. Agriculture still predominated but as a decreasing percentage of the GNP.

Romania's greatest error was to allow foreign investment to evolve in the direction of foreign dependence. Rather than learn from the Austrians, Czechs, and Germans, who by and large comprised the management and the skilled labor force, the Romanians came to rely on their foreign partners, happy to enjoy the profits while supplying the raw materials and the unskilled labor. After market saturation and import substitution had run their courses and world cereal prices began to fall, the economic momentum naturally slowed. With that slowdown, foreign investors lost interest and began to retrench.

The problem was suspended by WW I, from which Romania emerged with promising spoils. Despite its being a less than reliable ally, the diplomats at Versailles saw fit to award Romania a major portion of Transylvania from the defunct Austro-Hungarian empire and most of Bessarabia from the newly declared Soviet Union. The new territory meant a larger home market and even more natural resources. But a host of problems stymied economic development. The European financial community retrenched to their home markets, while Romanian government policy varied wildly between autarky and the pursuit of foreign investment. Economic recovery reflected recovery from the war, not expansion.

Rebuilding Romania was the most immediate challenge. Damage to the oil industry, the railroads, and bridges was extensive, and the reconstruction effort was challenged by the additional problem of extending the Romanian infrastructure into the newly acquired territories. The territory in the northeast, Bessarabia, was backward, and the territory in the northwest, Transylvania, though prosperous, had been run as a colony from Budapest. Dividing its attention and extremely limited funds among reconstruction, industrial investment, and rationalization of the new territories proved an unsustainable burden for the government.

The government hoped that a return to the gold standard would attract needed capital, but it drove Romania into even more serious debt problems by impeding its ability to repay its heavy wartime debt. The uncollectable old debts discouraged further European credit, and Romania found itself unable to attract either long- or short-term credit. In response, the government turned inward. Tariffs were consistently raised in the 1920s, and nationalization policies limited foreign ownership. The government took to purchasing foreign firms and granting monopolies to Romanian managers. Taxes on the peasants were raised steeply to finance these changes as agricultural surpluses diminished rapidly following the breakup of the large estates.

The burdensome policies of the government paved the way for the National Peasant Party to take office in 1929. Intending to restore Romania's former economic ties, the government cut tariffs and reaffirmed the equality of foreign capital. New programs were announced for the import of agricultural machinery, and an attempt was made to restore a more orderly process to the scattered industrial investment agenda.

No sooner did the new government achieve results when world depression dramatically reduced the prices of agricultural and oil exports, resulting in the regime's collapse. From that point forward, government policy was one of regulated industrial nationalism, with a new concentration on strategic industries. High tariffs were restored, and international trade was nearly exclusively conducted with Germany. In 1933, Germany agreed to buy Romanian oil and cereals at above world prices and in return sold industrial machinery and munitions. The relationship intensified throughout the 1930s, with Germany assisting Romania's development in chemicals, metallurgy, and timber, while Romania increased its exports of oil, minerals, and foods to Germany. By 1939, Romania was deeply involved in Germany's war machine, stimulating economic growth.

The relationship seemed ideal to Romania. As Romania fell under the influence of its homegrown fascists, the Iron Guard, and expanded its concern for defense, it is no wonder that it drifted into an exclusive relationship with Germany. The terms were simply too good for a country struggling with development, desirous of foreign assistance, and wanting at the same time to control both.

Being the most active Balkan country on the European scene proved to have both benefits and costs. Romania had attracted more foreign investment than any of its neighbors and had been awarded vast lands at Versailles. But having large minority groups within its borders and a nationalistic government increasingly more concerned with defense than with development, Romania epitomized the Balkan problem. In the 1930s nationalist politicians played on peasant insecurities, inclined to see their abject situation as a result of the previous foreign economic presence and the prosperity of ethnic minorities. Transforming peasant economic frustrations into national violence was hardly difficult for the politicians, whose audience was ignorant, poor, and provincial. Between the wars and under the communism that followed World War II, the nation's economic potential was tragically squandered.

Economy from 1945 to 1990

During the communist period, the economy reflected the hostility of Romania's political leadership towards its imperial overlord, the Soviet Union. In retrospect, this was all the more strange, given that Romania's economy became the most centralized and most inflexible in the entire East bloc. No other country so completely mirrored the Soviet model in planning and development. It was the only CMEA state to avoid undertaking even a hint of reform during the communist period. Excepting Albania, however, Romania was the first state determined to go its own way and the last to change its ways. Romania refused to become a natural resource provider for the more industrialized states of East Germany, Poland, and Czechoslovakia. It insisted on developing its own heavy industries, in the grand Soviet tradition.

Refusing to meet Moscow's wishes, Romania's relationship with the USSR was continually strained. With little Soviet support, Romania turned to the West for trade, loans, and aid, and found them. The monies were inconsequential for the Western economies but nonetheless sufficient to buttress the total transformation of Romania's economy. Industrial growth for the decades from 1960 to 1980 were stunningly high. But Romania entered the 1980s with an unmanageable hard-currency debt. In less than a decade, Romania made good on its debt, managed only by the nation's virtual ruin. The violence that brought Ceausescu down was an outpouring of popular frustration against the regime's political brutality and against the savage manner in which it managed the economy.

The initial stages of Romania's transformation to communism were uneventful. Though little fighting took place on its soil, Romania was slow to recover from the war, due in part to its wartime collusion with fascist Germany. Having occupied the country in 1944, the Soviet Union reclaimed Bessarabia, which accounted for one-fifth of Romania's territory, and seized the better part of Romania's industries—oil, metallurgy, and chemicals—under the pretext that they were German-owned, or built with German capital, and hence legitimate war reparations. Of those firms not wholly taken, the Soviets formed joint companies with the industries newly nationalized by the Romanian communist party and continued to exact heavy reparations until the end of 1948. The resulting decline in industrial output was dramatic. In 1945 output was not even 60 percent of its 1938 level, and for major manufacturers the number was closer to 30 percent. Only small artisans managed to maintain their production, thus raising the national statistics considerably.

When the Soviet confiscations had run their course, Romania settled into an economic system based totally on the Soviet model of rapid industrialization financed by draconian rates of capital accumulation and, of course, the collectivization of agriculture.

For the period 1950 to 1960, industrial production increased by 340 percent, driven by investment that had increased for the same period by 431 percent. Almost all Soviet investment for Romania went into the existing centers of manufacturing—oil, engineering, metallurgy, and chemicals—allowing nothing new development, while exports to the Soviet Union to repay the investments consisted of cereals, timber, and oil. Romania had never traded with the USSR before WW II, but by 1958 over 50 percent of Romania's foreign trade was with the Soviet Union, while another 20 percent was with its CMEA partners.

Romania's secondary position in the East bloc is indicated by the paltry loans it was able to win from Moscow. On average, from 1950 to 1960 Romania obtained 17 percent less in loans than Bulgaria, a nation less than half its size. It was apparent from the outset that Stalin had every intention of using Romania exclusively as a source of natural resources and food.

Khrushchev hoped that Romania's raw materials base could be developed for light industry, thus rationalizing Comecon development. But Romania adamantly maintained the primacy of its national concerns. Rather than conforming to CMEA integration, Gheorghiu-Dej rejected domestic de-Stalinization and continued on a course of extensive economic development, reducing exports of raw materials to the northern tier states and using those resources for internal development. Until Western trade opportunities opened, Romania continued to trade with the Soviet Union, but only to the minimum degree necessary to acquire needed parts and equipment. In effect, Romania returned to its interwar policy of autarky, concentrating on the oil and metallurgy industries in hopes of generating new sources of foreign exchange. Once Soviet troops left Romania in 1958 and the Sino-Soviet rift blossomed, Romania seized the opportunity to realign its position in the CMEA. Its quasi-independent position was never again in question.

Romania made a formal declaration asserting its independence from the bloc and from the Soviet Union in April, 1964. But the "New Course" for the economy had been operational since the late 1950s. Even then, trade with the socialist bloc was declining. In 1959 alone, trade with the West increased by 80 percent and grew dramatically throughout the decade. As of 1965, the Soviet portion of Romania's total trade had declined to 38 percent, while Western trade had increased to 36 percent. By 1970, over 50 percent of Romania's trade was outside the CMEA, and in another decade, socialist trade was no more than one-third of Romania's total.

Relative to its neighbors, Romania seemed in an exceptional position. Having 80 percent of Eastern Europe's total oil as well as other resources, Romania earned hard currency from the West and imported machinery, while continuing to buy and sell soft goods in the CMEA for which there was no market in the West. From 1960 to 1968, Romania actually managed to keep a trade surplus with its new Western partners.

Romania's defiant position toward Moscow had the additional benefit of attracting Western diplomatic attention, which in turn became a source of economic benefits. Romania opened relations with West Germany in 1967, the first satellite state to have a Western relationship at that time, and with the United States in 1969 after Richard Nixon's visit. For the West, Romania was a negligible market, but was a wedge towards fragmenting Warsaw Pact unity. Along with an increasingly independent foreign policy, Romania's internal policies appeared to be liberalizing. The result was growing trade with West Germany and the United States, improved tariff status, and private Western bank loans.

These benefits had the effects desired by Romanian planners. By 1970 industry and construction accounted for 70 percent of national income, up from 57 percent in 1965. Chemicals, iron, steel, fuels, and even light industries did well, with declines registered only in the food industry, a sector of little priority for Ceausescu. After only a few years into the next decade, Romania passed Hungary and Bulgaria and had equaled Poland in size of industrial production. In less than two decades Romania closed the income gap between itself and the previously more industrialized East Germany, Poland, and Czechoslovakia.

But in the process, it had assumed a burdensome foreign debt which steadily accumulated. Romania needed reform if it was ever to repay the debt. It claimed to have started a reform process in 1969, allowing firms a greater say in their management. But central planning was strengthened rather than weakened. Having been successful in the 1960s, the regime saw no reason to change tactics. During the 1970s borrowing increased and centralization deepened. Under Ceausescu output targets were doubled in 1972 and 1977, and investment in industry grew to 40 percent of national income. More and more products came under the purview of central planners. While other East bloc communist parties were searching for ways to unlink their parties from detailed economic management without compromising their power, Romania's communist party grew more involved in direct economic management. Oddly enough, in the mid-1970s, when it became apparent that the economy was facing an unprecedented crisis, the regime redoubled its efforts to maintain a strict central plan.

Romania entered the 1970s in apparent robust economic health. It became a member of GATT in 1971 and the IMF in 1972, both firsts for an East bloc state. It gained Most Favored Nation (MFN) status from the United States in 1975. It managed to attract West European investors into joint ventures and secured long-term trade and aid arrangements with France and Germany. From 1950 to 1977, with chemicals and oil-related industries leading the way, industrial output boomed at an annual rate of 13 percent, labor productivity grew at 8 percent annually, and the industrial labor force increased by 5 percent annually, among the highest rates in the world.

In retrospect it is apparent that by the early 1970s, and despite increased Western financial contacts, the Romanian economy was running on borrowed time. Enlarging the industrial sector while ignoring agriculture and the consumer goods industries began to exhaust the economy, particularly the capital stock. Shortages of labor and supplies—essential fodder for a centrally planned economy—grew increasingly pronounced, requiring even greater imports of Western technology. For the period 1970 to 1975, nearly one-quarter of total investment came from Western imports of technology, notably producer goods equipment and industrial raw materials. But with every passing year, paying for these imported goods proved ever more difficult, since Romania concentrated its production in producer goods for which there was no real market in the West.

The vulnerability of Romania's trade position and the general weaknesses of the domestic economy became particularly evident following the 1973 oil shock. What little trade surplus Romania had previously managed to maintain vanished. Western imports were slowed, and goods intended for sale in the CMEA found Western buyers. For 1975 imports grew by 4 percent and exports by 14 percent over the previous year. Decreasing imports served to damage the industrial base, since fewer technologically advanced machines found their way into the domestic economy. With only a limited market in the West, having only the slightest desire to trade with fellow communists, and seeking to avoid domestic reform, Romania found the only available market for its goods in the Third World.

Romanian goods proved attractive to LDCs and some OPEC nations, since they could not afford high-priced imports from the West. Romania exported producer goods for which there was no Western market and imported raw materials because its domestic supplies could no longer provide the inputs demanded by Romanian heavy industry. For the entire decade Romania imported oil, refined it, and exported it, while selling more and more of its low-quality finished goods and weapons in Central Africa, the Middle East, and Asia.

Becoming more involved in Third World trade had the added dimension of allowing Romania to further exert its independence from the Soviet Union as a self-proclaimed champion of developing states. In the 1970s Romania became the largest provider of aid in the entire East bloc. Although still a member of the communist camp, Romania managed to maneuver remarkably well between the camps of the superpowers, claiming to be both liberator and innovator while being neither.

Need for oil was the primary reason for Romania's expansion into the Third World market. Domestic production had leveled off in the late 1960s, and given Romania's unreliability as a communist partner, the Soviet Union would not sell it oil below world market prices, as it did with other CMEA partners. Romania began importing oil from the smaller producing states in OPEC to feed its petrochemicals industry and expand its refining capacity for export sales. Refining increased from 18.5 million tons in the early 1970s to over 25 million tons by 1978. No sooner was refining expanded than Romanian heavy industry absorbed all the imported oil, which was intended for processing and re-export. By 1975, all of Romania's imported oil was being consumed in the home market. Thus another source of hard currency was lost.

It was then that Romania sought even further African trade, setting up numerous joint ventures and joining every possible Third World organization, most importantly the Group of 77 in 1976, which qualified Romania for tariff advantages in the Common Market. The resulting realignment had a dramatic effect on trade. LDCs accounted for slightly more than 8 percent of Romania's total trade by 1970 but increased to more than 25 percent by 1980 before peaking at 30 percent in 1981.

Had it not been for a natural disaster, it is conceivable that Third World trade could have sustained Romania's highly unstable economy for quite some time. In March, 1977, the nation experienced a tremendous earthquake, mutilating the better portion of Romania's industry. The immediate consequences were very serious. Trade loss in 1977 alone exceeded $1 billion. But more importantly, the quake's damage had the singular effect of exposing the general weakness of the economy as a whole. Romania never recovered from the tragedy of 1977, and its economic history from that point forward was one of burgeoning Western debt and incredible socioeconomic hardship. Ceausescu announced reforms in 1979, but there was little alteration in economic policy to accommodate the new and exceptional circumstances. In the process of rebuilding, investment continued to be concentrated in the areas of producer goods, petrochemicals, machine tools, and ferrous metallurgy, despite the fact in these sectors labor productivity was plummeting and, as a whole, these firms were plainly not profitable. Because of a serious decline in domestic oil production and another doubling of the world market price, oil related industries were losing just under $1 million a day on their exports.

In order to continue feeding its industrial base, Romania continued to borrow. By 1979 the hard-currency debt stood at $6.7 billion, increasing to $10.5 billion by 1981. With the economy still in ruin from the quake, two successive years of poor weather in 1980 and 1981 resulted in bread rationing in 1981, a hardship last seen in 1953. Driven by American policy, international interest rates rose, and Romania could no longer service its debt but joined Poland in requesting a rescheduling with IMF assistance. The Fund asked for conditions: Romania would have to cut imports, reduce agricultural exports, stabilize wages and prices, and make national statistics available to the West. Romania was already cutting imports, but reducing agricultural exports and providing internal economic information to the West proved impossible for Ceausescu.

Rather than yield to Western scrutiny, Ceausescu chose instead a radically austere program for recovery, more severe than any imposed on the Third World by the IMF. National sacrifice was the new program. Imports of everything requiring hard currency were slashed, and exports of food and oil-related products, the only items for which there was still a market, were maximized. The building of grandiose construction projects was continued. In 1982, food exports rose by 12 percent while imports declined by 67 percent. Formerly the largest importer of OECD goods in the entire East bloc, by 1983 Romania was the smallest. After a twenty-year hiatus, Romania sought increased economic relations with the Soviet Union, which begrudgingly complied. From its peak of $11 billion, debt declined to $6 billion by 1985 and continued declining until the end of the decade, by which point it had been repaid.

The cost of repayment on Romanian society was more severe than could be expressed in financial terms. Shortages of food, energy, and every basic consumer good were endemic throughout the 1980s. The prices for those goods that were available were raised by 200 percent. Electrical outages became commonplace, and heating oil was nonexistent in the winter. The military was routinely enlisted to maintain order in rationing lines, and strikes, labor violence, and general riots were numerous. In desperate economic conditions, Romanian nationalists explained the difficulties as a product of the Hungarian minority. The United States responded to the gross violations of human rights by canceling Romania's MFN status in 1988. By then, it could be said, the Ceausescu monarchy was too proud to care.

FURTHER READINGS

Braun, Aurel. *Romanian Foreign Policy since 1965: The Political and Military Limits of Autonomy.* New York: Praeger, (1978).

Fischer, Mary Ellen. *Nicolae Ceausescu, A Study in Political Leadership.* Boulder: L. Rienner Publishers, (1989).

Jowitt, Kenneth. *Revolutionary Breakthroughs and National Development: The Case of Romania, 1944–1965.* Berkely: University of California History Press, (1971).

Seton-Watson, R. W. *History of the Roumanians: from Roman Times to the Completion of Unity.* Cambridge: The University Press, (1934).

Sugar, Peter F., ed. *Native Fascism in the Successor States, 1918–1945.* (1971) See the articles by Emil Turczynski ("The Background of Romanian Fascism") and Stephen Fischer-Galati ("Fascism in Romania"). Santa Barbara: ABC-CLIO, 1971.

II ROMANIA

DATA AND VITAL STATISTICS

I. **Agriculture**
   1. Land use, 1991
   2. Agriculture production index
   3. Selected indicators of agricultural development, 1970–1985
   4. Total grain production
   5. Principal crops
   6. Yields for selected crops
   7. Livestock
   8. Slaughterings and production of selected animal products
   9. Agricultural labor force and tractors, 1988
   10. Agricultural output
   11. Growth per capita in agriculture and food

II. **Communications and Transportation**
   1. General facts, 1990
   2. Radio and television Receivers
   3. Percentage of households owning various consumer durables 1986–1989
   4. Daily newspapers
   5. Transport traffic
   6. Railroad freight
   7. Air cargo, 1986–1988
   8. Road traffic
   9. Ownership of vehicles and automobiles, 1985–1988
   10. Number of persons per automobile, 1985–1988
   11. Post, telephones, and telex lines

III. **Economy**
   1. Economic profile, 1989
   2. Estimated real gross national product
   3. Real gross national product growth
   4. GNP per capita in dollars, 1990
   5. GNP per capita as a percentage of OECD Average, 1988
   6. Exchange rate
   7. Savings
   8. Money in circulation
   9. Growth of GNP by producing and consuming sectors
   10. Growth of GNP inputs and productivity
   11. Consumer spending on various items as a percentage of personal income, 1989

IV. **Education**
    1. Schools, students, and teachers
    2. Public expenditures on education
    3. Expenditures and pupils per teacher, 1989
    4. Distribution of teachers and pupils by educational level, 1987
    5. Mean years of schooling, 1980
    6. School enrollment ratios
    7. School enrollment, 1989
    8. Books, newspapers, and library book loans, 1989

V. **Energy and Resources**
    1. History of primary energy production
    2. Complete energy use
    3. Electricity production
    4. Installed electricity-generating capacity
    5. Commercial energy use by sector, 1985
    6. Proved reserves of crude oil, natural gas, and coal, 1989
    7. Mineral production

VI. **Government and Defense Forces**
    1. State budget, 1989
    2. Hard-currency debt
    3. Armed forces totals, 1989
    4. Components of defense force, 1985
    5. Military expenditures

VII. **Industry**
    1. Industrial production index
    2. Industrial production index (official and adjusted)
    3. Production of selected industrial items
    4. Rank of industry, manufacturing and service sector share of GDP, 1990
    5. Industrial waste generation
    6. Emissions of air pollutants
    7. Environmental summary

VIII. **Labor Force**
    1. Workforce by selected areas of the economy
    2. Average monthly earnings by economic sector
    3. Economically active population by sex and industry, 1977

IX. **Population and Health**
    1. Geography and demographic profile
    2. Population
    3. Population by age
    4. Population of major cities
    5. Health indicators, 1990
    6. Registered illnesses
    7. Fatalities by selected causes of death
    8. Life expectancy by sex, 1991
    9. Medical care, 1983–1988
    10. Abortion rates

X. **Trade**
    1. Exports and imports, by commodity group
    2. Main destinations of exports and main origins of imports, 1990

3. Principal trading partners
4. Index of import and export prices, terms of trade
5. Major imports and exports
6. Trade with Western countries
7. Trade with the USSR, by commodity
8. Trade with the United States, by commodity

Note: Where possible and relevant, Romania is compared to the Netherlands and Sweden combined, because they are of comparable population. Also, data for the United States, France, USSR, and other East European countries is provided for comparison where relevant.

I. AGRICULTURE

TABLE 4.I.1 Land use, 1991

		(Percent)			
Arable Land	Permanent Crops	Forest and Woodland	Meadows and Pastures	Other	Irrigated Land
43	3	28	19	7	11

Source: U.S. Central Intelligence Agency, *World Factbook*, 1991.

TABLE 4.I.2 Agriculture production index (Romania and selected countries)

			(1980 = 100)		
Country	1965	1970	1980	1986	1990
Romania	58	78	100	114	88
USSR	83	99	100	120	118
United States	79	81	100	107	112
France	77	81	100	105	105[a]

[a] 1989 figure.

Source: U.S. Central Intelligence Agency, *Handbook of Economic Statistics,* 1991.

TABLE 4.I.3 Selected indicators of agricultural development, 1970–1985

	1971–1975	1976–1980	1981–1985
Agricultural land use (thousand ha[a])			
Arable	9,609	9,791	9,898
Natural grassland	4,455	4,448	4,424
Other agricultural land	867	712	659
Crop structure[b]			
Grain	65	67	68
Maize	32	34	34
Oilseeds	8	9	10
Fodder roots, silage maize	4	3	1
Cultivated grassland	12	10	8
Beet	2	3	3
Potatoes, vegetables	5	6	6
Other	4	2	2

[a] ha: hectare $= 10,000 \ m^2 = 2.471$ acres.
[b] Percent of sown area.

(*continued*)

TABLE 4.I.3 *(continued)*

	1971–1975	1976–1980	1981–1985
Total output[c] 1981 prices			
Gross[d]	4.9	5.4	2.3
Net[d]	3.6	3.9	−0.9
Arable output[c]			
Total (gross), 1981 prices	3.9	3.6	2.5
Grain	2.9	5.4	2.4
Oilseeds	4.8	2.5	−0.4
Coarse fodder	6.7	0.9	−1.7
Livestock output[c]			
Total (gross), 1981 prices	6.0	6.4	1.1
Meat	7.6	6.3	1.0
Milk	1.9	4.4	−0.4
Eggs	7.8	7.9	3.1

[c] Annualized percentage changes between five-year periods.

[d] Gross output is total yield before harvest. Net output reflects losses following processing.

Source: UN, *Economic Survey of Europe in 1987–1988.*

TABLE 4.I.4 Total grain production[a] (Romania and selected countries)

	(Million Metric Tons)					
	1960	1970	1980	1985	1989	1990
Romania	9.83	10.63	20.20	18.80	18.38	18.20
USSR[b]	125.49	186.80	189.09	191.67	211.10	238.00
United States	181.26	186.72	269.68	347.01	283.86	312.14
France	23.02	31.29	47.36	55.07	57.05	55.38

[a] Data are for the following products, where they are produced: barley, corn, oats, rice, sorghum, and wheat.

[b] Includes miscellaneous grains and legumes. For comparative purposes a discount of 11% should be applied, because USSR totals include excess moisture, unripe and damaged kernels, weed seeds, and other trash.

Source: U.S. Central Intelligence Agency, *Handbook of Economic Statistics,* 1990, 1991.

TABLE 4.I.5 Principal crops

	(Thousand Metric Tons)		
	1986	1987	1989
Maize	20,158	18,378	11,800[b]
Wheat and rye	7,386	9,727	6,063[c]
Potatoes	9,106	7,572	7,200[b]
Sugar beet	7,082	7,149	6,650[b]
Barley	2,497	3,231	1,800[a]
Grapes	2,272	1,800[b]	2,000[b]
Sunflower seed	1,004	1,102	1,100[b]
Plums	813	727	765[b]
Apples	1,201	716	780[b]
Rice	169[a]	154[a]	175[a]

[a] Unofficial estimate.

[b] FAO estimate.

[c] Wheat is an unofficial estimate. Rye is an FAO estimate.

Source: The Europa World Year Book, 1990.

TABLE 4.I.6 Yields for selected crops (Romania and selected countries)

| | | (ql/ha^a) | | |
		1985	1987	1989
Wheat	Romania	23.4	28.0	35.8^b
	Bulgaria	28.7	38.2	47.7
	Czechoslovakia	49.3	50.8	51.2
	Hungary	48.3	43.7	52.4
	Poland	34.3	37.2	38.5
	Yugoslavia	36.0	36.0	42.0^b
	Soviet Union	15.5	17.8	19.4
Barley	Romania	25.9	36.0	44.8
	Bulgaria	30.7	37.0	43.6
	Czechoslovakia	44.3	42.3	47.2
	Hungary	37.3	38.2	46.8
	Poland	32.9	33.7	33.3
	Yugoslavia	27.0	24.0	28.0^b
	Soviet Union	16.0	19.1	17.5
Maize	Romania	38.5	27.0	24.7
	Bulgaria	30.7	37.2	40.0
	Czechoslovakia	54.4	56.4	52.7
	Hungary	62.9	61.3	62.2
	Poland	43.0	46.0	47.8
	Yugoslavia	41.0	40.0	34.0^b
	Soviet Union	32.1	32.4	37.1
Rye	Romania	15.0	14.9	16.2^b
	Bulgaria	14.9	16.6	20.4
	Czechoslovakia	34.0	34.9	40.5
	Hungary	19.3	19.5	27.3
	Poland	24.7	25.8	27.3
	Yugoslavia	17.0	17.0	19.0^b
	Soviet Union	16.5	18.6	18.6
Oats	Romania	12.8	15.7	15.9
	Bulgaria	13.9	14.8	27.0
	Czechoslovakia	37.4	37.3	32.3
	Hungary	29.6	23.9	32.5
	Poland	27.0	28.4	27.2
	Yugoslavia	N/A	N/A	N/A
	Soviet Union	16.3	15.7	15.7
Potatoes	Romania	204	129	124
	Bulgaria	109	86	137
	Czechoslovakia	184	171	186
	Hungary	196	160	186
	Poland	174	187	185
	Yugoslavia	88	81	70^b
	Soviet Union	113	121	120
Sugar beets	Romania	223	201	265
	Bulgaria	168	188	246
	Czechoslovakia	377	355	352
	Hungary	379	363	440
	Poland	336	332	340
	Yugoslavia	418	380	349^b
	Soviet Union	241	266	291

^{a} ql: quintal = 100 kg (220.46 lbs).
^{b} 1988 data.

Source: EUROSTAT, *Central and Eastern Europe 1991,* 1991; *Comecon Data 1989,* 1990.

TABLE 4.I.7   Livestock (Romania and selected countries)

		(Thousand)		
		1980	1985	1989
Horses	Romania	555	672	663
	Bulgaria	120	120	119
	Czechoslovakia	45	46	42
	Hungary	120	98	76[a]
	Poland	1,780	1,324	992[a]
	Yugoslavia	N/A	N/A	N/A
	Soviet Union	5,563	5,782	5,920
Cattle	Romania	6,485	6,692	6,291
	Bulgaria	1,843	1,735	1,600
	Czechoslovakia	5,002	5,066	5,129
	Hungary	1,918	1,766	1,698
	Poland	11,337	11,774	10,277
	Yugoslavia	5,474	5,034	4,759[a]
	Soviet Union	115,057	120,888	118,429
Dairy cows	Romania	2,670	2,901	2,468
	Bulgaria	723	682	633
	Czechoslovakia	1,902	1,860	1,795
	Hungary	765	688	646
	Poland	5,666	5,331	4,964
	Yugoslavia	3,086	2,915	2,858[a]
	Soviet Union	43,389	42,863	41,716
Pigs	Romania	11,542	13,631	11,671
	Bulgaria	3,808	3,912	4,353
	Czechoslovakia	7,894	6,651	7,498
	Hungary	8,330	8,280	7,661
	Poland	18,734	19,170	18,686
	Yugoslavia	7,867	7,821	7,396[a]
	Soviet Union	73,382	77,772	79,033
Sheep	Romania	15,865	17,342	15,435
	Bulgaria	10,433	9,724	7,973
	Czechoslovakia	910	1,087	1,051
	Hungary	3,090	2,465	2,068
	Poland	3,490	4,720	4,196
	Yugoslavia	7,384	7,693	7,564[a]
	Soviet Union	141,573	14,850	138,443
Goats	Romania	347	828	1,070[a]
	Bulgaria	467	460	433
	Czechoslovakia	57	53	50[a]
	Hungary	15	16	16
	Poland	10	10	10
	Yugoslavia	N/A	N/A	N/A
	Soviet Union	5,925	6,480	6,974
Hens (million)	Romania	97.8	120.1	114.0
	Bulgaria	39.9	37.9	37.3
	Czechoslovakia	45.3	45.4	46.6
	Hungary	61.0	56.7	52.8
	Poland	76.1	66.2	55.6
	Yugoslavia	N/A	N/A	N/A
	Soviet Union	967.3	1,109.9	1,151.0

[a] 1988 data.

Source: EUROSTAT, *Central and Eastern Europe 1991,* 1991; *Comecon Data 1989,* 1990.

TABLE 4.I.8 Slaughterings and production of selected animal products (Romania and selected countries)

		Production of Selected Animal Products (Thousand Tons)				Slaughterings (Thousand)		
		1980	1985	1989		1985	1987	1989
Beef	Romania	285	240	230[a]	Cattle	1,772	1,570	1,510
	Bulgaria	167	163	159	and	704	651	601
	Czechoslovakia	468	467	460	calves	1,804	1,710	1,733
	Hungary	215	180	170		525	471	435
	Poland	866	900	789		4,290	4,049	3,425
	Yugoslavia	344	352	301[a]		N/A	N/A	N/A
	Soviet Union	7,367	8,278	8,780		36,659	41,800	43,300
Pork	Romania	975	900	840	Pigs	12,500	11,539	11,218
	Bulgaria	390	434	482		4,582	5,086	5,364
	Czechoslovakia	853	891	971		8,180	8,495	9,124
	Hungary	1,100	1,113	1,112		11,301	11,589	11,830
	Poland	1,526	1,773	1,880		16,169	19,082	19,210
	Yugoslavia	461	526	546[a]		N/A	N/A	N/A
	Soviet Union	5,835	6,299	6,737		72,248	77,000	78,000
Mutton	Romania	81	70	67[a]	Sheep	4,412	3,880	4,700[b]
and	Bulgaria	126	116	112	and	5,705	5,907	5,481[a]
goatmeat	Czechoslovakia	12	13	12	lamb	1,380	1,457	1,500[a]
	Hungary	23	18	21		429	261	285
	Poland	39	47	43		1,347	1,654	1,580[a]
	Yugoslavia	59	63	70[a]		N/A	N/A	N/A
	Soviet Union	827	905	993		52,646	56,579	57,600[b]
Poultry	Romania	475	425	390	Goats	468	508	547
	Bulgaria	158	169	188		385	413	404[a]
	Czechoslovakia	172	194	233		1,700	1,875	1,562[a]
	Hungary	405	469	445		50	54	53[a]
	Poland	290	345	381		23	15	15
	Yugoslavia	277	299	329[a]		N/A	N/A	N/A
	Soviet Union	2,811	3,166	3,357		N/A	N/A	N/A
Milk	Romania	5,411	5,165	4,667				
	Bulgaria	2,357	2,590	2,512				
	Czechoslovakia	6,942	6,982	7,150				
	Hungary	2,729	2,833	2,942				
	Poland	16,446	15,543	16,429				
	Yugoslavia	4,352	4,682	4,638[a]				
	Soviet Union	98,608	103,743	108,529				

[a] 1988 data.
[b] Including goats.

Source: EUROSTAT, *Central and Eastern Europe, 1991.* 1991; *Comecon Data 1989,* 1990.

TABLE 4.I.9 Agricultural labor force and tractors, 1988 (Romania and selected countries)

	Percent of Labor Force in Agriculture	Population Per km² of Arable Land	Output per Worker in $	Tractors per Km²
Romania	22.1	228	1,921	12.2
USSR	14.2	125	3,830	45.3
United States	2.5	131	33,519	10.8
OECD average	8.1	809	23,334	18.2

Source: The Economist, *Book of Vital World Statistics,* 1990.

TABLE 4.I.10 Agricultural output, 1988 (Romania and selected countries)

| | **(Thousand Tons)** | | | |
	Cereals	Meat	Vegetables	Fruit
Romania	31,090	1,559	6,839	4,321
OECD average[a]	12,362	1,830	3,685	3,272
East Bloc average[b]	19,125	2,024	3,523	2,582

[a] Excluding the United States.
[b] Excluding Albania.

Source: The Economist, *Book of Vital World Statistics,* 1990.

TABLE 4.I.11 Growth per capita in agriculture and food, 1977–1988 (Romania and selected countries)

| | **(Percent Growth)** | |
	Agriculture	Food
Romania[a]	1.0	1.0
USSR	0.4	0.5
United States	1.4	1.4
France	1.3	1.3

[a] Romania's government statistics are inflated. Following Ceausescu's death, the new government revealed that since 1985 Ceausescu has ordered government officials to exaggerate agricultural output totals. In his final two years, output totals were more than doubled.

Source: The Economist, *Book of Vital World Statistics,* 1990.

II. COMMUNICATIONS AND TRANSPORT

TABLE 4.II.1 General facts, 1990

1. Communications
   Telecommunications
   Stations   39 AM, 30 FM, 38 TV
   Radios (1987)   3,150,000 (1 per 7 persons)
   Televisions (1987)   3,801,000 (1 per 6 persons)
   Telephones (1985)   1,962,681 (1 per 11 persons)

2. Transport
   Railroads
     11,275 km total, of which
     10,860 km 1.435-meter standard gauge
        370 km narrow gauge
         45 km broad gauge

      3,411 km electrified, of which
      3,060 km double track (1987)

   Highways
     72,799 km total, of which
     15,762 km concrete, asphalt, stone block
     20,208 km asphalt treated
     27,729 km/gravel, crushed stone, and parcel sufaces
      9,100 km unpaved roads, 1985

   Inland Waterways
      1,724 km (1984)

(continued)

TABLE 4.II.1 *(continued)*

Pipelines
    2,800   km crude oil
    1,429   km refined products
    6,400   km natural gas

Airports
    165   total, including
     25   with permanent-surface runways
     15   with runways 2,440–3,659 m
     15   with runways 1,220–2,439 m

Source: U.S. Central Intelligence Agency, *The World Factbook,* 1991; *The Europa World Year Book,* 1990.

TABLE 4.II.2 Radio and television receivers (Romania and selected countries)

| | (Per Thousand Inhabitants) | | | | |
	1970	1975	1980	1983	1986–1988
Romania					
Radios	152	145	144	143	291
TVs	73	127	167	173	166
USSR					
Radios	390	481	490	514	686
TVs	143	217	305	308	314
United States					
Radios	1,415	1,857	1,989	2,043	2,120
TVs	413	560	684	790	811
France					
Radios	315	326	743	860	995
TVs	216	269	354	375	333[a]

[a] 1987 data.

Source: UN, *Statistical Yearbook,* 1988; UN, *Human Development Report 1991,* 1991.

TABLE 4.II.3 Percentage of households owning various consumer durables, 1986–1988[a] (Romania and selected countries)

| | | | (Percent) | |
	Televisions	Radios	Refrigerators	Vacuum Cleaners
Romania	77	45	30	49
USSR	45	96	N/A	N/A
United States	98	99	100	N/A
France	98	98	97	88

[a] Means data for each country may refer to 1986, 1987, or 1988.

Source: The Economist, *Book of Vital World Statistics,* 1990.

TABLE 4.II.4 Daily newspapers (Romania and selected countries)

Country	1970	1975	1979	1986
Romania	55	20	35	36
USSR[a]	639	691	N/A	723[b]
United States	1,763	1,775	1,787	1,657
France[c]	106	92	90	92

[a] Data include nondaily newspapers.
[b] 1984 data.
[c] Data shown for 1975 and 1979 refer to 1976 and 1978 respectively.

Source: UNESCO, *Statistical Yearbook,* 1989.

TABLE 4.II.5 Transport traffic

	1980	1987	1989
Road traffic			
Passengers (million)	1,034	869	879
Freight (million metric tons)	451	420	382
Passenger-km	24.0	22.4	23.1
Ton-km (million)	11,756	5,511	5,813
Railway traffic			
Passengers (million)	348	472	481
Freight (million metric tons)	275	304	306
Passenger-km (billion)	23.2	33.5	35.5
Ton-km (million)	65.0	66.1	67.2
Inland-waterway traffic[a]			
Passengers (million)	1.6	1.8	1.8
Freight (million metric tons)	12.3	24.1	37.4
Passenger-km (million)	79.0	73.0	72.0
Ton-km (million)	2,350	2,656	3,666
Sea traffic			
Passengers (million)	N/A	N/A	N/A
Freight (million metric tons)	16.2	30.0	35.9
Passenger-km (million)	N/A	N/A	N/A
Ton-km (billion)	80	116	149
Air traffic			
Passengers (thousand)	1,871	3,071	3,369
Freight (thousand metric tons)	33.0	31.0	51.0
Passenger-km (million)	2,790	3,851	3,842
Ton-km (million)	74.7	63.0	78.0

[a] On domestically registered ships.

Source: EUROSTAT, *Central and Eastern Europe 1991,* 1991.

TABLE 4.II.6 Railroad freight (Romania and selected countries)

Country	1960	1970	1985	1989
Romania				
Billion metric ton-km	19.8	48.0	74.2	78.1[a]
Million metric tons carried	77.5	171.3	283.4	N/A
Romania as a percent of Eastern Europe[b]				
Billion metric ton-km	10.6%	16.9%	20.2%	N/A
Million metric tons carried	8.3%	13.8%	18.4%	N/A
USSR				
Billion metric ton-km	1,504.3	2,494.7	3,718.4	3,924.8[c]
Million metric tons carried	1,884.9	2,896.0	3,951.0	4,000.0
United States				
Billion metric ton-km	868.5	1,141.0	1,288.3	1,473.9
Million metric tons carried	1,180.5	1,426.3	1,567.0	1,792.0
France				
Billion metric ton-km	56.9	70.4	58.5	52.7
Million metric ton carried	227.0	260.0	193.0	174.0

[a] 1987 data.

[b] Eastern Europe includes Bulgaria, Czechoslovakia, East Germany, Hungary, Poland, and Romania.

[c] 1988 data.

Source: U.S. Central Intelligence Agency, *Handbook of Economic Statistics,* 1990.

TABLE 4.II.7 Air cargo, 1986–1988[a] (Romania and selected countries)

Country	(Freight in Km Tons[b])
Romania	13
Netherlands and Sweden	2,057
USSR	2,721
United States	13,829
OECD average	1,622

[a] Means data for each country may refer to 1986, 1987, or 1988.
[b] Of national origin.

Source: The Economist, *Book of Vital World Statistics,* 1990.

TABLE 4.II.8 Road traffic

| | (Thousand Vehicles) | | | |
	1986	1987	1988	1989
Passenger cars	124	129	141	14.4
Trucks[a]	14.5	12.7	16.6	13.5
Buses[b]	1.6	2.0	1.8	1.6

[a] Data are for 1980, 1983, 1984, and 1989, respectively.
[b] Data are for 1978, 1979, 1980, and 1989, respectively.

Source: Comecon Data 1990, 1991.

TABLE 4.II.9 Ownership of vehicles and automobiles, 1985–1988[a] (Romania and selected countries)

Country	Vehicles (Thousands)[b]	Automobiles (Thousands)
Romania	1,100.0	850.0
Netherlands and Sweden	9,552.8	8,733.3
United States	183,468.0	140,655.0
USSR	21,500.0	12,500.0

[a] Means data for each country may refer to 1986, 1987, or 1988.
[b] Vehicles include passenger cars, trucks, and buses.

Source: The Economist, *Book of Vital World Statistics,* 1990.

TABLE 4.II.10 Number of persons per automobile, 1986–1988[a] (Romania and selected countries)

Country	
Romania	81.1
Netherlands and Sweden	2.7
OECD	2.6
USSR	22.8
United States	1.8

[a] Means data for each country may refer to 1986, 1987, or 1988.

Source: The Economist, *Book of Vital World Statistics,* 1990.

TABLE 4.II.11 Post, telephones, and telex lines, 1986–1988[a] (Romania and selected countries)

Country	Post Offices	Letters per Person	Persons per Telephone Line	Persons per Telex Line
Romania[a]	N/A	N/A	N/A	N/A
Netherlands and Sweden	4,429	275.22	1.3	416
USSR	98,445	217.81	10.3	162,875
United States	40,117	645.48	1.3	N/A

[a] Means data for each country may refer to 1986, 1987, or 1988.
[b] Romania has yet to release any figures.
Source: The Economist, *Book of Vital World Statistics,* 1990.

III. ECONOMY

TABLE 4.III.1 Economic profile, 1990 (Romania and selected countries)

	Romania	USSR	United States	France
Gross national product				
Billion 1990 U.S. $[a]	73.7	2,660.0	5,456.2[b]	873.6[b]
Percent real growth	−10.8	−2.4 to −5.0	1.0	2.8
Per capita (1990 U.S. $)	3,200	9,140	21,830	15,490
Industrial production[c]	−20.0	−2.8	1.0	1.1
Trade (billion U.S. $)				
Exports, f.o.b.	12.5[d]	109.3[e]	393.9	216.6
Imports, c.i.f.	10.6[d]	114.7[e]	516.2	234.4
Trade balance	1.9[d]	−5.4[e]	−122.3	−17.8
Living standard indicators				
Automobile registrations (per thousand persons)	11[f]	46[f]	571[g]	395[f]
Energy consumption[h]	23[e]	35[f]	57[e]	29[e]

[a] At U.S. purchasing power equivalents.
[b] Gross domestic product.
[c] Percent growth.
[d] 1986 data.
[e] 1989 data.
[f] 1987 data.
[g] 1988 data.
[h] Barrels oil equivalent per capita.
Source: U.S. Central Intelligence Agency, *Handbook of Economic Statistics,* 1991.

TABLE 4.III.2 Estimated real gross national product (Romania and selected countries)

		(Billion 1990 U.S. $)			
Country	1970	1980	1985	1989	1990
Romania[a]	50.0	73.9	77.5	79.8	68.6
USSR	1,726.9	2,257.0	2,440.9	2,663.7[b]	1,465.9[b]
United States	2,985.8	3,916.0	4,513.3	5,198.4	5,465.6
France	491.7	680.6	733.9	818.5	819.6

[a] Data for 1985–1989 are estimates based on available data.
[b] The 1989 GNP figure for the USSR is based on CIA statistics, while the 1990 GNP figure is based on PlanEcon statistics. The great disparity between the Soviet GNP in 1990 and 1988 is due to extremely high estimates by the CIA during the 1980s.
Source: U.S. Central Intelligence Agency, *Handbook of Economic Statistics,* 1989, 1990; and "PlanEcon Report," vol. 6, no. 52, December 28, 1990.

TABLE 4.III.3 Real gross national product growth (Romania and selected countries)

| Country | Percent Average Annual Rate of Growth | | Percent | | |
	1971–1980	1981–1985	1985	1989	1990
GNP growth					
Romania	5.3	1.0	−1.0	−3.7	−10.8
USSR[a]	2.4	1.8	0.9	1.5	−2.4 to −5.0
United States[b]	2.8	3.0	3.8	2.5	1.0
France[b]	3.6	1.5	1.9	3.6	2.8
GNP per capita growth					
Romania	3.5	−0.6	−1.4	−4.2	−11.3
USSR	1.5	0.8	−0.1	0.7	−2.9 to −5.5
United States[b]	1.7	1.8	2.8	1.5	0.3
France[b]	3.0	1.0	1.5	3.1	2.4

[a] At factor cost.
[b] GDP growth.
Source: U.S. Central Intelligence Agency, *Handbook of Economic Statistics,* 1990, 1991.

TABLE 4.III.4 GNP per capita in dollars[a], 1990 (Romania and selected countries)

Country	Commerical	(U.S. $) Purchasing Parity	Free Market
Romania	1,816	2,950	961
USSR	2,560	5,060	1,299
United States	21,732	21,732	21,732
West Germany	24,210	16,310	24,210

[a] Based on exchange rate, purchasing power parity, and free market rate.
Source: "PlanEcon Report," vol. 6, no. 52, December 28, 1990.

TABLE 4.III.5 GDP per capita as a percentage of OECD average, 1988 (Romania and selected countries)

Country	Percent of OECD
Romania	8.10
Netherlands and Sweden	107.35
USSR	12.10
United States	116.30

Source: The Economist, *Book of Vital Statistics,* 1990.

TABLE 4.III.6 Exchange rate

| | (Lei per $; Period Averages) | | | | |
	1987	1988	1989	1990	June 1991
Commercial	14.55	14.27	14.92	22.43	60.00

Source: U.S. Central Intelligence Agency, *The World Factbook,* 1991.

TABLE 4.III.7 Savings

1984	(Million Lei) 1985	1986
138,910	153,190	167,330

Source: Comecon Data 1990, 1991.

TABLE 4.III.8 Money in circulation

(Million Lei)			
1980	1984	1985	1986
39,700	49,200	55,130	60,360

Source: Comecon Data 1990, 1991.

TABLE 4.III.9 Growth of GNP by producing and consuming sectors

	(Percent Average Annual Rate of Growth)		
	1985	1987	1989
GNP	−2.0	−0.1	−1.7
Producing sector			
Industry of which	1.7	−0.3	2.6
Machinery	5.1	3.1	4.3
Agriculture and forestry	−8.5	−0.4	3.3
Construction	−5.8	−3.5	−1.4
Transportation and communications	−3.5	0.2	−0.3
Trade	1.6	2.7	1.4
Services	1.8	3.8	4.2
Other	0.9	−4.5	−0.1
Consuming sector			
Personal consumption	7.5	2.5	1.4
Government	−0.4	−5.4	−0.8
Gross investment	−9.7	−25.0	−5.5
Residual	−20.7	3.9	0.9

Source: U.S. Central Intelligence Agency, "Eastern Europe: Long Road Ahead to Economic Well-Being," May, 1990.

TABLE 4.III.10 Growth of GNP inputs and productivity

	(Percent Annual Average Rate of Growth)			
	1980	1985	1987	1989
GNP	−2.2	−2.0	−0.1	1.7
Combined inputs	3.1	3.2	2.7	3.4
Capital stock	8.6	8.0	6.7	8.9
Labor	0.3	0.6	0.6	0.5
Combined productivity	−5.2	−5.0	−2.8	−1.6
Capital productivity	−9.9	−9.3	−6.4	−6.6
Labor productivity	−2.5	−2.6	−0.8	1.2

Source: U.S. Central Intelligence Agency, "Eastern Europe: Long Road Ahead to Economic Well-Being," May 1990.

TABLE 4.III.11 Consumer spending on various items as a percentage of personal income, 1989 (Romania and selected countries)

	Total per Head $	Percent Food/ Drink	Percent Clothing	Percent Energy	Percent Household Goods	Percent Health	Percent Transport
Romania	1,557	31.7	10.0	2.9	5.5	3.9	4.0
USSR	2,820	43.2	19.0	7.0	8.0	2.7	2.9
United States	12,233	13.3	6.5	19.5	5.7	14.7	14.8
France	9,635	20.0	7.0	18.8	8.3	8.8	16.7

Source: The Economist, *Book of Vital World Statistics,* 1990.

IV. EDUCATION

TABLE 4.IV.1 Schools, students, and teachers

	1980–1981	1987–1988	1989–1990
Schools			
General schools[a]	14,381	13,895	13,357
Vocational schools[b]	603	764	798
Technical colleges[c]	1,271	1,303	1,020
Universities	44	44	44
Students (thousand)			
General-school pupils[d]	3,308	3,027	2,892
Vocational-school pupils	140	278	305
Technical-college students[e]	1,008	1,251	1,348
Day pupils	736	N/A	N/A
Pupils per 10,000 population	454	546	582
Technical-college graduates	178.0	200.4	205.7
University undergraduates	193	157	165
Day students	161	N/A	N/A
Pupils per 10,000 population	87	68	71
University graduates	37.8	28.1	27.6
Teachers (thousand)			
General-school teachers[f]	157	142	142
Technical-college lecturers[g]	46.8	43.9	42.5
University academic staff	14.6	12.0	11.7

[a]Includes general lower secondary schools and combined lower/upper secondary schools. General schools include the compulsory primary/lower secondary school (7–10 years' schooling) and an upper secondary stage of 2–4 years.

[b]Pupils here receive a job-oriented education.

[c]Includes distance-learning institutions for teaching certificates; technical colleges to train technicians, technical colleges to improve the qualifications of workers' and similar for craftsmen.

[d]Includes both day and evening school pupils and also those on correspondence courses.

[e]Includes pupils involved in distance learning to gain teaching certificates, at technical colleges for technicians, at technical colleges to improve the qualifications of workers and craftsmen.

[f]Includes general schools and combined lower/upper secondary schools; teaching staff includes those members of staff with secondary or higher education who work as teachers, instructors, and technical instructors in the school workshops.

[g]The academic staff includes those members of staff with secondary or higher education, as well as staff seconded from industry (engineers, technicians, craftsmen, etc.).

Source: EUROSTAT, *Central and Eastern Europe 1991,* 1991.

TABLE 4.IV.2 Public expenditures on education

Year	Lei	As Percent of GNP	Percent of Total Government Expenditures
1975	15,194,700,000	3.5	6.4
1980	19,930,200,000	3.3	6.7
1985	17,940,900,000	2.1	N/A

Source: UNESCO, *Statistical Yearbook,* 1989.

TABLE 4.IV.3 Expenditures and pupils per teacher, 1989
(Romania and selected countries)

Country	Percent of GNP	Pupils per Teacher Primary/Secondary
Romania	2.1	21/33
USSR	7.3	17/N/A
United States	6.7	21/13
France	5.7	19/17

Source: The Economist, *Book of Vital World Statistics,* 1990.

TABLE 4.IV.4 Distribution of teachers and pupils by educational level, 1987

Educational Level	Schools	Teachers	Percent Female	Pupils	Percent Female
Preschool	12,291	31,300	100[b]	829,079	49[b]
First-level	13,895	141,609	70[b]	3,027,196	49[b]
Second-level	2,067	46,270	48[b]	1,529,372	46[b]
General	981	6,280	55	102,553	70
Teacher training	N/A	717	62	4,851	95
Vocational[a]	1,086	39,273	46[b]	1,421,968	44[b]
Third-level[a]	101	12,036	29[b]	157,041	45[b]
Total	28,354	231,215		5,542,688	

[a] Includes evening and correspondence courses.
[b] 1985 data.

Source: UNESCO, *Statistical Yearbook,* 1989.

TABLE 4.IV.5 Mean years of schooling[a], 1980
(Romania and selected countries)

Country	Total
Romania	6.6
USSR	7.6
United States	12.2
France	9.4

[a] For adults over 25 years old.

Source: UN, *Human Development Report 1991,* 1991.

TABLE 4.IV.6 School enrollment ratios[a]

Year	First Level (Ages 6–13)	Second Level (Ages 13–17)	Third Level (Ages 20–24)
1975	107[b]	65	9.2
1980	102[b]	71	11.0
1987[c]	97	79	9.8

[a] Percent total enrollment of all ages divided by the population of the specific age groups that correspond to the age groups of primary and secondary schooling.
[b] Ratios exceeding 100 reflect instances in which the students at a given level are not necessarily in the age group delineated for that level.
[c] 1987 data represent new age ranges in the following categories: first level (ages 6–13) and second level (ages 14–17).

Source: UNESCO, *Statistical Yearbook,* 1989.

TABLE 4.IV.7 School enrollment, 1989 (Romania and selected countries)

| | (Percent) | | | | | |
| | Primary | | | Secondary | | |
	Total	Male	Female	Total	Male	Female
Romania	97	N/A	N/A	79	79	80
USSR	106	N/A	N/A	98	N/A	N/A
United States	100	101	100	98	99	99
France	113	114	113	92	89	96

Source: The Economist, *Book of Vital World Statistics,* 1990.

TABLE 4.IV.8 Books, newspapers, and library book loans, 1989 (Romania and selected countries)

	Books Published per Year	Newspaper Circulation (Thousand)	Library Books Loans per Year (Thousand)	Volume Stock (Thousand)
Romania	5,276	3,637	56,752.0	69,559
Netherlands and Sweden	24,845	8,980	240,568.0	84,346
USSR	83,011	12,982	2,634.3[a]	1,523,071
United States	48,793	62,502	197,328.1	523,493

[a]Soviet library regulations rarely allow the loaning of books, thus the low figure.

Source: The Economist, *Book of Vital World Statistics,* 1990.

V. ENERGY AND RESOURCES

TABLE 4.V.1 History of primary energy production (Romania and selected countries)

| Energy Type | Country | (Thousand Barrels per Day of Oil Equivalent) | |
		1970	1980
Coal	Romania	125	164
	USSR	6,080	6,370
	United States	7,359	9,785
	France	523	284
Crude oil	Romania	281	242
	USSR	7,060	12,030
	United States	11,380	10,170
	France	68	51
Natural gas	Romania	460	639
	USSR	3,270	7,170
	United States	10,686	9,838
	France	118	129
Hydro/nuclear	Romania	13	57
	USSR	660	1,170
	United States	1,394	2,774
	France	317	665

Source: U.S. Central Intelligence Agency, *Handbook of Economic Statistics,* 1990.

TABLE 4.V.2 Complete energy use

(Thousand Metric Tons)

	Year	Production	Consumption[a]	Exports	Imports	Soviet Portion of Imports (%)[b,c]	
Crude oil[e]	1985	10,718	25,344	0	14,626	2,360	(16)
	1988	9,389	29,789	0	20,400	4,016	(20)
	1990	7,929	23,929	0	16,000	2,642	(17)
Refined	1985	24,700	15,060	9,690	50	2	(4)
oil	1988	29,380	16,530	12,900	50	4	(8)
products	1990	23,664	15,364	8,400	50	8	(16)
Motor	1985	5,305	1,405	3,900	0	N/A	
and	1988	6,595	1,785	4,800	0	N/A	
aviation gas	1990	4,667	1,927	2,740	0	N/A	
Diesel oil	1985	6,842	4,071	2,771	0	N/A	
	1988	8,348	4,178	4,170	0	N/A	
	1990	6,232	3,312	2,920	0	N/A	
Fuel oil	1985	8,432	5,867	2,565	0	N/A	
	1988	9,903	6,583	3,320	0	N/A	
	1990	8,121	5,771	2,350	0	N/A	
Other	1985	4,131	3,717	454	50	N/A	
refined	1988	4,534	3,984	600	50	N/A	
products	1990	4,644	4,304	390	50	N/A	
Natural gas[d]	1985	36,875	38,709	0	1,834	1,834	(100)
(million cm³)	1988	33,000	36,995	0	3,995	3,995	(100)
	1990	28,336	35,727	0	7,391	7,391	(100)
Hard coal	1985	8,657	14,705	0	6,048	2,166	(36)
(including	1988	9,100	16,100	0	7,000	2,856	(41)
anthracite)	1990	5,200	10,200	0	5,000	770	(15)
Brown coal	1985	37,924	37,976	0	52 0		
(including	1988	49,660	49,550	0	0 0		
lignite)	1990	32,983	35,271	212	2,500	2,500	(100)
Coke	1985	5,182	7,080	0	1,898	152	(9)
	1988	5,950	7,350	0	1,400	8	(1)
	1990	4,200	5,000	0	800 0		
Electricity	1985	71,819	75,078	0	3,259	2,000	(61)
(million kWh)	1988	75,318	82,293	0	6,975	5,575	(80)
	1990	64,161	74,021	0	9,860	6,200	(63)

[a] Romania is the 17th largest energy consumer in the world.
[b] Soviet portion of imports as a percent.
[c] To the nearest 1%.
[d] Romania is ranked 7th in the world among nations whose energy is generated from gas. It is the 8th largest producer of dry natural gas in the world.
[e] 1 metric ton = 8.03 barrels of oil.
Source: "PlanEcon Report," vol. 7, March 6, 1991.

TABLE 4.V.3 Electricity production[a] (Romania and selected countries)

	(Billion Kilowatt-Hours)			
Country	1970	1980	1985	1989
Romania	35.09	67.49	71.82	76.25
USSR	740.93	1,293.88	1,544.10	1,722.00
United States[b]	1,742.73	2,437.82	2,634.65	2,970.21
France	146.97	243.29	325.73	378.00

[a] Data are for total (gross) production at generating centers and therefore include transmission losses and station use.
[b] Beginning in 1980, data are for public utilities only.
Source: U.S. Central Intelligence Agency, *Handbook of Economic Statistics,* 1990.

TABLE 4.V.4 Installed electricity generating capacity[a] (Romania and selected countries)

Country	(Million Kilowatts)		
	1970	1980	1988
Romania	7.35	16.11	21.73[b]
USSR	166.15	266.71	339.00
United States	360.33	630.94	677.65
France	36.22	63.66	100.62

[a] All plants for both public and industrial use.
[b] 1987 figure.

Source: U.S. Central Intelligence Agency, *Handbook of Economic Statistics,* 1990.

TABLE 4.V.5 Commercial energy use by sector[a], 1985 (Romania and selected countries)

	(Percentage of Commercial Energy Used)				
	Industry	Transport	Agriculture	Commercial and Residential	Other[b]
Romania	64	4	0	32	0
USSR	60	13	0	27	0
United States	31	35	1	30	4
France	33	26	2	35	3

[a] Includes all solid, liquid, and gaseous fuels, as well as primary and secondary electricity.
[b] Other includes nonenergy uses, military uses, and nonspecified uses.

Source: From *World Resources, 1988–1989.* Copyright © 1988 by the World Resources Institute and the International Institute for Environment and Development in collaboration with the United Nations Environment Programme. Reprinted by permission of Basic Books, a division of Harper Collins Publishers Inc.

TABLE 4.V.6 Proved reserves of crude oil, natural gas, and coal, 1989 (Romania and selected countries)

Country	Crude Oil (Billion Barrels)	Natural Gas (Trillion Cubic Feet)	Coal (Million Metric Tons)
Romania	1	9	N/A
USSR	50–80	1,450	182,000
United States	26	165	205,000
UK	4	21	4,200
France	0.03	0.18	1,070

Source: U.S. Central Intelligence Agency, *Handbook of Economic Statistics,* 1990; U.S. Department of Energy, Energy Information Administration, *International Energy Annual,* 1988; UN, *Energy Statistics Yearbook,* 1986.

TABLE 4.V.7 Mineral production

Mineral	1985	(Tons) 1987	1989
Alumina	548,000	584,000	610,800
Aluminum, primary	247,000	260,000	269,100
Antimony	600[d]	600[d]	500[d]
Barytes	75,000[d]	72,000[d]	N/A
Bauxite (and aluminum)	460,000	480,000	345,200
Bentonite	180,000[d]	180,000[d]	180,000[d]
Bismuth	80[d]	75[d]	65[d]
Cadmium	55[d]	50[d]	46[d]
Coal			
Anthracite and bituminous	10,472,000	11,693,000	8,293,854
Lignite	38,513,000	43,109,000	52,199,793
Brown	834,000	897,000	843,652
Copper			
Mine production	30,000[d]	38,000[d]	42,900
Smelter production	36,000	38,000[d]	43,000[d]
Refined	42,000[d]	41,000[d]	48,000
Diatomite	290,000[d]	280,000[d]	260,000[d]
Feldspar	86,000[d]	82,000[d]	59,960
Ferro-alloys, electric furnace			
Ferro-chrome	44,000[d]	42,000[d]	42,000[d]
Ferro-manganese	80,000[d]	81,000[d]	80,000[d]
Ferro-silico manganese	39,000[d]	39,000[d]	40,000[d]
Ferro-silicon	50,000[d]	50,000[d]	50,000[d]
Silicon metal	4,500[d]	4,500[d]	4,500[d]
Fluorspar	20,000[d]	18,000[d]	16,000[d]
Gold, mine production of[a]	5,000[d]	5,000[d]	6,000
Graphite	12,000[d]	12,000[d]	10,000
Gypsum	1,620,000[d]	1,500,000[d]	1,600,000[d]
Iron ore	2,287,000	2,281,000	2,482,385
Iron, pig	9,212,000	8,673,000	9,500,000[d]
Kaolin	410,000[d]	400,000[d]	400,000[d]
Mineral production of lead	34,300[d]	30,200[d]	37,700[d]
Production of refined lead	48,636	43,186	45,000
Manganese ore, 22%[b]	68,000	65,000[d]	60,000[d]
Natural gas[c]	38,904	37,418	32,000
Petroleum, crude	10,718,000	9,504,000	9,237,000
Salt	5,019,000	5,395,000	5,500,000
Sillimanite minerals	70,000[d]	70,000[d]	70,000[d]
Silver[a]	25,000[d]	20,000[d]	25,000[d]
Steel inputs and castings	13,795,000	13,885,000	14,415,000
Sulfur and pyrites[b]			
Pyrites, 42%	200,000[d]	150,000[d]	150,000[d]
Recovered	150,000[d]	130,000[d]	N/A
Talc	65,000[d]	65,000[d]	60,000[d]
Zinc, mineral production	40,000[d]	40,000[d]	45,000[d]
Zinc, slab production	53,000	51,000	49,500

[a] Kilograms.
[b] Estimated average content.
[c] million m^3.
[d] Estimated.

Source: British Geological Survey, *World Mineral Statistics,* 1984–88; *World Mineral Production,* 1985–89.

VI. GOVERNMENT AND DEFENSE FORCES

TABLE 4.VI.1   State budget, 1989

| | (Billion Lei) | | |
	1987	1988	1989
Revenue:			
Tax revenue	86.87	89.46	94.88
Social security contributions	49.15	50.67	53.94
Taxes on payroll and workforce	37.72	38.79	40.94
Entrepareneurial and property income	280.17	244.21	255.37
Share of gross sales	48.72	144.71	150.61
Other receipts from social units	17.32	16.28	16.49
Share of net production	93.17	74.12	83.11
Administrative fees, charges and nonindustrial sales	.16	.24	1.02
Fines and forfeits	1.01	2.40	1.54
Other nontax revenue	35.64	27.77	33.52
Total	408.85	364.08	386.33
Expenditure			
General public service, including public order	1.87	1.88	1.90
Defense	25.28	27.54	29.33
Education	15.48	15.31	16.08
Health	14.80	15.09	16.20
Social security and welfare	66.89	69.82	75.40
Housing and community amenities	22.80	26.09	25.10
Recreational, cultural, and religious affairs	1.27	1.08	.28
Economic affairs and services	192.54	154.38	153.29
Fuel and energy	29.39	27.29	26.51
Agriculture, forestry, fishing and hunting	22.89	19.88	18.60
Mining, manufacturing, and construction	34.10	36.85	35.94
Transportation and communication	12.63	19.78	19.51
Other purposes	95.53	50.58	52.73
Total	343.79	314.09	320.55

Source: The Europe World Year Book, 1991.

TABLE 4.VI.2   Hard-currency debt

	(Billion in U.S. $)			
	1980	**1985**	**1988**	**1989**[a]
Gross debt, of which	9.4	6.6	2.2	0.4
Government	1.7	1.1	0.6	0.2
Commercial	6.5	3.0	0.4	0.2
Other	1.2	2.5	1.2	0.0
Reserves	N/A	0.2	0.8	1.2
Net debt	N/A	4.4	−1.1	−3.3
Debt service ratio[b]	N/A	32%	37%	23%

[a] Estimated.

[b] Debt service ratio is calculated as the share of principal and interest payments to total hard-currency earnings.

Source: U.S. Central Intelligence Agency, "Eastern Europe: Long Road Ahead To Economic Well-Being," May, 1990.

TABLE 4.VI.3   Armed Forces totals, 1991

Total armed forces	200,800	(127,200)[a,b]
Branches		
Army	161,800	(105,700 conscripts)
Navy	19,200	(10,800 conscripts)
Air Force	19,800	(10,700 conscripts)
Total reserves	626,000	
Army	565,000	
Navy	40,000	
Air Force	21,000	
Manpower	193,537	men reach the military age of 20 annually.
Budget	11.8	billion lei ($797.48 million)[c]

[a] Romania has not reduced its active duty personnel, though the majority are not considered combat-ready and are used primarily as an internal police.

[b] Excludes interior forces. Border Guards 18,400; Security Troops 34,800.

[c] Budget is for 1990. Budget based on 23.43 lei = $1.

Source: The International Institute for Strategic Studies, *The Military Balance 1991–1992,* 1991. Copyright IISS.

TABLE 4.VI.4   Components of defense force, 1985

Army
  Organization
      2   tank divisions
      8   motorized rifle divisions
      3   mountain regiments
      2   airborne
      4   artillery regiments
      5   antitank regiments
      2   antiaircraft artillery regiments
      2   surface-to-surface missile brigades
  Major equipment (1985)
    30+   battle tanks
   1,200   medium tanks
    400   BRDM-1/-2 reconnaissance vehicles
    900   heavy mortars
Navy
  Organization
    Naval bases at Mangalia, Constanta, Danube, Braila, Giurgiu, Sulina, and Tulcea
  Major Equipment (1985)
      3   Tetal frigates
     40   motor torpedo boats
     46   river patrol craft
     16   minesweepers

(continued)

TABLE 4.VI.4   *(continued)*

Air Force
  Organization
        6   fighter/ ground attack squadrons
       12   interceptor squadrons
        1   transport squadron
        1   helicopter regiment
  Major equipment (1985)
       70   MiG-17 fighter-bombers
      230   interceptor aircraft:
             30   MiG-23
            200   MiG-21
       33   transport aircraft
      110   helicopters
       18   reconnaissance aircraft
       80   training aircraft
       18   surface-to-air missile sites with 108 SA = 2

Source: Reprinted with permission from *World Defense Forces,* 2nd Edition, published by ABC-CLIO, 1989.

TABLE 4.VI.5   Military expenditures

	1979	1980	1985	1987
Billion lei	11.8	10.4	12.1	11.6
Constant price figures (million U.S. $)[a]	1,689	1,461	1,345	1,289
Military expenditures as a percent of GNP:				
Romania[b]	4.4%	4.3%	4.3%	N/A
USSR	12.9	13.0	12.5	N/A
United States	4.9	5.3	6.6	6.0
France	3.9	4.0	4.1	4.0

[a] 1986 exchange rates and prices.

[b] For Eastern European countries, the ratios of military expenditures to GNP in dollars are about twice the ratios that would obtain in domestic currencies.

Sources: SIPRI Yearbook 1988, 1989: World Armaments and Disarmament, Stockholm International Peace Research Institute, 1988, 1989; *World Military Expenditures and Arms Transfers,* 1987.

VII. INDUSTRY

TABLE 4.VII.1   Industrial production index[a] (Romania and selected countries)

				(1980 = 100)			
Country	1960	1970	1980	1986	1987	1989	1990[b]
Romania	N/A	54	100	104	103	97	179
USSR	38	68	100	113	116	118	115
United States	45	73	100	113	119	129	130
France	47	75	100	100	102	110	111

[a] Indexes for the noncommunist countries are value-added weighted indexes of industrial intermediate and final products. Industry includes manufacturing, mining, and, in most countries, public utilities. The indexes for the communist countries are estimates constructed by the U.S. Central Intelligence Agency, as nearly as possible on the same basis as the indexes for Western countries, and include manufacturing, mining, and public utilities.

[b] Preliminary.

[c] Index of gross values of output for individual commodities and branches are aggregated by 1982 value-added weights. This index is as comparable with the index of U.S. industrial production of the U.S. Federal Reserve Board as data will permit.

Source: U.S. Central Intelligence Agency, *Handbook of Economic Statistics,* 1991.

TABLE 4.VII.2 Industrial production index (official and adjusted)

	1960	1970	1980	1986	1987	1988[a]
			(1980 = 100)			
Official	10	35	100	140	147	156
Adjusted	18	52	100	97	93	90

[a] Preliminary.

Source: U.S. Central Intelligence Agency, *Handbook of Economic Statistics,* 1991.

TABLE 4.VII.3 Production of selected industrial items

	(Thousand Metric Tons, Unless Otherwise Noted)		
	1985	1986	1987
Agricultural and forestry products			
Canned fish	17	29	20
Canned vegetables	316	346	361
Canned fruits	163	183	167
Refined sugar	582	489	646
Margarine	33	39	42
Wine[a]	5,349	11,846	8,055
Beer[a]	9,847	10,603	10,364
Tobacco products	33	31	33
Cotton yarn, pure & mixed	170	181	172
Woollen yarn, pure & mixed	72	77	76
Flax and hemp yarn, pure & mixed	38	38	35
Chemical wood pulp	554	610	572
Paper and paperboard	741	768	712
Synthetic rubber	156	173	152
Fuels, minerals, metals, and chemicals			
Chemical filaments and fibers	257	303	287
Sulfuric acid	1,835	1,971	1,693
Caustic soda	814	846	817
Soda ash	836	895	894
Chemical fertilizers	3,097	3,278	2,897
Insecticides, fungicides, etc.	53	53	41
Plastics and resins	628	664	638
Gasoline	5,305	5,991	6,692
Distillate fuel oils	6,842	7,886	8,203
Residual fuel oils	8,432	8,198	10,330
Lubricating oils	572	568	554
Coke	5,182	5,670	5,826
Cement	11,189	13,054	12,435
Unworked glass[b]	61,994	68,584	72,990
Pig iron	9,212	9,329	8,673
Crude steel	13,795	14,276	13,885
Rolled steel products	9,900	10,207	9,675
Steel tubes	1,513	1,565	1,394
Aluminum, unwrought	265	269	275
Refined lead, unwrought	49	52	43
Machinery & equipment			
Electric motors[c]	8,065	9,226	9,107
Electric generators[d]	788	683	490
Tractors	70.2	39.2	37.9
Manufactured consumer goods			

[a] In thousands of hectoliters.

[b] In thousands of square meters.

[c] In thousands of kilowatts.

[d] In thousands of kilovolt-amps.

(continued)

TABLE 4.VII.3   *(continued)*

Cotton fabrics, pure and mixed[e]	700	731	710
Woollen fabrics, pure and mixed[e]	131	140	139
Linen & hemp fabrics, pure and mixed[e]	149	160	160
Silk fabrics, pure and mixed[e]	135	138	142
Footwear[f]	117,000	121,364	119,309
Rubber tires[g]	7,210	7,459	6,487
Passenger cars[g]	134.2	124.4	129.3
Radio receivers[g]	571	580	618
TV sets[g]	522	530	484
Washing machines[g]	210	263	242
Refrigerators[g]	400	404	420

[e] millions of square meters.

[f] In thousands of pairs.

[g] In thousands.

Source: The Europa World Year Book, 1990.

TABLE 4.VII.4   Rank of industry, manufacturing, and service sector share of GDP[a], 1990 (Romania and selected countries)

	Rank
Romania	4
Brunei	1
Angola	20
USSR	9

[a] All former East Bloc countries rank in the top 10 except Hungary. No OECD country is in the top 20. Additionally, no East Bloc state, nor the Soviet Union are among the top 20 countries in terms of manufacturing share of GDP or services share of GDP. This chart indicates the significant role of extractive industries in Eastern Europe and the USSR.

Source: The Economist, *Book of Vital World Statistics,* 1990.

TABLE 4.VII.5   Industrial waste generation

Romania has yet to release these figures.

TABLE 4.VII.6 Emissions of air pollutants, 1988[a]
(Romania and selected countries)

	Nitrogen Oxides		Sulfur Dioxide		
	Emissions (Thousand Tons)	Emissions per Unit GNP (Grams)	Emissions (Thousand Tons)	Emissions per Unit GNP (Grams)[c]	Greenhouse Index[b]
Romania[d]	390	4	1,800	19	2.2
USSR[e]	4,510	2	18,584	10	3.4
United States[f]	19,800	4	20,700	4	5.3
France	1,615	2	1,226	1	2.4

[a] Preliminary data.
[b] Carbon heating equivalents, metric tons per capita. 1988–1989 data.
[c] East European countries have a significantly higher emissions per unit GNP because of inefficient production. For example, on average, these countries use 50–100 percent more energy than the United States to produce a dollar of GDP, and 100–300 percent more than Japan.
[d] SO_2 estimate from 1980, NO_x estimate from 1985.
[e] Stationary sources only. 1987 data.
[f] Sulfur data are for sulfur oxides.

Source: State of the World 1991, A Worldwatch Institute Report on Progress Toward a Sustainable Society, 1991; UN, Human Development Report 1991, 1991.

TABLE 4.VII.7 Environmental summary, 1991

	Romania	Netherlands and Sweden[a]	USSR	United States	France
Energy					
Energy production					
Solids[b]	709	0	14,299	20,736	365
Liquids[b]	385	153	24,139	17,297	145
Gas[b]	1,050	2,146	25,541	16,280	115
Biomass[b]	31	115	742	1,150	97
Nuclear[c]	0	69,907	213,001	529,352	303,928
Hydroelectric[c]	12,627	72,146	222,803	272,023	51,158
Energy consumption					
Total[b]	2,887	3,925	52,027	69,496	6,119
Per capita[d]	132	226	193	307	149
Per capita (global rank)	27	13	12	7	22
Energy intensity					
BTUs/$1987 GNP	56,016	13,007	N/A	15,787	8,784
Global rank	14	108	N/A	99	120
Waste					
Access to sanitation services					
Urban population	100%	100%	100%	N/A	100%
Rural population	95%	100%	100%	N/A	100%
1988 Greenhouse emissions					
Carbon dioxide[e]	66,000	52,000	1,200,000	1,400,000	96,000
Methane[e]	1,900	1,590	35,000	40,000	2,800
CFSs[e]	N/A	16	110	190	50
Share of world emissions	0.7%	0.4%	13.6%	17.3%	1.7%
Global rank[f]	45	42	14	7	41

[a] Yugoslavia is compared to both the Netherlands and Sweden combined, because when combined, they are of comparable population.
[b] Trillion BTUs.
[c] Gigawatt hours.
[d] Million BTUs.
[e] Thousand tons.
[f] Per capita.

Source: From The 1992 Information Please Environmental Almanac. Reprinted by permission of the Houghton Mifflin Company.

VIII. LABOR FORCE

TABLE 4.VIII.1 Workforce by selected areas of the economy

	(Percent)		
	1980	**1986**	**1989**
Total (thousands)	10,350.1	10,669.5	11,070.0
Material production	87.6	87.3	87.0
of which			
Manufacturing industry	43.8	44.7	45.1
Agriculture and forestry	29.8	28.7	27.9
Transport and communications	7.2	7.1	7.1
Distributive trades, hotels, and restaurants			
Wholesale purchasing	6.0	5.8	5.9
Nonmaterial production	12.4	12.7	13.0

Source: EUROSTAT, *Central and Eastern Europe 1991,* 1991.

TABLE 4.VIII.2 Average monthly earnings by economic sector[a,b]

	(Lei)			
	1980	**1985**	**1989**	**1990**[c]
Total	2,238	2,827	3,063	N/A
of which				
Agriculture	2,160	2,752	2,981	N/A
Manufacturing sector	2,307	2,824	3,045	N/A
Construction	2,494	3,288	3,691	N/A
Transport	2,267	2,935	3,196	N/A

[a] State and cooperative sector; the average monthly wages and salaries of manual and nonmanual workers are calculated by taking 1/12 of total annual wages and salaries and dividing it by the average number of registered manual and nonmanual workers.

[b] Excluding taxes on wages.

[c] Average of first six months of the year.

Source: EUROSTAT, *Central and Eastern Europe 1991,* 1991.

TABLE 4.VIII.3 Economically active population by sex and industry, (from 1977 census)

	(Percent)		
	Males	**Females**	**Total**
Total	5,866,883	4,926,719	10,793,602
Agriculture and forestry	37.7%	62.3%	3,975,629
Industry	65.9	34.1	3,502,558
Construction	88.9	11.1	697,237
Utilities	77.1	22.9	115,560
Commerce	43.9	56.1	575,196
Transport, storage, and communications	87.5	12.5	556,505
Services	45.9	54.1	1,323,557
Other activities	53.6	46.4	47,360

Source: The Europa World Year Book, 1990.

IX. POPULATION AND HEALTH

TABLE 4.IX.1 Geography and demographic profile, 1990

Population	
Population in 1990	23,273,285
Population by 2000	24,400,000 est.
Population by 2020	25,400,000 est.
Current annual percent increase	0.5%
Population density per sq km	97
Net migration rate	−1 migrants/1,000
Urban/Rural (1986)	50.6%/49.4%
Ethnic Division	
Romanian	89.1%
Hungarian	7.8%
German	1.5%
Serb/Croat, Russian, Turk, Gypsy (combined)	1.6%
Religion	
Romanian Orthodox	70%
Roman Catholic	6%
Protestant	6%
Greek Orthodox	3%
Other	15%
Geography	
Total area	237,500 sq km (91,699 sq mi)
Land area	230,340 sq km (88,934 sq mi)
Coast line	225 km (140 mi)
Land borders with	
Bulgaria	608 km (378 mi)
Hungary	443 km (275 mi)
USSR	1,307 km (812 mi)
Yugoslavia	546 km (339 mi)
Disputes with	
Transylvania question with Hungary	
Bessarabia question with USSR	

Source: The Economist, *Book of Vital World Statistics,* 1990; U.S. CIA, *Atlas of Eastern Europe,* August 1990; Population Reference Bureau, *1989 World Population Data Sheet* (Washington, D.C.: Population Reference Bureau, Inc., 1989); U.S. CIA, *The World Factbook,* 1990.

TABLE 4.IX.2 Population (Romania and selected countries)

	(Million People at Midyear)				
	1960	1970	1980	1985	1990
Romania	18.4	20.3	22.2	22.7	23.3
Netherlands and Sweden	19.0	21.0	22.4	22.9	23.3
USSR	214.3	242.8	266.4	278.9	290.9
United States	180.7	205.1	227.8	239.3	250.9
France	45.7	50.8	53.9	55.2	56.4

Source: U.S. Central Intelligence Agency, *Handbook of Economic Statistics,* 1990, 1991.

TABLE 4.IX.3 Population by age (Romania and selected countries)

Age	Romania (1985) Total	Percent	Netherlands and Sweden (1987) Total	Percent	United States (1987) Total	Percent	USSR (1987) Total	Percent
<19	7,596,910	33.4	5,955,690	25.8	70,857,000	29.1	92,267,217	32.8
20–44	7,602,036	33.5	8,949,669	38.7	97,413,000	40.0	99,559,765	35.4
45–64	5,372,469	23.6	4,831,138	20.9	45,293,000	18.6	64,009,456	22.8
65+	2,153,421	9.5	3,367,020	14.6	29,836,000	12.3	25,501,353	9.0
Total	22,724,836	100.0	23,103,517	100.0	243,400,000	100.0	281,337,791	100.0

Source: UNESCO, *Statistical Yearbook,* 1989.

TABLE 4.IX.4 Population of major cities, 1986 (Romania)

Bucharest	1,989,823
Brasov	351,493
Constanta	332,676
Timisoara	325,272
Iasi	313,060
Cluj-Napoca	310,017
Galati	295,372
Craiova	281,044
Braila	235,620
Ploiesti	234,886

Source: The Europa World Year Book, 1990.

TABLE 4.IX.5 Health indicators, 1990 (Romania and selected countries)

Birth rate	16.0/1,000
of United States	15.0/1,000
of USSR	18.0/1,000
Death rate	11.0/1,000
of United States	9.0/1,000
of USSR	10.0/1,000
Infant mortality rate	22.0/1,000
of OECD and United States	9–10/1,000
of USSR	25.0/1,000
Maternal mortality rate[a]	150/100,000
of OECD and United States	10/100,000
of USSR	48/100,000
Life expectancy	68 male/73 female
of OECD	72 male/78 female
Fertility rate	2.2 children/woman
of United States	1.9 children/woman
of USSR	2.4 children/woman
Suicides[b]	6.6/100,000
of OECD and United States	14.6/100,000
of USSR	19.8/100,000

[a] Figures refer to live births. 1980–87 figures.

[b] 1987–88 figures.

Source: Population Reference Bureau, *1989 World Population Data Sheet,* (Washington, D.C: Population Reference Bureau, Inc., 1989); The Economist, *Book of Vital World Statistics,* 1990; UN, *Human Development Report 1991,* 1991.

TABLE 4.IX.6   Registered illnesses

Illness	1969	1975	1981
Influenza	538,245	235,584[a]	119,205
Mumps	79,912	64,333[a]	77,197
Viral hepatitis	56,296	54,488	53,877
Chicken pox	65,273	55,745[a]	53,527
Measles	147,859	10,476[a]	21,584
Gonococcal infections	22,143	34,774	18,929
Bacillary dysentery	19,118	27,751	17,768
Streptococcal angina and scarlet fever	14,813	14,416	9,559

[a] 1980 data.

Source: EUROSTAT, *Central and Eastern Europe 1991*, 1991.

TABLE 4.IX.7   Fatalities by selected causes of death

Cause of Death	1974	1981	1984
Circulatory illnesses	97,360	126,666	136,591
of which			
Illnesses of the cerebrovascular system	26,868	32,547	34,687
Ischaemic heart diseases	16,691	28,316	33,477
Hypertonia and hypertensive heart diseases	10,817	16,246	19,233
Arteriosclerosis	N/A	14,725	15,747
Acute myocardial infarction	N/A	9,552	9,790
Chronic rheumatic heart diseases	2,749	2,196	1,542
Malignant neoplasms	26,166	28,332	29,041
of which			
Windpipe, bronchi, and lungs	4,079	4,937	5,353
Stomach	5,226	4,215	4,065
Colon	823	1,117	1,173
Pneumonia	12,485	11,773	9,474
Bronchitis, emphysema, and asthma	15,958	10,738	9,198
Chronic liver disease and cirrhosis	4,472	6,702	7,519

Source: EUROSTAT, *Central and Eastern Europe 1991*, 1991.

TABLE 4.IX.8   Life expectancy by sex, 1991
(Romania and selected countries)

Romania	
Male	69
Female	75
USSR	
Male	65
Female	74
United States	
Male	72
Female	79
France	
Male	74
Female	82

Source: U.S. Central Intelligence Agency, *The World Factbook*, 1991.

TABLE 4.IX.9 Medical care, 1983–1988 (Romania and selected countries)

			(Number per Million)		
	Doctors	Dentists	Pharmacists	Beds (Thousand)	Total Health Expenditure[a]
Romania[b]	1,738.0	317.0	285.0	8.8	1.9
Netherlands and Sweden	2,630.0	790.0	144.6	12.6	8.8
USSR[b]	4,124.0	N/A	321.0	12.8	3.2
United States	2,035.0	560.0	641.0	5.9	11.2
OECD	2,199.5	453.8	559.2	8.0	8.3

[a] As a percent of GDP. 1987 figures.

[b] Figures for former communist countries are clearly misleading. According to the Soviet Ministry of Health, 1.2 million beds are in facilities with no hot water, 1/6 of the beds are in hospitals with no water, and 30 percent of the hospitals have no indoor toilets. Source: *Literaturnaya Gazeta,* February 3, 1988; and see also *World Affairs,* vol. 152, no. 1, Summer 1989.

Source: Population Reference Bureau, *1989 World Population Data Sheet,* (Washington, D.C.: Population Reference Bureau, Inc., 1989); The Economist, *Book of Vital World Statistics, 1990;* UN, *Human Development Report 1991,* 1991.

TABLE 4.IX.10 Abortion rates (Romania and selected countries)

Country	Number of Abortions	Rate per Thousand Women Aged 15-44	Ratio per 100 Known Pregnancies	Total Rate[a]
Romania[b] (1987)	421,400	90.9	56.7	N/A
Netherlands and Sweden (1986)	53,300	12.6	17.0	378
USSR (1985)	6,818,000	111.9	54.9	N/A
United States (1985)	1,588,600	28.0	29.7	797

[a] The number of abortions that would be experienced by 1,000 women during their reproductive lifetimes, given present age-specific abortion rates.

[b] Unlike the very liberal abortion laws in other East European countries, there are many legal restrictions in Romania. Despite such restrictions, the rate remains high, comparable to those around Eastern Europe. These legal restrictions and high abortion rates result in a number of illegal abortions. Such illegal abortions account for the high maternal mortality rates in Romania (between four and ten times the rate in other East European countries).

Source: Adapted with permission of The Alan Guttmacher Institute from Stanley K. Henshaw and Evelyn Morrow, *Induced Abortion: A World Review 1990 Supplement,* 1990.

X. TRADE

TABLE 4.X.1 Exports and imports, by commodity group

	(Million U.S. $)		
Commodity Group	1970	1980	1986
Exports:			
Machinery and equipment	422	2,791	4,338
Fuels, minerals, and metals	420	3,720	3,113
Agricultural and forestry products	496	1,962	1,488
Manufactured consumer goods	335	1,816	2,113
Other	178	920	1,450
Total	1,851	11,209	12,502
Imports:			
Machinery and equipment	790	3,153	2,830
Fuels, minerals, and metals	596	6,447	5,406
Agricultural and forestry products	306	1,884	1,166
Manufactured consumer goods	108	310	445
Other	160	1,124	753
Total	1,960	12,818	10,600

Source: U.S. Central Intelligence Agency, *Handbook of Economic Statistics,* 1990.

TABLE 4.X.2 Main destinations of exports and main origins of imports, 1990

Country	Percent of total
Destinations of exports:	
USSR	25.2
Italy	8.8
West Germany	10.2
United States	5.8
France	3.4
Socialist countries[a]	45.8
Nonsocialist countries[a]	54.2
Origins of imports:	
USSR	23.6
West Germany	11.4
Saudi Arabia	8.3
Iran	5.9
United States	4.6
Socialist countries[a]	57.4
Nonsocialist countries[a]	42.6

[a] 1987.

Source: EIU, "Romania, Country Report," No. 4, 1991. EIU, "Romania Country Profile," 1991–1992, 1991.

TABLE 4.X.3 Principal trading partners

	Exports to (Percent)		Imports from	
	1982	1985	1982	1985
USSR	17.0	21.4	18.4	22.4
United States	3.2	5.8	3.1	3.2
Western Europe				
France	3.1	2.6	N/A	1.3
Italy	N/A	7.5	N/A	1.7
United Kingdom	1.9	2.7	N/A	1.8
West Germany	7.9	7.5	4.9	3.4
Eastern Europe				
Bulgaria	N/A	1.7	N/A	3.0
Czechoslovakia	3.1	2.2	3.6	3.3
East Germany	4.6	4.2	6.1	5.8
Hungary	2.4	2.4	2.6	2.8
Poland	3.3	3.5	4.2	5.5
Other				
China	4.2	4.0	4.1	3.7
Egypt	2.1	3.6	2.5	10.4
Iran	4.4	2.1	8.9	8.6
Iraq	8.1	3.6	3.7	1.7
Libya	N/A	0.3	3.5	0.8
Saudi Arabia	N/A	0.1	N/A	0.2
Syria	N/A	1.1	4.9	4.3
Total including others	100.0	100.0	100.0	100.0
Total (lei billion)	151.8	192.3	124.9	148.4

Source: The Europa World Year Book, 1990.

TABLE 4.X.4 Index of import and export prices, terms of trade
(Romania and selected countries)

| | (1980 = 100) | | | |
	1984	1986	1987	1989
Romania				
Import prices	135	130	127	N/A
Export prices	124	114	114	N/A
Terms of trade	92	88	90	N/A
Bulgaria				
Import prices	128	125	124	112
Export prices	111	110	112	110
Terms of trade	86	88	90	98
Czechoslovakia				
Import prices	134	146	142	137
Export prices	112	119	119	129
Terms of trade	84	81	83	93
Hungary				
Import prices	125	136	139	163
Export prices	116	120	124	153
Terms of trade	93	88	89	94
Poland				
Import prices	139	198	279	1,281
Export prices	127	189	275	1,516
Terms of trade	91	95	99	118
Yugoslavia				
Import prices	116	108	109	124
Export prices	108	107	108	123
Terms of trade	93	99	100	99
Soviet Union				
Import prices	115	112	110	113[a]
Export prices	130	114	110	103[a]
Terms of trade	113	102	100	100[a]

[a] 1988.

Source: Comecon Data 1989, 1990, 1990, 1991.

TABLE 4.X.5 Major imports and exports[a]

Import Goods/Categories	(Thousand U.S. $) 1987	1988	1989
Meat and meat preparations	24,253	22,313	20,210
Paper, paper board, and articles of paper pulp	10,734	12,673	16,689
Nonmetalic mineral manufactures[b]	27,554	36,061	40,654
Iron and steel	24,342	58,788	52,364
Nonferrous metals	30,282	38,165	71,351
Manufactures of metals[b]	18,757	15,868	20,642
General industrial machinery and equipment[b]	11,982	10,184	16,193
Furniture and parts therof; bedding, etc.	176,189	177,298	191,221
Articles of apparel and clothing accesories	187,167	203,866	207,878
Footwear	39,634	37,262	23,617

Export Goods/Categories	1987	1988	1989
Meat and meat preparations	1,839	28	27,985
Organic chemicals	18,730	16,939	13,440
Dyeing, tanning, and coloring materials	16,584	16,631	14,602
Chemical materials and products[b]	15,582	21,312	15,089
Textile yarn, fabrics, made-up articles and related products[b]	84,845	99,492	106,063
Iron and steel	20,267	15,840	13,024

[a] According to SITC headings.
[b] Not elsewhere specified.

Source: EUROSTAT, *Central and Eastern Europe 1991,* 1991.

TABLE 4.X.6 Trade with Western countries[a]

	Importing Countries (Million U.S. $)				Exporting Countries			
	Jan–Dec 1985	1988	1989	Jan–Jun 1990	Jan–Dec 1985	1988	1989	Jan–Jun 1990
Austria	6.5	5.7	5.7	4.5	4.6	3.5	3.2	5.5
Belgium/Luxembourg	3.2	4.9	4.1	3.5[d]	4.3	2.2	2.2	6.2[d]
Finland	1.0	1.4	1.5	1.2	0.5	0.2	0.2	0.5
France	26.4	39.4	38.9	31.2	11.8	9.9	11.1	21.8
West Germany	45.4	65.8	68.2	56.8	26.4	27.3	25.9	60.3
Greece	4.7	4.8	5.9[c]	N/A	3.3	2.7	3.4[c]	N/A
Italy	75.4	69.1	79.9	42.0[d]	13.3	6.0	8.0	12.5[d]
Netherlands	10.5	11.2	10.5	8.7[d]	3.4	4.0	5.8	9.1[d]
Spain	5.0	8.8	9.6	8.3	1.4	0.2	0.5	2.1
Sweden	5.3	4.3	3.7	3.2[d]	1.7	1.4	1.8	2.3[d]
Switzerland	1.7	1.5	2.1	1.5	2.9	1.0	1.6	4.2
Turkey	5.3	16.5	19.8	18.2[e]	3.9	6.3	4.4	7.0[e]
UK	11.1	15.0	16.0	8.5	8.5	7.4	5.2	11.9
United States[b]	73.5	56.7	29.5	19.9	17.4	16.9	13.0	44.3

[a] Monthly averages from Western countries' trade accounts, in million U.S. $.
[b] Imports, fas.
[c] January–November.
[d] January–May.
[e] January–April.

Source: EIU, "Romania, Country Report," No. 4, 1990.

TABLE 4.X.7 Trade with the USSR, by commodity

Imports from the USSR	(Million Rubles[a])	
	1987	1988
Metal-cutting machine tools	42.4	37.6
Power-generating equipment	18.0	18.2
Mining, hoisting, excavating, etc., machinery	92.8	69.3
Tractors and agricultural machinery and parts	9.2	8.3
Motor vehicles and garage equipment	20.9	21.1
Aircraft and ships	23.0	29.4
Other machinery and transport equipment	183.0	192.8
Coal and coke	71.8	73.1
Petroleum and products	703.7	522.9
Fuel gas and electricity	489.1	560.1
Metal ores and concentrates	140.9	123.0
Pig iron and ferro alloys	43.6	43.0
Rolled ferrous products and pipes	100.5	103.0
Chemicals	59.6	65.7
Wood, paper, and manufactures	53.6	44.7
Raw cotton	55.3	57.7
Domestic appliances, clocks, and cameras	7.8	9.8
Total, including other items		
Million rubles	2,539.2	2,344.1
Million U.S. $	4,217.9	3,830.2

Exports to the USSR	1987	1988
Metal-cutting machine tools	57.3	61.4
Electrical equipment	50.1	46.1
Geology etc., equipment	346.3	425.8
Hoisting and conveying equipment	N/A	N/A
Computer equipment	N/A	N/A
Agricultural machinery	79.7	77.6
Railway equipment	241.8	215.2
Ships and boats	58.0	76.8
Other machinery and transport equipment	202.4	283.1
Rolled ferrous products and pipes	156.8	153.0
Chemicals	64.6	65.7
Fruit and vegetables	33.1	34.0
Wood	28.4	26.3
Raw tobacco	N/A	N/A
Tobacco manufactures	N/A	N/A
Textile cloth and manufactures	301.9	310.9
Footwear	70.4	60.8
Furniture	103.5	120.6
Beverages	N/A	N/A
Total, including other items		
Million rubles	2,347.2	2,431.2
Million U.S. $	3,899.0	8,524.9

Note: Commodity totals are additions of items in the trade accounts and may be incomplete.

[a]Noncommercial rate: end 1987 .602 rubles = $1.00, end 1988 .612 rubles = $1.00

Source: EIU, "Romania, Country Report," No. 4, 1990.

TABLE 4.X.8   Trade with the United States, by commodity

	(Thousand U.S. $)	
Imports from the United States	**1987**	**1988**
Cereals and preparations	61	2,610
Tobacco manufactures	289	N/A
Hides and skins, undressed	12,920	36,216
Oilseeds	81,829	59,320
Pulp and waste paper	3,004	185
Crude fertilizers and minerals	2,798	1,298
Coal	47,143	65,875
Petroleum and products	30	118
Chemicals	10,711	5,782
Iron and steel	80	75
Metal manufactures	367	550
Road vehicles	64	88
Other transport equipment	51	245
Scientific instruments, etc.	1,270	521
Machinery, including electric	23,365	20,292
Power-generating machinery	15,942	15,213
Total, including other items	192,107	202,245

Exports to the United States	**1987**	**1988**
Meat and preparations	15,996	9,480
Dairy products	440	447
Tobacco and manufactures	N/A	N/A
Crude rubber	186	1,458
Textile fibers and waste	3,196	1,466
Crude animal and vegetable materials	501	244
Petroleum and products	376,220	370,247
Chemicals	6,757	11,845
Paper, etc., and manufactures	3,945	1,798
Textile yarn, cloth, and manufactures	24,333	20,348
Nonmetallic mineral manufactures	17,175	18,866
Iron and steel	26,774	41,027
Nonferrous metals	39,214	6,638
Machinery, including electric	30,719	36,831
Transport equipment	2,986	1,858
Furniture	29,197	22,214
Clothing	95,580	72,335
Footwear	23,278	40,777
Total, including other items	715,347	680,623

Source: EIU, "Romania, Country Report," No. 4, 1990.

CHAPTER FIVE

BULGARIA

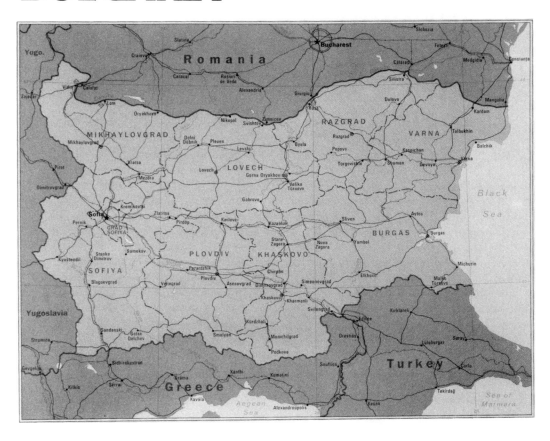

POPULATION:	8.98 million
SQUARE MILES:	43,325 mi², 110,912 km²
RELIGION:	Eastern Orthodox
CURRENCY:	Lev
EXCHANGE RATE:	Lv 31.0 : $1
DEBT:	$10.8 billion

I   BULGARIA

POLITICS, HISTORY, AND ECONOMICS

POLITICS

Bulgaria has a long and special relationship with the Soviet Union. In the ninth century, Bulgarians brought their civilization to the early Russians residing in the forests of Kiev— Kievan Rus'. Two Bulgarian missionaries, Cyril and Methodius, brought Christianity and the Cyrillic alphabet to those pagan Russians. This early relationship produced an exceptional tie between the Bulgarians and their Slavic brothers to the north, strengthened in the nineteenth century when Imperial Russia liberated Bulgaria from more than five hundred years of Ottoman rule. The result was an ambivalent relationship. The Bulgarians continue to believe they are still in Moscow's debt while simultaneously considering themselves the equal or even the superior of the pagan Russians they "civilized." Thus, the bond between Sofia and Moscow runs deeper than their common reading of Marx or Lenin. Their historical connections and their cultural similarities—their languages are similar and Sofia's state buildings, currency, and newspapers closely resemble Moscow's— all suggest the depth of the Slavic connection that exists between the two states.

During the communist period, Bulgaria was unquestionably the Soviet's most loyal ally while its leader, the obsequious Todor Zhivkov, saw the Soviet Union as his patron saint. So close and trusting was Bulgaria that in political circles, even communist ones, Bulgaria was referred to as the "Sixteenth Republic" of the Soviet Union. The allegiance went considerably beyond adulation. Bulgaria performed significant services for its idol. It peddled and transshipped Soviet arms and appears to have overseen the attempted assassination of Pope John Paul II. In every Soviet satellite, of course, there were sycophants eager to carry out the designs of Moscow. But remarkable in the Bulgarian case is the extent to which the Soviets were willing to entrust that satellite, extraordinarily more than its other fraternal allies, with the most sensitive and potentially embarrassing of its foreign policies. Lavish rewards were one of the products of this unique relationship. Soviet subsidies to Bulgaria, in per capita terms, were far higher than to other bloc states, while the weapons shipped to Sofia were always the most modern that Moscow was to let outside its borders.

From 1985, this close bond was strained as Gorbachev talked of reform, deeply unsettling Zhivkov, a man who had made his career espousing the latest Moscow doctrine. He could not accept Gorbachev's *glasnost* or his "new thinking" in foreign policy. Zhivkov believed that Gorbachev had violated 70 years of communist orthodoxy in order to enhance his own popularity with the Soviet people by criticizing his own communist predecessors, to whom Zhivkov had so steadfastly extended his loyalty. Gorbachev could break with the dead and depreciated Brezhnev, but Zhivkov remained a living Brezhnevite, the embodiment of the pure communist party system—fully corrupt, jealous of his prerogatives, effectively wielding power with a Mafia-like control that rewarded friends and family and destroyed those even vaguely suspected of disloyalty.

Zhivkov was different from the heads of the other communist states. He had outlasted and survived them all. Perversely, his longevity supplied a valuable legacy to his communist comrades not enjoyed by any other East bloc state. When Zhivkov finally fell in late 1989, the Bulgarian Communist Party (BCP) renamed itself the Socialist Party (BSP), placed the blame for the entire communist debacle on him, and managed to win a legislative majority in open elections. Outside observers saw this as a sure sign that even by eastern European standards, Bulgaria was hopelessly politically unsophisticated with no democratic tradition. Indeed, in the early months of 1990, the country remained politically adrift, without significant economic reform.

By the end of the year, however, Bulgaria appeared to be coming of age. The opposition could advance its own agenda as it finally outmaneuvered the dominant Socialist Party. Bulgaria began to follow the general pattern of political and economic reform established by the Hungarians and Poles. The ruling Socialists had neither the strength nor the inclination to derail that process.

Current Politics

The fall of the Berlin Wall on November 9, 1989, was only one, if the most powerfully symbolic, of the monumental events sweeping the East bloc. The very next day, the reverberations shook Sofia. After 35 years in office, 78-year old Todor Zhivkov, the longest-reigning party boss in the East bloc, was removed as the head of the Bulgarian Communist Party. Zhivkov's fall was a stunning turn. He had overseen the Party since 1954 and appeared in full control of the seemingly minor rumblings for change in Bulgaria. He had already proved himself a consummate survivor by his adept manipulations, both within and without the Party. Chosen by Khrushchev over more conservative rivals, Zhivkov used that endorsement to secure his political base. He survived an attempted coup in 1965 and settled into a long and comfortable tenure as party chairman and head of state during the Brezhnev period.

Like other communist directors, he had rewarded his family and friends. He promoted his daughter, Lyudmila, to Politburo status and kept her there, despite her eccentric mysticism, which was fully incompatible with Marxism-Leninism and a public embarrassment to her family and the party. Her brother, too, enjoyed similar promotions even in the face of his notorious pilfering of state funds.

Despite his nepotism, however, Zhivkov had extraordinary political skills. The most obvious was his ability to change with the times. Whether Khrushchev, Brezhnev, Andropov, or Chernenko ruled the communist capital, Todor Zhivkov nurtured his good standing in Moscow. As a result, his mentors gave him free reign to conduct business in Sofia as he saw fit. His skill at shuffling potential political rivals while maintaining continuity of policy seemed to improve with age. But once Gorbachev assumed the helm, Zhivkov's position as the loyal party boss in Sofia dramatically changed.

Initially, it appeared that Zhivkov could shift with the tide as he had done so many times before. Gorbachev's *perestroika* seemed an easy enough program to emulate. For Zhivkov a simple reshuffling of bureaucrats and party men was thought to be enough to satisfy Moscow. It was not, however, and in 1987, Moscow demanded a more determined reform effort. Zhivkov again complied, making deeper personnel changes and initiating genuine, although highly controlled, economic reform. The Bulgarian leader found he could deal with *perestroika*, Gorbachev's ideas for restructuring the economy and even the political system. But he could not respond effectively to Gorbachev's *glasnost*, or openness, which he equated with self-annihilation. In Bulgaria, the criticism of communism had totally different implications from the criticism of Soviet communism. Gorbachev, after all, could not be held directly responsible for the stagnation of the Brezhnev years or the terror of the Stalin era. But Bulgarian communism was synonymous with Zhivkov. Criticism of that system was an indictment of Zhivkov.

For short periods in 1987 and 1988, Zhivkov had flirted with tolerating independent associations and a more open press. But no sooner did he grant "socialist pluralism" than he withdrew it again. The slightest openness had then mushroomed quickly into bitter criticisms of the entire system. Zhivkov cracked down vigorously and was not about to repeat that experience under Gorbachev's renewed pressures. Yet in retrospect, it is doubtful that any degree of political liberalization could have saved the aged leader. Zhivkov embodied an historical legacy that symbolized for Bulgarians, and for Gorbachev, the fundamental flaws of communism.

Ultimately, two groups were responsible for Zhivkov's ouster—dissidents among the people and reformists in the Bulgarian Communist Party. Initially, the people merely encouraged BCP reformists; they weren't at the forefront of the social and political upheavals that had swept other communist parties from office. In the first contested elections in early 1990, they could not defeat the Bulgarian Socialist Party, the renamed BCP minus Zhivkov and his cronies. Nevertheless, as early as December 1989, they were setting the political agenda.

Overt dissidence had not been visible in Bulgaria until that year, because non-communists lacked organization and leadership in the face of Zhivkov's control. Several reform organizations appeared after the 1987 thaw, but they were all closely monitored and constantly harassed, including the independent trade union Podkrepa, the Federation of Clubs for Glasnost and Perestroika, Turkish rights groups, and various ecological clubs. Only those deemed harmless by Zhivkov were allowed to remain visible after the crackdown. The most visible of these were the ecological activists. The ecological activists evolved from critics of government environmental abuse to more general political dissent, all the while presenting their demands in an elliptical manner. Their transformation proved to be a crucial step in the downfall of the communist government and a major political force, with which the reformers had to deal after Zhivkov's departure.

In October and November of 1989, the Conference on Security and Cooperation in Europe (CSCE) sponsored an international ecological symposium in Sofia. The Bulgarian government sent its official environmental commission, but an unofficial ecological group, Ecoglasnost, demanded representation. Underestimating the impact of the environmentalists, Zhivkov agreed to their request. In his mind, allowing ecological activism was a perfect way to seize the high road of political reform and prove his conversion to *perestroika*. Emboldened by government recognition and shielded by the foreign journalists covering the CSCE conference, Ecoglasnost publicized its demands. It also initiated a petition campaign decrying two government hydroelectric projects.

Initially, the dissidents were allowed to collect signatures. But Zhivkov balked when they called for a petition-signing rally in a central Sofia park. On October 26, 1989, the Bulgarian police beat several of the protest leaders and arrested those who had come to participate in the rally. Yet under the scrutiny of the international press corps, the government soon released the detainees and described the arrests and beatings as a "misunderstanding." But its responsiveness to international scrutiny emboldened those Bulgarian reformists. On November 3, a huge crowd of demonstrators gathered outside the National Assembly to present Ecoglasnost's petitions to the government. And while a parliamentary group accepted the petitions without incident, the demonstration had stimulated soul-searching in the highest levels of the party.

Zhivkov's ouster on November 10, 1989, was not so much a revolution—the popular forces were peripheral to the event—but a palace coup, carried out by ranking but younger party members with the unabashed blessing of Gorbachev. Four of Zhivkov's associates were crucial in the changing of the guard. Two were dominant—Petar Mladenov, Foreign Minister since 1971, who replaced Zhivkov as Party chief and later became president, and Dobri Dzhurov, the Minister of Defense. They were joined by Aleksandar Lilov, who would become BCP chief in February, 1990, and Andrei Lukanov, Minister of Foreign Economic Relations, who became the Prime Minister.

Although Zhivkov's removal appeared almost offhand, a plan had been in the works for the better part of a year. On the very day the Berlin Wall was crumbling, Mladenov, returning from an official visit to China, stopped off in Moscow for discussions with his longtime acquaintance Gorbachev and other key officials. Mladenov was given permission, if not instructions, to replace Zhivkov. He returned to Sofia on the same day and that very evening gathered Zhivkov, as well as the rest of the Politburo, to inform them that Zhivkov was resigning. Zhivkov had sensed his end was near. Before the meeting he had engaged in frantic activities to stave off his betrayal; appreciative of the collapse of his political support, he conceded immediately and accepted the will of the "gang of four." Not lacking in grace, after acquiescing to his own ouster, Zhivkov, along with the rest of the Politburo, retreated to his study for drinks. The following morning, on national television, Mladenov read Zhivkov's resignation, an ironic, whimpering departure for the man who had for so long dominated the largest communist party in the East bloc.

The men who took power were true Gorbachev-style reformers. Their counterparts in East Germany and Romania claimed that mantle, but the new Bulgarian leaders deserved it. They intended to eliminate the endemic corruption of the former regime and to rescue Bulgaria from its economic torpor. Like Gorbachev, they certainly had no intention of surrendering the political monopoly of the party. Mladenov promised other reforms—gradual political liberalization and the increasing separation of the party from state functions.

To preserve the position of the party and secure their power, the new leaders distanced themselves from the former regime by developing a revisionist history, which placed the blame for communist failures on Zhivkov and his inner circle. After the political transition, they arrested Zhivkov and most prominent Politburo members, investigated their finances, and initiated prosecution for embezzlement and other outrageous misdeeds.

But the new leadership repeated the failings of Zhivkov by underestimating the power of the populace. Zhivkov's resignation and the changes sweeping other Eastern European capitals had emboldened independent political groups. Each day, they rallied in Sofia and other cities to demand multi-party democracy and a new constitution guaranteeing civil rights. Despite their varied political views, the most prominent dissident and anticommunist groups formed an umbrella organization, the Union of Democratic Forces (UDF), under the leadership of Zhelyu Zhelev. Some 16 different groups and parties had joined together, all prepared to bring their country to a complete standstill to achieve their common goals. For a country with no democratic tradition and no history of dissent, their challenge was impressive and dramatic.

After a month of demonstrations, Mladenov realized that his vague promises of reform were insufficient, and on December 13 he acceded to one of the demands of the UDF. He amended Article One of the Constitution, which had declared the Bulgarian Communist Party to be the only ruling power in the country. Later in the month, with independent trade unions still threatening strikes, the new leadership agreed to open Round Table talks to determine the future transformation of the country.

At the beginning of 1990, the communist reformers set up a government composed entirely of communists. The UDF, believing it had the upper hand, declined to join the new government, reasoning that its participation would merely enhance the legitimacy of the reform communists without giving it any leverage over communist-controlled bureaucracies. Even the Bulgarian Agrarian National Union, which Zhivkov had allowed to participate in past governments, seceded in order to assert its independence. In the face of the overwhelming momentum of events, the BCP convened an extraordinary congress in January, 1990, changed its name to the Bulgarian Socialist Party, and removed many of its most conservative members.

As happened throughout eastern Europe, the new direction resulted in mass defections from the communist party. But unlike the situation in other former satellites, the new leadership was able to maintain the BSP as a coherent organization and to run an impressive campaign in the later elections. There were constant disputes, but the party remained a viable force, at least until after the elections of June 1990.

Round Table talks among the BSP, the UDF, and the Agrarian Union (BANU) began in early 1990. The talks were televised, and their sessions became the effective policy-making body of the country, eclipsing the National Assembly, still controlled by the communists. But the Round Table talks did not go smoothly. The BSP bargained harder than expected; the BANU could not decide which group or platform to favor; and the UDF, in an uncompromising mood, walked out of the talks on several occasions. The UDF believed that its growing popular support entitled it to threaten the BSP with national strikes. In the end, a document was produced specifying the essentials necessary for a transition to democracy.

Free elections for a new legislature were scheduled for June 10. The new legislature, the Grand National Assembly, would have 400 members, half of whom were to be chosen by proportional representation from 28 constituencies, while the other half were to be elected from 200 single-member districts. A two-thirds majority of parliament would elect the president, who in turn, with parliamentary approval, would appoint a prime minister. The prime minister was empowered to appoint a government, also requiring legislative confirmation. According to the Round Table agreements, the first parliament would have 18 months to draft a new constitution in addition to its general responsibilities as a legislature.

After the initial agreements, in the period prior to the June elections, the Round Table continued to meet to negotiate further reforms. The negotiations mirrored the political turmoil engulfing the country. The BSP repeatedly attempted to reach agreements with the UDF on crucial economic matters, but the latter adamantly refused, just as it had refused to join the interim government. In the UDF's opinion, any gradual reform would inevitably fail. Given that belief, the UDF chose to boycott every reform measure, leaving the BSP to prove its ineptitude on its own. But the BSP, confronted with the need to bear full responsibility for economic reform, chose instead a safer course—to do practically nothing at all.

Bulgaria's economic progress in the first half of 1990 was the result of a relaxation on certain formerly prohibited economic practices rather than any significant administrative or legislative reforms. The BSP was fully aware of the precarious economic condition of the country. But as the election approached, it made public promises to avoid drastic measures. Lukanov and other reformers feared that instituting any fundamental changes would cost the BSP popular support, which had remained remarkably strong.

More than 30 parties, movements, and coalitions participated in the June 10 elections and in a second round of balloting, held a week later. Many of the groups had banded together under the umbrella of the UDF. As a result, only four parties—BSP, UDF, BANU, and the Movement for Rights and Freedoms (MRF)—were significant. The UDF managed to win the elections in October 1991, but the results indicated a new level of political complexity. The victory was modest because the UDF lost three of its major factions. Disintegration was to be expected given the diversity of the UDF, but their victory was only substantial enough to form a minority government. To maintain its position, the UDF requires the support of the Turkish party. Yet given the nationalist sentiment of the country, it will be difficult for the UDF to sustain Turkish support while at the same time satisfying the majority of the public.

The Movement for Rights and Freedoms (MRF) was created to protect the rights of the Turkish minority in Bulgaria. In the 1970s and 1980s, Zhivkov had initiated a brutal campaign to force their assimilation. In characteristically arrogant fashion, the regime had determined that only Bulgarians lived in Bulgaria. Thus all Turks were forced to renounce their Turkish names and adopt Slavic names. Muslims were harassed when they sought to practice their faith, and the remaining vestiges of Ottoman culture were extirpated.

MRF, headed by Ahmed Dogan, was founded after Zhivkov's fall to prevent further state-sponsored repression while restoring Muslim cultural and religious freedoms. Under Zhivkov, Dogan had been one of the few Turks to defy official policy. He had restored his Turkish name and covertly organized his community, for which he had been repeatedly punished. As a result, he now enjoys special moral authority as one of those who had been violently punished. Support for MRF is near universal among the Turkish Muslim minority, slightly less than 10 percent of the population.

The Bulgarian Agrarian National Union (BANU) was the only party other than the BCP allowed a legal existence before 1990. Formerly independent, it was forced to submit to Communist Party control following WW II. Its support in 1990 came largely from farmers and others who wished to reclaim their lands previously confiscated by the communists. Yet all through the campaign, BANU equivocated over the issue of land ownership. First it advocated restoration of legal title to those who had owned the land prior to collectivization. Later in the campaign it decided that the land should belong to those who cultivated it.

UDF support came from every social group dissatisfied with the communist party. Its members ran the gamut from the new agrarian union, the ecological group, a labor confederation, and a religious rights committee to former communists who had formed social democratic parties. The gathering of such disparate groups into one organization doomed UDF to weakness through the perpetual threat of disintegration. But that diversity also provided strength—support from a wide base of social groups: students, professionals, farmers, and workers. Through the election and the rest of 1990, the UDF managed to remain united, committed to a single political platform.

For all practical purposes, the UDF managed its unity only through a highly circumscribed set of electoral tactics, advocating a moderately rapid transition to a market economy while frequently recounting the sins of the Communist Party. Some of the more powerful UDF leaders were, in fact, committed to "shock therapy" to revive the economy. But in the interests of preserving unity, they avoided any reference to more radical measures for economic reform. The same moderate strategy had appeared to work elsewhere in the bloc. It seemed an appropriate strategy in Bulgaria as well.

Despite the widespread failures of both communism and the BCP, the Bulgarian Socialist Party retained surprisingly strong support. The party stood accused of the crimes of the Zhivkov era and had been weakened by internal divisions. But it had not been fatally weakened. The BSP succeeded in projecting responsibility for its past onto Zhivkov and his associates while papering over the splits within the party. Compared to its opponents, the BSP had ample financial resources and a powerful national organization. It was able to retain the support of older Bulgarians, die-hard communists, and most of the rural population. Thus, while 200,000 members left the party in the six months preceding the elections, nearly a million others retained their membership.

Perhaps most importantly, the BSP spoke to pervasive national fears over the economy. The party constantly argued that only they could engineer the country's gradual conversion to a market economy without the pain of unemployment, inflation, and deprivation. Ironically, by avoiding reference to the disgraced Zhivkov past, the BSP managed to communicate that it was the party of the future. UDF, by contrast, appeared mired in the hated past by harping on the failures of communism.

In stark contrast to other reforming communist parties, the BSP succeeded. The voters rejected rapid change, as had the Romanians and the Serbs of Yugoslavia. In an upset, the BSP fell just shy of an absolute majority of the popular vote, but won an absolute majority of legislative seats. In the two round election, the BSP won 211 of the parliament's 400 seats. The UDF won 144 seats. Equally as surprising, MRF, the Turkish party, won 23 seats, while BANU won only 16.

The BSP victory, combined with an agreement during the Round Table talks to give the presidency to the BSP's Petar Mladenov, meant that the reformed Communist Party retained its position of power. Observers concluded that Bulgaria was too immobile for change, that the nation was bound to go the way of Romania, and would fall into Byzantine political intrigue. For the BSP, though, there was little time for them to revel in what was the ultimate achievement for a communist party: victory in a freely contested election. The ballots had scarcely been counted before the BSP fell into an immediate and unsalvageable political decline. Like almost all major political developments in the East bloc in 1989 and 1990, its precipitous unraveling was entirely unexpected.

The postelectoral failure of the BSP to govern stemmed from three related components. First, the party was composed of unmanageable factions. Second, there was pronounced economic deterioration in the country. And third, the UDF adamantly refused to form a coalition government with the BSP or support any of its economic reforms. Over the course of less than six months, these forces interacted to devastate the BSP and eliminate it as a governing force.

No sooner had Mladenov been confirmed as president and Lukanov as prime minister than the new leaders were rocked by scandal. Between the June 10 and June 17 balloting, the UDF made public a damaging videotape of Petar Mladenov. In December of 1989, when the crowds in Sofia were celebrating the ouster of Zhivkov and demanding the resignation of all communists, Mladenov was captured on tape telling Defense Minister Dobri Dzhurov that the best way to deal with the crowd was to "let the tanks come." Mladenov proclaimed the tape an edited fake, but the UDF insisted on its authenticity. Angered by its electoral defeat in the face of evidence of vote fraud, the UDF continued to publicize the scandalous tape in order to discredit Mladenov and the BSP. The validity of the tape was soon established, and public protests demanding Mladenov's resignation grew. By early July, Mladenov, acknowledging his words while insisting they had been edited out of context, resigned to save his party.

But his withdrawal did little to shake the demands of the opposition. They wanted more. The center of Sofia was taken over by thousands of students and dissidents, who had already erected a tent city called the "City of Truth." There they carried on a near 24-hour-a-day vigil, demanding the end of socialist rule and investigations into all past communist atrocities. The notion of a tent "truth" city spread to other urban centers, attracting more and more sympathizers. At their most radical, the tent protesters went so far as to firebomb the Communist Party headquarters from which the BSP operated.

As support flowed to the protesters, the BSP fell into deeper disarray. Finding a BSP presidential candidate who could muster the necessary two-thirds legislative majority proved a nightmare. The National Assembly deadlocked for nearly a month while five rounds of voting failed to produce a president. Finally, in a rare moment of compromise, the BSP yielded the presidency to the UDF, and a deal was struck. The BSP accepted the leader of the UDF, Zhelyu Zhelev, as president in return for the UDF's support for General Atanas Semerdzhiev as vice-president. Consistent with the UDF's policy of not working with the socialists, Zhelev became an independent on entering the presidency.

Filling the highest offices still did not produce political order. The UDF refused to cooperate with Prime Minister Lukanov in filling his cabinet. More than two months passed before he was able to form a government, and even then several positions remained vacant. Except for a few independents, the government, like its predecessor, had no outstanding members and was socialist–conservative.

By the time the government was operational in late September, 1990, the Socialists were a spent force. Nine months had passed since Zhivkov's ouster, and no significant economic reforms had been adopted. Every sector of the economy had declined. Shortages were more pervasive and difficult than at any time since WW II. The people finally turned against the newly elected BSP, which came to be seen as responsible for the nation's problems themselves and the coverup of their magnitude.

At the same time, the BSP leaders turned against each other. In an effort to preserve unity, the leadership hastily convened another congress, which proved disastrous. The hardliners accused the reformers of cowardice in compromising with the opposition and demanded the resignation of Lilov, the reformist party head. The reformers demanded that the hardliners be more supportive of liberalization. But the reformers were woefully outnumbered, and the BSP fell completely under the sway of the conservatives. Rather than preserving the unity of the party, this caused its collapse. The most reactionary faction broke from the party, while the remaining members split into at least seven factions.

In October, Prime Minister Lukanov made a last-ditch effort to salvage the BSP. With the tent city still challenging the government, the economy still in ruins, and the UDF still refusing to join in a coalition, Lukanov offered the legislature an exceptional economic reform proposal. With the assistance of the U.S. Chamber of Commerce, the prime minister called for freeing the majority of prices, eliminating the majority of state subsidies to industry, establishing the real value of the currency, setting real interest rates, stimulating private economic activity, and beginning privatization.

Privatization was the only area in Lukanov's program where the BSP wished to proceed more slowly than the UDF had insisted. But still the bold program was not to be. Knowing that the BSP was desperate, the UDF refused its support in the legislature.

Instead, the UDF announced that it was ready to take over the premiership and unseat the BSP government. The UDF called for more protests, and the public converged on Sofia under a rallying cry from none other than the Beatles "Let It Be." Every loudspeaker, stereo, and phonograph was enlisted to the cause. In the course of a month, the protests spread throughout the country to become the largest show of discontent ever seen in Bulgaria. The country was once again brought to a complete standstill. The independent trade union Podkrepa instituted a general strike. When workers from the former communist labor union joined the students and activists in the streets, the BSP received its deathblow. The strikers refused to return to work until the BSP resigned. Lukanov had no choice but to negotiate with the UDF, which was finally prepared to talk with the BSP on its knees. After two weeks of fierce bargaining, the Lukanov government collapsed. The state radio station, recently converted to protest through rock and roll, celebrated Lukanov's resignation by playing Pink Floyd's "The Wall."

The BSP agreed to give up the premiership to an independent political figure, and the economic ministries to the UDF. It agreed to serve as an interim government until 1991, when the Grand National Assembly would conclude the drafting of a constitution and step down for new elections. Dimitar Popov, a widely respected independent, was chosen by the UDF as prime minister. The office of deputy prime minister was expanded to three individuals, with one to each of the main parties, the BSP, UDF, and BANU. The two key economic ministries, the Ministry of Industry, Trade, and Services and the Ministry of Finance, went to the UDF's economists, Ivan Pushkarov and Ivan Kostov.

Bulgaria is now governed by a coalition, though the UDF, maintaining at least the facade of refusing to cooperate with the BSP, refers to the present governing arrangements as "a team of specialists and experts." But no one was pleased with the coalition during the first half of 1991. Political and economic change was stymied by a raucous political struggle over the drafting of the new constitution and over the claim of the UDF that the BSP has sabotaged effective economic reform. The growing tension manifested itself in the UDF's call in March—backed by a huge rally in Sofia—for the resignation of the legislature and early elections. The BSP managed to preserve the coalition but agreed to elections in the early fall of 1991. There will be little progress on resolving the major challenges confronting the country until after the elections.

Nonetheless, the country has finally joined the general trend of reform in the former East bloc and signs of a new political era are evident. Popov's government has enacted the beginnings of an economic reform package. A farm bill has been adopted, expanding private plots and establishing a framework to disassemble collective farms. Other inhibitions to private economic activity have been removed. State subsidies have been cut and price controls, except on staples, have been lifted.

Bulgaria in 1991 is very different from what was anticipated following the BSP election victory in June, 1990. The BSP plays an ever-diminishing role. While it still dominates the bureaucracy, its political power is spent and its membership has plummeted from nearly a million members to under a quarter of a million. Its popularity has plummeted in equal measure. Opinion polls show that only 10 to 15 percent of the people intend to vote for BSP candidates.

The political forces of the future will come from the UDF, but not from the same UDF that overthrew the BSP. Opinion polls show that more than 55 percent of the eligible voters are now prepared to support UDF candidates, but its unity is tenuous and began unraveling in 1991. The most powerful parties within the UDF are developing their own political agendas and are likely to split from the UDF. To the UDF's credit, there has been no effort to mask its divisions but its disintegration appears to ensure that no single party will achieve a majority in the next elections. Bulgaria is likely to be ruled by a coalition government.

There is ample opportunity for the collapse of the UDF, now comprising more than 19 organizations. The Bulgarian Agrarian National Union–Nikola Petkov, led by Milan Drenchev, represents the UDF's agricultural interests but is not to be confused with the other Bulgarian Agrarian National Union (BANU). BANU broke from the communists after Zhivkov fell. At the same time, several noncommunists also decided to form a BANU party in the tradition of the original precommunist BANU. They gave their party the name of BANU–Nikola Petkov in honor of its precommunist leader. BANU–Nikola Petkov is more liberal than the BANU, but the two have common agricultural interests and merged into a parliamentary group in May, 1991, creating a major political force.

Ecoglasnost is an exceptionally strong UDF organization. Its leaders, Georgi Avramov and Petar Staykov, remain widely popular for their role in the ouster of Zhivkov. Since then, the public has become increasingly concerned with Bulgaria's badly damaged environment. Another UDF member, the Green Party, led by Aleksandar Karakachanov, also the mayor of Sofia, is distinct from Ecoglasnost. But the two organizations have nearly the same interests and could merge after resolving personality conflicts among the leaders.

The Federation of Clubs for Glasnost and Democracy includes the nation's most prominent dissidents and intellectuals, President Zhelyu Zhelev, and Petko Simeonov. The Club is likely to remain the core of the UDF as other organizations break away.

The Podkrepa Independent Labor Confederation, led by the firebrand Konstantin Trenchev, claims membership among workers, artists, and intellectuals. Podkrepa already has moved away from the UDF in an effort to assert itself as a labor organization rather than a political party. Though not yet as large as the former communist Bulgarian Trade Unions (BTU), Podkrepa has grown tremendously and now has more than a half million members and over 60 branch offices. Trenchev has somewhat damaged his popularity by expressing sympathy with the Turks and calling for a radical transition to a free market. But defections to Podkrepa from the communist labor federation are likely to make it the largest of the two unions in 1991.

The Bulgarian Social Democratic Party, led by Petar Dertliev, and the Citizens' Initiative Association, led by Lyubomir Sobadzhiev, played important roles in the ouster of Zhivkov. They may take several of the smaller social democratic parties under their wings.

One institution other than the UDF retains enormous popular support—the military. Dobri Dzhurov, the Minister of Defense since 1964, was instrumental in the removal of Zhivkov and remains one of the most popular leaders in Bulgaria. The military is perceived as the principal stabilizing force in the country, while the widely hated Ministry of Internal Affairs is held responsible for the repression under the communists.

The monarchists also remain a political force. No sooner was the "communist monarch" Georgi Dimitrov, founder of the communist state, removed from his mausoleum and cremated in July, 1990, than the royal monarchists reappeared. In the past election, monarchist parties won only about 10,000 votes. But since then, the reappearance of former King Boris III's daughter and son, Princess Maria-Louise and King Simeon II, has been widely applauded. Princess Maria, now a resident of New Jersey, returned to Bulgaria in May, 1991, in an effort to test her brother's popularity, and was showered with affection. Her brother, now a resident of Spain, was emboldened by the visit and has asserted that he is still king until the people declare otherwise. Bulgaria is unlikely to become a monarchy, but Simeon appears popular and could seek political office.

Bulgaria faces formidable challenges. Its per capita hard-currency debt is close to the level of Poland and half the level of Hungary. But its economy is far more troubled. It defaulted on its debt payments in 1990, while the economy nearly collapsed under the weight of ceaseless strikes. It will not be revived without substantial Western capital, which may follow a new debt repayment schedule. Bulgaria's economy was more deeply intertwined with the depleted economies of the Soviet Union and its satellites than any other bloc state. The country will experience further hardship in locating new sources of energy and new trading partners.

After the economy, the most pressing problems concern regional foreign policy matters—the Turks, the Macedonia question, and relations with Romania. None of these presents an immediate crisis, but all of them have the potential to frustrate political stability.

Relations between the Turkish minority and the Bulgarian majority reached an all-time low in the mid-1980s during Zhivkov's forced assimilation campaign. More than 300,000 Turks fled to Turkey. After Zhivkov's ouster, more than half of them returned, but the ethnic tension was never resolved. Turks remain a decidedly depreciated group, and the nationalist majority, including some UDF liberals, have virtually no concern for their well-being. Even the new prime minister, Dimitar Popov, exposed his anti-Muslim and anti-Turkish sentiments in a tactless interview shortly after assuming office. Nevertheless, relations with Turkey have improved following the ouster of Zhivkov, and Turkey has helped Bulgaria make up its oil shortfall. Nonetheless, ethnic strife retains the potential to damage Bulgaria's political stability and international reputation.

The Macedonia problem dates from the Ottoman period. Bulgaria was awarded most of Macedonia in the San Stefano Treaty of 1878, only to lose it three months later at the Congress of Berlin. Bulgaria tried to reclaim the territory in the Balkan Wars prior to WW I, after which it was divided between Bulgaria, Greece, and the Kingdom of Serbs, Croats, and Slovenes (now Yugoslavia). Having failed again during WW II to reclaim the land, Bulgaria's communist rulers ignored the issue. But since 1989, a nationalist reawakening in Yugoslavia and Bulgaria has focused attention once again on the issue of Macedonia.

Relations with Romania are tense, largely because of environmental issues. Bulgaria claims that Romania's chemical-processing plants release vast amounts of toxic gases and chemicals, which drift into Bulgarian territory. Romania, in turn, has argued that Bulgarian nuclear plants are operated with reckless disregard for safety. While both countries appear guilty as charged, the strong ecological movement in Bulgaria has managed to keep the issue boiling, straining relations between the two states.

In short, Bulgaria faces a number of threats. The new government appears to have realized that caution has become a luxury it can no longer afford. Prices have been freed, and a farm bill has passed the legislature. The new commitment to reform appears certain to bring IMF and World Bank assistance, allowing Bulgaria to refinance its debt and begin a genuine process of economic and political transformation.

HISTORY

From Origins to 1900

The Bulgars were a people of Turkic origins who migrated to the Balkans in the seventh century. They mixed with the Slavic tribes, which had begun to settle the land now known as Bulgaria in the sixth century A.D. Over time, the Bulgars were assimilated, adopting

Slavic culture and language. The main remnant of the Bulgars' Turkic heritage is the name Bulgaria. The First Bulgarian Kingdom was established in 681, and from that time onward, Bulgarian history was marked by a cycle of expansion followed by invasion and periods of foreign rule. Bulgaria became a powerful military force in the ninth century, expanding into territories now part of Greece, Yugoslavia, Romania, and the USSR. By the early eleventh century, however, its power began to decline, and in 1018 the First Bulgarian Kingdom fell to Byzantium's expansion.

The Bulgarians freed themselves from the Byzantine empire in the twelfth century, establishing the Second Bulgarian Kingdom in 1186. Like the First, it began to expand its influence through a series of wars. It defeated the Western crusaders in 1205 and succeeded in extending its domains to include eastern Thrace, the Aegean coast, Albania, and Macedonia in succeeding years.

By the mid to late 1200s, Bulgaria was again in decline. Its autonomy was contested by its neighbors, of which the last and most powerful was the Ottoman Empire. The Ottoman Turks began raiding the Balkans in the early fourteenth century and succeeded in totally defeating the Bulgarians by 1396.

The period under Turkish rule is known in Bulgaria as the darkest time in Bulgarian history. Bulgarian culture, which had thrived in the two previous kingdoms, was stifled, and the Bulgarian Orthodox Church was repressed as the Turks placed it under Greek Orthodox control. The Bulgars reacted to this repression in various ways. Some fled to the mountains while others remained, but in sullen silence. Still others, who came to be known as Pomaks, improved their situation by converting to Islam. The Ottoman conquest struck a heavy blow to the Bulgarian sense of national pride.

In the eighteenth and nineteenth centuries, the Bulgarians began to regain some of their lost confidence. In 1762, Father Paisi wrote the first Bulgarian history and called for the Bulgars to reclaim their national culture. By the nineteenth century, revolutionary sentiments grew, and in 1866 a secret committee to foment revolution within Bulgaria was formed in Bucharest. Inspired by uprisings throughout the Ottoman Empire, the Bulgarians staged their own in 1876. The uprising led to thousands of deaths and Turkish reprisals but mobilized Western sentiment in favor of the Bulgarians in the face of Turkish brutality. In 1877, the Russians invaded Bulgaria to help liberate their fellow Slavs from Turkish rule, defeating the Turkish army and dictating a peace treaty at San Stefano in March of 1878. The treaty unsettled the European powers because it both created a large autonomous Bulgaria, including most of Macedonia, and specified that Russia would occupy Bulgaria for two years. These two factors led to the calling of the Congress of Berlin, where the Bulgaria created at San Stefano was divided into three parts. The Macedonian portion and Eastern Rumelia reverted to Turkish control, while the remainder of Bulgaria was made autonomous. Once again, Bulgarian national pride was wounded.

Bulgarian culture languished under Ottoman rule, leaving it with a social structure that was to shape the course of events in the liberated country. The Turks had destroyed the native Bulgarian aristocracy, so that when Bulgaria finally became independent it had no indigenous, experienced political leaders, but it did have a highly egalitarian social structure.

From 1900 to 1945

In the postliberation period, Bulgaria struggled with four interrelated problems: creating a workable constitution, limiting the Russian domination of Bulgarian politics, fostering economic development, and recovering former territories.

The Turnovo Constitution of 1879 was the most significant success story of the period. It established an advanced democracy by vesting power in a popularly elected legislative assembly, specifying civil liberties and religious rights, and creating a system of universal primary education. The democratic nature of the Turnovo Constitution was shaped by the deeply felt sense of egalitarianism. Despite this, Alexander of Battenberg, chosen by the European powers as prince of Bulgaria, worked diligently to dismantle the basic system. In 1881, he succeeded in suspending the constitution and demanded extraordinary powers for himself. Battenberg was successful in his anticonstitutional coup primarily because of the support from Tsar Alexander III of Russia. But as relations between Russia and Bulgaria soured, Prince Alexander realized that he would have to gain broad support in Bulgaria in order to maintain his position. In 1883, he agreed to restore the constitution.

The relations between Bulgaria and Russia were often marred by such power struggles in the decades before the World War. In 1886, for example, Alexander of Battenberg was deposed by a putsch, which had been encouraged by the tsar. A new prince, Ferdinand, took control of Bulgaria in August of 1887, but the power struggle between Russia and Bulgaria continued as the tsar refused to recognize Ferdinand as Bulgaria's legitimate ruler. Unlike his predecessor, Ferdinand chose to remain in the country, producing a stalemate which lasted until 1896, when Russia's new tsar, Nicholas II, recognized Ferdinand's legitimacy.

Between the times of Ferdinand's succession and Russia's recognition, the distribution of political power had been significantly altered. The powers of the executive had dramatically increased, while political parties had fragmented. In addition, the state apparatus had become suffused with corruption, leaving Ferdinand to rule with a heavy hand for 31 years.

After he had consolidated his power, one of Ferdinand's main goals was the industrialization of what had been an underdeveloped agricultural region within the Ottoman Empire. At the time of liberation, most Bulgarians were landless laborers dependent on Turkish overlords. With the liberation, however, many Turks fled Bulgaria, leaving large landholdings available for Bulgarian ownership. Since there was no native aristocracy to take over the estates, Bulgaria became a country of small landowner cultivators.

Abolishing feudalism and creating peasant landowners did not eliminate the country's agricultural problems. The peasants assumed high levels of debt in order to pay for the land they had acquired. Furthermore, their landholdings were fragmented through inheritance to the extent that nearly half of the land holdings were considered too small for subsistence. High debt levels and small plots made the use of advanced farming techniques or machinery unfeasible. As a result, agricultural yields did not increase, and Bulgarian crops were not competitive on the world market. Because the agricultural sector produced little or no capital surplus, economic development was hindered, leaving Bulgaria impoverished.

Prince Ferdinand, nonetheless, was intent on modernizing the country and committed to developing Bulgaria's railway system, which he financed through substantial foreign borrowing. The state was left with massive foreign debt payments, higher internal taxes, and an extensive railway network ill suited to the needs of the economy. Ultimately Ferdinand's attempts to modernize the country failed, and Bulgaria remained dependent on its inadequate agriculture structure.

To compound these political and economic problems, Bulgaria was swept up in its fourth major challenge: irredentism, the belief that the former territories must be recovered. It is no exaggeration to suggest that from 1878 until World War II, Bulgaria was dominated by the theme of irredentism. Bulgarians refused to forsake their claims to the lands taken from them at the Congress of Berlin and returned to the policy of territorial expansion that had characterized the two Bulgarian kingdoms. In 1885 Bulgaria annexed Eastern Rumelia, and in 1912 Bulgaria became involved in the First Balkan War, meant to drive Turkey out of the Balkans. In 1913, the Bulgarians, along with Greece and Serbia, defeated Turkey. Most of the captured Turkish territory was divided among the three victorious countries, but they could not agree on Macedonia. Finally, a compromise was reached, wherein Macedonia was divided between Serbia and Bulgaria. However, another Balkan War began in the same year. Greece and Serbia allied with the

Montenegrins, Romanians, and Turks to defeat Bulgaria. Bulgaria lost the section of Macedonia it had so recently acquired, as it was partitioned between Serbia and Greece. Unwilling to admit defeat, the Bulgarians maintained their irredentism and their hostility to the victors of the Second Balkan War. These factors were dominant influences in Bulgaria's involvement in the two succeeding World Wars.

In World War I, the Bulgarians nurtured the dream of defeating Serbia and Greece in order to regain both Macedonia and their honor. When those states joined the Entente, Bulgaria joined the Central Powers against them. With the defeat of the Central Powers, Bulgaria signed a treaty of peace that not only denied it Macedonia but Thrace as well, including the portion it had gained after the Balkan wars.

The same four problems that troubled Bulgaria prior to World War I persisted in one form or another during the interwar period. While Bulgaria did not have to grapple with the problem of writing a constitution, it still faced political instability. Relations with Russia became less burdensome as the Bolshevik revolution produced an inward turn in Russia, preoccupied by its internal problems. When Russia did try to influence politics in Bulgaria, it was through Bulgaria's own Communist Party. This proved to be both less heavy-handed and less successful than previous Russian interventions.

While those traditional problems of Bulgaria were moderated, others retained their intensity. Bulgaria remained an underdeveloped agricultural country. The challenge of industrialization had not been solved. Nor had Bulgaria dealt successfully with its territorial aspirations. The loss of territory following the war heightened irredentist feelings, focused particularly on attempts to recover Macedonia.

The main grievance with the post–World War I Treaty of Neuilly, which had stipulated peace terms for Bulgaria, was that it forced Bulgaria from all but a small part of Macedonia. Furthermore, it gave the grain-producing region of the Southern Dobrudja to Romania. Bulgarian national sentiment was wounded once again. A revolutionary organization, the Internal Macedonian Revolutionary Organization (IMRO), took on the burden of reminding politicians of the Macedonian problem. IMRO terrorized government officials and carried out raids on Yugoslavia and Greece, making irredentism as troublesome as it had been previously.

The political instability of this period helped shape the events that followed World War II. There were dramatic changes on the surface of political life. Ferdinand abdicated in 1918 in favor of his son Boris. In the first elections after the war, the bourgeois parties lost to the antiwar parties, the Bulgarian Agrarian National Union (BANU), and the Communist Party.

Aleksander Stamboliiski, the leader of BANU, who had radical ideas for agrarian reform, formed a coalition government in 1919. Believing that an East Central European federation of agrarian states could be formed as an alternative to the capitalist West and the communist East, he willingly accepted the Treaty of Neuilly. Because of his internationalist vision, he believed that Macedonia and Bulgaria would eventually be joined into one union. The same radical approach to agrarianism also extended to domestic politics. Stamboliiski was suspicious of cities and of all those who drew their livelihood from them. He revised taxes in favor of peasants; he housed the poor in the large residences of the rich; and while he made education available and compulsory to age 14, he discouraged the higher study of academic disciplines. In short, he put his faith in the village. His approach to domestic politics, too, proved no more successful than his approach to international relations. He failed to establish a common ground for cooperation with the Communist Party. The Party maintained an ideology based on industrialization which he refused to accept. As a result, the communists refused to come to his support when he most needed allies. Boris, now King Boris, was equally hostile, since Stamboliiski had threatened his right to rule.

Ultimately, in 1923, Stamboliiski was murdered and the government overthrown by a coalition of IMRO and military elites. The coup marked a shift in Bulgarian politics. The new government reasserted traditional Bulgarian irredentist claims, while the bourgeois parties reasserted their dominance and excluded the communists and the agrarians from participation in government.

The bourgeois parties outlawed communist party organizations and gave free rein to IMRO to assassinate radical agrarians. Meanwhile, the Great Depression struck Bulgaria with particular ferocity and eroded support for the government. In 1934, the military seized power with no popular mandate other than the general disillusionment with the previous government. King Boris seized the initiative and staged a royal coup. He outlawed all political parties and suspended the constitution in an effort to impose political quiet across the country.

But the King could not still Bulgarian politics, because he could not resolve the two dominant challenges of its twentieth-century history—irredentism and economic development. Internal political forces demanded the return of Bulgaria's "lost" territories, driving the country to an alliance with Germany, the major continental revisionist state. Bulgarian politics were also energized by the failure of economic development.

Agriculture, remaining a subsistence enterprise, showed few substantial gains. Individual plots remained small and became increasingly arid and infertile. The number of plots increased 17.9 percent between 1926 and 1934, while the average landholding actually decreased by 14 percent during the same period. In order to provide land for redistribution, Stamboliiski had instituted a land reform program with rigorous upper limits on the size of landholdings. But virtually all rural land already fell within the limits he established.

Following the First World War, Bulgaria lost the Dobrudja, its chief grain-producing region, to Romania, further exacerbating its agricultural crisis. The Dobrudja comprised only 8 percent of the territory of prewar Bulgaria, yet it produced 20 percent of the country's grain. Its loss significantly diminished the country's agricultural surplus.

Several measures were proposed to solve the agrarian crisis, given that land reform had already been carried out. These included the modernization of agriculture and an increase in industrialization to absorb excess rural workers. While there was little or no change in terms of farm machinery, Bulgarian peasants did shift to more intensive and more highly profitable crops. The shift helped to maintain agricultural income in the face of the declining prices of the world depression.

The move toward industrialization produced virtually no results. There were few skilled laborers or managers who could work in Bulgarian factories. More importantly, industrialization was hindered by an absence of indigenous capital and the difficulties of raising foreign investments. Most foreign capital came from Germany, Bulgaria's most significant trading partner. Exports to Germany grew from 17 percent of total exports in 1921 to 66 percent in 1939. The close economic ties influenced the King's decision to ally with Nazi Germany in World War II.

When war broke out in September of 1939, Bulgaria declared its neutrality. But it feared the economic consequences of offending Hitler and saw ties with Germany as the most likely way to regain its lost territories. But given its traditionally strong ties with Russia, dating from the liberation from the Ottoman Empire, it did not wish to be involved in a war with the Soviet Union. When Bulgaria finally did enter the war on the side of the Germans, it did not declare war on the Soviet Union. In 1944, as Soviet troops were poised to invade Bulgaria, the USSR issued a declaration of war. The Bulgarians, however, chose to offer no resistance to the Soviet troops.

From 1945 to 1990

The presence of the Soviet Army was a necessary element for the seizure of control by communist parties in post–World War II Eastern Europe. But other factors were significant as well. Liberal democracy had been discredited throughout Eastern Europe in the interwar period. Because of the enormous problems of the East European states in the interwar period and their lack of experience with democracy, virtually all the experiments in liberal democracy failed. Bulgaria was no exception. Voting, for instance, was not the means by which governments were changed. Even the myth of parliamentary politics was discarded when the King carried out a royal coup and declared political parties illegal.

The rise of the communist party was also facilitated by Bulgaria's long socialist tradition. In the interwar period, the Bulgarian Communist Party had been the second largest party after the BANU, only to be outlawed after participating in a failed coup in 1923. By 1926, however, communist-backed organizations began to reappear. The Bulgarian Workers Party, the front party for the illegal communist party, was founded in 1927. It gained such widespread support that in 1932 it won the largest number of votes in the Sofia elections. The government panicked and drove the communist movement underground, where it prospered, developing a disciplined cadre as did the Bolsheviks in Russia before 1917. The party was prepared to reemerge after WW II under the mantle of the occupying Soviet army.

Bulgaria's traditional relationship with Russia was also influential in later relations between the two countries. The two countries had close cultural ties and a developed web of relationships based on mutual historical experiences. Moreover, the Russian Army was still fondly remembered for having liberated Bulgaria from the Ottomans in 1878. Thus, Bulgarian communists were not hampered by the anti-Russian feelings which plagued communists elsewhere in Eastern Europe. In addition, although the Soviet Union did declare war on Bulgaria near the end of World War II, there was little fighting between the two countries. Despite its alliance with fascist Germany, Bulgaria never did declare war on the Soviet Union.

But Bulgaria's restraint had not been motivated solely by mutual Slavic admiration. It had entered WW II for the same reason it had entered WW I: to gain territory from its European neighbors. A declaration of war on the Soviet Union would have more effectively provoked the Soviets.

Bulgaria, then, was favorably predisposed to the communist takeover on September 9, 1944. One day after the Soviet Army had entered Bulgarian territory, the Fatherland Front, the antifascist coalition founded by the communist party, came to power. The takeover, however, did not yet represent a total communist victory in Bulgaria. The Fatherland Front was a coalition of parties of which the Communist Party was the strongest. Its dominant position gave it control of the Ministries of Justice and Interior, which were essential for the gradual cooptation and elimination of rival parties. Of the several parties comprising the Front, the main competitor to the Communists was BANU. The Communist Party decided to break BANU's popularity. Until 1945, the Fatherland Front operated as a coalition, allowing the head of the BANU, Giorgi M. Dimitrov, to present his party as an independent alternative to the Communists. (Giorgi M. Dimitrov should not be confused with the head of the BCP at the time, also named Giorgi Dimitrov.) Dimitrov thought that Bulgaria should attempt to maintain ties with both the Soviets and the West. But as the international situation grew increasingly bipolar, his fence-sitting position became untenable, forcing him to resign under pressure in January of 1945.

The removal of Dimitrov marked the end of the coalition of the Fatherland Front. The Communist Party began choosing the leaders of the other parties in the coalition. Eventually, it began suppressing its partners. Finally, the party held a series of show trials, in which defendants, accused as traitors and spies, were sentenced to either death or life imprisonment.

The BCP consolidated its power by reorganizing the Fatherland Front. Beginning in 1948 and continuing in 1949, the other parties within the Front were absorbed or destroyed, the only exception being the weakened BANU, which formally maintained independence while accepting the dominant role of the Communists. BANU and several other parties allowed to exist after the full establishment of Communist control were sham parties, used to legitimate "socialist democracy."

The Communist Party, then, came to power in Bulgaria partly through happenstance and partly through a series of well-thought-out moves. It received its greatest boost from the occupying Red Army. Both the army and the party used brutal force to eliminate its competitors. In those formative years, the party was notoriously ruthless to its enemies, comparable only to the Polish party in the punishment administered to its opponents.

For years, the party demonstrated that it could maintain its power, but by the mid-1980s its power base had eroded. Prior to World War II, Bulgaria's backwardness meant low living standards as well as a sense among the Bulgarians that they were not part of the modern world. They viewed the 500 years of Turkish rule as a period of cultural and economic stagnation that had almost fatally ruined Bulgaria's possibilities for development. After World War II, there was a desperate desire for industrialization—quickly and at almost any cost.

While Bulgarians might have chosen the capitalist West as their model for development, the communist Soviet Union was seen as the more viable alternative. Stalin's industrialization drive had at least created a country advanced enough to win World War II. This, in addition to strong historical ties with Russia, moved many Bulgarians to look eastward for a model for their future. The success of the BCP was partly based on its commitment to an ideology of industrialization.

That commitment was first evident in the adoption of the Two-Year Plan in 1947. Elsewhere in eastern Europe, plans were introduced in order to rebuild after the destruction of the war. Since Bulgaria escaped significant war damage, it did not need to focus on reconstruction. The immediate and primary postwar goal was to industrialize the country. The Two-Year Plan was meant to begin the industrialization process through the implementation of a Stalinist economic model of state-owned industry and collectivized agriculture. The plan advanced Bulgaria rapidly. Prior to World War II, about 20 percent of the population was urban. By 1960, that figure had risen to 38 percent, and by 1985 it had reached 64.8 percent. Likewise, the percentage of the population employed in industry jumped from 7.7 percent in 1934, to 21.9 percent by 1960, and 37.2 percent by 1985.

Despite the initial successes of the Stalinist model, a number of problems had emerged by the end of the 1950s. These problems were not peculiar to Bulgaria but were true for all the states of Eastern Europe. First, the Stalinist model directed major investments to industry at the expense of agriculture. Since Bulgaria had a strong agricultural tradition and an amenable climate, it would have made sense to develop the agricultural sector. But given the developmental model, agriculture was largely ignored. The model also specified the allocation of inputs to heavy industry at the expense of the production of consumer goods. Heavy industry and industrial employment grew rapidly, and as a result neither agricultural production nor the living standards of the people matched the gains of heavy industry. When Stalin died in 1953, there was a move for reform.

In 1954, during the search for new ways to stimulate the Bulgarian economy, Todor Zhivkov became head of the BCP. After 10 years of minor changes, Zhivkov finally announced a comprehensive set of economic reforms aimed at producing consumer goods and fulfilling consumer needs. The scheme decentralized economic decision making, restructured wages to link them more closely to profits, and instituted a more flexible pricing system.

The economic reform program began to take hold, but in the face of a severe economic downturn it was abruptly halted in 1968. In force for only four years, the new plan could hardly have solved Bulgaria's economic problems. But a return to the Stalinist model, even a revised Stalinist model, would also not speak to the fundamental weaknesses of the economy. To counter those weaknesses, Zhivkov continued to tinker with the economy throughout the 1960s and 1970s, but by the end he had made relatively few significant changes and had failed to pull the country out of its mounting economic crisis. As the domination of the USSR over its satellites began to loosen in the latter half of the 1980s, Bulgaria once again moved in the direction of more comprehensive change.

The reforms of the 1980s were meant to devolve power to workers and managers and lead to the production of more marketable goods. The administration of the country was reorganized, and greater authority over prices and wages were once again given to individual firms, as distinct from the central planning authorities. But in 1988 Zhivkov repeated himself by abruptly canceling his own reforms. He announced that because they were not producing the results he had expected, they were rescinded.

The BCP had come to power with a commitment to industrialization. Although Bulgaria did make great strides, it failed to match the economic performance of other Eastern European states, let alone the West. Even worse, the party demonstrated that it was incapable of providing its people with a steadily advancing standard of living, producing instead periodic economic crises and shortages of goods. By 1989, the people appeared to have grown weary of failed economic reforms, focusing less on how far Bulgaria had come since 1945 but on how far Bulgaria had still to go to catch up to the West.

In May of 1989, violent protests broke out among Bulgaria's ethnic Turkish population. The government's campaign to force the "Bulgarianization" of its Turkish minority had failed and the government sent its special forces to control the protests. At the end of the month, the government announced that all Turks would be allowed to leave Bulgaria for Turkey.

An immediate mass exodus began. Some 300,000 Turks fled across the border. The repression of the Turks had exacerbated ethnic tensions. So did their flight. The majority of Bulgarian people took the exodus of the Turks as a sure indication of their greater loyalty to Turkey than to Bulgaria. But the exodus also caused immense hardships for the already floundering economy, as the Turks constituted a significant proportion of the agricultural work force. As they left the fields and orchards, even normally available foodstuffs such as milk and fruit began to disappear from the market. To counter the growing food crisis, the government announced that many firms would remain open on Saturdays, vacations would be canceled, and youth brigades would serve longer tenures.

During the summer of 1989, the flight of the Turks continued, the economic crisis sharpened, and social turmoil spread. Spurred by the disintegrating domestic situation and democratization in Eastern Europe and the Soviet Union, a number of party members determined that dramatic action was mandatory. What followed was the reorientation of the communist party; the elections in 1990, in which the reformed party won a governing majority; and then their abrupt disintegration as a unified and powerful force. Bulgaria faces certain political turmoil as its two principal political groupings, the BSP and the UDF, fragment into new political parties. The movement towards Western democracy does not appear to be what the communist reformers meant for their country in 1989. But it is the goal towards which the country has steadily progressed.

DIAGRAM OF GOVERNMENTAL STRUCTURE

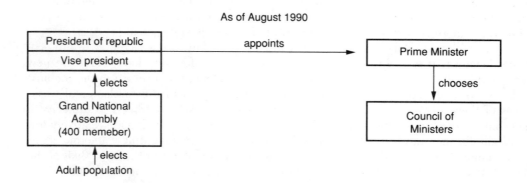

As of August 1990

ECONOMICS

Bulgaria may prove one of the best-kept economic secrets of Eastern Europe. In 1989, in all of Eastern Europe, only Poland imported more American manufactured goods than Bulgaria, while Bulgaria's exports to the United States increased more than 100 percent over the previous year. Although lacking mineral resources and energy supplies, Bulgaria had significant economic growth until the 1980s. By then its policy of concentrating investments almost exclusively in heavy industry was producing significantly diminishing returns. At the same time, its forty-year-long relationship with Moscow had become less beneficial as the Soviet economy fell into disarray.

In 1981, 1983, and 1985, the Bulgarian government announced reforms in an effort to stimulate its faltering economy. But Zhivkov faltered and scrapped all reform in 1987. In an effort to please Gorbachev, Zhivkov initiated a slight move to the market in 1987. But despite his interest in maintaining close ties to the reformist Soviet leader, Zhivkov had unwittingly pried open the system, laying the ground work for the collapse of his regime and of communist control.

The Bulgarian economy continued to decline in spite of his introduction of new reform measures, as did the economies of other socialist states as they were subject to reforms. In the face of the decline, Zhivkov never retreated. His government initiated new measures of economic decentralization and liberalized the already generous joint venture laws. The economy failed to respond.

With the dismissal of Zhivkov in late 1989, the resignation of Mladenov in mid-1990, the fall of Lukanov's socialist government in late 1990, and the assumption of responsibility for the key economic ministries by UDF in December, 1990, even greater acceleration in the transformation of the economic structure appears certain, especially following the September 1991 elections.

But that remains for the future. Now Bulgaria suffers from many of the economic ills of its former allies. Poverty is pervasive, with at least 40 percent of the population living below the poverty levels established by the government. Consumer goods and basic foodstuffs have been severely rationed, and housing is in short supply. A chronic budget deficit has unleashed sporadic but spiraling inflation since 1990. The government suspended repayment of principal on its $11 billion foreign debt in the first quarter of 1991 and suspended interest payments in the second quarter, thus ensuring that no additional short-term credits would be forthcoming. A labor shortage has also developed as the population has grown by less than 1 percent per annum while hundreds of thousands of Turks have fled. At least half the industrial firms are counted prime candidates for bankruptcy and extinction.

Despite the government's political confusion, the UDF and its coalition partners share similar objectives regarding the economy. The government appears committed to rapid economic reform, sensing that "shock therapy" is the last remaining option. Reforms are seen as necessary to attract foreign investment, eliminate the trade dependency on the USSR, and most important, break the stranglehold of the communist bureaucratic system. Bulgaria has reached its new consensus in a remarkably peaceful fashion, suggesting it may yet have a smoother transition from communism to a still uncertain future than will its neighbors.

Current Economic Reforms

The first contemporary economic reform to have lasting effect came in December, 1987, with the passage of a decree entitled "Regulations on Economic Activity." Far short of a market-type conversion, the decree was an attempt to institutionalize a host of partial reforms that had been implemented at the beginning of the Gorbachev era. More substantial reforms, resembling Hungary's, were instituted in January of 1989. The reforms have not been as sweeping as in other bloc states, but they have been consistent and suggest the existence of a firm base for future changes.

The "Regulations of 1987" took the crucial step of uncoupling government planning agencies from corporations and enterprises. The central economic plan of the Ministry of Economy and Planning was no longer compulsory. The state did, however, maintain policy measures for controlling the economy through the use of incentives—subsidies, interest rates, tax rates, prices, customs rates, and so forth. In addition, the new proposal maintained that 35 percent of Bulgaria's Net Material Product (NMP) would be made up of essential products, which the state would order directly from individual firms. The decree mandated that such orders would be made on a competitive basis and that firms which won the contracts would be entitled to special government benefits. While the decree revealed the government's inability to abandon the administrative command system, it was a milestone towards that end.

For the first time, market principles of self-management were partially applied at the level of the firm. In theory, firms were put on a self-supporting basis to foster initiative in decision making and to enhance management responsibility. Firms could determine their own internal restructuring, output, contractual relationships, sales channels, investment and banking relationships, labor remuneration, and if desired, foreign partners. Without seeking the consent of the government's powerful foreign trade organization (FTO), which had frustrated international trade agreements for years, firms were permitted to initiate and enter into foreign contracts, including methods of payment. It was a milestone, inasmuch as FTO regulation had been a near-sacred device for Communist Party economic control.

Under the more recent provisions, rules on the ownership of the means of production were also expanded beyond the state. Foreign firms, Bulgarian firms with foreign investors, and private persons or groups were granted the right to own the means of production. The 1987 Decree also made firms liable for their activities, while subsequent bankruptcy legislation denied government bailouts to all but a few firms.

The Zhivkov regime was reluctant to reveal the extent of Bulgaria's hidden inflation, common in communist systems. After his ouster, it was learned that inflation had exceeded 11 percent annually since 1985. From 1988 through 1989, the communist government introduced new wholesale prices for nearly 75 percent of the economy's output. A complete reform of retail and wholesale prices has been promised for 1991, to bring wholesale prices in line with world market prices. This would create a more competitive environment for trade while gradually introducing greater efficiency to the domestic economy.

To encourage enterprise self-financing, the Decree of 1987 introduced a new tax system. Previously, a system of negative taxation had served to subsidize poorly performing firms, while those that showed a profit faced rates as high as 90 percent. The new system set the profit tax at 40 percent, the fixed-capital tax at 3 percent, the working-capital tax at 4 percent, and the municipal tax on profit at 5%. It also unified the tax code and ended discrimination by region, industrial sector, or form of property. To encourage investment, firms were allowed to deduct investments and interest payments before calculating profit taxes. The entire system of taxes was slated for a major revision in 1991 to a value-added tax system. Hard currency has been made more widely available since 1987, especially because of new legislation that codified the laws for joint ventures and established free trade zones on the Black Sea and on the Danube in Burgas, Plovdiv, Ruse, Varna, and Vidin, with another possible zone in Sofia. In the zones, foreign firms, either alone or with Bulgarian partners, may engage in virtually any economic activity intended for export. All financial activities of the zone must be conducted in convertible currencies, and all profits from the economic activity in the zone are exempted from taxes. Profits on the import of goods and services from the zone into Bulgaria are taxed at 30 percent on that portion of hard currency that is transferred abroad and at 20 percent for those profits that are invested or reinvested in economic activity within the zone or in other joint ventures in the country. Revisions to joint venture legislation have formally guaranteed foreign ownership rights and granted priority treatment for the venture's construction and permit requirements. In addition, joint venture profits may now be transferred abroad, in the form of goods produced either by the venture or by Bulgarian firms.

The 1987 Decree also changed the banking system, creating eight new investment banks partially free of the Bulgarian National Bank. These new banks are able to extend credit and accept hard-currency deposits. They also have the right to deposit hard currencies in Western banks and accept currency credits from them. The National Bank retains its role as overseer—it has the power to set annual credit limits and interest rates. Firms may choose among the banks and are free to borrow directly from foreign banks. The legislation has been particularly effective in forcing firm managers to look toward independent financial institutions rather than the state as the source of capital. At the end of 1989, the National Bank was more thoroughly decentralized when its directors announced that its 130 branches would be granted greater autonomy. From their ranks, and from the eight investment banks created in 1987, more than 20 independent commercial banks have begun operations. The banking sector now has an independent footing vis-à-vis the state.

Property rights have undergone alteration, although private property rights are still limited. State and collective ownership take preference. The state maintained its hold on the largest production units and infrastructure operations, while new decrees extended oversight responsibilities to the legislature. Private ownership expanded, particularly in banking, insurance, and pension funds and in small and medium-size state production units. By the 1987 decree, the private sector was first encouraged to expand only in services and agriculture; individuals were still not permitted to hire individuals other than family members in their private activities. While individuals and firms may now employ the labor of others, they may still not own land and capital goods. Individuals may lease land for up to 50 years, and machinery and capital goods for a term equal to their amortization period.

Common to other reforming communist states, the first wave of substantial reforms in Bulgaria were more significant for their antiMarxist character than for their market orientation. As a result, tangible results have been limited. The great majority of enterprises and firms failed to adapt effectively to the reformed economy. Those that did were frustrated by the state planning agencies which continued their intervention in economic life. "Old" and "new" prices persisted, and firms operated under the burden of buying wholesale goods at the new prices while selling their goods at the old retail prices.

Economic indicators turned flat in 1988. But rather than retreat, the government enacted further economic reforms, similar to what had earlier been seen in Hungary. The regime had begun to come to terms with the fact that Bulgaria was losing its special benefits from Moscow and had to attract Western investment. In order to do that, it came to realize, the entire economy had to rest on a secure legal base. A flood of new legislation followed in 1989, dramatically improving and deepening the reforms, while amendments in 1990 enhanced the sway of the market.

Though the 1989 reforms known as Decree 56 were bold in their efforts to make Bulgaria a part of the world economy, they failed to settle the ambiguity of the economic role of the state. While more stringent limits were placed on the state, its power over the economy remained immense. Decree 56 consolidated the earlier "statement in principle" that the state was no longer liable for the financial obligations of its firms, by instituting concrete procedures for dealing with insolvency and establishing guidelines for the restoration or liquidation of firms. A firm may now be declared insolvent by its members, its creditors, or its servicing banks if it cannot meet its financial responsibilities within 60 days. The new regulations are a major step on the road to ending state subsidies for firms and creating genuine self-financing.

The new decree also broadened the scope of market prices. Prices are to be contracted freely between firms, while the state reserves the right to continue setting prices in raw materials, transport, and other areas that most affect Bulgarian living standards.

Investment laws for Western firms were substantially refurbished in hopes of expanding countertrade and replacing Bulgarian state borrowing with direct Western investment. Foreign firms may now have full ownership of their subsidiaries in Bulgaria and are no longer required to deal through the state representative, Interpred, which did more to frustrate commercial activity than encourage it. Joint ventures may appoint their own foreign management and directors. Foreigners may also own as much as 20 percent of a Bulgarian firm with no special state authorization and without a joint venture declaration, though joint ventures are, of course, still welcomed. Rather than requiring firms to earn their own hard currency, the new decree allows joint ventures to buy hard currency for leva from the Bulgarian state bank or currency auctions. The auction exchange rate remained at 9 leva to $1 in 1989 and 1990. The rate is still unrealistic, however, since in 1991 the leva traded unofficially at an average of 18–20 leva to $1. In terms of joint venture taxes, Bulgaria has outdone its neighbors. Firms may now carry tax losses forward, and the tax holiday period has been extended to five years.

Decree 56 also fortified the role of Bulgarian private and cooperative firms vis-à-vis the state. All firms have been granted equal status and may issue shares. State firms will no longer operate under preferential conditions. A value-added tax system was unveiled for domestic and foreign firms and will be applied in late 1991.

New laws for implementing Decree 56 quickly followed the original legislation, codifying the entire undertaking. Virtually every month since late 1989 has seen new steps towards a full market economy. Bankruptcy laws have been toughened, price decentralization advanced, rights for foreign firms upgraded, and the role of private economic activities enlarged. Newly registered firms now conduct foreign trade without seeking the permission of the state. Firms may freely hire (and fire) employees and buy and sell capital goods. By the end of 1990, 25,000 private firms were registered as such. Most of these had joined the Union of Citizens' Economic Initiative, an advocacy group for entrepreneurs.

Not directly covered in the 1989 Decree was agriculture. Piecemeal reforms had been introduced during the final months of Zhivkov's tenure and broadened after his departure. The state's administrative role in agriculture has begun to wither away and agriculture is now rapidly being turned over to private hands. The notion of the "firm" has been applied to agriculture. The state seeks to expand small private plots into more efficient production units and to privatize state farms, which are being reorganized for sale or lease. State farms not directly transferred to private control will be converted to stock-holding firms with shares to be held by the cultivators. Production bonuses have been announced for farmers who increase their output, and hard-currency exchange rights have been made available to them.

Agriculture is regaining its precommunist preferential treatment. Individual farmers may now own 20 hectares of farmland (30 hectares in mountainous regions), so long as they work the soil. The Bank for Agricultural Credit has been established to provide financing to private farmers. The state no longer specifies agricultural crops; cooperative farm debts have been forgiven; and prices have been liberalized, with complete decontrol scheduled for the end of 1991. Considering the disastrous farm outputs of 1989 and 1990—when some 50 percent of all food items were in short supply—these changes have been precipitously late. But the result should still be a dramatic increase in output.

Agriculture is the one area where Bulgaria can most rapidly achieve self-sufficiency. Even during the communist period it accounted for more than a quarter of GNP, despite receiving less than 7 percent of total investment. Since all of the political parties understand Bulgaria's agricultural potential, this sector will enjoy future attention regardless of which party is in power.

Outside of agriculture, the Lukanov government was short on specific economic changes in 1990, although it reasserted its commitment to a steady, if gradual, transition to a market economy. Nor was the Lukanov government especially successful at curtailing the control of the powerful state bureaucracy over economic life. Additional legislation is necessary to restrain the control of the bureaucrats.

Following Bulgaria's default, Lukanov sought to satisfy foreign creditors by applying for membership in the IMF and the International Bank for Reconstruction and Development (IBRD) as well as the General Agreement on Trade and Tariffs (GATT). Officials from the Organization for Economic Cooperation and Development (OECD) have also been asked to provide financial and economic expertise. To sustain and attract more foreign investment, Lukanov's government began drafting legislation to allow full private foreign ownership.

The Soviets worsened Bulgaria's economic plight in 1990. In late September they withdrew their promise that Bulgaria would have three years to convert its trade with Moscow to hard-currency, putting all trade on a hard-currency basis as of January 1991. By then, all political forces in Bulgaria acknowledged that the country's economy was in ruins, foreign credit largely nonexistent, and shortages had become endemic. Lukanov responded with a program of major budget cuts, the privatization of small firms and services to raise the output of consumer goods and foodstuffs, a devaluation of the lev, and major tax breaks for private firms during the first three years of operation. The reform program was largely designed by an international team headed by Richard Rahn, chief economist of the U.S. Chamber of Commerce. The New York Stock Exchange has also been commissioned to design a stock exchange, planned to open in Sofia by the summer of 1991.

But the changes were not enough to save the Lukanov government. An independent took the prime ministership in December 1990, while the UDF, with Zhelyu Zhelev as president, took the economic ministries. All the members of the UDF coalition asserted their commitment to the more rapid dismantling of socialism and the reorienting of Bulgaria more decisively to the economies of the West. Even labor signed on. Podkrepa, the 500,000-member trade union, supported, in the words of its leader Konstantin Trenchev, "a dash to the market." In the first six months of a UDF government, the legislature, still dominated by socialists, devalued the lev twice, passed an impressive Land Reform Law, raised foodstuff prices several hundred percent, and made additional moves towards a market. But the implementation of these reforms were blunted by the BSP, thus pushing off the transformation of the economy until after the 1991 elections. With a new government, IMF pressure, new loans, and most important, a clear sense among the leadership that without major reform the nation will not gain the Western assistance it desperately needs, Bulgaria is likely to surprise Balkan watchers.

Current State of the Economy

National income began a recovery in 1986, growing 5.5 percent over 1985, but industrial production remained weak. In 1987, the key industrial sectors, accounting for 60 percent of the economy, had modest gains of 1 percent to 2 percent, still not at their 1984 level of output. Zhivkov's departure was followed by the release of data indicating that previous economic figures were specious. The economy was in much more serious trouble than the Communist Party had been willing to admit. Some analysts claim that new data reveal that total economic growth in the entire decade of the 1980s was no more than 8 percent or 9 percent. Zhivkov had bought time by borrowing hard currency and then increasing Western imports to satisfy consumer needs. But the indigenous economy never managed to produce the goods necessary to satisfy domestic demand, nor to generate the hard-currency earnings necessary to pay for imports.

By 1990, Bulgaria could no longer meet its debt obligations. Higher wages failed to increase living standards, because a greater supply of new money was chasing the same output of consumer goods. The most positive development had been the establishment of at least a partial legal foundation for the transition to a market. There were also indications that private businesses had begun to respond to the new opportunities.

The country's attempts to enhance efficiency by importing new technologies proved unsustainable. Indigenous output of agricultural machinery and transport equipment failed to increase. Although two new nuclear reactors were activated in 1988 and the energy sector as a whole received priority investments, output increased only 3.6 percent, while coal output actually declined 7 percent. The results were especially serious in light of the hard-currency payments demanded by the Soviets for energy supplies in 1991. Industrial construction was stymied by shortages of basic building materials, and housing unit construction has remained 20 percent below planned targets. The biotechnology and chemicals industries have been exceptions, recording steady expansion, while the electronics industry alone has accounted for more than 30 percent of the economy's total output growth.

Bulgarian agriculture has continued to perform poorly, reflecting its thorough exhaustion after years of socialist control and state ownership. Output for the second half of the decade did not equal that of the first half. For 1988, with no particularly bad weather to blame, output actually declined by 0.7 percent. Corn, cotton, tobacco, sunflower, sugar beet, and other vegetable output all declined, with wheat and barley showing small increases. Traditionally self-sufficient in agriculture, Bulgaria began importing substantial quantities of feed grain from the United States.

Perhaps the country's greatest problem has been its failure to control its burgeoning imports, driving up its debt while damaging its once excellent credit rating. In 1988, for example, Bulgaria's imports from the West increased 16 percent, while exports declined 8 percent, although a huge surplus with its former communist trading partners gave the appearance that Bulgaria's trade was balanced. Its net debt with the West reached $7 billion, driving its convertible-currency debt service ratio up to 45 percent.

The positive news in this grim account of economic decline remains the commitment of the government to reform. By 1991, the transition to a market appears to have generated an unstoppable momentum.

The greatest threat to the economy appears unrelated to the government's commitment or its legislative reform program. The Turkish exodus brought about a severe labor shortage in excess of 150,000 workers. The 1989 harvest was disrupted and construction projects canceled. But the shortage had an impact on industry as well, because Bulgarian workers were forced out of their factories and into the fields to aid the harvest. The new government of Prime Minister Lukanov expended vast resources repairing Bulgaria's severely damaged international reputation to protect its applications for Western money and assistance.

Economic growth was negative for all sectors in 1989 and 1990 and is unlikely to turn positive until 1992 at the earliest. Bulgaria's Net Material Product fell 0.4 percent in 1989 and more than 11 percent in 1990, with investment dropping by at least 8 percent. Most investment capital was channeled into energy, heavy machinery, and raw materials, all of which performed poorly and all unlikely to be sources of future growth. Energy output fell from 2 percent to 4 percent, due to lower Soviet oil deliveries and the deterioration of the refining industry. Heavy machinery output dropped by at least 1 percent, while industrial production as a whole increased by 1 percent in 1989 only to fall by 14 percent in 1990. The construction sector completed less than half of its planned targets for the year, suffering from the shortage of Turkish labor as well as materials—notably bricks and cement.

The 1989 year was a disaster for agriculture despite a good growing season. Output declined by 0.4 percent, while close to 50 percent of all food items were in short supply.

Grain output remained steady and animals for slaughter marginally increased, but production of milk, eggs, cheese, cooking oil, and sugar all fell and continued to fall through 1990. This created panic buying, which in turn gave rise to further shortages in foods and consumer goods. Produce from private plots and even state farms was held off the market in anticipation of state price increases, which came too late to save the government or correct the shortages. The winter of 1990 saw the most severe deprivations in decades, with the average home enjoying neither dependable heating supplies nor fresh food. The Lukanov government declared the economy on the "verge of collapse."

Bulgaria's domestic woes were compounded by its poor export performance and overwhelming debt, neither of which will be resolved easily. In the mid-1980s, Bulgaria had extended credits to Third World countries to finance the export of huge quantities of Bulgarian goods. The vast majority of those countries never paid for their imports, and Bulgaria holds billions of dollars of their debt. In search of higher hard-currency earnings, Bulgaria cut its exports to developing countries. For the same reason, Bulgaria cut its exports to the states of the Council for Mutual Economic Assistance (CMEA), the Moscow-based communist trading bloc, also known as Comecon. Bulgaria consistently ran sizable surpluses with its communist trading partners, which were cleared only through barter trade. Bulgaria also lost markets following the Iraqi invasion of Kuwait. Iraq had promised to repay its $1.5 billion debt in oil, now unlikely in the foreseeable future.

After searching for new markets, Bulgaria has been unable to secure a market in the West. Its goods are deemed of insufficient quality to satisfy Western buyers. As a result, foreign trade turnover for 1990 dropped 8.1 percent. Hard-currency imports declined by 16 percent, but hard-currency exports dropped 18 percent. Bulgaria added another billion dollars to its $11 billion debt. In March 1990, the government suspended payments on debt principal, while interest payments consumed nearly 50 percent of the country's hard-currency export earnings. In June it defaulted on interest payments as well. The Foreign Trade Bank, which holds 90 percent of the debt, has been exploring the possibility of negotiating a 2-year delay in principal payments while seeking additional new credits.

The economy is almost totally dependent on the former Soviet Union for energy supplies and faces major future energy shocks. All of Bulgaria's natural gas and over 90 percent of its crude oil and coal have come from the Soviet Union. But those supplies have become ever more erratic. In 1990, Moscow informed Bulgaria that its export of oil would be cut from one million tons of oil per month to no more than 400,000 tons. Oil was in such short supply in the winter of 1990–1991 that whole cities could not keep dwellings above the freezing mark. Oil refining was off by more than 40 percent for 1990 and 1991, and it will be lower for 1992. Bulgaria is searching for alternative suppliers of oil and gas, but potential suppliers demand what the Russians demand—hard currency. Instead, the country is pursuing countertrade arrangements with Libya and Iran.

Bulgaria produces close to 40 percent of its electrical needs with five nuclear reactors at Kozloduy and is building six more reactors at Belene, once the home of a concentration camp. But the nuclear industry does not appear to have a promising future in Bulgaria. Kozloduy's Soviet-designed reactors have been repeatedly shut down for a variety of operational and technical difficulties. The new reactors, also Soviet-designed, are slated for startup in late 1992. Past failures and the Chernobyl disaster have created impressive political and popular support against a continuation of the Belene project. Construction was halted several times in 1990, postponing the completion date and putting the entire nuclear program in doubt.

Bulgarian economic growth in 1989 and 1990 was largely the result of price increases, not increases in physical output. There were, however, pockets of real growth, particularly in the electronics industry, where output of industrial automation systems and automatic telephone switching systems continued to expand. Electronics appears to be the most promising sector of the Bulgarian economy, likely to grow rapidly when the economy finishes its passage through the inevitably precarious straits of high inflation, food shortages, debt refinancing, and the closing of antiquated enterprises—a category that is estimated to comprise nearly 50 percent of all the state's firms.

A consensus has been generated for a more rapid transition to a market economy. The state has begun the process of auctioning off the majority of its industries, opening the country to foreign investments and private financing, lifting centrally controlled prices, and encouraging growth in light industry, food processing, agriculture, services, and tourism. The tax system will be revised to provide for substantial tax incentives for business. The state's investment policy will be altered to end subsidies for money-losing heavy industry while shifting funds to high-technology enterprises. Agriculture will be fully privatized through the breaking up of agro-industrial farms. Farm prices will be fully freed by the close of 1991.

The economic transformation will change Bulgaria's trade relationships. At the time of Zhivkov's fall, over 60 percent of Bulgaria's trade was conducted with the USSR. His successors began the transformation of the country's foreign economic relationships with the West. In May, 1990, Bulgaria signed an agreement with the EC that promised to remove, by 1995, all restrictions on Bulgarian goods and provide assistance to all areas of Bulgaria's economy. Desperate for investment, Bulgaria has promised a total opening to EC and American firms.

Like other reforming states, Bulgaria faces formidable challenges in its transition to a market economy. Inflation will continue to rise while the real income of Bulgarian workers is certain to fall. Evidence of poverty is widespread, and recent government disclosures indicate that the majority of pensioners now live below the poverty line on less than 100 leva per month. The interest on Bulgaria's foreign debt will exceed $1 billion for 1991. Hard-currency exports will remain inadequate to offset the debt burden. Agricultural output is likely to expand quickly as private farmers seize the incentives offered by their private plots. Industry, which accounts for 60 percent of National Material Production, faces the most formidable challenges. Like the industrial plants of other communist states, Bulgarian firms are energy-inefficient. World market prices for energy will, alone, push a good portion of the larger firms into bankruptcy. A full 45 percent of all state firms are considered technologically obsolete, and when the state eliminates the subsidies, industry will be very hard pressed.

Bulgaria now offers generous terms for duty-free zones and joint ventures. The government is seeking joint venture partners for the country's most successful industries— electronics, biotechnology, chemicals, and light machine building—as well as food processing, electric power generation, environmental protection, and transportation. The government has also dramatically increased trade ties with the United States.

There is no hope for a solution to the country's debt crisis without substantial international assistance. The government unveiled a write-down proposal to the West in April of 1991. But it will not get the 50 percent reduction it is asking for. While a full 75 percent of Poland's debt was owed to foreign governments, Bulgaria owes only 7 percent of its total debt to Western governments. Private debt holders of the London Club hold the other 93 percent of Bulgaria's Western obligations and are interested only in a rescheduling. However, new IMF guidelines and full GATT membership, expected in 1991, will facilitate Bulgaria's access to new capital. Likewise, the United States granted "Most Favored Nation" status in 1991 and with it, Overseas Private Investment Corporation insurance was made available.

Given its relatively small labor pool and few resources, Bulgaria will not be a large market for U.S. goods. It will never be able to compete with Czechoslovakia or Poland, for example. Nevertheless, it presents attractive economic opportunities still untapped.

Economy from Origins to 1900

When Bulgaria gained its independence from the Ottomans in 1878, the overwhelming majority of its population was engaged in primitive farming, without metal farming equipment or fertilizers. For the next seventy years and through two world wars, Bulgaria failed to change. While it was no longer an extension of the Middle East, it remained on the periphery of Western advancement. Being neither Eastern nor Western, Bulgaria seemed frozen in time. At the beginning of communist rule, the percentage of peasant farmers with small land holdings was the same as it had been in 1878. Neither had the ratio of urban to rural dwellers changed.

What had changed was the state bureaucracy. After independence, it expanded and centralized. It founded Bulgaria's modern industrial base, small as it was. At the time of its independence, Bulgaria had one factory, a textile firm in Sliven abandoned by the departing Ottomans. Within 10 years, 90 new factories were created, mostly in milling, textiles, leather works, brewing, and tobacco. European industries were already well developed, making it far cheaper to import tools and even finished goods than to produce them locally. As a result, Bulgarian manufacturers were essentially home industries manned by craftsmen and artisans.

Ironically, the Ottoman exit had impeded industrialization. Waves of Turkish farmers fled their farms for the Ottoman heartland. Bulgarian peasants and impoverished town and city dwellers immediately seized and occupied Turkish farms. Urban settlements were depopulated, producing a shortage of manufacturing labor. The land proved so fertile that even as the population grew, migration to the cities was limited.

Industrialization was also hindered by the loss of Ottoman markets. Bulgarian goods were produced for Eastern tastes and proved less popular when attempts were made to expand sales to the West.

Despite Bulgaria's urban and industrial decline, the new state was successful at establishing a substantial national bureaucracy. In part because of Western examples, and even more out of a desire to shed its Ottoman past and ensure its future independence, Bulgaria rapidly fashioned a highly centralized civil service. The bureaucrats in Sofia, for example, accounted for a full one-quarter of the city's population after only twenty years of independence. The urbanization of Bulgaria was singularly driven by bureaucratization as was industrialization. The primary explanation for the smooth transition to communism had its historical antecedents in the bureaucracy already deeply involved in national economic management.

Newly independent Bulgaria was quick to involve itself in economic matters, creating a Ministry of Trade and Agriculture, a Ministry of Education, which contained a Committee for Industry, and a National Agriculture School. After six years of independence, the state nationalized the railroads and banks while actively participating in developing coal and lignite mines and building railroads. In later years, the state stimulated industry by relying on subsidies and granting monopolies to favored industries. Before the turn of the century a new set of laws was adopted, the Encouragement of Industry Acts. The state's "encouragement" came in the form of free land, free water power, reduced railroad rates, and tax exemptions. At the same time, the definition of an enterprise worthy of state assistance was broadened. Smaller and smaller businesses were granted aid, but few could be considered industries. Most were workshops, employing a handful of laborers.

Home industries grew, but the initiative failed to transform Bulgaria's economic landscape. By 1911, nearly 90 percent of all manufacturing was food- and agriculture-related. But because the Encouragement Acts ignored agriculture, domestic production increased only fitfully and proved insufficient for the expanding industries. The failure of coordination between agriculture and industry was evident in Bulgaria's stable pattern of exports. Until World War I, 80 percent of its exports were raw agricultural products, mostly low-priced bulk grains shipped to Turkey, France, Britain, and Germany.

The state sought industrial development to reduce dependence on foreign countries, yet foreign monies played a significant role in establishing manufacturing. Originally, external interest centered on insurance, but once foreign banks were allowed, investment shifted to industry. By 1900, more than a quarter of all industrial capital was foreign. Belgian investors held 60 percent of the foreign capital, followed by Britain with 21 percent.

The Balkan Wars of 1912 and 1913 had little effect on Bulgaria. World War I, despite limited conflict within the country itself, was far more severe. Some 40 percent of Bulgarian men were mobilized, a higher percentage than any other warring state. The Entente blockaded Bulgaria to deny it raw materials and fuel imports. The combination of labor shortages and blockades diminished industrial and agricultural production. By the end of the war, nearly half of all factories had failed, and the rest operated only sporadically. In agriculture, industrial crops, such as tobacco, rose oil, and sugar beets, replaced grain crops. An influx of refugees who had been tobacco growers, coupled with the loss of grain-producing areas, led to a surge in tobacco production to the point that Bulgarian exports dominated the European market.

In 1909 tobacco accounted for 10 percent of Bulgaria's exports. By 1917 it exceeded 70 percent.

Other than replacing grain with tobacco, however, Bulgaria showed little change. In 1920, three-quarters of the population were peasant cultivators. There was little urbanization and considerable social stability. Within a decade after the war, the ratio of state employees to total population was four times the European average. But Bulgaria was not a nation-state. The nation was peasant and conservative, resistant to change. The state was Sofia, where industrial and commercial interests predominated, but where capital and raw materials were lacking. Having little say in agricultural production, while being deeply embedded in the limited infrastructure and industrial bases, the state was primarily a monopoly seller of grains and tobacco.

Bulgaria did experience some change, despite its largely stable social structure, in the two decades before the outbreak of World War II. Industry experienced a substantial boom before being crushed by the world depression. Agricultural production grew increasingly diversified and more productive with the creation of cooperatives, an Agriculture Bank, and direct state aid. Germany came to be a new and nearly exclusive purchaser of Bulgarian exports. The government, not surprisingly, was inclined to further centralization and increased control of economic activity as foreign interest declined.

Bulgaria managed the highest rate of industrial growth of the Balkan states for a decade and a half following World War I. That growth, only a comparative achievement, limited the technological base and the potential for future growth. Textiles and food processing accounted for some 70 percent of industrial output in 1930, while metals and machinery accounted for only 8 percent. Under the domination of workshops and small factories, a tiny domestic market, and the promise of higher returns in banking, industry remained an unattractive investment. Yet through the depression, there was a move towards import substitution, and real output continued to grow at an annual rate of 3.7 percent, higher than the European average. Domestic consumption of industrial output went from 61 percent in 1929 to 88 percent in 1938. But the marginal role of industry is demonstrated by the fact that by 1938 only 5.6 percent of national income came from the industrial sector.

In the interwar period, the countryside showed itself more receptive to change, stimulated by the newly emerging cooperatives and higher profits for industrial crops. Not only did tobacco cultivation boom, but so did sunflower, sugar beet, and later cotton production. After Turkey recovered a portion of its tobacco market, driving down world prices in the 1930's, Bulgaria turned to the cultivation of fruits, vegetables, and wine. On the eve of World War II, Bulgaria was devoting more land to industrial and cereal crops than any of its Balkan neighbors and less area to feed crops and pasture.

The rapid expansion of cooperatives and the state's grain-purchasing agency, the Hranoiznos, did much to assure the profitability of agriculture, given the stunted size of the average farm. The cooperatives kept the smallest of farms productive by offering credits, consolidating fields, and sharing agricultural machinery, while the Hranoiznos maintained artificially high prices for grains by purchasing domestic crops above world market prices. The resulting higher profits on the farm led to an increase in modern agricultural machinery. Nonetheless, the small size of the farms limited progress in other areas, which ensured continued primitive farming. In 1940, in comparison to its neighbors, Bulgaria was using essentially no fertilizers, and productivity per laborer was extremely low. To produce an equal portion of wheat, six times more labor was required in Bulgaria than in the Soviet Union. Living conditions in both were dismal. By 1941, only one in nine villages had electricity.

The most dramatic economic interwar change for Bulgaria was the rise of Germany as its key trading partner at the expense of Belgium, Britain, and France. In part because of their mutual estrangement at Versailles, Bulgaria and Germany developed a trading relationship similar to Bulgaria's later relationship with the Soviet Union. In 1939 Germany was buying 68 percent of Bulgaria's exports, increasing to 88 percent by 1944. For the same years, Bulgaria's imports from Germany were 65 percent of all its imports, increasing to 72 percent. Bulgaria entered and left World War II economically backward by all comparative standards, bureaucratically centralized, and fully dependent on Germany.

The social structure remained untouched except in one crucial respect. After independence, Bulgarians, in comparison to the minorities, increased as percentage of the total population. Bulgarian birth rates increased. Bulgarian refugees from other Balkan states entered the country and Turks left, until they fell below 10 percent of the total population—where the number remained until 1989—while the Greeks fell below 0.5 percent. Bulgaria, unlike its neighbors, Yugoslavia, Hungary, and Romania, was spared the menacing Balkan problem of large minorities. More than any other factor, this explains Bulgaria's relative social tranquility, both then and now.

Economy from 1945 to 1990

Until the 1980s, Bulgarian economic growth surpassed that of its Balkan neighbors. At the end of World War II, 80 percent of its workers were employed in agriculture, and its per capita income exceeded only that of Albania. But Bulgaria had been only slightly scarred by the war, and the communists took power with only slight internal disruption in a bloodless coup on September 9, 1944. Bulgaria's special relationship with Moscow led to favorable terms of trade and credit, producing substantial capital for investment. Bulgaria was able to adopt an ambitious industrialization drive, which produced impressive results. For twenty years, Bulgarian economic growth exceeded that of its Balkan neighbors. Per capita income growth averaged 5.6 percent per year from 1960 to 1979.

Bulgaria's impressive growth also reflected the early adoption of economic reforms that moved the country away from the Stalinist model. Because of its relative labor shortage, Bulgaria could not mimic the Soviet practice of achieving growth by increasing the size of the labor force. Instead, it had to concentrate on ever more intensive development, focused on creating huge enterprises.

Following the communist coup, the USSR began sending Bulgaria industrial and agricultural machinery as well as oil and cotton. In turn it imported agricultural produce, principally tobacco, which constituted 80 percent of Bulgaria's exports to the Soviet Union by 1947. Prior to the war, over 80 percent of Bulgaria's foreign trade was conducted with the West, but by its end virtually all its trade had been reoriented to the Soviet Union.

The Bulgarian Communist Party did not create any new institutions to operate the economy. It simply took over the already existing levers of control. In the financial sector, for example, the nationalized banks held almost all bank capital. The merger of the small private banks into the state sector was scarcely noted. The nationalization of agriculture and industry moved more slowly and was not completed until 1960, because both sectors were overwhelmingly composed of large numbers of small producers—artisans, craftsmen, and peasants.

Initially, Bulgaria mimicked the Soviet economic model more closely than any other bloc state. Steel, chemicals, machinery building, coal and lignite mining, and hydroelectric dam projects were all targeted for development. As the peasants fled the newly collectivized farms, they were mobilized for work in heavy industry. The state poured capital into the targeted sectors at twice the Western European average.

The result was an industrial transformation more dramatic than in any of the European satellites. In a decade of communist rule, Bulgaria underwent a striking conversion. Before communism, Bulgaria's industrial enterprises were the smallest in the Balkans, averaging 24 employees. By 1960, it had the largest, averaging 372 laborers, concentrated in 1,650 firms. Agriculture was transformed as dramatically. Bulgarian collectivization proceeded at the fastest pace in Eastern Europe, merging into larger and larger farms.

To pay for the machinery and industrial goods it imported from the Soviet Union, Czechoslovakia, the GDR, and the FRG, Bulgaria exported more and more foodstuffs and chemical fertilizers. Thus Bulgarian economic planners had to devote resources to increasing both agricultural and industrial production.

Comecon was committed to increasing industrial productivity and "intensification" through concentrating responsibility for certain industries in particular countries. Bulgaria specialized in the production of fork lift trucks, factory handling equipment, and agricultural machinery. But the quality of its manufactured goods was abysmal. As a result, Western demand for its goods was limited and Bulgaria had to seek credits to finance its Western imports. By and large, Bulgaria could export its manufactured goods only to other Comecon countries. By the end of the communist period, Bulgaria was more dependent on the Soviet Union than any other Comecon member.

During the 1970s, Bulgaria continued to maintain higher growth than other Comecon states. Yet signs of decline—slumping industrial productivity and agricultural output— began to appear after 1966. The country had begun to run up against the limitations of its communist system and development pattern. Yet the leadership merely increased the pressure for industrial growth. Planners assumed that higher levels of investment, computerization, and technology could solve the dilemmas of communist industrialization. The state continued to pour investment into chemicals, machine building, oil refining, and ferrous metals. On average, investment in industry from 1965–1975 exceeded 40 percent of total investment. (The foremost precommunist industry, textiles, declined to less than 4 percent of total industrial investment.)

Most detrimental to the economy in the 1970s was the regime's desire to "fine-tune" its socialist planning system. It introduced State Economic Associations, later renamed National Economic Complexes, borrowed from the Soviets. Similar industries were grouped to facilitate planning. State bureaucracies exercised increasing power as they came to control the Associations and through them, industrial firms.

This same commitment to concentration found its way into agriculture, initially producing reasonable returns. After collectivization, Bulgaria had the largest farms in all of Europe. But in the late 1960s, agricultural productivity began to decline. In the early 1970s, the regime responded with a characteristic communist answer–"bigness." The government began to merge state and cooperative farms with agriculture processing plants, creating Agro-Industrial Complexes (AICs) overseen by a new bureaucratic management, the National Agro-Industrial Complex. The complexes strained the national infrastructure, absorbed all surplus land, and raised costs. Growth continued to slow, and per capita consumption of fruits, vegetables, and meat fell throughout the 1970s. Moreover, since agricultural products were major inputs for the food-processing industry, that industry was further depressed.

One solution was to increase borrowing from the West. In 1972, Bulgaria's Western debt stood at $25 million. By the end of the decade, the sum stood at $4 billion. As a percentage of NMP, Bulgaria had the largest debt in the East bloc. Bulgaria had little difficulty servicing its burgeoning debt, however, since it was able to import more subsidized Soviet oil and resell it at world market prices in the West for hard-currency. Through oil sales, Bulgaria cut its hard-currency debt in half by 1982.

Following the Soviet lead, Zhivkov ordered reform. Labeled the "New Economic Mechanism" (NEM), a term of Hungarian invention, the reforms introduced limited market phenomena—freer prices, some competition, enterprise self-sufficiency, and a measure of decentralization. The program showed some limited results, and importantly, Bulgaria abandoned its commitment to concentration in favor of smaller and more rational enterprises directed towards consumer markets. Along with the NEM, joint venture laws allowed foreigners to take a majority equity stake in state-owned firms and to export profits in hard currency. While few foreign firms were attracted by the new legislation, the groundwork for a more substantial transformation had been established.

By the early 1980s, Bulgarian NMP growth was second only to that of East Germany. By 1985, however, the economy crested, and Soviet economic deterioration would soon have significant effects upon Moscow's most reliable ally. In a sense, Bulgaria's situation was no different from that of the other East bloc states confronting the limitations of a command economy. But its privileged position had disguised the shortcomings of the system and cushioned their impact. When the day of reckoning did appear, the regime was unprepared. The Soviets began reducing their generous terms of trade and limited the amount of oil Bulgaria could import, sending shock waves throughout the economy. Simultaneously, Moscow began to reduce its imports from the East bloc, damaging Bulgaria in particular, which conducted more than 60 percent of its trade with the Soviet Union. Nowhere was the effect of being the favorite ally and greatest dependent more abruptly and deeply felt than in Bulgaria. The rewards for abiding loyalty had proved advantageous only so long as the Soviet economy maintained its vitality. Thereafter, Bulgaria's greatest strength became its mortal enemy.

FURTHER READINGS

Crampton, R.J. *Bulgaria 1878–1918.* New York: Columbia University Press, 1983.

Crampton, R.J. *A Short History of Modern Bulgaria.* Cambridge: Cambridge University Press, 1986.

Feiwel, George. *Growth and Reform in Centrally Planned Economies: The Lessons of the Bulgarian Experience.* New York: Praeger, 1977.

Grothusen, Klaus-Detlev. *Handbook on South Eastern Europe, Bulgaria.* Göttingen: Vandenhoeck & Ruprecht, 1990.

McIntyre, Robert. *Bulgaria.* London: Pinter Publishers, 1988.

II BULGARIA

DATA AND VITAL STATISTICS

I. **Agriculture**
1. Land use, 1991
2. Agriculture production index
3. Selected indicators of agricultural development, 1970–1985
4. Total grain production
5. Principal crops
6. Yields for selected crops
7. Livestock
8. Slaughterings and production of selected animal products
9. Agricultural labor force and tractors, 1988
10. Agricultural output, 1988
11. Growth per capita in agriculture and food, 1977–1988

II. **Communications and Transport**
1. General facts, 1990
2. Radio and television receivers
3. Percentage of households owning various consumer durables, 1986–1988
4. Daily newspapers
5. Transport traffic
6. Railroad freight
7. Air cargo, 1986–1988
8. Road traffic
9. Ownership of vehicles and automobiles, 1985–1988
10. Number of persons per automobile, 1985–1988
11. Post, telephones, and telex lines, 1986–1988

III. **Economy**
1. Economic profile, 1990
2. Estimated real gross national product
3. Real gross national product growth
4. GNP per capita in dollars, 1990
5. GDP per capita as a percentage of OECD average, 1988
6. Exchange rate
7. Savings
8. Money in circulation
9. Growth of GNP by producing and consuming sectors
10. Growth of GNP inputs and productivity
11. Consumer spending on various items as a percentage of personal income, 1989
12. Cost-of-living price index

3. Principal trading partners
4. Index of import and export prices, terms of trade
5. Major imports and exports
6. Trade with Western countries
7. Trade with the USSR, by commodity
8. Trade with the United States, by commodity

Note: Where possible and relevant, Bulgaria is compared to Belgium, because they are of comparable population. Also, data for the U.S., France, USSR, and other East European countries is provided for comparison where relevant.

I. AGRICULTURE

TABLE 5.I.1 Land use, 1991

		(Percent)			
Arable Land	Permanent Crops	Forest and Woodland	Meadows and Pastures	Other	Irrigated Land
34	3	35	18	10	11

Source: U.S. Central Intelligence Agency, *The World Factbook*, 1991.

TABLE 5.I.2 Agriculture production index (Bulgaria and selected countries)

			(1980 = 100)		
Country	1965	1970	1980	1986	1990
Bulgaria	78	107	100	96	90
USSR	83	99	100	120	118
United States	79	81	100	107	112
France	77	81	100	105	105[a]

[a] 1989 figure.

Source: U.S. Central Intelligence Agency, *Handbook of Economic Statistics*, 1991.

TABLE 5.I.3 Selected indicators of agricultural development, 1970–1985

	1971–1975	1976–1980	1981–1985
Agricultural land use (thousand ha[a])			
Arable	3,647	3,722	3,733
Natural grassland	1,512	1,698	1,974
Other agricultural land	852	782	469
Crop structure[b]			
Grain	61	60	57
Maize	17	18	15
Oilseeds	8	9	9
Fodder roots, silage maize	8	8	10
Cultivated grassland	12	12	13
Beet	2	2	1
Potatoes, vegetables	4	4	4
Other	5	5	6

[a] ha = hectare = 10,000 m^2 = 2.471 acres.

[b] Percent of sown area.

(continued)

TABLE 5.I.3   (continued)

	1971–1975	1976–1980	1981–1985
Total output ^{c} 1980 prices			
Gross^d	2.2	2.1	1.2
Net^d	−0.6	−0.9	−2.9
Arable output^c			
Total (gross) 1982 prices	1.3	0.7	0.2
Grain	3.0	1.3	0.7
Oilseeds	0.4	1.5	1.1
Coarse fodder	2.6	3.1	1.4
Livestock output^c			
Total (gross) 1982 prices	3.8	4.0	2.4
Meat	2.9	5.3	2.1
Milk	1.8	3.3	4.0
Eggs	2.3	4.3	3.9

^{c} Annualized percentage changes between five-year periods.

^{d} Gross output is total yield before harvest. Net output reflects losses following processing.

Source: UN, *Economic Survey of Europe in 1987–1988.*

TABLE 5.I.4   Total grain production^a (Bulgaria and selected countries)

	(Million Metric Tons)				
	1960	1970	1980	1985	1990
Bulgaria	4.97	6.91	7.81	5.49	7.85
USSR^b	125.49	186.80	189.09	191.67	238.00
United States	181.26	186.72	269.68	347.01	312.14
France	23.02	31.29	47.36	55.07	55.38

^{a} Data are for the following products, where they are produced: barley, corn, oats, rice, rye, sorghum, and wheat.

^{b} Includes miscellaneous grains and legumes. For comparative purposes, an average discount of 11 percent should be applied, because USSR totals include excess moisture, unripe and damaged kernels, weed seeds, and other trash.

Source: U.S. Central Intelligence Agency, *Handbook of Economic Statistics,* 1989, 1990, 1991.

TABLE 5.I.5   Principal crops

	(Thousand Metric Tons)		
	1984	1985	1989
Wheat	4,836	3,086	5,402
Maize	2,994	1,350	2,421
Barley	1,279	800	1,568
Grapes	1,120	905	754
Sugar beets	1,133	832	912
Tomatoes	905	781	850
Apples	526	336	398
Potatoes	418	439	538
Sunflower seeds	462	365	447
Watermelons	274	260	79

Source: The Europa World Year Book, 1989, 1990, 1991.

TABLE 5.1.6 Yields for selected crops (Bulgaria and selected countries)

		(ql/ha[a])		
		1985	**1987**	**1989**
Wheat	Bulgaria	28.7	38.2	47.7
	Czechoslovakia	49.3	50.8	51.2
	Hungary	48.3	43.7	52.4
	Poland	34.3	37.2	38.5
	Romania	23.4	28.0	35.8[b]
	Yugoslavia	36.0	36.0	42.0[b]
	Soviet Union	15.5	17.8	19.4
Barley	Bulgaria	30.7	37.0	43.6
	Czechoslovakia	44.3	42.3	47.2
	Hungary	37.3	38.2	46.8
	Poland	32.9	33.7	33.3
	Romania	25.9	36.0	44.8
	Yugoslavia	27.0	24.0	28.0[b]
	Soviet Union	16.0	19.1	17.5
Maize	Bulgaria	30.7	37.2	40.0
	Czechoslovakia	54.4	56.4	52.7
	Hungary	62.9	61.3	62.2
	Poland	43.0	46.0	47.8
	Romania	38.5	27.0	24.7
	Yugoslavia	41.0	40.0	34.0[b]
	Soviet Union	32.1	32.4	37.1
Rye	Bulgaria	14.9	16.6	20.4
	Czechoslovakia	34.0	34.9	40.5
	Hungary	19.3	19.5	27.3
	Poland	24.7	25.8	27.3
	Romania	15.0	14.9	16.2[b]
	Yugoslavia	17.0	17.0	19.0[b]
	Soviet Union	16.5	18.6	18.6
Oats	Bulgaria	13.9	14.8	27.0
	Czechoslovakia	37.4	37.3	32.3
	Hungary	29.6	23.9	32.5
	Poland	27.0	28.4	27.2
	Romania	12.8	15.7	15.9
	Yugoslavia	N/A	N/A	N/A
	Soviet Union	16.3	15.7	15.7
Potatoes	Bulgaria	109	86	137
	Czechoslovakia	184	171	186
	Hungary	196	160	186
	Poland	174	187	185
	Romania	204	129	124
	Yugoslavia	88	81	70[b]
	Soviet Union	113	121	120
Sugar beets	Bulgaria	168	188	246
	Czechoslovakia	377	355	352
	Hungary	379	363	440
	Poland	336	332	340
	Romania	223	201	265
	Yugoslavia	418	380	349[b]
	Soviet Union	241	266	291

[a]ql: quintal = 100 kg (220.46 lbs).
[b]1988 data.

Source: EUROSTAT, *Central and Eastern Europe 1991*, 1991; *Comecon Data 1989*, 1990.

TABLE 5.I.7 Livestock (Bulgaria and selected countries)

| | | Thousand | | |
		1980	1985	1989
Horses	Bulgaria	120	120	119
	Czechoslovakia	45	46	42
	Hungary	120	98	76[a]
	Poland	1,780	1,324	992[a]
	Romania	555	672	663
	Yugoslavia	N/A	N/A	N/A
	Soviet Union	5,563	5,782	5,920
Cattle	Bulgaria	1,843	1,735	1,600
	Czechoslovakia	5,002	5,066	5,129
	Hungary	1,918	1,766	1,698
	Poland	11,337	11,774	10,277
	Romania	6,485	6,692	6,291
	Yugoslavia	5,474	5,034	4,759[a]
	Soviet Union	115,057	120,888	118,429
Dairy cows	Bulgaria	723	682	633
	Czechoslovakia	1,902	1,860	1,795
	Hungary	765	688	646
	Poland	5,666	5,331	4,964
	Romania	2,670	2,901	2,468
	Yugoslavia	3,086	2,915	2,858[a]
	Soviet Union	43,389	42,863	41,716
Pigs	Bulgaria	3,808	3,912	4,353
	Czechoslovakia	7,894	6,651	7,498
	Hungary	8,330	8,280	7,661
	Poland	18,734	19,170	18,686
	Romania	11,542	13,631	11,671
	Soviet Union	73,382	77,772	79,033
	Yugoslavia	7,867	7,821	7,396[a]
Sheep	Bulgaria	10,433	9,724	7,973
	Czechoslovakia	910	1,087	1,051
	Hungary	3,090	2,465	2,068
	Poland	3,490	4,720	4,196
	Romania	15,865	17,342	15,435
	Soviet Union	141,573	14,850	138,443
	Yugoslavia	7,384	7,693	7,564[a]
Goats	Bulgaria	467	460	433
	Czechoslovakia	57	53	50[a]
	Hungary	15	16	16
	Poland	10	10	10
	Romania	347	828	1,070[a]
	Yugoslavia	N/A	N/A	N/A
	Soviet Union	5,925	6,480	6.974
Hens (million)	Bulgaria	39.9	37.9	37.3
	Czechoslovakia	45.3	45.4	46.6
	Hungary	61.0	56.7	52.8
	Poland	76.1	66.2	55.6
	Romania	97.8	120.1	114.0
	Yugoslavia	N/A	N/A	N/A
	Soviet Union	967.3	1,109.9	1,151.0

[a] 1988 data.

Source: EUROSTAT: *Central and Eastern Europe 1991,* 1991; *Comecon Data 1989,* 1990.

TABLE 5.I.8 Slaughterings and production of selected animal products (Bulgaria and selected countries)

		Production of Selected Animal Products (Thousand Tons)				Slaughterings (Thousand Tons)		
		1980	1985	1989		1985	1987	1989
Beef	Bulgaria	167	163	159	Cattle	704	651	601
	Czechoslovakia	468	467	460	and	1,804	1,710	1,733
	Hungary	215	180	170	calves	525	471	435
	Poland	866	900	789		4,290	4,049	3,425
	Romania	285	240	230[a]		1,772	1,570	1,510
	Yugoslavia	344	352	301[a]		N/A	N/A	N/A
	Soviet Union	7,367	8,278	8,780		36,659	41,800	43,300
Pork	Bulgaria	390	434	482	Pigs	4,582	5,086	5,364
	Czechoslovakia	853	891	971		8,180	8,495	9,124
	Hungary	1,100	1,113	1,112		11,301	11,589	11,830
	Poland	1,526	1,773	1,880		16,169	19,082	19,210
	Romania	975	900	840		12,500	11,539	11,218
	Yugoslavia	461	526	546[a]		N/A	N/A	N/A
	Soviet Union	5,835	6,299	6,737		72,248	77,000	78,000
Mutton	Bulgaria	126	116	112	Sheep	5,705	5,907	5,481[a]
and	Czechoslovakia	12	13	12	and	1,380	1,457	1,500[a]
goat	Hungary	23	18	21	lamb	429	261	285
meat	Poland	39	47	43		1,347	1,654	1,580[a]
	Romania	81	70	67[a]		4,412	3,880	4,700[b]
	Yugoslavia	59	63	70[a]		N/A	N/A	N/A
	Soviet Union	827	905	993		52,646	56,579	56,600[b]
Poultry	Bulgaria	158	169	188	Goats	385	413	404[a]
	Czechoslovakia	172	194	233		1,700	1,875	1,562[a]
	Hungary	405	469	445		50	54	53[a]
	Poland	290	345	381		23	15	15
	Romania	475	425	390		468	508	547
	Yugoslavia	277	299	329[a]		N/A	N/A	N/A
	Soviet Union	2,811	3,116	3,357		N/A	N/A	N/A
Milk	Bulgaria	2,357	2,590	2,512				
	Czechoslovakia	6,942	6,982	7,150				
	Hungary	2,729	2,833	2,942				
	Poland	16,446	15,543	16,429				
	Romania	5,411	5,165	4,667				
	Yugoslavia	4,352	4,682	4,638[a]				
	Soviet Union	98,608	103,743	108,529				

[a] 1988 data.
[b] Including goats.
Source: EUROSTAT, *Central and Eastern Europe 1991*, 1991; *Comecon Data 1989*, 1990.

TABLE 5.I.9 Agricultural labor force and tractors, 1988 (Bulgaria and selectected countries)

	Percent of Labor Force in Agriculture	Population per km² of Arable Land	Output per Worker in $	Tractors per 10 km²
Bulgaria	13.2	235	4,612	8.7
USSR	14.2	125	3,830	45.3
United States	2.5	131	33,519	10.8
OECD average	8.1	809	23,334	18.2

Source: The Economist, *Book of Vital World Statistics*, 1990.

TABLE 5.I.10 Agricultural output, 1988 (Bulgaria and selected countries)

	Cereals	(Thousand Tons) Meat	Vegetables	Fruit
Bulgaria	7,858	788	1,973	1,747
OECD average[a]	12,362	1,830	3,685	3,272
East Bloc average[b]	19,125	2,024	3,523	2,582

[a]Excluding the United States.
[b]Excluding Albania.

Source: The Economist, *Book of Vital World Statistics*, 1990.

TABLE 5.I.11 Growth per capita in agriculture and food, 1977–1988 (Bulgaria and selected countries)

	Percent Growth Agriculture	Food
Bulgaria	0.9	1.2
USSR	0.4	0.5
United States	1.4	1.4
France	1.3	1.3

Source: The Economist, *Book of Vital World Statistics,* 1990.

II. COMMUNICATIONS AND TRANSPORT

TABLE 5.II.1 General facts, 1990

1. Communications
   Telecommunications
Stations	15 AM, 16 FM, 13 TV
Radios (1987)	1,982,929 (1 per 4.5 persons)
Televisions (1987)	1,692,411 (1 per 5.3 persons)
Telephones (1987)	2,073,271 (1 per 4.3 persons)

2. Transport
   Railroads:
      4,300 km total, all government-owned (1987)
      4,055 km 1.435-meter standard gauge
       245 km narrow gauge
       907 km double track
      2,510 km electrified

   Highways:
      36,908 km total (1987), of which
      33,535 km hard surface (including 242 km superhighway)

   Inland waterways:
      470 km (1987)

   Pipelines:
       193 km crude oil
       418 km refined products
      1,400 km natural gas (1986)

   Airports:
       380 total, including
        20 with runways 1,220–2,439 m
        20 with runways 2,440–3,659 m

Source: U.S. Central Intelligence Agency, *The World Factbook,* 1991; *The Europa World Yearbook,* 1990.

TABLE 5.II.2 Radio and television receivers (Bulgaria and selected countries)

	1970	1975	(per Thousand Inhabitants) 1980	1983	1986–88
Bulgaria					
Radios	270	160	242	230	357
TVs	121	173	186	189	189
USSR					
Radios	390	481	490	514	686
TVs	143	217	305	308	314
United States					
Radios	1,415	1,857	1,989	2,043	2,120
TVs	413	560	684	790	811
France					
Radios	315	326	743	860	995
TVs	216	269	354	375	333[b]

[a] 1987 data.

Source: UN, *Statistical Yearbook,* 1988; UN, *Human Development Report 1991,* 1991.

TABLE 5.II.3 Percentage of households owning various consumer durables, 1986–1988[a] (Bulgaria and selected countries)

	Televisions	Radios	(Percent) Refrigerators	Vacuum Cleaners
Bulgaria	93	95	96	30
USSR	45	96	N/A	N/A
United States	98	99	100	N/A
France	98	98	97	88

[a] Means data for each country may refer to 1986, 1987, or 1988.

Source: The Economist, *Book of Vital World Statistics,* 1990.

TABLE 5.II.4 Daily newspapers (Bulgaria and selected countries)

Country	1970	1975	1979	1986
Bulgaria	12	13	12	17
USSR[a]	639	691	N/A	723[b]
United States	1,763	1,775	1,787	1,657
France[c]	106	92	90	92

[a] Data include nondaily newspapers.

[b] 1984 data.

[c] Data shown for 1975 and 1979 refer to 1976 and 1978 respectively.

Source: UNESCO, *Statistical Yearbook,* 1989.

TABLE 5.II.5 Transport traffic

	1980	1987	1989
Road traffic			
Passengers (millions)	1,950	2,384	2,283
Freight (millions metric tons)	319	323	312
Passenger-km	21.6	27.7	26.8
Ton-km (millions)	10,078	10,090	10,411
Railway traffic			
Passengers (millions)	125	135	124
Freight (millions metric tons)	78	83	77
Passenger-km (billions)	8.0	9.2	8.7
Ton-km (millions)	17.7	17.8	17.0
Inland-waterway traffic[a]			
Passengers (millions)	0.4	0.3	0.1
Freight (millions metric tons)	4.9	4.1	3.4
Passenger-km (millions)	38.5	16.9	12.2
Ton-km (millions)	2,614	1,971	1,946
Sea traffic			
Passengers (millions)	0.7	0.5	0.4
Freight (millions metric tons)	24.7	25.9	25.5
Passenger-km (millions)	36	27	21
Ton-km (billions)	62	67	74
Air traffic			
Passengers (thousand)	2,187	2,183	2,722
Freight (thousand metric tons)	24.6	24.2	20.5
Passenger-km (millions)	2,670	3,578	3,876
Ton-km (millions)	38.8	41.7	39.5

[a] On domestically registered ships.

Source: EUROSTAT, *Central and Eastern Europe 1991,* 1991.

TABLE 5.II.6 Railroad freight (Bulgaria and selected countries)

Country	1960	1970	1985	1989
Bulgaria				
Billion metric ton-km	7.0	13.9	18.2	17.8
Million metric tons carried	38.4	68.2	82.9	80.0
Poland as a percent of Eastern Europe[a]				
Billion metric ton-km	3.8%	4.9%	5.0%[b]	N/A
Million metric tons carried	4.1%	5.5%	5.4%[b]	N/A
USSR				
Billion metric ton-km	1,504.3	2,494.7	3,718.4	3,924.8[c]
Million metric ton carried	1,884.9	2,896.0	3,951.0	4,000.0
United States				
Billion metric ton-km	868.5	1,141.0	1,288.3	1,473.9
Million metric ton carried	1,180.5	1,426.3	1,567.0	1,792.0
France				
Billion metric ton-km	56.9	70.4	58.5	52.7
Million metric ton carried	227.0	260.0	193.0	174.0

[a] Eastern Europe includes: Bulgaria, Czechoslovakia, East Germany, Hungary, Poland, and Romania.

[b] Latest available data.

[c] 1988 data.

Source: U.S. Central Intelligence Agency, *Handbook of Economic Statistics,* 1989, 1990.

TABLE 5.II.7 Air cargo, 1986–1988[a] (Bulgaria and selected countries)

Country	Freight (in km-tons[b])
Bulgaria	9
Belgium	651
USSR	2,721
United States	13,829
OECD average	1,622

[a] Means data for each country may refer to 1986, 1987, or 1988.
[b] Of national origin.

Source: The Economist, *Book of Vital World Statistics,* 1990.

TABLE 5.II.8 Road traffic

| | (Number of Vehicles) | | |
	1980	1987	1989
Motor cars	816,000	1,138,000	1,270,000
Motor cars per 1,000 inhabitants	91.9	126.9	141.2
Buses	21,000	26,000	26,000[a]
Motorcycles and mopeds	428,000	478,000	490,000[a]

[a] 1988.

Source: EUROSTAT, *Central and Eastern Europe 1991,* 1991.

TABLE 5.II.9 Ownership of vehicles and automobiles, 1985–1988[a] (Bulgaria and selected countries)

Country	Vehicles (Thousands)[b]	Automobiles (Thousands)
Bulgaria	1,150.0	1,000.0
Belgium	3,936.6	3,573.3
United States	183,468.0	140,655.0
USSR	21,500.0	12,500.0

[a] Means data for each country may refer to 1985, 1986, 1987, or 1988.
[b] Vehicles include passenger cars, trucks, and buses.

Source: The Economist, *Book of Vital World Statistics,* 1990.

TABLE 5.II.10 Number of persons per automobile, 1985–1988[a] (Bulgaria and selected countries)

Country	
Bulgaria	7.9
Belgium	2.8
OECD	2.6
USSR	22.8
United States	1.8

[a] Means data for each country may refer to 1985, 1986, 1987, or 1988.

Source: The Economist, *Book of Vital World Statistics,* 1990.

TABLE 5.II.11 Post, telephones, and telex lines, 1986–1988[a] (Bulgaria and selected countries)

Country	Post Offices	Letters per Person	Persons per Telephone Line	Persons per Telex Line
Bulgaria	3,112	58.20	4.5	359
Belgium	1,838	262.73	2.2	1,459
USSR	98,445	217.81	10.3	162,875
Unites States	40,117	645.48	1.3	N/A

[a] Means data for each country may refer to 1986, 1987, or 1988.

Source: The Economist, *Book of Vital World Statistics*, 1990.

III. ECONOMY

TABLE 5.III.1 Economic profile, 1990 (Bulgaria and selected countries)

	Bulgaria	USSR	United States	France
Gross national product				
Billion 1990 U.S. $[a]	49.9	2,660.0	5,465.2[b]	873.6[b]
Percent real growth	−6.0	−2.4 to −5.0	1.0	2.8
Per capita (1990 U.S. $)	5,600	9,140	21,830	15,490
Industrial production[c]	−10.7	−2.8	1.0	1.1
Trade (billion U.S. $)				
Exports, f.o.b.	16.0[d]	109.3[d]	393.9	216.6
Imports, c.i.f.	15.0[d]	114.7[d]	516.2	234.4
Trade balance	1.0[d]	−5.4[d]	−122.3	−17.8
Living standard indicators				
Automobile registrations (per thousand persons)	122[e]	46[e]	571[f]	395[e]
Energy consumption[g]	29[d]	35[d]	57[d]	29[d]

[a] At U.S. purchasing power equivalents.
[b] Gross domestic product.
[c] Percent growth.
[d] 1989 data.
[e] 1987 data.
[f] 1988 data.
[g] Barrels oil equivalent per capita.

Source: U.S. Central Intelligence Agency, *Handbook of Economic Statistics*, 1991.

TABLE 5.III.2 Estimated real gross national product (Bulgaria and selected countries)

	(Billion 1990 U.S. $)				
Country	1970	1980	1985	1989	1990
Bulgaria	35.6	47.0	48.9	51.2	48.1
USSR	1,726.9	2,257.0	2,440.9	2,663.7[a]	1,465.9[a]
United States	2,985.8	3,916.0	4,513.3	5,198.4	5,465.6
France	491.7	680.6	733.9	818.5	819.6

[a] The 1989 GNP figure for the USSR is based on CIA statistics, while the 1990 GNP figure is based on PlanEcon statistics. The great disparity between the Soviet GNP in 1990 and 1988 is due to extremely high estimates by the CIA during the 1980s.

Source: U.S. Central Intelligence Agency, *Handbook of Economic Statistics*, 1989, 1990; and "PlanEcon Report," vol. 6, no. 52, December 28, 1990.

TABLE 5.III.3 Real gross national product growth (Bulgaria and selected countries)

	Percent Average Annual Rate of Growth		Percent		
	1971–1980	1981–1985	1985	1989	1990
GNP growth					
Bulgaria	2.8	0.3	−3.0	−1.2	−6.0
USSR[a]	2.4	1.8	0.9	1.5	−2.4 to −5.0
United States[b]	2.8	3.0	3.8	2.5	1.0
France[b]	3.6	1.5	1.9	3.6	2.8
GNP per capita growth					
Bulgaria	2.3	0.1	−3.2	−1.0	−5.6
USSR	1.5	0.8	−0.1	0.7	−2.9 to −5.5
United States[b]	1.7	1.8	2.8	1.5	.3
France[b]	3.0	1.0	1.5	3.1	2.4

[a] At factor cost.
[b] GDP growth.
Source: U.S. Central Intelligence Agency, *Handbook of Economic Statistics,* 1989, 1990, 1991.

TABLE 5.III.4 GNP per capita in dollars,[a] 1990 (Bulgaria and selected countries)

	(U.S. $)		
Country	Commercial	Purchasing Parity	Free Market
Bulgaria	2,219	5,430	1,773
USSR	2,560	5,060	1,299
United States	21,732	21,732	21,732
West Germany	24,210	16,310	24,210

[a] Based on exchange rate, purchasing power parity, and free market rate.
Source: "PlanEcon Report," vol. 6, no. 52, December 28, 1990.

TABLE 5.III.5 GDP per capita as a percentage of OECD average, 1988 (Bulgaria and selected countries)

Country	(Percent of OECD)
Bulgaria	13.0
Belgium	90.4
USSR	12.1
United States	116.3

Source: The Economist, *Book of Vital World Statistics,* 1990.

TABLE 5.III.6 Exchange rate

	(Leva per $; Period Average)[a]				
	1987	1988	1989	Nov. 1990	March 1991
Commercial	0.9	0.82	0.84	0.74	16.13

[a] Floating exchange rate since February 1990.
Source: U.S. Central Intelligence Agency, The World Factbook, 1991.

TABLE 5.III.7   Savings

(Million Leva)			
1984	**1986**	**1987**	**1989**
11,524	13,954	14,658	16,223

Source: Comecon Data 1990, 1991.

TABLE 5.III.8   Money in circulation

(Billion Leva)			
1980	**1985**	**1988**	**1989**
10	16	18	19

Source: EUROSTAT, *Central and Eastern Europe 1991,*
1991.

TABLE 5.III.9   Growth of GNP by producing and consuming sectors

	(Percent Average Annual Rate of Growth)		
	1985	**1987**	**1989**
GNP	−3.0	−1.0	−0.1
Producing sector			
Industry	0.2	1.4	0.3
Agriculture and forestry	−15.4	−10.3	−1.4
Construction	−2.3	−1.5	−3.2
Transportation and communications	−0.7	0.7	0.9
Trade	2.5	1.5	0.3
Services	2.6	2.4	−4.2
Other	1.5	1.8	−0.8
Consuming sector			
Personal consumption	1.3	1.5	2.1
Government	1.1	1.2	1.3
Gross investment	−9.7	−36.6	−5.1

Source: U.S. Central Intelligence Agency, "Eastern Europe: Long Road Ahead to Economic Well-Being," May, 1990.

TABLE 5.III.10   Growth of GNP inputs and productivity (Bulgaria)

	(Percent Average Annual Rate of Growth)			
	1980	**1985**	**1987**	**1989**
GNP	−2.9	−3.0	−1.0	−0.1
Combined inputs	2.0	1.1	1.3	1.9
Capital stock	7.0	5.8	6.4	8.0
Labor	0.7	−0.2	−0.1	0.2
Combined productivity	−4.8	−4.0	−2.2	−1.9
Capital productivity	−9.2	−8.3	−6.9	−7.5
Labor productivity	−3.5	−2.8	−0.8	−0.3

Source: U.S. Central Intelligence Agency, "Eastern Europe: Long Road Ahead to Economic Well-Being," May, 1990.

TABLE 5.III.11 Consumer spending on various items as a percentage of personal income, 1989 (Bulgaria and selected countries)

	Total per Head $	Percent Food/ Drink	Percent Clothing	Percent Energy	Percent Household Goods	Percent Health	Percent Transport
Bulgaria	2,647	32.9	10.1	4.2	16.5	4.0	9.0
USSR	2,820	43.2	19.0	7.0	8.0	2.7	2.9
United States	12,233	13.3	6.5	19.5	5.7	14.7	14.8
France	9,635	20.0	7.0	18.8	8.3	8.8	16.7

Source: The Economist, *Book of Vital World Statistics,* 1990.

TABLE 5.III.12 Cost-of-living price index[a]

	(1980 = 100)		
Index Group	1985	1987	1989
Total	115	121	132
Food, drink, and tobacco	112	115	119
Other consumer goods	118	127	143

[a] Annual average.

Source: EUROSTAT, *Central and Eastern Europe 1991,* 1991.

IV. EDUCATION

TABLE 5.IV.1 Schools, students, and teachers

	1980–1981	1987–1988	1989–1990
Schools			
General schools[a]	3,590	3,503	3,620
Vocational schools[b]	300	264	245
Technical colleges[c]	242	256	276
Universities	31	33	33
Students (thousands)			
General-school pupils[d]	1,096	1,263	1,166
Vocational-school pupils	151	108	106
Technical-college students[e]	107	125	149
Day pupils	82	92	111
Pupils per 10,000 population	120	139	165
Technical-college graduates	33.4	26.6	33.5

[a] Includes general lower/secondary schools and combined lower/upper secondary schools. General schools include the compulsory primary/lower secondary school (7–10 years' schooling) and an upper secondary stage of 2–4 years.

[b] Pupils here receive a job-oriented education.

[c] Includes distance-learning institutions for teaching certificates; technical colleges to train technicians, technical colleges to improve the qualifications of workers and similar for craftsmen.

[d] Includes both day and evening school pupils and also those on correspondence courses.

[e] Includes pupils involved in distance learning to gain teaching certificates, at technical colleges for technicians, at technical colleges to improve the qualifications of workers and craftsmen.

(continued)

TABLE 5.IV.1 *(continued)*

	1980–1981	1987–1988	1989–1990
University undergraduates	87	119	137
Day students	67	89	101
Pupils per 10,000 population	98	113	152
University graduates	20.0	17.4	19.6
Teachers (thousands)			
General-school teachers[f]	60	73	71
Technical-college lecturers[g]	9.7	10.5	11.6
University academic staff	10.7	12.3	14.7

[f] Includes general schools and combined lower/upper secondary schools; teaching staff includes those members of staff with secondary or higher education who work as teachers, instructors, and technical instructors in the school workshops.

[g] The academic staff includes those members of staff with secondary or higher education, as well as staff seconded from industry (engineers, technicians, craftsmen, etc.).

Source: EUROSTAT, *Central and Eastern Europe 1991,* 1991.

TABLE 5.IV.2 Public expenditures on education

Year	Leva	As a Percent of GNP	Percent of Total Government Expenditures
1975	787,599,000	5.5	8.5
1980	1,145,118,000	5.6	N/A
1985	1,784,008,000	7.0	N/A
1986	1,911,982,000	7.1	N/A
1987	1,967,367,000	6.9	N/A

Source: UNESCO, *Statistical Yearbook,* 1989.

TABLE 5.IV.3 Expenditures and pupils per teacher, 1989 (Bulgaria and selected countries)

Country	Percent of GNP	Pupils per Teacher Primary/Secondary
Bulgaria	6.9	18/14
USSR	7.3	17/N/A
United States	6.7	21/13
France	5.7	19/17

Source: The Economist, *Book of Vital World Statistics,* 1990.

TABLE 5.IV.4 Distribution of teachers and pupils by educational level, 1987

Educational Level	Teachers	Percent Female	Pupils	Percent Female
Preschool	28,659	100	344,396	48
First-level	62,105	76	1,093,540	48
Second-level	27,862	58	389,445	49
General	9,837	67	167,845	64
Vocational	18,025	53	221,600	38
Third-level[a]	16,900	37	135,852	56
Total	135,526		1,963,233	

[a] Includes evening and correspondence courses.

Source: UNESCO, *Statistical Yearbook,* 1989.

TABLE 5.IV.5   Mean years of schooling[a], 1980 (Bulgaria and selected countries)

Country	Total
Bulgaria	7.0
USSR	7.6
United States	12.2
France	9.4

[a]For adults over 25 years old.

Source: UN, *Human Development Report 1991,* 1991.

TABLE 5.IV.6   School enrollment ratios[a]

Year	First-level (Ages 7–14)	Second-level (Ages 15–17)	Third-level (Ages 20–24)
1975	99	89	19.2
1980	98	84	16.1
1987[b]	104[c]	76	22.6

[a]Percent total enrollment of all ages divided by the population of the specific age groups which correspond to the age groups of primary and secondary schooling.

[b]1987 data represent new age ranges in the following categories: first-level (ages 6–13) and second-level (ages 14–17).

[c]Ratios exceeding 100 reflect instances in which the students at a given level are not necessarily in the age group delineated for that level.

Source: UNESCO, *Statistical Yearbook,* 1989.

TABLE 5.IV.7   School enrollment, 1989 (Bulgaria and selected countries)

	(Percent)					
	Primary			Secondary		
	Total	Male	Female	Total	Male	Female
Bulgaria	104	105	103	75	75	76
USSR	106	N/A	N/A	98	N/A	N/A
United States	100	101	100	98	99	99
France	113	114	113	92	89	96

Source: The Economist, *Book of Vital World Statistics,* 1990.

TABLE 5.IV.8   Books, newspapers, and library book loans, 1989 (Bulgaria and selected countries)

	Books Published per Year	Newspaper Circulation (Thousand)	Library Books Loans per Year (Thousand)	Volumes Stock (Thousand)
Bulgaria	4,583	2,834	34,094.6	56,042
Belgium	8,327	2,186	N/A	24,100
USSR	83,011	12,982	2,634.3[a]	1,523,071
United States	48,793	62,502	197,328.1	523,493

[a]Soviet library regulations rarely allow the loaning of books, thus the low figure.

Source: The Economist, *Book of Vital World Statistics,* 1990.

V. ENERGY AND RESOURCES

TABLE 5.V.1 History of primary energy production (Bulgaria and selected countries)

| Energy Type | Country | (Thousand Barrels per Day of Oil Equivalent) | |
		1970	1980
Coal	Bulgaria	125	111
	USSR	6,080	6,370
	United States	7,359	9,785
	France	523	284
Crude oil	Bulgaria	7	5
	USSR	7,060	12,030
	United States	11,380	10,170
	France	68	51
Natural gas	Bulgaria	8	3
	USSR	3,270	7,170
	United States	10,686	9,838
	France	118	129
Hydro/nuclear	Bulgaria	12	53
	USSR	660	1,170
	United States	1,394	2,774
	France	317	665

Source: U.S. Central Intelligence Agency, *Handbook of Economic Statistics,* 1989, 1990.

TABLE 5.V.2 Complete energy use

| | Year | (Thousand Metric Tons) | | | | Soviet Portion of Imports(%)[b,c] | |
		Production	Consumption[a]	Exports	Imports		
Crude oil[d]	1985	110	13,210	0	13,100	11,570	(88)
	1988	75	13,114	0	13,039	11,471	(88)
	1990	100	11,100	0	11,000	8,424	(77)
Refined oil products	1985	12,824	12,351	2,463	1,990	1,520	
	1988	12,634	11,841	2,347	1,554	1,184	
	1990	10,776	10,226	1,750	1,200	893	
Motor and aviation gas	1985	2,235	1,495	780	40	N/A	
	1988	2,190	1,477	743	30	N/A	
	1990	1,872	1,342	550	20	N/A	
Diesel oil	1985	4,690	3,600	1,590	500	N/A	
	1988	4,595	3,468	1,517	390	N/A	
	1990	3,928	3,098	1,130	300	N/A	
Fuel oil	1985	3,585	4,835	0	1,250	N/A	
	1988	3,512	4,488	0	976	N/A	
	1990	3,002	3,752	0	750	N/A	
Other refined products	1985	2,314	2,421	93	200	200	(100)
	1988	2,337	2,408	87	158	N/A	
	1990	1,974	2,034	70	130	N/A	
Natural gas (million cm³)	1985	21	5,419	57	5,455	5,456	(100)
	1988	10	6,238	23	6,251	6,249	(100)
	1990	5	6,956	15	6,966	6,966	(100)

[a]Bulgaria is the 29th largest energy consumer in the world.

[b]Soviet portion of imports as a percent.

[c]To the nearest 1%.

[d]1 metric ton = 8.03 barrels of oil.

(continued)

TABLE 5.V.2 *(continued)*

(Thousand Metric Tons)

	Year	Production	Consumption[a]	Exports	Imports	Soviet Portion of Imports(%)[b,c]	
Hard coal	1985	223	7,748	529	8,054	7,038	(87)
(including	1988	196	6,648	23	6,475	6,734	(98)
anthracite)	1990	185	6,262	0	6,077	5,818	(96)
Brown coal	1985	30,657	30,657	0	0	0	
(including	1988	33,951	33,951	0	0	0	
lignite)	1990	30,000	30,000	0	0	0	
Coke	1985	1,087	1,751	0	664	143	(22)
	1988	1,457	1,652	0	195	52	(27)
	1990	1,375	1,489	0	114	50	(44)
Electricity	1985	41,629	46,124	2,956	7,451	4,500	(60)
(million kWh)	1988	45,036	49,413	849	5,226	4,500	(86)
	1990	41,400	44,932	1,500	5,032	4,130	(82)

[a] Bulgaria is the 29th largest energy consumer in the world.
[b] Soviet portion of imports as a percent.
[c] To the nearest 1%.
[d] 1 metric ton = 8.03 barrels of oil.
Source: "PlanEcon Report," vol. 7, March 6, 1991.

TABLE 5.V.3 Electricity production[a] (Bulgaria and selected countries)

	(Billion Kilowatt-Hours)			
Country	1970	1980	1985	1989
Bulgaria	19.52	34.83	41.63	44.20
USSR	740.93	1,293.88	1,544.10	1,722.00
United States[b]	1,742.73	2,437.82	2,634.65	2,970.21
France	146.97	243.29	325.73	378.00

[a] Data are for total (gross) production at generating centers and therefore include transmission losses and station use.
[b] Beginning in 1980, data are for public utilities only.
Source: U.S. Central Intelligence Agency, *Handbook of Economic Statistics,* 1989, 1990.

TABLE 5.V.4 Installed electricity-generating capacity[a] (Bulgaria and selected countries)

	(Million Kilowatts)			
Country	1970	1980	1985	1988
Bulgaria	4.12	8.20	10.24	11.31
USSR	166.15	266.71	315.00	339.00
United States[b]	360.33	630.94	656.12	677.65
France	36.22	63.66	86.56	100.62

[a] All plants for both public and industrial use.
[b] Beginning in 1982, data are for public utilities only.
Source: U.S. Central Intelligence Agency, *Handbook of Economic Statistics,* 1989, 1990.

TABLE 5.V.5 Commercial energy use by sector[a], 1985 (Bulgaria and selected countries)

	(Percentage of Commercial Energy Used)				
	Industry	**Transport**	**Agriculture**	**Commercial and Residential**	**Other**[b]
Bulgaria	53	13	0	34	0
USSR	60	13	0	27	0
United States	31	35	1	30	4
France	33	26	2	35	3

[a]Includes all solid, liquid, and gaseous fuels, as well as primary and secondary electricity.

[b]Other includes nonenergy uses, military uses, and nonspecified uses.

Source: From *World Resources 1988–1989.* Copyright © 1988 by the World Resources Institute and the International Institute for Environment and Development in collaboration with the United Nations Environment Programme. Reprinted by permission of Basic Books, a division of Harper Collins Publishers Inc.

TABLE 5.V.6 Proved reserves of crude oil, natural gas, and coal, 1989 (Bulgaria and selected countries)

Country	Crude Oil (Billion Barrels)	Natural Gas (Trillion Cubic Feet)	Coal (Million Metric Tons)
Bulgaria	0.015	.25	3,656
USSR	50–80	1,450	182,000
United States	26	165	205,000
UK	4	21	4,200
France	0.03	1.84	1,070

Sources: U.S. Central Intelligence Agency, *Handbook of Economic Statistics,* 1990; U.S. Department of Energy, Energy Information Administration, *International Energy Annual,* 1988; UN, *Energy Statistics Yearbook,* 1986.

TABLE 5.V.7 Mineral production

Mineral	(Tons)		
	1985	**1987**	**1989**
Asbestos	400	400	300[e]
Cadmium	175[e]	170[e]	160[e]
Coal, hard	223,000	198,000	193,000
Coal, brown	30,657,000	36,621,000	34,095,000
Copper			
Mine production	58,000[e]	60,000[e]	50,000
Smelter production	50,000	60,000	57,000
Refined	53,000[e]	56,000[e]	55,800
Ferro-alloys			
Ferro-manganese and ferro-silico manganese	30,000[e]	31,000[e]	31,000[e]
Ferro-silicon	10,000[e]	10,000[e]	16,000[e]
Other ferro-alloys	1,000	1,000	1,000
Gypsum	388,000	306,000	499,600[e]
(Anhydrite)	113,000	103,000	N/A
Iron ore	1,985,000	1,850,000	1,613,400
Iron, pig	1,713,240	1,657,647	1,484,000
Kaolin	257,000	281,000	N/A
Lead	97,000	85,000	85,000
Lead, refined	116,000[e]	110,000[e]	99,000
Manganese ore, 30%[a]	38,000	38,000	18,000
Molybdenum	190[e]	200[e]	200[e]
Natural gas[b]	21	13	10[e]

[a]Estimated average manganese content.

[b]Million cm^3.

(continued)

TABLE 5.V.7 *(continued)*

	(Tons)		
Mineral	1985	1987	1989
Petroleum, crude	280,000[e]	280,000[e]	303,000[e]
Salt	89,000[e]	92,000[e]	77,500
Silver[c]	26,000	26,000	20,000
Steel inputs and castings	2,944,000	3,045,000	2,899,000
Sulfur and pyrites			
Pyrites, 42%[d]	65,000[e]	80,000[e]	N/A
Pyrites recovered	53,000[e]	65,000[e]	N/A
Zinc	68,000	68,000[e]	56,900
Zinc, slab	90,000	93,000[e]	86,900

[c] Kilograms.
[d] Estimated average pyrite content.
[e] Estimated.

Source: British Geological Survey, *World Mineral Statistics, 1984–88; World Mineral Production,* 1985–89.

VI. GOVERNMENT AND DEFENSE FORCES

TABLE 5.VI.1 State budget

	(Million Leva)		
	1986	1987[a]	1988[a]
Revenue			
National economy	20,384.8	19,011.8	21,109.0
Other receipts	1,622.7	1,661.0	1,843.0
Total	22,007.5	20,672.8	22,952.0
Expenditure			
National economy	11,377.6	9,590.1	10,842.0
Education, health, science, art, and culture	3,736.8	3,884.1	4,304.0
Social security	3,631.7	3,726.9	3,914.0
Administration and other	3,163.6	3,461.7	3,892.0
Total	21,909.7	20,662.8	22,952.0

[a] Approved budget proposals.

Source: The Europa World Year Book, 1989, 1990.

TABLE 5.VI.2 Hard-currency debt

	(Million U.S. $)			
	1980	1985	1988	1989
Gross debt	3.5	3.7	7.5	10.0
of which				
Government	0.3	0.6	1.0	1.2
Commercial	3.2	3.1	6.5	8.8
Other	N/A	N/A	N/A	N/A
Reserves	N/A	2.1	1.8	1.4
Net debt	N/A	1.6	5.7	8.6
Debt service ratio[a]	N/A	15%	38%	45%

[a] Debt service ratio is calculated as the share of principal and interest payments to total hard-currency earnings.

Source: U.S. Central Intelligence Agency, "Eastern Europe: Long Road Ahead To Economic Well-Being", May, 1990.

TABLE 5.VI.3 Armed forces totals, 1991

Total armed forces	107,000	(70,000 conscripts)[a]
Branches		
Army	75,000	(49,000 conscripts)
Navy	10,000	(5,000 conscripts)
Air Force	22,000	(16,000 conscripts)
Total reserves	472,500	
Army	420,000	
Navy	7,500	(to age 55/to ages 60–65 for officers)
Air Force	45,000	(to age 60)
Budget	1.65 billion leva/($1.98 billion)[c]	

[a]Bulgaria reduced its active duty personnel in 1990 by 10%. In 1991 active duty personnel was estimated at 100,000 but will not decline further because of the large neighboring Turkish forces.

[b]Expenditures include internal police and security, but all figures are estimates, since no budgets existed in the 1980s.

[c]Budget based on 16 leva = $1.

Source: The International Institute for Strategic Studies, *The Military Balance 1991–1992*, 1991. Copyright IISS.

TABLE 5.VI.4 Components of defense force, 1989

Army
Organization
3 military districts
5 tank brigades
8 motorized rifle divisions
1 parachute regiment
4 artillery regiments
3 antiaircraft regiments
3 surface-to-surface missile brigades
2 surface-to-air missile regiments
Major equipment (1986)
1,800 medium tanks
310 armored fighting vehicles
100-122mm and 130mm multiple rocket launchers
66 FROG-7 and Scud surface-to-surface missiles

Navy
Organization
Naval bases at Varna, Burgas, Sozopol, and Atiya
2 helicopter squadrons
2 coastal artillery regiments
3 naval guard companies
Major equipment (1986)
2 ex-Soviet R-class submarines
3 Poti-class corvettes
2 Riga-class frigates

Air Force
Organization
8 interceptor squadrons
6 fighter/bomber squadrons
1 reconnaissance squadron
1 transport regiment
1 helicopter regiment
1 air defense division
1 paratroop regiment
Major equipment (1986)
100 MiG-23
20 MiG-23 Flogger B interceptor aircraft
70 MiG-17 fighter/bomber/interceptor aircraft
36 MiG-17/-21 reconnaissance aircraft

Source: Reprinted with permission from *World Defense Forces*, 2nd Edition, published by ABC-CLIO, 1989.

TABLE 5.VI.5   Military expenditures

	1979	1985[a]
Million leva	700	1,010
Constant price figures (million U.S. $)[b]	680	828
Military expenditures as a percent of GNP		
Bulgaria	7.0%	8.0%
USSR	12.9	12.5
United States	5.0	6.6
France	3.9	4.0

[a] Latest available data.

[b] 1986 exchange rates and prices.

Source: SIPRI Yearbook 1989: World Armaments and Disarmament, Stockholm International Peace Research Institute, 1989.

VII. INDUSTRY

TABLE 5.VII.1   Industrial production index[a] (Bulgaria and selected countries)

Country	(1980 = 100)						
	1960	1970	1980	1986	1987	1989	1990[b]
Bulgaria	22	64	100	111	115	116	102
USSR[c]	38	68	100	113	116	118	115
United States	45	73	100	113	119	129	130
France	47	75	100	100	102	110	111

[a] Indexes for the noncommunist countries are value-added weighted indexes of industrial intermediate and final products. Industry includes manufacturing, mining, and, in most countries, public utilities. The indexes for the communist countries are estimates of CIA, constructed as nearly as possible on the same basis as the indexes for Western countries, and include manufacturing, mining, and public utilities.

[b] Preliminary.

[c] Index of gross values of output for individual commodities and branches are aggregated by 1982 value-added weights. This index is as comparable with the index of U.S. industrial production of the U.S. Federal Reserve Board as data will permit.

Source: U.S. Central Intelligence Agency, *Handbook of Economic Statistics,* 1991.

TABLE 5.VII.2   Industrial production index (official and adjusted)

	(1980 = 100)					
	1960	1970	1980	1986	1987	1988[a]
Official	16	49	100	148	155	166
Adjusted	22	64	100	110	112	113

[a] Preliminary.

Source: U.S. Central Intelligence Agency, *Handbook of Economic Statistics,* 1989.

TABLE 5.VII.3 Production of selected industrial items

| | (Thousand Metric Tons, Except as Noted) | | |
	1985	1986	1987
Agricultural and forestry products:			
Refined sugar	457	N/A	N/A
Wine[a]	3,859	N/A	N/A
Beer[a]	5,838	6,025	6,209
Cigarettes and cigars[b]	93,975	90,000	90,300
Cotton yarn[b]	82,700	85,100	83,900
Flax and hemp yarn[b]	9,500	8,500	8,200
Wool yarn[b]	35,100	35,200	32,200
Chemical wood pulp	174.3	162.0	141.6
Paper	370.4	377.2	366.6
Fuels, minerals, metals, and chemicals:			
Sulfuric acid (100%)	810.1	806.6	688.5
Caustic soda	157.1	143.6	108.6
Soda ash	1,036.6	1,054.2	1,070.2
Nitrogenous fertilizers[b]	837,736	817,900	801,400
Phosphate fertilizers[b]	171,705	132,400	130,800
Coke	1,087	1,156	1,314
Unworked glass–rectangles[c]	23,459	19,500	20,300
Clay building bricks[d]	1,122	1,145	1,077
Cement	5,296	5,640	5,589
Pig iron and ferro-alloys	1,754	1,651	1,706
Crude steel	2,944	2,965	3,044
Electric energy[e]	41,629	41,817	43,464
Machinery and equipment:			
Tractors - 10 h.p. and over[f]	5,350	5,094	4,751
Metal-working lathes[f]	5,477	5,912	4,888
Cranes[f]	1,457	N/A	N/A
Fork-lift trucks[f]	85,432	84,852	85,160
Manufactured consumer goods:			
Woven cotton fabric[g]	351,300	349,500	351,900
Woven woollen fabrics[g]	41,900	42,022	40,803
Woven fabrics of man-made fibers[g]	36,400	37,200	37,800
Leather footwear[h]	22,800	N/A	N/A
Rubber footwear[h]	8,217	N/A	N/A
Rubber tires[i]	1,659	1,668	1,851
Soap	25,800	N/A	N/A
Refrigerators, household[f]	122,100	118,000	110,500
Washing machines, household[f]	155,900	159,200	171,700
Radio receivers[f]	41,500	38,000	56,100
Television receivers[f]	110,600	153,700	198,500

[a] Thousand hectoliters.

[b] Metric tons.

[c] Thousand square meters.

[d] Million.

[e] Million kilowatt-hours.

[f] Units.

[g] Thousand meters.

[h] Thousands pairs.

[i] Thousands.

Source: The Europa World Year Book, 1989.

TABLE 5.VII.4   Industrial output by main sector

| | (Percent Change on Year Earlier Period) | | | |
| | 1987 | | 1988 | |
	Jan–Jun	Jan–Sep	Jan–Jun	Jan–Sep
Electronics	11.7	13.4	18.9	16.9
Transport, agricultural, and building equipment	4.7	3.8	−0.7	−0.1
Machine building for investment purposes	8.7	8.4	8.5	4.3
Biotechnical and chemical industry	2.6	1.1	6.6	6.3
Metallurgy and mineral resources	0.7	0.1	3.7	3.0
Construction and building materials	N/A	0.6	3.6	2.2
Power industry	N/A	6.1	0.2	0.5
Agro-industry	1.4	0.7	4.8	5.6
Wood products	1.4	−0.4	5.2	6.0
Consumer goods	5.2	4.7	4.6	4.3
Total industrial output	3.7	3.5	6.2	5.4

Source: EIU, "Bulgaria, Country Report," No. 4, 1988.

TABLE 5.VII.5   Rank of industry, manufacturing, and service sector share of GDP,[a] 1990 (Bulgaria and selected countries)

	Rank
Bulgaria	5
Brunei	1
Angola	20
USSR	9

[a] All former East Bloc countries rank in the top 10 except Hungary. No OECD country is in the top 20. Additionally, no East Bloc state, nor the Soviet Union is among the top 20 countries in terms of manufacturing share of GDP or services share of GDP. This chart indicates the significant role of extractive industries in Eastern Europe and the USSR.

Source: The Economist, *Book of Vital World Statistics,* 1990.

TABLE 5.VII.6   Industrial waste generation

Bulgaria has yet to release these figures.

TABLE 5.VII.7 Emissions of air pollutants, 1988[a] (Bulgaria and selected countries)

	Nitrogen Oxides		Sulfur Dioxide		
	Emissions (Thousand Tons)	Emissions per Unit GNP (Grams)	Emissions (Thousand Tons)	Emissions per Unit GNP (Grams)[c]	Greenhouse Index[b]
Bulgaria[d]	150	3	1,030	21	3.0
USSR[e]	4,510	2	18,584	10	3.4
United States[f]	19,800	4	20,700	4	5.3
France	1,615	2	1,226	1	2.4

[a] Preliminary data.

[b] Carbon heating equivalents, metric tons per capita. 1988–1989 data.

[c] East European countries have a significantly higher emissions per unit GNP because of inefficient production. For example, on average, these countries use 50–100 percent more energy than the United States to produce a dollar of GDP, and 100–300 percent more than Japan.

[d] The very high pollution rates in Bulgaria have had deleterious consequences for the population. According to research conducted by Dr. Kiriaki Basmadjieva of the Bulgarian Health Ministry, asthma and ulcer rates among people living near heavy industrial complexes in Bulgaria are nine times those of people living in relatively pristine areas; rates of skin disease are some seven times higher, or rickets and liver diseases four times higher, and of hypertension and nervous system diseases three times as high.

[e] Stationary sources only. 1987 data.

[f] Sulfur data are for sulfur oxides.

Source: State of the World 1991, A Worldwatch Institute Report on Progress Toward a Sustainable Society, 1991; UN, *Human Development Report 1991,* 1991.

TABLE 5.VII.8 Environmental summary, 1991

	Bulgaria	Belgium	USSR	United States	France
Energy					
Energy production					
Solids[a]	479	92	14,299	20,736	365
Liquids[a]	3	0	24,139	17,297	145
Gas[a]	0	0	25,541	16,280	115
Biomass[a]	7	6	742	1,150	97
Nuclear[b]	2,695	41,218	213,001	529,352	303,928
Hydroelectric[b]	2,697	366	222,803	272,023	51,158
Energy consumption					
Total[a]	1,222	1,588	52,027	69,496	6,119
Per capita[c]	145	187	193	307	149
Per capita (global rank)	23	15	12	7	22
Energy intensity					
BTUs/$1987 GNP	47,794	12,097	N/A	15,787	8,784
Global rank	22	111	N/A	99	120
Waste					
Access to sanitation services					
Urban population	100%	100%	100%	N/A	100%
Rural population	96%	100%	100%	N/A	100%
1988 Greenhouse emissions					
Carbon dioxide[d]	37,000	28,000	1,200,000	1,400,000	96,000
Methane[d]	360	490	35,000	40,000	2,800
CFSs[d]	1	9	110	190	50
Share of world emissions	0.4%	0.4%	13.6%	17.3%	1.7%
Global rank[e]	29	26	14	7	41

[a] Trillion BTUs.

[b] Gigawatt hours.

[c] Million BTUs.

[d] Thousand tons.

[e] Per capita.

Source: From *The 1992 Information Please Environmental Almanac.* Reprinted by permission of the Houghton Mifflin Company.

VIII. LABOR FORCE

TABLE 5.VIII.1 Workforce by selected areas of the economy

| | (Percent) | | |
	1980	1986	1988
Total (thousands)	4,297.4	4,423.8	4,443.7
Material production	83.1	82.1	81.7
of which			
Manufacturing industry	43.2	46.0	46.7
Agriculture and forestry	24.6	20.5	19.2
Transport and communications	6.8	6.7	6.6
Distributive trades, hotels and restaurants,			
Wholesale purchasing	8.1	8.5	8.8
Nonmaterial production	16.9	17.9	18.3

Source: EUROSTAT, *Central and Eastern Europe 1991,* 1991.

TABLE 5.VIII.2 Average monthly earnings by economic sector[a]

| | (Leva) | | | |
	1980	1985	1989	1990[b]
Total	193	228	286	310
of which				
Agriculture	167	105	255	270
Manufacturing sector	197	235	292	307
Construction	223	260	324	342
Transport	218	252	304	343

[a] State and cooperative sector; the average monthly wages and salaries of manual and nonmanual workers are calculated by taking 1/12 of total annual wages and salaries and dividing it by the average number of registered manual and nonmanual workers.
[b] Average of first six months of the year.

Source: EUROSTAT, *Central and Eastern Europe 1991,* 1991.

TABLE 5.VIII.3 Economically active population by sex and industry, 1985

| | (Percent) | | |
	Males	Females	Total
Agriculture and hunting	16.0%	16.9%	771,862
Forestry, fishing, mining, quarrying,			
manufacturing electricity,			
gas, and water	38.7	37.0	1,777,759
Construction	13.4	3.5	406,719
Trade, restaurants, and hotels	4.9	12.4	397,431
Transport, storage, and communications	9.6	3.6	314,507
Financing, insurance, real estate,			
and business services	0.2	0.9	24,696
Community, social, and personal services	17.1	25.6	992,611
Other activities	0.1	0.1	555
Total	2,451,171	2,234,969	4,686,140

Source: The Europa World Year Book, 1990.

IX. POPULATION AND HEALTH

TABLE 5.IX.1 Geography and demographic profile, 1990

Population	
Population in 1990	8,933,544
Population by 2000	9,000,000 est.
Population by 2020	8,900,000 est.
Current annual percent increase	0.1%
Population density per sq km	81.1
Net migration rate	−4 migrants/1,000
Urban/Rural	66.4%/33.6%
Ethnic Division	
Bulgarian	85.3%
Turk	8.5%
Gypsy	2.6%
Macedonian	2.5%
Armenian	0.3%
Russian	0.2%
Other	0.6%
Religion	
Bulgarian Orthodox	85.0%
Islamic	13.0%
Jewish	0.8%
Roman Catholic	0.7%
Protestant, Gregorian-Armenian, Other (combined)	0.5%
Geography	
Total area	110,910 sq km (42,822 sq mi)
Land area	110,550 sq km (42,683)
Coast line	354 km (220 mi)
Land borders with	
Greece	494 km (307 mi)
Romania	608 km (378 mi)
Turkey	240 km (149 mi)
Yugoslavia	539 km (335 mi)
Disputes	
Macedonia question with Greece and Yugoslavia	

Source: The Economist, *Book of Vital World Statistics,* 1990; U.S. CIA, *Atlas of Eastern Europe,* August 1990; Population Reference Bureau, *1989 World Population Data Sheet* (Washington, D.C.: Population Reference Bureau, Inc., 1989); U.S. CIA, *The World Factbook,* 1990.

TABLE 5.IX.2 Population (Bulgaria and selected countries)

	(Million People at Midyear)				
	1960	**1970**	**1980**	**1985**	**1990**
Bulgaria	7.9	8.5	8.8	8.9	8.9
Belgium	9.1	9.6	9.8	9.9	9.9
USSR	214.3	242.8	266.4	278.9	290.9
United States	180.7	205.1	227.8	239.3	250.4
France	45.7	50.8	53.9	55.2	56.4

Source: U.S. Central Intelligence Agency, *Handbook of Economic Statistics,* 1989, 1990, 1991.

TABLE 5.IX.3 Population by age (Bulgaria and selected countries)

Age	Bulgaria (1986) Total	Percent	Belgium (1984) Total	Percent	U.S. (1987) Total	Percent	U.S.S.R. (1987) Total	Percent
<19	2,463,304	27.5	2,627,171	26.6	70,857,000	29.1	92,267,217	32.8
20–44	3,088,395	34.5	3,526,973	35.8	97,413,000	40.0	99,559,765	35.4
45–64	2,370,939	26.5	2,354,231	23.9	45,293,000	18.6	64,009,456	22.8
65+	1,035,000	11.5	1,346,997	13.7	29,836,000	12.3	25,501,353	9.0
Total	8,957,638	100.0	9,855,372	100.0	243,400,000	100.0	281,337,791	100.0

Source: UNESCO, *Statistical Yearbook,* 1989.

TABLE 5.IX.4 Population of major cities, 1988

Sofia	1,136,875
Plovdiv	364,162
Varna	306,300
Burgas	200,464
Ruse	190,720
Stara Zagora	158,151
Pleven	136,287
Dobrich	112,582
Sliven	109,432
Shumen	107,973

Source: The Europa World Year Book, 1991.

TABLE 5.IX.5 Health indicators, 1990 (Bulgaria and selected countries)

Birth rate	12.7/1,000
of United States	15.0/1,000
of USSR	18.0/1,000
Death rate	12.0/1,000
of United States	9.0/1,000
of USSR	10.0/1,000
Infant mortality rate	15.0/1,000
of OECD and United States	9-10/1,000
of USSR	25.0/1,000
Maternal mortality rate[a]	13/100,000
of OECD and United States	10/100,000
of USSR	48/100,000
Life expectancy	69 male/75 female
of OECD	72 male/78 female
Fertility rate	1.9 children/woman
of United States	1.9 children/woman
of USSR	2.4 children/woman
Suicides[b]	15.8/100,000
of OECD and United States	14.6/100,000
of USSR	19.8/100,000

[a] Figures refer to live births. 1980–1987 figures.

[b] 1987–1988 figures.

Source: Population Reference Bureau, *1989 World Population Data Sheet* (Washington, D.C.: Population Reference Bureau Inc., 1989); The Economist, *Book of Vital World Statistics,* 1990; UN, *Human Development Report 1991,* 1991.

TABLE 5.IX.6   Registered illnesses

Illness	1984	1986	1988
Influenza	6,119	7,041	39,330
Chicken pox	40,737	39,211	31,457
German measles	24,371	8,498	24,719
Viral hepatitis	12,833	11,931	10,956
Streptococcal angina and scarlet fever	18,150	13,697	9,413
Bacillary dysentery	4,797	4,878	3,956
Mumps	852	68,613	446
Measles	292	1,370	404

Source: EUROSTAT, *Central and Eastern Europe 1991,* 1991.

TABLE 5.IX.7   Fatalities by selected causes of death

Cause of Death	1983	1985	1987
Circulatory illnesses of which			
Illnesses of the cerebrovascular system	22,025	23,637	22,136
Ischaemic heart diseases	18,162	21,767	20,873
Arteriosclerosis	7,300	7,112	8,994
Acute myocardial infarction	6,953	7,157	6,414
Hypertonia and hypertensive heart diseases	2,210	2,278	2,768
Malignant neoplasms of which	14,054	14,679	15,037
Stomach	2,501	2,371	2,339
Windpipe, bronchi, and lungs	2,905	2,990	3,100
Mammary gland	916	1,059	977
Pneumonia	4,579	4,629	4,073
Bronchitis, emphysema, and asthma	2,506	2,600	1,894
Diabetes mellitus	1,314	1,507	1,642
Nephritis, nephrotic syndrome, and nephrosis	558	554	708

Source: EUROSTAT, *Central and Eastern Europe 1991,* 1991.

TABLE 5.IX.8   Life expectancy by sex, 1991
(Bulgaria and selected countries)

Bulgaria	
Male	69
Female	76
USSR	
Male	65
Female	74
United States	
Male	72
Female	79
France	
Male	74
Female	82

Source: U.S. Central Intelligence Agency, *The World Factbook,* 1991.

TABLE 5.IX.9 Medical care, 1983–1988 (Bulgaria and selected countries)

	Doctors	Dentists	Pharmacists	Beds (Thousand)	Total Health Expenditure[a]
			(Number per Million)		
Bulgaria[b]	2,749.0	625.0	471.0	9.4	3.2
Belgium	3,119.0	629.0	1,112.0	8.9	7.2
USSR[b]	4,124.0	N/A	321.0	12.8	3.2
United States	2,035.0	560.0	641.0	5.9	11.2
OECD	2,199.5	453.8	559.2	8.0	8.3

[a] As a percent of GDP. 1987 figures.

[b] Figures for the former communist countries are clearly misleading. According to the Soviet Ministry of Health, 1.2 million beds are in facilities with no hot water, 1/6 of the beds are in hospitals with no water, and 30 percent of the hospitals have no indoor toilets. Source: *Literaturnaya Gazeta,* February 3, 1988; and see also *World Affairs,* vol. 152, no. 1, Summer 1989.

Source: Population Reference Bureau, *1989 World Population Data Sheet* (Washington, D.C.: Population Reference Bureau, Inc., 1989); The Economist, *Book of Vital World Statistics,* 1990; UN, *Human Development Report 1991,* 1991.

TABLE 5.IX.10 Abortion rates (Bulgaria and selected countries)

Country	Number of Abortions	Rate per Thousand Women Aged 15–44	Ratio per 100 Known Pregnancies	Total Rate[a]
Bulgaria[b] (1987)	119,000	64.7	50.7	N/A
Belgium (1985)	15,900	7.5	12.2	N/A
USSR (1987)	6,818,000	111.9	54.9	N/A
United States (1985)	1,588,600	28.0	29.7	797

[a] The number of abortions that would be experienced by 1,000 women during their reproductive lifetimes, given present age-specific abortion rates.

[b] In contrast to women from Western European and English-speaking countries, who are young, unmarried women seeking to delay a first birth, women from Eastern Europe are married with two or more children, using abortion for spacing and ending childbirth. In addition, high rates in Eastern Europe, except Romania, may be attributed in part to the very liberal abortion laws, where abortion has been used as a form of birth control since the 1950s.

Source: Adapted with the permission of The Alan Guttmacher Institute from Stanley K. Henshaw and Evelyn Morrow, *Induced Abortion: A World Review 1990 Supplement,* 1990.

X. TRADE

TABLE 5.X.1 Exports and imports, by commodity group

Commodity Group	(Million U.S. $)			
	1970	1980	1986	1988
Exports:				
Machinery and equipment	581	4,657	8,279	12,372
Fuels, minerals, and metals	162	1,573	1,146	1,363
Agricultural and forestry products	870	2,559	2,435	3,235
Manufactured consumer goods	295	923	1,547	2,177
Other	96	777	1,111	1,202
Total	2,004	10,489	14,518	20,349
Imports:				
Machinery and equipment	743	3,461	5,826	8,854
Fuels, minerals, and metals	533	4,194	6,838	7,658
Agricultural and forestry products	291	948	1,324	1,951
Manufactured consumer goods	104	430	623	1,049
Other	160	743	966	1,469
Total	1,831	9,776	15,577	20,981

Source: U.S. Central Intelligence Agency, *Handbook of Economic Statistics,* 1989, 1990.

TABLE 5.X.2 Main destinations of exports and main origins of imports, 1989

Country	(Percent of Total)
Destinations of exports:	
USSR	65.8
Germany	5.6
Czechoslovakia	4.4
Poland	3.9
Romania	2.0
Socialist countries	86.3
Developed capitalist countries	7.3
Developing countries	6.4
Origins of imports:	
USSR	56.3
Germany	10.7
Czechoslovakia	5.0
Poland	4.8
Socialist countries	75.9
Developed capitalist countries	17.0
Developing countries	7.1

Source: EIU, "Bulgaria, Country Report," No. 4, 1991.

TABLE 5.X.3 Principal trading partners

	(Percent) Imports from		Exports to	
	1985	1987[a]	1985	1987[a]
USSR	56.1	57.3	56.6	61.1
United States	1.1	0.7	N/A	N/A
Western Europe:				
Greece	N/A	N/A	1.5	N/A
Italy	1.2	1.2	0.5	0.6
West Germany	3.9	4.9	1.4	1.2
Switzerland	1.4	1.4	1.0	1.0
United Kingdom	N/A	N/A	1.7	N/A
Eastern Europe:				
Czechoslovakia	4.2	5.0	4.6	4.9
East Germany	5.1	5.7	5.1	5.5
Hungary	N/A	N/A	1.9	1.8
Poland	4.5	4.8	3.5	4.3
Romania	N/A	N/A	2.1	2.1
Yugoslavia	N/A	N/A	0.9	N/A
Other:				
Cuba	1.7	1.8	1.7	1.4
Iran	N/A	N/A	0.9	0.6
Iraq	N/A	N/A	3.1	2.9
Japan	0.6	1.0	N/A	N/A
Libya	2.9	1.0	4.3	3.4
Turkey	N/A	N/A	1.1	N/A
Total including others	100.0	100.0	100.0	100.0
Total (million leva)	14,067	14,067	13,739	13,802

[a]Figures are provisional.

Source: The Europa World Year Book, 1990.

TABLE 5.X.4 Index of import and export prices, terms of trade
(Bulgaria and selected countries)

	(1980 = 100)			
	1984	1986	1987	1989
Bulgaria				
Import prices	128	125	124	112
Export prices	111	110	112	110
Terms of trade	86	88	90	98
Czechoslovakia				
Import prices	134	146	142	137
Export prices	112	119	119	129
Terms of trade	84	81	83	93
Hungary				
Import prices	125	136	139	163
Export prices	116	120	124	153
Terms of trade	93	88	89	94
Poland				
Import prices	139	198	279	1,281
Export prices	127	189	275	1,516
Terms of trade	91	95	99	118

[a]1988.

(continued)

TABLE 5.X.4   *(continued)*

	(1980 = 100)			
	1984	1986	1987	1989
Romania				
Import prices	135	130	127	N/A
Export prices	124	114	114	N/A
Terms of trade	92	88	90	N/A
Yugoslavia				
Import prices	116	108	109	124
Export prices	108	107	108	123
Terms of trade	93	99	100	99
Soviet Union				
Import prices	115	112	110	113[a]
Export prices	130	114	110	103[a]
Terms of trade	113	102	100	100[a]

[a] 1988.

Source: Comecon Data 1989, 1990, 1990, 1991.

TABLE 5.X.5   Major imports and exports[a]

Import Goods/Categories	(Thousand U.S. $)		
	1987	1988	1989
Dairy products	7,891	6,813	6,062
Vegetables and fruit	10,265	10,196	11,364
Tobacco and tobacco manufactures	8,688	3,800	5,625
Metalliferous ores and metal scrap	5,684	8,751	5,653
Crude animal and vegetable material[c]	5,002	4,810	5,828
Yarn, fabrics, made-up articles, and related products[c]	5,847	7,259	7,785
Iron and steel	17,006	14,683	17,383
Articles of apparel and clothing accessories	40,241	31,782	33,088

Export Goods/Categories	(Thousand U.S. $)		
	1987	1988	1989
Organic chemicals	27,090	24,235	21,350
Dyeing, tanning, and coloring materials	27,812	22,807	18,287
Plastics in primary form[b]	N/A	40,850	27,150
Chemical materials and products[c]	27,856	33,955	24,696
Textile yarn, fabrics, made-up articles, and related products[c]	33,021	31,668	31,148
Nonmetallic mineral manufactures	19,203	14,684	14,567
Iron and steel	55,955	60,009	52,274
Nonferrous metals	25,982	25,599	17,246
Manufactures of metals[c]	18,883	19,306	22,373
Goods for complete production plants, Div. 84, 85, 87	16,415	19,240	28,485
Machinery specialized for particular industries	99,761	79,255	104,654
Metalwork machinery	95,139	72,098	46,986
General industrial machinery and equipment[c]	100,903	90,556	77,547
Electrical machinery, apparatus and appliances[c]	45,535	45,967	43,439
Road vehicles (incl. air-cushion vehicles)	24,040	50,393	31,616
Professional instruments and apparatus[c]	33,933	30,530	30,413

[a] According to SITC headings.

[b] Classification changed in 1988; figures for previous years not applicable.

[c] Not elsewhere specified.

Source: EUROSTAT, *Central and Eastern Europe 1991,* 1991.

TABLE 5.X.6 Trade with Western countries[a]

	(Million U.S. $)				(Million U.S. $)		
	1985	1988	1989		1985	1988	1989
Importing countries:				Exporting countries:			
Austria	3.1	2.4	3.1	Austria	11.0	16.4	12.9
Belgium/Luxembourg	1.6	1.7	1.3[b]	Belgium/Luxembourg	5.1	6.6	5.6[b]
Finland	0.4	1.0	1.1	Finland	3.2	2.7	2.9
France	4.7	5.2	6.1	France	13.3	12.7	12.6
West Germany	13.4	15.2	14.6	West Germany	47.2	74.3	65.3
Greece	2.8	3.9	4.5[c]	Greece	3.7	2.8	3.6[c]
Italy	7.0	9.3	10.6	Italy	13.9	17.0	23.9
Netherlands	2.9	2.9	3.3	Netherlands	3.8	7.0	7.0
Spain	4.1	4.3	3.4	Spain	3.7	2.9	2.4
Sweden	0.7	0.9	1.0[d]	Sweden	4.4	4.8	5.1[d]
Switzerland	1.1	1.2	1.2	Switzerland	7.9	10.3	12.7
Turkey	8.3	1.3	0.3[b]	Turkey	0.6	2.3	2.0[b]
UK	2.4	4.2	4.7	UK	11.9	12.2	11.8
United States	3.0	2.3	4.9	United States	8.7	10.6	15.1
Yugoslavia	7.2	10.5	14.0	Yugoslavia	9.0	12.1	12.5

[a]Monthly averages from Western countries' trade accounts, in million U.S. $.

[b]January–October.

[c]January–August.

[d]January–November.

Source: EIU, "Bulgaria, Country Report," No. 4, 1990.

TABLE 5.X.7 Trade with the USSR, by commodity

Imports from the USSR	(Million Rubles[a]) 1987	1988
Metal-cutting machine tools	64.4	62.2
Power-generating equipment	222.4	197.8
Mining, hoisting, excavating, etc., machinery	105.3	108.9
Tractors, agricultural machinery, and parts	209.3	248.9
Motor vehicles and garage equipment	275.1	317.8
Aircraft and ships	52.8	80.7
Other machinery and transport equipment	530.0	495.9
Coal and coke	315.0	270.0
Petroleum and products	1,910.4	1,559.6
Fuel gas and electricity	808.1	752.3
Metal ores and concentrates	37.2	28.9
Pig iron and ferro alloys	39.5	38.6
Rolled ferrous products and pipes	156.6	159.8
Chemicals	78.3	89.3
Wood, paper, and manufactures	99.2	83.3
Raw cotton	67.3	69.0
Domestic appliances, clocks and cameras	28.6	28.2
Total, including other items		
Million rubles	6,276.3	6,093.7
Million U.S. $	10,425.7	9,923.9

Exports to the USSR	1987	1988
Metal-cutting machine tools	246.3	268.0
Electrical equipment	145.0	131.7
Geology etc., equipment	N/A	N/A
Hoisting and conveying equipment	781.9	745.8
Computer equipment	979.0	1,084.6
Agricultural machinery	198.7	178.0
Railway equipment	N/A	N/A
Ships and boats	133.9	86.5
Other machinery and transport equipment	1,179.2	1,289.4
Rolled ferrous products and pipes	7.9	14.5
Chemicals	514.8	514.2
Fruit and vegetables	215.0	215.4
Wood	N/A	N/A
Raw tobacco	131.4	120.5
Tobacco manufactures	417.3	405.7
Textile cloth and manfactures	224.2	219.2
Footwear	22.6	24.5
Furniture	60.9	63.0
Beverages	96.2	116.7
Total, including other items		
Million rubles	6,551.7	6,873.1
Million U.S. $	10,883.2	12,966.8

Note: Commodity totals are additions of items in the trade accounts and may be incomplete.

[a]Noncommercial rate: end 1987 0.602 rubles = $1.00, end 1988 0.612 rubles = $1.00.

Source: EIU, "Bulgaria, Country Report," No. 4, 1990.

TABLE 5.X.8 Trade with the United States, by commodity

Imports from the United States	(Million U.S. $)	
	1987	1988
Cereals and preparations	33,274	73,146
Tobacco manufactures	5,023	2,462
Hides and skins, undressed	N/A	854
Oilseeds	9,118	13,258
Pulp and waste paper	246	N/A
Crude fertilizers and minerals	5	393
Coal	N/A	N/A
Petroleum and products	N/A	8
Chemicals	9,256	5,856
Iron and steel	N/A	30
Metal manufactures	631	894
Road vehicles	20	200
Other transport equipment	35	180
Scientific instruments, etc.	2,031	4,298
Machinery, including electric	24,529	14,230
Power-generating	N/A	40
Total, including other items	88,344	126,446

Exports to the United States	1987	1988
Meat and preparations	N/A	N/A
Dairy products	1,897	2,399
Tobacco and manufactures	20,001	9,395
Crude rubber	N/A	N/A
Textile fibers and waste	N/A	N/A
Crude animal and vegetable materials	171	72
Petroleum and products	3,737	N/A
Chemicals	5,736	9,889
Paper, etc., and manufactures	23	N/A
Textile yarn, cloth, and manufactures	1,358	113
Nonmetallic mineral manufactures	99	138
Iron and steel	70	454
Nonferrous metals	233	263
Machinery, including electric	1,241	889
Transport equipment	1,533	42
Furniture	116	225
Clothing	3,272	1,085
Footwear	11	N/A
Total, including other items	41,968	27,123

Source: EIU, "Bulgaria, Country Report," No. 4, 1990.

CHAPTER SIX

YUGOSLAVIA

POPULATION:	23,841,608
SQUARE MILES:	98,764 mi², 255,804 km²
RELIGION:	Eastern Orthodox, 50%; Roman Catholic, 30%
CURRENCY:	Dinar
EXCHANGE RATE:	Yud 20.36: $1
DEBT:	$ 18 billion

I   YUGOSLAVIA

POLITICS, HISTORY, AND ECONOMICS

POLITICS

Yugoslavia is now disintegrating, alternating between sporadic bursts of bloody civil conflict bordering on civil war and eerie moments of disingenuous calm. Before the tragic fighting erupted in 1991, the country had begun political and economic reform similar to the rest of the East bloc. But little international attention had been focused on the country's transformation. That process had been exceedingly complex because of the federal structure of the state. Moreover, Yugoslavia was not an official member of the East bloc and did not quite seem a part of collapsing communism in Eastern Europe. Also, there had been no singular crystallizing moment, such as the destruction of a wall or the assassination of an old-line communist leader. As a result, world attention focused on the more dramatic and more easily comprehensible events in Poland, East Germany, or Romania.

Nevertheless, in Yugoslavia as in those states, the communist party abandoned its political monopoly and free elections were held. Voters in four of the country's six republics elected noncommunist leaders. A new economic agenda establishing the basis of a market economy had been introduced by the prime minister, Ante Markovic, seeking economic growth through fiscal responsibility at all levels of the economy and an end to four-digit hyperinflation.

The 1991 collapse of the center and the outbursts of violence have meant the end of progress towards reform. No matter what the outcome of the present strife, Yugoslavia will never return to its previous political or economic structures. The forces that destroyed the state and its reforms have antecedents in the country's precommunist history. Combined with the failures of the communist era, the mix proved explosive. A single state had been created out of disparate ethnic, national, religious, and linguistic groups that had been part of two different, dissolving empires. World War II was particularly destructive of any sense of an emerging Yugoslav nationalism. The political and economic changes that Marshal Tito introduced into the conventional communist system were heralded as introducing the true potential of socialism. But soon after his death, the reforms were exposed as chimerical. The increasingly troubled and declining Yugoslav economy, coupled with the reappearance of nationalist sentiment, paved the way for the rise of Slobodan Milosevic as the ardent and dangerous president of Serbia. Serbian expansion and Croatian and Slovenian efforts to assert their independence followed. Violence was not far behind.

Now in the throes of civil war, Yugoslavia appears to be an Eastern European Lebanon. But in Lebanon the battles indicated a decades-long shift in power and the need to modify the political system to accommodate that shift. Yugoslavia is more like a USSR without nuclear weapons—a collection of highly diverse peoples, living under a withered socialist banner, who seized the first opportunity to declare their independence.

The dissolution has proved bloody. It is estimated that between a quarter and a third of the population of Yugoslavia is armed. None of them appear ready to renounce violence, despite the deaths of more than 2,000 of their fellows; the aerial bombardments of Zagreb, the second largest city in the country; and the creation of hundreds of thousands of refugees.

Current Politics

Before the drift into bloody chaos, Yugoslavia, or "the land of the South Slavs," was a loosely organized, multi-national federation that consisted of six republics—Serbia, Croatia, Slovenia, Bosnia-Hercegovina, Montenegro, and Macedonia—and two provinces part of Serbia but considered autonomous—Kosovo and Vojvodina. Yugoslavia was a multi-national state, with two alphabets, three religions, and four major languages. Because of the constitutional powers exercised by the individual republics and because of the tensions among the various political, national, and religious groups, Yugoslav politics have been among the most complex in the world.

The roots of the Yugoslav problem are painfully apparent. Serbo-Croatian is the language most commonly used by the vast majority of the Yugoslavs, but otherwise the peoples of the state have very little in common. Before joining in the formation of the Yugoslav state, Slovenia and Croatia were members of the Austro-Hungarian empire. Serbia, in contrast, had lived for centuries under Ottoman rule. Serbs comprise some 36.3 percent of the country's population; Croats, 19.7 percent; Muslim Slavs, 8.9 percent; Slovenes, 7.8 percent; Albanians, 7.7 percent; Macedonians, 6 percent; Montenegrins, 2.6 percent; and Hungarians, 1.9 percent. The Slovenes and Croats are Roman Catholics. Serbs, Montenegrins, and Macedonians are Eastern Orthodox Christians. Some 70 percent of the Albanians are Muslim, while 20 percent are Roman Catholic and 10 percent Eastern Orthodox. All the republics, and both autonomous provinces, have substantial ethnic and national minority groups within their borders.

Income inequalities between the Yugoslav republics are greater than in any other state of Europe. The differences in political sophistication are at least as great. The root of the present crisis is the failure to harmonize these immense differences among the peoples of Yugoslavia after the creation of a single state.

At its inception in 1918 the state was held together by the sheer will of its largest member, Serbia. But Serbian domination never translated into meaningful unification. In World War II, Serbia cast its lot with the Allies. Croatia sided with fascist Germany. While the rest of Europe fought a world war, Yugoslavia fought a civil war that cost an estimated one million lives. Following that devastating civil war within the punishing world war, Yugoslavia was united again under the domination of a communist party. But with the death of its charismatic chief, Marshal Josip Broz Tito, the communist party proved unable to maintain the unity he had forged. Another civil war is underway, with the Serb and the Croatian protagonists drawing on their diverse pre-Yugoslav histories and their World War II experiences to legitimate their claims.

While imposing unity from above, Tito actually compounded the problems of the Yugoslav state. He was committed to creating a workers' state, a laboratory of socialism, where the distinctions among peoples would pass into oblivion. In the end, however, he codified a system that was its antithesis. Communist Yugoslavia was meant to end Serbian domination, but because it was established as a system of federated republics, the differences among peoples were legally preserved and actually magnified. The constitution was revised in 1974 to grant greater rights to the republics, while the Serbian provinces of Kosovo and Vojvodina were extended republic status for all practical purposes. Moreover, in 1978, Tito established a "collective leadership" system, whereby the presidency and other federal offices would rotate among the republics. After his death in 1980, federal action was taken only with the consent of republic officials.

Tito's worker self-management economic system has been an additional complicating factor. The reforms adopted to transform the system proved ever more unworkable. By the 1980s, Yugoslavia had an $18 billion foreign debt as well as rampant inflation and unemployment. Worker "self-management" failed to create equality among workers and eventually bankrupted the state, a major factor in its collapse. Yet each republic saw itself as a victim of the old system, and none was willing to come to the aid of the federal state. The wealthier republics believed themselves taxed unfairly, while the poorer republics believed themselves exploited. Much like the Russian Republic, Serbia believed itself exploited by all the other republics and appreciated by none. The dramatic decline of the economy added fuel to the upsurge in nationalist sentiment.

The situation was ripe for exploitation by a nationalist demagogue, and the Serbian president seized the opportunity. Slobodan Milosevic had been a banker known in the West. In 1987 he took control of the Serbian Communist Party, largely through the betrayal of his own political allies. Having achieved control of the party, he began to destroy the fragile system erected by Tito to satisfy the eight major Yugoslav groups.

Milosevic, of course, is a symptom of the problems of Yugoslavia rather than the problem itself. Nonetheless, he has put the entire future of the state at risk. Believing that the interests of "Greater Serbia" were under assault from all sides, he demanded that all of the Serbian people be gathered into a single state. The current civil war is the result of his commitment to change the relation of the Yugoslav peoples, leading several republics to conclude that only full independence would preserve their national existence.

The Serbian president first promoted a mini-cult of personality in Serbia by exploiting the notion that Serbia had long been the victim of the Yugoslav federation. Enjoying the allegiance of the Serbian press, the Orthodox Church, and the Serbian intelligentsia, Milosevic first directed his nationalist attacks at Vojvodina and Kosovo. According to Milosevic, the autonomy granted them in the 1970s was an affront to Serbia.

He sacked the Communist Party leaders of Vojvodina and Kosovo and installed his puppets. He also unleashed widespread public protests, demanding the reincorporation of the provinces into Serbia. In the face of hundreds of thousands of Serbian protestors massed in Vojvodina, the region was easily subdued in 1988. At the same time, the leadership of Montenegro was replaced with Milosevic supporters. Kosovo fell soon after with the exercise of more populist tactics. The construction of greater Serbia had begun.

However, while Milosevic was solidifying his control over the Communist Party, the party itself was being challenged by the emergence of democratic forces. Although democratic sentiments were still quite fragile in 1989, many non-Serb communist leaders feared Milosevic's aggressive behavior to the point where they renounced the party and cast their lot with the emerging democrats. The initial popularity of the democrats stemmed not so much from their commitment to democracy as much as their opposition to Serbian dominance. Milosevic had effectively radicalized and unified the opposition to Greater Serbia.

At the Fourteenth Party Congress of January, 1990, Milosevic attempted to consummate Serbian control over the party. The Slovenians responded with demands for the separation of state and party; broader autonomy for the republics; and a declaration of human rights for all of Yugoslavia's peoples. Serbia and Montenegro refused that challenge, and Slovenia, joined by Croatia and Bosnia-Hercegovina, staged a walkout. The Congress quickly collapsed, followed by the ouster of the communist parties in four of the six republics, with Slovenia, Croatia, and Macedonia declaring their independence in 1991.

Center-right coalitions defeated communist and other left-wing parties in the elections in Slovenia and Croatia. In Slovenia, a coalition called the Democratic United Opposition of Slovenia (DEMOS) won the election. DEMOS is committed to private enterprise, the establishment of an independent judiciary, and multi-party democracy. Including the Christian Democrats, the most powerful member, as well as the Green Alliance, the Democratic Alliance, the Social Democrats, and the Craftsmen's Party, DEMOS controlled 126 seats in the 240-seat Slovenian national assembly. The opposition coalition consists of the League of Communists of Slovenia–Party of Democratic Renewal (LCS–PDR), the League of Socialist Youth–Liberal Party, and the Socialist Alliance of Slovenia.

The Slovenian national assembly elected Lojze Peterle, a 41-year-old Christian Democrat, as the republic's prime minister, while Milan Kucan, a communist but a staunch defender of Slovenian interests, was elected Slovenia's state president.

Before the outbreak of fighting, the principal political issues in Slovenia were its relation to the Yugoslav state, to Serbia, and to the federal army. Like the Croats, the Slovenes have long objected to the use of the revenues they contribute to the central government to build nonprofitable projects in the less developed southern Yugoslav republics. Many Slovenes favored the replacement of the present loose, federal system with an outright confederation. They proposed that Slovene military recruits serve only in Slovenia under the command of Slovene officers. They also proposed that the Yugoslav parliament be reformulated to contain an equal number of delegates from each republic, giving the 1.7 million Slovenes a vote equal to 8 million Serbs.

By the summer of 1991 the Slovenes became convinced that Serbia would never agree to a confederation. The republic formally declared its independence and set about building the structures of a state, including its own military and police forces and the establishment of a new currency.

But while Slovenia was acting against the federal republic, DEMOS was losing power within the republic, thus lessening its ability to mobilize Slovenians for the dual challenges of building state structures and countering Serbian opposition. Slovenian workers have become irate over the faltering economy, which may shrink by as much as 50 percent during the transition process, while others protest the influential role of the Roman Catholic clergy within DEMOS.

Shortly after the Slovenian elections, in April, 1990, the Croatian Democratic Community (CDC) won a decisive victory over the League of Communists of Croatia–Party for Democratic Changes. General Franjo Tudjman, CDC's leader, became the president of the Croatian republic. Tudjman had been a hero with Tito's Partisans in World War II, a former political prisoner, and a noted historian. Like DEMOS, the CDC is firmly committed to democracy and civil rights. But also like DEMOS, the CDC includes many strident nationalists, whose ardent defense of Croatian interests angered the Yugoslav military and fueled bloody clashes between the Croats and the Serbian minority living in Croatia. Many of these Serbs belong to the Serbian Democratic Party (SDP), whose leader is a psychiatrist with strong political skills, Dr. Jovan Raskovic.

President Tudjman struggled initially to calm the escalating violence in Croatia. Even after narrowly avoiding assassination by a Serbian gunman, Tudjman demonstrated deep sympathy for the Serbs in Croatia. Nonetheless, he has continued to advance the cause of Croatian nationalism. He restored the World War II Ustaši national anthem and flag. Evocative of Croatian independence for the Croats, those earlier Croatian symbols represent fascism and civil war to the remainder of the country. He has also moved to build the instruments of Croatian power. According to Tudjman, 60 percent of the police officers in Croatia were ethnic Serbs. He set about to dilute their influence through the massive recruiting of Croat officers. Whatever his earliest stance, Tudjman quickly adopted the Croatian nationalist agenda. Voicing fears of repression at the hands of Croatian nationalists, Serbs in Croatia continuously protested the rise of Croat nationalism and held their own referendum to demonstrate their commitment to autonomy. Armed Serbs seized local power and challenged the Croatian center. Serbian villages in those parts of Croatia adjacent to Serbia fell into armed clashes, attracting their fellow Serbians to cross into Croatia to join the fighting. The federal army then joined the conflict, first to control the fighting and then to fight the Croats.

The Croatian government attempted to limit the weapons in the hands of the Serbs. Prior to being ousted from power, the Croatian Communist Party had granted vast numbers of weapons permits to Serbian and Croatian communists. The Serbian uprisings were initially sustained by weapons acquired with those permits as well as by gun smuggling across the Serbian border. As a result, both the Croats and the Serbs in Croatia appear to have sufficient equipment to sustain an indefinite guerilla conflict.

The future of Yugoslavia is unknown, but the bitter war between Croatia and Serbia has dramatically altered its future. It appears that a federal government will continue in Belgrade. If Slovenia and Croatia, and even Macedonia, succeed in winning their independence, the remaining peoples of the country would still constitute a broad diversity of peoples, who would insist on representation in the central government. Even with Serbian hegemony in the future of Yugoslavia, many of its institutions are likely to remain.

Those institutions include a national bicameral legislature. The members of the Federal Assembly were chosen in countrywide, direct elections. The members of the Chamber of the Republics and Autonomous Provinces were chosen by the republican assemblies. Slovenia and Croatia have withdrawn their representatives to the legislature, while the other republics maintain their active participation.

The most important governing body was meant to be the Federal Executive Council (FEC), whose members were selected by the Federal Assembly. Yugoslavia's prime minister serves as president of the FEC. He is elected by the Federal Assembly for a four-year term and is also responsible for dealing with foreign creditors.

A collective, rotating, state presidency was to be composed of eight members, each of whom was meant to serve as president for one year. The country's six republics and two autonomous provinces were to be represented in the presidency. Although the president formally controls the military and oversees foreign policy, he has not been a powerful figure, in part because of his short tenure in office. Nonetheless, the office of state president was swept up in Yugoslavia's political crisis. The outgoing Serbian president, Borisav Jovic, and his allies succeeded in blocking access to the state presidency of Stipe Mesic, the Croatian representative and state vice president. Mesic and his allies from Slovenia and Macedonia walked out.

After more than six weeks of petty politicking, the Serbs backed down under pressure from the European Community, and Mesic assumed his post. By then relations between the Serbs and the Croats had disintegrated to the point that the military under Defense Minister General Veljko Kadijevic took orders only from the Serbian president, Slobodan Milosevic. The state presidency had become ineffectual.

Prime Minister Ante Markovic had been the country's most important politician. But the civil conflict, the eroding economy, and the rise of Milosevic have weakened his power. After his election in March 1989, the prime minister had initiated radical economic changes, supported by international institutions and foreign states. He drastically reduced the rate of inflation and increased the foreign exchange reserves. Most importantly, Markovic had insisted that the federal government would no longer be subordinate to the League of Yugoslav Communists (LCY). After the premature adjournment of the communist party Congress in January 1990, Markovic had insisted that "there is nothing to fear, Yugoslavia will function with or without the League of Communists." His boldness had served, however temporarily, to fill the power vacuum following the disintegration of the LCY.

Before the disintegration into violence, the prime minister and the Federal Executive Council were in the process of establishing a new political party, "The Alliance of Reform Forces." They intended to compete in countrywide Federal Assembly elections under its banner. The party was committed to preserving Yugoslavia's federal structure, a move resisted by many Slovene and Croatian politicians.

By the fall of 1991, the country was at war with itself, and Markovic's future was unclear. His economic reforms and his peacemaking efforts had been destroyed. But Markovic continued to embody the concept of a federal Yugoslavia. If that structure were to be restored (an unlikely prospect), he might emerge as a dominant actor to forge a postwar Yugoslavia.

Colonel General Veljko Kadijevic wielded more effective power than any other Yugoslav, including Serbian President Milosevic. On the eve of their 1990 elections, General Kadijevic made widely publicized official visits to Slovenia and Croatia. He meant to stress the significance of national unity, but his presence was intimidating to many republican nationalists. General Kadijevic and other officers at the senior level of the Yugoslav Peoples' Army (YPA) fear that democracy will destroy the country's cohesion. The breakaway republics have only served to confirm their judgment that democracy in Yugoslavia spells the end of the country.

But the YPA officer corps is no longer fully united in its purpose, and the intense fighting since mid-1991 is in part explained by the division. General Kadijevic, at least initially, understood the potential for conflict and restrained the military, reflecting his personal conflicts. A half-Serb, half-Croat who fought as a Partisan against Fascist Germany, he supported Prime Minister Markovic's reforms. Several months before the declarations of independence by Slovenia and Croatia, Kadijevic fell ill, allowing his chief of staff, the ardent Serbian nationalist Blagoje Adzic, to command the YPA. When Kadijevic was able to return, he used the army forcefully in order to stave off the challenge from Adzic. Though decidedly not in the Milosevic camp, he committed himself to the preservation of some kind of Greater Serbia and ordered the army to action to force a solution.

But the future of the army as a Serbian force appears to be in the hands of Adzic and his followers. Adzic is a Serbian hardliner, allied with Milosevic and the conservative League of Communists–Movement for Yugoslavia. He has made no secret of his hatred for Croatians and has repeatedly drawn on his own family history—his entire family was killed by Croatian Fascists—to justify and incite Serbian hysteria. With his power base in the First Army District of Belgrade, he has repeatedly defied the President, the Croat Stipe Mesic, by ordering the army to action. His increasing power is indicated by his sending air force planes to bomb the offices in which the Yugoslav president was meeting with Croatian President Tudjman in an effort to stop the fighting. The group only narrowly escaped death. Kadijevic was originally blamed for the incident, and he was clearly involved. But it appears that the military has come under the authority of the most hardline officers, led by Adzic.

The officer corps was always dominated by Serbs, and since the summer of 1991 their power has increased, as non-Serbs have been purged. But below the officer corp, the YPA has been dependent on conscripts for its recruits. In order to promote stability in the multi-national country, the armed forces posted its conscripts outside the borders of their national homelands. In an effort to promote autonomy, Slovenian and Croatian leaders demanded that their nationals serve within their own borders. Their demand was followed by the immediate defection of non-Serbs, who returned to their own republics. Additionally, the Slovene and Croat leaders demanded that the army be depoliticized, claiming that the domination of the officer corps by Serbs and Montenegrins makes the YPA an instrument of Serbian nationalism rather than Yugoslavian unity.

That claim has been borne out in the intensification of the fighting. The armed forces appear to have acted, initially at least, as an instrument of Milosevic and Greater Serbia. The military helped the Serbs of Croatia win autonomy from the fledgling Croatian state. It acted militarily against Croatia to force the subjection of president Tudjman to the federal will. The Croatians fought back, blockading federal military bases within Croatia, both to prevent those troops from joining the war against Croatia, and also to capture their arsenals of military equipment. With the deepening of the conflict, it has become more difficult to determine the military objectives of the army. But it appears most likely to be fighting to capture Slavonia and Krajina, the Serbian-inhabited areas of Croatia, in order to realize Milosevic's vision of Greater Serbia. It remains difficult to believe that the military believes it possible at this late date to force Croatia back into the Federal Republic.

There are several ways in which the YPA could be denied a victory. The European Community may be able to threaten the imposition of sanctions sufficiently vigorously to force a cease fire and negotiations. A Croatian military triumph appears possible only with the disintegration of the federal armed forces. The Serbian population appears to have begun to question the costs of realizing a greater Serbia, and many Serbs have begun to demand that their sons not be sacrificed in the fighting. But Serbian dissent appears insufficient to shatter the YPA, whose greater numbers and sophisticated weaponry gives it a powerful advantage over the Croatians.

Slobodan Milosevic, the charismatic and authoritarian president of Serbia, remains the country's most powerful politician. He both stimulated and capitalized on Serbian nationalist fervor, which had originally been directed against the Albanians in Kosovo, who were struggling to make their republic independent. Although he won a free election against fellow communists in November, 1989, and changed the name of his party to the Socialist Party of Serbia, Milosevic has never been committed to multi-party democracy. A growing number of Serbians across the party spectrum have protested his unilateral domination of Serbian politics. Nevertheless, he remains popular among most Serbian workers and peasants, based largely on his populist defense of Serbian nationalism, the repression he has imposed on the Albanians, the "liberation" of the Serbian districts of Krajina and Slavonia, and the war against the independence-minded Croatians. He has defended his use of force against the Albanians and the Croatians on the grounds of protecting the well-being of Serbians while safeguarding Serbian monasteries and other historical treasures from Albanian and Croatian nationalists.

In July, 1990, the Serbs voted in a referendum by a ratio of 9 to 1 to postpone multi-party elections. They were supporting Milosevic, who demanded a change in the Serbian constitution to diminish Kosovo's autonomy. The Albanians of the Kosovo assembly responded by announcing their independence, whereupon the Serbian police shut down the assembly and other Albanian institutions, including most of the Albanian news media. Prime Minister Markovic, even appreciating his need for Serbian support, criticized both the Serbian and Albanian positions on Kosovo, outraging the Albanians. When the Serbian election was held in December, 1990, Milosevic won the presidency, built on the popularity of his aggressive policies.

Montenegrin and Macedonian leaders supported Milosevic on the Albanian issue, fearing the large numbers of restive Albanians within their borders. Despite their support, in 1990 he threatened to redraw Yugoslavia's internal borders. By June, 1990, Montenegro, Macedonia, and Bosnia-Hercegovina seemed ready to explode in nationalist outrage.

Yugoslavia's foreign relations are less confused than its internal situation. Some 78 years ago, the Crown Prince of the Austro-Hungarian Empire, Archduke Ferdinand, was assassinated in Bosnia. That murder activated a system of European alliances and unleashed the European conflagration. But now the states of Europe, as well as the United States and the Soviet Union, agree on the need for a peaceful resolution to the problems of Yugoslavia. Initially, Western leaders supported Belgrade against the demands of the republics. Billions of dollars in aid were promised for national economic reform, and Slovenia and Croatia were warned not to proceed with their intentions to declare independence. U.S. Secretary of State James Baker, while visiting Yugoslavia in May, 1991, reiterated the common Western position. The strong support for the federal system emboldened Belgrade and Milosevic, who acted to enhance the interests of Serbia under the federal mantle. Not long after the Secretary's departure, however, Slovenia and Croatia issued their declarations of independence. The two wealthiest republics were determined to break from Belgrade, and the federal government was determined to fight to preserve the union under Serbian domination. Serbia, failing a common Yugoslavia dominated by Serbia, was determined to seize Croatian territories inhabited by Serbs.

With Serbia intent on advancing its interests, Croatia and Slovenia committed to advancing their independence, Bosnia frightened by the Serbian threat to seize its territories inhabited by Serbs, Macedonia demanding independence, and Croatia in the thick of war, the European states have been unable to bring peace to Yugoslavia. They have been unwilling to mobilize a Europe-wide military force to impose peace on the country, insisting that no European troops would be dispatched until a lasting cease-fire is in place—precisely what their intervention would be meant to accomplish.

Besides the internal agonies of the country, there are dangers from Yugoslavia's neighbors. Seven other countries, many with historical animosities and territorial disputes, border Yugoslavia. Bulgaria, for example, has announced that it will not countenance an independent Macedonia, which it views as rightfully Bulgarian. Greece has insisted that it will not tolerate the incorporation of Macedonia into Bulgaria.

Once it became clear that the Yugoslav conflict would not be peacefully or quickly settled, the EC agreed in 1991 to coordinate its policies, to speak with a single voice, and to favor no side. Even the former Soviet satellites, not EC members, adopted the EC policy. Still, that commitment has not been fully realized, as Yugoslavia's neighbors have occasionally adopted policies to advance their individual interests. Austria has warmly courted Slovenia and Croatia in anticipation of their permanent independence. Hungary sold arms to Croatia in 1990 and was embarrassed by the public disclosure. It prohibited any additional arms sales, but it clearly favors a weak Serbian state to ensure the relative autonomy of the more than 400,000 Hungarians who live in Vojvodina. Bulgaria has carefully navigated the question of Macedonia but is trying to advance its claims. Romania has been relatively aloof, but widespread speculation has Bucharest selling weapons to any side with hard currency. Italy's most immediate concern has been to control the Albanian problem, both in Albania itself and in Kosovo, as a means of limiting the number of Albanians fleeing to Italy. Greece, of all the surrounding states, has most ardently maintained the general EC position.

For the foreseeable future, it seems likely that Yugoslavia will be at war. When the war is finally halted, new political borders will need to be drawn.

Serbia is most likely to emerge from the conflict intact and strong. Milosevic, as long as he can maintain his ties to the federal army, will be the most powerful leader. By annexing the territories of other republics with large Serbian minorities, Serbia will find its territories significantly enhanced. But its economy, never robust, will not be able to provide economic well-being for its people.

Slovenia, the most homogeneous and prosperous of the republics, is especially fortunate in being geographically removed from the fighting. In the process of establishing its political independence, it is likely to take its place as a European mini-state.

Croatia faces a more troubled future. With more than 600,000 Serbs within its borders, Serbia will never accept Croatian independence without generous provisions for the Serbs. Croatia could give up its Serbian-dominated regions in return for full independence. But with Tudjman at the helm, as much seized by the Croatian nationalist awakening as is Milosevic with the Serbian, territorial surrender is now impossible. Given the apparent power of the federal army, it could continue its offensive and subdue the entire republic. However, any sustained occupation of Croatia is likely to produce continuous low-level terrorism against the occupiers.

The remainder of the republics and regions of Yugoslavia—Bosnia-Hercegovina, Vojvodina, Macedonia, Kosovo, and Montenegro—are equally troubled. They have little in common save their poverty. Only Montenegro, given its foreign enemies, is likely to remain voluntarily allied to Serbia.

Bosnia-Hercegovina appears to face cantonization. Approximately 40 percent of its population is Serbian, with the rest evenly divided between Croats and Muslims. If the Croats and Serbs each join their fellows in the other republics, the future of the Muslims appears bleak. Independence is impractical, but subjugation to either Serbia or Croatia would be detested. Vojvodina has a large Serbian population and has refused to seek independence. But at the least it will demand cultural and political autonomy. Moreover, its 400,000-strong Hungarian minority, some 20 percent of its population, will themselves seek autonomy within Vojvodina.

Macedonia declared its independence in September, 1991. It did so not to break from Yugoslavia but to exert its claim for significant autonomy in any future confederation.

Even though severe fighting is now sweeping Croatia, no settlement has ever been fashioned with Kosovo, the center of Yugoslav ethnic conflict in the 1980s. Given that nearly 90 percent of its population is Albanian, continued Serbian dominance is certain not to be accepted. The situation in Kosovo parallels the problem of Soviet Moldavia and Romania. So long as Ceausescu ruled, the Romanian enclave of Moldavia saw little gain from independence from Moscow and closer ties to Bucharest. It seemed then as a trade of the bad for the worse. Similarly, as long as Enver Hoxha tyrannized Albania and ensured its poverty, Kosovo's drive for autonomy was inwardly defined. With the passing of the last communist government in Europe, however, the possibility of joining Tirana has been renewed.

Serbia is certain not to let Kosovo go without a fight. The Serbians depreciate the Albanians as inferior and consider Kosovo—the site of a battle in 1389, marking the beginning of 500 years of Ottoman rule—the birthplace of the original Serbia. On the 600th anniversary of the battle in 1989, Milosevic demanded permanent Serbian control of Kosovo. With no military capability and Albania offering only poverty, Kosovo is likely to remain in what remains of Yugoslavia for the indefinite future. But in time, fighting in Kosovo could become even more vicious than the current Croatian–Serbian conflict.

The political fate of Yugoslavia is in the hands of ill-defined forces, no more clear within Yugoslavia than without. None of the key players, perhaps not even Milosevic, appreciated the consequences of their attempting to secure the most favorable conditions for their own republican ambitions. With the institution of democracy, and in the absence of the towering figure of a Tito or a strong communist party, unity could be neither imposed nor voluntarily maintained.

The tragedy of Yugoslavia is that after centuries of repression, and on the verge of instituting true democracy, its peoples appear determined to continue their feuds. The most likely future is that Yugoslavia will dissolve and that its successor states will fall dramatically short of what so many had so ardently hoped for so long.

HISTORY

From Origins to 1900

To understand contemporary Yugoslav politics, it is important to appreciate the deep religious and historical roots that have molded the world views of its different peoples. The Serbs and the Croats are both south Slavs but had long and dramatically different historical experiences. In the sixth century A.D., the region inhabited by the Serbs fell within the jurisdiction of the Eastern Roman Empire and its people converted to the

Eastern Orthodox faith. The Croats and Slovenes, by contrast, inhabited lands that came under the domination of the Western Roman church, which led to their adoption of Roman Catholicism. At the heart of the present Yugoslav struggle, in short, is a religious conflict.

The Yugoslav republics have distinct and ancient historical memories. Each of its peoples hearkens back to a different "golden age" when its rulers dominated vast territories. The Serbs, for example, grow nostalgic at the memory of Emperor Stephen Dušan, whose rule from 1331 to 1355 was the high-water mark of Serbian domination. The Croats recall the tenth- and eleventh-century reigns of their Dalmatian Kings, including Tomislav, Peter Kresimir, and Zvonimir, when Croatian power was ascendant. There is no common past to unite the peoples of the country.

In addition to diverse religions and historical memories, the Yugoslav peoples were differentially influenced by the states that dominated their territories. The Ottoman Empire administered Serbia between its victory in the epic Battle of Kosovo in 1389 and its withdrawal from Serbian soil in 1867. Many Serbs escaped Ottoman rule by fleeing to Hapsburg-controlled territories. There they were formed into a warrior band known as the Frontiersmen, or as they are known in German, *die Grenzer*. The *Grenzer* played a role in Yugoslavia comparable to that of the Cossacks in Russia, defending Christian Europe from the Muslim incursions. In exchange for their service to the Austrian Empire, they were granted land and the right to practice their religion. They are the ancestors of the Serbian population of Croatia, whom President Milosevic seeks to incorporate back into Serbia.

Other Serbs found refuge from the Ottomans in Montenegro, which remained a citadel of Serbian independence, thanks to its rugged terrain and the tenacity of its defenders. Meanwhile, Ottoman authorities encouraged Albanians to migrate to Kosovo and to other areas that had been part of Stephen Dušan's medieval Serbian empire.

Ottoman troops were stationed in Bosnia-Hercegovina until 1878, and formal Ottoman control of Macedonia and Albania continued into the early 20th century. Under the Ottomans, many Slavs in Bosnia and Hercegovina converted to Islam, retaining much of their wealth and influence as Muslims even after the Hapsburgs occupied those regions in 1878.

The experience of the south Slavs in the Ottoman Empire stood in stark contrast to that of their brethren living in the Hapsburg Empire. Croatian leaders had abandoned their independence to enter a union with Hungary in 1102 and later sought support from the Hapsburg Empire against the Ottomans. Despite Croatia's long-standing relations with Hungary, the Hapsburgs recruited Serbs to guard the Empire's borderlands against Ottoman encroachments.

Dalmatia was saved from the Ottoman threat when its Adriatic coastline was defended by powerful naval forces sent by Venice. Many Dalmatian coastal cities remained under Venetian control until 1797, when Napoleon's forces arrived. In 1805, French forces also occupied the city-state of Ragusa, today's Dubrovnik, which for centuries had used gold, high walls, trade, and its strong navy to resist the Venetians and the Ottomans. When Russia defeated France in 1812, the Hapsburg Empire was granted all of Dalmatia, which it governed until 1918.

History from 1900 to 1945

World War I, which gave birth to Yugoslavia, was preceded by eleven years of intensive maneuvering between the Austro-Hungarian Empire, the successor to the Hapsburg Empire, and the Kingdom of Serbia, which had gained its independence in 1878. The two states contested for control of all the south Slavs. From 1900 to 1914, Slovenia and Dalmatia were parts of Austria, and Croatia and Slavonia were parts of Hungary. In 1908, Austria unilaterally annexed Bosnia-Hercegovina, an area it had administered since its occupation in 1878. The Austrian annexation enraged Serbia, nearly led to a world war, and led the Serbian leaders to dedicate themselves to the unification of all Serbs.

Due to its vigorous opposition to Austro-Hungarian rule, Serbia became an inspiration to Serbs in Croatia and Bosnia-Hercegovina. Croatia remained less positive, but many Croatian intellectuals came to see the possibility of a future Yugoslav state with Serbia at its nucleus. They assumed that the powerful Serbian army would be a vital component of such a state but that Croatian politicians, steeped in the traditions of the Hapsburg Empire, would be its rulers. The Slovenes were generally less interested in the future Yugoslav state or in Serbia, preferring parliamentary maneuvers in Vienna to win greater autonomy.

On June 28, 1914, World War I was ignited by events in an obscure city on the periphery of Europe. On the anniversary of the battle of Kosovo, the heir to the Austrian throne, Archduke Franz Ferdinand, was assassinated in Sarajevo by Gavrilo Princip, a Serbian from Bosnia. Serbia fought with the Allies, including France, Britain, Russia, and eventually the United States, against the Central Powers, including Austria-Hungary, Germany, the Ottoman Turks, and Bulgaria.

The Kingdom of Serbia enjoyed early military successes against the Austrian army. But the combined forces of Germany, Austria, and Bulgaria compelled the retreat of the Serbian forces through the Albanian mountains, where Allied ships evacuated them to the island of Corfu in January, 1916. Then Serbian leaders began supporting the idea of a Yugoslav, rather than a pan-Serbian, state.

Nikola Pasic, the leader of the Serbian Radical party and the chief representative of the Serbian government in exile, negotiated with Slovene and Croatian leaders favoring the establishment of a Yugoslav state. Fearing Italian ambitions in Slovenia and Dalmatia, the Croatian and Slovene leaders sought support and protection through a merger with the more powerful Serbia. In July, 1917, in the Declaration of Corfu, the Serbian government committed itself to work for the unification of Serbs, Croats, and Slovenes in one state.

On December 1, 1918, the Serbian King, Alexander Karadjordjevic, proclaimed the Kingdom of Serbs, Croats, and Slovenes. The new state was to be a constitutional monarchy, with free elections and Western-style civil liberties. A committee of Montenegrin representatives overruled their own king by deciding to join the new state. But at the heart of the newly established Kingdom was a flaw that would ultimately prove fatal. Neither in the declaration of Corfu nor in the royal proclamation of 1918 was a political structure specified for the new state.

In November, 1920, fifteen political parties competed in an election for seats in a constituent assembly to adopt a constitution establishing that political structure. Seven parties won substantial numbers of seats.

1. Democrats, 92 seats
2. Serbian Radicals, 91 seats
3. Communists, 58 seats
4. Croatian Peasant Party, 50 seats
5. Agrarians, 39 seats
6. Slovene (Catholic) People's Party, 27 seats
7. Muslims, 10 seats
8. Other, 20 seats

The Democrats and the Communists constituted the only countrywide, Yugoslav parties, since their ranks included Serbs, Croats, Slovenes, and others. The Democrats enjoyed especially strong support from the Serbs of Croatia, led by Svetozar Pribicevic. Most importantly, the Democratic party adamantly supported the establishment of a strong central government that would work to unify Yugoslavia's various peoples.

On June 28, 1921, an alliance consisting chiefly of the Democrats, Serbian Radicals, and Muslims approved a constitution creating a centralized, constitutional monarchy, with universal male suffrage. But only 223 out of the 419 members of the constituent assembly voted in favor of the new constitution. Indeed, only 258 of the delegates even voted. The assembly had already banned the Communist party after a communist assassinated the former interior minister. Led by Stjepan Radic, the Croatian Peasant Party (CPP) had chosen to boycott the vote, because it advocated the establishment of a confederacy granting Croatia its own army and constitution. Using a procedural pretext, the CPP withdrew from the assembly and was joined by the Slovene People's Party, led by a Roman Catholic priest, Father Anton Korosec.

The new state constitution never earned the support of the leading parties of Croatia or Slovenia; thus, daunting political problems arose that would exacerbate the already formidable tasks of governing and modernizing the country. These were made even more formidable by the tendency of Serbian officials to treat Macedonians and Albanians as subject peoples. Having had an independent identity as the kingdom of Serbia and having lost one-fifth of its population to the ravages of World War I, the Serbs felt entitled to political primacy in the new kingdom. To the disappointment of the Croatians, the Serbs did occupy the vast majority of key positions in the state bureaucracy, the banks, the diplomatic corps, the army, and the police. As in other Balkan states at the time, government corruption was blatant and police intimidation, especially of communists, common. All political problems were exacerbated by widespread poverty, illiteracy, low levels of public health, and a huge rural population, some four-fifths of the total. Most villagers hated the central government because of what they perceived as confiscatory taxes and inadequate state services, especially the shortage of agricultural credits.

Prime Minister Pasic was astute at manipulating the commitment of the Democratic Party to a united Yugoslavia in order to establish a centralized Serbian state. Like the Hungarian government in the 19th century, Pasic played Pribicevic and the Serbs of Croatia against the Croats. When the Serbs in Croatia left the government to form their Independent Democratic party, Pasic deftly brought Radic and the Croatian Peasant Party into the Belgrade government. Pasic obtained support from the Muslims and eventually also from the Slovene People's Party; both received political concessions in return.

After Pasic's death, in 1927, Radic and Pribicevic joined forces to defend their mutual economic interests, but the alliance was not to hold. Radic was assassinated in 1928 by a Montenegrin parliamentary deputy. The new CPP leader, Vladimir Macek, failed to reach agreement with Serbian leaders. King Alexander asserted his authority, dissolved parliament, and abolished the constitution. He offered Croatia and Slovenia complete independence. But fearful of how Hungary, and especially Fascist Italy, might exploit their vulnerability, Croatian and Slovene leaders declined the King's offer. Alexander then renamed the country the Kingdom of Yugoslavia.

Although Alexander's royal dictatorship was initially popular, its rigged elections and police repression soon alienated the CPP, the Democrats, and others. Some Croat leaders fled to form opposition groups in exile, one of which, the Ustaši, engaged in violent terrorist attacks. On October 9, 1934, a Macedonian terrorist, acting with support from Italy, Hungary, and the Ustaši, assassinated King Alexander in Marseilles. Since Alexander's son was only eleven, a three-man regency was established, led by the late king's cousin, Prince Paul, who, unfortunately, never attempted to win back the allegiance of the Croats.

The new government, led by a Serbian businessman, Milan Stojadinovic, drew support from a number of parties, but by 1937 an opposition bloc had formed. In August, 1939, Prince Paul followed the example of Hitler, who had established a Slovak state following the German occupation of Czechoslovakia. Prince Paul established an independent Croatian state in order to attract the Croatian democratic opposition to his rule away from the Serbian democrats.

On March 25, 1941, with an economy dependent on Germany and surrounded by Axis states, Yugoslavia signed an alliance with Germany, Italy, and Japan. The pact was highly unpopular in Serbia, and within two days Yugoslav air force officers overthrew the government, immediately seeking an understanding with Hitler. He responded within two days—with an invasion. Most senior government officials fled the country, including the young king. (He was to return briefly to Yugoslavia for the first time in October, 1991, to test the possibilities of a restoration of the monarchy.) Within days of their invasion, Italian, German, Hungarian, and Bulgarian forces divided Yugoslavia. Mussolini invited Ante Pavelic, the leader of the Ustaši fascists, to rule the so-called Independent State of Croatia, which included Croatia and Bosnia-Hercegovina but excluded Dalmatia, an Italian acquisition.

The Ustaši regime, bolstered by many Muslim supporters, embarked on a campaign to annihilate the Serbs, Gypsies, and Jews of Croatia and Bosnia-Hercegovina. The Ustaši massacred an estimated 350,000 Serbs. These genocidal acts, to which the German army objected, gave Serbs in fascist Croatia a stark choice. They could fight the Croat fascists and risk death, or they could let themselves and their families be murdered. They had the choice of joining one of two resistance movements—the Četniks, led by a Serbian officer, Colonel Draža Mihajlovic, or the Partisans, led by Josip Broz Tito, the Croatian secretary general of the Yugoslav Communist Party.

Josip Broz had been born into a poor peasant Croatian family in a town located near the border with Slovenia. He became a steel worker before fighting with the Austrian army in World War I. As a prisoner of war in Russia, Broz became a communist, and in 1937 he rose to head the Yugoslav party. During World War II, he took the name Tito and continued to exhibit extraordinary leadership abilities that elicited fierce loyalty despite his insistence on imposing stern discipline. (The name *ti to* means "You! (Do) that!") A true Yugoslav nationalist, the Croatian Tito married a Serbian woman named Jovanka.

Tito's Partisans were unpopular in Serbia, where they instigated Nazi reprisals. As a result, Mihajlovic determined not to fight but to keep his irregular Serbian army in reserve, knowing resistance would result only in German atrocities against the Serbs. The Četniks, Mihajlovic planned, would wait for an invasion by Allied forces to end the Nazi occupation and then take control of the country. The Germans had already demonstrated their policies when German troops massacred 8,000 helpless people in the town of Kragujevac in retaliation for guerrilla raids. But they usually would not commit atrocities except in response to guerilla attacks.

The situation was different in Croatia and in Bosnia-Hercegovina. The Ustaši imposed a constant reign of terror. By November 1941, however, Mihajlovic had begun fighting, not the Germans, but the Partisans and the Ustaši. At times, his forces coordinated their campaigns with the Germans and Italians, also intent on eliminating the Partisans. A Yugoslav civil war had begun.

The Partisans had many advantages over the Četniks. They championed communism, an internationalist ideology, rather than Serbian nationalism, enhancing their appeal to a multi-national Yugoslav population. Their leadership included some of Yugoslavia's brightest intellectuals, many of whom had strong ties to the peasantry. During the interwar period, they had operated underground, developing skills that proved invaluable in wartime. Tito appealed to members of all Yugoslav nations, promising them a federal state, religious freedom, and free elections after the war.

Perhaps most importantly, the popularity of the Partisans was enhanced because they actively fought occupation forces, in spite of, and some claimed because of, the near certainty of brutal reprisals. Tito knew, for example, that enemy atrocities forced terrified villagers to seek refuge in the mountains of Bosnia-Hercegovina, where they often joined the Partisans. One of Tito's greatest assets was the barbarism of the Ustaši regime, which guaranteed him a steady stream of Serbian recruits, thirsting for retribution against those who had brutally murdered their family members and friends.

Tito also received important support from abroad. In 1943, the British government began strengthening the Partisans both militarily and diplomatically. The fall of Italy in September, 1943, enabled the Partisans to obtain valuable weapons and supplies. In addition, the Soviet army played an important role in liberating eastern Yugoslavia from German control in the autumn of 1944.

From 1941 to 1945, then, there were two wars—the war against the enemy occupation forces and an internal civil war. Atrocities were abundant in the civil war, committed by both sides. But the Partisans had unassailable advantages. Their countrywide appeal, superb organization, clear political program, and willingness to fight *both* wars by attacking the foreign armies and the Ustaši attracted vast numbers of followers.

Once in power in Belgrade, however, the Partisans abandoned their promises of free elections and instituted a police state. Nevertheless, Tito's popularity was high. Democracy in royal Yugoslavia had been a sham, and communist rule, with its internationalist and federal approach, seemed to offer a chance for peace in a multi-national state that had been ravaged by foreign intervention and civil war.

History from 1945 to 1990

The war had ended with a victory of the forces from the countryside over the cities. The communist victors, many of whom had until recently been peasants, were intent on curing the ills of capitalism, which had barely developed in northwestern Yugoslavia and not at all in the southeast. Yugoslav communists sought a shortcut to rapid industrial development that would simultaneously foster economic equality.

From 1945 to 1950, the communist dictatorship in Yugoslavia was harsher than in the other Soviet-dominated countries of Eastern Europe. Yugoslavia was formally a federal state, complete with six republics and two autonomous provinces within the Serbian republic. But in reality, Tito ruled Yugoslavia with strong and ruthless central powers. As early as 1945 in opposition to the wishes of Stalin, the Yugoslav communists had begun to destroy their opposition. Police terror was common. The communists captured the Četnik leader, Draža Mihajlovic, and tortured him for days before executing him. They imprisoned the Roman Catholic Archbishop of Zagreb, Cardinal Aloysius Stepinac, for not confronting the Ustaši regime during the war.

Initially, the communists satisfied the wishes of the peasants even as Belgrade embarked on a massive push for rapid industrial growth. Avoiding the forced collectivization of agriculture, Tito approved land reform, enabling hundreds of thousands of poor peasants to own property for the first time. He planned to develop heavy industry through massive assistance from the USSR.

But Stalin had become increasingly disenchanted with the Yugoslav communist leader and the independent stance Tito had demonstrated as early as 1942. Tito insisted that he retain unfettered control over Yugoslavia, the strictest police state in Eastern Europe. He also insisted on pursuing a far more aggressive policy towards the West than Stalin believed prudent. In 1946, for example, the Yugoslav military shot down an American transport plane, killing five crew members. The Soviet government convinced Tito to release the crew of another plane the Yugoslav military had forced down.

Immediately after the war, the Soviet government moved the headquarters of the Communist International, or Comintern, to Belgrade. Soviet intelligence officers used it as a front for operations meant to increase Soviet influence in Yugoslavia. But by 1948, Stalin's fury at Tito led to the expulsion of Yugoslavia from the Cominform (the successor to Comintern) and the call for "healthy forces" in Yugoslavia to overthrow Tito. Yugoslav authorities quickly arrested most of Stalin's supporters.

Yugoslavia's expulsion from the Cominform and its economic isolation from the Soviet bloc brought two immediate changes. Tito's rule, after some wavering, shifted towards an authoritarian system, oppressive but far less extreme than had initially been the case. In addition, there was a rapid shift to support of the West. A Yugoslavia independent of the Warsaw Pact and the USSR became a major contributor to the security of Italy, Greece, and Turkey. It also limited Soviet influence in the Adriatic Sea in particular and in the Mediterranean and Middle Eastern regions as a whole. Western planners welcomed Tito's shift, hoping that Yugoslavia's independent example would help splinter the international communist movement and weaken Soviet prestige and political control in the other Eastern European countries.

In immediate response to the break with Moscow, the Yugoslav leadership attempted to demonstrate their commitment to communist orthodoxy, both to the world and to their own ranks. They implemented massive, forced collectivization of agriculture and wildly optimistic five-year planning. Economic disaster was not long in coming, and by 1949 Tito accepted Western economic aid to save his rule.

Following the North Korean invasion of South Korea, Yugoslav leaders feared a Soviet invasion of their country, particularly since the peasants were seething with resentment over collectivization. U.S. military advisors soon arrived in Yugoslavia, and Tito began searching for ways to gain public support without abandoning his communist ideals. The break with Stalin had been a traumatic experience, even for the Yugoslav communists who remained loyal to Tito. Many had sided openly with Stalin, not just because they believed he would force Tito from power, but because they could not imagine defying Stalin or the Soviet Union. Pro-Soviet feeling was particularly strong in the Montenegrin communist party, where friendship with Russia had deep roots.

Between 1950 and 1953, the Yugoslav leadership abandoned much of its communist economic system. In the first years of communism, the country had remained predominantly agricultural, and even by 1947, 70 percent of the population were peasants. To maintain a popular base after the break with Stalin, Tito determined to win them over. He abruptly reversed collectivization. Only 1,000 collective farms of the original 7,000 remained by 1954, with some 80 percent of the agricultural land returned to private owners, although a maximum landholding was set at 10 hectares (about 25 acres).

In factories and other organizations, the communists established a system of "worker self-management," where management councils were elected biennially by the workers. Council members gained significant control over the internal administration and working conditions in industrial and commercial establishments. According to Yugoslav communists, these councils were the first step in what Karl Marx had called "the withering away of the state," a development that had not occurred in the Soviet Union, they insisted, because the Soviet government had revised Marx.

As the Yugoslav Communist Party moved away from Stalinist centralism, it was rechristened the League of Yugoslav Communists, meant to enhance the independence of the communist parties in the republics. Yugoslav communists, especially those from the southern republics, continued to pursue the classical communist aim of achieving equality. In its pursuit, the federal government financed hundreds of economically unsound "political" factories, especially in the south. The communists used northern money to create jobs in the south, but they also produced abundant resentment in the north.

After Stalin's death in 1953, Soviet and Yugoslav leaders made periodic attempts to improve relations, with only occasional successes. The high point came in May, 1955, when Nikita Khrushchev visited Belgrade and recognized separate roads to socialism. But the Hungarian revolution of 1956 quickly cooled Soviet–Yugoslav relations. Tito did not criticize the actual Soviet invasion but Soviet policies that, he argued, contributed to the revolution. Tito feared that the Hungarian revolution might spill over into Yugoslavia. He sealed the estrangement in 1957, when he refused Khrushchev's claim that the Soviets should play the leading role in the world communist movement.

Yugoslavia, of course, had played a highly visible and influential role, considerably out of proportion to its power, as one of the leaders of the Non-Aligned Movement, supporting Third World causes. It sent aid personnel to teach worker self-management in far-flung corners of the world, from Africa to the Middle East. Thousands of foreign students obtained scholarships, learned Serbo-Croatian, and completed degrees at Yugoslav universities. Tito gained great prestige at home and abroad. His pursuit of the Third World often angered officials both in Moscow and Washington, but U.S. leaders supported Yugoslav independence for strategic reasons.

By 1963, Croatian and Slovene leaders had convinced their comrades in the south—Macedonia, Kosovo, and Bosnia-Hercegovina—that the funds they had been receiving from Belgrade would result in Serbian demands for political support. That same year, they managed to institute a new constitution, increasing the power of the republics at the expense of the center. Only Montenegro sided with Serbia in the so-called reform crisis of 1960 to 1966. Internal political alignments were shifting from the previous north–south divide.

In 1966, the chief of the secret police, the Montenegrin Aleksandr Rankovic, fell from power. A former Partisan and likely heir to Tito, Rankovic used the security service to sabotage decentralization and market-oriented reforms and to wiretap Yugoslav leaders, including Tito. With his fall, the expectations of the reformers for additional changes gained momentum. Bosnian Muslims obtained official recognition as a republic, and Kosovo Albanians began voicing demands for autonomy. Yet Rankovic had many supporters in his native Montenegro and especially among Serbians, traditionally the most ardent defenders of the power of the center. They launched new efforts to preserve their positions, and Yugoslav politics became subject to ever more internecine strife and centrifugal forces.

The Soviet invasion of Czechoslovakia in 1968 increased Tito's popularity and heightened Yugoslav resolve to fight if attacked. Tito had visited Prague just before Soviet troops invaded, and he warned the Yugoslavs that it would be unconstitutional for anyone in Yugoslavia, even himself, to capitulate to an occupying force. He then carried on with his annual tradition, spending his birthday hunting for bear in the Bosnian mountains—a likely center of Yugoslav resistance had the Red Army invaded.

The advocates of change were by then in the ascendancy. The tangible success of small private businesses contrasted sharply with the performance of the socialist sector. State workers felt exploited, while the private sector demanded more freedom. Meanwhile, tens of thousands of guest workers, who had spent years in West Germany and elsewhere in Europe, began to return to visit or to settle in their home towns and villages. They had seen the wealth of the capitalist, democratic Western countries. They wanted for Yugoslavia what they had seen in those countries.

The economic tensions exacerbated nationalist sentiments. In 1968, following revelations about Rankovic's oppression, demonstrations took place in Kosovo. In addition to requesting cultural autonomy, an independent university, and the right to fly the Albanian flag, protesters demanded that Kosovo be freed from Serbian control to become a republic. The riots spread to the Albanian areas of Macedonia and the police cracked down. But the government granted many of the demands while it refused republic status to Kosovo for fear of alienating the Serbs.

In 1971, the "Croatian Spring" posed a direct challenge to the Yugoslav state and foreshadowed contemporary events. In 1970, on the momentum of Rankovic's fall, Croatian communists and students demanded greater autonomy, including control of their foreign-currency earnings, military service in Croatia for Croatian conscripts, and the use of their language in government offices. Other protests were lodged against the disproportionately high Serbian representation in the Croatian Communist Party, the Croatian police, and in the officer corps of the federal army.

In addition, Matica Hrvatska, a Croatian patriotic organization, gained political support among Croats in Bosnia-Hercegovina. Serbs, frightened by memories of the Ustaši massacres, prepared for war. In addition, communist leaders in Serbia, Bosnia-Hercegovina, Vojvodina, Macedonia, and Montenegro all objected to the Croatian demands. During November, 1971, students began demonstrating in Zagreb. The following month, Tito ordered a police crackdown and army maneuvers in Croatia. A purge of communists and students followed. The police arrested thousands, among whom was Dr. Franjo Tudjman, now the president of the Croatian republic, who was sentenced to a two-year prison term. In 1971 and 1972, Tito also purged advocates of political change in Serbia.

Even while ruthlessly suppressing all political demands, Tito again granted many of the economic demands of the reformers. He was careful, however, to appoint conservative communists to implement the changes. But the fundamental problems of Yugoslavia remained unaddressed. The republics and autonomous provinces were gaining power at the expense of the center. The people of Slovenia and Croatia, in particular, were swept up in significant economic change. Yet overall, the economy, particularly the socialist sector, failed to grow vigorously. Still, the regime refused to grant meaningful political rights or economic reforms.

After the death of Tito in May 1980, the country braced for political turmoil. Long-suppressed demands for change were bound to surface with the removal of the legendary father of Yugoslav communism. The economic deterioration made the succession period even more dangerous. In March and May 1981, Albanians in Kosovo and Macedonia rioted, and the Federal Executive Council sent federal police, including many Croats and Slovenes, to quell the revolt. In Kosovo, the Albanians again demanded republic status, including the constitutional right to secede from Yugoslavia. Some Albanians desecrated Serbian graveyards and monasteries, attacked Serbian men and women, and sabotaged power stations and railways. The police responded brutally, but Albanian unrest continued.

The Albanian protests and violence created a steady stream of Serbian and Montenegrin refugees, who fled from Kosovo to Belgrade, where their stories filled newspapers and fueled Serbian nationalism. The safety of Serbian women in Kosovo became a major issue. The Serbian communist party under its local chief, Slobodan Milosevic, was a principal beneficiary. Few Serbs in Serbia had been notably procommunist. But neither had they ever felt threatened as a national entity. Events in Kosovo changed that. The communist party in Serbia seized the Serbian cause, as did the Serbian Orthodox church.

The 1980s were years of immense pressures. Demands for fundamental economic and political changes were made with ever greater urgency. The economy faltered, and the economic crisis stimulated even more political demands. The communist party of Serbia became more strident, while other communist parties, particularly in Croatia and Slovenia, mellowed. Just as Yugoslav stability became less predictable, Yugoslav youth made demands that no communist system could satisfy. The worldwide success of market economies, improved communications, travel, videotapes, foreign radio broadcasts, Austrian TV, returning guest workers, Western rock music, and pro-American sentiment transformed the younger generation. They and many of their parents increasingly asked why many communist party members should be able to "live like Americans" while the rest of the population lived in relative poverty.

Simultaneously, Yugoslav fears about Soviet intervention declined. The Soviets were clearly preoccupied by their seemingly endless war in Afghanistan and a relentless decline in their economy. American foreign policy, meanwhile, had been reinvigorated, giving Yugoslavs additional reason to feel secure from Soviet invasion.

A major contributing factor to the transformation of the 1980s was the continuing death of the Partisan generation. They had argued that their wartime sacrifices and those of their fallen comrades precluded any shift from socialism. Many of them had sought to insure their beliefs by becoming the pillars of the security forces and the secret police. The 45 years of repression, for which they had been largely responsible, led them to fear for their lives should a free society emerge.

Even as the old order in Yugoslavia came to an end, serious problems remained, many of which existed before the formation of the communist government and many of which will persist after the emergence of its successor republics. The most persistent problem is the divide between the rich and the poor republics, a divide that falls almost entirely along the old military frontier between the Hapsburg and Ottoman Empires. Whether a free Yugoslavia can make progress towards developing its southern regions without sacrificing the prosperity of the northern republics will largely determine the country's future.

ECONOMICS

In an effort in 1936 to explain the economy of Yugoslavia, its foreign trade office began an information document: "It has been evident for some time past that foreign business circles have been insufficiently informed of economic conditions in the Kingdom of Yugoslavia." Foreign ignorance of the Yugoslavian economy is as real today as it was then. Some information has been made available because of the country's partial membership in the OECD. But Yugoslavia's economic complexities, even before the present civil war, were arcane and deep, and the war has heaped confusion on top of the complexity.

No economy of the former Soviet satellites is as paradoxical as the Yugoslav. The early communist economic policies of the other states, despite their numerous distinguishing economic characteristics, were similar. Moreover, their present economic challenge as they move towards market economies is to dismantle nearly identical bureaucratic structures formed to execute command economy initiatives. But Yugoslavia detoured early from the standard socialist model.

The particularity of Yugoslavia's formation as a single state, coupled with Marshal Tito's break with Stalin following WW II, resulted in a unique political-economic system that has gone its own way for four decades. The economy is predominantly state-directed; thus, Yugoslavia is socialist, a cognate of the East bloc. But Yugoslavia's structure of quasi-independent republics within a federal state has resulted in less centralized control at the federal level. One result is pronounced economic redundancy, in which each region boasts large industrial conglomerates, coupled with its own banking institutions, operating under near-monopoly conditions.

Yugoslavia's particularity is also demonstrated by the fact that it was never a member of the major East bloc economic or military institutions. But neither has it been a part of the West, even though its economic and political relations with the West surpassed those of the other socialist states. It has had quasi-official status in the OECD since 1961 and a lengthy history with the IMF and World Bank. If Yugoslavia never spoke the language of the market, at least it comprehended that language.

Yugoslavia's internal political diversity is reflected in its economic structure. Slovenia and Croatia in the northwest produced, before the civil war, almost half of the nation's hard-currency exports. Those republics had virtually no unemployment, and Western investments were numerous. Slovenia had a per capita GNP in excess of $12,000, which compared favorably with Western Europe. Yet in Kosovo and Macedonia, in the southeast, unemployment ranges from 25 percent to 50 percent, while hard-currency exports are negligible. In Kosovo, for example, hard-currency exports account for only 1 percent of the country's total, while its GNP per capita is in the range of $1,500.

With such broad regional economic autarky and disparities, it is remarkable that the government managed to produce any national program of reform. But it did, first haltingly, and finally with impressive resolve in 1988 and 1989. The challenge now is to determine which of many possible approaches to change would most effectively bring the reluctant republics to adopt reform while fashioning a new economy absent Slovenia and Croatia, so determined to achieve their independence, especially following the war.

The heart of reform in the entire former East bloc has been the destruction of the power of the bureaucracies. In Yugoslavia the challenge is immensely complicated by the power of bureaucracies at the federal, republic, and regional levels. To the present, the bureaucracies have largely preserved their power. Some 75 percent of Yugoslavia's foreign debt is owed by individual enterprises and banks, indicating the power of bureaucracies at the local level. Other ex-bloc states are depoliticizing the economy to decentralize economic control. But in Yugoslavia, to depoliticize the economy seems to require a recentralization of authority, at least at the republic level to create a republic-wide market or at the federal level to create a Yugoslavia-wide market.

The challenge of the economy is further complicated by the fact that any concentration of power in Belgrade now entails the reassertion of Serbian political control. The impossible challenge for Prime Minister Markovic was to find the political strength to reassert central control to inaugurate reform within a system of powerful centrifugal forces. He never managed to do so before the outbreak of the civil war. Without significant and rapid reform and an end to the fighting, the state structure is likely to collapse. If he or his successor can persuade the remaining republics that some unity is necessary to foster economic reform, Yugoslavia may well demonstrate its potential for economic growth. If he cannot, the fragile system will disintegrate, fostering further violence and decentralization.

Current Economic Reforms

Before the outbreak of the civil war, Yugoslavia was a leading reformer among the socialist states. Much of what was introduced in late 1989 was similar to what Poland introduced in 1990. But in the absence of a dramatic political revolution comparable to the events in Warsaw and Prague, Yugoslavia's economic transformation went largely unnoticed in the West. In addition, economic reform occurred piecemeal over a five-year period. Further, the reform effort was not accepted by all the republics and never became a unified national program. A recognition of the desirability of countrywide reform came just as Slovenia and Croatia determined they could no longer tolerate being in a union with Serbia. They came to understand national reform as a means for the Serbian-dominated federal government to exercise financial control over them. Serbia was also reluctant to accept reform, from fear that it would cost them more than the other republics. With the opposition of the three most powerful republics, a unified reform program was doomed. It is no surprise that the reform program—widely supported by the EC, the World Bank, and the IMF— would fail. Once fighting broke out in the summer of 1991, any hope for a unified program was lost. The certainty of economic ruin never appeared more apparent.

It is relatively clear that Yugoslavia will be succeeded by a number of states. At a minimum, there is likely to be three states: Slovenia, Croatia, and Serbia. Serbia will clearly be the largest successor state to the present Republic of Yugoslavia. Independence for other republics, Kosovo and Montenegro in particular, is certainly plausible.

Though Slovenia and Croatia are prosperous relative to the other republics, they do not yet have economies competitive with European standards, and if they succeed in winning their independence, they will face the challenge of creating state structures. An independent Serbia will contain some of the poorest regions of Yugoslavia. All the republics will be burdened by the extraordinary expenses of the war, not only in the form of direct outlays but also from the lost tourism revenues and from disruptions of the economy, such as the end of trade between fighting republics. Official estimates by the

Slovenian government predict that in a best-case scenario, the cost of independence alone will result in a decline of more than 50 percent of the republic's national wealth.

Despite their present inability to live within the confines of a single state, the republics faced similar economic problems in the past. As a result, irrespective of the outcome of the present conflict, the republics seem likely to adopt, however modified, the reforms that have already been offered by Prime Minister Ante Markovic.

Yugoslavia has been engaged in a process of soul searching for many years. In 1981, the government formed the Kraigher Commission to confront the unmanageable foreign debt of the 1970s. The Commission recommended market-oriented reforms. Their conclusions became part of the abundant advice that the country received from the IMF, the World Bank, and Western governments and economists, including the United States and the EEC states. As a result, Yugoslavia learned, earlier than any other state in Eastern Europe, the steps necessary to rescue its economy.

While the regime resisted the advice, it did begin to make changes, and the Kraigher Commission recommendations were finally adopted, following long debate and several revisions, in the summer of 1983. The government was under intense pressure to act because the economy was on the verge of collapse. Double-digit inflation and unemployment led Prime Minister Planinc Mikulic to begin the reform process.

The economic reforms of 1987, 1988, and especially 1989 were other significant attempts to cure the economic sickness of the country. The reforms were sufficiently disruptive to force the ouster of Prime Minister Mikulic, but the new prime minister, Ante Markovic, continued the course. In December 1989, as the West watched the violence of the death throes of communism in Timisoara and Bucharest, a little-noticed new round of economic reforms began in Belgrade. Enacted in January, 1990, they dramatically altered Yugoslavia's economic course. The prime minister's challenge was to persuade all the republics to embrace the federal program lest all their economies fail collectively. But the course of reform was erratic at best and its outcome uncertain, even before the violence of 1991.

Although hopes had been high following the 1988 liberalization of prices, imports, and foreign exchange rules, the economy continued to falter. By 1989, living standards declined to the levels of the mid-1960s; inflation reached an annual rate of 2,700 percent; unemployment was counted at 17 percent; and the foreign debt exceeded $20 billion and was growing. Yugoslavia could still boast the largest share of Western investment among the socialist states, but Western investors were reluctant to make the new investments required for growth. Answering its critics, the government under Markovic adopted rigorously restrictive monetary and fiscal policies and devalued the dinar. Bank reforms were deepened, and bankruptcy laws were given more teeth. Western investors were offered new incentives, including the right of complete foreign ownership and the full repatriation of profits.

Yugoslavia, of the former bloc states, has had the longest tradition of accepting Western investors. Joint ventures were first legislated in 1967, and the state understood the expectations of foreign investors. Although the original laws imposed considerable restrictions, the country attracted 371 joint ventures in two decades—an enviable number compared to the bloc states.

The most dramatic change for foreign investment came on December 31, 1988, with the passage of the Enterprise Law and the Foreign Investment Law. Seeing the reform movement taking root in the other states, Yugoslavia amended its foreign investment laws to remain competitive. The new laws were so attractive to foreign investors that by mid-1988 over 150 additional foreign ventures were sealed. At the close of 1990, the number of signed ventures stood at 2,300, making Yugoslavia the leader among socialist countries.

Foreign investment to date represents $1 billion in total capital investment, of which two-thirds is in joint ventures, with the rest divided between wholly foreign-owned firms and direct foreign investment in Yugoslav firms. No single investment is particularly large—they range from $300,000 to $1.75 million—and most are in entertainment, restaurants, and shops in lucrative tourist areas. Per capita, Slovenia and Croatia are the most heavily-invested republics, particularly from Germany, Italy, and Austria, which together hold more than 50 percent of the total foreign investment. The U.S. investment share is approximately 14 percent.

"Mixed enterprises," as joint ventures are called, may be in several forms, including the use of a private Yugoslav firm for the purpose of founding a 100 percent foreign-owned subsidiary. Foreign investors may act individually or through foreign firms, and they may contract both with Yugoslav firms and with individuals.

Completely foreign owned firms may take any form—joint stock, limited-liability, limited-partnership, or others. The founding firm has exclusive rights in hiring and firing its personnel, and no worker councils are involved. Instead, agreements with employees are contractually arranged independently or with trade unions. Most privately employed labor is nonunion.

The only major restriction on firms are limitations on the production of certain products or participation in specific industries. At present, the manufacture of military equipment and armaments is forbidden, and firms in communications, telecommunications, publishing, mass media, air and rail transport, and insurance are off limits to foreigners. It is highly likely that except for weapons production, the other restrictions will be lifted, especially since the more aggressively reformist republics are inclined to allow foreign investment in these areas. Western investments in Yugoslav firms have already been allowed in insurance, commerce, and other services.

Foreign firms involved with Yugoslav enterprises may take any number of legal forms. Joint stock firms are required to possess at least 150 million dinars in founding capital. Converted to dollars, the sum is approximately $5,000, adjusted annually for inflation. Provisions for limited-liability firms are nearly identical to the joint stock firm, except that the smallest share of founding capital for the limited firm is 20 million dinars, less than $700 at current exchange rates. In the unlimited joint firm those partners holding the unlimited liability have management rights or the right to appoint management, while in limited partnerships liability is limited to the value of the investment.

The new foreign investment law also significantly simplified the approval procedure for foreign ventures. After the parties to the venture reach agreement, they have 30 days to submit their charter to the Secretariat for Foreign Economic Relations. Accompanying the agreement must be an "outline of the expected investment results," a feasibility study. The Secretariat has 45 days to assess the venture's compatibility with Yugoslav law. If it issues no statement, the venture is thus approved, and if it is refused, the parties may appeal. After the venture is operational, it may still have to report to the Secretariat concerning the reinvestment of its profits, which are then taxed at a reduced rate.

The rights and privileges of the foreign investor are firmly secured by the legislation. According to the Yugoslav constitution, the foreign investor has "grandfather clause" protection. Subsequent laws or regulations following the establishment of a venture do not alter the original joint venture agreement. But if the new laws prove more attractive to a foreign investor, the venture is allowed to apply those laws.

Accounting procedures and profit calculations are in line with OECD and general international standards. All profits of foreign investors may be fully repatriated without restriction. In the event of a venture's liquidation or the expiration of its contract, foreign partners are guaranteed that their net assets, liquid or otherwise, are also free for repatriation without restriction.

Taxes on foreign ventures can be confusing, since they are levied at the federal, republic, provincial, and sometimes communal level. Before the initiation of the fighting, federal taxes were in the process of comprehensive revision to conform to European standards. Tax policies below the federal level are all conducive to foreign investment. Withholding taxes on a foreign partner's profits have been unified at the republic and provincial level and do not exceed 10 percent. There is a reduced tax rate on profits reinvested in the venture or in other ventures or if the profits are deposited in Yugoslavia. But the reduced rates vary by republic. Tax reductions are also available during the initial stages of the establishment of a foreign venture. Foreign investors may invest in a publicly, or "socially," owned Yugoslav firm without any management involvement. Article 5 of the Foreign Investment Law allows the foreign investor the right to negotiate management participation and a portion of the profits in proportion to the foreigner's invested capital.

Debt-for-equity swaps are also permitted to foreign investors. The government is clearly interested in selling its external debt in return for equity stakes in Yugoslav firms. It is encouraging a secondary market, where the national debt is offered at very high discount in relation to its nominal value.

There are no restrictions on foreign participation or investment in Yugoslav banks. There are no legal differences in the commercial banking codes between banks with foreign partners and exclusively Yugoslav banks, which are in the process of conversion from nonprofit institutions into limited-liability and joint stock firms. With the changes, several new joint venture banks have been created. At the close of 1990, two joint ventures were announced between U.S., French, and Yugoslav banks; the combined equity stakes of the banks from these three nations exceeded $30 million. The spread of Western banking institutions will clearly facilitate the financial dealings of foreign investors. Western participation, along with the foreign exchange law's guarantee a "permanently maintained convertibility of the dinar," removes much of the previous financial uncertainty.

On the heels of the new foreign investment laws, regulations for the establishment of "free trade zones" have been adopted. Any area open to international traffic—sea, air, or river—may be founded as a free trade zone and can conduct business in banking; insurance and reinsurance; tourist services; and manufacturing, primarily for export. Permission to establish a free trade zone requires at least $30 million in annual exports and the export of at least 70 percent of the goods and services produced in the zone.

Domestic reforms have been adopted over several years but unified in 1990 by the Federal Executive Council under the heading, "The Laws on Economic Reform in Yugoslavia." The Laws contain all the provisions necessary to convert the socialized economy. The government also initiated major fiscal, monetary, and price reforms in 1990, which were not fully implemented by all the republics before the beginning of the political and military struggles now engulfing the country.

The government has had a two-track approach to economic reform. In addition to establishing the legal basis for a market-driven economy, it attacked its economic problems at the level of the enterprise. Vertically integrated industrial conglomerates had to be broken of their habit of spending to increase wages and benefits irrespective of productivity. The funds to pay higher wages had been readily available because enterprises were allowed to establish and manage banks, from which they could borrow. The National Bank (NBY), in turn, guaranteed the solvency of the local banks.

Additionally, the economy was riddled with local protectionism. Firms offered credits to each other and favored their own network of local industries under the control of local communist party elites. The most recent OECD survey offers a startling example. Over 80 percent of the bread sold in Belgrade is produced by one firm. Yugoslavia has been a nation of monopolies, with the monopoly profits distributed as higher wages and corruption payments to local party elites.

In June 1989, the first major reforms to correct these abuses strengthened the ability of the central bank to refuse subsidies to local and regional banks and prohibited enterprises from controlling them. The Federal Assembly retained final say on monetary targets, but the NBY's control over the money supply was enhanced. It will no longer grant cheap credits for regional development programs, nor can the government simply borrow from it. Moreover, the Bank previously required unanimous agreement from all the republics, but now decisions can be taken with a simple majority, making it impossible for any one republic to hold up national policy. The extension of credits to commercial banks has been made dependent on their own creditworthiness, as defined by the NBY.

The Law on Bank Rehabilitation, passed in December, 1989, also gave the NBY control over bank solvency ratios, risk ceilings, and the licensing of banks. The National Bank has the right to force an insolvent bank into a program of rehabilitation that requires it to take on new investments and sell more shares while the NBY takes on some of its liabilities. The NBY will also require insurance deposits from the banks. Earlier legislation had required banks to convert themselves into shareholding firms, thus making them available for investors. But shareholders do not yet have voting rights on bank boards.

On the whole, the new laws are a significant step in converting Yugoslav banks into financial institutions resembling their Western counterparts. They are not yet totally divorced from their enterprise founders, nor do they face substantial competition. But with foreign competition, the legalization of private banks, and the enforcement of profitability on enterprises, Yugoslav financial institutions are moving in the right direction. The key determinant of the future of the country's banks will be the willingness of the republics to enforce the legislation, coupled with the full demarcation of banks from their founding enterprises.

The most important legislation in the transformation of socialized industry came in December, 1988, and in February and December, 1989. The new laws were attempts to break local, provincial, and republic monopolies. Those monopolies have been so effective that no more than a fifth of all commercial trade in the country crosses the borders of any one republic. Even telecommunications and railroad industries are overwhelmingly concentrated within individual republics. Additionally, the local monopolies served as powerful barriers to entry. Not only did the barriers limit the establishment of private enterprises, but even socialized industries were inhibited if they threatened the monopolies and cartels, which controlled the movement of goods from raw materials to manufacturing to the retail outlet.

The 1988 legislation attempted to force more competition by legalizing every kind of private and public business, either by individuals or groups of investors, Yugoslav or foreign. Private or public corporations and cooperatives were legalized without employment restrictions. Mergers were authorized within and across republic boundaries. The law also eliminated the Basic Organizations of Associated Labor (BOALs), quasi-independent management units, which operated independently in firms and blurred management authority and responsibility.

The February, 1989, law sought to enhance the efficiency of socialized firms by initiating bankruptcy procedures. The Social Accounting Service (SDK) was empowered to define a firm's viability in terms of its liquidity. Bankruptcy will be forced if agreement cannot be reached between a firm and its creditors. In 1989, according to OECD, the SKD found one in fifteen Yugoslav firms insolvent. But due to local resistance, only a fifth of the nonviable firms were subject to bankruptcy proceedings. In December, 1989, more legislation was passed, making local bodies responsible for bankruptcy proceedings and the rehabilitation or dissolution of illiquid firms. Despite the federal requirements, the pace of bankruptcies has been agonizingly slow, given the interest of local authorities in maintaining their region's firms.

The December legislation, Yugoslavia's first attempt at privatization, also provided for the conversion of publicly owned firms into stock and mixed-ownership firms. Firms were given the right to sell their equity wholly or in part to other firms, individuals, or foreigners. Local authorities were mandated to sell the equity of insolvent firms to the public.

The government liberalized the majority of prices, removed most import restrictions, and unified foreign exchange, all in an attempt to make enterprises come to terms with market realities. Since 1988, prices have been gradually freed from administrative control. Furthermore, in 1989 the federal government tried to reassert its control over regional authorities in the control of prices still set by the state. By the close of 1989 nearly 80 percent of producer prices were freed from state control.

Measures to liberalize imports, as one way to force domestic efficiency and break local monopolies, were equally dramatic. Stiff licensing and import requirements were abolished, quotas on imports were eliminated from nearly half of all goods, and the right to import was extended from socialized industries to private firms and individuals. Since the legislation, nearly 90 percent of all goods fall under the category of free imports, in contrast to 10 percent previously. The government also ended its administrative control over the allocation of foreign currency and authorized the National Bank to control exchange rates.

The most important domestic reform, however, and the first of its kind for a socialist economy, was the stabilization program of December, 1989, which made the dinar convertible. A new dinar was introduced, at the rate of one new to 10,000 old dinars, and fixed to the D-Mark at 7 new dinars to 1 mark. The exchange rate was set from December, 1989, to June, 1990, after which the NBY would periodically revise the rate. Wages were frozen for the same time period as well as the prices for a quarter of all industrial goods. The dinar was further strengthened when the NBY raised real interest rates. All these measures sent a jolting message to enterprises that they could no longer count on the continued devaluation of the dinar to accommodate their reckless economic behavior.

The strategy was a success. The government assumed that the new exchange rate would draw at least $1.5 billion from the private holdings of individual Yugoslavs. Instead, they converted nearly $7.5 billion to dinars, dramatically raising the government's foreign exchange reserves. By the end of 1990, the inflation rate had fallen to 13 percent, higher than intended but lower than it had been in years. More importantly, confidence in the dinar had been restored, allowing the federal government more leverage in controlling the money supply.

Yugoslavia's tax codes have been periodically but still insufficiently revised. More than 150 different tax rates are in use, while more than 50 percent of the government revenues are generated from sales taxes. The federal government has been revising the sales tax and has planned to introduce a new value-added tax system, compatible with the EC, between 1991 and 1995. The new system will group goods into eight categories, applying VAT rates equally to all goods in each category. It specifies that all taxes be separately indicated from the price of the goods, allowing the public to know what it pays in taxes. The new practice will contrast to the socialist system, which concealed taxes in the total price of goods. The new VAT taxes are not intended to provide the state with new revenues but to facilitate a broad reduction in taxes.

Current State of the Economy

The Yugoslav economy is hostage to the military, political, ethnic, and economic differences among the various republics. Reforms, no matter how well conceived or substantial, will have no lasting effects on the national economy until the feuding republics remake the federal state or create new independent countries. The political hatreds of the republics, exacerbated by the military conflict between the federal army (effectively allied with Serbia) against Croatia, and their wide disparities in levels of well-being make the very existence of a federal Yugoslavia problematic.

The country's political turmoil makes it impossible to assess the effectiveness of the reform legislation. The losses in production reflect the reforms taking hold as well as the political tensions and the conflict. Since 1987, production has been hampered by seemingly endless strikes, in which close to 1,700 enterprises and approximately 300,000 workers have participated each year. The strikes have become so commonplace that it is difficult to separate their economic, political, and ethnic roots.

Another challenge to understanding the economy is rooted in the difficulty of interpreting national economic figures. Given wide discrepancies in the development of the republics, statistical data for the entire country have only limited use, at least until a national economy forms. Economic indexes for the entire country reduce crucial differences between the republics, understate the well-being of the wealthier north, overstate the well-being of the poorer south.

The most traumatic shock to the economy has been the civil war. The costs of the fighting are now impossible to reckon, but it is estimated to have already cost in excess of several billion dollars. Direct war damage has been mounting, and the losses in economic productivity during the fighting have been staggering. The economy has been further damaged by the confiscations that occurred in the midst of the fighting. Serbs have taken over Croat businesses located in Serbia, and Croatia and Slovenia have done the same. Western financial support has been negligible during the fighting. Finally, and most importantly, private Western investment has been at a complete standstill and some has been withdrawn. Clearly, with other options now available in the former East bloc states, private investors will avoid Yugoslavia until a workable peace can be implemented. The costs of a continuation of the fighting will grow and are now impossible to calculate. It appears plausible, however, that the economy declined by more than 35 percent in 1991.

The Yugoslav economy has fallen relentlessly in previous years. The country underwent a debt crisis at the beginning of the 1980s, followed by an immediate fiscal crisis. Public sector demand was suppressed, setting off a general economic decline. Over the decade, public and private consumption fell by more than 1 percent per year. Only exports improved as foreign markets were rediscovered. In both 1987 and 1988, demand and output declined. In 1989, the economy fell sharply after the introduction of the Markovic plan but recovered modestly by the end of the year. The economy fell again in 1990 and collapsed in 1991.

Fixed investments in 1987 and 1988 declined more than 5 percent per year. Agriculture was hurt by two successive years of drought. Where agricultural output had increased 11 percent in 1986, output declined 4.5 percent in 1987 and 3.5 percent in 1988. Construction, the hardest-hit economic sector in the 1980s, fell 6 percent in 1988 (the worst annual decline since 1982) and continued to fall by 3 percent in 1989. Manufacturing output fell by 1 percent per year—a clear indication of the economic difficulties, since industry was at the center of the socialist economy. Even services declined in both years, falling more than 2.5 percent and then another 1.3 percent. Overall GNP fell 1.1 percent in 1987 and 1.7 percent in 1988. The economy was saved from collapse by external sources. Tourism brought in $1.5 billion, and Yugoslavs working abroad repatriated twice that amount.

Despite the dismal economic performance, market-oriented reforms were broadly successful in increasing foreign trade opportunities. When price controls were lifted in mid-1988, however, inflationary pressures erupted. Price decontrol was accompanied by the devaluation of the dinar, soon followed by wage decontrols and the search by workers for higher wages to match the price rises. By the close of 1988, inflation was above 250 percent. In 1989, the rate skyrocketed with the annualized rate of increase for the first quarter of 1989 above 500 percent, which rose to 13,000 percent by the fourth quarter. Hyperinflation had swept the economy. Yugoslavia was spared a liquidity crisis only through IMF support and agreements with foreign creditors.

The inflation of 1989 damaged but did not cripple the economy. Agricultural output increased by 5 percent. Beef, pork, and poultry production as well as grapes and wheat declined, but double-digit increases in fruits, corn, potatoes, and especially sugar beets, kept the aggregate statistics robust. Industrial output actually managed a slight gain of 1 percent. Shipbuilding, iron ore mining, and tobacco, industries of traditional importance, all fell by 7 percent. Textile yarns, beverages, chemicals, oil processing, and oil and gas extraction declined by smaller margins. But the majority of consumer and producer goods industries maintained positive growth. Tourism, spurred by the weak dinar, again provided important economic gains. Hard-currency earnings from tourism topped $2 billion in 1989, while remittances from Yugoslavs living abroad increased to above $3 billion. GNP was able to recover from the two years of losses, registering a modest gain of 0.7 percent.

Another positive sign in 1989 was an increase in machine tool imports from the West, as firms increased capital investment in modern equipment. While the state's tight fiscal policies kept investments in the socialized sector depressed, restrictions on the private sector were eased, stimulating private investment. In 1990 the economy declined, largely as a result of the sporadic ethnic fighting that engulfed the country. One of the few positive indicators was a precipitous fall in the number of labor strikes. Perhaps the violence served as an outlet for passions that had formerly been reflected in labor stoppages. But worker incomes in 1990 were only 60 percent of 1980 levels in real terms and heading lower. The government claimed an unemployment rate of 15 percent, but the actual rate was closer to 25 percent. More than a third of the 27,000 state firms were candidates for bankruptcy, and by the end of the year more than 800 firms, employing more than half a million laborers, were in bankruptcy.

Total GNP shrank 11 percent in 1990. Agricultural output fell as a result of a dev-astating drought, which in turn led to smaller animal herds due to a shortage of feed grains. Yugoslavia became a net food importer. Industrial output declined nearly 11 per-cent. The heavy industry and construction sectors both shrank substantially, while capital goods output decreased by approximately 20 percent. Machinery output fell by 19 per-cent. Shipbuilding fell by 12 percent. Chemicals were off by 10 percent. Coal processing dropped 30 percent. Consumer goods industries fell by 7 percent.

The most positive economic aspect of 1990 was the government's continuing efforts to control inflation. The inflation rate had dropped from over 2,000 percent per month to less than 60 percent by the end of December, 1989. Despite the hostilities between the republics, which emerged in 1990, the central government retained considerable power, and its efforts to control inflation were abetted by the quasi-independent National Bank and by the support and pressure of the IMF. As a result, inflation continued to fall in 1990 until it slipped below an *annual* rate of 4 percent by April.

After the midyear removal of the temporary price and wage controls and the oil price spurt following the Gulf crisis, inflation again accelerated. The federal government had no control over the monetary policies or banks of the republics, and inflation spurted to more than 120 percent by the end of the year.

The violence of civil war has led to a near-general collapse of the economy in 1991 and the explosion of inflation. Economic output fell through the summer of 1991 at an annualized rate of 30 percent.

National GNP statistics mask several important realities. Yugoslav industries are replicated in each of the republics. If free trade were instituted across republic borders within the country, Yugoslav industries would face more extreme plant closings and un-employment than Poland, Hungary, and Czechoslovakia. The private sector, historically much larger than in other socialist states, has continued to expand.

The hard-currency debt problem appears to have been brought under control. Total foreign debt has declined from its record high of $21 billion, near the end of 1987, to $16.8 billion. Remittances from Yugoslav laborers abroad, hard currency earned in the tourist industry, debt rescheduling, and new IMF and World Bank loans reduced the urgency of the debt burden. As confidence in the dinar plummets, however, the debt crisis is likely to become acute once again.

Yugoslavia's trade with countries with nonconvertible currencies has been dramatically reduced. By 1990, the West accounted for nearly 60 percent of all imports and exports, while nonconvertible-currency trade declined to 22 percent of exports and 13 percent of imports. Trade with the Soviet Union has long been assessed on a hard-currency basis at world market prices. Yugoslavia has thus avoided the currency shock of other former East bloc states suddenly forced to pay for Soviet energy supplies with hard currency at world market prices. Also in contrast to other former East bloc states, Yugoslavia has managed to find export markets for its machinery and manufactured goods, comprising more than 70 percent of its total exports. Yet Yugoslav consumers went on a Western shopping binge in 1990 and managed to generate a trade deficit of nearly $3.4 billion.

The economy of the future is dependent above all else on politics. Other bloc states are struggling to break central control. Belgrade has virtually none. Substantial economic reforms have been initiated. Impediments to private economic activity have been lifted, and the economy has been opened to foreign competition. But the determining factor will be the political resolution of the violence, which has done so much to make permanent the hatred between the peoples of Yugoslavia.

Economy from Origins to 1945

Before its political independence, the territories that would become Yugoslavia were profoundly heterogeneous. They were on the periphery of European development and dominated by peasant pursuits. Industrialization was concentrated primarily in the northwest areas of Slovenia, Croatia, and Vojvodina, which had been parts of the Hapsburg Empire. The development was typical of an imperial border territory—poor by the standards of the empire, yet prosperous compared to more distant lands. The southeast regions of Bosnia-Hercegovina, Serbia, Montenegro, Kosovo, and Macedonia were held by the Ottomans until the 1860s and 1870s. As the fortunes of the Ottomans declined, so too did those of its territories. The prosperity of those territories came from the limited trade that flowed between the Hapsburgs and the Ottomans. The distinguishing characteristic of Yugoslavia, its division between two empires, left Yugoslavia at economic odds with itself. Even after winning independence and even after its communist experience, it never managed to shed its internal economic differences. Yugoslavia remains defined by its place and its history.

Of the Yugoslav republics, Slovenia's prestatehood development was the most advanced. Before the area came under Hapsburg control, the Venetians used Ljubjana, the capital of Slovenia, as its northern trading outpost. Even after Hapsburg suzerainty in the 14th century, the Venetians continued to maintain Slovenia's ports and to develop the region until the 1700s. Because of its mountainous terrain, agriculture was not important to its economic development. The peasants raised animals, especially sheep, which served as the basis for the establishment of small textile manufacturers. With access to the Hapsburg market, cotton milling developed rapidly, as did glass production and timbering, which developed with Austrian money and German engineering.

Slovenia also possessed large deposits of coal and iron ore, which were significant to the economic fortunes of the province. In 1854, the Austrians built a railroad that joined Trieste, Slovenia's major port city, with the Hapsburg capital, Vienna. They also reduced tariffs so that the Slovenian industries were subject to competition from other parts of the empire. But the region was so richly endowed that foreign credits and investments were attracted and the economy boomed. The mines were being exploited, iron works had been built, and the railroads moved the products to distant markets.

The Slovenians suffered less discrimination from the Hapsburgs than did the other Balkan territories and were largely left alone. On the edge of the empire, Slovenia was relatively poor, yet in comparison to its fellow south Slavs, its economy was far superior.

National awareness developed among the south Slavs in the mid-1800s, though not until 1914 was there support in Slovenia for leaving the Hapsburgs.

Whereas Slovenia was controlled by the Austrians in the Austro-Hungarian Empire, Croatia was controlled by the Hungarians. Croatia's development was more sporadic than Slovenia's. It was divided into three subregions, each with distinct development patterns. Dalmatia, along the Adriatic coast, was initially dominated by Venetian traders. Its ports were lucrative trading centers. Croatia proper was split by the Hapsburgs into Civil Croatia and Military Croatia, which served as a buffer from the Ottomans. Military Croatia was mountainous and not well suited to farming, but many of the Serbians who had fled Ottoman rule accepted the Hapsburg offer of land there in exchange for military service. Despite its utility to the Hapsburgs as a military redoubt against the Ottoman enemy, the region's infrastructure was never developed, on the logic that if it fell to the Ottomans, the Turks would gain strategic advantage.

In Civil Croatia, with land more suitable for farming, large estates predominated. But the estates were not prosperous, because they often consisted of scattered tracts of land. Still, Croatia had access to a European empire and enjoyed steady development. Livestock raising, forestry, paper, and sugar milling were developed, because the Hungarians had an interest in their development. But whereas Slovenian development was encouraged by the Austrians, Hungary always held Croatian development in check, fearful of its threat to the home economy. The economic development of Serbia was considerably delayed because of the Ottoman occupation. Before the arrival of the Turks in the mid-14th century, Serbia, most notably under Stephen Dušan, enjoyed exceptional prosperity. A Roman-built road network and the Drima and Danube rivers facilitated trade in agricultural goods and mining. But under the military-feudal system of the Ottomans, the region fell into decay. Ottoman policies hindered Serbia's economic development, as did the obstacles to trade between the Hapsburg and Ottoman empires. The Turks seemed intent only in collecting taxes and not in developing its economy. The communications infrastructure—roads and canals—as well as the irrigation system were ignored and deteriorated.

As Ottoman central control weakened, Serbia's impoverishment was exacerbated by periods of regional violence. Once Serbia gained its independence through the Treaty of Berlin in 1878, large numbers of Turkish peasants were left on Balkan soil, predominantly in Bosnia, practicing small-scale subsistence farming. The pattern of small-plot farming hindered Serbian development and explains, more than any other factor, the poverty of Serbia and other Balkan territories.

Following independence, the Germans, French, and Austrians sought economic advantage in the region. They offered credits, particularly for the development of mines and the construction of a railroad linking Constantinople to Europe. But Serbia spent the majority of its credits to acquire arms. By 1910, only 7 percent of the work force were craftsmen, and only 16,000 workers in all of Serbia were employed in the mines and small factories. Its factories, largely established with German capital, were in brewing, milling, sugar refining, and textiles. A full one-third of the farms had no livestock, and another 10 percent had no means of transport. By the initiation of WW I, nearly 90 percent of the farmers possessed no tools other than hand-made wooden implements. The government was overwhelmed by foreign debt.

Following World War I and the formation of the Kingdom of Serbs, Croats, and Slovenes, later to be called Yugoslavia, the new state found itself in unenviable economic circumstances. Four factors interacted to shackle the country's development. First, the war had caused substantial physical damage. Second, the Kingdom was established with a large foreign debt, which grew with loans secured to restore the war-damaged economy. Third, like Poland at unification, the country had to meld distinct bureaucratic systems, the legacy of different colonial empires. Fourth, the unified economy was overwhelmingly agricultural, with only the most limited development in mining and extractive industries.

Damage from the war was immense. One million died in Serbia alone, and it is estimated to have lost somewhere near one-half of its prewar wealth. Serbia's livestock, its most important farming sector, had been devastated. More than half of the country's animals were lost—over 6 million sheep, nearly 2.5 million pigs, and over 1 million goats. More than one-third of the horses were destroyed—some 500,000 animals, which were the chief source of transport and plowing. Over 1.5 million cattle perished, one-quarter of the total stock. It required a decade to restore the animal stock to its pre–WW I levels. The losses were especially debilitating, because livestock had comprised one-quarter of all exports as well as a major source of supplies for the small domestic industries.

The foreign debt compounded these losses and proved exceedingly difficult to service, given the limited economy of the interwar period. Serbia brought more than 25 outstanding major international loans to independence, one-third of which had been used to cover government budget deficits. Another third funded the establishment of a national army, and only one-third were used for economic projects, the majority of which went to raw material–exporting industries. With the coming of the world Depression, raw materials plummeted in value.

Prewar loans had totaled 3.2 billion dinars, which required a full third of the state budget to finance. Following the War, the state borrowed nearly 16.5 billion dinars, primarily from the United States, France, UK, and Switzerland. The fivefold debt increase proved nearly impossible to service even before the Depression. Yet the country's need to borrow never diminished. Neither did the willingness of lenders to provide new funds. By the early 1930s, Yugoslavia owed 33 billion dinars—some $600 million—and was forced into rescheduling. Foreigners held more than 80 percent of the state's debt and owned close to 45 percent of all private capital by the outbreak of World War II.

Foreigners dominated mining, chemicals, shipping, and electrical power generation. Desperate for capital, Belgrade allowed foreign investors to establish firms to extract and export raw materials without domestic processing, ensuring that the country would become a source of inexpensive and unskilled labor. Only a tiny percentage of the country's zinc, lead ore, bauxite, silver, and copper were refined inside the country. Copper, for example, was financed largely with French capital. Nearly one million tons of copper were mined annually in Yugoslavia, making it the third largest producer in the world. Yet with only limited internal processing facilities, the country had to import refined copper products made abroad from its own raw materials.

Economic development was also hindered by the strain put on the central government to create a unified country and a unified market. The provinces of the country had been dominated by different foreign powers—Austria, Hungary, the Ottomans, the Italians, and the Greeks. Melding such disparate regions, peoples, and economies proved beyond the bureaucratic and economic capacities of the Serbian government, while exhausting a considerable share of its resources. Moreover, having become independent, Yugoslavia was cut off from the market and the capital of the former Hapsburg empire. It was forced to turn inward in search of indigenous sources of development from a population of just 12 million, the vast majority of whom were poor peasants. Merely coordinating the challenges proved a nightmare, and unlike Poland, which also had to piece itself together from three empires, Yugoslavia did not have the good fortune of one dominant majority people to serve as a unifying force.

Despite the emergence of a strong monarchy, the constitutional base of the country was always held in doubt, if not contempt, by many. The economy was never able to develop free from profound political and social tensions.

The republics bitterly disagreed on the economic policies of the state. Landlocked and poor, Serbia favored autarky, while Slovenia and Croatia favored liberal trade, at which they had been so adept before independence. The dispute was never decisively settled in the interwar period. Serbian dominance eventually prevailed and high tariffs were imposed, ranging from 50 percent on foodstuffs, stone, and glass products to 40 percent on iron and to almost 30 percent for textiles and nonferrous metals.

The high tariffs hindered development in Slovenia and Croatia. They did little to stimulate domestic industry, though they did protect agriculture. Foreign investors, who controlled the industrial concerns, were among the greatest beneficiaries, while the indigenous population was left paying above-world prices. The high tariffs helped control inflation and stabilized the dinar, thus restoring international confidence in Yugoslavia. Once this was restored, credits were again forthcoming.

Despite large foreign credits, the economy remained peasant-based. At the creation of the Kingdom, nearly 80 percent of the population earned their livelihoods on farms. At the start of WW II, three-quarters of the people continued to do the same. With the high rural birth rate and low rate of industrialization, farming productivity was stunted by rural overpopulation. The size of the average farm plot declined throughout the interwar period. In the early 1920s, the average plot was slightly below 10 acres, but by 1940, the average was closer to 5 acres. Slovenia and Croatia were exceptions, as large landowners preserved their estates through political leverage.

Diminishing farm size was also stimulated by the land reform policies of the new republic. After unification, Serbia, with mostly small farms, chose to divide the landed estates it inherited. Over six million acres were seized by the state and divided among close to 650,000 peasant families. The policy was popular with the former serfs, but it made rational, mechanized farming impossible. Agricultural productivity actually declined, leaving the poorer peasants in constant need of credits.

Yugoslavia's most widespread crops were corn and wheat. Tobacco, sugar beet, hemp, cotton, and wine grapes were more important for export earnings and state revenues. By 1930, animal breeding had recovered from the devastation of WW I and accounted for just under a quarter of export earnings. Pigs and cattle were raised for export, while sheep were used for domestic consumption. Goats were nearly as important as sheep. Food shipments ranged between 50 percent and 60 percent of total exports. Timber and raw materials were another 30 percent of exports.

Industry failed to develop appreciably in the interwar period. Immediately following the conclusion of the Great War, there was a sharp increase in workshops established to produce consumer goods. As these businesses began to take root, the government slowed growth to control its balance-of-payments problems. That was accomplished just as the Germans discontinued WW I reparation payments and the world Depression took effect. So badly was the economy hit that many factories went bankrupt and the government suspended payment on its foreign debt. The firms that survived were largely the foreign-owned mining operations, of little significance for the domestic economy.

Belgrade did manage one significant economic achievement—the construction of a limited network of railroads connecting the country. But it was completed only after 1935, too late to save the economy from German domination. From 1935 to 1939, Germany bought more than 50 percent of Yugoslavia's exports and supplied more than 50 percent of its imports.

During the two and a half decades between the wars, there were few jobs outside of agriculture in Yugoslavia. Only some 2,000 workplaces existed in the entire country, employing 150,000 laborers. Another 250,000 workers had railroad and mining jobs, while 170,000 entered the service sector. The state employed close to 650,000 persons in largely nonproductive projects. Testimony to the weak performance of the industrial sector was the fact that only about 5 percent of the rural workforce left their farms to work in industry, and no more than 10 percent of the total population was employed in industry at the outbreak of the Second World War. The small and largely impoverished urban industrial workforce proved as ready an audience for Tito's plea for a communist transformation as did the impoverished peasantry.

Two significant economic problems characterized the interwar precommunist period. The country was perpetually troubled by the mismanagement of its foreign debt and by the economic disparities of its regions. Yugoslavia had been forced to deal with the demands of foreign lenders and had attempted to stimulate development in the poorer regions long before Tito's rule. In the interwar period, Belgrade's efforts to direct industrial development to the regions of the southeast were met with outrage in the industrialized regions, which resented subsidizing their poorer countrymen.

Economy from 1945 to 1990

Communist development policies were complex and largely subordinated to the nationalities question. In theory, of course, communism was to have resolved both the nationality problem and the problem of industrial and agricultural backwardness. In practice, the nationality issue was never resolved but served to complicate economic planning and development, and communist planners actually exacerbated both the problems of the economy and the nationalities.

Milovan Djilas, once a key aide to Tito, observed that the party had created an administrative system far more beholden to regional interests than was politically necessary. Yugoslav political leaders did, of course, fight for their ethnic interests, but Tito exacerbated regional differentiation as an instrument of his rule long after its destructive consequences became overwhelmingly clear. That policy took on a life of its own, sustaining destructive economic decentralization—"dinar nationalism," as it was known in the country.

Economic nationalism was first centered in the six republics and the two autonomous regions. But even those economies came to be divided and subdivided over time, creating large numbers of antagonistic administrative units. For all the economic travesties created by the highly centralized socialist system of economic planning, Yugoslavia would have benefited from more central control. The economic regionalism contributed greatly to the ethnic conflicts now destroying the country.

Only during its first few years under communism, from 1945 to 1951, did Yugoslavia's economic development resemble the Moscow model. In fact, initially Yugoslavia had embraced Moscow's doctrines wholeheartedly, while the majority of the bloc states did so only reluctantly and after considerable resistance. Belgrade adopted Moscow-style central planning, large-scale nationalizations, and the subordination of all economic activity to the control of the communist party. Central control was justified on the grounds of overcoming the legacy of the vicious civil war that had taken more lives than the war against Germany and Italy. The only way, it seemed, to preserve and enrich the underdeveloped, agricultural, and war-torn state was to harness and direct its potential from the center. Tito's primarily peasant Partisan army also argued that only communist control of the economy offered the means to solve the vast economic inequalities between northwest and southeast.

Over 20 percent of national income was invested in those early years, leading to an output boom. Industrial production rose by 24 percent and agriculture by 16 percent in 1948. Exports and imports for the year both jumped by more than 80 percent, while employment rose by 30 percent. The sizable increases came on the abysmal postwar economic base but seemed to presage the transformation that communist economic centralization could accomplish. The country had not yet reached its pre-1939 production levels when the 1948 break with Stalin occurred. The Soviets, dutifully followed by their satellites, imposed a trade blockade on Yugoslavia, interrupting its growth and sending the economy into decline. Exports, the bulk of which had been directed eastward, fell by more than 33 percent in 1949. By 1950, exports, imports and agricultural productivity all had declined by more than 20 percent, while industrial production had managed to grow by less than 1 percent. In the following two years, industrial output registered declines of more than 1 percent, and employment dropped by at least 5 percent. As late as 1952, labor productivity in industry had still not reached 1939 levels.

The official communist line attributes all the declines to the Soviet-led boycott. The disruption of trade was very real and was a major factor in the decline. Yet the United States, seeing an opportunity to divide the bloc, granted aid and credits in amounts nearly matching those withdrawn by Moscow. Belgrade, sensing heightened needs for national security, increased defense spending by more than 20 percent, but most of the military supplies were financed by Western military aid.

The most powerful explanation for the economic decline following the break with Stalin was not the Soviet-imposed embargo but Tito's response to the break. For a brief period, Tito determined to prove his communist legitimacy by adopting policies "more communist than the Soviets." He redoubled his efforts for the complete nationalization of the economy and forced the collectivization of agriculture, producing instant economic decline.

Tito had directed his ideologues to find within Marxism the rationale for asserting Yugoslavia's independence from Moscow while justifying the legitimacy of its communist credentials. They concluded that Yugoslavia had actually reached a higher form of Marxist development than the USSR—"free associations of producers," as Marx termed it, which came into law in 1950 as the Workers' Self-Management Act. But central planning did not immediately disappear. It faded throughout the 1950s, while workers' management was codified and implemented.

Despite its grand name, the workers never actually gained the power to manage firms. What did occur was the dispersal of power away from the communist party center to republic, provincial, and local communist elites who were given authority for their economies. The pronounced decentralization of economic decision making intensified the tensions and rivalries among the republics and regions, establishing the foundation for the recent lurch to civil war.

The power acquired by the workers in the new self-management system was essentially the right to participate in seemingly endless meetings, which deteriorated to debates on the need to raise workers' wages. Members of workers' committees were frequently rotated to prevent the rise among them of any real leaders. The enterprise director, a political appointee, and his management team held power at the level of the firm. The enterprise was held in check at the local level by the party commune, which monitored the enterprise's compliance with the law, and by the trade union structure, also an instrument of party control.

While the federal government did give up central planning that specified output quotas, it continued planning that set development targets, leaving the firm to determine output and production mixes. But the central planners managed to retain all their other former powers. They retained the right to specify the disposition of nearly all the revenues of the firm. Every enterprise was required to contribute the majority of its earnings into a variety of funds, which it could not control. Additionally, Belgrade controlled depreciation and interest rates as well as wage standards. The planners also maintained a commitment to the goal of rapid industrialization, considered critical for the welfare of the poorer southeast. By championing the idea of regional industrialization, they retained the power to determine, either directly or indirectly, upwards of 80 percent of the allocation of investment.

So onerous were the "indirect" regulations established by the purportedly irrelevant central planners in Belgrade that prices were set with little attention to the costs of production. The market that was to have been created never materialized. By the end of the 1950s, the center was once again setting prices on more than 70 percent of production.

Workers' self-management in agriculture proved more troublesome. When farmers were offered the choice, they voted with their feet. They fled the agricultural cooperatives they had earlier been forced to join, resulting in the decimation of the socialized agricultural sector. By the end of 1960, no more than 10 percent of the land was cultivated through socialist cooperatives. Still, all state aid to agriculture, in the form of reduced taxes and of credits, was channeled to the cooperatives. Private farming was left to fend for itself.

Yugoslav theorists had argued that the new system would remain socialist but be guided by market phenomena and would produce both economic growth and socialist equality—true Marxist utopia. Ultimately, of course, the theorists proved wrong. The state did not wither away, nor did the workers gain power. Equality was never achieved. Still, the idea of workers' self-management gained widespread currency, particularly in the West. Economists with socialist leanings and many others believed that Yugoslavia had managed to eliminate the alienation of workers without compromising economic productivity.

The new economic program was doomed by two interrelated features of the old economic system—the irrational financing of investments and the unbridled desire to continue rapid industrialization. Prior to the self-management reforms, Belgrade's investment program was simple enough. The poorer regions were allowed to retain a larger portion of federal taxes than were the richer regions, and they were given direct grants-in-aid from the federal budget. There was, however, little supervision from the center of the ways in which the poorer regions spent their investment funds. Nor, for that matter, did the center monitor the expenditures of the more prosperous regions. At the level investments were actually made, there was no regard for the profitability of an investment project.

The poorer regions, believing they had been exploited as the suppliers of raw materials to the wealthier regions, built show projects. The supply of skilled labor and the availability of markets were irrelevant considerations. As the projects ran over budget or operated with vast deficits, federal subsidies were needed. The central bank responded with loans financed by expanding the money supply. The pattern of abuse grew worse as the republics and smaller political units were given more legal authority from the center, starting projects they could not possibly afford to finish.

In many cases, the funds were never used for development projects but to meet the budget deficits of the republics. Federal authorities were aware of the fiscal mismanagement. But they chose to win the political loyalty of the provinces by allowing them virtual economic autonomy.

The problems were hardly limited to the poorer regions. Even the most successful firms in the more prosperous republics frequently acted outside the realm of economic sense. Firms that produced economic surpluses were not allowed to invest those surpluses outside the enterprise or to lend surplus funds to banks, practices considered examples of "exploitation" by the communists. Directors responded by paying higher salaries and making capital investments in their own plants, creating ever larger enterprises beyond the economies of scale. Smaller firms merged and expanded through constant investments in their own plants, irrespective of demand for their products. By the 1960s, slightly more than 200 firms accounted for more than 50 percent of the nation's fixed capital and net product. The average number of their employees was nearly three times the number in the largest firms of West Germany. Yet gross output per unit of capital in 1960 was estimated at only 85 percent of what it had been in 1939.

Having secured the funds and erected huge enterprises, regional and local party bureaucrats acquired the ambition to protect the industries they had built no matter what the economic consequences. Each republic favored its own industries, and even within republics, ethnic groupings protected their own industrial conclaves. Competition was obstructed between regions and republics, as each group or local commune set out to integrate its own collection of industries, trade networks, and farms while excluding the products of other republics. A factory director would not think of seeking suppliers outside his region even if better prices and quality were available elsewhere. Yugoslavia was not an integrated market but a collection of competing economies made explosive by ethnic hostilities.

By 1960, personal consumption had yet to equal its 1939 level, and Yugoslavs gradually became aware of the magnitude of their economic problems. For the next thirty years, socialist officials attempted to revamp the economic system without yielding their socialist ideals. Their reforms did not reverse the economy's direction.

The government first concentrated on the financial system, attempting to control inflation and the growth of credit by devaluing the dinar and strengthening income and price caps. But the planners believed that the fundamental problems were at the enterprise level, where, they argued, "business discipline" had failed to take root. Their diagnosis was correct, but managers could hardly be expected to be sensitive to market forces. The government had long since determined to subsidize heavy and engineering industries, most notably metal refining, electrical equipment, and shipbuilding, and offer them multiple exchange rates to make substantial profits from guaranteed rates of currency conversion. As a result, many industries were showing profitability on the exchange rate alone. In order to maintain the subsidies, wages were kept low and justified as necessary for creating equality. The result was to penalize the workers in firms that actually showed a profit.

In 1963, the state responded to the poor conditions of the workers and the rise of unemployment by lifting the ban on migration. The country was shocked by the departure of hundreds of thousands of workers. For those who remained, tax rates on income was raised to 80 percent of gross earnings.

Recognizing the need for a genuine decontrol of the economy, a major economic reform program, known simply as the "Reform," was passed in 1965. The program called for reducing administrative oversight at the federal and republic level by applying only indirect monetary and fiscal controls. The share of firm revenues allotted to the state was reduced from 50 percent to 30 percent. The role of the central government in investments and subsidies was diminished, and tariffs were dropped to stimulate competition. The dinar was devalued close to the open market rate, and the national bank began a five-year process of replacing 100 old dinars with one new dinar. The individual enterprise was established as the source of decision making for savings, investment, and income distribution.

While the Reform reduced the power of the central party elites, it did not always lead to enterprise behavior in conformity with market forces. Enterprises became sensitive to material costs, but not necessarily to labor and capital costs. Moreover, since the nation was now comparing itself to international market standards, firms took to pricing their own goods at international levels irrespective of quality differences. Two weeks after the implementation of the reforms, the program was so thoroughly abused that the government had to impose price ceilings, gradually lifting them for about 40 percent of producer goods by 1967. Despite the controls, enterprises continued to raise prices at every opportunity, making inflation endemic. In the 1960s it averaged just below 8 percent, increasing to nearly 20 percent annually in the 1970s, after which it never declined.

Nor did the Reform reduce the power for meddling in the economy by republic, regional, and commune political elites. Once the central government withdrew its control, officials below the federal level moved to fill the vacuum. An elaborate system of formal and informal networks, which have continued to the present, allowed party and government officials and enterprise managers to obstruct the operation of market forces. Once banks were freed from the control of the NBY, for example, they fell under the control of local elites. By intensifying decentralization, the Reform of 1965 stimulated particularism, allowing regional authorities to enforce their own interests. The disaster of the 1965 Reform stemmed from the central government's abandoning its power to address national needs. The very differences in regional incomes, which were to be erased by the

Reform, produced policies that exacerbated the differences. The north prospered relative to the south, and ethnic tensions were heightened.

There were other attempts to reform the socialist system that were primarily responsible for driving the economy to a complete standstill in the 1980s. The reforms of 1974 and 1976 created a new worker-management organization, the Basic Organizations of Associated Labor (BOALs). The BOALs were meant to stimulate market forces through establishing an economic system based on contractual arrangements. In addition, workers were to become more active in the productive process, and thus more responsible for their actions. The regulations and responsibilities of the BOALs were, however, no small undertaking. The laws for their creation ran to more than 650 articles of confusing by-laws, restrictions, obligations, and requirements. Rather than stimulating responsibility, the reforms nearly strangled enterprises, while creating another layer of bureaucracy that reinforced nonmarket behavior.

With Tito's death in 1980, it was clear that workers' self-management had died as well. No further reform efforts were made until 1988, when Ante Markovic attempted to break the hold of the entrenched local bureaucracies. His reforms also failed to produce economic growth. Yet Yugoslavia survived. Massive Western loans flowed to Belgrade as a reward for its remaining outside the East bloc. The Europeans and Americans also believed that aid would ameliorate the endemic ethnic tensions and prevent civil war.

The economy also survived because the private sector was given greater leeway. Despite the restrictions under which it operated, private economic activity accounted for more than 20 percent of the nation's social product as early as 1960. Most agriculture had become private, as had the majority of small restaurants and tourist-related activities. In addition, by the mid-1960s as many as 150,000 private workshops had become suppliers to state enterprises. Finally, more than 1 million Yugoslavs went to Europe, notably Germany, as guest workers and annually remitted more than $2 billion to their families. The country had been sustained in ways not enjoyed by the other socialist states.

By combining aspects of socialism with those of the market, Yugoslavia managed to achieve the worst features of both. There was enough socialism to inhibit rational investment criteria and to facilitate hoarding financed by a valueless currency. There was enough market to produce unemployment and inflation. By drawing on both systems, a perverse structure of incentives had been established.

Looking back on the efforts at economic reform, it would be easy to conclude that the fundamental error was in decentralizing power in a nation of great ethnic diversity. But the crucial mistake was elsewhere. The country created a huge industrial sector, which could not be sustained by its human and raw material resources and which was unnecessary to its needs. The decentralization helped each republic protect its piece of the economic pie. With the central authority interested primarily in gross output, the local authorities interested in protecting their own firms regardless of profitability, and the workers in keeping their incomes above inflation, a vicious spiral was created, which eventually spun out of control.

AFTERWORD

Since the writing of this chapter, the situation has continued to deteriorate in the former Yugoslav state. In the bloodiest fighting on the European continent since WWII, by the Spring of 1992, it is estimated that between 6,000 to 10,000 died in the civil war. Nearly 1 million have been displaced and of these, nearly one quarter have left the country permanently. The United Nations proffered a cease-fire between Croatia and Serbia in January 1992, but the agreement has been violated by both sides leading to more than 100 casualties.

Slovenia, the most removed from the fighting, will be the first to recover from the morass. At this point, Croatia's independence is assured, but it will likely loose a portion of its Eastern border to Serbia or it will remain occupied by the Serbs. And, rebuilding the country will last in excess of a decade.

Attention in 1992 has turned increasingly to Bosnia-Hercegovina. Despite a boycott by the Serbian population, the republic declared its secession from Yugoslavia in a referendum on March 1, 1992, followed by Macedonia. The three-way ethnic division of Bosnia—1.9 million Muslim Slavs, 1.4 million Serbs and 750,000 Croats—has the potential to be even more explosive than what has been witnessed in Croatia. The ethnic mix in urban areas is deep. Remarkably, the three ethnic groups agreed to an EC plan in mid-March which would preserve the independence and borders of the republic while dividing the interior into three regions all with equal status. However, the presence of the Yugoslav army numbering more than 100,000 men (for all practical purposes, a Serbian army) is certain to complicate the fragile arrangement. Moreover, since Milosevic still intends to gather all Serbs into a Greater Serbia, it will be miraculous if the agreement actually endures.

With their limited options, the European Community and the UN have shown a concerted effort to contain the violence. Trade and economic sanctions were imposed on the entire region in November 1991 and were later lifted for all but Serbia and Montenegro. They have been assured the resumption of free trade and economic assistance when and if they agree to settlement of all national disputes by peaceful means. In an effort to apply leverage, the EC has also recognized each of the breakaway republics. The UN January cease-fire plan has been violated, but the historic introduction of a 14,000 member peace keeping force has gone forward nevertheless. The force, however, is concentrated in Croatia and thus does not guarantee the containment of fighting were it to break out in Bosnia. In addition, relations in the EC have the potential for conflict since the formerly quiet Greece has refused to recognize Macedonia for fear that the latter will make claims on Greek territory.

Serbia, throughout, has remained adamant in its determination to gather all Serbs. Despite the loss of life and the incredible economic damage, its determination is a clear indication that Serbia will continue to fight, conceivably until it is exhausted militarily.

FURTHER READINGS

Darby, H. C., R. W. Seton-Watson, Phyllis Auty, R. G. D. Laffan, and Stephen Clissold. *A Short History of Yugoslavia: From Early Times to 1966.* Cambridge: Cambridge University Press, 1966.

Jelavich, Barbara. *History of the Balkans.* Vol. 2: *Twentieth Century.* Cambridge: Cambridge University Press, 1983.

Ramet, Pedro. *Nationalism and Federalism in Yugoslavia, 1963–1983.* Bloomington: Indiana University Press, 1984.

Rothschild, Joseph. *Return to Diversity: A Political History of East-Central Europe since World War II.* New York: Oxford University Press, 1989.

West, Rebecca. *Black Lamb and Grey Falcon: A Journey through Yugoslavia.* New York: The Viking Press, 1941.

DATA AND VITAL STATISTICS

X. **Trade**
   1. Exports and imports, by commodity group
   2. Main destinations of exports and main origins of imports, 1990
   3. Principal trading partners
   4. Index of import and export prices, terms of trade
   5. Major imports and exports
   6. Trade with Western countries
   7. Trade with the USSR, by commodity
   8. Trade with the United States, by commodity

Note: Where possible and relevant, Yugoslavia is compared to both the Netherlands and Sweden combined, because they are of comparable population. Also, data for the United States, France, USSR, and other East European countries are provided for comparison where relevant.

I. AGRICULTURE

TABLE 6.I.1 Land use, 1991

		(Percent)			
Arable Land	Permanent Crops	Forest and Woodland	Meadows and Pastures	Other	Irrigated Land
28	3	36	25	8	1

Source: U.S. Central Intelligence Agency, *The World Factbook,* 1991.

TABLE 6.I.2 Agriculture production index (Yugoslavia and selected countries)

			(1980 = 100)		
Country	1965	1970	1980	1986	1990
Yugoslavia	65	77	100	117	104
USSR	83	99	100	120	118
United States	79	81	100	107	112
France	77	81	100	105	105[a]

[a] 1989 figure.
Source: U.S. Central Intelligence Agency, *Handbook of Economic Statistics,* 1991.

TABLE 6.I.3 Selected indicators of agricultural development, 1970–1985

	1974–1976	1981	1985
Agricultural land use (thousand ha[a])			
Arable	7,322	7,126	7,046
Permanent crops	713	738	734
Permanent pasture	6,342	6,417	6,444
Forest and woodland	9,028	9,310	9,294[b]
	1982	**1984**	**1985**
Total output[c]	7.0	1.5	−7.4

[a] ha = 1 hectare = 10,000 m^2 = 2.471 acres.
[b] 1984 data.
[c] Annualized percentage changes.
Source: EIU, *Yugoslavia Country Profile,* 1987–1988.

TABLE 6.1.4 Total grain production[a] (Yugoslavia and selected countries)

	1960	1970	(Million Metric Tons) 1980	1985	1990
Yugoslavia	10.93	11.61	15.66	15.81	14.06
USSR[b]	125.49	186.80	189.09	191.67	238.00
United States	181.26	186.72	269.68	347.01	312.14
France	23.02	31.29	47.36	55.07	55.38

[a]Data are for the following products, where they are produced: barley, corn, oats, rice, rye, sorghum, and wheat.

[b]Includes miscellaneous grains and legumes. For comparative purposes, an average discount of 11 percent should be applied, because USSR totals include excess moisture, unripe and damaged kernels, weed seeds, and other trash.

Source: U.S. Central Intelligence Agency, *Handbook of Economic Statistics,* 1990, 1991.

TABLE 6.1.5 Principal crops

	1985	(Thousand Metric Tons) 1987	1989
Maize	9,896	8,863	9,415
Sugar beet	6,268	6,238	6,797
Wheat	4,859	5,272	5,599
Potatoes	2,413	2,210	2,359
Grapes	962	1,325	1,022
Plums	484	757	819
Barley	748	504	702
Apples	368	423	546
Oats	252	232	279
Tobacco (leaves)	80	76	57

Source: The Europa World Year Book, 1991.

TABLE 6.1.6 Yields for selected crops (Yugoslavia and selected countries)

		1985	(ql/ha[a]) 1987	1988
Wheat	Yugoslavia	36.0	36.0	42.0
	Bulgaria	28.7	38.2	40.0
	Czechoslovakia	49.3	50.8	53.0
	Hungary	48.3	43.7	54.0
	Poland	34.3	37.2	35.0
	Romania	23.4	28.0	35.8
	Soviet Union	15.5	17.8	18.0
Barley	Yugoslavia	27.0	24.0	28.0
	Bulgaria	30.7	37.0	38.0
	Czechoslovakia	44.3	42.3	43.0
	Hungary	37.3	38.2	44.0
	Poland	32.9	33.7	30.0
	Romania	25.9	36.0	44.8
	Soviet Union	16.0	19.1	15.0
Maize	Yugoslavia	41.0	40.0	34.0
	Bulgaria	30.7	37.2	32.0
	Czechoslovakia	54.4	56.4	53.0
	Hungary	62.9	61.3	55.0
	Poland	43.0	46.0	51.0
	Romania	38.5	27.0	24.7
	Soviet Union	32.1	32.4	36.0

[a]ql: quintal = 100 kg (220.46 lbs).

(continued)

TABLE 6.I.6 *(continued)*

			(ql/ha^a)	
		1985	1987	1988
Rye	Yugoslavia	17.0	17.0	19.0
	Bulgaria	14.9	16.6	18.0
	Czechoslovakia	34.0	34.9	37.0
	Hungary	19.3	19.5	26.0
	Poland	24.7	25.8	24.0
	Romania	15.0	14.9	16.2
	Soviet Union	16.5	18.6	18.0
Potatoes	Yugoslavia	88	81	70
	Bulgaria	109	86	97
	Czechoslovakia	184	171	207
	Hungary	196	160	185
	Poland	174	187	186
	Romania	204	129	124
	Soviet Union	113	121	103
Sugar beets	Yugoslavia	418	380	349
	Bulgaria	168	188	161
	Czechoslovakia	377	355	337
	Hungary	379	363	393
	Poland	336	332	341
	Romania	223	201	265
	Soviet Union	241	266	261

^{a}ql: quintal = 100 kg (220.46 lbs).

Source: EUROSTAT, *Central and Eastern Europe 1991,* 1991; *Comecon Data 1989,* 1990.

TABLE 6.I.7 Livestock (Yugoslavia and selected countries)

		(Thousand)		
		1980	1985	1988
Cattle	Yugoslavia	5,474	5,034	4,759
	Bulgaria	1,843	1,735	1,637
	Czechoslovakia	5,002	5,066	5,705
	Hungary	1,918	1,766	1,690
	Poland	11,337	11,774	10,100
	Romania	6,485	6,692	6,416
	Soviet Union	115,057	120,888	119,580
Dairy cows	Yugoslavia	3,086	2,915	2,858
	Bulgaria	723	682	659
	Czechoslovakia	1,902	1,860	1,815
	Hungary	765	688	663
	Poland	5,666	5,331	4,737
	Romania	2,670	2,901	2,858
	Soviet Union	43,389	42,863	41,809
Pigs	Yugoslavia	7,867	7,821	7,396
	Bulgaria	3,808	3,912	4,119
	Czechoslovakia	7,894	6,651	7,384
	Hungary	8,330	8,280	8,327
	Poland	18,734	19,170	20,169
	Romania	11,542	13,631	14,351
	Soviet Union	73,382	77,772	78,143
Sheep	Yugoslavia	7,384	7,693	7,564
	Bulgaria	10,433	9,724	8,609
	Czechoslovakia	910	1,087	1,047
	Hungary	3,090	2,465	2,216
	Poland	3,490	4,720	4,336
	Romania	15,865	17,342	16,210
	Soviet Union	141,573	14,850	140,685

Source: EUROSTAT, *Central and Eastern Europe 1991,* 1991; *Comecon Data 1989,* 1990.

TABLE 6.I.8 Slaughterings and production of selected animal products (Yugoslavia and selected countries)

		(Thousand Tons)		
		1980	**1985**	**1988**
Beef	Yugoslavia	344	352	301
	Bulgaria	167	163	160
	Czechoslovakia	468	467	460
	Hungary	215	180	160
	Poland	866	900	871
	Romania	285	240	230
	Soviet Union	7,367	8,278	8,616
Pork	Yugoslavia	461	526	546
	Bulgaria	390	434	459
	Czechoslovakia	853	891	950
	Hungary	1,100	1,113	1,110
	Poland	1,526	1,773	1,870
	Romania	975	900	840
	Soviet Union	5,835	6,299	6,595
Mutton and goatmeat	Yugoslavia	59	63	70
	Bulgaria	126	116	107
	Czechoslovakia	12	13	12
	Hungary	23	18	18
	Poland	39	47	46
	Romania	81	70	67
	Soviet Union	827	905	960
Poultry	Yugoslavia	277	299	329
	Bulgaria	158	169	183
	Czechoslovakia	172	194	226
	Hungary	405	469	485
	Poland	290	345	368
	Romania	475	425	390
	Soviet Union	2,811	3,116	3,235
Milk	Yugoslavia	4,352	4,682	4,638
	Bulgaria	2,357	2,590	2,570
	Czechoslovakia	6,942	6,982	7,024
	Hungary	2,729	2,833	2,886
	Poland	16,446	15,543	15,643
	Romania	5,411	5,165	5,396
	Soviet Union	98,608	103,743	106,754

Source: EUROSTAT, *Central and Eastern Europe 1991,* 1991; *Comecon Data 1989,* 1990.

TABLE 6.I.9 Agricultural labor force and tractors, 1988 (Yugoslavia and selected countries)

	Percent of Labor Force in Agriculture	Population per km^2 of Arable Land	Output per Worker in $	Tractors per 10 km^2
Yugoslavia	23.6	335	2,329	39.8
USSR	14.2	125	3,830	45.3
United States	2.5	131	33,519	10.8
OECD average	8.1	809	23,334	18.2

Source: The Economist, *Book of Vital World Statistics,* 1990.

TABLE 6.I.10 Agricultural output, 1988 (Yugoslavia and selected countries)

| | (Thousand Tons) | | | |
	Cereals	Meat	Vegetables	Fruit
Yugoslavia	14,996	1,567	2,197	3,078
OECD average[a]	12,362	1,830	3,685	3,272
East Bloc average[b]	19,125	2,024	3,523	2,582

[a] Excluding the United States.
[b] Excluding Albania.

Source: The Economist, *Book of Vital World Statistics,* 1990.

TABLE 6.I.11 Growth per capita in agriculture and food, 1977–1988 (Yugoslavia and selected countries)

| | (Percent Growth) | |
	Agriculture	Food
Yugoslavia	−0.5	−0.4
USSR	0.4	0.5
United States	1.4	1.4
France	1.3	1.3

Source: The Economist, *Book of Vital World Statistics,* 1990.

II. COMMUNICATIONS AND TRANSPORT

TABLE 6.II.1 General facts, 1990

1. Communications
   Telecommunications
   Stations (1990)   199 AM, 87 FM, 50 TV
   Radios (1990)   4,700,000 (1 per 5.1 persons)
   Televisions (1990)   4,107,846 (1 per 5.8 persons)
   Telephones (1987)   3,909,000 (1 per 5.9 persons)

2. Transport
   Railroads
      9,349 km total (all 1.435-meter standard gauge)
         931 km double track
      3,760 km electrified (1988)
   Highways
   122,062 km total, of which
      73,527 km asphalt, concrete, stone block
      33,663 km macadam, asphalt treated, gravel, crushed stone
      14,872 km earth (1988)
   Inland Waterways
      2,600 km (1982)
   Pipelines
      1,373 km crude oil
         150 km refined products
      2,900 km natural gas
   Airports
      179 total, including
         54 with permanent-surface runways
      None with runways over 3,659 m
         23 with runways 2,440–3,659 m
         20 with runways 1,220–2,439 m

Source: U.S. Central Intelligence Agency, *The World Factbook,* 1990; *The Europa World Year Book,* 1990, 1991.

TABLE 6.II.2 Radio and television receivers (Yugoslavia and selected countries)

| | (per Thousand Inhabitants) | | | | |
	1970	1975	1980	1983	1985–88
Yugoslavia					
Radios	166	196	218	238	344
TVs	88	144	200	211	175
USSR					
Radios	390	481	490	514	686
TVs	143	217	305	308	314
United States					
Radios	1,415	1,857	1,989	2,043	2,120
TVs	413	560	684	790	811
France					
Radios	315	326	743	860	995
TVs	216	269	354	375	333[a]

[a] 1987 data.

Source: UN, *Statistical Yearbook,* 1988; UN, *Human Development Report 1991,* 1991.

TABLE 6.II.3 Percentage of households owning various consumer durables, 1986–1988[a] (Yugoslavia and selected countries)

| | (Percent) | | | |
	Televisions	Radios	Refrigerators	Vacuum cleaners
Yugoslavia	61	85	N/A	N/A
USSR	45	96	N/A	N/A
United States	98	99	100	N/A
France	98	98	97	88

[a] Means data for each country may refer to 1986, 1987, or 1988.

Source: The Economist, *Book of Vital World Statistics,* 1990.

TABLE 6.II.4 Daily newspapers (Yugloslavia and selected countries)

Country	1970	1975	1979	1986
Yugoslavia	24	26	27	28
USSR[a]	639	691	N/A	723[b]
United States	1,763	1,775	1,787	1,657
France[c]	106	92	90	92

[a] Data include nondaily newspapers.
[b] 1984 data.
[c] Data shown for 1975 and 1979 refer to 1976 and 1978 respectively.

Source: UNESCO, *Statistical Yearbook,* 1989.

TABLE 6.II.5 Transport traffic

	1983	1987	1989
Road traffic			
Passengers[a]	1,016,929	1,009,547	804,260
Freight[b]	177,249	148,239	124,563
Passenger-km[c]	31,212	31,733	26,235
Ton-km[c]	18,840	21,516	21,796
Railway traffic			
Passengers[a]	116,866	119,731	117,018
Freight[b]	89,558	84,188	84,821
Passenger-km[c]	11,643	11,827	11,653
Ton-km[c]	27,860	26,070	25,921
Inland-waterway traffic			
Passengers[a]	204	20	29
Freight[b]	20,916	18,997	19,268
Passenger-km[c]	37	1	1
Ton-km[c]	4,088	4,175	5,007
Sea traffic			
Passengers[a]	6,749	8,055	8,274
Freight[b]	25,493	34,846	38,294
Passenger-km[c]	182	208	210
Ton-km[c]	167,291	224,859	250,400
Air traffic			
Passengers[a]	4,728	6,871	5,585
Freight[b]	38	43	49
Passenger-km[c]	4,901	8,342	7,985
Ton-km[c]	85	112	154
Totals			
Passengers[a]	1,145,476	1,144,224	935,166
Freight[b]	313,254	286,313	266,995
Passenger-km[c]	47,975	52,111	46,084
Ton-km[c]	218,164	276,732	303,278

[a]Thousands.
[b]Thousand metric tons.
[c]Million.
Source: Statisticki Godisnjak Jugoslavije, 1990.

TABLE 6.II.6 Railroad freight

	1986	1987	1988
Passenger journeys (million)	132.0	120.0	116.0
Passenger-km (billion)	12.4	11.8	11.4
Freight carried (million metric tons)	89.8	84.2	83.6
Freight ton-km (billion)	27.6	26.1	25.4

Source: The Europa World Yearbook, 1990.

TABLE 6.II.7 Air cargo, 1986–1988[a] (Yugoslavia and selected countries)

Country	(Freight in km Tons)[b]
Yugoslavia	124
Netherlands and Sweden	2,057
USSR	2,721
United States	13,829
OECD average	1,622

[a]Means data for each country may refer to 1986, 1987, or 1988.
[b]Of national origin.
Source: The Economist, Book of Vital World Statistics, 1990.

TABLE 6.II.8   Road traffic

| | (Number of Vehicles) | | |
	1985	1987	1989
Passenger cars	2,824,267	3,023,693	3,323,940
Buses	26,013	29,241	29,407
Special vehicles	46,042	53,942	58,601
Motorcycles and scooters	112,648	96,198	89,950

Source: The Europa World Yearbook, 1989, 1990, 1991.

TABLE 6.II.9   Ownership of vehicles and automobiles, 1985–1988[a] (Yugoslavia and selected countries)

Country	Vehicles (Thousand)[b]	Automobiles (Thousand)
Yugoslavia	3,855.2	3,023.7
Netherlands and Sweden	9,552.8	8,733.3
United States	183,468.0	140,655.0
USSR	21,500.0	12,500.0

[a] Means data for each country may refer to 1985, 1986, 1987, or 1988.

[b] Vehicles include passenger cars, trucks, and buses.

Source: The Economist, *Book of Vital World Statistics,* 1990.

TABLE 6.II.10   Number of persons per automobile, 1985–1988[a] (Yugoslavia and selected countries)

Country	
Yugoslavia	7.8
Netherlands and Sweden	2.7
OECD	2.6
USSR	22.8
United States	1.8

[a] Means data for each country may refer to 1985, 1986, 1987, or 1988.

Source: The Economist, *Book of Vital World Statistics,* 1990.

TABLE 6.II.11   Post, telephones, and telex lines, 1986–1988[a] (Yugoslavia and selected countries)

Country	Post Offices	Letters per Person	Persons per Telephone Line	Persons per Telex Line
Yugoslavia	N/A	N/A	7.6	1,790
Netherlands and Sweden	4,429	275.22	1.3	416
USSR	98,445	217.81	10.3	162,875
United States	40,117	645.48	1.3	N/A

[a] Means data for each country may refer to 1986, 1987, or 1988.

Source: The Economist, *Book of Vital World Statistics,* 1990.

III. ECONOMY

TABLE 6.III.1   Economic profile, 1990 (Yugoslavia and selected countries)

	Yugoslavia	USSR	United States	France
Gross national product				
Billion 1990 U.S. $[a]	126.6	2,660.0	5,465.2[b]	873.6[b]
Percent real growth	−6.3	−2.4 to −5.0	1.0	2.8
Per capita (1990 U.S. $)	5,300	9,140	21,830	15,490
Industrial production[c]	−10.9	−2.8	1.0	1.1
Trade (billion U.S. $)				
Exports, f.o.b	13.9[d]	109.3[d]	393.9	216.6
Imports, c.i.f.	14.8[d]	114.7[d]	516.2	234.4
Trade balance	−0.9[d]	−5.4[d]	−122.3	−17.8
Living standard indicators				
Automobile registrations (per thousand persons)	130[e]	46[e]	571[f]	395[e]
Energy consumption[g]	16[d]	35[d]	57[d]	29[d]

[a] At U.S. purchasing power equivalents.
[b] Gross domestic product.
[c] Percent growth.
[d] 1989 data.
[e] 1987 data.
[f] 1988 data.
[g] Barrels oil equivalent per capita.

Source: U.S. Central Intelligence Agency, *Handbook of Economic Statistics,* 1991.

TABLE 6.III.2   Estimated real gross national product (Yugoslavia and selected countries)

Country	(Billion 1990 U.S. $)				
	1970	1980	1985	1989	1990
Yugoslavia	72.7	118.8	126.7	129.5	123.1
USSR	1,726.9	2,257.0	2,440.9	2,663.7[a]	1,465.9[a]
United States	2,985.8	3,916.0	4,513.3	5,198.4	5,465.6
France	491.7	680.6	733.9	818.5	819.6

[a] The 1989 GNP figure for the USSR is based on CIA statistics, while the 1990 GNP figure is based on PlanEcon statistics. The great disparity between the Soviet GNP in 1990 and 1988 is due to extremely high estimates by the CIA during the 1980s.

Source: U.S. Central Intelligence Agency, *Handbook of Economic Statistics,* 1989, 1990; and "PlanEcon Report," vol. 6, no. 52, December 28, 1990.

TABLE 6.III.3 Real gross national product growth (Yugoslavia and selected countries)

Country	Percent Average Annual Rate of Growth		Percent		
	1971–1980	1981–1985	1985	1989	1990
GNP growth					
Yugoslavia	5.0	1.3	0.6	−1.1	−6.3
USSR[a]	2.4	1.8	0.9	1.5	−2.4 to −5.0
United States[b]	2.8	3.0	3.8	2.5	1.0
France[b]	3.6	1.5	1.9	3.6	2.8
GNP per capita growth					
Yugoslavia	4.1	0.4	0.2	−1.6	−6.9
USSR	1.5	0.8	−0.1	0.7	−2.9 to −5.5
United States[b]	1.7	1.8	2.8	1.5	.3
France[b]	3.0	1.0	1.5	3.1	2.4

[a] At factor cost.

[b] GDP growth.

Source: U.S. Central Intelligence Agency, *Handbook of Economic Statistics,* 1990, 1991.

TABLE 6.III.4 GNP per capita in dollars, 1990[a] (Yugoslavia and selected countries)

Country	Commercial	(U.S. $) Purchasing Parity	Free Market
Yugoslavia	6,210	5,140	6,380
USSR	2,560	5,060	1,299
United States	21,732	21,732	21,732
West Germany	24,210	16,310	24,210

[a] Based on exchange rate, purchasing power parity, and free-market rate.

Source: "PlanEcon Report," vol. 6, no. 52, December 28, 1990.

TABLE 6.III.5 GDP per capita as a percentage of OECD average, 1988 (Yugoslavia and selected countries)

Country	(Percent of OECD)
Yugoslavia	13.40
Netherlands and Sweden	107.35
USSR	12.10
United States	116.30

Source: The Economist, *Book of Vital World Statistics,* 1990.

TABLE 6.III.6 Exchange rate

	(Dinars per $; Period Averages)[a]				
	1987	1988	1989	1990	Jan. 1991
Commercial	0.074	0.252	2.876	11.318	13.605

[a] As of January 1991 the new dinar is linked to the German deutsche mark at the rate of 9 new dinars per 1 deutsche mark.

Source: U.S. Central Intelligence Agency, *The World Factbook,* 1991.

TABLE 6.III.7 Savings

(Million Dinars)			
1984	1986	1988	1989
553,700	2,079,000	12,273,100	333,794,996

Source: Comecon Data 1990, 1991.

TABLE 6.III.8 Money in circulation

(Million Dinars)			
1980	1985	1988	1989
116,000	551,300	5,851,400	123,752,000

Source: Comecon Data 1990, 1991.

TABLE 6.III.9 Growth of GNP by producing and consuming sectors

	(Percent Average Annual Rate of Growth)		
	1985	1987	1989
GNP	0.9	−0.6	−1.0
Producing sector			
Industry of which	2.3	0.5	−0.9
Machinery	9.5	N/A	N/A
Agriculture and forestry	1.0	−5.2	0.6
Construction	−6.9	−4.3	2.0
Transportation and communications	4.5	4.2	−4.8
Trade	0.7	−7.4	−10.6
Services	2.7	3.7	1.6
Other	3.0	2.3	0.7
Consuming sector			
Personal consumption	−0.4	0.6	−3.6[a]
Government	2.5	2.7	1.4[a]
Gross investment	4.3	−17.0	2.0[a]

[a] 1988 data.
Source: U.S. Central Intelligence Agency, "Eastern Europe: Long Road Ahead to Economic Well-Being," May 1990.

TABLE 6.III.10 Growth of GNP inputs and productivity

	(Percent Average Annual Rate of Growth)			
	1980	1985	1987	1989
GNP	4.8	0.9	−0.6	−1.0
Combined inputs	3.4	1.6	1.8	3.4
Capital stock	4.8	1.7	2.3	4.9
Labor	1.4	1.3	0.9	1.1
Combined productivity	1.3	−0.7	−2.3	−4.3
Capital productivity	0.0	−0.8	−2.9	−5.6
Labor productivity	3.4	−0.5	−1.5	−2.1

Source: U.S. Central Intelligence Agency, "Eastern Europe: Long Road Ahead to Economic Well-Being," May, 1990.

TABLE 6.III.11 Consumer spending on various items as a percentage of personal income, 1989 (Yugoslavia and selected countries)

	Total per Capita $	Percent Food/ Drink	Percent Clothing	Percent Energy	Percent Household Goods	Percent Health	Percent Transport
Yugoslavia	557	55.2	8.1	9.5	8.1	3.6	9.1
USSR	2,820	43.2	19.0	7.0	8.0	2.7	2.9
United States	12,233	13.3	6.5	19.5	5.7	14.7	14.8
France	9,635	20.0	7.0	18.8	8.3	8.8	16.7

Source: The Economist, *Book of Vital World Statistics,* 1990.

TABLE 6.III.12 Cost-of-living price index

	(Previous Year = 100)		
Index group	1983	1986	1989
Total	140.9	189.1	1,351.9
Goods	142.2	188.5	1,361.4
Services	131.0	194.9	1,287.7
Food	144.9	190.4	1,355.1
Tobacco and drinks	139.6	191.3	1,578.1
Apparel	140.6	189.3	1,379.7
Housing and household operations	133.6	187.9	1,270.3
Rent	134.4	177.1	1,069.4
Fuel and light	134.7	186.3	1,318.6
Household furnishings	131.9	197.0	1,368.7
Hygiene and health	135.8	189.0	1,278.0
Culture and entertainment	132.7	204.7	1,254.1
Transport and communications	143.0	178.1	1,389.4

Source: Statisticki Godisnjak Jugoslavije, 1990.

IV. EDUCATION

TABLE 6.IV.1 Schools, students, and teachers

	1986–1987	1987–1988	1988–1989
Schools			
General schools[a]	13,317	13,238	13,126
Universities	322	314	310
Students (thousands)			
General-school pupils	3,735	3,732	3,722
University undergraduates	346,787	338,577	341,341
Day students	126,990	127,436	130,487
Teachers (thousand)			
General-school teachers	197	199	200
University academic staff	25,673	25,969	26,301

[a] General schools are primary and secondary schools combined.

Source: Statisticki Godisnjak Jugoslavije, 1990.

TABLE 6.IV.2 Public expenditures on education

Year	Dinars	As Percent of GNP	Percent of Total Government Expenditures
1975	28,897,000	5.4	24.4
1980	84,051,000	4.7	32.5
1985	419,799,000	3.4	N/A
1986	935,793,000	3.8	12.1
1988	5,438,621,000	4.3	N/A

Source: UNESCO, *Statistical Yearbook,* 1989.

TABLE 6.IV.3 Expenditures and pupils per teacher, 1989 (Yugoslavia and selected countries)

Country	Percent of GNP	Pupils per Teacher Primary/Secondary
Yugoslavia	3.8	23/17
USSR	7.3	17/N/A
United States	6.7	21/13
France	5.7	19/17

Source: The Economist, *Book of Vital World Statistics,* 1990.

TABLE 6.IV.4 Distribution of teachers and pupils by educational level, 1987

Educational Level	Teachers	Percent Female	Pupils	Percent Female
Preschool	40,315	94	396,889	48
First-level	62,537	71	1,432,452	48
Second-level	135,888	52	2,358,064	48
General	N/A	N/A	1,653,929	48
Teacher training	N/A	N/A	25,330	86
Vocational	N/A	N/A	678,805	44
Third-level	25,927	27	348,068	47
Total	264,667		4,535,473	

Source: UNESCO, *Statistical Yearbook,* 1989.

TABLE 6.IV.5 Mean years of schooling[a], 1980 (Yugoslavia and selected countries)

Country	Total
Yugoslavia	6.0
USSR	7.6
United States	12.2
France	9.4

[a] For adults over 25 years old.

Source: UN, *Human Development Report 1991,* 1991.

TABLE 6.IV.6 School enrollment ratios[a]

Year	First-level (Ages 7–10)	Second-level (Ages 11–18)	Third-level (Ages 20–24)
1975	103[b]	76	20.0
1980	100	83	21.8
1987[c]	95	80	18.6

[a]Percent total enrollment of all ages divided by the population of the specific age groups that correspond to the age groups of primary and secondary schooling.

[b]Ratios exceeding 100 reflect instances in which the students at a given level are not necessarily in the age group delineated for that level.

[c]1987 data represent new age ranges in the following categories: first-level (ages 6–13) and second-level (ages 14–17).

Source: UNESCO, *Statistical Yearbook,* 1989.

TABLE 6.IV.7 School enrollment (Yugoslavia and selected countries)

	(Percent)					
	Primary			Secondary		
	Total	Male	Female	Total	Male	Female
Yugoslavia	95	95	94	80	82	79
USSR	106	N/A	N/A	98	N/A	N/A
United States	100	101	100	98	99	99
France	113	114	113	92	89	96

Source: The Economist, *Book of Vital World Statistics,* 1990.

TABLE 6.IV.8 Books, newspapers, and library book loans, 1989 (Yugoslavia and selected countries)

	Books Published per Year	Newspaper Circulation (Thousand)	Library Book Loans per Year (Thousand)	Volume Stock (Thousand)
Yugoslavia	10,619	2,508	N/A	28,954
Netherlands and Sweden	24,845	8,980	240,568.0	84,346
USSR	83,011	12,982	2,634.3[a]	1,523,071
United States	48,793	62,502	197,328.1	523,493

[a]Soviet library regulations rarely allow the loaning of books, thus the low figure.

Source: The Economist, *Book of Vital World Statistics,* 1990.

V. ENERGY AND RESOURCES

TABLE 6.V.1 History of primary energy production (Yugoslavia and selected countries)

Energy Type	Country	(Thousand Barrels per Day of Oil Equivalent)	
		1970	1980
Coal	Yugoslavia	164	254
	USSR	6,080	6,370
	United States	7,359	9,785
	France	523	284
Crude oil	Yugoslavia	56	85
	USSR	7,060	12,030
	United States	11,380	10,170
	France	68	51

(continued)

TABLE 6.V.1 *(continued)*

Energy Type	Country	(Thousand Barrels per Day of Oil Equivalent) 1970	1980
Natural gas	Yugoslavia	18	31
	USSR	3,270	7,170
	United States	10,686	9,838
	France	118	129
Hydro/nuclear	Yugoslavia	93	162
	USSR	660	1,170
	United States	1,394	2,774
	France	317	665

Source: U.S. Central Intelligence Agency, *Handbook of Economic Statistics,* 1989, 1990.

TABLE 6.V.2 Complete energy use

	Year	Production	Consumption[a]	Exports	Imports	Soviet Portion[b] of Imports (%)[c,d]
			(Thousand Metric Tons)			
Crude	1985	4,149	12,749	0	8,600	4,500 (52)
oil[e]	1988	3,681	15,742	0	12,061	6,038 (50)
	1990	3,152	15,793	0	12,641	6,060 (48)
Refined oil	1985	12,575	13,292	989	1,706	1,650 (97)
products	1988	16,386	16,477	1,124	1,215	N/A
	1990	15,943	15,693	1,330	1,080	N/A
Motor and	1985	1,868	1,748	124	4	N/A
aviation fuel	1988	2,462	2,617	6	161	N/A
	1990	2,347	2,437	10	100	N/A
Diesel oil	1985	4,002	3,964	48	10	N/A
	1988	4,339	4,442	38	81	N/A
	1990	3,902	3,882	120	100	N/A
Fuel oil	1985	3,762	5,119	9	1,366	N/A
	1988	6,122	6,583	140	601	N/A
	1990	6,290	6,517	250	477	N/A
Other refined	1985	2,943	2,461	808	326	N/A
products	1988	3,403	2,835	940	372	N/A
	1990	3,404	2,857	950	403	N/A
Natural gas	1985	2,400	6,612	12	4,224	3,919 (93)
(million cm³)	1988	3,015	7,084	58	4,137	4,440 (78)
	1990	2,648	7,167	66	4,585	4,104 (51)
Hard coal	1985	400	4,680	0	4,280	3,093 (72)
(including	1988	362	4,219	0	3,587	2,803 (78)
anthracite)	1990	292	3,522	0	3,230	1,640 (51)
Brown coal	1985	69,100	68,761	508	169	151 (89)
	1988	72,228	72,207	46	25	9 (36)
	1990	76,300	76,305	20	25	0
Coke	1985	3,545	3,428	152	35	0
	1988	3,008	2,821	447	60	0
	1990	2,275	2,215	100	40	0
Electricity	1985	74,802	75,429	2,306	2,663	0
(million kWh)	1988	83,651	82,239	2,559	1,147	0
	1990	83,340	83,330	2,600	2,500	0

[a] Yugoslavia is the 26th largest consumer of energy in the world.

[b] Yugoslavia has paid the world market price for its Soviet oil for several years. Thus, it will not suffer the readjustment shock that other states presently face.

[c] Soviet portion of imports as a percent.

[d] To the nearest 1%.

[e] 1 metric ton = 8.03 barrels of oil.

Source: "PlanEcon Report," vol. 7, March 6, 1991.

TABLE 6.V.3   Electricity production[a] (Yugoslavia and selected countries)

Country	(Billion Kilowatt-Hours)			
	1970	1980	1985	1989
Yugoslavia	26.02	59.44	74.80	82.78
USSR	740.93	1,293.88	1,544.10	1,722.00
United States[b]	1,742.73	2,437.82	2,634.65	2,970.21
France	146.97	243.29	325.73	378.00

[a]Data are for total (gross) production at generating centers and therefore include transmission losses and station use.
[b]Beginning in 1980, data are for public utilities only.
Source: U.S. Central Intelligence Agency, *Handbook of Economic Statistics,* 1989, 1990.

TABLE 6.V.4   Installed electricity-generating capacity[a] (Yugoslavia and selected countries)

Country	(Million Kilowatts)			
	1970	1980	1985	1989
Yugoslavia	6.97	14.51	20.19	20.18[b]
USSR	166.15	266.71	315.00	346.00
United States	360.33	630.94	656.12	683.99
France	36.22	63.66	86.56	100.62[c]

[a]All plants for both public and industrial use.
[b]1987 data.
[c]1988 data.

Source: U.S. Central Intelligence Agency, *Handbook of Economic Statistics,* 1989, 1990.

TABLE 6.V.5   Commercial energy use by sector[a], 1985 (Yugoslavia and selected countries)

	(Percentage of Commercial Energy Used)				
	Industry	Transport	Agriculture	Commercial and Residential	Other[b]
Yugoslavia	47	20	2	13	18
USSR	60	13	0	27	0
United States	31	35	1	30	4
France	33	26	2	35	3

[a]Includes all solid, liquid, and gaseous fuels, as well as primary and secondary electricity.
[b]Other includes nonenergy uses, military uses, and nonspecified uses.
Source: From *World Resources 1988–1989.* Copyright © 1988 by the World Resources Institute and the International Institute for Environment and Development in collaboration with the United Nations Environment Programme. Reprinted by permission of Basic Books, a division of Harper-Collins Publishers Inc.

TABLE 6.V.6   Proved reserves of crude oil, natural gas, and coal, 1989 (Yugoslavia and selected countries)

Country	Crude Oil (Billion Barrels)	Natural Gas (Trillion Cubic Feet)	Coal (Million Metric Tons)
Yugoslavia	Negligible	1	7,900
USSR	50–80	1,450	182,000
United States	26	165	205,000
UK	4	21	4,200
France	0.03	0.18	1,070

Source: U.S. Central Intelligence Agency, *Handbook of Economic Statistics,* 1990; U.S. Department of Energy, Energy Information Administration, *International Energy Annual,* 1988; UN, *Energy Statistics Yearbook,* 1986.

TABLE 6.V.7 Mineral production

Mineral	1985	(Tons) 1987	1989
Alumina	1,138,926	1,113,000	1,240,000
Aluminum, primary	306,346	280,633	337,800
Antimony	1,088	834	798
Asbestos	6,918	10,964	9,111
Barytes	35,488	19,270	52,400
Bauxite	3,249,794	3,394,000	3,252,000
Bentonite	148,752	154,288	139,693
Bismuth	68	73	40
Cadmium	279	284	475
Coal			
Bituminous	400,321	379,444	293,000
Lignite	56,635,336	59,359,000	62,276,000
Brown	12,460,541	12,135,000	12,063,000
Copper			
Mine production	142,479	130,470	139,631
Smelter production	137,073	103,399	101,606
Refined	135,442	138,867	151,035
Diatomite	7,927	5,458	6,081
Feldspar	49,480	45,000	36,000[d]
Ferro-alloys, electric furnace			
Ferro-chrome	73,308	56,276	90,429
Ferro-silico-chrome	7,199	6,240	3,815
Ferro-manganese	35,775	38,041	33,869
Ferro-silico manganese	43,374	42,528	52,737
Ferro-nickel	9,248	9,556	17,102
Ferro-silicon	91,702	98,843	122,153
Other ferro-alloys	5,539	8,071	11,199
Silicon metal	33,094	31,915	15,897
Gold, mine production[a]	4,460	5,348	4,349
Gypsum	600,000	553,000	543,819
Iron ore	5,478,154	5,983,000	5,080,000
Iron, pig	3,120,000	2,868,000	2,899,000
Kaolin	243,826	255,772	254,949
Lead, mine production	115,115	106,670	105,161
Lead, smelter production	99,954	112,417	117,300
Magnesite	417,407	403,000	364,000
Magnesium, primary	4,918	5,932	6,106
Manganese ore, 34%[b]	31,800	41,297	41,000[d]
Mercury[a]	88,000	67,000	51,000
Mica	644	887	794
Natural gas[c]	2,400	2,887	2,871
Nickel, mine production	2,800[d]	3,500[d]	6,300[d]
Nickel, smelter/refinery production	2,800	3,500	6,300
Palladium	87	132	199
Petroleum, crude	4,149,259	3,867,000	3,392,000
Platinum	3	22	23

[a] Kilograms.

[b] Estimated average content.

[c] Million m^3.

[d] Estimated.

(continued)

TABLE 6.V.7 *(continued)*

Mineral	1985	(Tons) 1987	1989
Salt			
Rock	149,151	153,067	133,597
Sea	67,897	67,672	50,376
Other	193,194	282,650	184,461
Selenium	44	66	55
Silver	156,451	151,129	133,000
Sulfur and pyrites			
Pyrites, 42%	212,785	255,723	350,000
Recovered	173,000[d]	178,000[d]	178,000[d]
Talc	27,534	30,993	26,614
Uranium	29	70	70
Zinc mine production	89,347	74,000	73,000[d]
Zinc, slab	83,398	118,067	119,400

[d] Estimated.

Source: British Geological Survey, *World Mineral Statistics, 1984–88; World Mineral Production, 1985–89.*

VI. GOVERNMENT AND DEFENSE FORCES

TABLE 6.VI.1 State budget

	(Million Dinars) State Budgets			Other Budgets[a]		
	1987	1988	1989	1987	1988	1989
Revenue:						
Total receipts	300.8	813.1	11,376.5	288.6	745.9	8,782.3
Expenditure:						
Schools	N/A	N/A	N/A	4.1	12.7	155.2
Science and culture	N/A	N/A	N/A	1.6	4.4	39.3
Public health and social welfare	58.5	118.4	1,105.7	14.4	33.4	308.9
National defense	197.0	524.7	6,112.4	2.5	5.0	37.2
Noneconomic investment	0.8	1.5	44.1	8.7	19.7	154.8
Government	14.8	45.4	1,163.4	120.6	323.4	5,140.4
Investment and interventions						
in the economy	N/A	N/A	1,579.1	31.4	95.6	351.9
Other	29.6	69.6	822.1	98.1	220.4	2,487.9
Total	300.9	759.7	10,826.9	281.5	714.9	8,675.6

[a] Republican, provincial (Vojvodina and Kosovo), and communal budgets.

Source: The Europa World Yearbook, 1990, 1991.

TABLE 6.VI.2 Hard-currency debt

	(Billion U.S. $) 1980	1985	1988	1989
Gross debt	17.5	18.8	18.2	16.2
of which				
Government	2.6	7.1	5.4	5.5
Commercial	12.8	7.5	7.8	6.9
Other	2.1	4.2	5.0	3.8
Reserves	N/A	1.1	2.3	7.5
Net debt	N/A	17.7	15.9	14.9
Debt service ratio[a]	N/A	44%	31%	28%

[a] Debt service ratio is calculated as the share of principal and interest payments to total hard-currency earnings.

Source: U.S. Central Intelligence Agency, "Eastern Europe: Long Road Ahead To Economic Well-Being," May, 1990.

TABLE 6.VI.3 Armed forces totals, 1991

Total armed forces[a]	164,000	(95,000 conscripts)
Branches		
Army	129,000	(87,000 conscripts)
Navy	11,000	(4,500 conscripts)[b]
Air Force	29,000	(3,500 conscripts)
Total reserves	510,000	
Army	440,000	
Navy	43,000	
Air Force	27,000	(to age 55/to age 60 for officers)
Manpower	188,028	men reach the military age of 19 annually.
Budget	39.81	billion dinars ($3.52 billion)[c]

[a]Total armed forces declined because of the disillusionment of the state. Not shown in the totals, Croatia is estimated to have a National Guard in formation in excess of 22,000 men. Slovenia has a Territorial Defense estimated at 60,000–70,000 men.

[b]Includes 900 marines and 2,300 coast guards.

[c]Budget is for 1990. Budget based on 11.32 dinars = $1.

Source: The International Institute for Strategic Studies, *The Military Balance 1991–1992*, 1991. Copyright IISS.

TABLE 6.VI.4 Components of defense force, 1987

Army
  Organization
    12 infantry divisions
    11 antitank regiments
     8 independent tank brigades
     3 mechanized infantry brigades
     4 surface-to-air missile regiments
  Major equipment (1987)
    1,040 tanks
      170 reconnaissance armored fighting vehicles
      500 armored personnel carriers
    2,574 artillery guns/howitzers
    3,782 antitank recoilless rocket launchers
           SA-6, SA-7 surface-to-air missiles

Navy
  Naval bases, located at Lora/Split, Sibenik, Kardeljevo, and Kotor.
  Major equipment (1987)
    Submarines include
       3 Heroj class, 714 tons
       2 Sava class, 964 tons
       2 S-11 Una class, 88 tons
       4 frigates
       3 corvettes
      17 gun fast attack craft

Air Force
  Organization
    12 fighter/ground attack squadrons
     2 transport aircraft squadrons
     1 transport helicopter squadron
    14 surface-to-air battalions
     1 airborne brigade
  Major equipment (1987)
    145 fighter/ground attack aircraft
    140 interceptor aircraft, including 120 MiG-21F, 20 MiG-21U
     80 reconnaissance aircraft
    260 helicopters

Source: Reprinted with permission from *World Defense Forces,* 2nd Edition, published by BC-CLIO, 1989.

TABLE 6.VI.5   Military expenditures

	1979	1980	1985	1987
Million dinars	55.1	76.3	465	1,320
Constant price figures (million U.S. $)[a]	2,480	2,623	2,328	1,577
Military expenditures as a percent of GDP				
Yugoslavia	4.7%	4.9%	3.9%	2.4%
USSR	12.9	13.0	12.5	N/A
United States	5.0	5.4	6.6	6.4
France	3.9	4.0	4.0	4.0

[a] 1986 exchange rates and prices.

Source: SIPRI Yearbook, 1989: World Armaments and Disarmament, Stockholm International Peace Research Institute, 1989.

VII. INDUSTRY

TABLE 6.VII.1   Industrial production index[a] (Yugoslavia and selected countries)

Country	(1980 = 100)						
	1960	1970	1980	1986	1987	1989	1990[b]
Yugoslavia	N/A	54	100	111	111	111	98
USSR[c]	38	68	100	113	116	118	115
United States	45	73	100	113	119	129	130
France	47	75	100	100	102	110	111

[a] Indexes for the noncommunist countries are value-added weighted indexes of industrial intermediate and final products. Industry includes manufacturing, mining, and, in most countries, public utilities. The indexes for the communist countries are estimates constructed by the U.S. Central Intelligence Agency as nearly as possible on the same basis as the indexes for Western countries, and include manufacturing, mining, and public utilities.

[b] Preliminary.

[c] Index of gross values of output for individual commodities and branches are aggregated by 1982 value-added weights. This index is as comparable with the index of U.S. industrial production of the U.S. Federal Reserve Board as data will permit.

Source: U.S. Central Intelligence Agency, *Handbook of Economic Statistics,* 1991.

TABLE 6.VII.2   Industrial production index (official and adjusted)

	(1980 = 100)					
	1960	1970	1980	1987	1988	1989[a]
Official	23	49	100	120	119	120
Adjusted	N/A	61	100	111	112	111

[a] Preliminary.

Source: U.S. Central Intelligence Agency, *Handbook of Economic Statistics,* 1989, 1990.

TABLE 6.VII.3 Production of selected industrial items

	(Metric Tons)	
	1985	1988
Agricultural and forestry products		
Mechanical wood pulp	129	129
Chemical wood pulp	578	582
Semi-chemical wood pulp	141	132
Cotton yarn	133	136
Woolen yarn	51	50
Sugar	933	636
Canned vegetables	126,000	112,000
Canned meat	91,000	83,000
Canned fish	38,000	33,000
Edible oil	237,000	236,000
Wine[a]	3,473	3,665
Beer[a]	10,656	11,970
Cigarettes[b]	59,034	59,698
Fuels, minerals, metals, and chemicals		
Electric engine[c]	74,802	83,651
Gasoline	3,508	4,168
Distillate fuel oils	3,397	3,834
Residual fuel oil	4,525	6,122
Pig iron	3,120	2,916
Steel	4,480	4,485
Electrolytic copper	135	145
Refined lead	100	110
Zinc	83	127
Aluminum	316	313
Iron castings	470	433
Sulfuric acid	1,489	1,731
Calcined soda	200	214
Clay building bricks[c]	3,773	4,047
Roofing tiles[c]	444	487
Cement	9,027	8,840
Machinery and equipment		
Construction machinery	52	42
Industrial machinery	77	60
Agricultural machinery	141	114
Tractors[d]	56,565	58,267
Trucks[d]	15,772	13,747
Railroad freight cars[d]	2,236	643
Rotating machines[e]	4,728	5,543
Power transformers[f]	11,490	7,771
Thermal apparatus	84,000	63,315

[a]Thousand hectoliters.
[b]Million units.
[c]Million kilowatt-hours.
[d]Units.
[e]Kilowatts.
[f]Kilovolt-amperes.

(continued)

TABLE 6.VII.3 *(continued)*

| | (Metric Tons) | |
	1985	1988
Manufactured consumer goods		
Motor cars[g]	228,000	305,000
Bicycles[h]	666	808
Stationery and newsprint	329	320
Woven cotton fabrics[i]	344	351
Sole leather	3,879	2,081
Upper leather	20,733	19,477
Footwear, excluding rubber[j]	93,063	86,336
Radio receivers[h]	152	130
Television receivers[h]	666	549

[f] Kilovolt-amperes.
[g] Including cars assembled from imported parts.
[h] Thousand units.
[i] Million square meters.
[j] Thousand pairs.

Source: The Europa World Yearbook, 1989, 1990.

TABLE 6.VII.4 Industrial waste generation

Yugoslavia has yet to release these figures.

TABLE 6.VII.5 Industrial output

	1988				1989			
	1 Qtr	2 Qtr	3 Qtr	4 Qtr	1 Qtr	2 Qtr	3 Qtr	4 Qtr
Total volume	−0.9	−2.4	N/A	0.5	2.7	3.5	0.4	−1.6
of which								
Investment goods	−3.0	−12.6	−8.6	−3.0	5.7	9.5	N/A	−1.0[a]
Consumer goods	−10.0	0.8	N/A	−4.7	2.0	1.7	6.4	5.5[a]
Intermediate goods	−0.8	−1.7	0.4	1.0	2.6	3.0	−2.2	1.0[a]

[a] October only.

Source: EIU, "Yugoslavia, Country Report," No. 4, 1990.

TABLE 6.VII.6 Rank of industry, manufacturing, and service sector share of GDP[a], 1990 (Yugoslavia and selected countries)

	Rank
Yugoslavia	10
Brunei	1
Angola	20
USSR	9

[a] All former East Bloc countries rank in the top 10 except Hungary. No OECD country is in the top 20. Additionally, no East Bloc state, nor the Soviet Union, is among the top 20 countries in terms of manufacturing share of GDP or services share of GDP. This chart indicates the significant role of extractive industries in Eastern Europe and the USSR.

Source: The Economist, *Book of Vital World Statistics,* 1990.

TABLE 6.VII.7   Emissions of air pollutants, 1988[a] (Yugoslavia and selected countries)

| | Nitrogen oxides | | Sulfur dioxide | | |
	Emissions (Thousand Tons)	Emissions per Unit GNP (Grams)	Emissions (Thousand Tons)	Emissions per Unit GNP (Grams)	Greenhouse index[b]
Yugoslavia	N/A	N/A	N/A	N/A	1.4
USSR[c]	4,510	2	18,584	10	3.4
United States[d]	19,800	4	20,700	4	5.3
France	1,615	2	1,226	1	2.4

[a] Preliminary data.
[b] Carbon heating equivalents, metric tons per capita. 1988–89 data.
[c] Stationary sources only. 1987 data.
[d] Sulfur data are for sulfur oxides.

Source: State of the World 1991, A Worldwatch Institute Report on Progress Toward a Sustainable Society, 1991; UN, Human Development Report 1991, 1991.

TABLE 6.VII.8   Environmental summary, 1991

	Yugoslavia	Netherlands and Sweden[a]	USSR	United States	France
Energy					
Energy production					
Solids[b]	658	0	14,299	20,736	365
Liquids[b]	155	153	24,139	17,297	145
Gas[b]	81	2,146	25,541	16,280	115
Biomass[b]	34	115	742	1,150	97
Nuclear[c]	4,689	69,907	213,001	529,352	303,928
Hydroelectric[c]	23,731	72,146	222,803	272,023	51,158
Energy consumption					
Total[b]	1,678	3,925	52,027	69,496	6,119
Per capita[d]	81	226	193	307	149
Per capita (global rank)	39	13	12	7	22
Energy intensity					
BTUs/$1987 GNP	29,657	13,007	N/A	15,787	8,784
Global rank	46	108	N/A	99	120
Waste					
Access to sanitation services					
Urban population	78%	100%	100%	N/A	100%
Rural population	46%	100%	100%	N/A	100%
1988 Greenhouse emissions					
Carbon dioxide[e]	39,000	52,000	1,200,000	1,400,000	96,000
Methane[e]	830	1,590	35,000	40,000	2,800
CFSs[e]	5	16	110	190	50
Share of world emissions	0.4%	0.4%	13.6%	17.3%	1.7%
Global rank[f]	64	42	14	7	41

[a] Yugoslavia is compared to both the Netherlands and Sweden combined, because when combined, they are of comparable population.
[b] Trillion BTUs.
[c] Gigawatt hours.
[d] Million BTUs.
[e] Thousand tons.
[f] Per capita.

Source: From The 1992 Information Please Environmental Almanac. Reprinted by permission of the Houghton Mifflin Company.

VIII. LABOR FORCE

TABLE 6.VIII.1 Workforce by selected areas of the economy

	(Percent)		
	1980	1986	1989
Total (thousand)	5,798	6,716	6,876
Industry	37.3	39.1	39.5
Agriculture and forestry	4.4	4.6	4.6
Construction	11.1	9.1	8.1
Transport and communications	6.9	6.7	6.7
Commerce	10.0	9.8	10.0
Housing and local administration	2.2	2.0	2.0
Education and culture	6.9	6.5	6.7
Health and social welfare	5.4	5.9	6.2
State administration and finance	7.8	8.0	7.9

Source: Comecon Data 1990, 1991.

TABLE 6.VIII.2 Average monthly earnings by economic sector

	(Dinars)			
	1980	1985	1987	1989
Total	7,368	40,661	173,965	8,010,000
of which				
Agriculture	6,731	38,879	157,157	7,169,297
Industry	6,955	39,952	167,886	7,650,000
Construction	7,022	34,904	152,838	6,450,000
Transport, post, and communication	7,904	43,358	185,892	8,860,000

Source: Comecon Data 1989, 1990, 1990, 1991.

TABLE 6.VIII.3 Economically active population by sex and industry, 1988

	(Percent)		Total
	Males	Females	(Thousand)
Agriculture, hunting, forestry, and fishing	76.6	23.4	338
Mining and quarrying	89.8	10.2	147
Manufacturing	60.9	39.1	2,597
Electricity, gas, and water	83.9	16.1	143
Construction	89.2	10.8	563
Trade, restaurants, and hotels	45.6	54.4	922
Transport, communications, and storage	80.7	19.3	522
Financing, insurance, real estate, and business services	43.8	56.2	208
Community, social and personal services	42.9	57.1	1,277
Total (thousand)	4,178	2,706	6,884

Source: ILO Yearbook of Labour Statistics, 1989–1990.

IX. POPULATION AND HEALTH

TABLE 6.IX.1 Geography and demographic profile, 1990

Population	
Population in 1990	23,841,608
Population by 2000	25,000,000 est.
Population by 2020	26,200,000 est.
Current annual percent increase	0.6%
Population density per sq km	104.0
Net migration rate	0/1,000
Urban/Rural (1981)	46.1%/53.9%
Ethnic division	
Serb	36.3%
Croat	19.7%
Muslim	9.0%
Slovene	7.8%
Albanian	7.7%
Macedonian	5.9%
Yugoslavia	5.4%
Montenegrin	2.5%
Hungarian	1.9%
Other	3.8%
Religion	
Eastern Orthodox	50%
Roman Catholic	30%
Protestant	1%
Other	10%
Muslim	9%
Geography	
Total area	255,800 sq km (98,764 sq mi)
Land area	255,400 sq km (98,610 sq mi)
Coast line	3,935 km (2,445 mi)
Offshore islands	2,414 km (1,500 mi)
Land borders with	
Albania	486 km (302 mi)
Austria	311 km (193 mi)
Bulgaria	539 km (335 mi)
Greece	246 km (153 mi)
Hungary	631 km (392 mi)
Italy	202 km (126 mi)
Romania	546 km (239 mi)
Disputes	
Kosovo question with Albania	
Macedonia question with Bulgaria and Greece	

Source: The Economist, *Book of Vital World Statistics,* 1990; U.S. CIA, *Atlas of Eastern Europe,* August 1990; Population Reference Bureau, *1989 World Population Data Sheet* (Washington, D.C.: Population Reference Bureau, Inc., 1989); U.S. CIA, *The World Factbook,* 1990.

TABLE 6.IX.2 Population (Yugoslavia and selected countries)

	(Million People at Midyear)				
	1960	**1970**	**1980**	**1985**	**1990**
Yugoslavia	18.4	20.4	22.3	23.1	23.8
Netherlands and Sweden	19.0	21.0	22.4	22.9	23.4
USSR	214.3	242.8	266.4	278.9	290.9
United States	180.7	205.1	227.8	239.3	250.4
France	45.7	50.8	53.9	55.2	56.4

Source: U.S. Central Intelligence Agency, *Handbook of Economic Statistics,* 1989, 1990, 1991.

TABLE 6.IX.3 Population by age (Yugoslavia and selected countries)

Age	Yugoslavia (1987)		Netherlands and Sweden (1987)		United States (1987)		USSR (1987)	
	Total	Percent	Total	Percent	Total	Percent	Total	Percent
<19	7,278,911	31.1	5,955,690	25.8	70,857,000	29.1	92,267,217	32.8
20–44	8,637,490	36.9	8,949,669	38.7	97,413,000	40.0	99,559,765	35.4
45–64	5,434,708	23.2	4,831,138	20.9	45,293,000	18.6	64,009,456	22.8
65+	2,066,079	8.8	3,367,020	14.6	29,836,000	12.3	25,501,353	9.0
Total	23,417,188	100.0	23,103,517	100.0	243,400,000	100.0	281,337,791	100.0

Source: UNESCO, *Statistical Yearbook,* 1989.

TABLE 6.IX.4 Population of major cities, 1981[a]

Belgrade	1,470,073
Split	882,050
Sijek	867,646
Zagreb	855,568
Rijeka	540,485
Skopje	504,932
Sarajevo	448,519
Ljubljana	305,211
Novi Sad	257,685
Nis	230,711

[a] Latest available data. The last census in Yugoslavia was conducted in 1981.

Source: The Europa World Year Book, 1991.

TABLE 6.IX.5 Health indicators, 1990 (Yugoslavia and selected countries)

Birth rate	15.0/1,000
of United States	15.0/1,000
of USSR	18.0/1,000
Death rate	9.0/1,000
of United States	9.0/1,000
of USSR	10.0/1,000
Infant mortality rate	24.0/1,000
of OECD and United States	9-10/1,000
of USSR	25.0/1,000
Maternal mortality rate[a]	22/100,000
of OECD and United States	10/100,000
of USSR	48/100,000
Life expectancy	69 male/75 female
of OECD	72 male/78 female
Fertility rate	1.9 children/woman
of United States	1.9 children/woman
of USSR	2.4 children/woman
Suicides[b]	16.1/100,000
of OECD and United States	14.6/100,000
of USSR	19.8/100,000

[a] Figures refer to live births. 1980–1987 figures.

[b] 1987–1988 figures.

Source: Population Reference Bureau, *1989 World Population Data Sheet,* (Washington, D.C.: Population Reference Bureau, Inc., 1989); The Economist, *Book of Vital World Statistics,* 1990; UN, *Human Development Report 1991,* 1991.

TABLE 6.IX.6 Registered illnesses

Illness	1987	1988
Diseases of the respiratory system	5,879,317	5,827,499
Diseases of the circulatory system	3,050,479	2,992,458
Diseases of the nervous systems and sensory organs	1,879,484	1,789,677
Diseases of the digestive system	1,699,835	1,682,492
Mental disorders	1,358,117	1,298,704
Diseases of the genitourinary system	1,057,971	1,037,110
Infectious and parasitic diseases	506,482	480,265
Diseases of blood and blood-forming organs	336,590	326,168
Diseases of endocrine glands, avitaminosis and other nutritional deficiency, metabolic diseases, and immunity deficiency	323,959	319,684
Neoplasms	90,415	91,515

Source: Statisticki Godisnjak Jugoslavije, 1990.

TABLE 6.IX.7 Fatalities by selected causes of death

Cause of Death	1984	1986	1988
Diseases of the circulatory system	108,078	111,298	109,291
Neoplasms	31,696	33,597	36,878
Injury and poisoning	13,711	13,163	13,709
Symptoms of ill-defined conditions	19,635	19,147	16,491
Diseases of the respiratory system	12,083	11,326	9,296
Diseases of the digestive system	9,301	7,588	8,648
Certain diseases of early infancy	4,407	4,052	3,510
Diseases of the genitourinary system	3,852	3,467	3,524
Infective and parasitic diseases	2,998	3,024	2,997
Endocrine, nutritional, and metabolic diseases	2,980	2,188	3,381

Source: Statisticki Godisnjak Jugoslavije, 1990.

TABLE 6.IX.8 Life expectancy by sex, 1991
(Yugoslavia and selected countries)

Yugoslavia	
Male	70
Female	76
USSR	
Male	65
Female	74
United States	
Male	79
Female	79
France	
Male	74
Female	82

Source: U.S. Central Intelligence Agency, The World Fact-book, 1991.

TABLE 6.IX.9   Medical care, 1983–1988 (Yugoslavia and selected countries)

	Doctors	Dentists	(Number per Million) Pharmacists	Beds (Thousand)	Total Health Expenditure[a]
Yugoslavia[b]	1,794.0	802.0	261.0	6.1	4.3
Netherlands and Sweden	2,630.0	790.0	144.6	12.6	8.8
USSR[b]	4,124.0	N/A	321.0	12.8	3.2
United States	2,035.0	560.0	641.0	5.9	11.2
OECD	2,199.5	453.8	559.2	8.0	8.3

[a] As a percent of GDP. 1987 figures.

[b] Figures for the former communist countries are clearly misleading. According to the Soviet Ministry of Health, 1.2 million beds are in facilities with no hot water, 1/6 of the beds are in hospitals with no water, and 30 percent of the hospitals have no indoor toilets. Source: *Literaturnaya Gazeta*, February 3, 1988; and see also *World Affairs,* vol. 152, no. 1, Summer 1989.

Source: Population Reference Bureau, *1989 World Population Data Sheet* (Washington, D.C.: Population Reference Bureau, Inc, 1989); The Economist, *Book of Vital World Statistics,* 1990; UN, *Human Development Report 1991,* 1991.

TABLE 6.IX.10   Abortion rates (Yugoslavia and selected countries)

Country	Number of Abortions	Rate per Thousand Women Aged 15–44	Ratio per 100 Known Pregnancies	Total Rate[a]
Yugoslavia (1987)	358,300	70.5	48.8	N/A
Netherlands and Sweden (1986)	53,300	12.6	17.0	378
USSR (1987)	6,818,000	111.9	54.9	N/A
United States (1985)	1,588,600	28.0	29.7	797

[a] The number of abortions that would be experienced by 1,000 women during their reproductive lifetimes, given present age-specific abortion rates.

[b] In contrast to women from Western European and English-speaking countries, who are young, unmarried women seeking to delay a first birth, women from Eastern Europe are married with two or more children, using abortion for spacing and ending childbirth. In addition, high rates in Eastern Europe, except Romania, may be attributed in part to the very liberal abortion laws, where abortion has been used as a form of birth control since the 1950s.

Source: Adapted with the permission of The Alan Guttmacher Institute from Stanley K. Henshaw and Evelyn Morrow, *Induced Abortion: A World Review 1990 Supplement,* 1990.

X.   TRADE

TABLE 6.X.1   Exports and imports, by commodity group

Commodity Group	(Percent of Total; fob/cif) 1980	1984	1988
Exports by commodity group			
Food, live animals	9.5	8.6	7.5
Beverages, tobacco	1.9	1.4	1.0
Other raw materials	7.4	4.7	5.5
Fuel, lubricants	2.6	3.6	1.6
Vegetable oils	0.2	0.1	0.1
Chemicals	11.2	9.7	9.1
Manufactures[a]	22.2	22.8	28.5
Machinery, transport equipment	28.4	31.0	30.8
Manufactures, miscellaneous	16.2	17.9	15.6
Other	N/A	N/A	0.1
Total	100.0	100.0	100.0
Total (million U.S. $)	8,978	10,254	12,779

[a] Of which clothing and footwear are the most important subcategories.

(continued)

TABLE 6.X.1 *(continued)*

Commodity Group	(Percent of Total; fob/cif)		
	1980	1984	1988
Imports by commodity group			
Food, live animals	6.4	3.4	6.1
Beverages, tobacco	0.2	0.1	0.2
Other raw materials	10.2	11.9	11.0
Fuels, lubricants	23.6	29.3	18.0
Vegetable oils	0.6	0.8	0.2
Chemicals	12.1	14.6	17.3
Manufactures	15.6	15.2	15.9
Machinery, transport equipment	28.0	22.1	27.0
Manufactures, miscellaneous	3.3	2.5	4.3
Others	0.7	N/A	N/A
Total	100.0	100.0	100.0
Total (million U.S. $)	15,064	11,996	13,329

Source: EIU, "Yugoslavia, Country Profile," 1989–1990.

TABLE 6.X.2 Main destinations of exports and main origins of imports, 1990

Country	(Percent of total)
Destinations of exports:	
USSR	18.6
Italy	17.3
Germany	17.1
France	5.3
United States	4.8
OECD[a]	51.4
Developing countries[a]	13.6
EC[a]	36.9
Origins of imports:	
Germany	19.3
USSR	13.0
Italy	13.0
Austria	5.8
France	5.3
United States	4.5
OECD[a]	54.8
Developing countries[a]	18.8
EC[a]	38.9

[a] 1989.
Source: EIU, "Yugoslavia, Country Profile," No. 4, 1991.

TABLE 6.X.3 Principal trading partners

	(Percent)					
	Exports			Imports		
	1983	1986	1988	1983	1986	1988
USSR	27.2	30.3	18.7	20.6	16.0	17.9
United States	3.5	5.5	5.8	6.4	5.7	5.5
Western Europe						
Austria	2.2	2.2	3.4	3.5	3.4	4.6
France	2.7	2.9	3.9	3.4	3.6	4.2
Germany	8.1	8.6	11.3	13.4	14.6	17.2
Italy	8.1	8.8	15.0	8.1	8.2	14.3
UK	N/A	1.8	2.6	2.0	2.2	2.3
European Community	N/A	28.8	N/A	N/A	37.1	N/A

(continued)

TABLE 6.X.3 (*continued*)

	(Percent)					
	Exports			Imports		
	1983	1986	1988	1983	1986	1988
Eastern Europe						
Czechoslovakia	6.5	4.1	4.2	5.6	4.9	3.4
East Germany	3.8	3.2	2.6	3.5	3.3	2.7
Hungary	2.9	2.6	2.0	2.4	2.2	2.3
Poland	3.1	4.1	3.9	2.6	3.3	3.3
Socialist countries	47.8	44.3	34.4	38.0	28.6	27.7
Other						
Iraq	4.5	3.3	3.1	5.8	6.8	4.8
Nonsocialist countries	52.2	55.7	65.6	62.0	71.4	72.3
of which						
OECD	31.9	41.3	51.5	44.7	54.8	56.1

Source: EIU, "Yugoslavia, Country Report," 1989–1990.

TABLE 6.X.4 Index of import and export prices, terms of trade
(Yugoslavia and selected countries)

	(1980 = 100)			
	1984	1986	1987	1989
Yugoslavia				
Import prices	116	108	109	124
Export prices	108	107	108	123
Terms of trade	93	99	100	99
Bulgaria				
Import prices	128	125	124	112
Export prices	111	110	112	110
Terms of trade	86	88	90	98
Czechoslovakia				
Import prices	134	146	142	137
Export prices	112	119	119	129
Terms of trade	84	81	83	93
Hungary				
Import prices	125	136	139	163
Export prices	116	120	124	153
Terms of trade	93	88	89	94
Poland				
Import prices	139	198	279	1,281
Export prices	127	189	275	1,516
Terms of trade	91	95	99	118
Romania				
Import prices	135	130	127	N/A
Export prices	124	114	114	N/A
Terms of trade	92	88	90	N/A
Soviet Union				
Import prices	115	112	110	113[a]
Export prices	130	114	110	103[a]
Terms of trade	113	102	100	100[a]

[a] 1988.

Source: Comecon Data 1989, 1990, 1990, 1991.

TABLE 6.X.5 Major imports and exports

Import Goods/Categories	(Million U.S. $) 1986	1987	1988
Food and live animals	780	701	813
Beverages and tobacco	34	29	28
Crude materials (inedible), except fuels	1,271	1,160	1,441
Mineral fuels, lubricants, and related materials	2,437	2,195	2,317
Animal and vegetable oils and fats	58	18	27
Chemicals and chemical products	1,862	2,055	2,280
Basic manufactures	2,091	2,092	2,100
Machinery and transport equipment	3,907	3,843	3,574
Miscellaneous manufactured goods	466	506	573
Commodities and transactions not classified by kind	9	4	2

Export Goods/Categories	1986	1987	1988
Total	12,914	12,603	13,154
Food and live animals	888	881	941
Beverages and tobacco	116	114	122
Crude materials (inedible), except fuels	447	563	690
Mineral fuels, lubricants, and related materials	208	220	199
Animal and vegetable oils and fats	6	11	33
Chemicals and chemical products	1,246	1,291	1,142
Basic manufactures	2,465	3,015	3,606
Machinery and transport equipment	3,603	3,476	3,874
Miscellaneous manufactured goods	1,853	1,825	1,964
Commodities and transactions not classified by kind	19	31	25
Total	10,852	11,425	12,597

Source: Comecon Data 1989, 1990.

TABLE 6.X.6 Trade with Western countries

Importing Countries	(Million U.S. $) 1985	1988	1989
Austria	528.7	564.3	600.4
France	534.0	573.7	554.8
West Germany	2,308.8	2,302.9	2,256.8
Italy	1,209.2	1,294.1	1,370.6
Netherlands	211.8	209.0	236.9
Sweden	202.0	173.2	198.2
Switzerland	289.2	315.9	271.7
UK	283.5	322.6	297.3
United States	690.4	716.2	727.4

Exporting Countries	1985	1988	1989
Austria	281.8	413.9	431.8
France	371.3	417.8	490.8
West Germany	1,142.0	1,330.4	1,429.2
Italy	1,125.7	1,489.9	1,885.7
Netherlands	103.2	116.5	134.1
Sweden	89.5	104.7	109.2
Switzerland	107.1	109.3	101.9
UK	213.5	269.1	321.4
United States	573.2	733.3	724.9

Source: Comecon Data 1989, 1990.

TABLE 6.X.7 Trade with the USSR by commodity

Exports, fob	(Million U.S. $) 1987	1988
Food	110	45
Live animals	0	0
Meat and products	31	10
Cereals and products	50	8
Fruit and vegetables	7	12
Beverages and tobacco	1	1
Wood, lumber, and cork	0	1
Metal ores and scrap	6	30
Petroleum and products	2	2
Chemicals	152	152
Rubber manufactures	37	56
Wood and cork manufactures	10	11
Paper, etc., and manufactures	20	23
Textile yarn, cloth, and manufactures	42	63
Nonmetallic mineral manufactures	9	15
Iron and steel	13	10
Nonferrous metals	11	7
Metal manufactures	65	65
Machinery, including electric	926	964
Transport equipment	265	335
Furniture	128	26
Clothing	148	133
Footwear	309	295
Total, including other items	2,222	2,354

Imports	1987	1988
Food	19	13
Meat and preparations	0	0
Metal ores and scrap	79	87
Petroleum and products	576	370
Chemicals	117	141
Coal, coke, and briquettes	137	146
Gas	346	317
Textile fibers and waste	98	94
Textile yarn, cloth, and manufactures	21	20
Nonmetallic mineral manufactures	3	2
Iron and steel	50	67
Nonferrous metals	63	69
Metal manufactures	8	3
Machinery, including electric	117	114
Transport equipment	N/A	97
Scientific instruments	7	3
Total, including all other items	1,926	1,748

Source: EIU, "Yugoslavia, Country Report," No. 3 and No. 4, 1990.

TABLE 6.X.8 Trade with the United States, by commodity

	(Million U.S. $)	
Exports, fob	**1987**	**1988**
Food	35	41
Live animals	0	0
Meat and products	23	28
Cereals and products	0	0
Fruit and vegetables	5	6
Beverages and tobacco	23	34
Wood, lumber, and cork	0	0
Metal ores and scrap	0	0
Petroleum and products	8	1
Chemicals	29	34
Rubber manufactures	12	15
Wood and cork manufactures	1	2
Paper, etc., and manufactures	1	2
Textile yarn, cloth, and manufactures	16	18
Nonmetallic mineral manufactures	18	21
Iron and steel	23	53
Nonferrous metals	56	43
Metal manufactures	18	24
Machinery, including electric	55	68
Transport equipment	122	47
Furniture	135	128
Clothing	62	58
Footwear	39	52
Total, including other items		
(million U.S. $)	734	708
Imports	**1987**	**1988**
Food	107	40
Meat and preparations	0	0
Coal, coke, and briquettes	46	76
Metal ores and scrap	0	0
Petroleum and products	17	13
Chemicals	92	81
Gas	0	0
Scientific instruments	43	43
Textile fibers and waste	20	37
Textile yarn, cloth, and manufactures	7	8
Nonmetallic mineral manufactures	1	3
Iron and steel	2	2
Nonferrous metals	1	1
Metal manufactures	5	5
Machinery, including electric	198	202
Transport equipment	75	102
Total, including all other items		
(million U.S. $)	717	728

Source: EIU, "Yugoslavia, Country Report," No. 3 and No. 4, 1990.

Bibliography

Annual Bulletin of Transport Statistics for Europe. New York: United Nations, 1989.

Atlas of Eastern Europe. Washington: U.S. Central Intelligence Agency, August 1990.

Book of Vital World Statistics. New York and London: The Economist, 1990.

Bulgaria, Country Profile. London: The Economist Intelligence Unit, 1988, 1989, 1990, 1991.

"Bulgaria, Country Report." Nos. 1-4, 1990, 1991. London: The Economist Intelligence Unit, 1990, 1991.

"Bulgaria: Foreign Economic Trends Report." Sofia: U.S. Embassy, April, 1990.

Central and Eastern Europe 1991. Country Reports. Luxembourg: EUROSTAT (Statistical Office of the European Communities), 1991.

Comecon Data 1989, 1990. New York: The Vienna Institute for Comparative Economic Studies, 1990, 1991.

Czechoslovakia, Country Profile. London: The Economist Intelligence Unit, 1988, 1989, 1990, 1991.

"Czechoslovakia, Country Report." Nos. 1-4, 1990, 1991. London: The Economist Intelligence Unit, 1990, 1991.

1988 Demographic Yearbook. New York: United Nations Statistical Office, 1990.

"East Europe Business Information Center Fact Sheet." Washington: U.S. Department of Commerce, International Trade Administration, Feb. 7, 1989.

The East European & Soviet Data Handbook: Political Social & Developmental Indicators, 1945–1978. Paul S. Shoup. New York: Columbia University Press; Stanford: Hoover Institution Press, 1981.

"Eastern Europe: Long Road Ahead to Economic Well-Being." Washington: U.S. Central Intelligence Agency, May, 1990.

Economic Survey of Europe in 1987–88. New York: United Nations Economic Commission for Europe, 1989.

"1990 Economic Trends, Czechoslovakia." Washington: U.S. Department of Commerce, January, 1990.

Energy Statistics Yearbook. New York: United Nations, 1981, 1986.

"Export Information: Czechoslovakia." Washington: U.S. Department of Commerce, International Trade Administration, January 1, 1990.

The Europa World Year Book. London: Europa Publications, Ltd., 1989, 1990, 1991.

FAO Production Yearbook. Rome: Food and Agricultural Organization of the United Nations, 1962, 1971, 1981.

"Foreign Economic Trends and their Implications for the United States: Czechoslovakia." Washington: U.S. Department of Commerce, May, 1990.

"Foreign Economic Trends and their Implications for the United States: Romania." Washington: U.S. Department of Commerce, May, 1990.

"Foreign Economic Trends Report: Bulgaria." Sofia: U.S. Embassy, April 1990.

"Foreign Economic Trends Report: Hungary." Budapest: U.S. Embassy, September, 1989.

Handbook of Economic Statistics. Washington: U.S. Central Intelligence Agency, 1985, 1989, 1990, 1991.

Human Development Report 1991. New York and Oxford: United Nations Development Programme, 1991.

"Hungarian Economic Reform: Status and Prospects." Washington: U.S. Department of State, September, 1989.

Hungarian Statistical Yearbook. Budapest: Hungarian Central Statistical Office, 1986.

Hungary, Country Profile. London: The Economist Intelligence Unit, 1988, 1989, 1990, 1991.

"Hungary, Country Report." Nos. 1-4, 1989, 1990, 1991. London: The Economist Intelligence Unit, 1989, 1990, 1991.

Induced Abortion. A World Review 1990 Supplement. S.K. Henshaw and E. Morrow, New York: The Alan Guttmacher Institute, 1990.

The 1992 Information Please Environmental Almanac. compiled by World Resources Institute, editor Allen Hammond, Boston: Houghton Mifflin Co., 1992.

International Energy Annual. Washington: U.S. Department of Energy, Energy Information Administration, 1988.

International Energy Statistical Review. Washington: U.S. Central Intelligence Agency, 1990.

International Financial Statistics. New York: International Monetary Fund, 1989.

International Information Annual. Arlington, VA: U.S. Department of Energy, Energy Information Administration, 1988.

ILO Yearbook of Labour Statistics. Geneva: International Labour Office, 1988.

The Military Balance 1991-1992. Published by Brassey's. London: The International Institute for Strategic Studies, 1991.

"PlanEcon Report." Edited by Jan Vanuous, Vol. VI, Nos. 1-52; Vol. VII, Nos. 1-52. Washington: PlanEcon, Inc., 1990, 1991.

Poland, Country Profile. London: The Economist Intelligence Unit, 1988, 1989, 1990, 1991.

"Poland, Country Report." Nos. 1-4, 1990, 1991. London: The Economist Intelligence Unit, 1990, 1991.

"Quarterly Economic Review of Romania, Bulgaria, Albania." Annual supplement. London: The Economist Intelligence Unit, 1983.

"Reform in Eastern Europe: Implications for Trade, Aid, and Commercial Relations." Washington: The Library of Congress, Congressional Research Service, May 23, 1990.

"Report on Eastern Europe." Various issues. New York and Munich: Radio Free Europe/Radio Liberty Research, 1985–1991.

Romania, Country Profile. London: The Economist Intelligence Unit, 1989, 1990, 1991.

"Romania, Country Report." Nos. 1-4, 1990, 1991. London: The Economist Intelligence Unit, 1990, 1991.

"Selected Countries' Trade with the USSR and East Europe." Washington: U.S. Central Intelligence Agency, 1990.

Social Indicators of Development. Washington: World Bank, 1989.

The Soviet Union and Eastern Europe. George Schopflin, ed. New York: Facts on File Publications, 1986.

State of the World. A Worldwatch Institute Report on Progress Toward a Sustainable Society. New York and London: Worldwatch Institute, 1991.

Statistical Yearbook. New York: United Nations, 1985–86, 1988.

Statistical Yearbook. Paris: UNESCO, 1985–86, 1989.

Statisticki Godisnjak Jugoslavije. Belgrade: Federal Socialist Republic of Yugoslavia, 1990.

Stockholm International Peace Research Institute (SIPRI) Yearbook, World Armaments and Disarmament. Stockholm & Cambridge, MA: Almquist & Wiskell International, 1988, 1989.

The World Almanac and Book of Facts. Mark S. Hoffman. New York: Newspaper Enterprise Association, 1989.

World Defense Forces. 2nd ed. Rose Schumaker, ed. Santa Barbara, CA: ABC-CLIO, 1989.

The World Factbook. Washington: U.S. Central Intelligence Agency, 1990, 1991.

World Military Expenditures and Arms Transfers. Washington: U.S. Arms Control and Disarmament Agency, 1987.

World Mineral Production 1985–1989. Supplement to World Mineral Statistics. London: British Geological Survey, Her Majesty's Stationery Office, 1989.

World Mineral Statistics 1984–1988. London: British Geological Survey, Her Majesty's Stationery Office, 1988.

World Resources 1988–89. New York: The World Resources Institute, Inc., 1988.

1989 World Population Data Sheet. Prepared by PRB Demographers, Carl Haub and Mary Mederios Kent. Washington: Population Reference Bureau, Inc., 1989.

Yearbook of International Financial Statistics. Washington: International Monetary Fund, 1989.

Yearbook of International Labour Statistics. Washington: International Labour Organization, 1988.

Yugoslavia Country Profile. London: The Economist Intelligence Unit, 1987, 1988, 1989, 1990, 1991.

"Yugoslavia Country Report." Nos. 1–4, 1990, 1991. London: The Economist Intelligence Unit, 1990, 1991.

Name Index

Adamec, Ladislav, 74, 75, 76
Adzic, Blagoje, 359
Agnes of Bohemia, 71
Alexander of Battenberg, 297
Alexander, King, 365
Alexander III, Tsar, 297
Andropov, Yuri, 2, 287
Antall, Jozsef, 148, 151, 152, 153, 162, 165, 167
Antonescu, Ion, 227
Ascherson, Neal, 32
Ash, Timothy Garton, 32, 102
Auty, Phyllis, 389
Avramov, Georgi, 294

Baba, Ivan, 149
Baker, James, 360–361
Balcerowicz, Leszek, 4, 5, 8, 18, 19, 22
Baroszcze, Roman, 8
Benes, Edvard, 82, 83, 84, 85
Bethlen, Istvan, 156
Bierut, Boleslaw, 14
Bilák, Vasil, 86
Bismarck, Otto von, 10
Boleslaw II, 9
Boris III, King, 294, 298, 299
Braun, Aurel, 248
Brezhnev, Leonid, 85, 86, 160, 286, 287
Brucan, Silviu, 221
Bujak, Zbigniew, 5, 16

Calfa, Marian, 75
Campeanu, Radu, 219
Čarnogurský, Jan, 76, 77, 78
Carol I, King, 224, 225
Carol II, King, 226
Ceausescu, Elena, 217, 230
Ceausescu, Nicolae, iv, 23, 95, 144, 153, 216, 217, 218, 219, 220, 221, 222, 223, 225, 226, 229–231, 232, 233, 234, 236, 237, 238, 239, 242, 244, 245, 246, 247, 248, 362
Chernenko, Konstantin, 287

Cimoszewicz, Wlodzimierz, 7
Clissold, Stephen, 389
Coposu, Corneliu, 220
Crampton, R. J., 315

Daranyi, Kalman, 156
Darby, H. C., 389
Davies, Norman, 32
Demszky, Gabor, 148
Dertliev, Petar, 294
Dienstbier, Jiri, 76
Dijmarescu, Eugen, 235
Dimitrov, Georgi, 294, 300
Dimitrov, Georgi M., 300
Djilas, Milovan, 384
Dlouhy, Vladimir, 75, 88
Dogan, Ahmed, 290–291
Dragon, Pal, 149
Drenchev, Milan, 294
Dubeček, Alexander, 70, 72, 73, 74, 76, 85, 86, 100
Dulles, Allen, 158
Dušan, Stephen, 363, 381
Dutsch, Tamas, 150
Dzhurov, Dobri, 288, 292, 294

Farkas, Mihaly, 158
Feiwel, George, 315
Ferdinand I, 80–81
Ferdinand, Archduke, 360
Ferdinand, Archduke Franz, 364
Ferdinand, King, 225
Ferdinand, Prince, 297
Fierlinger, Zdenek, 84
Fischer, Mary Ellen, 248
Fischer-Galati, Stephen, 248
Fiszbach, Tadeusz, 7
Fodor, Gabor, 150
Fojtik, Jan, 74
Frasyniuk, Wladyslaw, 5, 16
Friedrich, Istvan, 155

Gerasimov, Gennadi, 72
Gero, Erno, 158, 159, 173

Subject Index